HIGH STRANGENESS

Other books by Laura Knight-Jadczyk

*The Secret History of the World
and How to Get Out Alive*

*9/11: The Ultimate Truth
(with Joe Quinn)*

The Wave

HIGH STRANGENESS

HYPERDIMENSIONS AND THE PROCESS OF ALIEN ABDUCTION

Laura Knight-Jadczyk

with
Harrison Koehli

Red Pill Press
2008

Published by Red Pill Press,
10020-100 Avenue, Grande Prairie,
Alberta, T8V 0V3, Canada.
www.redpillpress.com

Some material in this book appears in a slightly
different form in *Amazing Grace* (out of print),
and *The Secret History of the World.*

Printed and bound in Canada.

table of contents

Preface

It's sad but true that most people don't like inconvenient realities to upset their pleasant illusions and prejudices. I see this all the time in my own daily interactions with people. Once someone reaches a point in his or her life when they feel they "understand" the world well enough—often around the age of thirty—they spend the rest of their life filling in the blanks of what they think they already know. It's a tendency that usually becomes more extreme over time. Ideas and worldviews seem to harden in tandem with the arteries.

The friends people make, television shows they watch, the internet sites they visit—the very world they create for themselves—all of these usually support the circumscribed worldview they themselves have adopted.

Obviously, it's the same with books. It's a rare book that has the ability to truly change one's mind about the world. Rarest of all are those gems with the ability to change one's life.

Laura Knight-Jadczyk's *High Strangeness* is such a book.

It follows that such a book can only be written by those rarest of thinkers, someone possessing profound insights, freedom from convention, and the utter fearlessness necessary to tear down illusions and stare down the face of the abyss. Laura Knight-Jadczyk is such a person.

I believe that Laura understands, better than probably anyone you will ever know, just how dire is the plight of our civilization—the plight of our species. She also understands that to change one's life, one must be willing to fight.

"Fight what?" one might ask. The answer may seem strange within the context of our post-post-post modern 21st century setting, but it is … to fight evil.

Crazy? No. Not at all.

High Strangeness is a book that lays out provocatively and passionately the hidden slavery of the human race. The problem is that this situation is so far removed from what most people have come to accept about their world, that Knight-Jadczyk's analysis and information will meet with tremendous resistance. Calling this book a "new paradigm" is a gross understatement. Understanding it will require most readers to discard nearly everything they think they know about how the world works. I realize this is a significant claim, and I do not make it lightly.

My problem in reviewing this book is amplified by how much of its information was obtained, and therein lies the core controversy surrounding Laura Knight-Jadczyk. Because for more than a decade, she has obtained information—lots and lots of information—from a group of people she calls "the C's": short for Cassiopaeans. In other words, this is information that has

preface

been gathered in sessions using a Ouija board and planchette, over and over, year after year.

This is not an easy thing for me to comment on. When my own work focuses so extensively on open source documentation, "proven" data that brooks no argument from established sources, when I have spent my public career with the meticulous caution of a historian to make a careful and reasoned argument on the UFO cover-up, delving into the world of "channeled" information can make me decidedly uncomfortable.

But here is why I feel what the Cs are genuine. In the first place, I have had the pleasure of knowing Laura, of spending time with her in deep conversation, as well as with many people who belong to her global salon, the *Signs of the Times* (SOTT). In other words, I don't just think that Laura is honest—I know she is. I know that she is a down-to-earth mother of five, who just happens to be brilliant and totally relentless. I have been fortunate indeed to meet many extraordinary people in my life, but even among these people, Laura is special.

So, yes, there is a personal connection here, one of friendship, and a detached reader might wonder if my own judgment is clouded in this review.

But the real issue, as I see it, when reviewing the content of this book, is twofold. First, how can we be sure that the communications from "The Cassiopaeans" are genuine; and second, is there inherent value in those communications?

To answer the first question, all I can say is that her channeled information is not the first, and will certainly not be the last. My attitude on most claimed channeled information usually ranges from extreme caution, to skepticism, to outright disbelief. But I cannot say that all such information is bunk or must be dismissed out of hand. My own research into the history of Remote Viewing (RV) has convinced me beyond any reasonable doubt that there is another dimension to our existence other than the straightforward material one. There is something more. Call it non-local, call it spiritual, it does not matter. There is an important aspect to our existence that conventional minds and "official culture" do not recognize.

Taken in that context, when I read the incredibly rich, detailed—and logical—statements coming from "the C's," I find it unlikely that Laura (or anyone, for that matter) could convincingly fake them. In the first place, the process for obtaining this information is from a Ouija board, with several people touching the planchette, and one person in charge of recording the letters, which come in at a furious pace. I have learned enough about the process of using the Ouija, and known enough people who have described this experience to me in detail, that I am satisfied something real is going on in that process. Moreover, the "dialogue" between Laura and the Cs also frequently includes other members of the channeling session who are present. Frequently the transcripts record very active discussions that include the comments and questions of many people in attendance.

I am inclined to think that the C's are real. Yet, we all must recognize that their existence does not pass the test of scientific evidence. We can take their existence as, let us say, an interesting working hypothesis.

But it is the message of the Cassiopaeans that really matters. What they tell us is that the world we live in is an illusion not unlike that of the movie, *The Matrix*. The human race is being manipulated physically and spiritually by a race of beings that we know as the Reptilians, whom Laura refers as "The Lizzies" (her down-to-earth way of stripping them of their terror and putting them in their place). They can manipulate time with ease, they control "the Greys," and they live in what is known as the Fourth Density.

What is a density? I confess I don't quite understand the physics, and I am not sure that physics is the right path here in any case. But animals live in the second density, and we humans live in the third. It is, therefore, more of a state of consciousness than, say, a "dimension" of existence. The Reptilians are able to manipulate and control us in just the way that we can control cattle. But simply because the Reptilians live in a state of consciousness that is higher than ours does not mean they are ethical. They are, in fact, what we would refer to as pretty evil. They exist in what is called a "Service to Self" (STS) state of being. Humanity also exists in STS. There are other beings, however, such as the Cs, who live in a "Service to Others" (STO) state of being (and incidentally on the Sixth Density).

But the Reptilians can indeed do many things by virtue of being Fourth Density. For one, they can "appear" into our reality at will, in essentially any guise or form. They "need" us as food, both psychically/spiritually and physically. They have farmed us throughout our very existence. They have shaped our religious and political systems. Indeed, in many crucial ways, they have "made" us in their own image. Breaking free of their oppressive control is humanity's paramount task if it is ever to achieve true personal and spiritual liberation.

Incidentally, the abduction process comes into play here as one of several mechanisms by which "the Lizzies" control us. Using their creations, the Greys, to conduct most of the abductions, these events seldom occur in our Third Density reality. Instead, they take place in the Fourth Density, which effectively means it occurs in a timeless, spiritual realm. Yet while in the Fourth Density, life seems just as physical to us as always, and the return to Third Density is like the process whereby one copies and pastes a file back to one's hard drive. That is, the changes (and implants) that occur in the Fourth Density reality are effectively copied to one's Third Density body.

This is certainly a lot to take, and merely scratches the surface. Reading the book is really the only way to grasp it all.

I should point out that not all of this book deals with the Cassiopaeans, although this is its core. But there is a great deal of trenchant analysis by Knight-Jadczyk throughout, something that her readers have come to expect over the years.

The overall message of the book is grim. But the situation is not hopeless. I am very much taken by the motto of the C's, stated several times in the book: "knowledge protects; ignorance endangers."

No matter what the final truth is regarding the existence of the C's, or the Reptilians, or any other entities, I think all of us could use this as a personal motto. We live in a very dangerous world, far more dangerous, far worse, than most people realize. Yet, there is a way to safety, and it lies in understanding the nature of the reality in which we exist. This is hard work, but easily worth the effort.

I am also grateful to Laura Knight-Jadczyk for her courage in facing some of the most difficult issues human beings can face. She is a shining light in a world of darkness.

—Richard Dolan

Richard M. Dolan is author of UFOs *and the* National Security State: Chronology of a Coverup *(Hampton Roads, 2002). He speaks at conferences around the world and has appeared on numerous television and radio programs. Visit his website at http://keyholepublishing.com.*

foreword

High Strangeness is a radical work. It weaves together threads from the fields of history, religion, psychology, physics, and philosophy in an attempt to provide an objective understanding of our reality. Its subject is controversial, having been blindly accepted by some and categorically denied and derided by others, both of which groups seem to lack the attitude of healthy skepticism, critical thought, and open scientific inquiry that befits a true *philosopher*.

Since the mid- to late-1940s, when the UFO phenomenon entered strongly into public awareness, a public effort to analyze and understand the reality behind so-called "flying saucers" has been long coming. Despite the efforts of a few fearless scientists and researchers, official denial, media ridicule, and scientific bullying have harried the matter throughout the ensuing decades. As such, the greatest scientific minds have either felt the subject unworthy of close attention, or have felt the need to keep their research and thoughts on the subject private, for fear of destroying their reputations and careers. Those few who confronted this pressure met strong resistance.

High Strangeness is Laura Knight-Jadczyk's attempt to answer questions ignored by both "skeptics" and "believers". First and foremost, is there really a UFO phenomenon? Even if we only cursorily examine the literature, we are forced to admit something is happening. Aside from credible civilian witnesses, military personnel have observed anomalous craft repeatedly violate sensitive airspace, tracking them both visually and on radar, since at least World War II. (An historical analysis suggests the phenomenon is much older than that.) With the release of long-classified documents thanks to the Freedom of Information Act, we now know that officials in military, intelligence, and government took the subject very seriously, and continue to do so, while publicly denying any official interest. Knight-Jadczyk quotes historian Richard Dolan's seminal analysis of this documentary evidence, *UFOs and the National Security State: Chronology of a cover-up 1941-1973* (Keyhole Pub., 2000). One such document, the 1947 "Twining Memo" calls the phenomenon "real and not visionary or fictitious." The objects observed are identified as moving with "extreme rates of climb, maneuverability … and motion which must be considered evasive when sighted…" As for the objects themselves, they are "circular or elliptical in shape, flat on bottom and domed on top … metallic or light-reflecting…" They travel in "well-kept formation" of three to nine objects.

Who or what operates such "craft"? Is the phenomenon related to so-called "alien abduction"? Can it be said to influence human affairs? In short, what is its true *nature*? Each question leads to numerous avenues of inquiry, of which not one is solely sufficient to give adequately objective answers. A valid theory of the nature of UFOs and the beings controlling them must take into account *all* data: both the *signal* and the *noise*.

And there is a lot of noise, as anyone familiar with the subject will know: 'contactees', benevolent space-brothers, ubiquitous 'grays', shape-shifting reptilians, psychic powers, mind-controlling implants, vast government conspiracies... We must also take into account the possibility that some of this noise is deliberate, and here the subject becomes maddeningly complex. We know that intelligence agencies have treated the subject with intense interest. We also know that such agencies have reputations for extreme secrecy and deception, to the point of creating elaborate propaganda and disinformation: PSYOPS. Knight-Jadczyk cites the infamous FBI COINTELPRO operations as one such example. And so, the subject cannot be studied without an adequate understanding of the psychology and motivations of "behind-the-scenes" players.

The answers Knight-Jadczyk provides are both comprehensive and disturbing. If they are true, the UFO phenomenon has far-reaching implications for both our past and future, and to deny the matter outright would be a great disservice to science and humanity.

A Multilevel Approach

Knight-Jadczyk proposes a *multilevel* perspective of the universe, challenging the widely held *unilevel* worldview. Put simply, our natural conceptual understanding of the world is conditioned by our species-specific perceptual apparatus and the experience of everyday life. It operates as if the world is simply *as we see and experience it*; if we do not see something and thus cannot subject it to analysis, then it must not exist. Intrinsic to this natural worldview is the perception of time as strictly *linear*. We see reality on a single "level"—the visible universe—that changes and evolves over time (evolution being a process whereby matter becomes more complex and increasingly more conscious). This view is in opposition to that of a *multilevel* universe that is experienced subjectively, i.e., according to the perceptual limits of a specific unit of consciousness. Hyperdimensional physics posits "higher" levels of reality than those perceptible to us, and time that is non-linear. Levels, as such, are not temporal *stages*—they are not necessarily related to, or limited to, periods of time—they exist *simultaneously*.

> "The illusion of the passage of time arises from confusing the given with the real. Passage of time arises because we think of occupying different realities. In fact, we occupy only different givens. There is only one reality." (Kurt Gödel)

> "The standard big-bang theory depicts a homogeneous universe that looks like a single bubble. But if we take into account quantum effects, the self-reproducing inflationary universe is a bubble producing new bubbles producing new bubbles

producing new bubbles and so on. This kind of repeatedly branching pattern is what mathematicians call a fractal. ... According to the branch of physics called quantum cosmology, the universe is best represented as a pattern called a wave function that does not depend on time. But then why do I see the universe evolving in time? The answer may be that as long as I am observing the universe, the universe breaks into two pieces: me and the rest of the universe. And it turns out that the wave function for each of these separate pieces does depend on time. But if I merge with the universe, my time stops." (Physicist Andrei Linde interviewed by Rudy Rucker in "Big Bang Bust", *wired.com*)

Multilevelness is empirically observable both *within* any given level, and *between* any two levels. For example, humanity is on a qualitatively higher level than other forms of animal life, its greater degree of autonomy and consciousness being a function of the increasing complexity of the cortical regions of the human brain. At the same time, one human can be at a higher level than another. Most obviously, this can be observed in the difference between a psychopath and a fully developed human being (this idea will be expanded upon below). This, too, suggests that higher levels are characterized by an increase in autonomy, as observed in the levels of, and harmony between, emotion, intellect, and behaviour; and a decrease in automatic, instinct-driven behaviour characteristic of lower levels of life. Such a view suggests that as matter and life become increasingly conscious, evolution becomes increasingly *self-directed*. Higher levels of autonomy bring higher levels of responsibility, both for ourselves and others.

The limits that biology places on perception of reality seem to block awareness of higher levels. A dog cannot conceive of the differences between its own way of thinking and ours, nor can it perceive that such differences exist. Similarly, a psychopath lacks the normal brain functions[*] to be aware of the differences between *its* way of thinking, and that of a normal human being. This gives new insight into J. S. Mill's aphorism: "It is better to be a human being dissatisfied than a pig satisfied; better to be Socrates dissatisfied than a fool satisfied. And if the fool, or the pig, are of a different opinion, it is because *they only know their own side of the question*. The other party to the comparison knows both sides."

Taken further, we would not necessarily perceive higher levels, and if we did, would not necessarily see them *as* higher. Perception of a higher level from a lower level seems to see higher-level activity as deviation from the norm, as *anomalous*—not for what it truly is. It sees *surface*, not *reality*. A dog senses activity—movement, sounds, the interaction between owners—and the result is 'magical': food has been produced, seemingly from nowhere, the dog unaware of the meaning of the words communicated between higher, and more autonomous, beings. Similarly, a psychopath views normal emotional reactions

---

[*] Dysfunction in the psychopath is particularly related to the amygdala and frontal lobe regions. See James Blair, et al., *Psychopath: Emotion and the brain* (London: Blackwell Pub., 2005) for the most up-to-date research on the subject.

as anomalous and incomprehensible—facial contortions with no emotional content. Such content is outside the limits of his awareness. How might activity from a higher level than our own—a higher dimension—appear to us?

> Postulates and conjectures from Chinese mathematician Linfan Mao (*Smarandache Multi-Space Theory*, Phoenix: Hexis, 2006):
>
> *Postulate 6.2.1* At the beginning our cosmos is homogenous.
>
> *Postulate 6.2.2* Human beings can only survey pseudo-faces of our cosmos by observations and experiments.
>
> *Conjecture 6.3.1* There are infinite many cosmoses...
>
> *Conjecture 6.3.2* There must exists a kind of beings who can get from one cosmos into another. There must exists a kind of being who can go from a space of higher dimension into its subspace of lower dimension, *especially, on the earth.*

While the mineral, plant, and animal kingdoms are not, and cannot, be aware of the existence of higher levels, humans, endowed with a greater degree of reason, and while still lacking direct perception of higher levels, can at least accept their existence mathematically and analyze anomalies suggestive of their existence. A multilevel perspective strongly suggests the existence of beings *at a higher level than humanity*, and hyperdimensions are a natural place to look for them. However, such beings will not necessarily be directly visible to our perception, except through the lens of the aforementioned "anomalies". Even in the event of direct interaction, such beings may very well appear "human", or at least recognizable in a physical sense (humanoid, animalistic). However, we would be much like psychopaths trying to comprehend normal humanity's higher emotions—a futile effort.

One way to comprehend this hyperdimensional dynamic is by visualizing a two-dimensional world interacting with an encompassing three-dimensional one. We can then translate this experience to a 3D–4D level by analogy. For example, imagine the observable universe existing entirely on/in the two-dimensional surface of a bubble, like a pencil drawing on a piece of paper. To the inhabitants of this 2D reality, the world is a closed system—all that exists are the two-dimensional geometric objects and beings within the closed system—and they cannot perceive anything outside their 2D field of vision. Nothing enters or leaves the system, at least not to the awareness of its inhabitants. A circle existing on the surface—which would appear as a single straight line, the ends further away then the center—is an obstruction to movement, just as a spherical rock is in 3D.[*]

Life progresses naturally and without incident until a 3D being observes the large bubble and decides to experiment. She takes a pin and inserts it into the bubble. To its inhabitants this is a miraculous event. From 'nowhere' an

---

[*] For an excellent introduction to higher dimensions, see Rudy Rucker's *The Fourth Dimension: A guided tour of the higher universes* (Boston: Houghton Mifflin Co., 1984).

impassable point has appeared in their world: an anomalous metallic 'circle'. As the 3D being further inserts the pin, passing a rusted section through the surface of the bubble, its denizens watch as the object changes color, seemingly of its own accord. She then removes the pin completely, and it disappears from their reality.

The 3D woman in this thought exercise has a greater, multidimensional perception of reality. She can understand the 2D world and the effect she has on it. She also has a greater amount of control over the 2D realm on account of her greater awareness. The 2D beings, with a less expansive perception of reality, cannot conceive of the existence of a higher world, let alone a higher being. Certainly those who observed the frightful intrusion into their reality were scoffed at by the more rigidly dogmatic of their species. And perhaps a little understood mystic spoke of the "gods", who could enter and leave their world at will; of life as an 'illusion'; and theorized higher worlds perceptible only with higher degrees of awareness.

Hyperdimensional physics posits that our world exists enmeshed in higher dimensions. Einstein explained gravity as the effect of hyperdimensional 'curvature' of spacetime. Some theorists, like physicist John Wheeler, have proposed that matter itself is a 3D 'projection' from a higher dimension, much like billiard balls will 'project' protrusions when placed upon a rubber sheet. Many of these theories see the universe as existing within a hyperdimensional 'film' or membrane, like Linde's bubbles. Just as we exist on the thin film of a dimensional bubble, so can other bubbles exist, and bubbles within bubbles— higher worlds. And just as bubbles can collide, perhaps cosmic bubbles also do so, causing our worlds to intersect. In such moments, contact between universes is possible.

Multilevelness and Psychopathy

Polish psychiatrist Kazimierz Dąbrowski pioneered the study of multilevelness in human development with his theory of "positive disintegration", which has a direct bearing on this work. The impetus for his theory came from the observation that gifted individuals are often psychoneurotic, i.e. they experience intense inner conflicts, or "disintegrative" states, from which they grow, while most others live a relatively stable or "integrated" life, without much inner conflict and growth. An expert in child development and psychopathology, Dąbrowski identified several qualitatively distinct levels of human development, both in his historical research of famous personalities and his extensive clinical work.[*]

---

[*] The results of Dąbrowski's extensive studies are presented in his encyclopedic *Multilevelness of Emotional and Instinctive Functions* (Lublin: Towarzystwo Naukowe Katolickiego Uniwersytetu Lubelskiego, 1996). His *Personality-shaping Through Positive Disintegration* (Boston: Little Brown & Co., 1967) is an excellent introduction to the theory of positive disintegration and its implications for the evolution of individuals and societies.

While the theory cannot be adequately summarized within the confines of this space, some generalities will suffice for our purpose. According to the theory, higher levels of development cannot be achieved without the disintegration of lower mental structures, lower structures tending to be automatic and habitual, higher structures increasingly autonomous and conscious. At lower levels, especially psychopathy, the intellect is merely an instrument used in the pursuit of primitive drives; at higher levels it is influenced by empathy and a hierarchy of values. 'Will' progresses from biological/environmental determination to something higher and *self*-directed.

Knight-Jadczyk uses Castaneda's term "predator's mind" to refer to the lower structures innate to us all—the base "names of God" (which is the Sufi term for the same thing). We are at our weakest and most vulnerable to manipulation when we act under the influence of such drives, or when our lack of discernment prevents us from seeing their manifestation in others, especially our leaders. (Dąbrowski was very aware of the consequences of such blindness. He suffered under the Nazi and Soviet regimes—both characterized by the disproportionate influence of psychopathic individuals—in his homeland, Poland.) Luckily we have the ability to identify higher and lower levels *within ourselves*, sublimating the lower levels and choosing to embody higher ones. Dąbrowski called this universal or *global* development, psychopathic identification with lower levels being *one-sided* development. The former could be called the path of "service to others", as it is grounded in selflessness, empathy, and understanding others; the latter, the epitome of "service to self", as it is grounded in selfishness, narcissism, self-importance, and arrogance.

These concepts, grounded in an empirical study of human development, provide a rich scientific framework for contemplating the material presented in the final chapters of this work. Terms such as "death", "second birth", "authentic self", "objective love", and the "shamanic ascent" acquire deeper meaning, as do the concepts of spiritual entropy and creativity, the "names or faces of God", and the "higher self". A multilevel approach to human development also puts the hyperdimensional aspects of Knight-Jadczyk's theory into perspective. If the universe is multidimensional; if we are, in fact, multidimensional beings whose awareness is limited to our *present* level, a "future self" and our possible interaction with it becomes intelligible. The implications of such a conception of reality are far-reaching.

A hyperdimensional being—more specifically, a *multidimensional* being with a greater awareness of reality, i.e., with less limits on perception—would most likely have the understanding, and ability, to manipulate the causal laws of our world at will. An event artificially manufactured, influenced, or exploited (e.g. a staged miracle, a stage-managed conflict, a convenient natural disaster) in our "past" can have a predicted effect in our "future".[*] An understanding of such

---

[*] As Dr. Arkadiusz Jadczyk points out in his afterword to this book, causal (time) loops are a necessary aspect of many hyperdimensional theories. Put simply, time travel is theoretically plausible in such theories.

laws would undoubtedly delight a cosmic Machiavellian (a hyperdimensional being of "one-sided" development). Only with such a hyperdimensional understanding does "conspiracy" begin to make sense.

As Knight-Jadczyk observed in her study of conspiracies over twenty years ago, 'conspiracy researchers' hypothesize grand conspiratorial traditions, passed down through the ages in some super secret society or brotherhood—Freemasons, Templars, Jewish Mystics, holy bloodlines, the Illuminati, etc. However, an analysis of key players involved in such conspiracies shows that such individuals are most often psychopathic—they are ruled by primitive instincts and short-term gratification, lacking the emotions that promote social bonds and love. In short, they are ruthless, and *reckless*, in their pursuit of power. How do we reconcile a trans-millennial blueprint for world domination with the extremely selfish, and shortsighted, nature of those who *seek* world domination? How do we reconcile what appear to be teleological ends to long chains of events, with the unlikely possibility that the criminal-minded people who influence such events can actually envision and manage such a "selfless" plan? It appears that the observable phenomena of conspiracy are merely proximate mechanisms, while the ultimate cause lies elsewhere.

Not only that, the traces of such conspiracies often lead to dead ends. One group is destroyed and another seemingly takes its place, with no obvious connection to suggest an honorary "passing of the torch". Rather, the roots of Machiavellian groups seem more like a social disease, adapting to and infecting those societies whose immune systems are weak. In other words, it is a 'natural', causative, and automatic process that can be understood and, with knowledge of these processes, either prevented or *manipulated to reach a desired end*. The question then becomes, how is this done if those who occupy the inspirational roles of such conspiracies—psychopaths—are themselves unaware of such 'ends'?

In this regard, the work of Andrzej Łobaczewski, a contemporary of Dąbrowski , and author of *Political Ponerology: A science on the nature of evil adjusted for political purposes* (Grande Prairie: Red Pill Press, 2006), provides important details. Not only does he correctly identify the pathological nature of totalitarian systems of government and their key features—the inspirational role of psychopathy, the necessity of total war on two fronts for the system's survival (i.e. a well-armed external threat, and the internal threat posed by its own people), double language to cloak its true motives, etc.—he also describes the social processes by which such groups gain influence and eventually rule nations. These processes provide a possible explanation for how conspiracies appear and why they seem, on the surface, to be so vast in scope.

Simply put, the statistical presence of psychopathic individuals (1-4% of any given population) and normal people's inability to detect them inevitably causes the moral deterioration of any social group (religious, political, corporate). Psychopaths, well known for their ability to mask their own predatory nature with a convincing "mask of sanity", infiltrate such groups, using their ideology as a Trojan Horse with which they rise to power. In such a way, crimes against humanity are cloaked in moral and humanistic terms. It is therefore likely that the traces observed by conspiracy researchers of long-term conspiracies by "secret societies" are merely the naïve and exploited ideological garments cloaking a more sinister reality; perverted morality couched in high-sounding ideals and magnanimous goals. Meanwhile, the "true believers" of such groups are viewed with contempt by the inner circle. The psychopaths, characteristically operating behind the scenes, use normal people's inherent benevolence and concern for their descendants' future as a body in which to keep their social cancer alive. When such a group dies, or ceases to provide adequate cover for psychopathic ends, the seeds will already have been sown in some other well intentioned, but inadequately protected, ideology.

Ufology and the 'Alien' Threat

The implications of this reality should be clear, for both UFO science and the UFO cover-up. Even a well-intentioned cover-up, due to its inherent secrecy, is ripe for ponerogenesis (the genesis of evil). The same goes for UFO study groups dealing with such a controversial topic. Without an adequate multilevel understanding of humanity, we are left vulnerable to the whims of con men in all areas of life. And without the experience of *seeing* such manipulations on our own level, we are left vulnerable to the manipulations of hyperdimensional beings of even more cunning—like so-called 'authoritarian personalities' who will defend our leaders, no matter how corrupt and abusive, rationalizing the behaviour of established authorities.* Knight-Jadczyk cites some disturbing examples of such "Stockholm syndrome" within ufology. Unfortunately, blindness to pathological behavior is the first criterion for its genesis.

Dr. David Jacobs, Associate Professor of History at Temple University, is one of the few prominent researchers to see the alien abduction phenomenon for what it is. His book, *The Threat: Revealing the secret alien agenda* (New York: Fireside, 1999), is the result of his experience with numerous abductees. Interestingly, he provides a description of 'alien' and 'hybrid' behavior that is startlingly familiar. While abductees report that their abductors display normal human emotions (love, happiness, anger, laughter, sadness),

> There is ... an emotional component of some hybrids that is unacceptable—and out of control. It is as if some hybrids have been *improperly socialized* and are running loose, *doing whatever they please*. They have strong sexual drives, but they are *not controlled by social constraints*. ... Intentional cruelty is an important component of hybrid interaction with abductees—especially in sexual situations. ... Some hybrids demonstrate such cruelty that their "projects" live in fear of being subjected to it again. Deborah's case is a good example of an

---

* Dr. Bob Altemeyer's free online book on the subject, *The Authoritarians*, is an insightful and disturbing look at the thought patterns of "Right Wing Authoritarians".
<http://home.cc.umanitoba.ca/~altemey/>

abusive relationship in which the hybrid *rules through fear, intimidation, and punishment.* (Jacobs, 177, 197-8, emphasis added)

Jacobs describes episodes of psychopathic behaviour that could have come directly from the pages of Cleckley or Hare.[*] In a word, sadism. Jacobs speculates:

> It is also possible that the malevolent behavior of hybrids toward abductees is necessary. Perhaps they need to generate fear, intimidation, guilt, shame, and humiliation to fulfill the objectives of their agenda ... it is possible that the *human genes* in the hybrids might be responsible [for this behavior]. Because the late-state hybrids are mainly human, they have strong sexual drives but *little conscience.* It is as if they have human attributes but *lack human controls.* (Jacobs, 206-7, emphasis added)

Jacobs is describing psychopathy, a very "human" disorder. Psychopaths are known above all else for their charm, to appear as "normal" as anyone else. But it is all an act. Beneath the surface they are ruthless, sadistic, and callous. As Łobaczewski describes, psychopaths will often present themselves as the ideal lover and companion, only to "transform" after the wedding into an abusive authoritarian.[*] Once they have their prey (i.e. wife) cornered, they can safely remove their mask of sanity. After all, who would believe that such a charming, healthy, stable husband would do the things his wife says he does?

If Jacobs is correct in his observations, the "aliens" do not seem to be creating a "new" race. They are increasing the number of one that already exists. This is interesting considering the periods of time at which this has occurred 'naturally', in the periods of time Łobaczewski refers to as "pathocratic" (e.g. 'Nazi' Germany, 'Soviet' Russia). If such beings, like human sadists, *feed* on the suffering of others, they seem to be manipulating the laws of ponerogenesis for a maximum payoff. They are doing so by manipulating human psychology and promoting psychopathy, that is, beings "like them". Unless we want to be "saved" by such beings—as the population of ancient Palestine was "saved" by the Assyrian empire, or pagans were 'saved' by the Christian empire—the first step *must* be an education on the nature of human psychopathy. All else follows.

—Harrison Koehli

Harrison Koehli is an internet essayist and co-editor of the alternative news website sott.net. His writings deal with psychopathy and politics, and he is

---

[*] The first comprehensive work on psychopathy was Hervey Cleckley's *The Mask of Sanity: An attempt to reinterpret the so-called psychopathic personality* (St. Louis: The C. V. Mosby Company, 1941). It is available for download at <www.cassiopaea.org/cass/ sanity_1.pdf>. Robert Hare is one of the present authorities on psychopathy. His *Without Conscience: The disturbing world of psychopaths among us* (New York: Guilford Press, 1999) is an excellent introduction.

[*] Sandra Brown's comprehensive work, *Women Who Love Psychopaths* (Health and Well-being Publications, 2008), deals with this very subject.

currently collaborating on a graphic novel dealing with these subjects entitled When Psychopaths Rule. *An authority on ponerology, he has appeared on Dr. Kevin Barrett's "Dynamic Duo" radio program and Dustin Cantwell's "Fane of the Cosmos". He studied jazz performance and religious studies at Grant MacEwan College and the University of Alberta. He also maintains the website <http://ponerology.com>.*

introduction

ufo science and religion

Almost thirty years ago, I received my first formal training in hypnosis. Over the years, I not only sought out additional training, I employed this skill on behalf of many troubled individuals. Until 1994, I had never encountered what is popularly known as an "abductee"—that is, an individual claiming to have been abducted by alleged aliens. I have to admit that when I did, it presented certain problems both in terms of having a well-established technique to deal with it, as well as my own categories of what is or is not possible.

I often tell people in a sort of joking way: of all the people who *never* wanted to know anything about aliens and UFOs, I deserve a place at the head of the line. Very few people really understand how deeply serious this remark is. When I opened the door to consider the possibility—quite remote as I thought—of the *possibility* of "other worldly" visitors, life as I knew it ended. That was thirteen years ago. But then, a completely new life was born from the ashes. And so, here I am producing a book about UFOs and aliens. The road from there to here has been difficult, to understate the matter, and complicated by all the high strangeness that seems to surround the subject.

The term *high strangeness* is attributed to Dr. J. Allen Hynek who addressed the United Nations on the subject of UFOs on November 27, 1978 in the following way:

> Mr. Chairman, there exists today a world-wide phenomenon... indeed if it were not world-wide I should not be addressing you and these representatives from many parts of the world. There exists a global phenomenon the scope and extent of which is not generally recognized. It is a phenomenon so *strange and foreign to our daily terrestrial mode of thought* that it is frequently met by ridicule and derision by persons and organizations unacquainted with the facts...
>
> I refer, of course, to the phenomenon of UFOs... Unidentified Flying Objects... which I should like to define here simply as "any aerial or surface sighting, or instrumental recording (e.g., radar, photography, etc.) which remains unexplained by conventional methods even after competent examination by qualified persons."
>
> You will note, Mr. Chairman, that this definition says nothing about little green men from outer space, or manifestations from spiritual realms, or various psychic manifestations. It simply states an operational definition. A cardinal mistake, and a source of great confusion, has been the almost universal

substitution of an interpretation of the UFO phenomenon for the phenomenon itself.

This is akin to having ascribed the Aurora Borealis to angelic communication before we understood the physics of the solar wind.

Nonetheless, in the popular mind the UFO phenomenon is associated with the concept of extra-terrestrial intelligence and this might yet prove to be correct *in some context...*

We have on record many tens of thousands of UFO reports... they include extremely intriguing and provocative accounts of strange events experienced by highly reputable persons... events which challenge our present conception of the world about us and which may indeed signal a need for a change in some of these concepts...

Mr. Chairman, any phenomenon which touches the lives of so many people, and which engenders puzzlement and even fear among them, is therefore not only of potential scientific interest and significance but also of sociological and political significance, especially since it carries with it many *implications of the existence of intelligences other than our own...*

Speaking then for myself as an astronomer, and I believe for many of my colleagues as well, there is no longer any question in my mind of the importance of this subject...

Mr. Chairman, I have not always held the opinion that UFOs were worthy of serious scientific study. I began my work as Scientific Consultant to the U.S. Air Force as an open skeptic, in the firm belief that we were dealing with a mental aberration and a public nuisance. Only in the face of stubborn facts and data similar to those studied by the French commission... have I been forced to change my opinion...

The UFO phenomenon, as studied by my colleagues and myself, bespeaks the action of some form of intelligence... but whence this intelligence springs, whether it is truly extra-terrestrial, or bespeaks *a higher reality not yet recognized by science*, or even if it be in some way or another a strange psychic manifestation of our own intelligence, is much the question. We seek your help, Mr. Chairman, in assisting scientists, and particularly those already associated with the many formal and informal investigative organizations around the world, by providing a clearing house procedure whereby the work already going on globally can be brought together in a serious, concentrated approach to this most outstanding challenge to current science. (Emphasis added.)

I would like to draw your attention to particular remarks made by Dr. Hynek in the passage quoted above:

[A] global phenomenon ... *so strange and foreign to our daily terrestrial mode of thought...* it carries with it many implications of the existence of intelligences other than our own... [It] bespeaks the action of some form of intelligence... but whence this intelligence springs, whether it is truly extra-terrestrial, or bespeaks a higher reality not yet recognized by science, or even if it be in some way or another a strange psychic manifestation of our own intelligence, is much the question...

These remarks address the high strangeness factor. High strangeness describes those UFO cases that are not only peculiar but that can often be utterly absurd.

high strangeness

In some cases, there are events before, during, and after the "sighting proper" imbued with elements of time and space distortion, bizarre synchronicities, strange states of consciousness, beings that act absurdly, strange 'creatures' associated with the sighting, but not necessarily part of the sighting, anomalous phone calls, electronic glitches, paranormal events including poltergeist type activity, and what are popularly known as *men in black* (MIBs). Researcher John Keel's book *The Mothman Prophecies* deals with all these subjects, and is an excellent introduction to the subject of high strangeness.

In a paper on high strangeness, French scientist Jacques Vallee and Eric Davis write:

> A primary objection to the reality of Unidentified Aerial Phenomena events among scientists is that witnesses consistently report objects whose seemingly absurd behavior "cannot possibly" be related to actual phenomena, even under extreme conditions... Skeptics insist that superior beings, celestial ambassadors or intelligent extraterrestrial (ETI) visitors simply would not perpetrate such antics as are reported in the literature.

In one case, a farmer in Minnesota, Mr. Simonton, claimed that a craft hovered in his barnyard and strange swarthy oriental looking men offered him a jug which he filled with water and then gave him pancakes. Dr. Hynek had the little cakes analyzed and found they lacked any salt content. Vallee noted that saltless cakes are often a feature of fairy myths, a connection which would appear again and again in his research (see Vallee, 1969).

Another case was that of a Belgian farmer who saw a UFO land in his field. He approached the craft and a small "alien" came up to him and asked him for the time! The farmer replied with the requested information. The alien told him he was wrong and pointed a wand at him which paralyzed him until the alien had departed in his craft. When the authorities investigated the case, they found a circle of destroyed flora on the landing site, and it was reported that even the soil was damaged from something like extreme heat exposure.

When you read enough raw data from the many thousands of cases, you get the deep impression that the witnesses are telling the truth about what they have experienced. Why would a couple of farmers make up such ridiculous, nonsensical stories? Testimony was obtained to show their mental stability and competence. They never made any money from their stories, and they certainly weren't after fame. In fact, they suffered more from telling their stories than if they had just kept quiet.

Such cases are not isolated. There are many with such bizarre elements. Something is certainly happening to these people, and it is something that has both physical and psychological components. Nevertheless, this high strangeness factor is a problem because it's all too easy to dismiss or ignore such "reports" because of these ridiculous claims. One has to wonder if this "high strangeness" isn't deliberate—and for that very reason. This brings us to consider the signal to noise factor.

introduction

Dr. Hynek wrote in a paper presented at the AIAA 13th Aerospace Sciences Meeting Pasadena, Calif., January 20-22, 1975, entitled "The Emerging Picture of the UFO Problem":

But one element that is common to all scientific endeavor is the problem of signal-to-noise ratio; in the UFO phenomenon this problem is a major one. The UFO problem is, initially, a signal-to-noise problem. *The noise is, and has been, so great that the existence of a signal has been seriously questioned.* Isaac Asimov, whom no one could accuse of lacking in imagination, writes:

"Eyewitness reports of actual space ships and actual extraterrestrials are, in themselves, totally unreliable. There have been numerous eyewitness reports of almost everything that most rational people do not care to accept—of ghosts, angels, levitation, zombies, werewolves, and so on... The trouble is, that whatever the UFO phenomenon is, it comes and goes unexpectedly. There is no way of examining it systematically. It appears suddenly and accidentally, is partially seen, and then is more or less inaccurately reported. We remain dependent on occasional anecdotal accounts". (*From the December 14, 1974 issue of TV Guide, a media magazine with a very great circulation and hence powerful in forming public opinion.*)

Here we see a very important part of the UFO problem, that of the presentation of data to men of science, and to men, like Asimov and others who excel in writing about science.

Scientific efforts can be seriously hampered if the popular image of a subject is grossly misleading. Funds can be curtailed and good men of science who wish to give time to the subject are apt to face misrepresentation whenever their work receives any public attention. Ball lightning is just as much an unknown as the UFO phenomenon, yet scientists can openly discuss these "balls of light" but are likely to be censured if they talk about similar unidentified lights which last much longer, are brighter, and move over greater distances, but are labeled UFOs. Proper presentation of the UFO phenomenon to the media may not seem an integral part of the UFO problem, per se, but its effects loom large.

The signal-to-noise aspect of the UFO problem is aggravated to a high degree because the signal is a totally unexpected signal, and represents an entirely new set of empirical observations which do not fit into any existing framework in any of the accepted scientific disciplines. One may even contemplate that the signal itself signals the birth of a new scientific discipline.

I return to the out-of-hand dismissal of the UFO phenomenon by persons like Isaac Asimov, in part, because of the poor presentation of the data to such persons. This is an important facet of the UFO problem itself and must be taken into account if we are to make any progress with the study of the signal.

An analogy may be useful here: In the isolation of radium, Mme. Curie was obliged to work through tons of pitchblende to obtain a minuscule amount of radium. Yet there was no question of the signal in the "pitchblende noise". The radioactivity of the pitchblende was unquestioned. Let us suppose that instead there had been a rumor—an old wives' tale, or an alchemist's story—that there existed a miraculous unknown element which could be used in the transmutation of elements, and which had miraculous healing powers and other exotic properties. Would any scientist, on the basis of such an alchemist's tale, have done what Mme. Curie did to lift the signal out of the noise of tons of pitchblende? Hardly. Mme. Curie *knew* that there was a signal—it wasn't a rumor. And although the labor was immense, there was a definite, scientifically accepted methodology for separating the signal from the noise.

Now, in the UFO problem we did not know at the start that there was a signal—there were merely tales, unacceptable to scientists as a body. Only those of us, through a long exposure to the subject, or motivated by a haunting curiosity to work in the field and to get our hands dirty with the raw data, came to know there was a signal.

We *know* that we cannot find a trivial solution to the problem, i.e., a common sense solution that the phenomenon is either entirely a matter of misidentification, hallucinations, and hoaxes, or a known phenomenon of nature, e.g., of a meteorological nature. We know that there exists a subset of UFO reports of high strangeness and high witness credibility for which no one—and I emphasize—*no one*, has been able to ascribe a viable explanation. But the Isaac Asimovs and the trained scientists, as well as large segments of the public, do not know this. And we cannot expect them to know this unless we present data to them properly and thus provide motivation to study the subject. We who have worked in the UFO field are somewhat in the position of Einstein who wrote to Arnold Sommerfeld in response to Sommerfeld's skepticism of the General Theory of Relativity:

"You will accept the General Theory of Relativity when you have studied it. Therefore I will not utter a word in its defense."

Emotional defense of the UFO phenomenon is pointless; the facts, properly presented, must speak for themselves.

With the noise level so high, and with the popular interpretation of UFOs as visitors from outer space rather than simply what their initials stand for, Unidentified Flying Objects—an unidentified phenomenon whose origin we do not know—it is very difficult for one to be motivated to study the subject.

The noise in the UFO problem is two-fold. There is the obvious noise, and also the more "sophisticated" noise, which *might even be part of the signal*. The obvious noise is akin to that well known to any scientist. An astronomer recognizes the noise of errors of observation, of instrumental errors, or that introduced by atmospheric distortion, by photon statistics, etc.

In our problem the noise is likewise comprised of errors of observation (though to a much greater degree), but also to wishful thinking, deliberate substitution of interpretation of an event for the event itself, as, "I saw a space ship last night" for "I saw a light in the sky last night", and the totally extraneous noise of the unbalanced imaginations of the pseudo-religious fanatics who propagate unfounded stories and who uncritically accept anything and everything that appeals to their warped imaginations...

The question of whether the UFO phenomenon is a manifestation of some type of intelligence, whether extraterrestrial, "meta-terrestrial", or indeed some aspect of our own, is a critical one.

Certainly, in those close encounter cases in which creatures or occupants, ostensibly the pilots of the craft, are reported, intelligent behavior of some sort seems obvious. Even if the occupants are robots, a more distant intelligence is implied. The almost universally reported response to detection by these occupants is an important part of the picture; upon detection the creatures are reported to disappear quickly and take off. Except in certain cases, there appears to be no desire for any involvement with the human race...

5

introduction

Given the elements of the present picture of the UFO phenomenon, it is clear that any viable hypothesis that meets these picture elements satisfactorily will be, according to present views, "far out".

There have been other times in the history of science when striking departures from classical concepts were necessary. Since new hypotheses must in some way use present knowledge as a springboard, it is a sobering thought to contemplate that the gap between the springboard of the known and a viable UFO hypothesis might even be so great as to prevent the formulation of an acceptable hypothesis at present.

Thus, for example, only a century ago, an inconsequential period of time in total history, the best scientific minds could not have envisioned the nuclear processes which we now feel certain take place in the deep interiors of stars. The question of energy production on the sun capable of maintaining the sun's prodigious outflow of energy for hundreds of millions of years—a time period demanded by the fossil history millions of years—was simply not answerable by any hypothesis conceivable to the scientists of a century ago.

It is indeed sobering, yet challenging, to consider that the entire UFO phenomenon may be only the tip of the proverbial iceberg in signaling an entirely new domain of the knowledge of nature as yet totally unexplored, as unexplored and as unimagined as nuclear processes would have been a century ago.

Dr. Hynek is often referred to as the father of rigorous scientific UFO investigation. He was a scientific consultant for the Air Force's UFO investigation, Project Bluebook which later research shows to have been intended to debunk the subject (see Dolan, 2002). But after studying so many credible cases, Dr. Hynek went on to found the Center For UFO Studies (CUFOS). He also invented the classification for UFO sightings, terming the phrase *close encounter*. He is the author of the landmark UFO book, *The UFO Experience: A Scientific Study*. Dr. Hynek served as director of CUFOS until his passing in 1986.

Regarding Hynek's idea that we may be dealing with "an entirely new domain of the knowledge of nature", his friend and associate, Jacques Vallee has interesting comments to make:

[C]urrent hypotheses are not strange enough to explain the facts of the phenomenon, and the debate suffers from a lack of scientific information. Indeed, from the viewpoint of modern physics, our Cosmic Neighborhood could encompass other (parallel) universes, extra spatial dimensions and other time-like dimensions beyond the common 4-dimensional spacetime we recognize, and such aspects could lead to rational explanations for apparently "incomprehensible" behaviors on the part of entities emerging into our perceived continuum.

As it attempts to reconcile theory with observed properties of elementary particles and with discoveries at the frontiers of cosmology, modern physics suggests that mankind has not yet discovered all of the universe's facets, and we must propose new theories and experiments in order to explore these undiscovered facets. *This is why continuing study of reported anomalous events is important: It may provide us with an existence theorem for new models of physical reality.*

6

Much of the recent progress in cosmological concepts is directly applicable to the problem: Traversable wormholes (3-dimensional hypersurface tunnels) have now been derived from Einstein's General Theory of Relativity (Morris and Thorne, 1988; Visser, 1995). In particular, it has been shown that Einstein's General Theory of Relativity does not in any way constrain spacetime topology, which allows for wormholes to provide traversable connections between regions within two separate universes or between remote regions and/or times within the same universe.

Mathematically it can also be shown that higher-dimensional wormholes can provide hypersurface connections between multidimensional spaces (Rucker, 1984; Kaku, 1995).

Recent quantum gravity programs have explored this property in superstring theory, along with proposals to theoretically and experimentally examine macroscopic-scale extra-dimensional spaces (Schwarzschild, 2000).

Thus it is now widely acknowledged that the nature of our universe is far more complex than observations based on anthropocentric self-selection portend...

No experiment can distinguish between phenomena manifested by visiting interstellar (arbitrarily advanced) ETI (extra-terrestrial intelligence) and intelligent entities that may exist near Earth within a parallel universe or in different dimensions, or who are (terrestrial) time travelers...

If we must formulate a view of the problem in a single statement at this point, that statement will be:

Everything works as if UAPs (Unidentified Aerial Phenomenon) were the products of a technology that integrates physical and psychic phenomena and primarily affects cultural variables in our society through manipulation of physiological and psychological parameters in the witnesses. (Vallee and Davis)

As I have written in my books and publications on our website, www.cassiopaea.org, I have *never* seen an "alien" that I know of as an alien with any certainty. I have no conscious awareness or memory of any such thing as a "typical abduction" or an encounter with an alien in any semblance of a conscious state of mind. Indeed, in this book I am going to talk about certain "encounters" that are "highly suggestive", but there is a certain ambiguity about them that relates directly to this issue of "state of mind", and this ambiguity leaves the event always in question as far as I am concerned. I certainly have as good an imagination as the average person if I need it to solve a problem, but after raising five children, there is little "imaginative flying" going on in my head and a lot of being practical and finding out what is really going on.

In my book, *Amazing Grace*, I chronicled a number of my own experiences of surpassing strangeness, though I never thought of these events in terms of "aliens". Until I was 41 years old, I never saw anything that I might have thought—by any stretch of the imagination—could be a UFO, and when, at that late date, I finally did see something of such extraordinary configuration and behavior, I immediately tried to find a "plausible excuse" for it so I could "go back to sleep". But, as Hynek said, there are certainly things for which we cannot find a common sense solution. It is at such a point, when all avenues of identification and explanation have been exhausted, that the individual who is "motivated by a haunting curiosity" goes to work in the field, gets their hands dirty in the raw data, and realizes that there is, most certainly, a signal even if it is a signal that suggests an intelligence so strange and foreign to our daily terrestrial mode of thought that we are stunned by the implication. That implication can be shattering to our sense of safety: that the UFO phenomenon may be signaling "*an entirely new domain of the knowledge of nature as yet totally unexplored,* as unexplored and as unimagined as nuclear processes would have been a century ago". It was partly as a consequence of this event that I began the experiment that resulted in the "Cassiopaean transmissions". After a certain amount of research, after facing the high strangeness factor repeatedly, I understood clearly something that Jacques Vallee proposes in his paper cited above:

> The cognitive mismatch or Incommensurability Problem between human and ET cultures will guarantee that the latter will develop communication techniques *other than radio*. ET cultures may be sending radio and optical signals to Earth now but they may also be sending signals in a variety of other forms such as holographic images, psychic or other consciousness-related signals, modulated neutrinos, gamma ray bursters, wormhole-modulated starlight caustics, signals generated by gravitational lensing techniques, modulated X-rays, quantum teleported signals, or some quantum field theoretic effect...

Vallee has touched upon the very issues that my husband, Arkadiusz Jadczyk, has discussed in the foreword to this book. Most of this material included in the Foreword was published by him long before Vallee wrote the above paper, though it seems likely that Vallee was moving in this direction for quite some time as evidenced in his book *Forbidden Science.* In the Epilogue, Vallee talks a little bit about physics, parallel realities, hyperspace:

> Cosmology now recognizes the possibility, indeed the inevitability, of multiple universes with more than four dimensions. Communication and travel within our universe are no longer thought to be absolutely constrained by the speed of light and a constant arrow of time. Even travel into the past may be considered without necessarily creating insurmountable paradoxes. This is a tremendously exciting development. It opens up vast new realms for theoretical and experimental endeavor...
>
> If we look at the world from an informational point of view, and if we consider the many complex ways in which time and space may be structured, the old idea of space travel and interplanetary craft to which most technologists are still clinging appears not only obsolete, but ludicrous. Indeed, modern physics has already bypassed it, offering a very different interpretation of what [an] "extraterrestrial" system might look like...
>
> For some time various knowledgeable friends have urged me to take my research behind the scenes again. I intend to follow their advice. I cannot justify remaining associated with the field of ufology as it presents itself to the public today. Furthermore, I suspect that the phenomenon displays a very different structure once you leave behind the parochial disputes that disfigure the debate,

confusing the researchable issues that interest me. The truly important scientific questions are elsewhere.

While it is true that Dr. Hynek, Dr. Vallee, and my husband, Dr. Jadczyk, were working for years in the direction of these ideas, what is amazing is that the Cassiopaean communications also discussed the same things in considerable detail with me, an amateur whose driving interest was in finding out why the world was the way it was and humanity's role within it. Certainly, this is often the same drive that operates in scientists—those scientists who actually do "good science" with an open mind—but it necessarily has different results from the efforts of the layperson in most cases. In my own case, however, the results have been quite similar: scientific theories and mind-expanding concepts regarding an "entirely new domain of the knowledge of nature". This was the gift of the Cassiopaeans.

At the same time, there is much in the Cassiopaean Material that is strikingly similar to philosophical concepts native to certain esoteric teachings, most particularly Sufi ideas and the system brought forward by Georges Gurdjieff and Boris Mouravieff, and most recently in the psychological theories of Polish psychologists Kazimierz Dąbrowski and Andrzej Łobaczewski. Gurdjieff and Mouravieff claim to be presenting something called *esoteric Christianity*. What I have discovered in my own research is that this esoteric Christianity is quite similar to Archaic Siberian Shamanism, the degraded remnant of what must have been the "religion" of the Northern Peoples—the Megalith builders—in prehistoric times. I have traced these developments and laid out all the clues in my book *The Secret History of the World*, also published by Red Pill Press.

How we view our world and our place in it is entirely dependent on what we know about what went before. What became overwhelmingly apparent as I continued in my research was that the true history of man has been so distorted by "official culture" as to make it almost impossible for the average person to really understand why the world is as it is, and what possible role humanity may play in the grander scheme of things.

Tracking the processes of history certainly gave me an uneasy feeling that there was some sort of "pattern" to it which certainly could not be a conspiracy in human terms. Until I opened my mind to the possibility of "alien interactions with humanity", and began to consider the many implications of such ideas—most particularly time loops and alternate universes—nothing about the history of mankind made any sense at all.

Most assuredly, historians of ancient times face two constant problems: the scarcity of evidence, and how to fit the evidence that *is* known into the larger context of other evidence, not to mention the context of the time to which it belongs. Very often historians have to use what could be described as a more or less "legal method" for deciding which bit of evidence has more or less weight than another. For example, most of what we know about ancient times comes to us in polemics written by adversaries of a particular group or idea—political propaganda of ancient times. These polemics survived because they were "favored" by the elite rulers or conquerors, and the "inside knowledge" of the group in question is lost because they may have been destroyed along with their material. In this respect, it is much easier to "refute than confirm". A difference of emphasis can be as telling as a new discovery.

Fortunately, ancient history is not "static" in the sense that we can say we know all there is to know now simply because the subject is about the "past". For example, the understanding of ancient history of our own fathers and grandfathers was, of necessity, more limited than our own due to the fact that much material has been discovered and come to light in the past two or three generations through archaeology and other historical sciences.

But more important to this process is the consideration of *manipulation* of facts. If you are judging history by a kind of legal method, it becomes crucial to know who is or is not likely to be telling the truth. Often, the only way to determine that is to evaluate what Georges Dumézil referred to as the "line of force". When we have taken a particular text apart and have ascertained, as much as possible, the approximate legitimacy of each element, there still remains another question that actually constitutes the essence of the matter: What are the main trends of the whole? What are the lines of force running through the *ideological field* in which the details are placed? This is often where religion enters the picture, acting as the lens through which we view our past and the scale by which we judge the merits of testimony.

Regarding religion, and most particularly the religions that hold sway over our world such as Christianity born of Judaism, we simply cannot overstress the importance of deep and serious study. We cannot ignore the question of whether or not Christianity, Judaism and Islam are "true", and why, if they are *not*, they have spread and persisted. If they are not true, we need to evaluate a proper response to them.

As many regular readers of our website know, due to our willingness to study and discuss the controversial subjects dealt with primarily in this book, we have been accused of being a "cult". I've had a lot of trouble dealing with that accusation because every such claim has been a lie, and they've all been made by members of *real cults*—scary ones, too. The Oxford English dictionary entry for 'cult' states: 1. a system of religious worship, esp. as expressed in *ritual*. 2. A devotion or homage to a person or thing. 2b. A popular fashion esp. followed by a specific section of society 3. denoting a person or thing popularized in this way.

It is clear that the above description could easily apply to any of the organized religions prevalent today. Christianity, Judaism, Islam, Buddhism (and others) are replete and indeed founded on ritual and "devotion to a person or thing". However, they are not generally referred to as "cults". The term cult, in its modern and widely understood form, is reserved for any group formed under a *hierarchical structure*, where some form of *coercion or manipulation* of the group members exists. Generally there is also some *focus of worship*, be it the group leader(s) or some other outside personage or thing such as Jesus, Jehovah/Yahweh, Allah or the Tooth Fairy.

The issue of *justification for worship or allegiance*—that is, *the coercion and manipulation*—is usually tied to the perceived or stated benefits or potential benefits to be derived from belief, worship or allegiance. In other words, promises are made of heavenly rewards that can never be demonstrated or proven (no one has ever come back to tell us that heaven exists, nor is there any proof), promises of survival of the end of the world—to be the "Chosen People" who rule—or wine bearing *houris* who minister to the martyr in paradise—are all included in the *promises of the main cults* that dominate our world: Judaism, Christianity and Islam.

We, on the other hand, take the approach of a sort of scientific mysticism—where mystical claims are submitted to rational analysis and testing, and the required scientific proofs are modified to allow for the *nature of evidence from theorized realms outside our own* where ordinary scientific proofs might not apply.

And yet, again and again, we have had to address this issue of being labeled a "cult" because the accusations and mud keep flying.

In the beginning, it was very hard for me to understand why—after all, I was just a mother of five kids with a hobby publishing the results of my studies on the Internet, and one would think that doing that was allowed in a democratic society—but it became obvious that there are some fairly powerful groups on the planet who must be scared to death of this ordinary housewife as is evident from the extraordinary amount of effort put into trying to shut me up!

So far, when we have tracked the origins and connections of our accusers, we generally end up at powerful Christian or Jewish organizations with covert government or military ties that have a vested interest in maintaining their cultic controls over peoples' minds. At this point, the Islamic groups haven't gone after us, but that's only because we have been pointing out that the Muslims are on the short end of the stick in this go-round.

The fact is, as far as I am concerned, Islam—as a monotheistic religion that promotes an "object of worship"—is no better than Christianity or Judaism—all three of them are, historically speaking, vile, bloody, violent cults. What is going on in the Middle East today—this conflict that threatens to blow up the whole planet (and if you don't know that this is the case, you have not been paying attention!), is just more of the same old cult nonsense that has been playing out for the past two millennia.

Faith that can "move mountains" is promoted by cults—also known as the standard monotheistic religions—as the necessary thing that the "faithful" must cultivate in order to receive the benefits that are promised by the hierarchy. The example of Abraham's willingness to sacrifice his son, Isaac, has been trotted out for ages as the supreme example of how one is to approach the "god". One must be willing to give the god anything and everything! This "faith" is an essential part of the "covenant" with the god—a sort of "act of trade", so to say.

The story about the almost sacrifice of Abraham in the Bible is actually nearly identical to the Vedic story of Manu. These acts of sacrifice were based on what was called *sraddha* which is related to the words *fides, credo, faith, believe* and so on.

The word *sraddha* was, according to religious historians Dumézil and Levi, too hastily understood as "faith" in the Christian sense. Correctly understood, it means something like the trust a workman has in his tools to "shape or create" reality and techniques of sacrifice were, in the way of tools, similar to acts of magic!

Such "faith" is, therefore, part of a "covenant" wherein the sacrificer knows how to perform a prescribed sacrifice correctly, and who also knows that if he performs the sacrifice correctly, it *must* produce its effect.

In short, it is an act that is designed to gain control over the forces of life that reside in the god with whom one has made the covenant. Such gods as make covenants are not "literary ornaments" or abstractions. They are active partners with intelligence, strength, passion, and a tendency to *get out of control if the sacrifices are not performed correctly*. In this sense, the sacrifice—the "faith"— is simply black magic.

In another sense, the ascetic or "self-sacrificer", is a person who is *striving for release from the bondage and order of nature* by the act of attempting to mortify the self, the flesh; testing and increasing the will for the purpose of winning tyrannical powers while still in the world. But again, we see that through this self-sacrifice, he or she seeks *mastery of the gods*. It is, in short, manipulation and coercion at its most subtle to promote "faith" as the bringer of salvation.

What seems to be so is that it is generally individuals who have been "disenfranchised" or who feel helpless and at the mercy of the forces of life— whether they manifest through other people or random events—who are those most likely to seek such faith, such a covenant with a god. They feel acutely their own inability to have an effect in the world, and they turn their creativity inward to create and maintain their subjective "faith" in opposition to objective reality.

What is crucial to understand in all this is that fundamentalists of all kinds are basically "giving their will" away in exchange for promised benefits. This free will is their own power of creativity—their own possibility for growth and development that can only commutate and expand in the process of uncertainty, taking risks, and making free and willing exchanges with others that do *not* include dominance and manipulation.

The "absolute certainty" of the fundamentalist locks them into *entropy*, and their creative energy goes to feed a vast system of illusion. These systems are the creation and maintenance of the idols they worship. Like the paranoid schizophrenic, they devise baroque and ingenious systems of perception and define them as "given by god". They then spend an enormous amount of energy editing out all impressions that are contrary to their system of illusion.

Another aspect of the Man who must be Right that manifests in religious beliefs is that fundamentalists look down on others who do not share their faith. It is, at root, an "us vs. them" system that focuses its ironclad preconceptions so rigidly on "future benefits", that its adherents simply lose sight of the here and now.

Fundamentalists are more interested in dogma than in actual deeds in the moment. It is extremely important to get others to believe in their illusion in order to confirm its "rightness", even if they claim, on the surface, that "everyone has the right to their own opinion". The fact is, they cannot tolerate anyone else's opinion if it is different from their own because it threatens their "rightness".

This rightness *must* be maintained at all costs because, deep inside, the Right Man (or woman) is usually struggling with horror at their own helplessness. Their rightness is a dam that holds back their worst fears: that they are lost and alone and that there really is no god, because how could there be a god who loves them if they have to suffer so much? Their inability to feel truly loved and accepted deep within is, in effect, like being stranded in a nightmare from which they cannot wake up.

Faith. This is the thing that a "charismatic leader" utilizes to induce his followers to engage in violence against other human beings. This "faith"—this "rightness" of one's views, of one's god, and what the god is supposedly "revealing" to the leader—can be induced by manipulations and promises of heavenly or other rewards, and this can then be used to manipulate other people to do one's bidding.

And so it seems that the requirement of "faith" and "worship" of an object of cultic value such as Jehovah, Yahweh, Jesus or Allah is the means by which human beings can be induced to commit atrocities upon other human beings.

We see that the image of Abraham, who was willing to sacrifice his own son, is not so compelling a picture after all. It merely symbolizes a sort of mindless belief in the orders of someone or something "out there" that certainly may not have the best interests of humanity at heart.

We can perceive, in the willingness of Abraham to sacrifice his son, the Right Man terror of Cain who killed his brother because his sacrifice was not accepted. A god who picks and chooses what sacrifice is "good enough"—setting brother against brother—is certainly a "jealous god", and such a god is a psychopath.

The main template of Christianity—received directly from Judaism—is that of *sin*. The history of *sin* from that point to now, is a story of its triumph. Awareness of the nature of *sin* led to a growth industry in agencies and techniques for dealing with it. These agencies became centers of economic and military power, as they are today.

Christianity—promoting the ideals of Judaism under a thin veneer of the "New Covenant"—changed the ways in which men and women interacted with one another. It changed the attitude to life's one certainty: death. It changed the degree of freedom with which people could acceptably choose what to think and believe.

Pagans had been intolerant of the Jews and Christians whose religions tolerated no gods but their own. The rising domination of Christianity created a much sharper conflict between religions, and religious intolerance became the norm, not the exception.

Christianity also brought the open coercion of religious belief. You could even say that, by the modern definition of a cult as a group that uses manipulation and mind control to induce worship, Christianity is the Mother of all Cults—in service to the misogynistic, fascist ideals of Judaism!

The rising Christian hierarchy of the Dark Ages was quick to mobilize military forces against believers in other gods and most especially, against other Christians who promoted less fascist systems of belief. This probably included the original Christians and the original teachings. The change of the Western world from Pagan to Christian effectively changed how people viewed themselves and their interactions with their reality. And we live today with the fruits of those changes: war without end.

Which brings us back to the Control System of our reality:

> [A] global phenomenon ... *so strange and foreign to our daily terrestrial mode of thought*... it carries with it many implications of the existence of intelligences other than our own ... [It] bespeaks the action of some form of intelligence... but whence this intelligence springs, whether it is truly extra-terrestrial, or bespeaks a higher reality not yet recognized by science, or even if it be in some way or another a strange psychic manifestation of our own intelligence, is much the question... It is indeed sobering, yet challenging, to consider that the entire UFO phenomenon may be only the tip of the proverbial iceberg in a signaling *an entirely new domain of the knowledge of nature as yet totally unexplored*, as unexplored and as unimagined as nuclear processes would have been a century ago.

It is this "*entirely new domain of the knowledge of nature*" that has been the concern of the Cassiopaean transmissions from the very beginning. It is the nature of this domain that is the subject of their communications regarding aliens, alien abductions, hyperdimensional realities, religious and political tyrannies, and related subject matter. This is the central core of the book you now hold.

The book is presented in three parts. The reader should be familiar with some of the literature on UFOs and aliens. Rich Dolan's and Jim Marrs' books, listed in the bibliography, provide a good introduction, along with those of John Keel, Karla Turner, Jacques Vallee and David Jacobs. Part One includes an account of the events leading up to, and during, the early days of the "Cassiopaean experiment" which resulted from our attempts in superluminal communication. It also includes the conclusions of my research at the time: the discovery that there is really very little in our world that does not, ultimately, lead back to this new domain of knowledge of the processes of nature.

Part Two is a presentation of a series of articles originally published on *cassiopaea.org* which deal with hyperdimensions, alien abduction, and conspiracy. They were removed after we came to understand that any attempt to discuss this subject in a rational and scientific way is almost doomed from the start. The reason for this state of affairs is a recurring theme of the book: COINTELPRO.

Part Three is adapted from my book *Secret History*. It consists in what I have learned through hard work, though certainly, I was given a direct initiation into Higher Knowledge via an ancient Cabalistic clue system of communications from "us in the future"—the "Gift of the Present".

PART ONE:
The High Strangeness Factor

chapter one
the call

the evil magician

After the death of my grandmother in 1984, the *high strangeness* factor of my life was bumped up a few notches. It is only in retrospect that I see that my grandmother's death was a "gift", because it was the impetus for asking deep and burning questions.

I was then 32 years old, and my grandmother had been an omnipresent part of my life. In the simplest of terms, my thoughts were: my grandmother is dead; how can I know she still loves me? What am I to do with the love I have to give her? What is the medium of exchange? Is it over? Is there no more? If so, then what's the point, damn it?

How can it be that such a bond, one that may be assumed to exist in platonic noumenal terms, yet which is expressed in physical manifestation, seems suddenly to end when the material body is sealed in the tomb? Why is there this dreadful veil that prevents our access to other realities in terms of certainty?

The answers offered by the Christian faith in which I grew up suddenly seemed not merely unsatisfactory, but downright insulting to the memory of my grandmother and the bond that had existed between us. The ideas of Spiritualism and the concepts of reincarnation were only slightly helpful, but as far as I was concerned, there was no proof. There was a lot of circumstantial or anecdotal evidence and conjecture; but there was also another side: such evidence was declared to be either psychologically unsound or a satanic delusion to lead us astray depending on whether you asked scientists or the church.

I was pregnant at the time my grandmother died, and the baby was born in the Spring of 1985. As a result of injuries I suffered during the delivery, I was bedridden for many months after.

Since I could no longer maintain my very active participation in life in a physical way, I was forced, by the universe, as it were, to find other outlets for my energy. I decided this would be the perfect time to not only catch up on my reading, but also to master the art of meditation which might assist in my investigation into this question of Eternal Life. I remembered a book that I had purchased some years earlier, *In Search of the Miraculous* by P.D. Ouspensky.

The blurb on the cover said: "The noted author of *Tertium Organum* combines the logic of a mathematician with the vision of a mystic in his quest for solutions to the problems of Man and the Universe". It seemed that a book that promised insight to the issues I was struggling with—even a very dry book—didn't seem like such a bad idea when I could do nothing else. I asked for it, and soon it was located and brought to me.

I realized pretty quickly that this book would go to the top of the list of "forbidden works" according to the elders of the church, but I didn't care. I was still "on guard" against "evil ideas", but I was sure that I could filter out anything too "dangerous" in a work that promised insight on the issues for which I was seeking answers.

Everything was fine for about 17 pages, and I found it to be deeply interesting and then—well—then this mysterious "G" (about whom I knew nothing), made a remark that completely knocked the wind out of my still mostly Protestant sails. In response to Ouspensky's speculation that, in the industrial age, humans were becoming more "mechanized" and had stopped thinking, Gurdjieff said:

> "There is another kind of mechanization which is much more dangerous: being a machine oneself. Have you ever thought about the fact that all people themselves are machines? ... Look, all those people you see are simply machines—nothing more. ... You think there is something that chooses its own path, something that can stand against mechanization; you think that not everything is equally mechanical."

At this point, Ouspensky raised the very argument that was forming in my own mind: "Why of course not! ... Art, poetry, thought, are phenomena of quite a different order." Gurdjieff replied: "Of exactly the same order. These activities are just as mechanical as everything else. Men are machines and nothing but mechanical actions can be expected of machines."

I was so enraged that I snapped the book shut and threw it against the wall!

How dare he say such a terrible thing about human beings! How dare he deny the reality of the spirit, the sublimity of music and mysticism and the salvation of Christ! I'm surprised that sparks from my eyes didn't set the bed on fire and steam didn't issue from my ears. I was hot with outrage!

But, it had been said. The seed of the thought had been planted in my mind. After awhile, my curiosity about such a concept came to the fore. I began to mull over the issue in an attempt to find ways to disprove it.

I mused over my own life, all my interactions with other people, and gradually, I began to realize that there was, indeed, something mysteriously "mechanical" about the interactions between human beings. I thought about the many people I had worked with therapeutically using hypnosis and how "mechanical" the therapy was; how the roots of most of their problems were rather like "mechanical" and conditioned reactions to their perceptions and observations. Generally, it seemed, these perceptions were erroneous, and it was the error of this "mechanical" thinking that created the problems in the first place.

But, over and over again I could see that such problems and the ways they formed and operated, as well as the therapeutic solutions themselves, were, essentially, mechanical. It was like a formula. With just a few "hints" from the person, I could almost immediately see the whole dynamic of their past and the formation of their problem, as well as the "mechanical" way to solve it. I applied the technique, and just like changing the wires and spark plugs in a car, it made them start "firing on all cylinders" again.

OK, so the guy has a point, I thought. I was curious to see what further remarks might be made about Christianity. Ouspensky asked the same question I would have asked myself:

"For a man of Western culture, it is of course difficult to believe and to accept the idea that an ignorant fakir, a naïve monk, or a yogi [i.e. the three *ways* of the body, emotions, and intellect] who has retired from life may be on the way to evolution while an educated European, armed with 'exact knowledge' and all the latest methods of investigation, has no chance whatever and is moving in a circle from which there is no escape".

Gurdjieff answered: Yes, that is because people believe in progress and culture. *There is no progress whatever.* Everything is just the same as it was thousands, and tens of thousands, of years ago. The outward form changes. The essence does not change. Man remains just the same. 'Civilized' and 'cultured' people live with exactly the same interests as the most ignorant savages. Modern civilization is based on violence and slavery and fine words...

What do you expect? People are machines. Machines have to be blind and unconscious, they cannot be otherwise, and all their actions have to correspond to their nature. Everything happens. No one does anything. 'Progress' and 'civilization,' in the real meaning of these words, can appear only as the result of conscious efforts. They cannot appear as the result of unconscious mechanical actions. And what conscious effort can there be in machines? And if one machine is unconscious, then a hundred machines are unconscious, and so are a thousand machines, or a hundred thousand, or a million. And *the unconscious activity of a million machines must necessarily result in destruction and extermination. It is precisely in unconscious involuntary manifestations that all evil lies.* You do not yet understand and cannot imagine all the results of this evil. But the time will come when you will understand.

Gurdjieff was right. He was speaking at the beginning of the First World War, in the opening rounds of a century of unprecedented warfare. My copy of *In Search of the Miraculous* was to fly across the room at least a dozen more times. I fumed and raged inside each time I was confronted with an idea that, upon reflection and comparison to my observations and experiences, seemed a far better explanation of the dynamics of human existence than anything I had ever read in my life.

As for this "unconscious evil" that Gurdjieff mentioned, he explained in the *Tale of the Evil Magician:*

A very rich magician had a great many sheep. But at the same time this magician was very mean. He did not want to hire shepherds, nor did he want to erect a

21

fence about the pasture where his sheep were grazing. The sheep consequently often wandered into the forest, fell into ravines, and so on, and above all they ran away, for they knew that the magician wanted their flesh and skins and this they did not like.

At last the magician found a remedy. He hypnotized his sheep and suggested to them first of all that they were immortal and that no harm was being done to them when they were skinned. On the contrary, it would be very good for them and even pleasant. Secondly he suggested that the magician was a good master who loved his flock so much that he was ready to do anything in the world for them. In the third place he suggested to them that if anything at all were going to happen to them it was not going to happen just then, at any rate not that day, and therefore they had no need to think about it. Further, the magician suggested to his sheep that they were not sheep at all; to some of them he suggested that they were lions, to others that they were eagles, to others that they were men, and to others that they were magicians.

And after this all his cares and worries about the sheep came to an end. They never ran away again but quietly awaited the time when the magician would require their flesh and skins.

Ouspensky wrote that "theoretically, a man could awaken. But in practice this is almost impossible. As soon as a man awakens for a moment and opens his eyes, all the forces that caused him to fall asleep in the first place begin to act on him with tenfold energy. He immediately falls asleep again, very often dreaming that he is awake."

I also thought about my study of the history of man in my search for the answers to why things are the way they are, and how I had come to see it as the biography of Satan. I was beginning to realize that something was very wrong with the picture of the world that we are taught from the moment we are born, and that is further implemented in our culture, our society and most especially our religions.

I thought back over my life and realized that all the events that had gradually maneuvered me into my present position could most definitely be perceived as the mechanical "forces that act to keep a person asleep". It was a certainty that some tremendous pressure had been applied to stop me from observing, from analyzing, and most of all from thinking and learning.

The question was: who or what was the true nature of the "Evil Magician"?

none dare call it conspiracy

Reading *In Search of the Miraculous* "jump-started" my thinking processes, which had lain fallow during the years when my first three children were small. Without really planning it, during this period of forced physical inactivity, I was establishing a regimen of deep and intense thinking, alternating with the deep contemplation and stopping of the chatter of meaningless thought that was achieved during meditation. My meditations seemed to progress quite rapidly and soon was able to enter a rather "timeless" state for what proved to be somewhat extended periods of time.

After my regular meditation exercises, I would sit up in bed, surrounded by piles of books and notebooks, reading and writing notes on what I read. As I did so, I would often stop and think about questions that occurred to me as I read. The instant these questions were framed in my mind, thoughts would simply pour into my head so fast that I was mentally leaping and jumping just to follow them. These thoughts always and only came in response to questions that I would pose mentally about whatever I was considering at the moment in my studies. The urge to write these thoughts down was so overwhelming that I spent literally hours a day, filling page after page in longhand. I still have boxes full of these notebooks. It didn't occur to me that I might be doing something called "channeling" at the time. In fact, such an idea would have horrified me. I was just "asking interesting questions" in an open way, with no attempt to impose any pre-conceived answers. What entered my mind in response to these questions just seemed like "thinking".

At some point, I decided that I must find out if these ideas that were coming to me had any basis in fact whatsoever. Just because a thought "came to me", didn't mean I intended to accept it as a valid answer to my question. I most definitely needed more data! So the answers that "came to me" actually served to point me in the direction of certain studies that otherwise might not have been part of my experience. I was compelled by my rational and reflective nature to research each idea that came to me in order to discover if there was any way it could be supported scientifically and objectively.

Getting more data was a problem. I subscribed to a library service by mail, and soon began ordering and reading book after book on subjects that ranged from geology to physics; from psychology to theology; from metaphysics to astronomy. As I read, I found many pieces that not only supported the ideas that came to me in response to my questions, but also expanded on many of the concepts in dramatic ways, leading to more interesting questions, more answers, and more data collection. I was both surprised and energized to find that the ideas I was getting weren't so crazy after all! If the "idea" I had was not supported by observation or scholarly opinion, I discarded it.

I eventually assembled my notes and ideas into a book I called *The Noah Syndrome,* which, after a few revisions, became *The Secret History of the World.* The main idea of the book was Macro-Cosmic Metamorphosis in Quantum terms, which I related to Matthew 24: "As were the days of Noah, so will be the coming of the son of man. For just as in those days before the flood they were eating and drinking, marrying and being given in marriage, until the day when Noah went into the Ark, and they did not know or understand until the flood came and swept them all away, so will be the coming of the Son of man."

This event, the End, was compared to the "Days of Noah"—the Deluge. The key seemed to be held *in the concept of the Ark.* My search for the true meaning of Love, Salvation, Faith and Eternal Life was, essentially, a search for the *meaning of the Ark.* Metaphorically speaking, there is no better expression of

23

this search than the story of Noah and the Ark. All quests of life and love and existence can be expressed in this story of a man, faced with the destruction of his world—and in this case, it was literally destruction of the entire world, or so the story goes—and he set about building an Ark.

The next question was, of course, exactly what is this process of Metamorphosis, and exactly what constitutes an Ark of safety? These were the questions I was asking when I came across a small paperback, Gary Allen's *None Dare Call it Conspiracy*. Everything in this book just slotted into place with the teachings of Gurdjieff and Ouspensky that Man is asleep and under the control of an "Evil Magician".

I realized that the Evil Magician was a metaphor, at least in part, for political and historical control systems. This realization was, once again, devastating to my illusions. As Gary Allen suggests, without any intelligent control, 50% of the time events would occur in social, cultural and political spheres leading to great benefit for all. Factoring in intelligent decisions to do good would bring this average even higher. I could clearly see this wasn't reflected in our reality. Man hasn't stopped killing his brother; he has just developed more efficient and mechanical means of doing it.

Why? Who or what is influencing events to the negative?

Putting Allen's ideas together with Gurdjieff's, it seemed merely the result of certain "mechanical" laws of the Universe that humans refer to as "good" and "evil". These laws were cyclical and could be better expressed in terms of physics. (This is one of the threads I followed to the idea of Cosmic Quantum Metamorphosis.) However, as we will see in later sections of this book, the idea of "control systems"—whether human or non-human—was to become more and more refined as we researched the topics.

skeptical channeling

Several years and a number of very strange events went by. In 1991 I met a young man, Frank, with whom I had many conversations about metaphysical and philosophical subjects. Frank frequently asked me to use hypnosis to help him "channel". He would say, "The one thing I *can* do is channel. I do it all the time.

I didn't have a very high opinion of "channeling", having read reams of it while writing *Noah*, but I decided it wouldn't be scientific to discard Frank's claims to be an "exception" without at least a trial. I suggested he just simply go into a relaxed state and try automatic writing. My opinion of channeling was not changed. Frank produced the same "cosmic word salad" that's been around for years. Nevertheless, in discussing the matter with Frank, I began to think about my own experiences in "getting answers", as well as the historical fact that "channeled" material can often be so close that it is clear that something other than just chance is operating. The little glimpses of truth intrigued me. So, Frank and I continued to discuss it and a theory began to take shape in my mind in response to the question.

Part of the theory I hammered out was that the reason other sources proved, in the end in case after case, to be so human and fallible, was because an initial error was made in the thinking of the various individuals who acted as channels or mediums. They assumed that a higher source could just be dialed up on the phone, so to speak, and that was that. I theorized, from the few flashes of light I could discern in the vast body of material, that an occasional truly higher source would manage to connect momentarily, or in a skewed or corrupted way, but that, for the most part, it was either discarnate entities who didn't know a whole lot more than humans did, or that the phenomenon was produced by psychological pathology. I studied the matter from a number of directions trying to discover a clue as to what the obstruction was, if higher sources did, in fact, exist.

The chief obstruction seemed to be this very cloud of theoretical lower level beings and/or thoughts that apparently surrounded our realm like a curtain. My research into this area led me to the work of Drs. William Baldwin, Edith Fiore, Carl Wickland, and others who had worked directly with possession and exorcism and related therapeutic techniques. Since studying these matters had long been on my agenda of "things to do", it seems that it manifested in my life at precisely the right moment.

Taking into account the leading questions and subtle mind manipulation of many popular hypnotherapists, it seemed to me that there are a lot of "dead dudes"—or personality fragments—who will come forward in various ways during hypnosis (including using the vocal instruments of a medium), who describe the "afterlife" in glowing and ephemeral terms. Upon deeper inspection, it seems that there is a very great deal more to the matter.

I began my own experimental work in this area with a major attitude of skepticism. That was good because, as it turned out, having started as a skeptic, I was quite taken aback to discover the reality that the so-called astral planes are a veritable jungle. Even though I conducted my sessions with extreme care to avoid any possibility of contaminating my subjects, over and over again, I discovered that all was not well in the "higher" realms. It seems that there are "powers" in these realms that are most definitely *not* beneficial to humanity and do not have our best interests at heart.

That led, of course, to the question as to why so much nonsense is propagated by so-called channeled sources that are, clearly, in many instances, lying? In other cases, they are, at the very least, guilty of a serious lack of attention to crucial details. In my opinion, at this point in time, the lack of knowledge about this single issue is one of the chief reasons that it continues to build and perpetuate, increasing and amplifying the sufferings of humanity. How "good" are channeled sources that do not inform us of the truth of the "higher realms"? If anything, the so-called "New Age" movement has been so heavily inculcated with the idea that one must not ever think about negative things, that they, above all other people, are most subject to its predations. *If you don't know about*

25

something, you cannot defend yourself against it. The consistent deflection from the truth of the state of the so-called higher realms by masses of published material over many years, almost suggested a *program* of disinformation. It was beginning to look to me as though there was something or someone "out there" who didn't want us to know something.

Yes, I know that this flies in the face of standard "New Age" philosophies. But let me just say that, over and over again, this has been proven to be so in clinical experience of a sufficient number of trained researchers that before anyone dives into denial, they ought to give it consideration as a working hypothesis to be tested. If it's wrong, no harm can be done by having considered it. If it's right, it could save our lives.

William Baldwin wrote: "With limited, if any, knowledge and distorted perceptions of the nature of the spirit world, the non-physical reality, many people leave themselves open and create their own vulnerability as part of creating their own reality!" This remark contains within it the description of the trap into which millions upon millions of human beings have been imprisoned for millennia. Lack of true knowledge of the spirit worlds is, essentially, the philosophical foundation of "faith" as taught by the three major monotheistic religions, as well as the New Age religion. In other words: faith, as understood and practiced by most human beings, is merely another word for denial, and denial constitutes living a lie, and a lie, by the definitions of those very religions involved, is "Satanic". But without knowledge and an ability to discern, one is then subject not only to the vagaries of any passing entity who hears the "call", but also to cosmic laws of which most of humanity are abysmally ignorant.

Some surround themselves with light, or pray and specify "for my highest good" in their invocations. What they do not realize is that this actually constitutes permission and invitation to any discarnate spirit who truly *believes* that it is acting "for your highest good" in its realm of wishful thinking and earth-bound ego fixation.

Keep in mind that we are not talking about demonic possession here. That is an entirely different kettle of fish, though it follows the same rules. We are talking about your garden variety, well-meaning dead dudes wandering in the lower astral planes due to ignorance or some sort of affinity to the Earth. As Edgar Cayce remarked: a dead Presbyterian is just that—a dead Presbyterian!

In coming face to face with all of this material and experience, I have to admit that I attempted to formulate a rationalist theory to explain it all. I could see that the jungle-like nature of the astral realms might be merely another psychological drama invented by the endlessly creative mind as a means of sorting through some current life issue. But, in the same way that I have never really cared if reincarnation was real or not, I didn't really care if the fact that there seemed to be higher level negative beings on the astral planes was real or not; I only cared that the therapeutic applications worked.

And work they did; consistently, and remarkably. One of the most amazing things about it was the consistency of the symbolic or archetypal language of the subconscious. Subject after subject, from all walks of life, with all different levels of education and intellectual development, from different religions and belief systems, all of them, when asked the same series of questions, responded with the same types of symbols relating to similar issues and relationships.

Whether they were actually discarnate beings, or some split off aspect of human personality, or energy constructions of an etheric sort, which could be detected and symbolically assigned personality and history, didn't matter to me; I knew that the mind is infinitely creative, and I was reluctant to take a hard and fast position on the subject. I continued to work with the concepts, constantly on the lookout for new data that might help me to refine, prove or disprove my theory. To remain as open as possible for new information, my working hypothesis was that it was very likely that all that existed was an artifact of consciousness; the only thing I was giving a high probability to was that consciousness could and did exist independently of matter. Consciousness could be positive or negative. Whether it was, in all cases, or even in most cases, consciously aware, I didn't know.

Part of the difficulty presented by this work with exorcism-type activities, (though that is a misnomer for a procedure that is more akin to "discarnate counseling"), indicated that most activity that passed for "channeling" could be immediately dispensed with as being merely the production of the so-called "astral realms" (leaving aside the issue of whether the astral realms were artifacts of consciousness). I began to wonder if there was anything truly "higher", and if so, what it was and how "high" could one really go?

This led to a second obstruction to achieving possible high-level contact that I called the "transducing factor". This hypothesis suggested that it was evidential that a truly higher level source simply could not make a full and secure connection with consciousness that was embodied in the physical state because it would be like trying to run a 110V appliance on 220V current. If it were a "higher" source, by definition, its energy would so overwhelm any human recipient that it could not be sustained.

I formulated this idea based on reading case histories. There were examples of people who clearly had lost their minds after contact with "higher sources". Like meteorites, they flashed across the sky of our collective psychological and spiritual domains, brief illuminators of the landscape, only to crash and burn in ignoble descent. For the most part, it was clear that such efforts posed many dangers as explicated in extensive readings in ancient literature, occult writings and various Eastern mystical teachings.

Another reason that I formulated this idea was based on the observations of Nature. The one thing we observe consistently in the world around us is *growth* occurring in *cycles*. For example, human consciousness begins to grow from the moment of conception. Whether or not this is the result of a merging of an *external* consciousness with a developing neurological/physical system—a "ghost in the machine" effect—consciousness grows. Let's take that as an observable given principle.

At the beginning of life, when there is less apparent consciousness, the being sleeps a great deal. In the prime of life, when the consciousness is most apparent

27

and active (within wide variation which may depend on richness of consciousness), the body sleeps less. At some point, consciousness begins to recede from the body in old age (again, with wide variation), and the body again reverts to longer periods of sleep. In other words, a "seed" consciousness is planted in a newly conceived/born human being; it grows according to the richness of the environment and the potentials of the DNA parameters that are present in the body. When it reaches optimum growth, it begins receding. The important thing to understand is that consciousness apparently recedes because it has grown to the maximum and it no longer "fits". It has achieved its fullest expression in that body, utilizing the available neurological/physical construct. We might conjecture that when this upper limit, or critical mass, has been achieved, then movement "out of the body" proceeds by stages.

This movement into and out of the body by stages suggested to me that the death process was a sort of "birth" into a "higher" or richer and denser state of being that was *not sustainable by the physical construct.* Had it been sustainable at a higher level, or at greater density and richness, the death process might not have been stimulated to begin at that point. That this might have something to do with genetic considerations occurred to me. Just as different plants and creatures have certain and definite genetic parameters that determine not only their configuration, function, learning potentials and life expectancy, so do individual humans, within certain ranges, have similar configurations, functions, learning potentials and life expectancy. That these potentials could relate in a symbiotic way to consciousness occurred to me as a strong possibility. In other words, consciousness can only grow to a certain limit that is determined by the genetic constraints of the body it occupies.

Thus, it seemed that it was logical to pursue this line to the conclusion that a truly "higher being", or one that has achieved great density and richness of consciousness, could not, by the very constraints of the genetic configurations of function and potential in the human body, actually enter into the human consciousness energy field and put on somebody else's body like a glove, for the purposes of direct interaction, unless it was of similar configuration and potential as the host body itself. It had "grown" and would no longer "fit".

The logical deduction then would be that, if a consciousness that was external was, in fact, able to enter or merge with a human being, or connect in a direct way, it could only be one that was not any more advanced than the normal consciousness potential of that human being, albeit without the constraints of space and time. This last consideration might give a different perspective to such a consciousness, but does not attest to its advancement in philosophical or spiritual terms.

In other words, a dead Presbyterian is just that: a dead Presbyterian. If the consciousness can use your body, it can't be much different from your own.

Going through the literature on channeling and spirit mediumship, I found some very interesting cases where the consciousness of the "possessing entity" (trance channeling *is* "possession", after all) appeared to be, at the very least, a small order of magnitude more dense and rich than the medium him or herself (who may or may not have achieved their consciousness/genetic potential). The curious thing about such cases was that there seemed to be a direct relationship between such potentials and body mass: mediums who seemed to be capable of making limited connection to seemingly higher beings were rather large. Not only that, but when subjected to scientific controls and measurements, as some of them were in the 19th and early 20th century, it was learned that such mediums could lose up to fifteen pounds of body mass in an hour or two of such contact. The Italian medium Eusapia Palladino is a case in point.

I naturally thought of the very ancient Goddess images found all over the world, where She is nearly always represented as a very fat woman! Well, I was definitely a qualified applicant for the job! The only thing was, I was not at all satisfied with the levels of contact achieved even in those cases described above.

I also came across stories of yogis and shamans who, in states of meditation or shamanic ecstasy where they claimed to have made some sort of "cosmic connection", lost incredible amounts of weight due to the "heat of the state". That this was a heat that did not necessarily register on a thermometer was clear, but heat of a certain kind was definitely present in these cases, as well as significant fluctuation in body mass.

This led me to the idea that, in terms of channeling truly higher beings, the mode itself presented significant problems. Relative to the theorized "high voltage" of such higher sources, I proposed that the only way to make such a contact was to combine the energies of two or more people as a "receiver", and then to attempt to "tune" the receiver with repeated acts of intent.

As I puzzled over the problem, I realized that the only real way to combine energies as a human "biocosmic" receiver was to use some form of communication that required more than one person and which also provided an immediate feedback checking mechanism. The obvious answer was a Ouija board-like instrument.

In my younger days I experienced modest success "playing" with such an instrument, though I had given it up as possibly "dangerous" or just merely childish. It was slow, tedious, and I wasn't exactly sure of the source of the replies, never mind how accurate they were. Nevertheless, now I was looking at it in a different way and considering the possibilities that it was a potential means of coordinating focus and intent as well as proximity of energetic biopsychic fields, with the added feedback loop for "tuning". I knew that I needed to research it to discover if, theoretically, it would suit the purpose.

There are two main theories about how the Ouija board is supposed to work. The first is called *automatism.* Automatism is also supposed to be the means by which dowsing, pendulums, table tipping, automatic writing and other movement of physical objects by purported spiritual forces are supposed to take place. What this means is that the participants may not realize that they are responsible for the movements of the indicator, but they are still doing it themselves. Conscious or unconscious expectations can signal nerves to fire thereby causing tiny, imperceptible motions of the fingers which produce the "answers". In this theory, the use of the "talking" board is similar to theories of automatic writing which claim that such messages originate in the conscious or unconscious mind of the medium. Defined within this context, the talking board is merely a bypass of the conscious mind, and a shortcut between the unconscious mind and the neuromuscular control system. "Collective automatism" occurs when more than one person is operating the board.

So we see that, psychologically speaking, automatism allows the subconscious mind temporary control of some part of the body without the interference of the conscious mind. At the same time, it leaves the conscious mind conscious for checking the feedback, monitoring the activity, and basically balancing the effort within the controls of experimental protocols.

Some "experts" claim that having a healthy unconscious mind is the key to protection since opening such a door without due care could most certainly trigger psychosis in certain individuals. I have a slightly different view. I don't think that bypassing the conscious mind in this way can "trigger" psychosis. What I do think is that it can open a door to reveal pathology that, with careful analysis, will be seen to have been present all along, manifesting in many symptoms of the body and life of the individual.

The issue of whether or not using a board, or any other type of unconscious accessing tool can "invite" possession is rather like asking which comes first, the chicken or the egg? Dr. Baldwin, although reasonable in so many other things, comes to some illogical conclusions on this issue. The evidence, as Baldwin describes it, tells us that the state of "possession" probably already exists in any given individual and the use of the conscious bypass only allows it to "speak" and reveal itself. But that presents its own set of problems. Obviously, anyone who is not trained in the techniques of Spirit Release should never open such a door. So, by the same token, an individual who has no knowledge of these techniques, who has not spent a considerable period of time learning about them and working with them, ought never to attempt channeling in any context! To do so is to invite disaster. (And that, of course, brings up the obvious question as to why "channeling" has become such a popular sport.)

The Spiritualist theory, of course, posits that discarnate spirits or other ethereal beings are contacted and channeled through the board. Nevertheless, even this concept depends upon the theory of automatism for actual operation. The discarnate spirit is able to connect to the operator via the subconscious or unconscious mind and take control of the ideomotor responses, bypassing the conscious mind, and generating movement of the *planchette* via stimulation of nerve impulses. Naturally, this theory posits that, as soon as the communication has ended, the spirit leaves, and all is well and good. The evidence, however, indicates that if certain knowledge is not available, and certain actions are not taken, the spirit does not leave! It merely withdraws into the "interstitial" spaces of the energy field of the host and becomes quiescent, continuing to drain life force for its own sustenance.

One of the more interesting theories I came across was developed by Barbara Honegger who was said to be the first person in the United States to obtain an advanced degree in experimental parapsychology. Honegger suggested that automatism was the result of "stimulation" of the right hemisphere of the brain so that it could overcome the suppression of the left hemisphere. It was never entirely clear what was doing the stimulating, however, and I could obtain no further information on her research.

The Chinese seem to have been the first to use spiritual automatism in the form of a *writing planchette,* called a *chi,* which was a sort of divining or dowsing rod used to write. It was said that the spirits came down into it, moving it, and the object of the activity was to use it to spell out the gods' messages on paper or in sand.

It seems that all "primitive" or preliterate cultures had some form of codified communication between spirits and the living. This phenomenon seems to have been universal in the ancient world, and only came under condemnation with the inception of monotheism around 1000 BC. In the sixth century BC the Thracian Dionysiac cults were known to be using shamans as trance channels to communicate with the spirits, or what were then known as *theoi* or gods: discarnate immortal beings with superhuman powers.

Some scholars suggest that rationalist philosophy was born out of the Dionysiac, Orphic, and Eleusinian mystery cults devoted to the channeling of these gods; certainly much ancient Greek philosophy, especially that of Pythagoras, Heraclitus, and Plato, was saturated with these mysteries. This brings up the question directly related to the control systems we will describing throughout this book: how could "channeled" information have been the basis of the Rationalist philosophy that there was nothing to channel? Could it be a progression of the monotheistic idea that there was only one god, and Yahweh was it? When Yahweh spoke through his channels, they were called prophets and the activity was "divine inspiration". When anybody else did it, it was deception, necromancy, or demonic possession. However, if the other gods actually *did* exist, and were actually communicating, as Yahweh presumably was, then what status does that suggest about Yahweh, who claimed to be the *only* god simply because he said so via channeling? The monotheistic idea seems to have succeeded in stripping away any spiritual support from the lives of human beings.

In Plato's *Theagetes* Socrates confesses, "By the favor of the Gods, I have since my childhood been attended by a semi-divine being whose voice from time to time dissuades me from some undertaking, but never directs me what I am to do."

The Greek oracles at Dodona and Delphi and other sites would prophesy by sinking into a trance during which they were possessed by discarnate spirits; some of the famous ones by a single spirit, or what we would today call a *spirit-guide.* Oracles often lived in caves and thought of the spirits they channeled as coming up to them from the underworld through fissures in the rock.

The most interesting item of all is the fact that Pythagoras used something like a Ouija board as early as 540 BC: a "mystic table" on wheels moved around and pointed toward signs that were then interpreted by the philosopher himself, or his pupil Philolaus. Even down to the present day, the mysteries of the

Pythagoreans are subjects of intense interest to scientists and mystics alike. And here there seems to be evidence that the advanced knowledge of Pythagoras may have been inspired by a Ouija board!

By the time the Romans had conquered Greece, the rationalist movement was turning against spirit-channeling. Cicero, the Roman rationalist whom the early Church Fathers highly revered, railed against spirit-channeling or necromancy on the grounds that it involved ghastly pagan rituals. But, as noted above, eventually, rationalism bit the hand that fed it and began to devour its father, monotheism, by further extending the argument to the idea that there is no god, there are no spirits, nothing survives the death of the physical body, therefore there is really nobody for us to talk to on the "other side"—so why bother? Science took the view that the whole thing was a con game, and that's pretty much the current mainstream scientific opinion of the phenomenon today.

After working with spirit attachment issues, I had a lot of questions. As I have already said, there was an open possibility in my mind that such "spirits" were merely fragments of the personality of an individual, sort of like little broken off circuits in the brain running in repetitive loops, created by trauma or stress. Perhaps an individual, when faced with a difficulty, entered a narcissistic state of fantasy, created a "dream", which was imprinted in the memory of the brain. If they then emerged from this state back into dealing with their reality, but not having dealt with the issue itself, it might become locked away in a sort of cerebral file drawer, sitting there, waiting to be triggered by the electricity or neurochemicals of the brain in some random unconscious scan. The same could be said for so-called past life memories; they were merely self-created memory files generated in a state of narcissistic withdrawal due to stress. Such neurological files could then be downloaded and read by using the conscious bypass method of either automatism or simply allowing the conscious mind to "step aside" as in trance channeling. For that matter, simple psychotherapy could be considered channeling in these terms.

Conscious channeling is more problematic because it suggests a definite pathological condition in which spirit attachment or multiple personality may play a part. In such cases, the "alter" ego, as either an alternate personality or an actual attached entity, is strong and well entrenched enough to establish a far stronger hold on the body of the host than those which can only manifest via automatism or trance.

Professor Douglas Robinson at Ole Miss (The University of Mississippi) suggests that an analogy can be drawn between the function of a translator and the channel or medium. Both the translator and channel must convey the ideas and meanings of the original author to a new audience, leaving out her own ideas, opinions, and arguments. The translator must be a neutral conduit and allow the original author to speak through them. In the ordinary sense, translation is done merely across linguistic or cultural barriers. In the sense of channeling, it is done across temporal, consciousness, or even hyperspatial barriers.

> The analogy suggests both (a) that the source author has the power to initiate communication with the target audience through the translator (the author is active, the translator is passive, or at the very most active only in the act of surrendering his/her activity to that of the author), and (b) that the translator possesses some means of gaining access to the author's voice and meaning, of reliably "opening up" to the intentional speaking of a person who is almost invariably other. Sometimes translators translate source texts they wrote themselves, but usually the source author is another person, most often distant in time and place, and not infrequently dead.[1]

In the present day, under the influence of rationalist Western technology, the idea that anyone can just sit down and begin to channel is very similar to the idea that translation can be done by machines with no human interface. This is a very subtle point. In terms of a computer program that translates from one language to another we see that the program attempts to execute an algorithm, or series of algorithms that consist of gathering intelligence, charting a course of action, giving a series of commands, and carrying them out. *The results are only as good as the algorithms.* And we see, from the literature, that the "channeling phenomenon" as it is widely practiced, omits reason from the algorithm. There is no feedback mechanism, and thus no possibility of accurate tuning. This means that it does not allow for an algorithm that can handle the fact that there may be competing forces inside the channel's mind. Excluding reason and the possibility of competing forces results in the algorithm: "I am the Lord your God and there is no other because I said so! And if you don't believe me, then it will be all the worse for you!" Not very productive, to say the least.

The fact is, machine translation researchers despair of ever programming a machine to produce a translation of professionally usable quality without human assistance. In the same way, it is likely impossible to produce channeled material of any usable quality without full consideration for the competing forces as well as the application of reason in dealing with them. Without application of knowledge and direct, rapid feedback, there is little possibility that anything other than useless psychobabble will emerge. And such seems to be the case. But of course, that excludes the narcissistic delusionals, the deliberate frauds, and the pathological cases of multiple personality. They are all out there in New Age Land, and it's a jungle!

In the end, those machine translation systems that do work are, effectively, cyborg translation systems: they all require a human-machine interface.

In science fiction movies, we often see a "machine translator" that enables the space traveler to just plug himself into a gadget via some brain electrode, and open his mouth and automatically speak in the language of the planet he is visiting. The words may start out in his brain in his own language, but by the time the come out of his mouth, the machine has altered the nerve impulses to the organs of speech causing them to produce correct words in the unknown tongue. Apparently, the machine also works in reverse, and the space traveler

---

[1] Professor Robinson's webpage. http://home.olemiss.edu/~djr/index.html

may hear words spoken in the unknown language, but he "experiences" them in his own. What is interesting to me is the fact that it is a prosthetic device that turns the space traveler into a sort of cyborg translator who becomes able to "channel" foreign speech.

The point I am trying to make in this funny "reverse analogy" is that by the use of prosthetics, we are in a position to employ an algorithm that includes both reason and feedback! Reason, when properly employed, posits an entire army of what Adam Smith called "invisible hands", which shape, direct, regulate, and control translation. Thus reason itself can be an "invisible hand": *Reason is an internalized form of ideological mastery.*

Just as the spirit seizes or possesses the channel and speaks—or otherwise operates through the channel's willing body—in the same way a text in a foreign language is fed into a computer to be translated, (often quite ineptly), so too does ideology and its agents—including reason—seize or possess the ideological subject and wield that subject's body as virtually its own. And in this sense, we discover that the channel, as a "translation machine", can become something far more interesting.

An individual who, via long and intensive study, comes to the idea that there is a possibility of communicating with higher consciousnesses, formulates a hypothesis of how to do it, and then experiments with that hypothesis—adjusting and modifying throughout the process—is, in a sense, being guided by invisible hands, or forces of the cosmos. But it is clearly a source of some greater complexity and deep need to communicate complex and new concepts that prepares such a translator. In terms of ordinary lower level channeling, we find that the spirits of such activities "hail" the channel through whom it wishes to speak by appearing before the clairvoyant, or welling up like verbal pressure inside the head begging to be released for the clairaudient. Sometimes the channel falls into unconsciousness and wakes up to find that something or somebody else had been using their organs of speech.

In the same way does the *cosmos at large,* via reason, knowledge and a questing spirit planted in a human form, "hail" a potential channel/translator of truly higher realities. The words "translate", "transfer" and "transduce" all have the same Latin root. And it is in the role of translator that we discover that just "plugging in and turning on the machine" is not enough.

Translators must be trained; they must not only know the other language, they must know how to regulate the degree of fidelity with the source text, how to tell what degree and type of fidelity is appropriate in specific use contexts, how to receive and deliver translations, how to find help with terminology, and so on. All of this suggests a long period of training and preparation.

A translator–channel is someone who has studied these things, who knows these things, and who, most importantly, governs their channeling–translating behavior in terms of this knowledge. This knowledge is ideological. It is controlled by cosmic ideological norms. To know, *via reason,* what those cosmic norms prescribe and act upon them is to submit to their control. To become a translator-channel of truly higher cosmic consciousness is to be hailed as a translator by "invisible hand" of the Universe.

If you want to become a translator–channel, you must submit to the translator's role of learning the language in an expert way; you must submit to being directed by what the cosmic ideological norms inform you is the true spirit of the source author, and to channel that spirit unchanged into the target language.

Thus it was, with all of these considerations in mind, I finally settled on the board type instrument as being the best mode of dealing with the issues. It is a prosthetic device that allows constant feedback between the algorithm of "machine translation" of the subconscious/unconscious, and the human interface of the conscious mind which must constantly employ reason for "tuning". This is possible only with a board due to the fact that the "channel" is using both the conscious bypass for reception, while at the same time is able to maintain constant conscious integrity. By being, at all times, in full possession of their own mind and having the ability to observe, control and direct acceptance or rejection of any material or sensation at any time, reason is brought in as part of the algorithm. In other words, used correctly, by an individual who is knowledgeable in the subjects under discussion, as well as the clinically demonstrated realities of "other realms", this is one of the finest tools available for developing contact with the subconscious, the higher self, and/or benevolent entities which wish to make telepathic contact. And that is the key word: telepathic. This type of device allows one to create a "separate line", so to speak, a "switchboard" where a new circuit is established through a minute thread of consciousness without giving up control in anyway.

Due to the influence of the movie *The Exorcist*, the device has acquired a negative reputation. Yet, this was not always the case! Funny how an entire "doctrine" can be created by Hollywood which people then accept is as gospel.

Some so-called "experts" will claim that being a "medium" is OK, but that using a board or automatic writing as a medium or even "trance channeling" can only bring in "lower level" entities. They base this wholly illogical statement on the claim that "no spirit of an advanced degree of spirituality, no ascended master or guardian spirit, would ever stoop to abusing the writing or speaking talents of another person, living or dead". Let me get this straight: it's OK to do any of the above as long as you call yourself a "medium". If you call yourself a "channel", or if you establish protocols whereby you are in constant, conscious control, you are, by definition, only in contact with "lower level entities?" Most peculiar; also most abysmally ignorant.

Contrary to the above "expert" opinion, one part of my hypothesis, based on years of research, was that sustained contact with true higher-level sources had rarely, if ever, occurred in the entire history of channeling. (At least not the type of sources I theorized to exist at truly higher levels of existence.) Thus, no one really "knew the language". It was absurd to think that one could just sit down, from their present human condition, download and translate something that, evidentially, had almost never been encountered before.

chapter one

At this point in time, I hypothesized that the "Universe at large", or the "source" I wished to contact, did, in fact, have the power to initiate communication with the target audience—humanity—because it was evident, through all the experiences of my life up to that point, that the universe speaks to us via the events of our lives. The many remarkable synchronicities in evidence, as well as close observation of the dynamics of my life itself, as well as the lives of other people I had observed, could only be interpreted as deliberate actions from some ultra-cosmic reality attempting to teach me the language of symbols. I felt that I had, most definitely, been "hailed" by the Universe which was asking me to undertake the task of learning the language and acting as translator–channel. Whether or not a more direct mode of communication could be established via myself as such a translator, I was not entirely certain. But I was most definitely anxious to make the attempt to gain access to the Voice of the Universe by "hailing" back via a long process of building a circuit into, and possibly even through, the deep unconscious mind.

Since it was clear that these interactions involved some level of being of which most of us are unaware, and to which we have little access, I realized that this amounted to the fact that I had to "learn the language" at some as-yet unknown level of my being. Not only was I proposing to learn this language that had never before been systematically studied, I knew that I had to learn how to "regulate the degree of fidelity with the source text, how to tell what degree and type of fidelity is appropriate in specific use contexts, how to receive and deliver translations, how to find help with terminology, and so on". This was the reasoning, or "ideological state apparatus" I was setting up as the protocol for the return "signal".

Reading through the literature on channeling, it was evident that the most respected and trustworthy material in the history of channeling had either come through a board type instrument, or had been initiated by a board type instrument. That it was a means of learning a new language in some internal place in the mind, like plugging in a translation matrix device, was evident. With the added information at my disposal regarding spirit attachment, multiple personality disorder and other pathological conditions, as well as the means of dealing with them effectively, I realized that, if I was correct in my hypothesis, I could possibly take channeling to a level never before achieved—or at least, only very rarely.

Of course, it all depended on a long period of "training" and applying the algorithm. And this meant a possibly very long period of using a board type instrument to "channel" not only one's own subconscious fragments through their series of dramas, but possibly an endless number of frequency related discarnates before all the "loops" had been played out and dealt with and brain synchrony was achieved.

In the end, I decided that even if that was all that we accomplished in the process, it was still a worthwhile activity. Purifying the mind by healing its fragments in whatever terms they manifest could only be good! The important thing I realized was to not give up using the board too soon. That would be like assuming one had a good mastery of a language just because one could use it for everyday purposes. To be a true translator, one must master a new language at the most subtle and refined levels imaginable.

At this point, I thought I had a pretty good theory, and it was time to put it into the test phase; so, we began. Frank and I met every week to sit and "Hail the Universe". I have notebooks which record every motion of the planchette for over two years. In the end, this material does, indeed, support my theory. We waded through endless loops of the unconscious mind, endless purported "discarnate" entities or past life scenarios; endless lost souls wandering in the astral realms seeking release into the light. At one point I realized that if any of this material had any factual basis, the board was an excellent tool for effecting spirit release, contrary to the opinions of Dr. Baldwin.

As our experiment in channeling proceeded, we discussed the many possible ways that a "true higher source" might be identified. We both thought that a higher source, by virtue of greater and more inclusive "cosmic perspective", would be able to make absolutely stunning "predictions" that would "hit the mark" every time. The problem was, in a short term feedback loop of testing, how to validate such a hypothesis?

Frank came up with a solution: Lottery. Well, that seemed reasonable enough. We could ask for a lotto prediction from every entity, then "grade" them based on their ability to predict. Since there were daily games, we concentrated on these.

Now, while I have been known to buy a lotto ticket or two based on a dream or just an impulse, and to win when I do, I have never been a real gambler. If I had the money to buy a soft drink and, instead, decided to give up the drink in favor of a lottery ticket, I felt that this was no more than I would spend on junk food or a movie, and for me that was all it was: entertainment. If I won, it was fun; if I didn't, I hadn't lost any more than I would have wasted otherwise. I never considered buying a lottery ticket as a way of getting out of any financial difficulty. If I was in a situation where I could not justify buying even a candy bar because money was that tight, I didn't buy a lottery ticket either.

For me, the "lotto test" was theoretical. I wasn't going out and buying tickets, but I discovered that Frank was. Not only that, he seemed particularly devoted to this aspect of the experiment. Doing it as a test was one thing, but doing it with intent to profit was somewhat disturbing to me.

In actual fact, we did have a few hits in that regard. They usually came up on a different day than predicted, sometimes even as long as several weeks after they were given. Frank claimed to have made money this way, but I reminded him that his overall expenditure on tickets ought to be deducted from his winnings to get a real picture.

But "testing" by getting lotto numbers was only part of what we were doing. We were also "chatting" with the various entities that came and went by, asking for details of their alleged lives and experiences, trying to get checkable data. In the end, Frank and I and other participants in the experiment were quite fascinated with the parade passing before us, and we joked that it was better than going to the movies, watching television, or going to parties! In full consciousness, we could peer into endless realms of otherworldly activity—dramas of tragedy and hope, despair and joy—and do it all while drinking coffee, eating cookies, and taking time out to chat. But what was really going on at other levels of being would prove to be more fascinating and mysterious than anything I had hypothesized.

chapter two
the signal

missing time

At the early stages of our channeling experiment I must admit that I was a flaming skeptic about UFOs and aliens. I'd decided that sightings and claims of abductions were strikingly similar to past life dramas, and after reading Whitley Strieber's *Communion* and Ruth Montgomery's patently ridiculous *Aliens Among Us*, I refused to give any serious consideration to the subject. The stories were so crazy I simply could not consider them to be real in any context other than as useful metaphors of psychological struggles.

In short, stories of aliens and abductions seemed an archetypal drama of the subconscious mind. I called it the Millennial Disease and saw it as a form of mass hysteria. I attributed the physical scars and traces of abduction to stigmata-like effects, or poltergeist type events. Clearly, there was very little about UFOs and aliens that couldn't be explained by these theories.

Even after finally reading some of the literature—courtesy of Frank and another period of being bedridden—I was impressed, but skeptical. Some were claiming that aliens had been visiting Earth since archaic times, others that they were gone now; we "let them in" by setting of the atomic bomb; they were here to save us from blowing ourselves up; they were highly evolved spiritual beings; they were demons from Hell, and we had better get ourselves back to church if we expected to survive the invasion. The only thing *certain* was that people were seeing and experiencing something singularly strange. It was hard to tell if the whole alien abduction thing was a "manipulation" by the government to make people think aliens existed, or if aliens did exist and were trying to make the government look guilty and stupid. What a morass of confusion!

Not to be intimidated by unexplained phenomena of any sort, I started working on a new theory to explain the UFO/alien abduction phenomenon. There was little in these stories that could not be explained by mass hallucination and hysteria, psycho-kinesis, stigmata, repressed memories of physical or sexual abuse, psychosis, schizophrenia—heck, just a whole cornucopia of tricks of the mind to choose from! I was actually pretty proud of my fiendishly clever solution! Pride goes before a fall, you know. This was in March of 1993.

Not long after I had been released from my sickbed and the inundation of UFO books, I answered an ad for some additional computer equipment I needed.

I called the number and began to chat with the woman, Patricia. As often happens, one thing led to another, and after an hour or so on the telephone, Pat asked to meet me so that she could consider scheduling a hypnosis session. There was something really strange that had happened to her back in 1987 that *still* bothered her and she wanted to know why, or at least get relief from the internal anxiety it had caused.

She and her 16-year-old son were returning home to Maryland on the Pennsylvania Turnpike after the funeral of an aunt. It had began to snow when she saw a very bright bluish white light ahead, and off to the side of the road. She thought that it was a light that had come on to illuminate a billboard since it was getting dark. She said that what happened next was so strange that, even in remembering it, she felt strange and uneasy. She said that she felt a paralysis come over her hands and arms as though someone had taken control of the car.

Having just read a grocery sack full of books on UFOs and "missing time" and all that, I immediately recognized the purported prodromal signs of a "missing time" experience as described by Budd Hopkins. It was rather creepy to be having this conversation right after having read those books. I managed to stay cool, however, and I casually asked what happened next.

Pat said that this was the crazy part because she couldn't remember! After seeing the light and feeling the paralysis, the next thing she remembered was sitting at a traffic light 50 or 60 miles down the road. She did not remember making the turn off the main highway, and her son had just cut his finger on a tin of cookies he was trying to open. He was bleeding, and she "came to herself" saying, "there's a towel in the back seat". To further add to her dismay, she arrived home much later than she should have, but, at the same time, had an almost full tank of gas.

She was sure that it had been her aunt attempting to contact her psychically, and she really needed to know what her aunt needed to tell her. The fact that she made no mention of aliens made the whole thing far more interesting to me because if she had claimed to have been abducted by little green men, I would have ended the conversation. Of course, I did not want to even suggest anything about "aliens", because I wanted to try to prove my theory about alien abductions being "psycho-dramas" in the same manner as past lives. I just told Pat that we could certainly clear the problem up quickly with hypnosis! She made an appointment.

It was the night of Thursday, April 15, 1993, when it began to storm terribly. I expected a cancellation on account of the rain, but surprisingly, she showed up. We went through the normal pre-session interview, and then talked a bit about the event again. I also wanted clues about areas of possible family conflicts that might be at the root of such a drama. Pat was a real estate agent and also owned a medical reports business working under government contract to transcribe social security records. She talked a bit about her children and her disabled husband, who was dying. I was sure the stress of caring for him was an exacerbation of her problems.

Nothing was said about "aliens" at any point whatsoever. I carefully inquired about her interests. She had never been interested in metaphysics, much less aliens. She was a formerly devout Catholic who was now in a state of doubt about her religion. While she was sure that I was not going to be able to hypnotize her, she turned out to be a good subject and quickly went under. I decided to make a videotape of this session rather than the usual audiotape. I wanted a record of my "proof" that the "alien abduction phenomenon" had another explanation!

I instructed Pat to go back to the time when she was driving the route of their return from the funeral. It was snowing so hard that they turned onto another highway, trying to find better driving conditions. She described seeing the light in front of what she thought was a billboard. She described it as iridescent blue, a pale oval of baby blue hanging there in front of the billboard. It made no sense to her, and she began to rub her eyes—firmly in the memory—saying that she must be imagining it. But, the light wouldn't go away and, still fully in the memory, she asked her son if he could see it. He couldn't, adding to her confusion. What was more, as she continued to describe it, the light kept getting bigger.

At this point, Pat was alarmed because she felt something taking over control of the car. She claimed that she wasn't driving anymore, something was driving the car, and the light was getting bigger.

Then the skip. All the drama and build-up to some dramatic climax just ended and she said, "I wish that damn light would change."

"What?" I asked.

"I'm just waiting for the light to turn green", she said. At this point, her voice became panicked. "Oh my God, Patrick! What did you do?"

It was clear that something was going on in her memory. Something was wrong.

"Oh my God, Patrick!" the woman was saying. "What did you do? There's a towel in the back seat. Get it."

I reassured Pat that everything was all right, and asked her to explain to me what was happening. She told me that she was sitting at a traffic light in a small town waiting for the light to change, and her son had been trying to open a tin of cookies someone gave them after the funeral. He couldn't open them, and she told him to get the penknife out of the glove compartment. Somehow he managed to cut his hand, and she was panicked by the copious amounts of blood. So, there they are, sitting at a traffic light all of a sudden, and Patrick's hand is bleeding—a lot.

Pat was agitated and upset all out of proportion to what was happening. Something was upsetting her, and not just the cut on her son's hand. She was breathing very fast and had raised her arms to her chest and crossed them, as though she was trying to protect herself. I reassured her that she and her son were safe.

I realized that we needed to understand how she skipped from the approach to the blue light to a little town fifty miles down the road. I asked her about this,

41

and she was distressed to not know how she suddenly arrived at this traffic light. How did she travel 50 miles without being aware of it? What happened to the blue light?

I stopped her and suggested that we start over again. I directed her to go back to the beginning, back to the turnpike, and start over. But it was futile. Every time we went through it, it skipped from the approach toward the blue light to the traffic light 50 miles down the road. I was pretty determined to find out what happened during those 50 miles. Since I considered it a real possibility that such scenarios were symbols of some sort of psychological drama, I decided to take my subject even deeper, for another replay. I planned to use my "secret weapon" for getting in the back door of the subconscious.

Well, it worked—partly. This time Pat managed to remember a parking lot. She could see the blue light growing, and she could feel the car leaving the highway. She described how she and her son stopped in the parking lot of a closed diner, just off the road, not far from the "billboard" from which the light emanated. "What happened next?" I asked.

"I wish that damn light would change", she said. Another skip. To say that I was surprised is putting it mildly. Whatever it was, it had something to do with an event somewhere between the parking lot and the traffic light: from a blue light to a red light.

I tried again. I spent a few minutes deepening the trance even more. I also decided to take Pat out of the event and have her view it at a remove, on a screen. In cases of very traumatic events, this often works to get a description of what happened, and then later, the emotional trauma can be dealt with. I asked her to see herself in a safe place, inside a room, sitting in a recliner, resting peacefully, and in front of her was a television on which she could view the events from that night without emotional attachment. I then told her to visualize a TV remote control in her hand with which she could control the "movie" on the television. She could fast forward, rewind, turn it off; whatever she needed to do to feel safe and in control. I asked her to go to the beginning of the story again, and push the "play button" and describe what she saw.

She was back on the highway driving through the snow. Along came the billboard and the light. I instructed her to use the remote and slow the action down, use the button that will advance the action one frame at a time. She saw the blue light in front of the billboard, growing. She felt some force taking control of the car. She felt the car leaving the road, turning into the parking lot while she was fighting the wheel. The car parked itself, and they were sitting there in the car, in the parking lot, outside the closed diner. They didn't know why; they were waiting for something; someone was approaching the car. I asked her to describe who it was.

"I can't", she said. She was twisting and fluttering her hands in agitation again. She began to hyperventilate. Her arms were twitching and jerking. She was rubbing them frantically with her hands as though she were in pain.

"What do you mean, you can't?" I asked.

"Because *THEY* won't let me." The word "they" was pronounced with such terror that a chill ran up my spine.

"What do you mean? Who is it stopping you from seeing, from speaking, from remembering? Who is *they*?" I asked, hoping she would blurt it out before the skip came again.

She just shook her head mournfully. "I can't tell", she said. "I can't."

If ever there was proof that a hypnotherapist with a pre-formed belief cannot influence the recall of a subject, this case is a classic in that regard! I am ashamed to admit my assumptions now, and I freely admit that it may not have been the proper approach to the problem, but then again, the subject was not claiming to have been abducted by aliens—at least not consciously. What's more, I *was* very careful not to "lead" in any way, so the "experiment" was, essentially, uncontaminated.

For a few moments I was completely nonplussed. I had never encountered a "they" who could so effectively block memory and cause pain and suffering when attempts were made to access it. I had never encountered a blocked memory that I could not find some way to access. This was one of my specialties. I could find the "back door" of the mind, ease the pain, and get to the root of the problem. I quickly theorized that I was dealing with a deeply repressed trauma. I wanted to believe that it related to something in childhood, or perhaps even a past life, but I couldn't shake the eerie sensation that washed over me when she cried *"They* won't let me!"

I knew that I could not lose the professional "control" and decided that it was not wise to push any further at this moment. Sometimes a subject must be "conditioned" over time. So I started the suggestions that would make her feel good, make her like hypnosis, make her want to do it again, and help her to go into a trance more easily in the future so that a deeper state could be achieved and we could "deal" with this thing. Then, I brought her out.

We discussed a future appointment and she agreed that she would like to try again and that was that, except for the fact that she called and cancelled on the day of the next appointment.

In considering the implications of this session, there were just too many unknowns, too many things that didn't make sense. What could happen on the side of a snowy highway that could be so dreadfully traumatic that it induced pain to even approach it? I could think of no scenario whatsoever that was so bad that it would not be remembered with emotional distance techniques in place. Even if the subject had just turned off the highway to rest, and a gang of psychopaths had grabbed them and forced them to participate in some bizarre Satanic ritual, that didn't compute because it could not explain why, against all laws of probability, they would let them go on their journey with only a cut hand. Was Frank right? Had this woman and her son been abducted by aliens? Did they have some technology that could implant a "pain block" to memory of the event? That was just too far-fetched. I didn't buy it. There had to be something else, but I simply could *not* imagine what.

chapter two

In the following weeks, a series of events occurred that really upset my self-assurance that all of this was just psychological suppression of ordinary human trauma. The newspapers and TV news shows began reporting multiple sightings of UFOs in the area. From the middle of April until the end of the month, more than a dozen people in Pasco, Hernando and Pinellas counties in Florida claimed to have seen a large, boomerang-shaped craft moving across the sky. The witnesses included a Hernando County sheriff's deputy, who said the craft carried no markings, had a row of blue lights and he estimated the wingspan at around 200 feet. He had observed it for several minutes before it accelerated to a speed that was impossible for any man-made craft.

Something about these stories bugged me. After the whole affair died down, I assembled the reports in chronological order, since some people gave their reports only after seeing that someone else had done so before them, and the order of the reports in the news was not the order of the sightings. I realized that the very first sighting of the black boomerang shaped objects had been made by a person who lived only a few blocks away from my home on the evening of Thursday, April 15, at the exact time I was conducting my hypnosis session with the woman who lost 50 miles between the blue light and the red light. (The woman had been watching a television program, and knew exactly at what point she had seen the UFO.) What was even more upsetting was that the witness's description seemed to place the black boomerang hovering directly over my neighborhood, maybe even right over my house.

The reports of the black boomerangs that came in conjunction with this session did not make me happy. In fact, it gave me the absolute creeps! It also made me think.

If we conjecture that this "alien phenomenon" is part of some deep government conspiracy designed to experiment on people—perhaps to make them think that they are being abducted by aliens so that they will assiduously seek greater controls and protection from "Big Brother"—we have a curious problem with this case: how could such a hypothesized group engineer the response to this session that did, in fact, manifest?

I was very careful not to mention the word "alien" or "abduction" to the woman on the phone prior to the session. If phone conversations are being monitored, how did this one get selected for special attention? Such monitoring, even for "key words" that would trigger a need for personal attention, suggests a conspiracy of such vast and complex proportions that the logistics of it stagger the mind.

Well, suppose it is a government conspiracy. Suppose that they do have such monitoring capabilities, that they are monitoring my phone, Pat's phone, or the phones of everybody by computer. As a result, suppose they knew I was going to hypnotize her and sent out a flotilla of stealth type aircraft to beam some wave at her (or something like that) which would prevent her from talking to me. Why would they go to all that trouble?

It seems to me that it would be easier to just send one of those nice white panel trucks we see in the movies to park a block away from my house for their "wave beaming" activities. Or perhaps they just thought it was a handy time to create a UFO flap at that moment for general purposes: to get everyone all excited, to reinforce the "alien phenomenon" scenario they are creating. We are still looking at logistics that stagger the mind.

The next question we have to ask is this: since this woman "appeared" in my life at precisely the moment I had been familiarized with the phenomenon sufficiently to recognize the symptoms, how do we deal with that synchronicity? If it is a government conspiracy that was aiming at taking me in by gradual degrees, by creating a series of events in my life that would lead me to give up my "rational explanations" of the phenomenon, what kind of surveillance and "human resources management" does that suggest? Again, it boggles the mind.

My conclusion was that it couldn't be human engineered, but I wasn't ready to seriously consider that it could be "otherworldly" either. In other words, *high strangeness* was everywhere. Thinking these thoughts produced a strange feeling in me of being "watched" in ways hard to describe. It was so strange a synchronicity that I couldn't help but think that the appearance of these craft related to our activities with the superluminal communication experiment. I tried to sweep this thought under the rug, but it kept coming back.

There was a final article in the *St. Petersburg Times* about this series of sightings and this last article was designed to put it all to rest; it was a suggestion that what had been seen was a "stealth bomber". It was all just a strange coincidence. My comfort zone was reestablished and I could rest at night—for a while.

Frank, of course, was ecstatic with this event. It was proof that Pat knew things that were dangerous to know—something the aliens—didn't want her to reveal. He theorized that the presence of the UFOs was an effort to reinforce a pain block, or even induce it remotely, and that this was what she meant when she said, "They won't let me [tell what happened]."

Even though this was a reasonable deduction, based on the observable evidence, I was not ready to buy Frank's theories. I was so determined to deny the evidence of so-called aliens, and to prove that the alien phenomenon was nothing more than a psychological aberration, that I decided that the rash of sightings was just another outbreak of millennial disease. As soon as one person claimed to have seen the giant boomerang, the public became excited and "infected", and everybody was imagining that they were seeing the same thing. After all, if there were so many aliens out there snatching people, where was the proof? "Where's the evidence?" I asked Frank. "Show me a damned alien, for God's sakes. *Habeas Corpus!*"

black boomerangs

At this point, health issues again moved to the forefront. All my life, it seemed that as soon as I recovered by sheer force of will from one assault, another would arrive seemingly out of nowhere. I could hardly walk, standing became excruciatingly painful, and the numbness, tingling, and bone-deep aching in my left arm nearly drove me crazy. The doctor diagnosed it as angina, related to heart damage I had suffered in 1981, and suggested exercise. Not being able to stand or walk for more than a few minutes, the obvious solution was swimming.

The only place to swim therapeutically was a stressful 30 minute drive away, and my legs swelled terribly after just ten or fifteen minutes of riding in the car. I began to think about how helpful it would be to have a swimming pool in the back yard, but I realized that there was just simply no way that we could manage in terms of our present situation. I would have to think of another way; perhaps the beach or the public pool. But, just in case, I said out loud to the empty room, "God, a swimming pool would help!"

One night, my number two daughter asked her father if she could pick the numbers as he was going out the door to buy his lottery tickets. She picked them, and we won! Fifteen grand.

The pool wasn't ready until August. I thought it was appropriate that the children and I could "baptize" the pool by floating on our rubber rafts and watching the Perseid meteor shower.

August 16, 1993: In the subtropics, it gets dark about nine o'clock in the evening, so it would not be until a couple of hours later that meteor viewing conditions would be optimal. The children were excited to stay up late and watch a meteor shower in the pool. They had rushed out at about ten o'clock, while I stayed in and struggled to clean up the kitchen before going out to join them at eleven. Three of the five children were out there with me. My eldest daughter was on a date, and the baby was in bed.

I slid into pool for the very first time, and was so happy and grateful to have it! I moved to the far side to lean my head against the ledge and float, looking in the direction the meteors were supposed to be found. The viewing conditions were favorable: no moon, clear sky with only a slight upper level haze from the humidity, and the ambient light was minimal. Suddenly, my twelve-year-old daughter cried out, "Look! Up there!"

This was no meteor. It was a 300 foot wide black boomerang, emanating a faint reddish glow, moving so slow and low that I knew if I had been standing on the roof of my two-story house, I could have reached up and touched it! We had plenty of time to observe it and note the "brushed matte black metal" appearance of its underside.

We watched as it moved ever so slowly overhead, utterly silent, seeming to float more than anything else. It continued south, seeming to skim the treetops.

We were looking at each other and saying "What was that?!" when my son shouted, "Another one!" And, sure enough, just to the west of the path of the first one, there was another. Every detail was identical: altitude, speed, reddish glow, and utter silence! I was, at this point, in sufficient possession of my senses to try to hear something! Dead silence. And that struck me as odd, since there are normally all kinds of night sounds: crickets, night birds, frogs and so forth. But there was no sound, no vibration, no hum. Nothing.

We stood there in amazement for a few frozen moments and then the kids began to shout for their dad to come out. He came to the door.

"What's all the excitement about?"

The kids were saying, all at once, "We saw a UFO!"

"That's nonsense", he said.

I will never be able to explain why I said this, but what came out of my mouth was, "Oh, it was just a flock of geese! I guess we are going to have bad weather because the geese are flying South early this year!" I laughed as I shoved it under the rug.

My husband looked at me like I was an idiot. "Geese", he said sarcastically, "do not fly South in August. And anyway, we are South!" Hearing a logical refutation had a strange effect on me: I became very upset and confused all out of proportion to the event.

The only thing I could think of to do was to go inside and call Frank. He was absolutely ecstatic, crowing with delight: "Finally you'll believe me! You saw a real UFO!" He then rewound his answering machine and played a message from an hour earlier. Another friend had called him to describe having seen the exact same thing! He had been out in his driveway at ten o'clock to see a few meteors and was also over-flown by the big black boomerang, with his neighbor as a witness.

At this point, I became so upset that I had to go in my bedroom and sit and consider the matter. It was clear to me that if I could not find a rational explanation for this thing, there was only one thing to think: either they were real, or I had contracted the "Millennial Disease" and was losing my mind.

This was certainly not a stealth bomber. The newspaper article had described them pretty thoroughly when the previous flap had occurred several months earlier. The writer had assumed that when people say they are seeing a "boomerang" shaped object, that they are really saying a "triangular" object. The description of the stealth bombers included a fuselage that the object we had seen simply did not have. It had been a boomerang shape. Not a triangle, not a diamond, a boomerang without any sort of "body" behind the bow shape. But how could I know this for sure? Maybe there were stealth bombers that were newer or different models.

Did anybody *else* see it besides Frank's friend and his neighbor and the kids and me? I wanted to get a consensus of descriptions. I wanted to know that I was not crazy. I wanted an explanation. That meant, of course, that with the weight of evidence from others, I would be able to consult with authorities and confirm that it was, indeed, easily explained as an experimental—but terrestrial—craft. Problem solved, case closed.

So, the next day, trying to act very casual in spite of my embarrassment at even asking such a question, I called a couple of the local television stations to inquire if there had been any reports of "strange objects" in the sky. One woman was very nasty and informed me that, of course there had been strange objects in the sky, it was called a meteor shower! Well, I was not talking about lights flashing across the sky, and I certainly knew a meteor from a 300 foot wide black boomerang, but damned if I was going to even utter those words! All I wanted to know was if there had been any reports of anything from all the meteor watchers that could not be explained.

The results were less than helpful. I was treated like a lunatic for even asking the question. That only served to heighten my dismay. But I wasn't ready to give up yet.

I received similar treatment from various other media sources I contacted in my effort to get some information. I was not comfortable enough to make a report of my own, so I was really trying to talk about the subject without even using the term "UFO". In retrospect, my reluctance to even say it is comical!

There didn't seem to be any information to be obtained until Frank called and told me that the weatherman on one of the television stations had mentioned that one of the "community weather observers" had reported several "flocks of geese" the previous night. Since I had tried to explain it to myself in these same terms, I thought that this might be a "hit". But that was all I was going to get from the "standard" sources.

I was frustrated at being blown off and treated like an idiot. This frustration only added fuel to the fire burning in me, driving the need to discover what it was I had seen. As I considered my options, I remembered an organization that collected reports of such things: MUFON (Mutual UFO Network). Maybe they would know. Even if they were somewhat to the left of rational in their belief that some sightings of strange craft were "alien", they were said to be trying to sort the real ones from the false reports. Perhaps they could help me confirm that I had seen an aircraft that was known, or conjectured to be, part of a secret government project?

I looked in the back of one of Frank's books and found the phone number for the national headquarters of MUFON. The person who answered gave me the number for the local chapter. An answering machine picked up. The director was going to be on vacation for the next two weeks. I hesitated, but finally left my name and number and the fact that I wanted some information about a "possible UFO sighting". I was using "UFO" in the literal sense of the word: it was unidentified, and I was seeking identification in a rational sense, not a confirmation of alien visitations and more mumbo jumbo.

It was well into September before anyone from MUFON called me back, with an apology for taking so long. Since the monthly meeting was the next day, perhaps I would come and give the report in person. Well, that was pushing me just a bit too far, too fast. I was not ready to hang out with geeks who believed in little green men and who probably wore plastic pocket protectors, coke-bottle glasses, and kept Mad Magazine rolled up in their back pockets!

I mean, get real!

The day of the MUFON meeting, I was definitely not going to go. I was going to drop the whole subject. But, as the clock rolled around, the kids disappeared to various activities, the baby went off with her father, and I was left at home alone. The need to know had not lessened one bit, and I tried to come up with any rational excuse not to go. Surprisingly, my usual state of exhaustion was at a minimum and, with no other apparent reason to hinder me, I thought that maybe, just maybe, I would go and check this MUFON bunch out. If it was creepy, or if I became too tired, I could always come right home.

I was surprised. There were no geeks. Not a single pocket protector. And these folks were certainly too old for Mad Magazine! I entered quietly, took a seat at the back of the room and listened to a discussion in progress. I was amazed at how extremely intelligent and rational these folks were; more so than average, in my opinion; and certainly brighter than the run-of-the-mill "New Age Groupie". No one was ranting a spittle flecked monologue about being visited by Venusians, taken aboard their craft, and transported to Looney-Land. Nobody was talking about aliens here to "serve mankind". In fact, it was a rather technical discussion of possible propulsion systems of UFOs, based on observed behavior by creditable witnesses whose stories were cited, along with some impressive documentation and credentials.

At the break, I was asked to sign a guest sheet. The director recognized my name and asked me to talk about my sighting. After the break I stood in front of the group and, with extreme embarrassment, began to tell my little story about the Black Boomerang. As I finished, all sorts of questions were asked. I made a drawing on a blackboard and that was that. I had said my piece and I sat down.

A discussion followed. The earliest known sighting of the Black Boomerang type object, as I had drawn it on the chalkboard, was in Albuquerque in 1951. They were also seen in Lubbock, Texas, and became famous as the "Lubbock

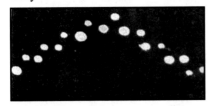

Lights" in the photo to the left.[2] It was noted, as a point of interest, that these early sightings also occurred in the month of August, which I thought was peculiar. What was most interesting to me was the fact that the same design was seen over 40 years previously. That sort of cancelled out my idea of a new design. No change in model in 40 years? Those boys in Black Ops are really slipping! No imagination at all!

There were also extensive reports of these types of craft being sighted repeatedly in the Hudson Valley of New York in a famous series of events that included all kinds of anomalous phenomena among the hundreds of witnesses.[3]

---

[2] One of five photographs taken by student Carl Hart in Texas, August 1952.

[3] The Hudson Valley Sightings actually comprises of a number of incidents which took place between 31st December 1982 and 10th July 1986. These truly remarkable sightings have never been explained and even "arch-debunker" Philip J. Klass admitted to being baffled by the whole series of incidents. Beginning in Putnam County, New York, the series of sightings eventually involved approximately 5,000 witnesses and covered the geographic area from Peekskill and Ossining, New York, in the west to New Haven, Connecticut in the east and from Brookfield, Connecticut in the north to Westport in the south. Many of the objects observed were described as V-shaped or "boomerang-shaped" but later triangular craft were also witnessed. A very large majority of witnesses claimed that the objects were truly colossal, at least 300 ft. in size and, in general, most of them were travelling much slower than a plane. On the whole the UFOs were described as being silent, although a hum was sometimes heard. All of the sightings were experienced at night and

49

A scientist had been involved in that situation, a Dr. Hynek. I had never heard the name before, but I was soon to hear it quite a lot. I would also come to respect his work and opinions.

Long after these events and discussions, I did more research on the "Black Boomerang" matter and discovered some very disturbing connections in an article in the book series *Mysteries of Mind, Space and Time*, written by Hamish Howard and Toyne Newton, edited by Peter Brookesmith (Westport: Stuttman, 1992). The authors give some of the history of Clapham wood, "a small densely-treed area nestling in the shelter of the South Downs in West Sussex, England." Reports of strange lights and high strangeness go back hundreds of years. One resident reporting seeing a Moon-sized light descend into the woods, which left the stench of burning matter. More recently, in October 1972, a telephone engineer saw a "flying saucer" hover over the woods before veering off, while at the same time a couple walking nearby saw a light in the sky approach Clapham Wood, sending a beam of light vertically into the woods below and then taking off at a high speed.

> Paul Glover of the British Phenomenon Research Group was walking ... along the downs toward Clapham Wood one clear starlit night in the summer of 1967. At about 10 p.m., both men suddenly became aware of a huge black mass low in the sky blotting out the stars as it moved very quickly toward them. The object was boomerang shaped and made no sound. As it passed overhead the displacement of air was so great they ducked into the bushes for safety. They vehemently denied it could have been a cloud, for it retained its shape, was on a definite course, and there was no wind to drive it. Minutes later, they saw two bright objects high in the sky, which they watched for several minutes. One of the UFOs released a smaller object that traveled across to the second object, seemed to enter it, and then re-emerged and veered off, disappearing from sight. An hour later, on their return in the opposite direction of their walk, two yellow lights descended in the region of the woods, followed just a few seconds later by two more, and then a final pair, making a total or three groups of two. Then at the point where they seemed to have dipped down into the woods, two white beams of light shot out horizontally—quite unimpeded by the contours of the downlands—followed by the next two beams and then the final two, all traveling very fast, before disappearing into the night sky. No craft of any kind could be seen behind the lights.
>
> During that same year, in the village of Rustington a few miles westwards along the coast, two schoolboys, Toyne Newton and John Arnold, who had never even heard of Clapham Wood, had a strange story spelled out to them on a Ouija board: that Clapham Wood was a base for spacecraft,[4] and that one had landed recently to fetch supplies of sulphur and other chemicals.

---

observers remarked that the objects showed between five and fifteen lights of a number of colours, sometimes the lights changed colour and turned off and on. On occasions these lights were bright enough to illuminate the ground below the craft.

[4] I found this reference to a Ouija board warning about UFO bases in conjunction with a sighting of a black boomerang to be quite coincidental considering my own sighting of a boomerang type craft, followed 11 months to the day by the "arrival" of the Cassiopaeans.

No one believed the boys, of course, but nearly 10 years later an investigation was carried out when soil samples were taken from the woods. From the report given in BBC-TV's Nationwide program at the time, it seems there was more than a grain of truth to the sulphur story. The investigation had been triggered by reports of dogs disappearing in the woods in 1975.

According to a local paper, the *Worthing Herald*, Wallace, a 3 yr. old chow belonging to Mr. and Mrs. Peter Love of Clapham, disappeared, as did a 2 yr. old collie belonging to Mr. John Cornford. Apparently the collie, although normally obedient, suddenly rushed off into a small copse between two trees in an area known locally as the Chestnuts, and was never seen again. The mystified owner searched thoroughly!

Mrs. H.T. Wells, who lives at nearby Durrington, said that when her collie gets near the woods, it becomes "desperate", and a golden retriever belonging to Mr. E.F. Rawlins of Worthing ran into the woods one day and returned "very distressed". Shortly afterwards it became paralyzed and had to be destroyed".

Another dog owner, who wished to remain anonymous, reported that when she took her dog to this area it ran around in circles, foaming at the mouth, with its eyes bulging as if in great pain.

The account goes on to say that a horseman (who also wished to remain anonymous, but his report was said to have been verified) tied his horse to a tree and stepped back a ways to have a pit stop. When he stepped back out of the bushes, he was amazed to find his horse missing. Although he searched the area extensively and made exhaustive enquiries, the horse was never found.

Several people have reported the feeling of being "pushed over by invisible forces" in this area and others have had spells of faintness. Two men walking through the wood reported that both were afflicted at the same moment: one doubling over in internal agony and the other clutching his head and screaming that his eardrums were "being pulled out of his head". They both staggered about 50 yards further and the effects ceased.

The body of a missing man was found two weeks after he went missing, but in an extremely advanced state of decomposition. Forensic evidence showed that the rate of decomposition had been greatly accelerated due to "unknown factors". This article continues:

A skeptical investigator, Dave Stringer of the Southern Paranormal Investigation Group, visited the area with a Geiger counter in August [there is that month again] 1977. The woods were silent and the air still. Everything appeared normal, but, as he pushed through heavy undergrowth, he had to lift the machine above his head. When he did so, it began to register an alarming high level. Mr. Stringer stopped and looked back at the area he had just passed through. He saw a dark shape about 12 feet in height; while not being distinctive in outline, it was very definitely not smoke and he could only describe it as a "black mass". Seconds later a large white disk shot out from behind nearby trees at a 45 degree angle and disappeared into the sky. Simultaneously, the dark mass disappeared. Stinger retraced his steps [braver than I!] and found at the spot where the form had appeared, an imprint of a four toed footprint similar to one found at a place called Devils' Dyke near Brighton, where there was known to be a black magic "coven".

51

Stringer made a quick sketch of the footprint. It was unknown to him at the time, that it matches a footprint reproduced in Collin de Plancy's *Dictionaire Infernal* published in 1863, and that this footprint is supposed to be that of the "Demon Amduscias".

UFO sightings continued at Clapham into 1978 and 1979. The spate of strange reports at that time concluded with the disappearance of the Reverend Neil Snelling, vicar of Clapham Church... One morning after shopping at Worthing, he decided to walk back to his Steyning home through Clapham Wood. He has not been heard of since and an exhaustive search of the area revealed nothing. [The retired Clapham vicar's remains were not discovered until three years later in August 1981 near Wiston Barn on the Downs and an Inquest subsequently declared an open verdict.]

All in all, I was coming to an awareness that this phenomenon was not only strange, it was possibly dangerous. Just how strange and dangerous I would discover soon enough. Two most disturbing things were taking place that are mirrored in the report about the Clapham Wood Black Boomerang and its effect upon animals. My collie, Danny-boy, went into a decline that nothing could reverse. The vet was completely baffled, and everything we tried failed. In the end, he could only suggest a congenital heart defect leading to cardiac insufficiency. Within three months of the Black Boomerang, he died with his head in my lap on the kitchen floor. Danny was only three years old, a gentle and wonderful dog. I was heartbroken. (At this point in time, I was making absolutely no connection between the Black Boomerang and Danny-boy's death.)

At the same time, my own physical condition, instead of getting better, had gotten worse from that first night in the pool. I was constantly sick. I had a terrible rashes, hives and welts. All the mucous membranes of my body kept swelling to the point that my throat and nose would almost shut completely. The undersides of my eyelids were so irritated they oozed yellowish, sticky fluids constantly. My ears itched deep inside which nearly drove me crazy.

These symptoms were always the precursor to an attack of severe nausea. I felt as though a fence post had been driven through my chest. My breathing was labored and painful; I broke out in a cold sweat. My doctor finally suggested that I was suffering allergies which exacerbated my already compromised cardio-pulmonary system. It was decided that I must have reached a sort of "critical mass" of allergen exposure at some recent time. I had some relief from Benadryl and other allergy medications, but that was not a long-term solution. My body simply did not seem to be able to handle the toxins anymore. The doctor wanted to run extensive allergy tests and begin a course of treatment designed to more or less desensitize me to whatever was affecting my system.

The symptoms were worse at night, starting at about 11:00 p.m. I reasoned this must be the time of "critical mass" of the day's exposure to whatever allergen was active at the moment. However, as long as I was sitting still and didn't try to move around too much, I was fine. Moreover, my brain hadn't died, so I continued to read and study to divert my mind. I also kept a schedule of hypnosis sessions. Without reading and my work, I would have felt completely useless. I would have had no life at all.

more missing time

All through the early months of 1994 we had continued our weekly sittings. We continued our lottery experiments, and also regularly "tested" various entities with questions about weather, politics, news items of various sorts, asked for predictions about this or that person and, admittedly, asked all kinds of snoopy questions just to see what would bounce back.

The point was to establish a "feedback" loop designed to access deep levels of consciousness at the least, or to "tune" the bio-cosmic receiver, at most. Most part-time participants had neither the patience nor the motivation to continue in anything that did not provide instant gratification or winning lotto numbers. They wanted to be able to just "turn on, tune in and channel now!" Working at it was too much like—well—like work!

Candy, who I met after another series of truly bizarre events, was a regular participant for almost half a year. When she learned that I worked with hypnosis, she immediately wanted to be hypnotized because she was convinced that she had been abducted by aliens. After dealing with Pat, I wasn't too anxious to dive into that arena again. Just because I was a good hypnotist and had good techniques and ideas, didn't mean that I knew beans from apple butter about handling an alleged alien abductions. All the reading I was doing wasn't going to give me the technical education I needed to handle it, either.

Well, naive bozo that I sometimes am, I thought it would just be a matter of making some calls to find who to go to for advice or training. I started at the logical place to begin: call the local psychologists and psychiatrists for guidance. Not a good idea. Nobody in our semi-backwater area would even consider such an idea, much less touch it with a ten foot pole!

As I continued to make calls on Candy's behalf, the enormity of the problem began to overwhelm me. From what I could determine, many, many thousands of people—a cross section of humanity—were coming forward and saying that they had experienced contact with aliens from other worlds. In all my reading of history and social phenomena, I had never encountered anything quite like this. And yet the general response they get from others, including professionals who are supposed to be providing help and support, is *ridicule*. But even if the phenomenon was bogus, didn't the people claiming such experiences deserve counseling?

In reviewing the cases available to me, I noted that the typical victim was almost frantically worried about a "loss of time", and some vague memory of being restrained or trapped. The person becomes hyper-irritable, suffers from loss of concentration and short-term memory. An "abductee" is generally hypersensitive to loud noises, claims to hear things no one else can hear, and to see things no one else can see, including getting "feelings" about others that are impossible to explain or quantify in any way. In short, they show signs of real trauma.

One of the more disturbing aspects of the phenomenon is that there are often physical traces—scratches, puncture wounds, bruises—and even missing segments of skin, generally in perfectly round configuration as though removed by a cookie cutter.

Candy was obviously suffering. She was almost hysterical in her desperation to find an answer to what was going on in her life. It was clear that she felt almost abandoned by her husband and friends in this matter, because it was so strange and out of keeping with the other, utterly normal, aspects of her life. It was clear that she was suffering from severe anxiety, and a very real fear of being alone for even a short while.

No matter what the explanation for their experiences, these people needed to be taken seriously; they needed to be validated; and most of all they needed a support system.

Basically, I had three choices to consider in regards to Candy.

1) She was purposely creating a hoax, no abduction occurred.

2) An abduction really occurred by persons or beings unknown.

3) No abduction occurred, but Candy believed it did.

I was rapidly giving up the idea that abduction stories were concocted for fame and glory. For most people, the event was one of great shame, and they most certainly didn't want anybody to know about it. That they were so desperate for help that they overcame tremendous reluctance indicates how severely they were traumatized.

The question of the sanity of people claiming to have been abducted was also rapidly being answered in the negative. If millions of people believed that a guy, 2000 years ago, died on a cross and arose three days later, and were considered sane, then people claiming abductions, with far more direct experience and evidence, were undoubtedly sane also.

I realized, however, that each individual case had to be considered separately. To assume anything from the beginning was not ethical. To begin an investigation of such an event meant that the only thing I would be dealing with was Candy's memory—either conscious or unconscious. Thus, a consideration of her life history was necessary. I was going to be far more thorough with Candy than I had been with Pat.

Candy was about 35 years old, the wife of a doctor, owner of her own fashion boutique, and mother to two girls. She had been born and raised in a very strict religious family, but, chafing at the restrictions, had left home at an early age to stay with a brother who worked in a designer clothing shop. There, she also began working in the same business and ended up marrying the owner. This man died, leaving her with a small child and a large inheritance.

A beautiful young widow with a baby and a lot of money does not remain on the marriage market very long. With her new husband, the doctor (the spitting image of Dudley Do-Right), she moved to Florida where they had a second child together. The object was to get away from the unhappy memories of the loss of her first husband and start a new life. The boutique she left in the care of her brother, who managed the business on her behalf.

After her youngest child started school, Candy became bored and decided to go to work for a different doctor in the large medical complex where her husband also had his offices. She took an administrative position and settled into her role with ease. She was very intelligent, charming and attractive.

At the same time, Candy began to attend a Metaphysical/Spiritualist church, probably more out of curiosity than anything else, but soon became deeply involved in the spiritualist beliefs and practices. At this point, strange things began to happen. She claimed that strange things had happened to her all her life, but she just had managed to suppress most of it. I certainly understood this approach!

First, she kept encountering a man in the building where she worked. He was employed by a practice on a different floor, so she only saw him in the elevators, the parking lot, and the local cafes. Every time she did encounter him, she was conscious of a strange electricity between them. Soon they were exchanging brief pleasantries.

One evening, Candy and a co-worker, her friend Edith, went out for drinks together when Candy's husband was at a medical convention. The man she kept running into coincidentally appeared in the same bar and stopped by their table. They invited him to sit down and soon were involved in a conversation on metaphysical topics. Candy said that she could not recall how the subjects followed one after the other, but what was true was that in a very short period of time, the three of them were discussing deeply held beliefs, feeling intense rapport, and it was somewhat "magical". The man said he knew the location of an old Indian mound, apparently a place of great power. He offered to show both ladies where it was. Feeling secure with a female companion, Candy wanted to see this Indian mound, and they all went together in the man's car. Keep in mind that it was well past dark when they made this plan. When they arrived at the location, a swampy, wooded area on the Gulf of Mexico, they all got out and proceeded to hike through the underbrush to this purported Indian mound.

Now, aside from the absurdity of the picture presented here, three adults in their business clothing, hiking out in the muddy swamps after dark, there is the consideration of what, in the name of all good sense, would have sent anyone off on such a hike?

Nevertheless, that is, apparently, what they did. Three professional adults of impeccable good sense decided to go stomping in the tidal swamps on the Florida coast at night. At some point, Edith was left behind and lost. Something happened to frighten Candy, but afterward she couldn't say what it was, only that she was very confused. She demanded to be taken home. The man cheerfully obliged, they located Edith wandering in the bushes, and he drove them back to their cars and off they went home.

The only problem was, when Candy got home, it was almost midnight. She had "lost" well over two hours.

I went over this point with her carefully, going over the exact chronology of that night. She should have been home no later than 9:30, yet, it was just a few minutes before midnight when she made it home. She was surprised because her children were already in bed sleeping, and the house was quiet and dark. When she saw the time, she became almost hysterical at the very thought that she had been gone so long. What might her children have thought?

At that point Candy's life began to fall apart. She was suddenly so emotional that she couldn't stay on an even keel from one minute to the next. She became almost uncontrollably obsessed with the man in the building, believing he was her "soul mate" one minute, and that he was a government spy the next. This was related to her belief that, somehow, the government was "watching" her. She felt that somehow she must find ways to be with this man because the government was using him against her, and they were really meant to be together. Then she felt he was watching her, and she had better avoid him.

Immediately following this event, her husband was in an auto accident with another woman in the car. Any reservations she might have had about the break-up of her marriage dissolved, and the relationship disintegrated rapidly. It was at this point that I first met her. In other words, she must have made her trip to the swamps at almost the exact time the series of synchronous events began to manifest in my own life that led me to meet Candy!

Candy apparently knew the abduction encounter scenario from reading or other sources. She thought she had experienced some sort of encounter with "Space Brothers". She was convinced that she had been given a message during her encounter, and that it was important for her to remember it to share with mankind.

Trying to get the story out of her in a linear way was like pulling teeth. The subject was so laden with emotion that it was difficult to make anything out of it without stopping her repeatedly, backing her up, and having her describe things in a sequential way. I didn't want to jump to any conclusions because I still held out for the possibility of other explanations. Based on the series of events, I thought it was also possible that she had been given some kind of "date rape" drug by this man who took her to the Indian mound with rather more ordinary— if reprehensible—intentions.

But Candy held firmly to the idea that the man had hypnotized her, that he was a government agent, and that the government was watching her because she was "chosen" by the aliens to deliver a message. Why or how he would be involved in her abduction if he were a government agent wasn't exactly clear, and certainly didn't make any sense. Candy knew it. She agreed with a rueful laugh that she knew she sounded crazy, and it was clear that she was close to the edge. She most definitely needed help, and if I couldn't find someone competent to send her to, or to instruct me, we might have been on our own with this one.

It also seemed to me to be important to find out how much Candy had read about alien abductions. She claimed that she had never read anything about it, that what she knew was just gossip and word of mouth, but I wasn't too sure. If she had spent a lot of time reading about the subject she was, in my opinion, "contaminated" as a true "test" subject. I could help her to deal with the trauma, but I could never consider her statements under hypnosis to be evidence of anything. After trying for weeks to find competent help without success, I finally agreed to do an "exploratory" session.

As might be expected, in Candy's subconscious mind, there were abductions galore. Candy was a veritable "chosen child" of the friendly Gray aliens. However, certain elements came up in her sessions that startled her. The abduction process was decidedly not as friendly as she'd thought. The following are extracts from a series of sessions done over a period of several months:

Q: OK. What's happening to you next?

A: I see this bright light and I'm alarmed... I see fingers like suction cups on the end of them... They're like touching my face...

Q: How many individuals are there with you?

A: Oh God, this is weird. (Sigh.) It's almost like I see a dinosaur or something. With little short arms... and its, um... it's got funny skin... it's like, it's like... brownish, slickish... it's got a real funny face... it's like a skull but the front of the skull is like going out, real far out...

Q: Like a snout?

A: Yeah.

Q: How tall was it?

A: Um...

Q: Taller than you?

A: Oh yeah, it looked bigger than me. It's just funny.

Q: What's funny?

A: Nothing, it's gone.

Q: Where did it go.

A: I don't know. It disappeared.

Q: What do you mean it disappeared?

A: I don't know, it's almost like an image. And then it just vanished.

Q: How many other beings are there with you?

A: Um... they're all busy all over.

Q: About how many are there?

A: Um... five or six.

Q: What do they look like? Do they all look the same?

A: Oh, they're funny looking... they're almost like, um... they remind me of the baby dinosaur... how puffy his face was with the eyes were like... smaller... not big eyes like him... like squinty eyes...

Q: What color are their eyes?

A: Um... I don't know... when I look at their eyes I see a green circle that keeps swirling... [...]

Q: What is happening to you?

A: Um. (Sigh.) It's hard to breathe.

Q: Do you smell something?

A: No. I see a little... it's almost like a little gold scorpion. It's right by my nose... my face...

Q: What is it doing?

A: I don't know. They have it on the end of some tweezers.

Q: Where is the scorpion going?

A: (Signs of distress.) Uh, this is weird... it's almost like it goes in my mouth... the back of my... my, um, throat...

Q: How does it get there?

A: They put it there.

Q: How do they put it there?

A: Um... it's almost like I see a machine with an arm on it. Almost like a dentist's arm... I don't know...

Q: What is it for?

A: I don't know... television comes to my mind...

Q: Did they tell you what it was for?

A: No, they don't tell me.

Q: Is it in place now?

A: Um.. They're working on it. They're moving my head... I hear ringing in my ears

Q: What happens next?

A: Um... the back of my neck hurts!

Q: Why does the back of your neck hurt?

A: I don't know, its like... I have these headaches...

Q: Where are you now?

A: I'm on the table.

Q: What are they doing to you?

A: They're rubbing my arms.

Q: Has the scorpion been put in?

A: Um hmm.

Q: Did it hurt?

A: Um hmm.

Q: It did?

A: I don't know... it's just... I got a headache now...

Q: Where did they put it into.

A: Well, you know, it's like... in the back of my neck... its through my mouth into the back of my neck... and my ears... I hear my ears ringing... they're like clogged up... and I feel... I don't know... like shh... shocks or... I don't know...

Q: Shocks?

A: Pain shooting through my head.

Q: Pain? What is the pain from?

A: It's like nerve something... I don't know...

Q: OK. You have a small mark above your ear... where did you get that mark?

A: I don't know, it's like, um... I don't know... I see this... I see a little tiny, um... metal box... I'm just gonna say what I see... I don't know...

Q: That's connected to the mark above your ear?

A: Yeah. It's almost like I feel like I'm being bit by an ant or something...

Q: Well, were you being bit by an ant?

A: Hm. When I thought... When you said that I see uh, um, it's almost like an ant made out of metal...

Q: OK.

A: With the stingers.

Q: What does it do?

A: What, the ant?

Q: Um hmm.

A: It has... I'm seeing a needle on it...

Q: Long needle, short needle...

A: Uh, I see a needle... its like it connects to something...

Q: What does it do?

A: Goes in and it connects to something... I don't know...

Q: Did this happen at the same time that the scorpion was put in your neck through your throat?

A: No... (Distress.)

Q: Let's go back to where you are on the table and they have just put the little scorpion in the back of your neck through your throat... Now, you said this hurt... Did it hurt when they put it in? Or did it begin hurting after they put it in?

A: After they put it in. I had a headache... I have a headache... [...]

Q: OK. How long have you been connected with this group?

A: Um... I just see a face in front of me...

Q: What does the face look like?

A: Um...

Q: Is it one of them?

A: Um hmm... it has real sad eyes... it doesn't want me saying anything... [...]

Q: Do they have any future plans?

A: I hear something saying yes.

Q: Do you know when?

A: No.

Q: Do you know what's in store... what will happen? Are you in cooperation with them?

A: Umm... I don't know... I don't feel good.

Q: What are you feeling right now...

A: I don't know... I'm feeling kind of sick to my stomach.

Q: Take a real deep breath and the nausea will pass.

A: Oh, God! (Sigh.)

Q: Now, Candy I'm here and I'll take care of you. You know we discussed beforehand that we want to know at the deepest level we can understand. Are these beings working with you with your permission?

chapter two

A: Umm... No.

Q: Is there action you can take, or that you can perceive in a broad way, to prevent this kind of action or activity?

A: Umm... I don't know what this is I'm seeing... a tunnel...

Q: You're seeing what, a tunnel?

A: A tunnel with like webs all on it... I don't know what it is... its... (Long pause, signs of distress.)

Q: A tunnel with webs in it?

A: Yeah... it's not a nice place... (Signs of extreme nausea and distress.) Mmmm...

Q: If the tunnel could speak, what would it say?

A: You don't want to be here.

Q: Where is here?

A: It's almost like "where we can put you if we want you".

Q: What is there?

A: Bad stuff.

Q: What kind of bad stuff?

A: Ah... this is weird... it's almost like see a crayfish eating like a red glob... but the crayfish has a mouth...

Q: If the crayfish could talk, what would it say?

A: They don't talk. (Signs of nausea and distress.)

Q: What is the red glob?

A: I don't know... (Gagging.)

Q: Alright, take a deep breath now...

A: I don't like this...

Q: Alright, I am going to count from five to one, and on the count of one you are going to move to your highest level of consciousness... a place of pure light and knowledge. (Countdown.) How do you feel now?

A: OK.

Q: Now, do you see the light?

A: Um hmm.

Q: Alright. I want you to merge with the light and the knowledge that is in the light. Is there any means by which you can stop these events or protect yourself? The knowledge will be there, you can access it easily.

A: (Long pause) It's almost like I'm hearing a voice say that we have something beautiful that they will never ever have.

Q: We as humans?

A: Um hmm.

Q: Is this what they wish to acquire?

A: Um... I don't know... they're just like, I would guess, parasites, or something like that. [...]

Q: What's going on around you.

A: I'm just going to tell you what I see... it's kind of weird. Umm... I see all these little white guys, they're like children... they're running around... a bunch of 'em... umm... I see this woman with gray umm... I don't know if I can see her... (Distress.) You know, it's like I'm trying to see and it's slipping. She's there but I can't see her.

Q: Take a real deep breath. I am going to count to three and on the count of three any blocks to your memory, any impediments, any distortions will dissolve away and you will see clearly and completely everything that occurred to you at that point in space time and forward. (Countdown.) What do you see? Look at this woman. What does she look like?

A: Umm... I'm in a different room. This room is a round room and it has almost like a glass dome over the top of it... ummm... I'm, uh... it's like a city I'm seeing. This is strange...

Q: Stop a minute... stop and take a real deep breath. Back up. Back up to the woman you couldn't see. On the count of three she will appear on the screen and you will be able to describe her clearly. (Countdown)

A: Umm... oooh... I see this woman... she's got long wiry white hair...

Q: What about her eyes?

A: I'm just going to tell you what I see. When I look in her eyes they are like circle green... circling green... spiraling... on one picture I see her as ugly but then I see a beautiful woman's face... I see her one way and when I look there is like a shadow over the face... it looks like a beautiful woman but when I first looked at her it wasn't but... when I look at it again it looks like a beautiful woman...

Q: What sensation do you get from this woman?

A: I just want to say she's hateful.

Q: Does she say anything to you?

A: No. It's like she's watching me real careful.

Q: What does her body look like?

A: Umm.. real thin and tall... really thin, thin, thin arms and long fingers.

Q: How many fingers?

A: I want to say four. She's real, real tall. Real skinny. But this big head with this wiry hair.

Q: Describe the head.

A: It's a triangle but kind of rounded on the edges.

Q: Does she have big ears or little ears?

A: No, I'm seeing little curves on the side of her head.

Q: What about her mouth?

A: Rows of teeth.

Q: What about a nose?

A: I'm seeing two little curves, real small... two holes, just holes.

Q: Does she say anything to you?

A: No. She's watching me though. Watching me as I'm walking by with these, these... she dislikes me for some reason.

Q: OK, you're walking by, what happens next?

A: We're sitting down.

Q: We who?

A: I'm sitting down and there is a small woman next to me and there's a man next to me. And this woman's like, right around behind me, standing up.

Q: Which woman is behind you?

A: The one with the, uh, the woman I don't like. She's bossy.

Q: Is she in charge?

A: Unh uh. But she's got, I don't know... she has a certain function or something... But, umm... I don't know, she's just not nice.

Q: You're sitting on a bench and there's a woman next to you.

A: Yeah. This is a person. A human.

Q: Do you recognize her?

A: Unh uh.

Q: Do you recognize the man?

A: I can't see him very clear.

Q: As you're sitting on the bench, what happens? Why are you sitting on the bench?

A: They're showing us a big screen.

Q: Tell me what you see on the screen.

A: (Sigh.) Umm... What we are looking at is the Earth and they are showing us different places on the Earth.

Q: What about those places?

A: Bases I guess is what they are.

Q: Bases?

A: Um hmm.

Q: Anything that you would recognize?

A: Unh uh. Just spots, just showing different areas for some reason.

Q: What is the reason for showing you this?

A: (Sigh.) They are preparing us.

Q: Preparing you for what?

A: Departures to these different bases.

Q: Departures to these different bases?

A: Um hmm.

Q: Has anybody told you anything? Details as to why?

A: They're showing us.

Q: What else do you see on the screen?

A: Umm... Well, its, its... it's like they show us this... oh, that's weird... (Long pause.)

Q: Describe it.

A: They show us different spots... they show it to us and then all this information comes into our heads like all about it and where it is... all the information about what it's about and what's going on and...

Q: Well, what is the information?

A: Umm... (Sigh.)

Q: Tell us what is coming into your head as you watch these pictures on the screen.

A: They are training us for a job or something. They want us to know how to do things.

Q: What kind of things?

A: Well, how to run things.

Q: Run what kind of things?

A: Things that, umm... how things work.

Q: What things. How what things work?

A: How these bases work. Where they're located. And they are training us to live there.

Q: Are these bases on the planet Earth?

A: Um hmm.

Q: Can you name any specific ones?

A: Umm... The Amazon jungle, umm... the North Pole... they're all over.

Q: This knowledge, this information is coming into your mind as you watch these visual images on this screen, can you determine how to access it?

A: (Sigh.) I would say, umm... continuous hypnosis and peeling away the layers...

Q: OK. Continue to describe what you are seeing on the screen. Anything else?

A: Umm... the only thing I see is that we're sitting there and it's like, umm... thought transfer, you know what I mean? It's like symbols and musical notes...

Q: You are seeing symbols?

A: Um hmm.

Q: And you are hearing music? Or sounds?

A: Well, I'm seeing the music.

Q: You are seeing the music?

A: Um hmm.

Q: Can you freeze frame any of these symbols and recall them and when you are awakened could you draw some of these symbols?

A: I don't know. They go real fast.

Q: Do they remind you of any kind of symbols you have seen at any place or time?

A: Um hmm.

Q: What do they remind you of?

A: Well, the crop circles.

Q: OK, what's happening next?

A: We're just learning.

Q: Can you tell us any more of what you are learning?

A: All about these bases. And what we need to be doing.

Q: Do you get any sense of when you are going to be doing this?

A: Umm... 1998 comes up for some reason. It's an important time for something... the countdown begins then...

Q: OK, do you get any sense of why it's going to be necessary to know how to do these things at these bases?

A: Oooh... we're in trouble...

chapter two

Q: We're in trouble?

A: Um hmm.

Q: What do you see, what do you hear, what do you know?

A: I don't see, I feel… I just feel really sad.

Q: Why do you feel really sad?

A: I don't know, I just feel real sad. (Begins to cry.)

Q: Why do you feel sad? Talk about what you know.

A: It's just… I don't know… so much destruction…

Q: There's destruction, what kind of destruction?

A: I don't know. It's almost like wars or something.

Q: Is it wars? Or something else?

A: (Sigh, distress.) It's like somebody's coming.

Q: Somebody's coming? Who's coming?

A: I don't know. It's like an army of ships or something I see.

Q: An army of ships is coming?

A: Um hmm.

Q: What kind of ships?

A: Spaceships. All I see is a group small discs flying in big squadrons or something.

Q: Are these…

A: Not nice.

Q: Not nice? Can you tell where they are coming from? Do you have that information from your screen?

A: Unh uh.

Q: Somebody's coming, and you see that there is going to be a war. Between who?

A: It doesn't make sense. It's almost… there's… these aliens are working with the government to prepare, plan for this upcoming… whatever these other people, these other beings that are coming. I know that doesn't make sense but that is what I am seeing or feeling or hearing.

Q: OK, are the beings you are with, would you judge them to be of positive or negative polarity.

A: Umm… they're nice… I think… Except that woman… I don't like that woman…

Q: Are the beings that are coming, do you think they are of positive or negative nature in relation to humans? Or, is it just what they are telling you, that they are nice and the ones who are coming are not nice?

A: It's just what they are telling me.

Q: Could it be possible that the beings that you are with are the negative beings and the ones that are coming are the positive beings?

A: (Sigh.) I don't know. I don't feel bad with these, these little white people… I don't like this woman, though.

Q: I want you to try a little experiment. I am going to count to three and on the count of three I want you to try to read her mind and see what she is thinking.

64

(Countdown.) Connect and describe what she feels and thinks. How does she perceive what's going on?

A: (Distress.) What I'm feeling right now is really hungry.

Q: Is that how she feels?

A: Um hmm.

Q: Hungry for what? What is she hungry for?

A: (Sigh.) She feeds off of us.

Q: How does she feed off of us? What does she do when she feeds? What is it she is wanting to do?

A: She feeds off of us... I don't know.

Q: What does she do physically to feed?

A: It's like she puts her mouth over you and sucks something... like your air out or something... and her eyes, you know what I mean? It's, you know... she drains you.

Q: And she is one of this group that you're with?

A: She's like lurking in the back. She isn't in charge, but she's, um, in the background. She's watching me. She's one of them.

Q: Let's move forward. They are continuing with the showing of the videos or the images. What happens when they finish these images?

A: I feel sick to my stomach.

Q: Why do you feel sick to your stomach?

A: I don't know. I just feel really bad.

Q: Talk about why you feel really bad.

A: They told us things that hurt us. I don't know, I just feel really bad. I hurt.

Q: Let's back up. Stop where you are and let's back up... They are telling you things that are hurting you. What are the things they are telling you?

A: They are showing us all kinds of destruction. Cities of mangled iron... things aren't going to be safe...

Q: What's not going to be safe?

A: The planet's not going to be safe.

Q: From what?

A: This destruction.

Q: Who is causing the destruction?

A: I don't know. I just see a wave generated.

Q: A wave that's generated?

A: Um hmm.

Q: What generates the wave?

A: I can't see anything.

Q: What does this wave do when it is generated?

A: Throws the axis off. The magnetic axis. It's magnetic and we have magnetic axis. Somehow it throws it completely out of harmony. It does something to it and throws it out of harmony.

Q: And what is the result of this throwing out of the axis?

A: I see the Earth spinning. Not normally, but out of balance.

Q: OK. And what it the result of this out of balance spinning?

A: Destruction.

Q: OK. And you can't detect from where this wave originates.

A: Can't see anything.

Q: Is it a natural wave? Or is it unnatural?

A: I don't know what this means. Somebody is causing... they're disrupting something. All those ships I saw...

Q: Are the ships causing this wave?

A: They are disrupting something. There's a disruption.

Q: Are the squadrons of ships you see coming, do they come before this destruction or after?

A: The only thing I can say is that they ride the wave in.

Q: They ride the wave in? And you can't see where the wave is coming from?

A: All I can see is we have to get prepared.

Q: How do we get prepared?

A: They are preparing us.

Q: Do we have to do anything ourselves?

A: We are programmed.

Q: How can one tell if one is programmed?

A: Things will be triggered. You are set up to do certain things... movies, books, different things trigger things that are in your subconscious... I see a key, or a wheel... how a wheel fits together... two wheels fit together and it clicks in...

Q: OK. This wave you speak of, do you sense that it is a wave coming from deep space or is it a wave coming from within our solar system?

A: It's on its way! We don't know about it but somebody knows!

Q: Who knows, does the government know?

A: Yes.

Q: Do they plan on telling anybody?

A: They are setting things in motion. This is why more and more information is being released.

Naturally, after reviewing these experiences, Candy had a whole different perspective on the abduction phenomenon. She became obsessed with reading everything about it she could find. In this respect, we were certainly on the same "path".

When we talked on the phone, there were strange clicks and buzzes on the line. I laughed at the thought of anybody tapping my line to see what we knew about "aliens", because it was a certainty very little. But Candy was convinced that she had "something" they were after—that the objective of any surveillance was herself. Her conviction that the man who had taken her out to the mounds was a government agent being intertwined with that bizarre conviction that he was also her soul mate led to her theory that he was being used to "lure" her into some kind of government conspiracy, and it was her job to "rescue" him in some way. I knew that it was going to take a lot more work to peel away the screens and false memories, not to mention the emotional programs that were still driving Candy.

In the period of time dealing with Candy's experiences, we continued our weekly channeling sessions. We chatted with various "dead dudes" and "space brothers" and notebooks full of "earth changes" and disaster prognostications. One source identified himself as "Jordan", and claimed to be on a ship near Mars, having just arrived there from an orbit around Neptune. He then went on to answer all kinds of questions that confirmed many of the theories of Zecariah Sitchin, claimed that he was a member of a "sister race" to mankind, and just generally performed like your standard "space brother". I was not impressed. Most of it was just nonsense piled upon nonsense.

I don't think the entities were deliberately lying to us, nor do I think that they were "evil". I just think that Cayce was right: a dead Presbyterian is just a dead Presbyterian. If a person dies with strong beliefs formed in the crucible of life on Earth, they take those beliefs with them. And it seems that souls congregate with other souls of similar "frequency" or belief. In this way, they support one another in their illusions and become convinced that what they experience is the whole banana. In this way, they can communicate with the living, absolutely convinced that what they are saying is truth, with the best of intentions; and in the end, it can be all lies.

I didn't want lies, however well-intentioned the source. I didn't want to hear the same tired old illusions that humankind has been fed for millennia that have never done anything to help us change our status on Earth and in the cosmos. I wanted one thing and one thing only: the objective truth, *if* it existed. Like a person playing blind man's bluff, I was groping for answers.

As I studied, the question inside me grew larger and larger. By this time I had read a few dozen books on UFOs and aliens, but their arguments were so contradictory and confusing that I despaired of ever making any sense of it all. Were the "lights in the skies" and the stories of fairy abductions the same phenomena that happened here and now in our world? If so, this raised even more questions and seeming contradictions. Why would an alien race experiment on and observe us for 10000 years? What is the point? To breed? To cultivate us as food? As one correspondent of mine humorously put it:

If they are twenty billion years more advanced than we, why haven't they figured out how to grow synthetic protein in culture dishes in their own labs on their own planet in their own star cluster? ... But wait! Why would creatures who can jump from Earth to Zeta Reticuli in a heartbeat keep their food supply in Nevada? Why don't they take it with them? If you were able to jump from one town to another or one state to another by thinking it, and you wanted to paint a house in say, Texas, would you keep the paint bucket in New York and jump back and forth every time you had to load the brush just because you could jump back and forth? If you could jump to the grocery store, would you jump forty times to buy forty items or would you get everything in one jump so you wouldn't have to bother?

People! That's why we have refrigerators and pantries! So we don't have to get in the car (flying saucer) and drive to the store (Nevada) every day! I can't believe we're more intelligent than our Gray owners! They must be humiliated.

The alternative—a human-engineered program of medical experimentation—is equally contradictory. If the government is behind all the abductions, surely they would have screwed up at least once in 60 years and we would know that fallible human beings were doing it! The fact that not one single incident, not one single abduction, not one single purported kidnapping event has ever resulted in a screw-up that led to anyone seeing the "man behind the curtain", should give us pause to think.

I'm sorry, I can't buy the idea that the U.S. government can pull off an enterprise of this kind, with evidence of world-wide activity, for so long, involving possibly millions of individuals, the logistics of which make the machinations of WWII look like the planning for a picnic. And so, even though many aspects of the phenomenon beg for explanation, I think that we have to look for a hypothesis that explains and predicts the phenomenon better than what he has suggested. And part of that hypothesis may be that such ideas are deliberately planted in the mind of the public for the very purpose of hiding a dreadful and sinister secret.

We can also see that, if the government is not involved, then public officials would be most interested in maintaining the cover-up. To admit certain possibilities could lead to worldwide chaos and anarchy. If we are, as Charles Fort was wont to say, "property"—if we "belong" to some race of advanced beings who use us for food and resources—then there is no point to anything we believe in at all. It is all a lie; a sham; a grand illusion; an enormous cosmic fraud. Who can live with that thought?

So there was no answer. Only clues to be followed. But following the clues, based on my work with spirit release and exorcism, I had an idea about why the purported aliens really wanted human beings. It had nothing to do with regenerating their race by stealing embryos or using human beings in their version of Hamburger Helper. From reading the cases, from the information about Candy's supposed alien abductors, I had the idea that their food was a type of energy: the energy of emotion.

The stories told about a "gazing process", where the abductee was subjected to a sustained and intense eye contact that generated a form of "life review". This drew forth extreme emotional response as the chief feature of the experience, and afterward, the victim often became ill, feeling drained or depleted in a significant way.

But this did not explain certain other reports filtering out here and there about aliens feeding on human blood, or bathing in ghastly vats of body fluids and parts to "absorb" nutrients. If they were creatures that fed on energy, what were they doing partaking of material nourishment, no matter how the process was accomplished?

Again, there were more questions in my mind than answers.

chapter three
the noise

'aliens' in myth

I began to concentrate on gathering every bit of data on the subject that I could get my hands on. What I found was that people have seemingly been visited by all sorts of strange beings throughout the ages. While some of these creatures have been utterly fantastic in description and activity, by far the most common type has been humanoid—having some semblance to the human physical

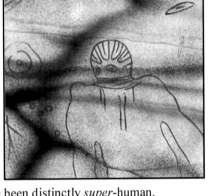

configuration. However, their powers have been distinctly *super*-human.

I read stories going back hundreds of years that told stories of these humanoid beings, but the fact is, there are images of them that are thousands of years old. In the picture above, we see a six meter high figure with a large round decorated head. The massive body, the strange clothing, the folds around the neck and on the chest suggest some ancient astronaut. The image is from Jabbaren, in the Tassili mountains, Algeria, south of the Hoggar, dated to about 6000 BC. Notice the disc like object over the shoulder of the figure on the right side of the image. The next image is from Kimberley, Australia, 3000 BC, and shows beings resembling modern "Grays".

Consider also the following report from the Gazette of the town of Nuremberg, Germany, written in 1561:

> At dawn of April 4, in the sky of Nuremberg, a lot of men and women saw a very alarming spectacle where various objects were involved, including balls

"approximately 3 in the length, from time to time, four in a square, much remained insulated, and between these balls, one saw a number of crosses with the color of blood. Then one saw two large pipes, in which small and large pipes, were 3 balls, also four or more. All these elements started to fight one against the other".

The events lasted one hour and artist Hans Glaser commemorated the event in a woodcut. Looking at the woodcut at right, it seems that it depicts some of the objects crashed on the ground outside the city.

Matthew Hurley, author of *The Alien Chronicles*, has collected many images of artwork that appears to depict UFOs. He writes:

> The artwork in my collection consists of frescos, tapestries, illustrations, oil paintings and early photographs... One can only guess at why these artists chose to insert UFOs into their artwork. Did they have UFO sightings in their day and decide to add them in? Perhaps they had an inner urge to insert them. Maybe they had some arcane knowledge about the relationship between UFOs and certain religious events. Whatever the truth is, there are UFOs in these pieces of artwork and one can ponder and reflect on this truth.

Dr. Karla Turner, professor of literature at North Texas University and vocal alien abductions researcher, wrote extensively about so-called abductees who did not fit into the "Gray alien scenario" promoted by Hopkins and Strieber. Dr. Turner addressed such issues as military abductions, reptilian aliens, relationship manipulations and general deceitful tactics of so-called aliens. Karla authored three books on the subject: *Into the Fringe, Masquerade of Angels* and *Taken*.

In 1995, Karla contracted a very dangerous form of breast cancer almost immediately after what she claimed was an abduction. She died at the age of 48. I really valued our internet friendship, and when she wrote me for the last time, telling me that she was too weak to continue our correspondence, I wept.

Looking back, of course, it's easy to speculate that Karla's death on January 9, 1996, might be an example of how certain "forces" might deal with someone who was getting entirely too close to the truth. She wasn't "martyred" in any obvious way. What she had been saying can be summed up in the following:

> It is a myth that alien abductions of humans follow a set pattern or agenda. Perhaps the best-known proponent of this theory is Budd Hopkins, who in his

books made the genetics and other cross-breeding scenario familiar to the public. Yet when you read back through those books, you'll notice that several of the alien encounters seem to have very little apparent connection to an interest in breeding of DNA. And even Hopkins, in the past couple of years, has had to expand his theory to include a definite alien interest in some other things, such as pleasure and pain in humans.

Other well-known UFO researchers also harbor restrictive theories about the abduction phenomenon. Jacques Vallee, David Jacobs, Whitley Strieber, Brad Steiger, John Lear, Raymond Fowler, Jenny Randles, Kevin Randle, John Keel and other writers hold a diversity of intelligent, often ingenious theories, yet each makes the same error. They ignore parts of the abduction evidence—whatever details don't support their ideas.

Yet it must be clear that any present theory which cannot account for all the known evidence is not acceptable. At best, it can be misleading, especially for victims of abductions who turn to these prominent researchers seeking answers...

As to researchers who claim that the ETs are here to help us evolve some higher consciousness or that they are here for some other positive purpose-saving our planet, promoting world peace, etc.—I challenge those researches to incorporate anomalous data in this view.

What about those people who suffer total breakdowns after their experiences? What about those who undergo wild personality changes, who find themselves obsessed with deviant sexual behavior they never had before, often leading to the breakup of marriages and friendships? These things have happened numerous times, but no researcher has yet explained the higher purpose behind such results.

Particularly disturbing are those cases where previously healthy individuals have an ET encounter and then develop debilitating or terminal illnesses. It is well known that many women suffer gynecological problems after their experiences, often leading to hysterectomies. But other instances have shown the development of severe fatigue, horrible swelling and itching, and even cancer. Where are the positive effects in these cases?

Theories are starting places for research, not proven conclusions, and UFO researchers must be willing to expand and alter their pet theories according to the data they uncover. It would be wonderful if we could shape ET experiences into something positive, but until the details of abduction encounters—all the details—are given serious consideration, I think it's dangerous to cling to theories that ignore data that will not fit. We owe it to ourselves to seek the whole truth. (*UFO magazine*, Vol. 8 No. 1 January/February 1993)

Karla's husband, Elton, later published the following remarks, published in *Contact Forum* (September/October 1994), which are more timely today than ever:

"186,000 M/Second—it's not just a good idea, it's the law", the bumper sticker read. Something about that statement irritated me. Here we were in the midst of a UFO conference and someone was selling an old reality!

The mixture of our notions of physical reality and our concept of law are keeping us in the dark ages of human thought. Modern science has brought us many new ideas about the nature of the universe, but those ideas are constantly being challenged and changed as our powers of observation sharpen and equipment improves. I thank our scientists for their contributions; I love air conditioning, airplanes, and the television waves that travel our air. What bothers me, is that we have not stopped to consider, "The Law."

What laws do the invaders (and I use that term intentionally) of our world abide by? I posit that we have no idea of the rules of the navigable universe by which these otherworldly entities operate. We continue to develop ideas of their intentions based on our own social rules and written laws. I asked a prominent author and researcher of the UFO phenomenon the other day why he thought the aliens could be trusted—why we should believe what they tell us. His reply was sincere, I think. He said they have demonstrated their truthfulness by predicting some future events, and, lo and behold, what they said came true. He said they have told us our planet is in ecological crisis and we know that is true. And, although they seem to have been here for thousands of years, they have not invaded us. What wonderful creatures they must be!

In the few years that I have been studying my own personal invasion by these creatures, I have come to understand that the invaders do not tell the truth unless it serves *their* purpose. They play on our fears, using pollution, war, nuclear holocaust and greed as backdrops for their warnings. But every day since I was a small child, I have been aware that those things are part of our world. We all know these things. It does not take a zillion-plus-IQ creature from the planet Orlon to make me aware that we have problems in our world that we must face. We have very human problems to deal with—problems that we can deal with.

The problems we cannot yet overcome is that of outside interference in our affairs. Some people may call it "benevolent intervention" and point to positive results. I respect the scientists and laymen of all disciplines who have been studying the alien phenomenon and artifacts for the past 50 or 60 years. It appears that they have made some progress, as witnessed by the rapid developments in the aerospace industry, medicine, communications, etc., a great deal of which seems to have come from such research. What is missing is a thorough and public study of the mission and rules of engagement in the war for our world.

I believe that our very thoughts and consequently, our behavior as a race of sentient beings are being *undermined* through the power of insinuation and the implantation of controlling devices in our bodies by non-human (most of the time) entities. This is truly the most effective way to invade and conquer. I do not trust such creatures no matter what I have been told about their altruistic motives.

Katherine Briggs' *An Encyclopedia of Fairies* (1978) gives many examples of fairy abductions. The similarities between fairy abductions and alien abductions are interesting to note: fairy abductees report marks on their bodies; a thick drink is often given to the abductee; the victim is paralyzed and then levitated away; the fairies traveled in circular globes of light. Another similarity to the UFO abduction scenario is the Bigfoot-type creature which was called a "bogie" in fairy lore.

In his classic study *Passport to Magonia*, French scientist Jacques Vallee presented many examples of similarities between fairy and UFO sightings. Jean Bastide, in *La memoire des OVNI* (1978) went further and said the "modern contacts established with extra-terrestrials respect precisely the same rules as contacts in the past with beings more or less human in form."

Many so-called fairies and aliens also look and act like what have been described throughout history as demons; both abductions exhibit striking similarities to activities of *incubi* and *succubi*. A fairly classic example of an alleged succubus interaction is presented in Robert Curran's *The Haunted*. The following is a transcript of a taped interview with the victim:

Q. How did you first know something was wrong?

A. The way I came awake, I guess.

Q. There was something different about it?

A. Yes, it was like I'd been—oh, thrown off a cliff or something. You know, as if some violent action woke me up.

Q. Can you describe what you saw?

A. At first I didn't see anything at all. I just felt this tremendous sort of panic—I wasn't sure if I was having a nightmare or not.

Q. What convinced you that you weren't having a nightmare?

A. Her scales.

Q. Her scales. You mean by that serpentine—snakelike—scales?

A. Yes.

Q. You said "she". These scales were on a woman?

A. Yes.

Q. Would you describe her?

A. To be honest, I even hate to think about her. Her skin was paper white, but it was covered in some places with the scaly surface I mentioned, and then in other places with open sores, the kind you'd think a leper would have or something, And these sores were running with pus.

Q. How old was she?

A. I would estimate around sixty-five or seventy. I can't be sure.

Q. What else did you first notice about her?

A. She had long, white, scrabbly hair and her eyes were all red and the inside of her mouth and her gums were green. Some of her teeth were missing but those she had were very long and vampire-like.

Q. What about her body?

A. That was the weird thing. Her body itself was firm, you know, like that of a younger woman.

Q. What did she do?

A. She paralyzed me in some way. I saw her walking out of the shadows to our bed and I sensed what she was going to do but I couldn't stop her.

Q. Then what?

A. Then she mounted me in the dominant position and she started riding me. That's the only way I can describe it.

Q. Was it pleasurable?

A. No, no. In fact, I don't remember feeling anything at all, other than panic and complete terror.

Q. What was Janet doing during all this?

A. Only after I'd been awake for a time did I realize that Janet had earlier gone downstairs to sleep on the couch, which she occasionally does in the hot months.

Q. What was the being doing next?

A. Coming to sexual climax. She just looked at me and smiled showing those incredible teeth. I tried to look away but something held my eyes to her. I could tell when she was having orgasms because she would give little jerks and her smile would broaden.

Q. She was having orgasms?

A. Oh yes, you could tell that by her expressions and her movements.

Q. Then what happened?

A. Then she vanished.

Q. Just like that?

A. Just like that. Just vanished. And that's when I noticed the sticky substance all over me.

Q. Sticky substance?

A. Yes. I suppose you'd have to compare it to semen, the texture of it, anyway. It was emitted from the creature's vagina. And I was sore, too.

Q. Sore?

A. Yes, as if I'd had prolonged sex, even though it had been only a few minutes. But then I began to wonder if I hadn't passed out during it or something because, as I said, my genitals were extremely sore.

Q. What happened next?

A. I went into the bathroom and looked myself over. The fluid on my body had a very pungent odor. I took a shower and washed it off as quickly as I could. I had to scrub very hard.

The belief that these are *supernatural* beings is to be found in every society around the world. This is a common theme in all religions and folklore. It seems that, in the guise of the UFO/alien abduction phenomenon, the reports are as frequent in our own day as they have ever been. One such modern incident with startling parallels to the above was reported in one of Karla Turner's books:

> This time, as he lay on the table, after having been made to drink a cinnamon smelling liquid, he saw a white haired woman walking over to him. He said she seemed gentle and perhaps caring. She got on top of him, initiating sex, and when it was over she left.
>
> He remembered once when he was thirteen waking up to see a strange woman, dark-eyed with white wispy hair, approach him in unfamiliar surroundings. She got on top of him and engaged in sex, yet it was not at all erotic for Casey. (Turner, 1992)

The point is that there is a tradition stretching back *thousands* of years of beings abducting humans and their offspring; these beings fly in globes of light, can paralyze their victims, induce amnesia about the event, force strange drinks on their victims, have sex with them and, in many cases, ultimately drive them to madness, physical ruin, or even take over their bodies for their own use.

An additional parallel has to do with *blood*. From beyond recorded history the ritual drinking and spilling of blood has been the vital element in sacrifice, gaining power and appeasing the gods. For life, one must have blood. This is a central idea of both Jewish and Christian theology. We have a right to ask: From what has this idea arisen?

The legends of the vampire have persisted since the beginning of recorded history. Modern occultists have been talking and writing about demonic bloodsucking materializations for years, and lately, we have the American "Chupacabra" and cattle mutilations. The problem, of course, lies in sorting fact from fiction. We know that Eastern European reports tell us that something called *vampirism* reached almost epidemic proportions in the 18th century.[5] The stories are quite lurid and many of the details must be attributed to the terrified imaginations of superstitious peasants, yet much of the documentation is so detailed and the witnesses so reputable that it seems impossible that *nothing* was going on there. The question is, what *was?* The idea of a corpse coming out of their coffin at night to suck the blood of the living seems pretty irrational, and I think we can discard it as confused reports of a phenomenon of an entirely different nature.

The cultic vampire, created largely by Bram Stoker in 1897, carries overtones of sexuality that may be more than mere accident. The blend of sexuality, violence, seduction and surrender, evil, and the promise of immortality has excited and fascinated many people ever since. Sex and the supernatural: an unbeatable combination!

British actor Christopher Lee explained the appeal of the vampire by saying: "He offers the illusion of immortality ... the subconscious wish we all have of limitless power ... a being of tremendous brain and physical strength..." The illusion of immortality! That is very similar to what has been offered to many UFO abductees. "Frank and James... both of them had been told that new bodies were somehow being made or prepared for us" (Turner, 1992).

While numerous individuals have been called or have called themselves vampires—engaging in sadistic rituals of murder and/or drinking blood—they were not vampires in the supernatural sense of the word. Nevertheless, the connection between supernatural vampirism and sex is profound.

Vampirism is believed to be contagious; the person who is vampirized, being depleted of vitality, is thought to be a psychic vacuum who then draws energy from the people they encounter in daily life. This energy is then available for the vampirizing entity on their next call to collect. The effect of this vampiric activity—unexplained physical exhaustion—occurs frequently in UFO abduction scenarios:

> Throughout the fall and winter, we felt literally under siege from forces and entities we couldn't fathom... the next morning, I simply couldn't wake up. No matter how hard I tried or how much tea I drank, I was in a daze the entire day, yet I had no reason to be so exhausted... but just as suddenly as she'd been

---

[5] We note that this was the century of the American and French Revolutions.

exhilarated, she was drained of all her energy and almost fell to the ground in a faint... Megan collapsed on the couch, unable to speak or even open her eyes for almost half an hour. (Turner, 1992)

In addition to the elements of abduction, sexual activity, and energy depletion, reports include both *poltergeist phenomena* and the related *invisible attacker*. Raised scratch marks frequently appear on the bodies of some poltergeist victims and I have read one report of an investigating police officer who saw cuts spontaneously appearing on the legs and chest of a screaming poltergeist victim. Turner's accounts of UFO abductions include all of these phenomena:

> [H]e woke up in his bed with a strange female alien being beside him. " She was trying to get me worked up", he said. "She got on top of me and tried to make me respond, you know, sexually. But I kept refusing, I pushed her away and begged her to leave me alone... she was naked, though, and she felt really cold when she touched me" ... "I found these marks this morning", he pointed... three large puncture marks on the skin on the back of his calf arranged in an equilateral triangle...
>
> He was staying alone in a friend's apartment, collapsing in bed after hours of walking the streets alone, and when he awoke he was covered with bruises and scratches all over his back...
>
> "I was sitting on the couch, and it was late at night. And all of a sudden, the couch started hopping up and down, and then this footstool started hopping, I mean, really hopping. It was shaking me!" ...
>
> "The whole bed started to shake, and when I tried to move, I found I was paralyzed. I couldn't even speak, but somehow I finally managed to whisper a prayer, asking the god of truth and love to make this frightening force go away. I repeated the prayer again and again, until the paralysis broke, but the bed shook even more violently as my strength increased... I tried to rouse Casey and tell him what had happened, but he rolled over sleepily without responding... at that point, three women came in and approached me. They held me comfortingly and told me, 'You did the right thing, You passed the test.'" (Turner, 1992)

This *high strangeness* is part and parcel not only of UFO and 'alien' encounters, but also mythical fairy, demon, and vampire encounters and even alleged cases of possession. When possessing entities are questioned during exorcism about how they selected a target for possession they often reply that the subject was chosen *before he was born*. In most cases, the line of contact and the gradually building assault can be traced back to childhood. It could be said, in general, that the process of possession has already begun before either the target or those around him are aware of the signs. The same may be true of so-called alien encounters.

In most cases there is a sensation of the presence before an actual encounter takes place. The Betty Andreasson alien abduction, the subject of Raymond Fowler's *The Andreasson Affair,* is a classic. The scenario described is quite common in abduction cases. For the sake of comparison, let's look at a condensed version.

A light appeared outside the window. The rest of her family appeared to go into a state of suspended animation. Four small creatures entered the room passing straight through a door. One of them communicated with her telepathically and led her outside where an oval craft was waiting. On board she was subjected to a painful physical examination. A probe was pushed up her nose. Another probe was inserted into her navel and she was told she was being measured for procreation.

Next she was made to sit in a glass chair where she was enclosed by a transparent cover and immersed in fluid; she could breathe through tubes attached to her nose and mouth. A sweet liquid oozed into her mouth. When she was released from the chair she found that she had traveled to the alien's planet.

Two of the creatures took her along a tunnel and through a series of chambers. The first was full of small reptile-like creatures; the second was a large green-colored space where they floated over pyramids to a city of mysterious crystalline forms. She was taken into one of the crystal shapes where she was confronted by a giant bird that burst into light and then collapsed into a pile of embers. A voice told her that she had been chosen for a special mission which would be revealed to her. When Betty stated she believed in God, the voice told her that that was why she had been chosen. The leader, Quazgaa, told her that secrets had been locked in her mind. She was then escorted back to her home where she saw the rest of her family still in a state of suspended animation. The aliens put the family to bed.

Now, consider the following condensed account of a case of alleged demonic infestation, obsession and possible possession which has been thoroughly documented and described in *The Demon Syndrome* by Nancy Osborn:

> The room was bathed in a hazy, luminous glow. A strong scent of ozone... a gust of cool wind burst through the open window... It seemed peculiar to Ann that the moon shone so brightly on a cloudy night.
>
> She started to get up. Three dark silhouettes materialized as if entering through the open window... her husband ... slept on, oblivious... Two of the figures stayed in the background but the third drew nearer... he was taller than the other two... As the leader advanced the two smaller creatures seemed to float in the background, chattering unintelligibly... the mysterious intruder did not have a complete body... It was clothed in a black flowing shroud with two arms and hands extending from the edges ... but they were not human appendages. Not normal, regular arms and hands, but cloven ones like those of a pig. The teeth and mouth seemed inhuman. Four fangs protruded where incisors should have been, and rough, thorn-like projections were the closest semblance of human teeth. Its face had an almond shape and the skin was tinted pink. But it was the eyes that frightened Ann most, for they burned crimson... The creature had only a small amount of wiry hair that stood straight up, and the ears were pointed... there were no feet... the thing moved by gliding and floating...
>
> [The entity speaks] 'I have come to take you with me, Ann Haywood. You have been chosen to be one with us. Turn to me and I will give you peace and comfort.' ... a sense of euphoria overcame her. It was a warm, calm sensation... she exerted effort and began to pray again... 'You and your damned God! He's no use to you anymore. Can't you understand? I have come for you. Relax and

let go. You will never be sick or worried again. It is a place of peace and warmth such as you experienced minutes ago. So let go, let go!'

As the monster cajoled, it came closer and closer to Ann. Finally its mouth opened wide and it began to cover her face with its sticky maw. The heat of its breath and the unbearable stench emanating from it seemed to weaken Ann. The being's saliva felt hideously cold and slimy as the monster sucked her life force out... Ann began to struggle violently... the creature hissed in disappointment: 'I am your peace, and I am your strength. I will take care of you from now on. There is no god.' All three entities left through the bedroom wall and into the night... (Osborn, 1982)

In a chilling similarity we find certain images in common which have also appeared in other cases of both alien abduction and demonic infestation: "An astral trip to some unknown, exotic place was standard fare. She saw the Egyptian pyramids... it was then that Ann felt that she was a part of eternity... immortal... safe, happy and free from pain."

In an interview with a member of the press, Ann Haywood was trying to explain how "the Lady" transported her in time to distant places.

"She puts the robe around me and then my mind separates from my body. I can look back and see it lying there. Then we go up through the ceiling, pop out the roof, and fly into space. One night the Lady took me back in time. We were in a foreign country and the people wore old-fashioned clothes. The Lady took on the appearance of a beautiful woman in a blue robe. She performed miracles for them..."

Suddenly Ann's face turned ashen and she asked to be excused. Her scream of pain was heard from the bathroom where she had taken refuge. When Ann came out, she was sniffling and holding her abdomen. The Lady had savagely attacked her for revealing that down through history, creatures like the Lady have taken the form of saints. They then use the gullibility of humankind to misguide and misinform people so that they believe they are seeing miracles performed. Ann begged the newsman to delete that portion of the interview. (Osborn, 1982)

And, reminiscent of the vampire and the Karla Turner case, Ann Haywood suffered too: contact with the 'Lady' was always physically draining. Ann felt used each time the creature took her, and her health deteriorated with each attack. The demon was slowly killing her both physically and mentally. If she wanted to make love with her husband the 'Lady' would tell her: "Ann do not waste your time in senseless copulation. I need your strength. You are mine..."

The alien abduction scenario follows the demon infestation syndrome up to a point: the aliens are rarely, if ever, forced to admit their nefarious intentions. The demons, when queried under certain circumstances, will become quite verbose. Ann's demon was also quite talkative, and we should pause to consider whether her statements are factual or simply more lies and deception.

The 'Lady' transformed herself into a leopard and then a wolf-like beast for Ann. "We can take any form we choose... My kind rules this world. Destiny is changed forever when one of us appears... *Soon, not just you, Ann, but the whole world will know us.* Before the year two thousand, no one will deny our existence. But before your soul returns to spirit, another must replace you. There is one now who is being influenced."

Mechanical failures have been prevalent whenever Ann is present. Eugene Wyatt conducted the original interview before assigning a reporter to the feature article that was prepared for publication in the *Tennessean* (June 4, 1978, issue). The recording was taped on professional equipment. Yet, the machine tore up the tape. Mr. Wyatt said on record, "The computer failed immediately and had to be reset twice. When we tried to edit the story on a video-display terminal, it also failed. The whole power-supply section had to be replaced. It just burned out." When a local television station did some footage with Ann at her home and later ran it through a monitor at the station, the film came out a dazzling red. The technician said he'd never seen a similar anomaly.

This is a condensation of Ann's remarks from several interviews:

I'm saying that there are invisible worlds and beings that populate them. Just because we can't see them doesn't mean they don't exist... Every animal has a natural enemy. And so does mankind. It's not disease or death, but terrible creatures that watch us all until we become weak. Then they hover around us like vultures picking at a corpse. When this happens, we become broken in spirit. That's when people do terrible, unspeakable things. They commit suicide or kill others and just create misery for everyone. Often, the victims end up in mental institutions...

One of those monsters lives inside of me... she only hurts me when I defy her. I try to stay on her good side. She's very temperamental and has a terrible temper. The Lady doesn't like religion, either. She doesn't believe in God as I do... the Lady doesn't communicate directly with anyone but me. Some have seen her, and she's left her voice on cassette tapes, but she's never spoken directly to anyone but me.

I can speak to her aloud or in my thought. She knows everything you and I are saying and thinking. When she speaks, she has a woman's voice. When she's angry the tone is deeper.

The Lady seems to know everything... sometimes we talk about the place she wants to take me to. She says I'll find peace and rest, no worry, no sickness and that I won't have to die a painful physical death like everybody else... I have never gone all the way to the place she wants to take me because I was afraid I wouldn't come back...

When I am with her it's usually a very pleasant feeling—when she's in a good mood—it's warm and peaceful... all my problems are blotted out... it's just a complete silence and we're together...

One thing the Lady doesn't like is that I pray a lot. She thinks I should never do that. If I don't stop when she asks me too she gets angry... my praying interferes with my relationship with her...

I don't think she's afraid of God. When I do go to church, she won't let me concentrate on what the preacher is saying... she distracts me somehow and she waits just beyond the church property line for me to come out... I thought at first that she was of the Devil...

I cry about it a lot... when I get depressed about it, the Lady snaps me right out of the bad mood... she tells me something about her side of the world— where I would go and what I would do and that changes my outlook and I just perk up... no suffering, no worrying, no death, a land that's filled with promise, where the idea that you can make something of yourself doesn't exist—you already are something... it feels like a tug-of-war and I'm in the middle. If I didn't love my family, I might have already gone with her. A lot of times I am tempted to give in...

She's also trying to convince me that I can't help anybody else who has a problem like mine. She says mine is not a mental illness... It's a reality conflict...

In the beginning I was really terrified. I would turn around and she would be there. I was afraid to go to sleep at night, because she would come mostly at night, when everything was quiet, or in the daytime when I was at home alone. But usually she appears at night, when I settle down.

She comes, and we go away together. She puts the cape around me and it seems like I go off into a dream world. The Lady takes me to beautiful places here on this planet or to other planets, and sometimes into the far, far past. Occasionally we even visit the future, but I don't understand any of it...

I still can't get used to the way she looks... she's not like we are. Not at all. She doesn't even seem to have the same body composition as humans. When she touches me with her hands, it's like touching dry ice... her hands just stick to my skin, and they leave red marks wherever she touches... The physical contact stings from the coldness and also burns a little...

When she wants to she can control my thoughts. If she wants me to say something about her while she listens to a conversation, she'll let me remember things. But if she doesn't like a person, all information about her is erased from my mind as if she doesn't exist.

She says it's time for me to talk about her. Also, she says that soon the whole world will know about her kind... she told me I was chosen... she needs people... she needs my breath. The Lady needs that in order to survive in the human world. She has to have it on a daily basis in order to exist on our plane. I supply her with the breath of life every day, sometimes as often as three or four times a day. More energy output on her part and mine requires more feedings of breath... its the same sensation as you get when you hyperventilate... the Lady has to have breath in order to stay down here...

I know that I'm going to have to give up my family because they're Christian. I was saved at one time until the Lady came into my life. She says 'I don't know why you believe in old books that tell about a God that you must worship. That God belongs to other people and not to you. Have you ever seen God? You see me and you know that I am real, that I exist.'... it seems as if there's something like an army buildup. A forceful thing on both sides... she said that she will convince me sooner or later that there is no God ... she thrives on wickedness. (Osborn, 1982)

a hyperdimensional control system

Considering the matter in depth, I could see a tradition stretching back thousands of years, of otherworldly beings abducting humans and their children. Along with most rationalists, I had always considered these stories to be "psycho-dramas", or "artifacts of consciousness". The study of anomalous

80

experiences, the paranormal, and related psycho-spiritual fields has occupied many of the brightest minds of our race for millennia. In the past two-hundred years or so explanations have tended to emphasize a particular reality—materialistic and anthropocentric—as being the arbiter of all that exists, and anything that does not fit into this belief system is discarded as either irrelevant or pathological. It's clear that strange things have continued to happen, despite the fact that they do not conform to the rationalist scientific reality construct.

However, what is distressing this repeated intrusion of another reality is that, for the most part, such events may be behind most of the world's *religious* belief systems. In those cases where the religious trappings are stripped away, the remaining phenomena do not seem to be favorable toward humanity. Jacques Vallee's control system hypothesis is interesting in this regard:

> I believe there is a system around us that *transcends time as it transcends space*. The system may well be able to locate itself in outer space, but its manifestations are *not spacecraft in the ordinary 'nuts and bolts' sense*. The UFOs are physical manifestations that cannot be understood apart from their psychic and symbolic reality. What we see in effect here is not an alien invasion. It is *a control system* which acts on humans and *uses* humans. (Vallee, 1979)

In other words, what Vallee was suggesting was something very similar to *The Matrix*, as represented in the movie by that name. I was considering this long before the movie was made and the idea popularized. The very idea that this might be a reality that dominated or controlled our own was staggering. What made the problem so terrifying was the fact that my studies and experiences in "spirit attachment" and demonic possession were also reflected in the so-called UFO and alien phenomena.

The fact that modern alien abductions mirror demonic infestation and vampirism is part of an historical pattern. A pattern implies a pattern maker. What we are concerned with is who or what that pattern maker is, and for what purpose it is operating the control system.

French ufologist Jean-Francois Boëdec, in his book *Fantastiques recontres au bout du monde* (1982), suggests that UFO sightings start long before the actual experience. He noted many cases in which the witnesses had premonitions that something was about to happen, or for some reason they went home by a different route, or took an unaccustomed walk. Somehow, it seems, the witnesses were being prepared for the experience they were about to undergo. In many cases, the abductee claims there is a sensation of a presence before an actual encounter takes place.

I can't say that any such "premonition" occurred in my own experiences. I walked out to that swimming pool thinking of nothing but floating, relaxing, and maybe catching a meteor or two streaking across the sky. But that simply may be due to a lack of sensitivity or awareness to certain subtle clues. Perhaps my rational approach acted as a barrier?

Nevertheless, Boëdec has a point. In my work with Spirit Release Therapy—which I should mention was a therapy I used because it worked, not because I "believed" in it—many so-called "attached entities" I conversed with during hypnosis sessions claimed that their host was chosen "before he was born". As I pointed out above, in most cases, a line of contact and the gradually building assault can be traced back to childhood. It might be said, in general, that the process of possession has already begun before the target or those around him are aware of the signs. But this flies in the face of many religious and philosophical teachings that tell us that we have "free will"—that we are in control of our lives.

The first thing I noticed in deeply studying the abduction phenomenon was that some encounters with entities seem accidental while others are clearly directed at a specific person. This led me to wonder whether the seemingly accidental encounters were as accidental as they appeared to be, or if they, too, were chosen well before the experience. In such cases, I had to ask: did the manifestation occur in response to some hidden need, a psychological state that calls for outside intervention of some kind?

In any case of psychic vampirism or actual possession, there is usually a point at which the entity enters into a relationship with the individual. A decision is made by the victim to allow that contact. This often occurs simply *because the victim is not aware of the significance of the event.* It seems to be a minor event and may come as the result of tiredness, mental excitation, frustration, or pain.

One relevant factor that emerged from my research was that these beings, whether demons, vampires or aliens, seem to have the ability to influence our thoughts, our physical bodies, the weather and even events in our lives, to the point that we can be worn down under such attack and give in to their control almost by default. In the case of alien abductions, these may be events staged as "alien abductions", designed for the very purpose of wearing down the victim and inducing acquiescence.

Another element of these abductions that is historically evident is the "physical exam". The famed Betty and Barney Hill case describes a simulated medical test in which a long needle is inserted into the navel. A fifteenth century French calendar, the *Kalendrier des bergiers*, illustrates the tortures inflicted by what were being called "demons" on the people they have taken. The demons are depicted piercing their victims' abdomens with long needles.

Jacques Vallee has expressed doubts that a material civilization with space and time travel capabilities would come in such numbers to do "stupid" things like abduct people and perform primitive experiments or examinations on them, suggesting some motive other than 'scientific research'.

stockholm syndrome

Many people report that their abductors are benevolent beings, but when we consider all the factors of the big picture of the phenomenon, it seems that such stories of benevolence may be misleading.

Kenneth Ring discovered that a large sample of people who reported near-death experiences (NDE) also tended to have had other, prior, "unusual experiences", including UFO sightings and/or abductions which were interpreted by them in a positive way. After their NDE, they generally reported a remarkable change very similar to a religious conversion. They also often reported the sudden acquisition of a new talent or interest. Ring tested his subjects in different ways, and most of them had high scores on what is called the *dissociative personality scale*. Such people are easily hypnotized and tend to daydream a lot. So, there does seem to be a correlation between dissociation and thinking that ET is "good".

The skeptics jumped for joy at this news. They leapt onto the idea that Ring's subjects were all simply inveterate daydreamers, or that previous trauma had led to a "need for attention and self-esteem" which caused them to fantasize these experiences. Since there was a clear correlation between those who had experienced "positive alien interactions" and clearly pathological states, the label was slapped on everyone who acknowledged the possibility that the alien reality was more than just a meme infection.

Ring suggested that childhood dissociation might be a technique that an abused person could develop to adapt to a difficult situation. Because these people become strongly dissociative at an early age, they find it easier to enter altered states of consciousness. Ring then proposed that since people in such altered states might have a wider range of perception than ordinary people, they might be more "prone" to experience paranormal events than a control group who might also be exposed, but unable to perceive them.

There is another way to look at Ring's findings, which we will return to in the next chapter: it may be that people who are *not* able to perceive more subtle realities are the ones who are viewing reality in a dissociated state—dissociated from what *is*, the objective world. Whether they are promoting the "alien reality" as a positive experience, or the SETI reality, or any other reality that does not take into account the broadest range of observable facts, such individuals may be operating in pathological states of dissociation, or cognitive dissonance. Contradictory information is compartmentalized. In this sense, the idea that "God is in heaven and all is right with the world" is as much a fantasy as the idea that mankind is the result of mindless evolution.

A person who is not aware of the subtext of the play of forces in our world, a person who, as I had done, compartmentalizes things so they do not have to see the implications, may be the one who has dissociated and identified with the rationalist, materialistic interpretation of reality. In other words, if there is a control system as Vallee suggests, an Evil Magician, as Gurdjieff called it, it very likely promotes this view in order to conceal itself.

A very simple way of looking at it is in terms of what is popularly called *Stockholm syndrome*. The term was coined in the early 70s to describe the puzzling reactions of four bank employees to their captors. On August 23, 1973, three women and one man were taken hostage in one of the largest banks in Stockholm. They were held for six days by two ex-convicts who threatened their lives but also showed them kindness. To the world's surprise, all of the hostages strongly resisted the government's efforts to rescue them and were quite eager to defend their captors. Indeed, several months after the hostages were saved by the police, they still had warm feelings for the men who threatened their lives. Two of the women eventually got engaged to their captors.

Psychologist Dee Graham has theorized that Stockholm syndrome occurs on a societal level. Since our culture is patriarchal, she believes that all women suffer from it—to widely varying degrees, of course. She has expanded on her theories in *Loving to Survive: Sexual Terror, Men's Violence, and Women's Lives*, which is well worth reading. In her book, *The Paranoia Switch: How Terror Rewires Our Brains and Reshapes Our Behavior—And How We Can Reclaim Our Courage*, clinical psychologist Martha Stout gives a similar theory: just as an abusive husband will use the trauma he inflicts on his wife to control her—she will paradoxically turn to her abuser for love and protection—authoritarian leaders will use societal trauma, like terrorism, to gain their subjects' support. The dynamics of Stockholm syndrome directly address the issue of those who view their "abductions" as "desirable". Victims have to concentrate on survival, requiring avoidance of direct, honest reaction to destructive treatment.

When there is a socially imposed mandate to "think nice thoughts" and view the world in a positive light, even in the face of evidence to the contrary, people generally find it necessary to become highly attuned to the approval or disapproval of the "social norms". As a result, they are motivated to learn how to think in social norms, and do not examine their own, honest experiences. As victims of societal Stockholm syndrome, we are encouraged to develop psychological characteristics pleasing to the system. These include: dependency and lack of initiative; inability to act, decide, think; strategies for staying alive, including denial, attentiveness to the system's demands, wants; and expressions of approval of the system itself. We are taught to develop fondness for the system accompanied by fear of interference by anyone who challenges the system's perspective. Most of all, we are conditioned to be overwhelmingly grateful to the system for giving us life. We focus on the system's kindnesses, not its acts of brutality. Denial of terror and anger, and the perception of the system as omnipotent, keep us psychologically attached to the Matrix Control System. High anxiety functions to keep us from seeing available options.

Psychophysical stress responses develop. Such persons might even think that ET would land on the White House Lawn to "serve mankind".

One person in ten says that they have seen a UFO. According to a recent survey I read, about ninety percent of us believe Earth has been visited by extraterrestrials. But it is the strangest thing I have ever observed that these statistics will lead ordinarily intelligent people to suggest that this is a "psychosocial phenomenon of huge magnitude", rather than addressing the broader "reality" of UFO-ET phenomena. Talk about Stockholm syndrome! I know whereof I speak because I tried that approach myself.

I had spent years studying psychic and psychological phenomena, and had come to the firm idea that any and all of it was simply a matter of understanding the nature of consciousness, perception, beliefs, memory, dreams, memory of dreams, the formation of images and its philosophical counterpart—it was all mind, and nothing else. I was convinced that our beliefs created our reality, and that "you spot it, you got it". If we didn't believe it to be possible, we don't see it.

In early 1994, as I was going through the research, and after another series of strange events which I have chronicled in some detail in my autobiography, *Amazing Grace*, I had a conversation with Frank that was extremely distressing. Frank began by listing the string of strange, synchronistic and even somewhat miraculous events that had brought me to this moment. He cited point after point through my life history, right up to the past few years when the strangeness of events, including bizarre synchronicities, had multiplied to the point that I felt like I was living in a madhouse where normal reality no longer held sway. The effect of having all of these things brought together in a sweeping view of my life history was overwhelming. It's one thing to have things happen sequentially, over a period of time, in more or less in isolation, which you can then shove under the rug and try to forget until the next incident, and quite another to have to look at it all in context. I had to admit that it certainly appeared that there were forces at work in life, in my own life particularly, that are not generally accounted for in the normal systems of explaining the order of the universe. In the face of the evidence, presented more or less as witness testimony in a courtroom might have been, I felt the formerly solid earth of my reference system slowly crumbling beneath my feet. With each point he made, I felt like another wave was washing over my foundation of sand. I seemed to be sinking into the mire of complete lunacy.

How can you deal with a life that has gone completely over the edge in terms of strangeness that you neither wish to experience, nor perpetuate?

As Frank pointed out, even though I was most definitely a "non-believer", as soon as I had been exposed to knowledge about the alien phenomenon, I encountered my first "alien abductee" case. Didn't I think this was unusual? And wasn't it a fact that UFOs had accompanied that first "abduction" session I'd conducted? Didn't I think this was an unusual phenomenon? Not everyone who might be an abductee under hypnosis attracts a whole flap of UFOs. The question was, of course: was it the abductee or the therapist in whom the denizens of UFO-land were interested?

I didn't like the way the conversation was going.

Frank then pointed out the obvious (to him) connection between my deteriorating physical state and my own UFO encounter. When I protested there may be no relation at all, he pointed out how my dog had suffered and died within a very short time after this "exposure", and how my symptoms always seemed to peak at exactly the time of night the UFO had come along. What was my explanation for that little item?

I had none. I was distressed for him even to put it in words. As long as it was unspoken, I could continue to ignore it.

He kept pressing his points (described in *Amazing Grace*): what about the 'face at the window'? What about the kidnapping when I was a child by an individual who had been connected to the Navy in some mysterious way? What about the light outside at boarding school? What about the incident when I awakened reversed in the bed? What about all the gynecological mishaps I had suffered? On and on he went. And as he ticked off each item, I felt more and more nauseated.

Frank's theory was that the whole drama of recent times—a series of events spread across several counties, including dozens of witnesses, most of whom I didn't even know—was "staged" to get my attention; to wake me up. What was more, even our meeting was obviously a "destined" event (also described in *Amazing Grace*).

I did not like what Frank was saying. I was really struggling to ignore the anomalies in my life and did not like the connotation Frank was putting on my experiences. In the first place, I had studied too much, seen too much, and worked with too many troubled people to overlook the dangers of ego and subconscious tendencies to distort. When anyone starts to think they are "special", that God is "talking" to them, it's a sure sign of descent into delusion and "magical thinking".

Nevertheless, I had read many cases by now of strange events similar to my own that were attributed to "aliens", and that was the problem. If it wasn't "aliens", who or what was it? If it was what people were calling "aliens", did this mean they were literally visitors from deep space? Or were so-called aliens merely artifacts—induced perceptions—of victims of some vast government mind control experiment? Most terrifying of all: were aliens what had been known as demons throughout history?

Of course, in my own mind, there was an additional twist to this line of logic: Why would anyone or anything go to so much trouble to set up so many bizarre things to get my attention if I wasn't supposed to do something about it? If I was supposed to do something, they had certainly picked the wrong person, because it was becoming pretty clear that I was probably not going to live a lot longer.

Considering "this UFO business" had another effect on me: I mourned the years I'd spent studying and digging for answers, only to have it all trashed in one night by a stupid black boomerang.

"Why me?"

"That's what you need to figure out", Frank said.

What I was figuring out wasn't very pleasant. Because of my experience as a hypnotherapist, I could detect the "signature" of a malevolent intelligences working in my life and my experiences in an effort to either destroy or divert me from something. If these beings had the power to interfere in my life with malicious intent, even when I was deeply involved with positive thinking and meditation—which one would suppose should act as a defense—what protection did anyone have? Were we, the human race, defenseless against these creatures?

The words of Gurdjieff came back to haunt me. Were the belief systems of metaphysics and religion useless drivel promulgated by an Evil Magician to convince people they were Lions, Men, Eagles or Magicians instead of sleeping sheep?

What kind of madhouse had I opened my eyes to see? Was the fact that I had seen it the very source of its existence? Was I, by noticing evil, more vulnerable to attack? Surely not: The evidence of the presence of evil threaded its way through the lives of others who denied all the clues. I saw clearly the "mechanical" or "accidental" nature of the Universe that Gurdjieff talked about. I realized that our own programmed refusal to see reality, our ignorance, was the chief door through which Evil entered into our lives.

Was it possible, as Gurdjieff suggested, to become free of this? To awaken? To see the projector behind the slide show of our lives? And, more importantly, to see who was running the projector and why?

I struggled with my thoughts and emotions for days. I was truly passing through the valley of the shadow of death. I had thoroughly convinced myself that UFOs and aliens could not possibly exist. In fact, even after the flap surrounding the hypnosis session with Pat, I had contemptuously declared that the "Millennial Disease" was spreading. Upon seeing the thing itself with my own eyes, I had pronounced it to be a flock of geese, in the same way I had rationalized the wet nightgown and grass seeds on the night I woke up reversed in my bed.

All those times, including the night I saw the strange light in the snow at boarding school, the events had been followed by protracted illnesses. If there were other incidents preceding any of my other physical disturbances, I certainly didn't remember them. But by now, from studying the literature, I was aware that many people might remember nothing at all.

After reading almost 15 hours a day for months—everything on the subject I could get my hands on—I began to realize: Some sort of "alien presence" on our planet *is real*, and everybody is telling lies about it. I was terrified.

If there is a psycho-spiritual or even literally physical "invasion" taking place before our very eyes, under our very noses, represented in the symbol system of our lives and experiences, interacting with this "control system" at some deep level, what kind of protection do we have?

Well, in thinking about it deeply, it does appear that these beings—whatever they turn out to be—can plunder our world, our lives and our very minds at will.

But I also have observed that they seem to be going to an awful lot of trouble to conceal their activities and to confuse observers with hundreds of crazy stories of different "races" and groups of semi-mythological "good guys and bad guys".

After spending some time attempting to prove that the ET hypothesis was essentially a psychic contagion, a meme, a "Millennial Disease", and failing, I came to the realization that the reality of the phenomenon of psychic contagion was an important part of the process, but in a completely opposite way of what was being suggested by the "experts". What I noticed was the fact that "memes" seemed to be significantly present *in the context of obscuring the issue.* What seems to happen is that false ideas about what is really happening spread from core "authorities", such as the authors of popular books about UFOs, alien abductions, and so on, and this is seemingly designed to create "attitudes", perceptual controls, "reinterpretations" of personal experiences *by the act of implanting ideas about oneself and about the nature of experiences* which, due to their hyperdimensional nature, are ambiguous. In short, "memes" are the essence of societal Stockholm syndrome!

As it happens, in spite of the many claims that only those who "believe in the phenomenon" tend to experience it, the fact is that those who report the most intense involvements frequently never "believed" in the phenomenon at all, and confronted with the traumatic nature of their experiences, do *not* want to even consider that it might be real.

Considering people who, as Hynek described them, "through a long exposure to the subject, or motivated by a haunting curiosity to work in the field and to get our hands dirty with the raw data, came to know there was a signal", such individuals begin to view the world *as it is,* defying the memes that are generated and released on society like a form of bio-semiotic warfare. Of course, there is a special type of "meme" that is propagated to "reduce" or macerate those who suggest a reality to the UFO phenomenon as were typically used historically against anyone who perceived a higher reality, including great saints and mystics of all kinds.

This meme aims to discredit states of mind that produce nonlinear shifts in the psychic landscape: a connection between sexual life and religious emotions is often drawn; conversion is a "crisis of puberty"; devotion is just the parental instinct of self-sacrifice run amok; the search for meaning to it all is merely a hysterical starvation for a more earthly object of affection, and so on. St. Paul had an epileptic seizure on the Road to Damascus, Saint Teresa was a hysteric, George Fox suffered a disordered colon, Carlyle had an ulcer. Those who are looking for a materialist explanation for everything will find all sorts of disordered glandular functions, and voila! All spiritual verities will be successfully disposed of and skepticism and the Blind Watchmaker will reign supreme!

The problem with these reductionist explanations is this: even if it is true that St. Paul had epilepsy, and that is the "materialistic account" of his vision on the road to Damascus, does that then negate the spiritual significance of the event?

Because, in point of fact, every single "spiritual condition"—positive or negative—probably does have an expression in physiology.

We would also like to note that the hard-core skeptic is as likely to be skeptical because he suffers liver disease as the born again Christian is likely to be converted because his ulcer drives him to seek relief. The evil magician can have a dirty colon and the psychic vampire can have false teeth. In short, raptures and rants can be equally represented by organic conditions. And if this is taken *as the model of verity*, then none of our ideas, our thoughts, feelings, scientific doctrines, beliefs or disbeliefs, have any value at all. If such an idea is the theory upon which we are to evaluate our reality, then we must theorize that *every* idea emanates from the state of the body of the originator. That is to say: what is sauce for the goose, is sauce for the gander.

As I continued my examination of the standard religions as well as the many and varied New Age teachings, I saw these systems being used as the very means of propagating memes. I could see individuals with no extensive knowledge of the history metaphysics being fooled by a belief in the "benefits" of alien abduction. We repeatedly see terms describing "light" or related phenomena. This tends to make the percipients regard the experience as "good". Gurdjieff was right: mankind *is* asleep and one of the conditions of this sleep is the absence of an active "B.S. meter".

Many people reporting "abductions", when the surface or screen memories have been probed in a competent way, reveal memories of events so chilling in their implications that the first interpretation must be looked at carefully. The fear evoked in these experiences is tangible. Yet, these other beings somehow convince their victims that all they do is for "the good of the planet" or "the enhancement of our race". Even the esteemed John E. Mack, M.D., professor of psychiatry at Harvard, seems to have been taken in by such a view. He writes in *Abduction*:

> The idea that men, women, and children can be taken against their wills from their homes, cars, and schoolyards by strange humanoid beings, lifted onto spacecraft, and subjected to intrusive and threatening procedures is so terrifying, and yet so shattering to our notions of what is possible in our universe, that the actuality of the phenomenon has been largely rejected out of hand or bizarrely distorted in most media account. ... My own work with abductees has impressed me with the powerful dimension of personal growth that accompanies the traumatic experiences ... especially when these people receive appropriate help in exploring their abductions histories... Let us suppose that [Cosmic Intelligence] ... is not indifferent to the fate of the Earth, regarding its life forms and transcendent beauty as one of its better or more advanced creations. And let us imagine that the imbalance created by the over growth of certain human faculties ... were diagnosed ... as the basic problem. What could be done as a corrective? The two natural approaches of which we can conceive would be the genetic and the environmental. Is it possible that through a vast hybridization program affecting countless numbers of people, and a simultaneous invasion of our consciousness with transforming images of our self-destruction, an effort is being made to place the planet under a kind of receivership?

This view is rooted in emotional beliefs that cling desperately to any straw offered that those more powerful than we are "good". If they are not, what are we to do? What *has* been done?

As I waded through the literature, I came across many controversial accounts said to originate from military intelligence officers, physicists hired to work on secret projects, and others claiming inside knowledge of a vast government cover-up. Some of these revelations match the reports of other individuals who claim to have recalled, either consciously or under hypnosis, scenes of unparalleled horror and abuse at the hands of some of the so-called alien visitors. This is generally taken as corroboration of one by the other. But we have to ask: why would participants in a cover-up be motivated to come forward? Is it that such individuals, having penetrated deeper into the veil of secrecy, have become horrified witnesses whose consciences prompted them to talk? Perhaps those in power began keeping their arrangements secret, only to discover they had a tiger by the tail and couldn't let go? Maybe they began sending "agents" out to "reveal" fragments of the truth, while the possibility of forced exposure looms ever closer? Or, perhaps, such individuals are part of a vast mind-control experiment designed like a monstrous crazy-making drama, where the government secretly promotes a belief in aliens while publicly denying it?

The book *Clear Intent* by Lawrence Fawcett and Barry J. Greenwood provides evidence based on the government's own documents that the highest ranking public officials and the elite of the U.S. security and intelligence organizations have deliberately and persistently lied about aliens and UFOs for the last fifty years. That is raw data. Interpretations ought to be made rather carefully.

On the other hand there are quite a number of people who claim to have a variety of psychic experiences: prophetic "dreams" or visions, channeling "space brothers". They claim they are being contacted by beings who are here to "help" us or to "save us" if only we will let them. However, they may in reality be victims of quite different processes. These stories are then spread around, increasing the level of confusion.

The bottom line seems to be that the idea that negative forces do not exist— and even if they did, there's no need to worry—is the greatest deception of all. We are repeatedly told: if we just think nice thoughts, or meditate regularly, or "get saved", or repeat our affirmations, nothing icky will ever enter our reality. However, the facts seem to be that, as Vallee says, "there is a system around us that *transcends time as it transcends space*... What we see in effect here is not an alien invasion. It is *a control system* which acts on humans and *uses* humans." We are not dealing with materialistic, Earth-based technology here! These guys walk through walls, float people out of their bodies and control minds—the abilities we have historically attributed to angels or demons or vampires. In the past, we dealt with ghosts and "gods" and demons. We are dealing with the same entities now, only we are calling them "aliens". They probably always *were* "aliens"! And maybe they want to be "gods" again.

One thing I knew for sure from doing the spirit release work: evil insinuates itself into our lives in the guise of goodness and truth. This problem is made even worse by the acceptance of the New Age teaching that "evil" simply does not exist unless an individual creates it in their reality. Evil follows the line of erosion of our spirituality *through the erosion of knowledge*. What better way to protect evil activities than to deny that they exist?

The New Age types say that putting one's attention on these ideas "gives them energy". This is true only if one focuses in this way with the intention of participation. However, a comprehensive understanding of these forces is absolutely necessary in order to know how to give them less energy.

It was a stunning and grotesque prospect for me to consider that humanity, as a whole, has been used and cunningly deceived for millennia. I realized that the UFO and alien business was truly nothing new. We have historical records of these phenomena stretching back thousands of years. This suggests that the terror and confusion is exactly what they want to generate. If these beings could get what they want simply by moving in and taking it, would they spend so much time creating terrorizing humanity? Why are they going to so much trouble to persuade us to accept their total control if they could take it at will? These guys would not be spending so much time terrorizing us and trying to sneak in the back door if it were possible for them to walk in directly. There is something we have that they want. There is some power we have that they don't want us to discover.

The act of facing the "pattern of activity" behind the events of my own life that bespoke such a hidden reality was absolutely soul searing and mind numbing. It acted as a conflict between my internal integrity, intellectual acuity, and all my emotional beliefs in a kind and loving god. While I was most definitely learning, I didn't like what I was learning. As I have said, of all people who never wanted to know anything at all about UFO's and aliens, I deserve a place at the head of the line. Yet, there it was.

To consider the idea of malevolent beings in control of our world that could prey on us at will, behind our ordinary reality, was utterly soul shattering. I began to see the possibility of an interpenetrating reality of more or less physical solidity that interacted with humans as we may interact with wildlife in a forest: the hunters and the hunted.

Standing back from my life in overview, there were the hints of some sort of pattern maker, and it wasn't God in any sense that I had ever conceived of Him. Yes, I could see both positive actions and negative actions; a dynamic interplay of forces that related in some direct way to my own thinking, seeking, and growth. But exactly what it was, and precisely how it operated, I couldn't tell yet. It was like a shadow show where the shadows are produced by certain angles of light behind objects which, when finally revealed, may bear no resemblance whatsoever to the form of the shadow. A balled up fist could as easily be interpreted as a bird or a dog, or—when expanded to its full shape—a hand. Just what was I seeing? What's more, why did it seem that I was being challenged to see it? Why me? I struggled until I was exhausted in my soul.

91

chapter four
conspiracy
is the only
reality

in science

As I have written, I've spent much of my life trying to find reasonable explanations for complex and mysterious events, struggling to fit the anomalous experiences of my own as well as other people into acceptable categories, trying to find prosaic explanations. The ironic consequence of this was that I was often compelled to shove logical observations under the rug of the mundane world, and in that sense, you could say that my imagination certainly was exercised! Because of these experiences and the fact that they did not "fit" into the "reality construct" of our society, I realized that part of our world is marginalized to an extreme degree, and this was troubling to me. I struggled mightily to bridge the gap between *high strangeness* and the reality that our culture accepts as valid and real, establishing reasonable categories into which I could pigeonhole anomalies so as to not deny the evidence, while still giving credibility to the social and cultural norms of what is or is not possible.

When a person knows that there are "strange things out there" on the one hand, and, on the other, that these strange things are regularly ridiculed and debunked, it becomes necessary to do something! The result is usually that a long list of terrestrial experiences are effectively fenced off from scrutiny for the simple reason that they may be considered abnormal or even sinful. That's not a healthy way to live.

Like many, many people, I never asked for strange things to happen in my life. I most definitely fought a losing battle to pretend they weren't happening or that there was a "normal explanation" for them. I often wondered how many other people in the world had suffered because their deep realities had been ridiculed? At the most extreme end are people considered insane because their perceptions are different. But there are also vast numbers of people who have had many odd experiences who are afraid to speak of them, who hold them close inside, wondering daily if they're losing their minds, or perhaps even whether they are being subjected to some sort of demonic torment.

Charles Fort, decrying the state of anomalies investigation, wrote in his book *LO!*:

> Our data have been bullied by two tyrannies. On one side, the spiritualists have arbitrarily taken over strange occurrences, as manifestations of the departed. On the other side, conventional science has pronounced against everything that does not harmonize with its systematizations. The scientist goes investigating, about as, to match ribbons, a woman goes shopping. The spiritualist stuffs the maws of his emotions. One is too dainty, and the other is gross. Perhaps, between these two, we shall some day be considered models of well-bred behavior.

How can we account for this? There is a little known fact about hypnosis that is illustrated by the following story, adapted from Hugh Lynn Cayce's book *Venture Inward*, and as confirmed by my own experimentation:

A subject was told under hypnosis that when he was awakened he would be unable to see a third man in the room who, it was suggested to him, would have become invisible. All the "proper" suggestions to make this "true" were given, such as "you will *not* see so-and-so." When the subject was awakened, lo and behold! the suggestions did *not* work.

Why? Because they went against his belief system. He did *not* believe that a person could become invisible. So, another trial was made. The subject was hypnotized again and was told that the third man was *leaving the room,* that he had been called away on urgent business, and the scene of him getting on his coat and hat was described. The door was opened and shut to provide "sound effects", and then the subject was brought out of the trance. Guess what happened? He was *unable to see* the Third Man.

Why? Because his perceptions were *modified according to his beliefs*. Certain "censors" in his brain were activated in a manner that was acceptable to his *ego survival instincts*—his psychological need for equilibrium.

The ways and means that we ensure survival of the ego is established pretty early in life by our parental and societal programming. This conditioning determines what *is* or is *not* possible; what we are "allowed" to believe in order to be accepted. Just as we avoid physical pain, we avoid information that will harm the beliefs with which we interpret the world around us. At first we learn what pleases our parents, then we modify our beliefs based on what pleases our society—our peers.

To return to our story, the Third Man went about the room picking things up and setting them down and doing all sorts of things to test the subject's awareness of his presence, and the subject became utterly hysterical at this "anomalous" activity! He could see objects moving through the air, doors opening and closing, but he could *not* see the *source* because he did not believe that there was another man in the room.

So, what are the implications of this factor of human consciousness? (By the way, this is also the reason why most therapy to stop bad habits does not work— they attempt to operate against a "belief system" that is imprinted in the subconscious that this or that habit is essential to survival.) One of the first things we might observe is that everyone has a different set of beliefs based upon their social and familial conditioning, and that these beliefs determine how much of the *objective* reality anyone is able to access.

In the above story, the *objective* reality *is what it is*, whether it is truly objective, or only a consensus reality. There is clearly a big part of that reality that is inaccessible to the subject due to a *perception censor* that was activated by the suggestions of the hypnotist. That is to say, the subject had a strong belief, based upon his *choice* as to who or what to believe. In this case, he had chosen to believe the hypnotist and not what he might be able to observe if he dispensed with the perception censor—even if that activation was fraudulent.

And so it is with nearly all human beings: we believe the hypnotist—the "official culture"—and we are able, with preternatural cunning, to deny what is often right in front of our faces. What is most disturbing in the case of the hypnosis subject described above is that he is entirely at the mercy of the "invisible man" because he chooses not to see him. Is it possible that—in a similar way—we are under the control of a "hypnotist" who does not have our best interests at heart?

Let's face it: we are all taught to avoid uncomfortable realities. Human beings—faced with unpleasant truths about themselves or their reality—react like alcoholics who refuse to admit their condition; the cuckolded husband who is the "last to know"; or the wife who does not notice that her husband is abusing her daughter. In *States of Denial: Knowing about Atrocities and Suffering*, Stanley Cohen discusses the subject of denial, which may shed some light on the context in which we find the "alien phenomenon" situated.

Denial is a complex "unconscious defense mechanism for coping with guilt, anxiety and other disturbing emotions aroused by reality". Denial can be both deliberate and intentional, as well as completely subconscious. An individual who is deliberately and intentionally denying something is acting from a level of lying, concealment and deception.

Believing anything that comes down the pike is not the opposite of denial. "Acknowledgement" of the probability of a high level of truth about a given matter is what should happen when people are actively aroused by *certain* information. This information can be 1) factual or forensic truth; that is to say, legal or scientific information which is factual, accurate and objective; it is obtained by impartial procedures; 2) personal and narrative truth including "witness testimonies".

I should add here that skepticism and solipsistic arguments—including epistemological relativism—about the existence of objective truth, are generally a social construction and might be considered in the terms of the hypnotized man who has been programmed to think that there "is no truth".

Denial occurs for a variety of reasons. There are truths that are "clearly known", but for many reasons—personal or political, justifiable or unjustifiable—are concealed, or simply not acknowledged "out loud". There are "unpleasant truths" and there are truths that make us tired because if we acknowledge them—if we do more than give them a tacit nod—we may find it necessary to make changes in our lives.

Cohen points out that "All counter-claims about the denied reality are themselves only maneuvers in endless truth-games. And *truth, as we know, is inseparable from power.*" Denial of truth is, effectively, *giving away your power.*

There are different kinds of denial. First, there is literal denial which is the type that fits the dictionary definition, the assertion that something did not happen or does not exist. This most often occurs in very painful situations where there are conflicts of love: the wife would say that the husband could not have molested his daughter, therefore the child must be making it up. This also seems to apply to denial of the state of our manipulated reality. Our love for our parents, our need for their approval, is often transferred to our peers, our employers, and the State. To think about stepping outside of the belief system that makes us "belong" is just too frightening. It assaults our deepest sense of security.

The second kind of denial is "interpretative". In this kind of denial, the raw facts that something actually happened are not really denied—they are just "interpreted". If a person is reasonably intelligent, and is faced with evidence of phenomena that do not fit into the belief system of one's family, culture, or peer group, there is nothing to do but to interpret—to rationalize it away. The Stockholm syndrome that abductees develop for their abductors is one example. Interpretive denial can provide a plausible explanation for any belief system. If one does not deny being abducted, the possible interpretations are endless: benevolent aliens, spirit guides, dead relatives, demons, military abductors, etc. For those who completely deny data outside the materialistic world view, "swamp gas" and the Planet Venus given as an explanation for UFOs are good examples.

I have to admit that this latter type of denial was the one that gave me the most "comfort". I couldn't deny many strange things, so I worked very hard to create acceptable categories for them. Sure, my categories were wider and more liberal than those of ordinary people who were not involved in the kind of work and research that engaged my thinking, but they were restricted categories nevertheless. I drew a line against "aliens and UFOs" and that line was, for many years, impassable.

The third kind of denial is termed by Cohen as implicatory denial where there is no attempt to deny either the facts or their conventional interpretation; what is ultimately denied are the psychological, political and moral implications that follow from deep acknowledgement. For example, the idea that America is being run by a madman with designs on the entire planet is recognized as a fact, but it is not seen as psychologically disturbing or as carrying any moral imperative to act.

Cohen discusses five different contexts of psychological denial: 1) perception without awareness, 2) perceptual defense 3) selective attention, 4) cognitive errors and 5) inferential failures. His conclusion is that "the scientific discourse misses the fact that the ability to deny is an amazing human phenomenon ... a product of sheer complexity of our emotional, linguistic, moral and intellectual lives".

As my husband, Ark, has written, science seems to be controlled by money. Scientists, for the most part, *have* to work on those things that get funding. There is nothing terribly unusual about that since it is a general rule for everyone. If you don't get money for your work, you starve, and then you don't do any work at all. Yes, that's somewhat simplistic, but still relevant to the subject here.

A few years back, our research group assembled a timeline[6] of secret and not-so-secret scientific projects—and those involved in them. The result was a compelling view of the fact that science has most definitely been used in a very detrimental way in our world. However, when such ideas—backed by the kind of extensive data we assembled—are brought to public attention, they are generally dismissed as "conspiracy theory" and are thus deemed unworthy of attention. So please, bear with me a moment here and let's apply a little logic to the problem.

The first thing we want to think about is the fact that the word "conspiracy" evokes such a strong reaction in all of us: nobody wants to be branded as a "conspiracy thinker"; it just isn't "acceptable"; it's "un-scientific" or evidence of mental instability. Right? That's what you are thinking, isn't it? In fact, I bet that the very reading of the word even produces certain physiological reactions: a slight acceleration of the heartbeat, and perhaps a quick glance around to make sure that no one was watching while you simply read the words "conspiracy theory" silently.

Have you ever asked yourself *why* the word evokes such an instantaneous emotional reaction? Have you ever wondered why it stimulates such strong "recoil"? After all, it is only a word. It only describes the idea of people in "high places" thinking about things and doing things that manipulate other people to produce benefits for themselves. Certainly, everyone "knows" that this happens all the time. No one would even raise an eyebrow if you said: "Well, everybody knows that politicians are corrupt and just playing politics to get rich". But if you really stop to consider the ultimate implications of such a statement, you would have to admit that this could be a real problem about which you might wish to do something. But then, of course, what could you do? We see here what Cohen has called "implicatory denial" where there is no attempt to deny either the facts or their conventional interpretation; what is ultimately denied are the psychological, political and moral implications that follow from *deep acknowledgement*. We can casually admit things in states of implicatory denial, which then leads us directly into "interpretative denial" where the raw facts that something may actually be happening—such as a conspiracy—are not really denied—they are just "interpreted" or rationalized away. We are then more easily able to slip into literal denial, that there is no "conspiracy", and then the

---

[6] http://www.cassiopaea.org/cass/timeline.htm

painful truth of our true condition is ameliorated and we can return to our sitcoms, ballgames and weekend barbeques.

Historian Richard M. Dolan studied at Alfred University and Oxford University before completing his graduate work in history at the University of Rochester, where he was a finalist for a Rhodes scholarship. Dolan studied U.S. Cold War strategy, Soviet history and culture, and international diplomacy. As an expert, his opinion of "conspiracy theory" is that *from a historical point of view, the* only *reality is that of conspiracy.* Secrecy, wealth and independence add up to power. Deception is the key element of warfare, (the tool of power elites), and when winning is all that matters, the conventional morality held by ordinary people becomes an impediment. Secrecy stems from a pervasive and fundamental element of life in our world, that those who are at the top of the heap will always take whatever steps are necessary to maintain the status quo.

And maintaining the "status quo" in science *has* to be one of the main objectives of the Power Elite. And how do they do that? By "official culture".

Official culture, understood this way, from the perspective of elite groups wishing to maintain the status quo of their power, means only one thing: COINTELPRO (Counter Intelligence Program). Here I do not mean the specific FBI program that was created to counter the anti-war movement of the 60s and 70s, but the concept of the program, and the likelihood that this has been the mode of controlling human beings for possibly millennia. Certainly, Machiavelli outlined the principles a very long time ago and little has changed since.

I like to call it "cosmic COINTELPRO" to suggest that it is almost a mechanical system that operates based on the *psychological nature of human beings*, most of whom *like* to live in denial. After all, "if ignorance is bliss, 'tis folly to be wise". This is most especially true when we consider the survival instinct of the ego. If the official culture says that there is no Third Man in the room, and if it works through the inculcated belief systems, there is little possibility that the "subject" will be able to see the source of the phenomena in our world. It will always be an "invisible Third Man." Using the model of the 70s COINTELPRO as a guide to what may be going on in our world, let us consider the fact that the FBI has been shown to have concentrated on *creating bogus organizations and promoting bogus ideas as a form of control.*

"There exists in our world today a powerful and dangerous secret cult." So wrote Victor Marchetti, a former high-ranking CIA official, in his book *The CIA and the Cult of Intelligence.* This is the first book the U.S. Government ever went to court to censor before publication. In this book, Marchetti tells us that there *is* a "Cabal" that rules the world and that its holy men are the clandestine professionals of the Central Intelligence Agency. (In our opinion, the CIA is but one "arm" of the cult, just as Benedictines were but one order of the Catholic Church.)

Borrowing from and paraphrasing Marchetti: This cult is patronized and protected by the highest level government officials in the world. Its membership is composed of those in the power centers of government, industry, commerce, finance, and labor. *It manipulates individuals in areas of important public influence—including the academic world and the mass media.* The Secret Cult is a global fraternity of a political aristocracy whose purpose is to further the political policies of persons or agencies unknown. It acts covertly and illegally.

The most effective weapons of COINTELPRO are ridicule and debunking. Notice that Marchetti points out that this is done via manipulation of individuals in areas of important public influence—including the *academic world* and the *mass media.*

Bottom line is: if you have bought into the emotionally manipulated consensus of "official culture" that there are no conspiracies, that there is no "Third Man", it is very likely that you are being manipulated by fear of ridicule. You are in denial. You have been hypnotized by the suggestions of the holy men of the Secret Cult. And you have chosen to believe them over your own possible observations and senses.

Why is it so that the very individuals who should be diligently studying the UFO/alien phenomenon do not? Why is it so that scientists—most particularly physicists and mathematicians of a good and honest disposition—seem to be the ones who most actively resist the very idea that their profession *may* have been taken over and "vectored" by conspirators who do not have humanity's best interests at heart? Why do scientists—those to whom the power elite *must* look for solutions to their "power problems"—think for one instant that their profession is exempt from conspiratorial manipulation and management?

That just isn't logical, is it?

In the physical sciences, very often machines and instruments are utilized to "take measurements". In order to achieve accuracy with even the most precisely tooled device, certain tests are undertaken to establish the "reading error" of the gadget. What we would like to suggest is that the "official culture" that establishes what may or may not be taken "seriously" is a planned and deliberate "reading error" built into the "machine" of science—our very thinking—the suggestions of the "hypnotist".

Without a historical context of science, there is little possibility that a sincere scientist—who is generally not much interested in history, based on my own experience—will ever be able to establish the "reading error" of his machine— his thinking.

There are only so many hours in the day, only so many days in the year, and only so many years in the life of a scientist. The amount of study that is necessary to discover the threads of "conspiracy", where they lead and what they lead to or away from, is actually overwhelming. I know: I've spent about 30 years doing it. What's more, I began my research from a skeptical point of view that "conspiracy" was paranoid thinking, and I was determined to find the way to demonstrate that there was *no* conspiracy. I wanted to create categories where anomalies could be discussed rationally within the accepted bounds of our social and cultural constructs. Unfortunately, not only did my plan fail—my hypothesis was utterly demolished by the hard facts.

One thing I did learn was that finding those "hard facts" was very difficult and time-consuming. And that is deliberate. After all, how good a conspiracy is it if it is so easily discovered? It is clear that in such a high stakes arena as the Global Control agenda now being overtly pursued by the Bush Reich—after years and years of the "secret science"—whatever conspiracies exist, will be managed with all the resources and power of those elitists who wish to retain control. That is a formidable obstacle.

I would also like to mention the fact that, even though I am the one who has collected and sorted data, my husband, a mathematical-theoretical physicist, *has* assisted me in analyzing it. At first he did it to humor me. And then, as he applied his knowledge of mathematics to the various problems I brought to him, he began to realize that science *can* be applied to these problems, and once that is done, it strips away the denial mechanism, and one is left with the inescapable conclusion that nothing is as it seems and never has been. We live in an ocean of lies, disinformation, manipulation, propaganda, and smokescreens.

Too bad more competent scientists do not bring their skills to the solving of these problems. But that is precisely what the "Secret Cult" does *not* want to happen. And that is precisely *why* the most subtle and far-reaching of the "COINTELPRO" operations have been run *on scientists themselves.*

Physics and mathematics are the *numero uno* professions that have been used—historically speaking—to support the power elite. They are the ones that give the elite their "tools of power", their bombs and mind control technology. It is logically evident that the governing elite have a vested interest in making sure that the money goes only to projects that 1) will augment their control; in which case such projects will be buried and no one will know about them; or 2) projects that do not threaten their control, in which case we may assume that they are funding research in the public domain that leads *away* from the "important" issues. In short, if it's popular, gets funded, is allowed out in the open, you can almost guarantee that it is smart but useless.

You can take that to the bank.

Here is where we come back to the context. If we take it as an operating hypothesis that there does exist a powerful elite whose interests are served by science, and who have a vested interest in public science never approaching the "secret science", we have adjusted our "machine tolerances" and can look at the problem in a different way. We then face the problem of what is *good* science?

A general definition would be that good science is that which contributes to the increase of knowledge within the scientific community overall, providing better methods of solving problems. By this definition, there is a *lot* of "respectable science" that is not "good science". Also, by this definition, there is a lot of "good science" that is not "respectable". In fact, based on our short review of "conspiracy", we might even think that most "respectable science" is deliberately vectored toward being very "smart but useless". Then we might suspect that the very best of the "good science" is deliberately ridiculed, attacked, or otherwise suppressed at a very early stage.

This, of course, brings us to the question: who, or what is behind it?

Actually, this would be a question that might be best answered by scientific analysis. When one is considering such things as COINTELPRO, the confusing elements of double and triple reverse psychology might be sorted out by those who are trained to use mathematically logical constructs. However, they are the very ones who are most turned off by the very idea. We suggest that is deliberate.

Why? Perhaps we can find an answer in something discussed by UFO researcher and writer, Don Ecker, in his article, "The Human Mutilation Factor":

> In the last forty years of UFO research, one of the most baffling questions that have plagued researchers has been "Is the UFO Phenomenon dangerous to humanity?"
>
> Over the years, there have been numerous cases where the phenomenon has figured into human deaths, but as a rule, most cases have been officially ruled accidental. When speaking of cases where death has resulted, usually most assume cases where military pilots have died as a result of "chasing" the phenomenon. One of the most famous of these military chases that is discussed whenever the subject of death and UFOs is raised, is the famous "Mantell Case". This case is so well known that I will not discuss it here, but there are many others. In one of the less well known cases, during the mid 1950's, a military jet interceptor was observed on radar being "absorbed" into a UFO over the Great Lakes. No trace of pilot or aircraft was ever found. ... [A]nother case reported in the excellent work "Clear Intent" was ... the "Cuban MIG Incident". In this case a Cuban MIG was locking on his weapons radar when the aircraft exploded in mid-air. The wing man was certain that the UFO had fired some type of weapon, but other than the jet exploding, no other smoke, flame or other obvious weapon firing was observed.
>
> The matter of either overt or covert hostility on the part of UFOs has always been treated warily by serious researchers. On the one hand, if the enigma is hostile, then several questions must be faced. What if anything should the powers in authority tell the public? Is the government capable of handling a threat of this type? Is the public ready to face an issue as potentially terrifying as a "possible threat from somewhere else?" Other than incidents involving military involvement, have there been cases where civilians have been injured or killed during some type of UFO encounter? Is it possible that the reported cases of UFOs and their occupants abducting unwilling humans for some type of medical or genetic experimentation could be true? Now, if any of this is factual, then what ramifications do the Human Race face in light of the above?
>
> According to Mr. Phil Imbrogno, during the research that led to the writing of *Night Siege: The Hudson Valley UFO Sightings* by Dr. J. Allen Hynek, Philip Imbrogno, and Bob Pratt, Imbrogno has stated that on several occasions, Hynek specified that he wanted no mention of the dozens of human abductions that they had already uncovered at that time, to be mentioned in the book. Hynek was afraid of the adverse publicity if word of this aspect leaked out to the public. After Hynek's death, Imbrogno stated publicly on Compuserve and other public forums, facts of abductions, animal mutilations, and EVEN several cases of mysterious deaths of humans, that he indicated COULD possibly be linked to the UFO Phenomenon.
>
> While researching several stories for UFO Magazine, I interviewed a number of prominent UFOlogists, over the last several months, and in each case, the question of human deaths, in connection with animal mutilations, invariably was raised. Most readers of this text will be familiar with Mr. John Keel, who many

regard as the last of the Great UFOlogists. From the earliest days of modern UFOlogy, Keel has been a force to reckon with. The author of numerous books that address various aspects of UFOlogy, and magazine articles too numerous to mention, Keel has a unique slant on the subject that most will never experience. According to Keel, *the phenomenon has always had an unexplained hostility towards humans*, that have led to untold numbers of deaths. While Keel will be the first to explain that he rejects the ET hypothesis, he does not doubt the phenomenon a bit. In what many UFOlogists consider as one of Keel's best works *The Mothman Prophecies*, Keel related report after report of animal mutilations involving cattle, dogs, horses and sheep, and also related what were called "vampire killings" of four humans in Yugoslavia, [where] the victims were "mutilated and drained of blood".

After having spoken to John Ford, the Chairman of the Long Island UFO Network, for a news story for UFO Magazine, I became even more convinced that the aspect of potential UFO hostility should be investigated. Ford relayed a numbing number of animal mutilations, human disappearances, human abductions, covert Federal involvement in areas that suffered high numbers of animal mutilations, and even armed military helicopters that chased UFOs over civilian communities. Ford, who is [an] officer of the Federal Court system, did investigations into the disappearances of mostly young adults over a year period, in areas of high UFO overflights, and after having several personal friends who were police officers of the local municipalities look into the situation, came to the conclusion that the facts were being suppressed. The reason given was that there was "no need to panic the public". Although no ironclad proof can be made for direct UFO intervention, the circumstances are extremely suspect.

After growing up in an age where the entire human race can be decimated by nuclear, biological and chemical weapons, the human race somehow manages to keep slogging on. I have seen more people "panicked" over a shortage of gasoline than imminent nuclear holocaust, yet somehow when the subject of UFOs crop up, the government doesn't want to panic anyone. It really makes me wonder what they know, that I should. I really don't think that they are going to talk to anyone soon...

In the new issue of *UFO Magazine*, I have written an update on the investigation of what appear to be more mutilations involving humans.

During the November 1989 Omega conference hosted by John White, Whitley Strieber castigated UFO Magazine for running my story on human mutilations in Vol. 4 Number 3. In that news story, I related the results of an investigation I was conducting on what appeared to be a series of human deaths that greatly resembled animal mutilations. Also, I included a report from Wm. "Bill" Knell of the Long Island Skywatch organization.

Knell had been conducting research into an inordinate number of missing children in the area of Westchester County. According to Strieber, he had received "hundreds" of phone calls from concerned citizens about the story. (That in itself is suspect, as anyone knows who has ever tried to call Strieber. Strieber has an answering service or secretary that screens each call, takes a message and then Whitley decides on whom he will speak with.) Anyway, I digress. Knell has many police contacts, and after checking with them, there were no contacts from Whitley. (One could surmise that what really had Whit in a snit was the way the print media had lambasted his flick, *Communion*, and his recent books, such as *Majestic*. He had just called all journalists "prostitutes".)

According to Knell and officers from the New York State Police, and the Connecticut State Police, the reported figures were in no way accurate, but the weirdest happening was when Knell received an inquiry from an Asst. Medical Examiner from Westchester County. The Asst. ME wanted to know everything Knell could relate on humans that had been mutilated. When Knell pursued this, it turned out that 3 morgues (2 in New York, 1 in Connecticut) had been "hit" in the middle of the night. Newly arrived human cadavers had been mutilated by removal of face, genitals, eyes, parts from the stomach, rectum, thyroids, etc. The morgues were immediately investigated by the police, but nothing could be placed on the employees. There were reduced staff at that time of night, and the events occurred in different areas. High Strangeness indeed. According to the Asst. ME, the incidents were immediately concealed from the media and public. More than likely the reasons were that there was no explanation, nor were the incidents going to be solved in the near future. As an aside, there were also quite a few animal mutilations that were occurring in New York and Connecticut, and once again no solutions were forthcoming for these events.

The Satanic explanation was examined, and according to the reporting witness, did not hold water.

Charles Fort, mentioned earlier, was an obsessive collector of anomalous events. Fort traveled to the major metropolitan libraries of his day where he would read through the various scientific journals of the day, looking for "damned data".

"Damned data" includes strange phenomena and experiences which included reports of strange things falling from the sky, strange things seen in the heavens, and strange disappearances. Fort was not just critical of the efforts of science to explain our reality, he was downright contemptuous of it. He would gleefully and fiendishly mock astronomers, meteorologists, and other scientists and their efforts to either deny or explain away anomalous occurrences. He derided their pompous attempts to deny what they could neither understand nor explain. His notes were published as *The Book of the Damned*. Fort once remarked that the only conclusions he could draw from all his research, was that Earth was "owned" by some beings who we could neither see nor comprehend. He said: I think we're property.

in religion

Now we want to look at one of the most troubling aspects of the UFO/alien problem that we have only touched on briefly: *what does it mean for religion?*

My answer is that it is not only science that is being vectored by COINTELPRO, but our general cultural experience which has been molded for millennia by religion. Nowadays, in the presence of widespread sharing of information relating to anomalous appearances of what are now being called UFOs and "aliens", we find that another form of disinformation has led to the identification of Jesus with the "interstellar astronaut" theory. Yes, apparently Jesus is an "alien". Dr. Vyatcheslav Saitsev of the University of Minsk claimed that Jesus came from outer space. His idea was that Jesus was a representative of a higher civilization, and that this is the explanation of his supernatural powers. He noted: *"In other words, God's descent to Earth is really a cosmic event."*

He may not be so crazy! Considering the work of COINTELPRO to conceal, distract, and disinform, the question is: *which God?*

In the past several years we have indeed been deluged with a tidal wave of books about ancient mysteries and purporting to reveal the "greatest secrets" of all time that have enthralled the world. All of them seem to have a similar, general trend, which is to support a certain derivation of the ancient mysteries in terms of Egyptian secrets, technology, and religion. The most widely promulgated of these books are by authors such as Henry Lincoln, Graham Hancock, Robert Bauval, John Anthony West, Robert Temple, Laurence Gardner, and a supporting cast too numerous to mention. This trend is the subject of *The Stargate Conspiracy* by Lynn Picknett and Clive Prince. The book is a useful overview for the novice in terms of achieving a basic understanding of the fact that there is, indeed, something very mysterious going on all over the planet in terms of shaping the thinking of humanity via books, movies, and cultural themes.

Picknett and Prince suggest that the central theme of the conspiracy is the *"manipulation of beliefs* about the origins and history of human civilization, in particular of beliefs about the existence of an advanced civilization in the ancient past and its influence on the earliest known historical civilizations, primarily that of Egypt". What Picknett and Prince fail to note is that the beliefs about the origins and history of human civilization have been manipulated *for millennia* to keep humanity in the dark. Anyone who doubts that this is often done quite consciously and deliberately ought to have a look at a few remarks of Cornelius Tacitus about the Roman Raj in Britain:

> The following winter was spent on schemes of the most salutary kind. To induce a people, hitherto scattered, uncivilized and therefore prone to fight, to grow pleasurably inured to peace and ease, Agricola gave private encouragement and official assistance to the building of temples, public squares and private mansions. He praised the keen and scolded the slack, and competition to gain honor from him was as effective as compulsion. Furthermore, he trained the sons of the chiefs in the liberal arts and expressed a preference for British natural ability over the trained skill of the Gauls. The result was that in place of distaste for the Latin language came a passion to command it. In the same way, our national dress came into favor and the toga was everywhere to be seen. And so the Britons were gradually led on to the amenities that make vice agreeable— arcades, baths and sumptuous banquets. *They spoke of such novelties as 'civilization', when really they were only a feature of enslavement.*

Just as the Roman empire—and the Assyrian and Persian empires before it— has manipulated beliefs, an in-depth examination of periods of history wherein great "advances" manifest, including the personal writings of the individuals involved, will show that such phenomena are just as present today. It is quite a revelation to discover that great "ideas" have been imposed upon us simply because the alternative view, which had more supporting evidence, was not useful to the control agenda of the authorities.

What is taking place at our present moment in history via what can only be called religious revivalism—including its manifestation as the so-called New Age movement with its subset of specialization in UFOs and aliens—is what is known in popular intelligence parlance as "damage control", a vast COINTELPRO operation against the revelation of truth in its proper context. In place after place, in all fields of scientific study, discoveries are being made that contradict what we have been taught to believe about our world, our history, religions and origins. The only way the Secret Cult that controls the world can deal with the emergence of truth in so many fields is to make a very powerful and concerted effort to divert these discoveries into a framework that will continue to serve the agenda of the control system.

Picknett and Prince astutely note that the writers listed above may not be conscious participants in the damage control system, but that they are most definitely being provided with the grist for mills of a massive cover-up operation—a shell-game of reality with moves so dexterous that unless the reader understands from the beginning that the hand is, indeed, quicker than the eye, they will be lulled by the obvious truths so that at the point the lie is introduced, they will swallow it at once without noticing that it is a lie. And make no mistake about it: these lies are intended to be a deadly poison—slow acting, but 100 percent lethal.

While Picknett and Prince rightly notice that the alternative history being proposed by the current spate of books, gurus, New Age mass market workshops and symposia, utilizes ideas and concepts born in the "occult world", they fail to distinguish the fact that what is "occulted" comes in two flavors: truth and just more and trickier lies. They are right about the fact that there is a lot of so-called occult, psychic, and New Age channeled material that is purely evil—part of this conspiracy to cover up the failures in the old belief systems. But they are wrong to believe that the system that is in place, the beliefs that have been promulgated on humanity for millennia, are the benevolent results of natural human evolution, or a benign and omniscient God who has our best interests at heart. In fact, Picknett and Prince do not even seem to notice the fact that the present Matrix of beliefs is crumbling, and *this* is what has necessitated the present co-opting and perversion of truth. If there was no failure of the old system, there would be no need for a new one. Picknett and Prince recoil in horror at the conspiracy they have uncovered, but they do not realize that the old system is exactly the same, and that they have fallen for the oldest of Machiavellian tactics: create an enemy by demonizing your opponent, and then step in as a savior to do exactly what you have accused the opponent of planning. Picknett and Prince do not seem to be fully cognizant of the subtle nature of disinformation tactics and how cleverly it has been used throughout the millennia to deliver lies wrapped in truth.

Meet the new boss, same as the old boss.

Giving them the benefit of the doubt, we do understand the position of Picknett and Prince. It's one thing to pursue conspiracy theories and to find them, track them and think that there are some very naughty folks here on the Big Blue Marble. It's an altogether different thing, after one has tracked enough of these theories, to come to the realization that they are all just different parts of the same elephant, and that the critter is really thousands of years old. When that fact smacks you in the face, either you run screaming in denial, or you begin to step back from the truly *big* picture—the global–millennial picture—and see that there is a very stinky rat somewhere. Having arrived at that, you realize that such a conspiracy could not be created or sustained by human beings—at least not alone.

I first started researching conspiracies after reading Gary Allan's *None Dare Call it Conspiracy*. I was so outraged that I decided to dig into the subject and prove it wrong, so I started following the trails of these various conspiracies. Two things were apparent. One was that while I could not disprove this idea of conspiracy, I could not find the *center* because every paper would come to a dead end. At a certain point in each group's history they would disappear, dissipate, be destroyed, and then another one would rise somewhere else and pretty much take over. Sometimes there are connections between the end of one and beginning of another, but not often.

The other thing I was thinking about was what I call the "payoff factor". The people who control this planet are generally power-hungry, greedy, selfish, self-centered. A benevolent person can do something self-sacrificing, so that their descendants—their children and grandchildren—will benefit, but a person who is greedy and selfish only do things for short-term rewards. But in the history of all these various conspiracies, the people involved are eventually decimated. There are no favors, no honor among thieves. This puzzled me because how can such an obvious conspiracy, if we take a broad view, be maintained? What drives it? Who is in charge if all the various groups are at each others' throats? How to maintain this cohesion without the obvious consciousness of the participants?

In studying conspiracy, you're left having to face the most difficult task of all: asking yourself who or what could be behind it. Having asked that question, you realize that you simply cannot answer it unless you open your mind to a whole constellation of possibilities that you would formerly never in your wildest dreams have considered. Then, if you work very, very hard, you may discover the "truth" that *they want you to believe*.

However, if you continue to work very, very hard and are very, very lucky, you will realize that you need help, and you will seek this help based on the knowledge you have acquired that such help can and does exist—only we generally do not have access to it because we are too easily duped and manipulated—and then you might begin to learn the rules of communicating with higher minds than our own. At such a point, following such an approach, there is some hope of sorting out the mess. But it isn't easy, and it can't be easy.

If it was, it would have been done hundreds or thousands of years ago, and the world would not be in the state it is in today.

Returning now to the disinformation campaign initiated by the Secret Cult, even if it is true that their goals are negative to humanity, the likelihood is that those negative goals are wrapped in layers of truth about humanity and human history—for a reason. And Picknett and Prince missed that one. The fact is, if many of the ideas and teachings of such groups about human history prove to be correct, how easy it will be for them to claim that since they are right about those things, they are also right about their political, social, and economic aims. And that is how the most effective disinformation works. By the same token, if Picknett and Prince are proven wrong about their claims *against* the alternative history aspects of the conspirators, then their related claims that there is a conspiracy will likewise be ignored. And that would be a terrible mistake.

Just what are the aims of such groups? *Synarchist* groups have been implicated in terrorism in the pre-World War II years. In the years leading up to the Nazi takeover of Germany, a Frenchman named Viven Postel du Mas wrote a notorious document, called the Synarchist Pact, which became their manifesto. In 1932, a society called the Synarchist Empire Movement was founded in France, which was described as "a secret society with very specific and limited membership, following a definite politico-economic programme". Picknett and Prince discovered that this group was behind right-wing terrorist gangs such as the CSAR (Secret Committee for Revolutionary Action), and that most of the CSAR membership were also part of the Synarchist Empire Movement. In 1941, a police report in Vichy France exposed a plot by Synarchists to take over the government, noting a close relationship between the Synarchist movement and the Martinist Orders.

It seems that after World War II, the Synarchists went even deeper underground in order to work on Plan B, since Plan A (Hitler's agenda) didn't pan out. In recent years Synarchist groups have come out into the open both in Europe and in Britain, and this leads us to Picknett and Prince's major research find: the connection between R. A. Schwaller de Lubicz and the Synarchist movement. Paraphrasing Picknett and Prince:

Given the nature of Synarchy one would probably never know the names of even the most powerful. But we do know quite a lot about one of them: R.A. Schwaller de Lubicz. It is curious that Schwaller de Lubicz has become the 'godfather' of Alternative Egyptology even though few have read his works first-hand. His ideas mostly come to us through the books of Graham Hancock, Robert Bauval and, of course, John Anthony West, all of whom have expressed their admiration for this scholar. They refer to him as a philosopher, or as a mathematician. What is interesting to us, however, is that, although Schwaller de Lubicz was those things, they never call him an occultist—which he was. And the never call him a Synarchist—which he was.

A leading figure in the Paris Theosophical Society, he broke away to form his own occult organization, which he called *Les Veilleurs*—the Watchers— specifically in order to carry his esoteric ideas into the political arena. Perhaps it will come as no surprise to discover that he has been described as a 'proto fascist.' He even claims to have designed the uniform for Hitler's SA ('Brownshirts'). Although it is not certain that his claim is true, Schwaller de Lubicz clearly had no problem with people thinking that it was. One of Schwaller de Lubicz's 'Watchers' was Vivien Postel du Mas, the man who wrote the Synarchist Pact of the 1930s. Through du Mas, Schwaller de Lubicz had a particular influence on Hitler's Deputy, the tormented and complex Rudolf Hess. Schwaller de Lubicz was anti-Semitic and racist—and, like the Nazis, thought that women were inferior to men. For example, he taught that women were intellectually incapable of understanding the Hermetica. All this is important, because it is impossible to separate Schwaller de Lubicz's political, Synarchist beliefs from his work as an Egyptologist, the work that certain authors so admire.

In the realm of cultural shaping, we find the *Holy Blood, Holy Grail* guys (Baigent, Lincoln, and Leigh) busy cooking up a "divine bloodline". This has now become the sensation of 2004 with Dan Brown's novel *The Da Vinci Code*, taking the cultural programming to another level. This idea is supplemented by the work of Laurence Gardner who has connected the Holy Grail bloodline to *reptilian aliens*. (At the same time, we have a host of true believers around the planet preaching the gospel of those cute and helpful Grays, and the reptilian Lord who really loves us and never did anything to humanity except teach them all about how to be civilized.) In other words, the stage has been set for the "new gods" to claim direct lineage from Jesus!

But there's a big problem with this faux lineage. As I wrote in my analysis of the Bible that can be found both on our website and in my book, *Secret History*, what seems to be true is that the writers of both the Old and New Testaments couldn't just toss out the oral traditions of the people. They used them in a very special way. With an awareness of how history can by mythicized and then historicized, and any combination thereof, we can look at the scriptures with a different eye. We can theorize that there must have been a real person around whom the legend of Jesus—the mythicized history—was wrapped. We can theorize that he was teaching something important and dramatic for it to have made such an impact. We can also theorize that this "impact" was seen as very dangerous at first, but later, after many twists and turns had been introduced, it was thought that the growing myth and popularization of Jesus could be utilized—with appropriate rulings on what was "holy writ"—as the centerpiece of a Control System. It often seems that whatever was positive was twisted and turned backward by the time Roman Emperor Constantine adopted Christianity for political purposes. What develops with a broad historical review, is the idea that whatever "Jesus" was really doing and saying, it was most certainly twisted, corrupted, and emphasis shifted in fairly predictable ways.

Put simply, the Bible as we know it was declared to be "holy and infallible" to justify any of a number of *political maneuvers*.

Regarding the creation of the Bible as it really happened, in examining this process, we find nothing of the "Holy Ghost" in there. That's the plain fact. And

107

a lot of people in the "business" of religion know it. Nevertheless, in our current day, we find an astonishing state of affairs: our institutions of higher learning generally have a special faculty allotment for the teaching of theology, financed by the taxpayer, whether Christian or Jew!

One assumes that the students who study this theology are also given exposure to other studies, such as math, languages, science, and so forth. The question then becomes: what kind of strange distortion, what incomprehensible corruption takes place in the minds of human beings, so that they can so completely separate their academic knowledge from what they hear preached at them from the pulpit? What kind of brainwashing can so effectively cause the simplest of facts to be forgotten?

How does this happen? It is literally staggering to a logical, intelligent human being, that the fairy tale of the Bible—as God's word—has endured so long. There is nothing to which we can compare this in the entire seven thousand years of human history of which we are aware. Calling it all a "pack of lies" seems rather harsh, but it is increasingly evident that it is certainly intentionally misleading. And, in that case, what shall we call it?

How about COINTELPRO?

When researching religious matters, one always comes across prophecy and miracles. It seems that those who are to be kept in fear of the Lord need an unequivocal sign from time to time. Miracles and visions can sway whole armies. We can think of the battle cry "Great is Allah!" and the claim of the salvific blood of Christ that was held up as a shield against the Saracens. We should also be reminded of the mandate of Yahweh to "utterly destroy" just about everybody who wasn't hanging out with Joshua and his gang.

Such "visions" go back into our primeval past. Around 5000 BC, the divine Ishtar was said to have appeared to Enme-Kar, the ruler of Uruk, telling him to overthrow the city of Aratta. But, at the moment, we are mostly concerned with visions in the context of the Bible since it is the Bible that underpins the beliefs of a staggering number of human beings on planet earth at the present time, including their "revised forms" in the New Age and Human Potential movement, and most particularly George Bush and the Gang. That alone should give us pause to consider the company we keep!

Additionally, when we step back from the situation, the one thing that we see is that prophecy is at the center of the Judeo-Christian-Islamic tradition. The prophets of these religions claimed to be in direct contact with the Creator of the Universe, and this creator seems to have been singularly "personal" in the sense of having personal traits, whims, likes and dislikes. His prophets are, naturally, privileged messengers, receiving his divine revelations and these revelations divide mankind into those who believe them and those who don't. Naturally, those who don't are damned depending on who has the upper hand.

The Christian religion, and its New Age offshoots, is the chief proponent of the many End of the World scenarios with which we are most familiar. Scenarios about the end times originate mostly in the body of apocalyptic, eschatological writings of the New and Old Testaments. It is in the final book,

Revelation, that most striking and symbolic representations about the end of the world are said by many to be depicted.

It is a difficult work to comprehend. Probably no other piece of writing in history has been examined more thoroughly and interpreted more widely. It is the end-of-the world legend, a doomsday tale on moldy bread with virtual reality special effects in abundance. It is the inspirational fountainhead for mad prophets, spittle spewing pulpit-pounders, apocalyptic Enochian magicians, fanatical true believers, grade-B movie makers, and knaves and snake-oil salesmen of every form and sort.

In William Bramley's book, *The Gods of Eden*, he noted that when we consider history, we can clearly see that the drive of human beings to have peace is as strong, if not stronger, than the drive to have war. But, when the issue of war is examined, one realizes that, most often, the "trigger" for war and the related "inhumanity to man" is that *the drive for spiritual freedom is twisted by manipulation.*

It's easy to look back on history and see where this or that group was "misled" in their beliefs and thereby fell into errors of thinking that led to the perpetration of unspeakable horrors. We can point to the genocide advocated by the God of the Hebrews, or the religious-zeal-run-amok of the Catholic church when it instituted the Inquisition. We can see the twisted version of the "genetic superman" that led to the holocaust of World War II. It's easy to discern these errors of the past, because we "know more now". Well, isn't that an interesting thing? We *know* more now. How much more can we learn?

It almost seems as if the game has just gotten more and more complex, but the same essential errors keep getting repeated. What is at the root? (Aside from the fact that we notice the above examples all relate to monotheistic exclusivity.)

Human beings have a sort of built in drive to be "insured" or "underwritten" regarding any choices they may make. This is due to a fundamental condition of our reality. This condition seems to be a sort of "randomness" or lack of control of our lives. Our observations of reality tell us that there is "something out there" that we need to know about because having this key can "make or break" us. We adopt religions because we are anxious. We are anxious because we realize, from our observations, that at any moment, this "randomness" which manifests as destruction, will fall upon us either physically or psychically. It would be oh so helpful if we could see the future in advance, be informed of the respective consequences in the choices confronting us in every moment.

Over and over again we can see that this need to be "insured" is what is used to manipulate human beings. What we see is that *a scientific view of spirituality is discouraged while at the same time, the inner desire for "salvation" is constantly being stimulated by various religious teachings.* As a consequence, a great many people can be led into doing a lot of cruel and stupid things. The perceived need to "save souls" is a prime example of how such a seeming positive polarization can be suddenly shifted to do the exact opposite of what the religious teachings explicate. And this is an important point to remember!

Zecharia Sitchin and William Bramley, following Von Daniken, have postulated that the ancient evidence demonstrates the actual, physical presence of an extraterrestrial race who came to earth to set up "controls" over humanity, with possible plans to return and "harvest the fruits" of their efforts. In both cases, their studies have indicated strongly that this "extraterrestrial race" does *not* have humanity's best interests at heart! Both of them did a lot of work, gathered a lot of *facts*, and were certainly not listening to some bug eyed Gray alien trying to convince them that "this is for *you*! We are here to help!" Yet, somehow, both of them did not deal with a crucial element of the problem.

The fact is, we find today those same "aliens" zipping about, sliding in and out of our reality like slippery eels, gazing and probing and "communicating" all kinds of excuses and scenarios to explain what they are doing based on how gullible or ignorant their victims are. This factor has to be considered. In other words, what Von Daniken, Sitchin and Bramley fail to factor into their arguments is the *continuing* evidence of "interaction" and "domination" from another "realm" of existence. The Annunaki, as defined by Sitchin, and the "Custodians" as defined by Bramley, may not be *physical beings*, (in our terms), who occupy, dominate, and then leave for some obscure reason. The evidence of those people, now numbering in the multiples of thousands, claiming "alien abduction" and "contact with aliens" and even "visions of the Virgin" and other miracles throughout history, seems to contradict this view. It seems far more likely that the ancient stories indicate a cultural openness that *permitted perception* of such beings, *acknowledged their reality*, and merely made the distinction between them and ordinary human beings by referring to them as "gods".

William Bramley also chronicled considerable historical evidence of a relation between the sightings of UFOs and the sudden onslaught of deadly diseases or plagues. We have similar concerns in the present time which indicates that this is not a "new thing", but merely part of a cycle. The Annunaki have never left, and the Brotherhood of the Serpent is still with us, active and growing stronger by the day.

Considering religion as COINTELPRO, during my reading, I came across a curious remark by the medieval Jewish commentator, Rashi, saying, in effect, that the Genesis narrative *was written to justify what we now call genocide!* The God of Israel, who gave his people the "promised land", had to be unequivocally supreme so that no one, not even the dispossessed, could appeal against his decrees (Isserlin, 1998).

In Umberto Eco's *The Search for The Perfect Language*, the idea is suggested, though subtly, that the development of the Hebrew Bible, even if there were some ancient texts involved, (though not nearly as ancient as most believers suppose!) was primarily a *"promotion" to validate Judaism*. This validation was necessary in order to then "validate" Christianity as the "one true religion". In other words, the "rights" of the Jews, the unappealable decrees of Jehovah/Yahweh, could be "inherited" by the Christian Church as instituted for political reasons by Constantine!

What we finally observe about Christianity can be summed up by saying that it is clear that it was taken over by a sort of counter intelligence program to be used as a control system. The Egyptian religion became the model of Christianity, and the "Stargate Conspiracy"—substituting essentially Synarchic ideas for the original Christianity—was a great success. It has been used to kill more people than any other ideology in recorded history. It is, as it happens, the foundation of the Bush Reich Agenda—agents of the Apocalypse. Christianity—and other monotheistic religions—are basically Draconian. They are the well from which much in our society, our mores, ethics, judgments, is drawn. It has been the justification for the greatest series of bloodbaths in "recorded" history.

Could there be a reason for this?

Simultaneously, there are those that claim there is a "gradual revelation" plan going on via the government and its space program, juxtaposed against a big push by George Bush and the Fundamentalists of both Christian and Zionist tendencies to institute a One World Government.

So, we have a right to ask: what the heck is really going on? What does it mean when Christian Fundamentalists talk about the "New Jerusalem" when, in point of fact, the evidence shows that anything and everything that had to do with the Old Jerusalem was lies and disinformation swirling around that crafty Yahweh/Jehovah guy with control issues?

The reality seems to be that Judaism, Christianity and Islam were specifically designed and created just to produce a particular situation that is desirable to someone at a certain point in time, and again, we see the same operation being run on humanity in the present day as the New Age–Human Potential movement. It's not that these religions and their prophecies accurately predict the future; they were set up so that their followers would unwittingly fulfill the plans of a group that feeds on destruction. The manipulation of belief systems by human agents for purposes of political control (which will be discussed more in depth in the next sections) leads to a system of mass suffering that is beneficial to the "aliens", who provide the otherworldly "proof" of the religion's validity.

Interestingly, there are ancient texts that refer to this very problem. In the book of Enoch, Jesus is recorded as saying:

> From the time when the devil fell from the glory of the Father and (lost) his own glory, he sat upon the clouds, and sent his ministers, even angels flaming with fire, unto men from Adam even unto Henoch his servant. And he [the devil] raised up Henoch upon the firmament and showed him his godhead and commanded pen and ink to be given him: and he sat down and wrote threescore and seven books. And [the devil] commanded that he should take them to the earth and deliver them unto his sons. And Henoch let his books down upon the earth and delivered them unto his sons, and began to teach them to perform the custom of sacrifice, and unrighteous mysteries, and so did he hide the kingdom of heaven from men. And [the devil] said unto them: Behold that I am your god and beside me is none other god. And therefore did my Father send me [Jesus] into the world that I might make it known unto men, that they might know the evil device of the devil.

111

chapter four

Let me repeat that part again:

> And Henoch let his books down upon the earth and delivered them unto his sons, and began to teach them to perform the custom of sacrifice, and unrighteous mysteries, and so did he hide the kingdom of heaven from men. And he said unto them: Behold that I am your god and beside me is none other god.

This is the god of Judaism, Christianity and Islam... the Devil.

in time

In a general sense, to almost everyone, including yours truly, the very idea of time traveling, mind marauding, hyperdimensional beings with full powers to create and maintain a reality of illusion and restriction in which we are confined like sheep, waiting daily to see which of our number will be "taken" for their wool, skins, or flesh, is so horrifying a concept that accepting it as a real possibility, is tantamount to being stripped of all hopes, dreams and comfort.

Like many of you, I began this work full of frustration with teachings that don't work or don't make sense when compared with honest observation of reality and experience. There was such a labyrinth of contradictions everywhere I searched, and I *knew* it was necessary to go beyond everything hitherto known or tried. I did have the idea that this knowledge had been available in ancient times, judging by the evidence of the megaliths and other incomprehensible structures all over the globe, but whether or not it would be possible to rediscover this path was uncertain.

It was *very* clear that there was a serious discrepancy between the observable reality and some "deeper reality" from which, presumably, ours derives something of its form and structure, but I knew there was something that separated "us" from "them". And again, when searching for answers, it always ended in a maze of insupportable assumptions and irreconcilable facts.

But when the Cassiopaeans began to communicate, to say things that *did* explain the problems I was finding in science, religions and philosophies, and those things they told us were *not* part of my expectations, I became furious and railed at such a bleak picture of our existence. I had already gone through some of this process in earlier years while reading Gurdjieff and Ouspensky, but I found that what the Cassiopaeans were saying was far more dispiriting than I was prepared to receive. I rejected ideas that suggested our "fairy tale" beliefs just *might* be imposed on us to keep us asleep and unaware because I didn't like them either! As time went by and evidence from other sources mounted, I raged at lessons that drove home these points in my personal life; and I have wept oceans for the loss of my innocence. So, believe me when I say to those of you who write to me struggling to grasp this reality, trying to reason and rationalize some way to hang on to the old, false belief systems—I *do* understand!

But, when all is said and done, I think I wept even more for all the years wasted in stupidity and blindness. After a time, I realized that we are only stupid

112

and blind exactly as long as we *need* to be stupid and blind, and not one second longer. I am enormously grateful for all those experiences because they *did* teach me in a very deep way.

If it is true that humans are being bred and raised like cattle in a global stockyard and fed upon both psychically and sometimes even physically, we have a truly serious situation going on here, to put it mildly. As I have explained before, I have never seen a "drachomonoid" being except in dreamlike states or almost hypnopompic semi-sleep states. So, when the Cassiopaeans began to talk about them, it was truly "Twilight Zone" time, in my opinion!

I have also stated that, whenever the Cassiopaeans have told us anything, I work very hard to discover if there is any form of what I call vertical or lateral corroboration. Vertical data is that which is located in history at any point different from the present. Lateral data consists of collecting reports, witness information, and other data that amounts to circumstantial evidence from the present time. It is always better if the two types of data "cross" or intersect. But it is still not the same as having a "smoking gun". But, when you are dealing with hyperdimensional realities, "smoking guns" are not very likely to be found.

In the case of the idea of man being "food" for hyperdimensional beings, there is an enormous amount of both vertical and lateral corroboration of *all* kinds. So much so that, in fact, it is almost impossible to understand why it is not generally known. Clearly, there have been deliberate efforts to hide this fact. And, the fact that it is hidden may itself tell us something.

The point is, when don Juan and Gurdjieff and the Cassiopaeans (and others) tell us that our religions, our social structure, our values, our beliefs about our spiritual nature and condition have been *deliberately created to perpetuate the illusion that we are free;* that we are (or can be) "special and adored children of a loving God"; that we are or can be "co-creators" with God, that we can *do* anything at all of a positive and powerful nature, we need to carefully examine this issue!

But it is *work* to examine it objectively. It is *hard work* because it consists of long and difficult self-examination in order to be able to overcome the emotions that prevent us from discovering what illusions we are hanging onto, what illusions are preventing us from seeing and acting in such a way as to *become free.*

And yet, we *can* see that *something* is evolving here! With the maturation of the "group mind", the stakes get higher and the deceptions deeper!

For many centuries, millennia even, simplistic religions and social dynamics were dominant over most of the world. This was possible because even when there was an "intrusion" by one of these hyperdimensional beings into our reality, when they did "drop in for dinner", so to speak, it was easy to conceal because of the lack of communication between tribes and peoples.

When we sit in our comfortable homes and look at our reality, including that which is outside our windows, we see a "stable" front. Cars pass on the street taking people to and from their homes in their varied daily activities. The sun shines, children pass by talking and laughing. Everyone is involved in their life in an immediate and identified way, believing that this life they are involved in is what *is*.

But, once in a while, something bizarre happens to someone, and they struggle to deal with this anomaly in the space/time continuum. Usually, it is sufficiently minor that they can "damp it" and forget about it, which they *must*, because it is too aberrant in the normal accepted course of events. It must be shoved under the rug and hidden.

Once in awhile, bigger things happen in the reality—evidence of the hyperdimensional control system intrudes, or the "screen" breaks down in some way—and it becomes news and gets reported. Charles Fort spent many years collecting these types of things from the newspapers and magazines all over the world.

When this happens, the "accepted belief system" hurries to "damp down" the item so that everyone can go along in their respective and collective illusions. And, since the events are localized, it is easy to cover it up. And, in the past, this was a *lot* easier than it is today.

When you read the collected works of Charles Fort, you see that the "alien reality" that is so widely reported today was just as active then as it is now. In fact, you see that it may even be somewhat "cyclical". Just as we have cycles of food production, planting, growing and harvesting, so may hyperdimensional beings harvest us according to some "seasonal" rule.

But, in any event, in the past it was a lot easier to keep the lid on the matter. But then, people began to become literate. Books and papers and magazines were published and distributed. Travel became easier and information from around the world about these "odd intrusions" into our reality could be collected giving an overall pattern that something was not right.

Before Charles Fort, there were some few people who already "smelled a rat". Mr. Fort kindly shoved it right under our noses and the reaction has been quite interesting. The "cover up" machine went into *full* operation through the most effective vectors of mainstream science and religion. But, the rat had been smelled and some people couldn't just shove it back under the rug. The stench kept wafting in the window that had been opened.

And so, certain people began to start searching for the source of this stinky rat. They began to gather knowledge and information.

We can even note *how* the "cover-up" machine began to do this "damage control". When you study the history of social and religious movement and change, you can see the "control mechanism" morphing with every discovery or realization made by human beings. As they outgrew the old religions, the simplistic explanations, new "religions" were put in place. At exactly the right time—the period of scientific expansion and growing knowledge of the nature of reality which brought the old religious views into serious question—the whole spiritualist movement began, leading to channeled information that was designed to patch up the holes in the control net. Newer and more elaborate explanations of the "higher realms" came into our reality. And, with each new question, the control system had a new answer to help everybody calm down, relax, and stop asking questions!

At the present time, this is even more amazingly evident. A few years ago, when we first began sharing the Cassiopaean information, many of the issues we dealt with were not even addressed by these other "sources". But, with everything we release, the "other side" brings some new candidate forward with new explanations to "patch the holes" we are tearing in the fabric of reality.

The story of the reality of spirit, of the play of forces that exist as a subtext to the lives of all human beings, can be told as a journey toward knowledge and understanding. My search for the existence of truth about our reality forced me to recognize the validity of perceptions beyond those of materialism. I learned to challenge my own beliefs and suffer the agony of surrendering my own dearly held reality constructs.

I suspected something was wrong with the "facts of life" as they were presented to me when I was a kid. Sure, I then spent a little over thirty years trying to be "normal" and make that square peg fit the round hole, "looking for a reason to believe". But then there was a memorable day when I finally grew up and admitted that maybe—just maybe—the Emperor was naked. And here it is, over twenty years later, and now—well, now I know that not only is something rotten in Denmark, I also know there is a dead elephant in the middle of the collective global living room, and I can never *not* see it again.

During that twenty plus years of uncovering that huge, dead critter that occupies a central place in our reality, I was driven by the idea that I just wanted to know what was *really* going on in this strange world I lived in where, on the one hand, science was moving so fast that we would soon be able to destroy our planet, while on the other hand, the varied religions were telling us not to worry, God was probably going destroy it for us, and we had better believe in the "right god" or we were toast.

How can a person live in a world where "the End of the World" is being predicted every minute? That's crazy!

But darned if that isn't what just about every religion—including the New Age versions—on the planet talks about!

You go to church, get scared to death in an hour and a half, warned about hellfire and damnation, and then they pass the plate so that you can pay the high priests to put in a good word for you with God so that maybe you won't suffer as much as that jerk down the street who goes to a different church! And even if you do suffer here on earth, if you believe hard enough, and prove it by putting your money where your faith is, at least you'll get your reward in paradise.

This was back in 1982 when I had three small children. As a mother, I wanted to know what to teach my children. I knew that what I had been taught to believe was frightening. I had grown up in a time when children were regularly taught what to do in case of an atomic bomb attack—Cuba was only 90 miles from Florida where I was born—and at the same time, the standard religious teaching of my family—mainstream Protestants—promoted the "suffer on Earth to get rewarded in Heaven" routine.

I knew I had certainly suffered from the state of the world and the teachings of my faith. I really, *really* wanted to know if this was something that I should pass on to my children.

When I held my babies and rocked them or looked into their sweet, innocent faces—untroubled by the concerns of the world around, certain that Mother would make them safe—I had to ask myself, *How can I tell them these things? How can I 'break it to them' that this world into which they have been born is so frightening and uncertain and full of traps that not only are their lives in constant danger, their very souls may be in peril?*

How could I tell that to my children???

If it was true, I *had* to tell them.

But what if it wasn't true?

What if it wasn't true?

I knew one thing and one thing only: I wanted more than anything in the world to tell my children the truth, to prepare them for whatever might lie ahead of them in their lives. And the question burned inside me: What if I told those little beings who I loved more than my own life a *lie*? What kind of a mother would I be? What kind of "Mother Love" is that?

The Cassiopaean communication was only a part of this process. Looking back on this experiment in accessing "higher consciousness", which, at that point, I only theorized might exist, there is a lot to be said for the idea that most of what has come "from the C's" could very well have come from my own subconscious. After all, I had spent nearly my whole life reading everything from history to psychology. The phenomenon of the scientist working on a difficult problem who then, after he has examined all the parameters, dreams of a novel way to put the different parts together that solves the problem is well known in the history of science. The discovery of the benzene ring is a case in point. So it isn't too much of a stretch to say that the material that came "from the C's", who clearly stated "we are *you* in the future", was merely a similar process.

The attentive reader who has read the many articles on our website that include material from the Cassiopaean experiment will notice that most of the C's material has to do with history and the hidden motivations for the events in our world. These were certainly the things that concerned me—events and choices of action and being that could lead to a positive future or a negative future either on a personal, or global, level—and so, perhaps my vast reading was sorted and assembled in novel ways by my own subconscious mind or superconscious mind.

Be that as it may, it does not, in my opinion, at all detract from the usefulness of the material. The discovery of the benzene ring came from a dream and led to a breakthrough in science. And so it has seemed that the concerted effort to examine all the parameters of reality, and then to "allow" it to sort itself and "come out" in a novel process of reassembly, has proven very fruitful in many respects.

Of course, there are still some items that the C's have come up with that obviously could *not* come from a "reordering" of the masses of material available to my subconscious from years of reading. In that respect, due to the novel way in which the material was obtained as a "group effort", perhaps some of the material was extracted from the subconscious databanks of the other participants? And perhaps some of the data was nonsense—my own and others? These are all questions we consider when we analyze the material and subject it to verification or testing.

There is still another category of material—that which later proves to be insightful in ways that simply could not come from the subconscious data of *any* of the participants.

Or could it?

Perhaps an awareness of what is going on politically and socially can be "sorted and reassembled" in the subconscious the same way the information that led to the discovery of the benzene ring was? Perhaps probabilities are calculated in the subconscious mind based on vast collections of data that we don't even realize we have? Perhaps lifetimes of observations of the world "out there" consisting of billions of databits can be stored in our subconscious and lead to very complex "data sorting" and "probability estimation"?

Perhaps there is, after all, a completely scientific and material explanation for the Cassiopaean material; except for just a few items that I am certain were *not* part of the conscious or subconscious data of any of the participants—items that were known to only a few people on the planet and which we had to dig deep to verify. But then, that is only evidence of an ability to access information that may be in the databanks of unknown others at a distance.

But, isn't that the point? That we search for that tiny clue that there *is* a reality beyond that which the materialist scientific view accepts as measurable?

Just as certain mechanical aids can augment the perception of certain ranges of light such as infra-red, ultra-violet, x-rays, and radio waves, so might our so-called psychic perceptions be similarly augmented. This was my theory at the beginning of the Cassiopaean Experiment though I never thought it would evolve into a dialogue with "myself in the future" or that "aliens" would be included in the subject matter discussed on a serious basis.

The material you are going to read in the next section used to be on our website, but we decided to take it all down. Why? One of the main reasons was because we experienced an extraordinary level of attack both personally and professionally as a consequence of publishing what you are going to read in this book. These attacks came from several sources including weirdoes, cranks, and derisive skeptics. The attacks that were most troubling to us, however, originated from what can only be called a gang of cyber-terrorists.

There was, of course, a third kind of reader who was interested in this material: people who were sincere and openly seeking information about strange experiences in their lives that were not only inexplicable, but which had left them with scars of the soul. I am certainly such a person myself, and it could be said that the material in this book exists because of my own seeking for answers to these most troubling of questions.

It is for this last type of reader that the decision was made to make the material available in the form of the book you are now holding in your hand.

PART TWO:
The Man Behind the Curtain

chapter five
the cassiopaeans

On July 16, 1994, at our weekly Saturday evening sitting, we were all a bit excited at the latest news from space. Fragments of Comet Shoemaker-Levy were soon to begin a series of collisions with the planet Jupiter, an extremely rare cosmic event. The impacts were supposed to continue for the next seven days, and I was very interested to see if this would have any noticeable effect on Earth.

We were just sitting there with our fingers lightly on the planchette, the "question" inside me growing larger and larger as it had been doing for months, when suddenly the planchette began to move in slow, deliberate circles in a way we had never before experienced. We jerked our fingers away and I asked Frank, "Did you just do that?"

"No", he replied indignantly. "Put your fingers back. Let's see what's going on!"

A funny pinching feeling and a tingle started at the back of my head that ran down my arm. The planchette began to move again slowly in a spiral. Spiral in and spiral out. We did the usual thing and said, "Hello!"

Slowly, the planchette precisely and deliberately spelled "Hello." That was not exactly usual. The usual response to "hello" was for the planchette to go to "yes". It always took a bit for each entity to get "warmed up" and be able to move comfortably around the board. As unusual as that opening was, we were not prepared for what was about to happen.

> Q: Do you have any messages for us?
> A: Keep doing what comes naturally.
> Q. (L) In what respect?
> A: Study.
> Q: (L) What is your name?
> A: Mucpeor.

This was an unusual name. Up to this point in time, the names we had been given had all been, more or less, familiar. Names like "Dave" or "John" or "Mary" were not uncommon with the "dead dude" crowd. Some of them even used archaic, but still familiar names like "Agamemnon" or "Aquila". So, a completely unfamiliar name with no known connection was another first. Since we had already been visited by a spate of "space brothers", the next logical question was:

Q: (L) Are you an alien from another planet?
A: Alien from your perspective, yes.

That was a funny answer. They were not "aliens", but were "alien from our perspective"? Well, Jordan and the other space brothers had belonged to one "alien" group or another. The Cosmic Confederation or the Galactic Brotherhood or whatever. So the next natural question was:

Q: (L) What is your group called?
A: Corsas.
Q: (L) Where are you from?
A: Cassiopaea.
Q: (L) Where is that?
A: Near Orion.
Q: (L) I heard that the Orions are the "bad guys". Are the Orion group bad?
A: Some bad.

I had read so much about different purported groups of "aliens", most of whom pointed the finger at a slew of them from somewhere in Orion who were here to do all kinds of nasty things. So this was certainly a "test question". The fact that the Cassiopaeans did not jump on the Orion bashing bandwagon was significant.

Candy had recently read a book on the channeled *Ra Material* which explained a concept of determining "good guys" from "bad guys". This consisted in asking if the entity served self or others. So, that was the next logical question:

Q: (L) Do you serve self or others?
A: I serve both.
Q: (L) Are you bad or good, in our terms?
A: Good.
Q: (L) What is your philosophy?
A: One.
Q: (L) What are you here for tonight?
A: Prophecy.
Q: (L) What prophecies?
A: Tornadoes Florida—several.
Q: (L) Where else?
A: Also Texas and Alabama.
Q: (L) When?
A: Sun is in Libra.
Q: (L) What planet are you from?
A: Carcosa.

The term "Carcosa" was one of the first signs we were dealing with something a bit different here. Up to this point, none of the discarnate entities we had dealt with had been able to read our minds. But here, there was a funny reference to a word that had been playing through my mind all day. I was a bit startled by this remark. It was from Jacques Vallee's book, *Revelations*. At the beginning of each section, there are quotes from Cassilda's Song in *The King in Yellow,* Act 1, Scene 2, by Robert W. Chambers. After the session, I opened the book to re-read the quotes. The song goes:

> Strange is the night where black stars rise,
> And strange moons circle through the skies,
> But stranger still is... Lost Carcosa.
> Songs that the Pleiades shall sing,
> Where flap the tatters of the King,
> Must die unheard in ... Dim Carcosa.
> Along the shore the cloud waves break,
> The twin suns sink behind the lake,
> The shadows lengthen... In Carcosa.

More interesting still, to those already familiar with the Cassiopaean material, is the reference to the "twin suns". Referring to Carcosa, I asked:

Q: (L) Where is that?
A: 2 D I L O R.

The planchette had begun to move very fast and we were not able to keep up. The last remark was lost and only a few of the letters written down.

Q: (L) What was that again?
A: You pay attention.
Q: (L) What else is going to happen?
A: Seattle buried; Japan buckles; Missouri shakes; California crumbles; Arizona burns.
Q: [Unknown question.]
A: Go to Denver airports.
Q: (L) When is all this going to happen?
A: Scandal—Scandal—Denver Airport.
Q: (L) What about the Denver airport?
A: Scandal.
Q: (L) I don't understand.
A: New Denver airport.
Q: (L) I don't understand.
A: Pay attention.
Q: (L) OK, we are paying attention. What are you trying to tell us?
A: Denver new airport big big big big scandal.
Q: (L) What kind of scandal?

123

A: Government.

Q: (L) Specifically what?

A: You will see Dallas airport is secret base Orlando too Miami too.

Q: (L) What about Denver airport and how does it relate to prophecies?

A: Denver reveals the government Look for it Pay attention.

Q: (L) What else do you have to tell us?

A: Montana: Experiment with human reproduction. All people there—rays—radon gas.

Q: (L) How are they doing this?

A: Compelled—Don't trust Don't ignore too strong urges sinister plots.

Q: (L) What do you mean? I don't understand?

A: Strong urge is directed by sinister plot.

Q: (L) Plot by whom?

A: Consortium.

Q: (L) Who are the members of the consortium? Aliens? The government?

A: All.

Q: (L) All who?

A: Government and other.

Q: (L) Who is the other?

A: Unknown.

Q: (L) Why can't you tell us who is the other?

A: You know who.

Well, all this was very interesting. Finally, an entity that could spell and didn't spend any time wandering around looking for the letters. Now was my chance, so I decided to ask the question that had been bugging me all day as a sort of test.

Q: (L) Bob Lazar referred to the fact that aliens supposedly refer to humans as containers. What does this mean?

A: Later use.

Q: (L) Use by who? How many?

A: 94 per cent.

Q: (L) 94 per cent of what?

A: Of all population.

Q: (L) What do you mean?

A: All are containers 94 per cent use.

Q: (L) I don't understand.

A: Will be used 94 percent.

Q: (L) Used for what?

A: Total consumption.

Q: (L) What do you mean by consumption? Ingested?

A: Consumed for ingredients.

Q: (L) Why?

A: New race. Important 13 years about when happens.

Q: (L) Why are humans consumed?

A: They are used for parts.

Q: (L) We don't understand. How can humans be used for parts?

A: Reprototype Vats exist. Missing persons often go there and especially missing children.

At this answer, I was in shock. What kind of entity would tell us such things? What kind of awful reality must such information proceed from? I was torn between terminating contact that very instant, and working my way through it to find some resolution.

Q: (L) Do we have any protection?

A: Some.

Q: (L) How can we protect ourselves and our children?

A: Inform them. Don't hide the truth from children.

Q: (L) How does truth protect us?

A: Awareness protects. Ignorance endangers.

Q: (L) Why tell children such horrible things?

A: Need to know.

Q: (L)I don't know how knowing this helps. This is awful. Why tell children such things?

A: Must know—ease pain with meditation.

Well, the very suggestion of frightening my children with such horror stories practically sent me into a fit! But, again, I was torn. More than anything I was curious as to what kind of being would be saying such dreadful things. The negative entities I had encountered most definitely had never said such things; in fact, they always presented themselves as really good but misunderstood and persecuted. Finding excuses for their evil was the hallmark of beings of darkness. Were we now addressing a different kind of dark being, one that was so dark it didn't care how many awful things it said? Or, were they telling me things designed to galvanize me—me, the mother of five children—to ask more questions designed to protect our children?

Q: (L) Why are you telling us this? It's awful!

A: We love you.

Swell. But what kind of love would tell us such awful things, I wondered. And then, immediately I realized that I was always warning my children about dangers. Even if I didn't like to admit that the world was a dangerous place, I knew that I had to tell them such things in order for them to be aware—to preserve them.

Q: (L) Are we supposed to tell others?

A: Don't reveal to public. You would be abducted.

That was a reasonable answer and certainly didn't suggest that they had an agenda for us to go around scaring people. I was curious about the so-called "project" mentioned as being completed in about 13 years (2007), for which this being was saying so many terrible human sacrifices were made. Even if it was an evil being, maybe I could get enough information in a hurry that I could tell others and maybe it would make sense to some of those who were more familiar with such details.

Q: (L) What is the purpose of this project?
A: New life here.

Since I had formulated my idea that the aliens feed on human emotion, I decided on this for a test question. An alien who fed on us would very likely deny it unless, as I already thought, we were being addressed by a being of such insouciant darkness that we had never encountered its ilk before.

Q: (L) Are the aliens using our emotions and energies?
A: Correct; and bodies too. Each earth year 10 percent more children are taken.

They weren't going to let that missing children issue alone. It was too horrible to contemplate. Why did they keep saying something that upset me so? I was a bit distraught, as a mother, and in a shaking voice I asked:

Q: (L) Do they suffer?
A: Some.
Q: (L) Do they all suffer?
A: Some.
Q: (L) What happens to souls? Is this physical only?
A: Physical—souls recycled.
Q: (L) Where do the souls go?
A: Back here—most.
Q: (L) Do some go elsewhere?
A: And go out of planet human.

Again, just in case this monstrous story was true, I wanted details—something I could check.

Q: (L) Who is responsible for this?
A: Consortium.
Q: (C) This is totally sick! I don't want to do this any more!
A: Sick is subjective.
Q: (L) But what you are telling us is so awful!
A: Understand, but all does not conform to your perspective.

With that answer, I realized that what we were being told, as crazy as it sounded, just might be the truth. But again, what kind of being tells such truths?

Q: (L) Why is this happening to us?
A: Karma.

Q: (L) What kind of Karma could bring this?

A: Atlantis. [I deal with the subject of "Altantis" extensively in *Secret History*.]

Q: (L) What can protect us?

A: Knowledge.

Q: (L) How do we get this knowledge?

A: You are being given it now.

Q: (L) What knowledge do you mean?

A: You have it.

Q: (L) How does the knowledge of what you have told us help us?

A: Gives great defense.

Q: (L) What knowledge gives defense?

A: Just gave it.

Q: (L) What specifically?

A: Don't ask that not important.

Q: (L) We don't understand.

A: Knowing about it gives psychic defense.

Q: (L) How do we tell other people? And who should we tell?

A: Inform indirectly only.

Q: (L) How?

A: Write.

Q: (L) Should we use hypnosis to uncover such memories?

A: Open.

Q: (L) Have any of us been abducted?

A: Yes.

Q: (L) Who of us sitting here?

A: All.

Q: (L) How many times?

A: Frank-57; Candy -56; Laura-12.

Q: (L) Why has Laura not been abducted as much? (Laura laughs)

A: It is not over.

Q: (Candy laughs.)

A: Candy was abducted last month. Laura—33—[years of age or years ago?]

Q: (L) Who is abducting us?

A: Others.

Q: (L) What is the name of the group?

A: Different names.

Q: (L) Are we all abducted by the same group?

A: Mostly.

Q: (L) What did they do to us?

A: Gave false memories. Made you inhibited child—headaches—sick at school.

Q: (C) Where is my implant?

A: Head.

Q: (L) Frank?

A: Same.

Q: (L) Laura?

A: Same.

Q: (L) What are the implants for?

A: Study device.

Q: (L) To study what?

A: Soul composition.

Q: (L) Do any of the rituals we perform provide protection against further abduction?

A: Don't need protection if you have knowledge.

Q: (L) How do we get this knowledge?

A: Deep subconscious.

Q: (L) When did we get it?

A: Before birth.

Q: (L) Is there anything else we can do for protection?

A: Learn, meditate, read.

Q: (L) Are we doing what we need to be doing at the present?

A: So far. Need awaken. Must go now. Out of energy. I must go.

I didn't know what to think. Indeed, again there was that injunction to learn. I was traumatized by the information given; that was a certainty. How was I supposed to process that? Over the years I had become so sensitive to the sufferings of others that I had to look away if we were forced to pass an auto accident. I had to leave the room if there was a sad story on the news. If a movie became sad, I couldn't continue watching it. If I read a story about an ill or abused child, I would become depressed for days afterward.

I had five beloved children of my own, and I was a sort of vicarious mother to every child on the planet. I didn't see grubby little boys as bratty kids, I saw them as the beloved child of their mother; and I identified with all mothers. I would take as much care for the child of a stranger as for my own; and would be grateful for any other mother to feel the same about my children. My children were my life. So why did they push this issue about children being taken and experimented upon? Was this designed to hurt me specifically so that I would feel bad and the entity, whoever he was, could feed on the energy of my suffering? Or was I being driven to learn something important; something crucial for all humanity?

There was only one thing to do: get some facts.

I thought it would be a relatively easy thing to buy a world almanac and discover what the statistics on missing children were: how many were missing, how many were successfully returned to their families.

Nothing.

OK, Plan B. I made calls to local law enforcement agencies. What government department kept track of such statistics? I was passed from one to the other and back again.

How about Plan C? I called agencies and said I was a freelance news reporter doing an article. In this country, that's a fair way to get public information. No special credentials are required.

But it didn't matter. No one knew much about missing children.

There are now dozens of organizations and agencies that are devoted to "missing and exploited children". The only problem is, you still can't get a straight, single answer to a simple question: how many children go missing every year and how many are returned safely and where's the proof? Everywhere you look you get a different figure, though, over time, a sort of "standard" figure has evolved. But getting any kind of hard copy on hard statistics with data to back it up is, as far as I have been able to tell, impossible. Nobody wants to talk about it in those terms.

And I began to ask myself, why?

What's more, during that week of trying to get answers to this one particular issue, I began to get a feeling that something was definitely not right with our world. Something was horribly wrong and nobody was admitting it, much less talking about it. I had no proof that what the communication from the board had told me was true. Yet I most definitely had been obstructed in trying to prove it to be false.

Maybe he or she was telling a simple truth. And wasn't that what I was after? Even though I was asking for Truth, like everyone else, I still had the idea that Truth ought to be "nice". The fact that Truth might not be all sweetness and light was not lost on me even if I still had that prejudice that "higher beings" would say only "lofty" things.

The next session, on the last day of the Comet Shoemaker-Levy impacts with Jupiter, the barrier between realms collapsed, quite literally with a thunderous crash. It was July 22nd.

Suddenly, upon sitting at the board, we heard three very loud and very close thunderclaps directly above the house. They sounded like a plane exploding right over the top of us, and were so strong they actually made the building shake. Fearing imminent destruction, we jumped up, throwing our chairs down backward behind us, and dashed madly to the door to see what was happening in the skies overhead.

The sky was completely clear, the moon was shining, stars were twinkling. After looking around and listening for a bit, we decided this must be one of those "out of the blue" lightning strikes we had heard about, even if there had been no flash of lightning accompanying it. (We would have noticed the light with the windows open.) We returned to the table in a state of extreme puzzlement and began to sit again, talking about this strange thunder and paying little attention to the board at all. Again, the planchette began to move in slow, deliberate spirals. And again, I said, "Hello!"

A: Hello.
Q: (L) Is anyone with us?
A: Listen, Look. Learn. Stop eating. (Candy was having a snack.)
Q: (L) What is the problem with eating?

A: Not good connection.

Q: (L) What is your name?

A: Ellaga.

Another unusual name; I was intrigued.

Q: (L) Are you discarnate from Earth?

A: No.

Q: (L) Are you from the same group we communicated with the other night?

A: Yes.

Q: (L) Are you from another galaxy?

A: No.

Q: (L) Where are you from?

A: Cassiopaea.

Q: (L) Is this the constellation we know as Cassiopeia?

A: Yes.

Q: (L) What can we do for a better connection?

A: Less noise.

There was activity in the next room. We shut the door.

Q: (L) Do you have information for us this evening?

With this question, the planchette took off, and I started calling out the letters for Candy to write, trying desperately to keep up. They were delivered in one long string with no word breaks so that we had to divide them into words afterward. It was impossible to try to follow word by word, putting the letters together in the mind, so I gave up and just pronounced each one as the planchette dashed around the board.

A: Space invasion soon. Four to six years. Battle between forces good and evil Wait near Look far Listen Mexico fall Ethiopia quake September both New Near January Paris bomb London Blizzard 109 die Plane down Tahiti Cholera Montana January 1995 government US behind California quakes Three soon Oklahoma political abduction February 95 Big news.

The curious thing about this last remark is that on February 25, 1995, we were given a warning of a terrorist bomb attack within a month. Connect that to Oklahoma "political abduction", the word February followed by "big news", and we find a curious relationship to the April 19, 1995 Oklahoma bombing of a federal building in which at least 168 people lost their lives. Later convicted in the bombing, Timothy McVeigh, a Gulf War veteran, told reporters he was under the control of an implant in his hip, and that he believed he had been abducted and programmed by the government.

It seems pretty clear that no "space invasion" has occurred on our planet within "4 to 6 years". At least, not in the terms we would understand a "space invasion". However, I was reminded of what Candy had said during one of her hypnosis sessions about 1998: "It's an important time for something... the countdown begins then..." I later came back to this point for clarification and the following exchange occurred:

Q: (L) Will there be a war in the sky with the aliens?

A: Yes.

Q: (L) Will it be between Orions and the Federation? (I had gotten these terms from the Ra Material.)

A: Yes.

Q: (L) Will it be visible on Earth?

A: Oh, yes.

Q: (L) When will this be?

A: It has already started. Will intensify steadily.

Q: (L) Why are we not aware that it has already started?

A: Disguised at this point as weather. Fighting part still in other dimension. Will go to this one within 18 years. Anytime within this period. Not determinable exactly when. Could be tomorrow or 18 years.

Q: (L) 18 years from now is 2012. Is there some special significance to that time?

A: By then.

I found it utterly fascinating that weather was being described as a mask for activities in higher realms. This idea is, in fact, very ancient. Continuing with that second encounter:

Q: (L) What is causing the Earth Changes?

A: Electromagnetic wave changes.

Q: (L) Can you be more specific?

A: Gap in surge heliographic field.

Q: (L) I don't understand.

A: Put Frank on processor channel open.

Q: (L) Do you mean that Frank can channel on the computer?

A: Yes. Do it now.

I thought then—and this was later confirmed—this was an attempt at side-tracking the process. I had the feeling that such a request was coming from Frank, who was not very enamored of the board process, though he patiently went along with me, or from some other source that would have very much liked to divert us from our controlled method. We had certain feedback loop tuning control. From wherever the request came, I was determined not to accede to any requests and just said "no" and pushed on.

Q: (L) Is a meteor or comet going to hit Earth?

A: Open.

Q: (L) What are the effects on us of the comet striking Jupiter?

A: Further field imbalance.

Q: (L) Was that comet meant for Earth as some psychics are saying?

A: Open.

chapter five

Internet rumors at the time of the Comet Shoemaker-Levy impacts on Jupiter held that this comet had been meant to hit Earth, but a certain group of aliens, and I don't remember which one, had decided to "save" the Earth by redirecting these comets to strike Jupiter instead. Naturally, all of mankind was supposed to be grateful to this particular group for saving our buns from the fire!

Q: [Unknown question, probably relating to missing children. I think I had brought the subject up again to "test" and see if we couldn't get a more "nice-nice" answer. Well, if that was what I was expecting, that was not what I got!]

A: Bits children's organs removed while wide awake—kidneys crushed—then next feet—next jaw examined on table—tongues cut off—bones stress tested—pressure placed on heart muscle until burst.

Q: (L) Why are you saying these awful things?!

A: Must know what consortium is doing.

Q: (L) What children are they doing this to?

A: Done mostly to Indian children.

Q: (L) Why am I getting this horrible feeling while you are telling us this?

A: Because subject is distressing.

Q: (L) Why do we need to know these things?

A: Very big effort on behalf of Orions and their human brethren to create new race and control.

Q: (L) Where are you from?

A: Cassiopaea.

Q: (L) Where do you live specifically?

A: Live in omnipresence.

Q: (L) What does that mean?

A: All realms.

Q: (L) Can you tell us what your environment is like?

A: Difficult.

Q: (L) Well take a stab at it.

A: What stab?

Q: (L) Do you serve self or others.

A: Both. Self through others.

Q: (L) Candy wants to know the details of her abductions.

A: Do you?

Q: (C) Yes.

A: Are you sure?

Q: (C) Yes.

A: Soon, vibrations not right at this time.

Q: (L) Does this mean Candy's vibrations are not right to receive this information?

A: Right.

Q: (L) Why was information about our abductions given last time?

A: Was not I.

Q: (L) And who are you?

A: Ellaga.

This last response only became clear later. We were soon to learn that each session brought forth a different "entity". As each "moment" in space time was totally unique, so were the energies surrounding us and our questions. Thus a different name of the communicating entity designated a different frequency, though we were told that there were really no "separate" entities communicating. Each session was unique in its question-answer energy exchange.

Since my cousin, Sam, had been so devoted to the ideas of Zecharia Sitchin's *The 12th Planet,* I decided that a couple of questions along that line might be interesting. Sitchin claims in his books that a superior race of alien beings once inhabited our world. He claims that they were travelers from the stars, that they arrived eons ago, and genetically engineered mankind to serve as their slaves. He claims that the "Sons of Anak" mentioned in the Bible are the Annunaki, and also that they are the same as the Biblical Nephilim. They are a race of gold-seeking giants from a renegade planet in our own solar system, known to the Sumerians as the "Planet of the Crossing". This planet "crosses" the plane of the ecliptic every 3600 years, and when it gets close enough, these beings make a "hop" to earth to check up on their creation. Supposedly, this will happen again soon. The title comes from the fact that Sitchin proposes twelve houses of the zodiac for twelve "planets"—including the Sun and moon—so it's really a tenth planet. He also fails to note that the Earth is excluded from zodiacal considerations due to the fact that astrology is geocentric. Since Sam was so "sold" on the Sitchin scenario of ancient astronauts, and I was equally convinced that it was a theory that was full of errors, I thought that this would be another good test question.

Q: (L) Is there a tenth planet as described by Zecharia Sitchin?

A: No. [OK, no point in pursuing that!]

Q: (L) Was Venus ejected from Jupiter?

This was proposed by Immanuel Velikovsky as an explanation why ancient astronomers and mythmakers claimed that Venus was born from Jupiter. The reader will most certainly wish to read *Worlds in Collision* because it is one of the most rational books ever written. Even if Velikovsky was wrong about some of the conclusions he drew regarding myth and legend, his observations and proposals of a new way at looking at the cosmos have yet to be fully appreciated. And, according to the Cassiopaeans, he was, at least, partly correct. But, in response to the question, was Venus ejected from the planet Jupiter, the answer was:

A: No.

Q: (L) Did Venus follow a cometary orbit for a time as theorized by Velikovsky?

A: Yes.

Q: (L) Did Venus appear in our solar system, from the area of Jupiter, coming from deep space as suggested by Velikovsky?
A: That is correct.

Q: (L) Was Venus the pillar of smoke by day and fire by night as seen by the Jews during the Exodus?
A: No.

Q: (L) What was seen by the Jews?
A: A Guideship.

Q: (L) Were Sodom and Gomorrah destroyed by nuclear weapons?
A: Yes and no.

Q: (L) How were they destroyed?
A: EMP

Q: (L) What is "EMP?"
A: Electromagnetic pulse.

This last remark about "Electromagnetic Pulse" energy was made long before any of us at the table were aware of anything called EMP. It was later described in some detail by Col. Corso in his book *The Day After Roswell.* But that was a few years ahead of us at this point in time.

Unfortunately, after the previous two years of mostly nonsense spirit interactions, we were not yet in the habit of taping, and we did not know if this communication was a fluke or not. So, we only have notes from the first half dozen or so early sessions. After a couple of weeks of repeated contact and apparent strengthening of the communication, I bought a special tape recorder to tape the sessions.

From this point on, we began what I intended to be a far more rigorous fine tuning and "testing phase" of the communication. This consisted in rapid questions that jumped from one subject to another across a broad range of categories. I was checking consistency, trying to confuse the source, and also trying to determine range and limits. I was most especially interested in questions relating to "unsolved mysteries" and spent days going through books looking for particular "mysteries" to ask about.

In one sense, this was a good thing, and in another it was not so good. One thing that became very evident during this process was that there was no way possible for any of the information to have been "beamed" into our heads from any human source. The questions were so random and the answers were so rapid—many of them checking out after later research—that it precludes the idea of being "beamed from a satellite" by human agents. If the information had been "beamed" via a satellite, whoever was there reading our minds in zero time, or tuning in to our questions via some listening device, would have had to have the fastest "look-it-up-quick" crew on the planet. We also had to really dig for the answers that invariably confirmed that the Cassiopaeans could tell us things that were most definitely not part of our own subconscious minds.

The Cassiopaeans were fast on the draw. And they soon began doing their own punctuation, accurately I might add, so that if anyone was "beaming info" into our heads, they were a stickler for grammar, as well as the fastest at looking up answers in the world's biggest library!

The very bad thing about my "testing phase" is the fact that there is almost no part of the material where the subjects do not just jump all over the place. Indeed, we would come back and ask follow-up questions at later times, but any one session could jump from higher cosmic realms to the perception of house cats.

Nevertheless, even though I was taking the experiment a bit more seriously, I still had no real idea what I had done. Even now, twelve years later, I try to keep an open mind, to always be aware of the fact that our own minds can fool us in myriad ways. We still research on a daily basis—often making amazing discoveries because we have been given a "clue" from the Cassiopaean transmissions. It is only in this context of hard research that the subject of the high strangeness of hyperdimensions and the process of alien abduction begins to make sense.

chapter six
dimensions and densities

In order to understand the Cassiopaean information on the process of alien abductions, it is necessary to have a little bit of background in the subject of dimensions and densities. This is a subject fraught with confusion in the present time primarily due to a conflict of semantics. The general public has a conception of "dimension" that is not the same as the mathematical models constructed by physicists and mathematicians, and, as a result, when the subject is approached in a serious way, most of those in the scientific community become frustrated and "toss the baby out with the bathwater".

The term *density* refers to qualitatively distinct levels of being. Each density has its own structure of life forms, perception, and lessons for the consciousness residing in it. For example, the first density is inanimate matter. This is the most materially "dense" level of reality. The second density—flora and fauna—is less dense, materially. It has more *free will* than first density and its lessons have more to do with biological life, survival, adaptation, competition. Humans reside in third density, and so on. The idea of densities implies beings at a higher level of being than humanity. We will discuss more of the science behind fourth density in chapter sixteen.

The Cassiopaean meaning of *dimensions* is closer to that of the understanding of the general public, such as "in another dimension" and "parallel or alternate dimensions":

> First of all, confusion abounds here due to incorrect interpretations. Dimensions are not densities!!!! Dimensions are strictly the result of the universal consciousness as manifested in the imagination sector of thought. Density means level of development as measured in terms of closeness to union with the One Cycle. Now, a shocker for you: You would not exist if someone didn't "dream you up". You literally are the "figments" of someone's imagination, and nothing more!!! Remember, "God" is really all existence in creation, in other words, all consciousness. This is because all existence in creation is consciousness, and vice versa. Remember, all there is is lessons!

What do the Cassiopaeans mean by "level of development"? The following dialogue may help to clarify the idea.

> Q: At seventh density there is union with the One. At sixth density there is... what? An equal balance of dark and light, or being and non-being, is that correct?
> A: Pure consciousness no need to physicalise.

Q: And, I think that there are the three ethereal densities, and the three material densities, and the middle, fourth density, the variable physical/ethereal density...

A: Close.

Q: And these densities are only distinguishable by virtue of the nearness to union with the One, is that correct?

A: Nearness?

Q: Well, you know I don't mean it in a that sense... Help me out here!

A: No, you are doing just fine.

Q: Now, I am seeing it sort of like the perpendicular reality image. There is a circle in the center, and each individual is like an outraying perpendicular realities which go out and out and out, and eventually come back to the center, because the gravity in the center brings them back. But, these are perpendicular. Something happens in a horizontal, concentric circle sort of way that distinguishes states of being, in relation to this center and these perpendicular realities. What is the demarcation of the realm levels, what is the relationship between the perpendicular reality and its moving outward that distinguishes it at certain relational points from the center itself? I understand that it is consciousness, but we are also dealing with non-being. Being and non-being. What is the relationship of these perpendicular realities to the seven realms of existence?

A: Not essentially correct. Perpendicular reality is knowledge/awareness/being matrix. Realms are merely *experiential divisions based upon consciousness energy directors.*

Q: What are consciousness energy directors?

A: Compare yourself to your backyard denizen. How do each of you view calculus?

Q: Well, I don't know exactly what calculus is, but I know it is important. I am sure that the dog would not only think it is not useful, he would not even be aware of it. How does that relate to consciousness energy directors?

A: All in nature seeks balance. One day, so to speak, "Percy" will indeed have an opinion of calculus.

Q: OK, so consciousness energy directors are like a horizontal reality in relation to the perpendicular ones?

A: Slots, my dear, slots.

Q: Now you have mentioned these "slots". What are these slots, and how does one move from one slot to another?

A: Picture this: you have 7 sizes of marbles. You have 7 widths of slots. Where do the marbles "fit in".

Q: Do the marbles represent units of consciousness?

A: Close. Or, *divisions of consciousness-level energy resonance profiles.*

Q: Do these divisions of consciousness grow and change?

A: Yes.

Q: And they grow and change through acquiring knowledge, is that correct?

A: Basically.

Q: And acquiring knowledge is akin to acquiring energy? Or light? Light energy?

A: Not exactly. That would be like saying that "filling up" at the gas station is akin to acquiring speed.

Q: So, knowledge and light are like the gas for the car, but speed comes from utilization?

A: Yes.

Q: And utilization means...

A: Knowledge application which generates energy, which, in turn, generates light.

Q: Let me back up. We have marbles in slots... What causes the marbles to go into the slots? What are the slots?

A: An analogy to depict realms for you.

Q: Do the marbles move from one slot to another?

A: When, and only when, they have acquired the proper fit.

Q: Oh. How do they acquire the proper fit?

A: How do you?

Q: I guess you grow?

A: Yes.

Now, going back to the idea of the three physical realms and the three ethereal realms which balance each other, with the intermediate realm of fourth density where physicality is "variable and selective", we have to consider the concept of realms of pure consciousness. Many scientists have discussed the idea of "aether" as the means by which material things are in contact with one another so that the evidence of "non-local" events could be explained in pseudo-material terms. The aether is conceptualized as "a little bit more than a vacuum" or a "vacuum that can vibrate". Einstein rejected the idea of aether on the basis of Occam's Razor as an "unnecessary" hypothesis. Dirac, later on, revisited the concept and tried to revive it in terms of the "Dirac Sea", or "animated quantum vacuum".

> Cassiopaeans: "Aether" is Terran material science's attempt to address ether. The trouble is, there is simply no way to physicalize a plane of existence which is composed entirely of consciousness. It is the union of perfect balance between the two "states" or planes, that is the foundation and essence of all creation/reality. You cannot have one without the other! Terran scientists have been programmed to believe that nothing can exist unless it can be measured, estimated, calculated and represented in some way in the physical material plane. Not true!!!!!!! For example: We are in NO WAY physical.

The "two states" referred to above, or *planes,* are referring to matter and consciousness. The Cassiopaeans say that the material universe and consciousness are so completely connected, intertwined, bonded, and merged that without the one the other would not exist either.

There are seven levels of *density* and this idea is represented also in many ancient teachings. It is the origin of the "Seven Days of Creation". All of these levels are connected—perfectly bonded and balanced. The three "higher" densities"—seventh, sixth, and fifth—are ethereal realms, and the three "lower" densities, which exist for balance to the three higher levels, are material. The intermediate density, fourth density, is where the balance can be "seen" or "realized" most fully. It is a level of both "dense" consciousness and yet is still material. Also, time as we understand it, does not exist at the higher densities.

Cassiopaeans: If there's no end and no beginning, then what do you have? The here and now which is also the future and the past. Everything that was, is and will be, all at once. This is why only a very few of your third density persons have been able to understand space travel, because even though traveling into space in your third density is every bit as third density as lying on your bed at night in your comfortable home, the time reference is taken away. Something that you hold very close to your bosom as if it were your mother. And, it is the biggest illusion that you have. We have repeatedly told you over and over that there is no time, and yet, of course, you have been so brainwashed into this concept that you cannot get rid of it no matter what you do, now can you? Imagine going out into space. You'd be lost when confronted with reality that everything is completely all at one? Would you not? Picture yourself floating around in space!

And now, when you merge densities, or traverse densities, what you have is the merging of physical reality and ethereal reality, which involves thought form versus physicality. When you can merge those perfectly, what you realize then, is that the reason there is no beginning and no end is merely because there is no need for you to contemplate a beginning or an end after you have completed your development. When you are at union with the One at Seventh density, that is when you have accomplished this and then there is no longer any need for difference between physical and ethereal forms.

Q: (L) OK, if you are in fourth density, for example, does everything move at the speed of light and is that why there is no time there and no gravity?

A: No. That is an incorrect concept. There is no speed of light in fourth density because there is no need for any "speed". Speed, itself, is a third density concept. You remember, all there is is lessons. That's it! There's nothing else. It is all for your perception. For our perception. For all consciousness. That's all there is.

You see, we speak to all of you when we say this. It's now time for you, as individuals, to try to move away, as much as possible, not to force yourselves, of course, but to try and move away at your own pace as much as possible, from the constraints of third density. You have all learned lessons to the level where you are more than ready to begin to prepare for fourth density. Third density involves a level of physicality and restriction and restraint and all of the things that go along with those, that you no longer need. So, therefore, even though we understand that at times it may feel comfortable to cling to this, there is time for you, and there is that word again, it is time for you to consider moving ahead and get ready for fourth density and not to be concerned with such things as time or how to free yourself from the illusion of time. That really is not important. That's like the third grade student delving into mathematics and stopping everything to go back and contemplate the ABC's and why it isn't CBA or BAC. There really is no point. It is what it is. They are what they are. Time is a nonexistent, artificial creation of illusion for the point of learning at the level where you are at or were, and once you have left that level, you no longer need it.

Imagine a conversation between two people: Billy and Gene. Billy says to Gene, "There is no such thing as time". Gene says, "Oh, really? But I want to know what it is". Billy says, "But I just told you there is no such thing. Time does not exist. It is not real in any form, in any frame of reference, in any form of reality, any level of density. It simply does not exist". And, Gene says: "Oh, that's interesting. Now, again, what is this time?"

While you are still in this third density it is still necessary for you to conform, to a certain extent, to the ways of others who are more comfortable within the realm of third density. But, as we have stated previously, perhaps it is "time" for you to begin preparing for fourth density and not concern yourself any more than is absolutely necessary with all the where's and why's and what for's of third density reality. This truly is behind you, now, and we know that because we can see from all levels six through one and back again in full cycle.

Picture it this way: we will access some of your memory banks and give you another reference which, interestingly enough, fits very closely with the perpendicular reality wheel that we described earlier. You know what a slide projector looks like? To give you some feeling of what this expanded nature of reality really is, picture yourself watching a big slide presentation with a big slide wheel on the projector. At any given point along the way you are watching one particular slide. But, all the rest of the slides are present on the wheel, are they not? And, of course, this fits in with the perpendicular reality, which fits in with the circles within circles and cycles within cycles, which also fits in the Grand Cycle, which also fits in with what we have told you before: All there is is lessons. That's all there is... and we ask that you enjoy them as you are watching the slide presentation... And, if you look back at the center of the projector, you see the origin and essence of all creation itself, which, is level seven where you are in union with the One.

Densities can be thought of as "vertical" and dimensions as "horizontal" and infinite. It is in this understanding of the structure of the universe that we can begin to comprehend the confusing and metamorphic nature of alien realities and the abduction process.

It is from fourth density that most abductions take place. But before we can even talk about that, the "cognition" of densities must be clear. Discussing them in abstract terms is all fine and good, but without a real grasp of what such a reality must be like will leave us with no comprehension of what can be taking place in trans-density interactions.

Cognition is the process by which we recognize the world around us. Certain things fall within our "realm of cognition", and we are aware of them. Other things don't and, when they "puncture" or "emerge" into our perception of our reality, they are considered anomalous, and we have no real comprehension of them. Most people respond to "anomalies" with fear or denial or half-baked theories that have no real raw data as a base.

The world of our cognition seems to rest on the interpretation of data we receive from our five senses. We consider solid things to be "solid", yet it is clear to those who study physics that everything that exists is subject to many and varied interpretations.

Since the contact with the Cassiopaeans began, I have been urged by them to study as many systems of knowledge as I can reasonably cram into a busy life. I have found numerous correspondences to the Cassiopaean comments on the various levels of reality in other works, most notably those of the Sufi Shaykh, Ibn Al-'Arabi, and the teachings of various Shamanic paths including that explicated by don Juan and recorded by Carlos Castaneda. I have also found hints in other sources, including myths and even the Bible.

A recent work by anthropologist Jeremy Narby entitled *The Cosmic Serpent* examines and discusses certain aspects of Shamanic perception that echo remarks made by the Cassiopaeans, probably at about the same time that this book was being written in Europe. This points up the fact that nobody has the "whole cheese" and that it is our job to search and learn and "put the pieces of Osiris" back together in terms of our understanding.

Dr. Narby remarks about the work of one of the foremost authorities in the history of religions, Mircea Eliade, who wrote *Shamanism: Archaic techniques of Ecstasy*, saying:

> Eliade, who was not a trained anthropologist... identified astonishing similarities in the practices and concepts of shamans the world over. Wherever these 'technicians of ecstasy' operate, they specialize in a trance during which their 'soul is believed to leave the body and ascend to the sky or descend to the underworld.' They all speak a secret language which they learn directly from the spirits, by imitation. They talk of a ladder—or a vine, a rope, a spiral staircase, a twisted rope ladder—that connects heaven and earth and which they use to gain access to the world of spirits. They consider these spirits to have come from the sky and to have created life on earth.[7]

Narby comments: "Eliade understood before many anthropologists that it is useful to take people and their practices seriously and to pay attention to the detail of what they say and do" (17).

Most of Dr. Narby's work concerns the shamanistic vision as perceived via hallucinogenic substances, and this relates to a brief series of remarks by the Cassiopaeans in an interesting way:

> Q: (L) J and I are very curious about artistic expression at fourth density. We experience art and music in a very positive and moving way, most of us, in this realm, and sometimes music can be very sublime and very transforming. It can move one in a lot of very unusual ways. What is it like in fourth density?
>
> A: In 4th, you can "see" sounds and "hear" colors, for example.
>
> Q: (L) This sounds a lot like the hallucinogenic visions of many shamanic paths. Is this what we are talking about here?
>
> A: Bingo!
>
> Q: (L) So, in other words...

---

[7] See Narby (1998) p. 17; also Eliade (1964), p. 5 (specializes in trance), pp. 96-97 (secret language), pp 126ff and 487ff (vines, ropes, ladders) and p. 9 (spirits from the sky).

A: The answer to your next question is yes, shamans experience a bleedthrough of 4th density.

Q: (F) In other words an LSD trip is like a glimpse into fourth density. (L) Do you recommend this method for accessing this type of reality.

A: Open. [This answer reflects a reluctance on the part of the C's to recommend anything in order to preserve free will.]

Q: (T) The problem is that most humans would want to do that all the time and not work on doing it in a natural way.

A: Yes.

Q: (J) Is that like the concept of adding additional dimensions to the three we normally experience?

A: Yes. 4th level density implies an additional dimension of experience, doesn't it?

Q: (T) The first dimension is a single point, the second is the movement of the point into a line, the third is the movement of the line into a plane and the addition of time gives solidity. What is the fourth?

A: Discover!

Q: (J) I've seen, we have all seen, the light spectrum. What we are able to perceive with our eyes is only a limited section. Is reality like that? What we are able to perceive is only a small section of the spectrum of vibrations?

A: Close.

Q: (T) When we move into fourth density will we be able to perceive more of this electromagnetic band?

A: Much.

Q: (L) A few years ago I was meditating on my bed and I did what I call "zoning". It is an indescribable state. I kind of bobbed back to the surface for a moment because I experienced a buzzing in my head that sounded like an electrical transformer. Words came into my head that were like: "The presence is approaching", and I thought immediately of Shekina, or the "forerunner" of the "presence of God".

I was a little agitated because I was not positioned in the way I would have liked to be to receive any experience or visitation. The last thing I remember is making adjustments in my position and then nothing more until I just sort of came to with an intense thirst. I don't know how much time passed, but it must have been a considerable period to be so thirsty.

The bed was adjacent to a wall between the bedroom and the bathroom with just a walk space. I had to be careful not to bump my head on the wall when I was getting up. I got out of the bed and was quite startled to discover that my head and shoulders passed right through the wall into the bathroom! As soon as I noticed that, I started to pay attention to what else I was experiencing.

I noticed that all physical objects appeared as transparent slides of shimmering and deeply intense color and light. The walls of the house were merely shimmering curtains of light. I could see the children in their beds in other rooms in the house, their bodies were light. I could see through the house to the outside and it was not darkness as we perceive it. I was aware that it was night, but trees, plants and other objects were apparent by their appearance as color and light. I had a brief thought of something distant and it was as though my vision was telescopic and zoomed onto it instantaneously. I was also aware that my vision was 360, that is, I could see in all directions at once.

All of this happened very quickly, or so it seemed, and I realized that I was not in the body. That thought startled me and the instant I was startled, that is, felt an inkling of fear, I snapped back in like a rubber band. I discovered myself exactly as I had been prior to hearing the buzzing, not having actually made those adjustments in my position that I remembered.

A: You experienced a bleedthrough of 4th density.

Q: (T) When you started to explain about the trance state, you said: "What I call zoned out, I can't explain it". That's the same thing the Cassiopaeans say when we ask them to explain what fourth density is like! (J) Yes, we have no physical frame of reference. (L) Yes, I can't say I wasn't unaware, because I was intensely aware of everything. And yet, I can't say I was focused on any one thing, because I'm not. (F) The last session we had we received some clues as to why it is they can't explain all these things. They said something when we were talking about plants and rocks at first density. Try to think of something in animal language to express what it is like to perceive the universe as a human. The thing that occurs to me is that, even though we share the same space with dogs, cats, etc., their perception of the universe is so radically different that for all intents and purposes, they might as well be on another planet. It isn't just what they physically can see and how they see it, but how they perceive and understand it and how they think. It is so radically different from a human being... and some people get all attached and all emotional and think that animals are almost human and the dog isn't even thinking, "Oh, I'm a dog, I think I'll just take a nap". So, if you think about the steps up density-wise, if they are merely equal, imagine the jump from third to fourth! In fourth, they may understand us entirely, but their view is radically different.

A: Precisely!

Dr. Narby comments, after his experiences with the Shamans of South America: "True reality is more complex than our eyes lead us to believe". He then describes an experience which helped him to conceptualize the reality of the shamanistic world.

> Five months into my investigation, my wife and I visited friends who introduced us during the evening to a book containing colorful 'three-dimensional images' made up of seemingly disordered dots. To see a coherent and '3-D' image emerge from the blur, one had to defocalize one's gaze.... After several attempts, and seemingly by magic, a remarkably deep stereogram sprang out of the page that I was holding in front of me. It showed a dolphin leaping in the waves. As soon as I focused normally on the page, the dolphin disappeared, along with the waves in front of it and behind it, and all I could see were muddled dots again. (45-46)

Narby next brings up some interesting things about cognition.

> We do not know how our visual system works. As you read these words, you do not *really* see the ink, the paper, your hands, and the surroundings, but an internal and three-dimensional image that reproduces them almost exactly and that is constructed by your brain. The photons reflected by this page strike the retinas of

your eyes, which transform them into electrochemical information; the optic nerves relay this information to the visual cortex at the back of the head, where a cascade-like network of nerve cells separates the input into categories (form, color, movement, depth, etc.). How the brain goes about reuniting these sets of categorized information into a coherent image is still a mystery. This also means that the neurological basis of consciousness is unknown. (48)

This highlights the fact that, if we don't even really know how we see things that we term "three-dimensional reality", how can we begin to conceptualize how we will perceive something as strange as the ideas of fourth density? It seems to be so that when a person hallucinates there is no "external source" of visual stimulation. This is seemingly proved by the fact that cameras cannot record hallucinations. The "enigma of hallucinations" can be reduced to a primary issue: are the hallucinations originating *inside* the human brain as the "third density" scientific studies suggest, or from *outside* as the shamans declare?

All around the world shamans of different pathways tell the same stories and see many of the same visions. And these visions nearly always include serpents which inform the percipient that they are the creators of the human race.

Dr. Narby concludes his study by hypothesizing that the serpentine images are representations of DNA. "To sum up, DNA is a snake-shaped master of transformation that lives in water and is both extremely long and small, single and double. Just like the cosmic serpent" (93).

> Mircea Eliade has shown that these different images form a common theme that he called the 'axis mundi,' or axis of the world, and that he found in shamanic traditions the world over. According to Eliade, the axis mundi gives access to the Otherworld and to shamanic knowledge; there is a 'paradoxical passage,' normally reserved for the dead, that shamans manage to use while living, and this passage is often guarded by a serpent of a dragon. For Eliade, shamanism is the set of techniques that allows one to negotiate this passage, reach the axis, acquire the knowledge associated with it, and bring it back.... According to my hypothesis, shamans take their consciousness down to the molecular level and gain access to biomolecular information. (93)

However, it may not be quite so simple. A distinction needs to be made between the *Serpent* and the serpentine representation of DNA and "waves of energy from the cosmos". Joseph Campbell (1968) discusses the ubiquitous snake symbols, saying:

> Throughout the material in the Primitive, Oriental and Occidental volumes of this work, myths and rites of the serpent frequently appear and in a remarkably consistent symbolic sense. Wherever nature is revered as self-moving, and so inherently divine, the serpent is revered as symbolic of its divine life. (154)

But, as Dr. Narby notes:

Campbell dwells on two crucial turning points for the cosmic serpent in world mythology. The first occurs 'in the context of the patriarchy of the Iron Age Hebrews of the first millennium B.C., [where] the mythology adopted from the earlier Neolithic and Bronze Age civilizations... became inverted, to render an argument just the opposite to that of its origin.' In the Judeo-Christian creation story told in the first book of the Bible, one finds elements which are common to so many of the world's creation myths: the serpent, the tree, and the twin beings; but for the first time, the serpent, 'who had been revered in the Levant for at least seven thousand years before the composition of the Book of Genesis,' plays the part of the villain. Yahweh, who replaces it in the role of the creator, ends up defeating 'the serpent of the cosmic sea, Leviathan....

Campbell writes regarding the twin beings in the Garden of Eden: 'they had been one at first, as Adam; then split in two as Adam and Eve. However, 'the legend of the rib is clearly a patriarchal inversion' as the male begets the female, which is the opposite of previous myths and of biological reality. Meanwhile, the damnation of the serpent is particularly ambiguous; Yahweh accuses it of having shown Eve the tree that allows one to tell the difference between good and evil... According to Campbell, these patriarchal inversions 'address a pictorial message to the heart that exactly reverses the verbal message addressed to the brain; and this nervous discord inhabits both Christianity and Islam as well as Judaism, since they too share in the legacy of the Old Testament.' (Narby, 65-66; Campbell, 1964, 17, 9, 22, 29, 30)

The second turning point for the serpent image occurs in Greek mythology where Zeus, originally represented by a serpent, becomes a killer of the serpent and defeats Typhon, the child of the goddess Gaia. Something apparently occurred at these times that may become clear as we proceed with this analysis.

But, let's turn our attention now to another interesting description of "another reality", and see if we find any relations between it and the purported "alien realm". In *The Active Side of Infinity*, Carlos Castaneda describes an experience in the wilderness of Mexico under the tutelage of his mentor, don Juan Matus.

He [don Juan] had described the energy body to me countless times, saying that it was a conglomerate of energy fields, the mirror image of the conglomerate of energy fields that makes up the physical body when it is seen as energy that flows in the universe. He had said that it was smaller, more compact, and of heavier appearance than the luminous sphere of the physical body.

Don Juan had explained that the body and the energy body were two conglomerates of energy fields compressed together by some strange agglutinizing force. He had emphasized to no end that the force that binds that group of energy fields together was, according to the sorcerers of ancient Mexico, the most mysterious force in the universe. His personal estimation was that it was the pure essence of the entire cosmos, the sum total of everything there is.

Now, before we continue with Carlos and don Juan, I want to insert a few remarks from the Cassiopaeans on this very subject.

A: And this, my dear, is another example of gravity as the binder of all creation... "The Great Equalizer!"

145

Q: (L) You have said that gravity is the binder of all reality.

A: Yes.

Q: And now you talk about perception bonding.

A: Yes. Now, try to picture how gravity is the binder of all reality!!!

Q: (L) If gravity is the binder, is gravity consciousness?

A: Not exactly. Did you know that there is no "right" or "left" in 4th density through 7th density? If you can picture this exactly, then you may be able to understand the responses to all the questions you are asking. If not, best "give it a rest". Because it will only be productive learning when you ponder and reflect/review "later".

Q: (L) Is gravity something from the center of dimensional windows to an opposite "construct" in the ethereal realm, rather than the attraction between objects in this material realm?

A: Gravity is the "binder" common to all imaginable existence. That is all you really need to know.

Q: (L) OK, binder. Does gravity bind in the same way that weak hydrogen bonds bind the DNA strands?

A: No.

Q: OK, then, does gravity bind the way the phosphate bond binds the carbon atom?

A: These are material. The missing link for all you folks is that gravity is as much antimatter as matter!!

Q: (A) Then, concerning this gravity, and the antimatter, is it a correct picture that there are two such domains; positive and negative, and the gravity has something to do with the exchange between the positive and negative?

A: Gravity is the "fuel", or "life blood" of absolutely everything that exists!!! Matter/antimatter. One features atomic particle based matter, the other features pure energy in conscious form. Gravity is the balancing binder of it all. First you must get a correct picture of gravity. Gravity is the binder between matter and antimatter.

Q: (A) You are using the word 'gravity.' Scientists are also using the word 'gravity.' Apparently there are two different meanings?

A: How so?

Q: (A) Because, according to science, gravity is a force, like other forces, is a field, like other fields, and being a field...

A: But it is the foundational field from which all other fields emanate.

Now, getting back to Carlos and don Juan. We left them discussing the force that binds energy fields together and how it may play a part in binding the energy body to the material body. Carlos continues:

Don Juan had said that by means of discipline it is possible for anyone to bring the energy body closer to the physical body. Normally, the distance between the two is enormous. Once the energy body is within a certain range, which varies for each of us individually, anyone, through discipline, can forge it into the exact replica of their physical body—that is to say, a three-dimensional solid being. ... By the same token, through the same processes of discipline, anyone can forge

146

their three-dimensional, solid physical body to be a perfect replica of their energy body—that is to say, an ethereal charge of energy invisible to the human eye, as all energy is....

Sitting at the back of his house in central Mexico that day, don Juan said that the energy body was of key importance in whatever was taking place in my life. He saw that it was an energetic fact that my energy body, instead of moving away from me, as it normally happens, was approaching me with great speed.

"What does it mean that it's approaching me, don Juan?" I asked.

"It means that something is going to knock the daylights out of you", he said, smiling. "A tremendous degree of control is going to come into your life, but not your control, the energy body's control."

"Do you mean, don Juan, that some outside force will control me?" I asked.

"There are scores of outside forces controlling you at this moment," don Juan replied. "The control that I am referring to is something outside the domain of language. It is your control and at the same time it is not. It cannot be classified, but it can certainly be experienced. And above all, it can certainly be manipulated. Remember this: It can be manipulated, to your total advantage, of course, which again, is not your advantage, but the energy body's advantage. However, the energy body is you, so we could go on forever like dogs biting their own tails, trying to describe this. Language is inadequate. All these experiences are beyond syntax."

Darkness had descended very quickly, and the foliage of the trees that had been glowing green a little while before was now very dark and heavy. Don Juan said that if I paid close attention to the darkness of the foliage without focusing my eyes, but sort of looked at it from the corner of my eye, I would see a fleeting shadow crossing my field of vision.

I did see some strange fleeting black shadow projected on the foliage of the trees. It was either one shadow going back and forth or various fleeting shadows moving from left to right or right to left or straight up in the air. They looked like fat black fish to me, enormous fish. It was as if gigantic swordfish were flying in the air....

"What is it, don Juan?" I asked. "I see fleeting black shadows all over the place."

"Ah, that's the universe at large," he said, "incommensurable, nonlinear, outside the realm of syntax. The sorcerers of ancient Mexico were the first ones to see those fleeting shadows, so they followed them around. They saw them as you're seeing them, and they saw them as energy that flows in the universe. And they did discover something transcendental. ... They discovered that we have a companion for life... We have a predator that came from the depths of the cosmos and took over the rule of our lives. Human beings are its prisoners. The predator is our lord and master. It has rendered us docile, helpless. If we want to protest, it suppresses our protest. If we want to act independently, it demands that we don't do so....

"You have arrived, by your effort alone, to what the shamans of ancient Mexico called the topic of topics. I have been beating around the bush all this time, insinuating to you that something is holding us prisoner. Indeed we are held prisoner! This was an energetic fact for the sorcerers of ancient Mexico."

"Why has this predator taken over in the fashion that you're describing, don Juan?" I asked. "There must be a logical explanation."

"There is an explanation," don Juan replied, "which is the simplest explanation in the world. They took over because we are food for them, and they squeeze us mercilessly because we are their sustenance. Just as we rear chickens in chicken coops, the predators rear us in human coops. Therefore, their food is always available to them."

I felt that my head was shaking violently from side to side. I could not express my profound sense of unease and discontentment, but my body moved to bring it to the surface. I shook from head to toe without any volition on my part.

"No, no, no, no," I heard myself saying. "This is absurd, don Juan. What your saying is something monstrous. It simply can't be true, for sorcerers or for average men, or for anyone."

"Why not?" don Juan asked calmly. "Why not? Because it infuriates you?"

"Yes, it infuriates me," I retorted. "Those claims are monstrous!" ...

"I want to appeal to your analytical mind," don Juan said. "Think for a moment, and tell me how you would explain the contradiction between the intelligence of man the engineer and the stupidity of his systems of beliefs, or the stupidity of his contradictory behavior. Sorcerers believe that the predators have given us our systems of beliefs, our ideas of good and evil, our social mores. They are the ones who set up our hopes and expectations and dreams of success or failure. They have given us covetousness, greed and cowardice. It is the predators who make us complacent, routinary, and egomaniacal."

"But how can they do this, don Juan?" I asked, somehow angered further by what he was saying. "Do they whisper all that in our ears while we are asleep?"

"No, they don't do it that way. That's idiotic!" don Juan said, smiling. "They are infinitely more efficient and organized than that. In order to keep us obedient and meek and weak, the predators engaged themselves in a stupendous maneuver—stupendous, of course, from the point of view of a fighting strategist. A horrendous maneuver from the point of view of those who suffer it. They gave us their mind! Do you hear me? The predators give us their mind, which becomes our mind. The predators' mind is baroque, contradictory, morose, filled with the fear of being discovered any minute now."

Don Juan continues: "I know that even though you have never suffered hunger... you have food anxiety, which is none other than the anxiety of the predator who fears that any moment now its maneuver is going to be uncovered and food is going to be denied. Through the mind, which, after all, is their mind, the predators inject into the lives of human beings whatever is convenient for them. And they ensure, in this manner, a degree of security to act as a buffer against their fear." (213-220)

Now, let's go back a moment to something that Dr. Narby found in the literature of shamanism. He quotes the subjective description of the ayahuasca experience written by an anthropologist named Michael Harner. In the early 1960s, Harner was studying the culture of the Conibo Indians. He was told by the Indians that if he really wanted to understand their religious system, he had to drink ayahuasca. He agreed with fear and trepidation, and the following account of his experience was the result:

After several minutes he found himself falling into a world of true hallucinations. After arriving in a celestial cavern where 'a supernatural carnival of demons' was in full swing, he saw two strange boats floating through the air that combined to form 'a huge dragon-headed prow, not unlike that of a Viking ship.' On the deck, he could make out 'large numbers of people with the heads of blue jays and the bodies of humans, not unlike the bird-headed gods of ancient Egyptian tomb paintings. ... Then he saw that his visions emanated from 'giant reptilian creatures' resting at the lowest depths of his brain. These creatures began projecting scenes in front of his eyes, while informing him that this information was reserved for the dying and the dead: 'First they showed me the planet Earth as it was eons ago, before there was any life on it. I saw an ocean, barren land, and a bright blue sky. Then black specks dropped from the sky by the hundreds, and landed in front of me on the barren landscape. I could see the 'specks' were actually large, shiny, black creatures with stubby pterodactyl-like wings and huge whale-like bodies... they explained to me in a kind of thought language that they were fleeing from something out in space. They had come to the planet Earth to escape their enemy. The creatures then showed me how they had created life on the planet in order to hide within the multitudinous forms and thus disguise their presence. Before me, the magnificence of plant and animal creation and speciation—hundreds of millions of years of activity—took place on a scale and with a vividness impossible to describe. I learned that the dragon-like creatures were thus inside all forms of life, including man. In retrospect one could say they were almost like DNA, although at that time, 1961, I knew nothing of DNA. (Harner, quoted by Narby, 54-55)

Going back to Castaneda for a moment, and keeping in mind these strange creatures described by Michael Harner, we find don Juan and Carlos out in the desert one day:

I really wanted to start for home right away ... but before we reached his house, don Juan sat down on a high ledge overlooking the valley. He didn't say anything for awhile. He was not out of breath. I couldn't conceive of why he had stopped to sit down.

"The task of the day, for you", he said abruptly, in a foreboding tone, "is one of the most mysterious things of sorcery, something that goes beyond language, beyond explanations. ... So brace yourself by propping your back against this rock wall, as far as possible, from the edge. I will be by you, in case you faint or fall down. ... I want you to cross your legs and enter into inner silence, but don't fall asleep".

It was rather difficult for me to enter into inner silence without falling asleep. I fought a nearly invincible desire to fall asleep. I succeeded, and found myself looking at the bottom of the valley from an impenetrable darkness around me. And then, I saw something that chilled me to the marrow of my bones. I saw a gigantic shadow, perhaps fifteen feet across, leaping in the air and then landing with a silent thud. I felt the thud in my bones, but I didn't hear it.

"They are really heavy", don Juan said in my ear. He was holding me by the left arm, as hard as he could.

I saw something that looked like a mud shadow wiggle on the ground, and then take another gigantic leap, perhaps fifty feet long, and land again, with the same ominous silent thud. I fought not to lose my concentration. I was frightened beyond anything I could rationally use as a description. I kept my eyes fixed on the jumping shadow on the bottom of the valley. Then I heard a most peculiar buzzing, a mixture of the sound of flapping wings and the buzzing of a radio whose dial has not quite picked up the frequency of a radio station, and the thud that followed was something unforgettable. It shook don Juan and me to the core—a gigantic black mud shadow had just landed by our feet.

"Don't be frightened", don Juan said imperiously. "Keep your inner silence and it will move away".

I was shivering from head to toe. I had the clear knowledge that if I didn't keep my inner silence alive, the mud shadow would cover me up like a blanket and suffocate me. Without losing the darkness around me, I screamed at the top of my voice. Never had I been so angry, so utterly frustrated. The mud shadow took another leap, clearly to the bottom of the valley. I kept on screaming, shaking my legs. I wanted to shake off whatever might come to eat me. (231-233)

This is pretty scary stuff, to say the least. But, can it be true? Before we think that this is just a phenomenon or hallucination of shamans and anthropologists, let's have a look at another event in a slightly different context.

This is just a short segment of an account obtained under hypnotic regression. The hypnotist is Barbara Bartholic, and the subject is "David", the son of Dr. Karla Turner.

Something was obviously missing in David's recollection of events, so Barbara asked him more about what he had seen by the fir tree.

"I'm looking at a shadow", he replied. "Maybe it's the cat, he likes that tree. Rustling, pomegranate tree. At the bottom? But how? This, there's something moving, but I can't see it. It's a dark spot, a black spot, moving around the tree. And it's gone".

Barbara asked him to expand his description, so David continued.

"I saw, it looks irregular. Is it a shadow? It's black. It's on the ground. It's moving around and away, quickly, rustling. Like walking on leaves. And it's very faint with a whisper... a snake sound, real faint. ... My brain's not working", he said. "I'm just tramping behind her to the car. Ah, ah. But I want to go look at that. I heard a noise."

"What did the noise sound like?" [Barbara asked.]

"A rope, pulled real fast", he replied. "Whoooo, kind of like a top. But soft, so it was muted. And that's when I see the thing. The black. It's just blackness, on the ground. Very quick. Something hit me before".

"Where?" Barbara inquired.

"Shocked me", he answered. "In the back. In my hip, at the bottom of my spine... I'm bouncing, mechanically, towards the satellite dish, I think. ... It's big.... It hurt, all over, the shock. Tingles real loud. All over my bones it's tingling, shaking. ... I'm walking around the tree, and I hear a noise. Like a top, a spinning top. It starts high-pitched and goes lower, and goes away pretty fast. So I look towards it. I can't see very well. ... It's like a blot on the ground, ... a black towel? Or a garbage bag? Kind of odd-shaped. It's flat, flat-flat. It, it is on the ground, it's no different than the ground, but it's just black and moving fast. And it's making a little noise. ... I'm looking at the thing. ... A blackness. A 'not.' Like a 'not-there.' Like a moving oil puddle on the ground. ... And it's moving, but changing, too. Not much, just the edges, not very stable. And it's gone quick. ... I feel strange. ... I'm just not me. ... I feel blank ... like a remote unit..." (Turner, 1992, 132-139)

It's rather strange that this victim of an "abduction" has described something similar to what don Juan talks about as the "predator". It is also worthy of note that David experiences some strange sound effects similar to those described by Castaneda while interacting with this "black shadowy" thing that looks like a puddle of oil on the ground. Castaneda, in fact, entitled the chapter that discussed these things "Mud Shadows".

But how can we begin to attempt to understand these "energy constructs" that appear in both shamanic visions as well as purported "alien abductions". What do these things have in common? In the next several chapters we will attempt to answer these questions.

TDARM

Before we get into presenting the Cassiopaean information about the abduction process, there is a particular technology of fourth density that they introduced in 1994 as a result of our questions about the creation of mankind that I would like to bring forward. The following excerpts, extracted from numerous sessions and merely arranged in chronological order, are self-explanatory.

Q: (L) You said something the other night about the expansion of a star being conducive to creation. Could you give us a little bit on that aspect?

A: Transdimensional atomic remolecularization.

Q: (L) What is remolecularization.

A: Being reassembled.

Q: (L) Reassembled from what to what?

A: Mode of 4th density assembly into 3rd density. It is a form of "density collision".

Q: (L) Does this mean that this was a point in space time when pure energy could form around a framework of a thought pattern and thus become solid matter?

A: Close.

Q: (L) Is this transitioning of energy from higher densities into third density or solid matter kind of a traumatic event for universal energy?

A: Subjective.

Q: (L) Is it a form of death?

A: Death and birth are the same.

Q: (L) Was it a requirement to be on a planet with a dying star for this remolecularization to take place?

A: If 3rd density remolecularization is the objective, yes.

Q: (L) Is energy moving down when it comes into third level?

A: No. It is upward movement of Molecules, atomic matter. Light is first density and unifies all densities.

Q: (L) Does that mean that by us moving from third density into fourth density that we are getting farther away from unification with the source?

A: No. Light and darkness unify all densities.

151

chapter six

Q: (L) Does light become electricity via a change in density?

A: Yes.

Q: (L) Is it from first to third when it becomes electricity?

A: Yes.

Q: (D) Is transdimensional atomic remolecularization the same as teleportation?

A: Close.

Q: (D) OK, is this the way we will transfer from third to fourth density?

A: It is technology for this purpose.

Q: (L) What procedure or technology do the Grays use to pass through solid matter?

A: Transdimensional atomic rearrangement.

Q: (L) How do aliens transport themselves or others on beams of light?

A: By electron focusing and previous answer.

Q: (L) Who or what are the individuals called "Men in Black"?

A: Lizard projections.

Q: (T) Does that mean that they are just projecting an image of a being?

A: Yes.

Q: (T) The MIBs are not real, then, in our physical terms?

A: Partly correct. You do not understand technology but we will describe it if you like.

Q: (L) We like. Please describe this.

A: First we must explain further time "travel" which is Transdimensional transfer utilizing electromagnetic adjustment of atomic structure to alter speed of time cycle convergence, because the two concepts are closely related. The first step is to artificially induce an electromagnetic field. This opens the door between dimensions of reality. Next, thoughts must be channeled by participant in order to access reality bonding channel. They must then focus the energy to the proper dimensional bridge. The electrons must be arranged in correct frequency wave. Then the triage must be sent through realm "curtain" in order to balance perceptions at all density levels.

Q: (L) What is the interpretation of triage as you have used it?

A: Triage is as follows: 1. Matter, 2. Energy, 3. Perception of reality.

Q: (L) Why do you refer to a technological device that supposedly transports someone from one density to another, as a 'trans-dimensional remolecularizer?'

A: In order to reconstruct 3rd density into 4th density physical, other dimensions must be utilized in the process. Remember, we are talking about exact duplicates which are merged.

Q: (T) It is like a program loading onto a computer. Some programs just load straight in. Others need to create a space on the hard drive to put files that they need to *load* the program, but are not *part* of the program, and when it is finished loading, it erases all the "loading instructions". The hard drive is still the hard drive, but for a time, the program used a sector of the hard drive, and created a temporary dimension, let's say. Is this what we are looking at here?

A: Close. And remember, we said "true" dimension!

Q: (L) So, it is like one hard drive, many programs, loading instructions for new programs that are then erased, etc. If there is one "true dimension", and infinite universes within it, does one particular universe exist, of and by itself, at any given time, until it is merged into a new one, or is there within this one true dimension, multiple universes as real as ours is, to which we could go, and could be there alongside ours, so to speak?

A: Yes to the latter.

Q: (L) And, can infinite numbers of "dimensions" exist within each level of density, even if temporary?

A: Yes. If you want to go back and change "history", either for individuals or for universal perception, you must first create an alternate universe to do it. Your 4th density STS "friends" have been doing this a lot.

Q: (L) If you, being a general term, create an alternate universe, does the former one continue to exist, or does the former one merge into the new one?

A: Both.

Q: (L) Is déjà vu a result of some sensation of the universe having changed?

A: Or... some sensation of reality bridging.

Q: (L) What is reality bridging?

A: What does it sound like?

Q: (T) A bridge is something you put between two things...

A: You wish to limit, wait till 4th density, when the word will be obsolete!

Q: (L) That still doesn't help me to understand déjà vu as a "sensation of reality bridging". Is déjà vu because something comes into our reality from another?

A: One possibility...

Q: (T) It's a bleed through from other dimensions... that when we think we have been someplace before, it is because in another dimension we have...

A: Yes.

Q: (L) If you are now in a particular universe that has been created and merged by fourth density STS, and there is still the old universe existing, can you feel a connection, or a bridging, because some alternate self is in that alternate universe, living through some experience... or a similar thing?

A: No limits of possibilities.

Q: (L) So it can be any and all of those things, and bridging realities of "past" and "future", as well. Is it possible to change the past within a particular, selected one of the universes; can you go back in time, within that universe, change the past, and have it change everything forward, still within that selected universe, like a domino effect?

A: In such a case, yes.

Q: (L) But, you said that if you want to change the past, you have to create an alternate universe... (T) No, you asked about changing the past, and they said you have to create a temporary place to work from, a position from which you can manipulate the reality...

A: *That is for specialized activities such as abductions.*

Q: (L) So that creating of an alternate universe was for special things, and not for a general historic change?

A: What was described is not the same as an "alternate universe".

Q: (L) It is like a temporary file that will go away when you are finished loading the program. And that is not creating an alternate universe, but rather a temporary dimension...

A: Close.

Q: (L) In our particular universe, what is the primary mode? Are we constantly shifting and merging universe to universe, or is our past being changed and reacting like the domino effect... at least in the past few years... Is it that any and all possibilities and will and do take place?

A: Closer.

Q: (L) Can you clarify that any further for me?

A: No, because you would simply not grasp it.

Q: (T) It is part of the infrastructure of the universe which we are in no way capable of understanding at this point. We can't even get quarks right.

A: Yes.

Q: (L) Are the words "universe" and "dimension" synonymous?

A: Yes and no.

Q: (L) In what sense yes?

A: For you, these are "Gray" areas, and no matter how hard you try, until your perception shifts fundamentally, you ain't gonna get it!

Keeping all of this in mind, let us now turn our attention to the Cassiopaean description of the abduction process. The question and answer format will be adhered to for the sake of clarity.

Q: (L) A couple of nights ago I did a hypnosis session with J___ to examine the events that took place on August 16, 1993, over my pool, wherein two 300 ft wide black boomerangs were seen by all of us, kind of casually drifting by. In this hypnosis session, after two or three passes through the events, he indicated that, in fact, that was not merely a sighting of something going overhead, but was actually an abduction situation. One remark he made during this session, and this startled me a little, and I would like to get a little amplification on the subject, was that toward the end when I asked what happened, he said that he was "taken apart and beamed back down without benefit of a pain suppressor". This meant that when he was demolecularized some sort of device that is used to suppress pain was not used, and the process of atomic demolecularization or remolecularization can actually be painful, and can cause distress. Is this correct?

A: Possibly. The whole process of abduction can be stressful, but, to varying degrees and, of course, we must remind you that, as with everything else, it is your own perception of reality that is the most important factor, not some notion of your own perception of reality.

Q: (L) I don't understand what you mean. Is there some device that... does it hurt to be taken to pieces molecularly, beamed aboard a space ship and then sent back. (J) Can this be painful to the body?

A: Well, first of all, you are getting way ahead of yourself. Do you honestly believe that a beam of light came down and "took you to pieces", moved your body physically onboard a space vehicle, did some form of examination or some such thing and then reassembled your entire body without a pain suppressor? Is this what you believe?

Q: (L) Well, he didn't say it happened to me, he said it happened to him. (J) We have never heard the term "pain suppressor" before. (L) Yes, we have never heard anything about anything like this; and do I believe a beam of light could have come down and disassembled him and reassembled him, and then something was done to him. From all the abduction cases I have studied I would say it is possible. I mean, knowing about the time manipulation capabilities of said entities, it is entirely possible that it could have happened without any awareness of any loss of time whatsoever.

A: Yes, this is true, however, your description of it is not completely correct as referenced in the hypnosis session you speak of, or at least your interpretation of the information given during the hypnosis session given is not correct. Now, it must be noted here, that when we make such clarifying statements such as "this is not correct" or "that is not correct", it is unusual for us to do this because the nature of your state of being and all others is one involving various degrees of bonded illusion. Therefore any and all possibilities are present in most instances. However, when two or more of these bonds of the illusion are misaligned, then, indeed, absolute correctness or absolute incorrectness is possible. In this case, there is a misalignment of the bonding. Therefore, it is, in fact, completely incorrect. We will now describe the process in more detail. This knowledge is very important not only for what, perhaps, has happened in your reality as you would refer to it as your past, but also in possible variations of your present and in what you refer to as your future. These experiences must be known in their entirety as to what they really are.

You are not normally removed as a physical third density being from one locator to another. What happens is very simple. The time frame is normally frozen, and we use the term "frozen" for lack of a better term. What this means is that your perception of time in your physical locator, third density body, ceases to pass during this period of time that is called "zero time" variously by members of your human race. What happens is that the soul imprint occupying of that particular host body is removed forcibly, transported to another locator, and remolecularized as a separate physical entity body for purpose of examination, implantation, and other. The soul imprint is used for the purpose of duplication process; it is then demolecularized and the soul imprint is replaced in the original body at the original locator. That is the process that takes place.

On occasion, the fourth density beings doing the abduction can actually make a mistake in the time referencing points of the third density illusion. This may create the effect of the appearance of an alternate or duplicate experience, when, in actuality there has only been one experience. This was what happened in your case. As you perceived the passage of two "ships" for lack of a better term, when in actuality, there was only one. That is because the time frame reference illusion was not completely matched from beginning of event to the end of the event in zero time. Normally, however, that is not a problem. On rare occasions, the host, or the subject of the abduction can actually find themselves replaced in the time frame illusion in what could appear to be several hours, day, weeks, or even, sadly, years prior to the beginning of the event, which, of course, could cause side effects such as total insanity and other such things. Fortunately that did not occur in your case, but there was some fracturing of the time frame reference illusion. This is why you thought you saw two ships when in actuality you only saw one.

Now, it is most important that you understand that this is not a physical, third density experience in its entirety. There is the soul imprint that all first density, second density, third density, and fourth density beings possess, as you already know; that is extracted. From that soul imprint a duplicate copy or clone, if you will, which appears on fourth density, can then be made and studied and the soul imprint is then replaced into the original body at whatever density it was taken. This is normally how the process is done.

Most often, if the third density being is removed in total physicality, there is no return of that being to third density. They are permanently removed to fourth density. Most often that is what takes place although on rare occasions there can be return. However, there is no need for this as complete duplication for all purposes of examination, alteration of sensate, and implanting; need not be done on third density; can be done completely in the fourth density duplication process. Do you understand?

Q: (T) How does the implant come back to the third density body that's originally still here?

A: The process we are describing, which involves the remolecularization; it is very complex to try and describe how the fourth density is translated into third density, except that once the duplicate, the fourth density clone, is present, all fourth density realities surrounding that fourth density duplicate will be matched in third density whenever and wherever desired. Because, in effect it is the entire density level which is being exchanged, not just the object contained within.

Q: (L) So, in other words, just as the soul imprint, when it goes into fourth density, can be used as a template to create a carbon copy, so to speak, then anything that is done to the carbon copy then becomes a template that recreates that same manifestation when it is sent back into the third density?

A: Precisely. With the only variance there being that technology is used to make sure that implants, or added material that comes from fourth density, is such that it will also translate equally into third density through the remolecularization process.

Q: (L) Is there any method that we could or should know about to remove or deactivate implants.

A: No, you are not capable of doing that without causing death of the host. And, by the way, please don't believe those who claim that they can do such things as they cannot. Any implants that are claimed to have been removed are those which have been placed by 3rd density beings for purposes of disinformation and confusion.

Q: (L) So, in this particular case, something was done, something occurred here, which affected me. My subsequent physical condition makes me curious as to whether the physical reactions I had for six to nine months, and still have occasionally, following this event, were a third density reaction to the, what you call, fracturing of time. Was this an aberration or was this intentional?

A: It does not occur as a result of the "fracturing" of the time frame reference illusion. It occurs as a result, simply and merely, of your psychic impression imprint of the experience itself reflecting back into your third density physical reality.

Q: (T) Is the pain that J___ described not what he said it was, but rather the pain that is related when the fourth density being removes the life force?

A: Life force is never removed. The soul is extracted. In answer to your question: J___ is merely expressing the discomfort and distress that most third and second density beings experience when abducted by fourth density Service To Self entities.

Q: (L) Now, what we would like to know is, if our souls are abducted from our bodies and then used as a pattern for remolecularization in fourth density, is there ever, at any time, a remolecularized clone that is retained in fourth density even after the soul has been returned to its original body?

A: No, it's not possible.

Q: (L) So, they don't keep a pattern or clone of any of us after they have abducted us, "they" being a general term?

A: No.

Q: (L) Do any of the STS beings have the ability to cause us physical problems, or mental or emotional problems when not in direct contact with us?

A: Certainly.

Q: (L) How is this done?

A: A number of different methods used.

Q: (L) So any and all methods may be used at any given time?

A: That is correct.

Q: (L) Could you give us one or two examples of how this is done?

A: There are many: sound wave manipulation of the ultra high frequency range would be one.

Q: (L) What do these sound waves in the ultra high frequencies do?

A: They can alter chemical balances within the body of the subject, thereby also the brain, using the physical path to cause distress by altering these chemical imbalances into place.

Q: (L) Do these ultra-high frequency sound waves ever carry messages in terms of pre-coded suggestions that are triggered by these waves?

A: Messages are not carried in ultra-high frequency sound waves. Now, you are talking about an entirely different method.

Q: (L) Alright then, moving on to another subject, how are pre-coded information signals sent? Can messages be sent via sound-wave focusing?

A: No, sound wave focusing is designed to alter body and brain chemistry in order to alter such things as feelings, emotions, and so forth, which then may lead to the altering of mental thought patterns. But messages are not sent by ultra-high frequency sound waves.

Q: (L) How are they sent?

A: Messages are sent by something called Free Formal Imaging which means that a thought is formed in one realm and sent to a second realm, which is yours.

Q: (L) OK. Can it be sent to a directed target?

A: Absolutely.

Q: (L) Now, the question has arisen that, since other dimensional beings have the ability to kidnap or abduct or forcibly extract souls, do they also have the capability of manipulating our soul essences after they have left our bodies during the transition to fifth density?

A: Not correct.

Q: (L) They do not?

A: No, you see when your physical body expires, and you enter fifth density, this is done one way and one way only: by passing through a conduit which opens specifically for the purpose of transference from third density to fifth density. Now, something often referred to in your terminology as a silver thread, is like a closed line which opens when this conduit is needed. That's rather awkward, but it's the only way to describe it. So that when the physical body terminates, this line is opened forming a conduit through which the soul passes naturally. However, part of the existence of this conduit is that it is absolutely impenetrable by any force from any density level. Therefore, souls in the process of transferring from third density to fifth density are not in any way able to be molested or tampered with. And it should be mentioned here, also, that the soul imprint of the physical body always has a connection to fifth density and that is through the so-called "silver thread". That always exists as the third density soul's doorway to fifth density. It can be opened at a moment's notice whenever needed. When it is opened it becomes a conduit. Through that conduit the soul passes. And it is not subject to interference by anything. This is not a deliberate construction, it is merely the natural process similar to what could be described as the protection mechanisms existing on second level density for creatures which are not capable of protecting themselves through their own conscious thought processes. For example, your turtle is contained within a shell that protects it. That shell is impenetrable by any natural forces, therefore nothing that is natural can harm that turtle. However, the same can exist for any creature when it is connected by the silver thread to fifth density. Once it is passing through the conduit produced by the opening of the silver thread, then, of course, it cannot be tampered with. Do you understand?

Q: (L) Yes, but why do so many souls, when they leave the body, not traverse this conduit, and why do they stay earthbound, and why do they attach to other bodies? Why does this condition exist?

A: That is a complicated question, however the best answer is choice is involved there for those souls who wish not to leave the plane of third density. The only possibility to do this is to be detached from the now expired physical body but still be within the third density plane, which, of course, is not natural, but nonetheless can occur. In situations such as this, though it has been incorrectly reported, the silver thread is still attached and still remains a thread rather than a conduit. The soul is still attached to the silver thread but detached from the host body which has now expired. So the effect is very similar to being consciously aware of third density surroundings without a third density unit to accompany. Also, please be aware of the fact that once the soul leaves the confines of the physical body, the illusion of time passage is no longer apparent even when the soul remains on the third density plane. Therefore, it appears to that soul that no time whatsoever has passed. And, we mention this merely for you to contemplate all of the various meanings behind this.

What the C's have proposed is that what we have come to know as alien abduction is not a purely physical process. It is conducted from a realm that is invisible to the naked eye and undetectable by current scientific methods of observation. The aliens use a type of technology (transdimensional atomic remolecularization) to extract the *soul imprint* of a person, perform their examinations, implants, and "alteration of sensate" while in a temporary realm of their creation, and then to reinsert the "soul" into the body. This process takes place outside of our perception of time, and thus—depending on how accurate they are—can appear to take place in minutes, hours, or days. They may even miscalculate and insert the modified soul imprint *before* the time of abduction.

To help with this process, and the control of their subjects, they also have technology that would nowadays be called "non-lethal weaponry". Similar technology is already being developed and used by our almost human controllers: crowd control weapons like the long range acoustic device (LRAD) can cause extreme physical reactions and disorientation. We even suspect that something like "free formal imaging" is being used on the U.S., which we will expand on in chapter twelve. Using such a method, an image or scenario can be broadcast, which is then received and interpreted by the person using their own framework of ideas and possibilities.

These technologies could account for a lot of the high strangeness surrounding the phenomenon, for example, the "time-specific" nature of "close encounters"—faeries, demons, explorers in airships, spacemen in spaceships—and "screen memories"; the "invisibility" of the craft during abduction; missing time; their seeming ability to manipulate space-time.

chapter seven
gods of old

grays, lizzies, and the 'plan'

Q: (L) What or who, precisely, are the Gray aliens?

A: Cybergenetic probes and decoys created by the Reptoids.

Q: What is being done in the "gazing process" that so many abductees report from their interactions with the Grays?

A: Study brain. Reflective remolecularization imaging via energy focusing.

Q: (L) What is behind their eyes?

A: Camera like system.

Q: (L) Is that system also able to send signals?

A: Yes. This induces thought paralysis.

Q: (L) Do they implant thoughts with their eyes also?

A: Can.

Q: (L) What do they do with implants?

A: Monitor and control your total sensorium.

Q: (L) I have drawn a sort of conclusion about some of the activities of the Lizzies and their abductions through the Grays and so forth, and it seems to me that these excessive numbers of exams, gynecological, reproductive or whatever, might possibly be a screen for a process that is used to extract life force or energy from the human being, through the basal chakra, the sexual chakra, which is where, as I understand it, the life force enters in. Is this idea correct or on track?

A: Close.

Q: (L) It does seem that the Grays and Lizzies are abnormally interested in sexual activities of human beings, is that correct?

A: Yes.

Q: (L) Do they have tremendous sex drives even though they are in fourth density?

A: No.

Q: (L) Are they interested in sexual energy simply because it is life force?

A: Partly and they are also desperately working to stave off change in order to retain control.

Q: (L) What changes are they desperate to stave off?

A: The transition to 4th level.

Q: (L) They are trying to stave off the fourth level change. Can they do that?

A: No. But they are also hoping to retain control even if change occurs.

Q: (L) By what means do they do this through these gynecological exams? Is there some technical activity they undertake?

A: Yes.

Q: (T) OK, in this Krill document there was a statement made that the Grays and other aliens use glandular substances extracted during physical exams of human beings, what they would call the gynecological and the sperm extraction exams, that they used these glandular substances to get high or to feed on, that they are addicted to these, is this a correct assessment?

A: No. They use it as a Medicine which helps them cope with 3rd density; it helps them to manifest in a more solid physical manner during their visits to your realm.

Q: Do they also use sexual energy given off by individuals to maintain their status in three dimensions?

A: No. That feeds them in 4th density. Most orgasmic energy drains to 4th density.

Q: (L) So, these supposed memories people have from their abductions of these exams just screens of procedures used to take life force from them?

A: Yes.

Q: (L) When they sample an abductee's tissue and take the little scoops or chunks out of them, what do they take these chunks of flesh for?

A: Cloning.

Q: (L) If they clone, why do they need such large chunks?

A: You don't know all details of cloning process yet.

Q: (L) Do they take twins, or one of a pair of twins, and raise one artificially?

A: Have done so.

Q: (L) What is the purpose of taking one of a pair of twins?

A: Study to determine which is best soul receptacle: one of twins or clone.

[This raises the question as to why the choice has to be either. Is there some connection between clones and the original body and one twin and another that is vital to the purpose of the Lizzies?]

Q: (L) For what purpose are they trying to decide which is the best receptacle, the clone or the twin? Receptacle for what?

A: Future project to switch physical realities.

Q: (L) They are going to enter into the bodies themselves so that they can switch their reality?

A: Yes.

Q: (L) So, they are preparing a bunch of soulless bodies into which they can enter in themselves?

A: Will try.

Q: (L) And could you tell us what the Reptoids look like?

A: Upright alligators with some humanoid features in face.

Q: (L) Do they have tails?

A: Yes.

Q: (L) How tall are they?

A: Six to eight feet tall.

Q: (L) Do they wear clothing?

A: Yes.

Q: (L) I know this is a silly question, but does their clothing have an opening for the tail?

A: Yes.

Q: (L) Do they defecate?

A: No. They are 4th level.

Q: (L) So, when you are fourth level you neither eat nor defecate in the third density way?

A: Correct.

Q: (L) Do the Lizzies have the ability to change their shape or appearance?

A: Temporarily.

Q: (L) The comment was made at one point that certain alien beings abduct humans and subject them to cruel and torturous deaths in order to create "maximum energy transfer". In this respect, what is this maximum energy transfer that occurs during a long, slow, torturous dying process?

A: Extreme fear and anxiety builds up fear/anxiety energy which is of a negative nature which fuels the beings that you speak of in that they draw from that and produce a sort of a fueling energy which keeps them going as one of their forms of nourishment based on their metabolic structure.

Q: (L) What is their metabolic structure?

A: That is very complex and very difficult to describe because it is on the fourth level of density which you do not understand. But, part of their reason for existence on the fourth level is their ability to nourish themselves both through ethereal methods and through physical methods. Therefore, this energy transfer of pain and suffering would represent the ethereal method of nourishment and other means are achieved physically.

Q: (L) What other means?

A: Well, the drinking of blood and blood by-products would be an example of that. [This suggests an interesting connection to Vampire tales as perhaps representations of the same hyperdimensional beings.]

Q: (L) Do they do that?

A: Yes, but the manner of intake is different than what you may be thinking. It is done through pores.

Q: (L) In what manner?

A: Bathing and then absorbing the necessary products and then disposing of the remaining product. [This image was later on related by Dr. David Jacobs in his book *The Threat*. An abductee described walking into a vaulted room with 40 tanks in which the Grays "ate and slept."]

Q: (L) What beings, in specific, do this?

A: Both those that you describe as the Lizard Beings and those you describe as the Grays. This is necessary for their survival in each case. Even though the Grays are not natural parts of the short wave cycle, but rather an artificial creation by the Lizard Beings, but nevertheless they mimic the nourishment functions.

Q: (L) Since they are artificially created by the Lizard beings, does this mean they have no souls?

A: That's correct.

Q: (L) How do they function? Are they like robots?

A: They function by interaction with the souls of the Lizard beings. This technology is extremely far in advance of that with which you are familiar, but the Gray beings are not only built and designed artificially, but also function as a projection mentally and psychically of the Lizard beings. They are like four dimensional probes.

Q: (L) As four dimensional probes, what are their capabilities?

A: They have all the same capabilities of the Lizard beings except for the fact that their physical appearance is entirely different and they do not have souls of their own and also their biological structure is internally different. But, their functioning is the same and in order to remain as projection beings they also must absorb nutrients in the same fashion both spiritually and physically as the Lizard beings do. The reason the negative energy is necessary fuel is that the Lizard beings and the Grays are both living in the fourth level of density, which is the highest level of density one can exist in serving only self as these entities do. So, therefore, they must absorb negative energy because the fourth level of density is the highest example of self service which is a negative thought pattern. The fourth level of density is a progression from the third level of density. With each progression upward in density level, the existence for the individual conscious entity becomes less difficult. So, therefore, the fourth level of density is less difficult to exist in that the third, the third is less difficult than the second and so on. It puts less strain on the soul energy. Therefore, beings existing on the fourth level of density can draw from beings existing on the third level of density in terms of absorption of negative soul energy. Likewise, beings on the third level of density can draw from beings on the second level of density, though this type of drawing is not as necessary but is done. This is why human beings existing on the third level frequently cause pain and suffering to those of the animal kingdom who exist on the second level of density because you are drawing negative soul energy as beings who primarily serve self, as you do, from those on the second level, and on the first, and so on. Now, as you advance to the fourth level of density which is coming up for you, you must now make a choice as to whether to progress to service to others or to remain at the level of service to self. This will be the decision which will take quite some time for you to adjust to. This is what is referred to as the "thousand year period". This is the period as measured in your calendar terms that will determine whether or not you will advance to service to others or remain at the level of service to self. And those who are described as the Lizards have chosen to firmly lock themselves into service to self. And, since they are at the highest level of density where this is possible, they must continually draw large amounts of negative energy from those at the third level, second level, and so on, which is why they do what they do. This also explains why their race is dying, because they have not been able to learn for themselves how to remove themselves from this particular form of expression to that of service to others. And, since they have such, as you would measure it, a long period of time, remained at this level and, in fact, become firmly entrenched in it, and, in fact, have increased themselves in it, this is why they are dying and desperately trying to take as much energy from you as possible and also to recreate their race metabolically.

Q: (L) Well, if we are sources of food and labor for them, why don't they just breed us in pens on their own planet?

A: They do.

Q: (L) Well, since there is so many of us here, a veritable smorgasbord, why don't they just move in and take over?

A: That is their intention. That has been their intention for quite some time. They have been traveling back and forth through time as you know it, to set things up so that they can absorb a maximum amount of negative energy with the transference from third level to fourth level that this planet is going to experience, in the hopes that they can overtake you on the fourth level and thereby accomplish several things.

1: retaining their race as a viable species;

2: increasing their numbers;

3: increasing their power;

4: expanding their race throughout the realm of fourth density.

To do all of this they have been interfering with events for what you would measure on your calendar as approximately 74 thousand years. And they have been doing so in a completely still state of space time traveling backward and forward at will during this work. Interestingly enough, though, all of this will fail.

Q: (L) How can you be so sure it will fail?

A: Because we see it. We are able to see all, not just what we want to see. Their failing is that they see only what they want to see. In other words, it's the highest manifestation possible of that which you would refer to as wishful thinking. And, wishful thinking represented on the fourth level of density becomes reality for that level. You know how you wishfully think? Well, it isn't quite reality for you because you are on the third level, but if you are on the fourth level and you were to perform the same function, it would indeed be your awareness of reality. Therefore they cannot see what we can see since we serve others as opposed to self, and since we are on sixth level, we can see all that is at all points as is, not as we would want it to be.

dispelling myths

Q: (L) Is the amnesia related to UFO abductions deliberately induced or is it a product of the mind's inability to deal with the event?

A: It is an equal commingling of both.

Q: (L) The part that is deliberately induced, how is that accomplished?

A: By using a cosmic energy flow to influence memory function through a combination of spiritual and chemical interaction.

Q: (L) Can you be more specific?

A: Being more specific would be in another way less specific, but a good way to put it is altering the flow of electromagnetic energy in the brain. Electromagnetic energy, electromagnetism, is the life force that exists within all that evolves through long wave or short wave cycles.

Q: (L) Now, I have some articles in this magazine here: This is a gal who has "channeled for thousands around the globe since 1985. Her books and magazine articles are published in six languages worldwide," etc., etc. Her "source" says here: "The human consciousness is roughly divided into three different areas for the sake of this illustration: the conscious mind, the subconscious mind and the unconscious mind". Now, are these labels generally correct?

A: Roughly.

Q: (L) The material says further: "The unconscious mind is a link to your greater self, it is also used as a wasteland where scary, dark things are stored that you really don't want to bring up". Is this a fairly accurate statement?

A: Semi-accurate.

Q: (L) Is there anything you can say to make the statement more accurate?

A: The unconscious mind is also a conduit for connecting with the higher self, other selves, and the universal mind.

Q: (L) She goes on to say: "When you are a child and have a traumatic event, the subconscious not only finds a way to immediately process the information and store it, but also to protect you from further fragmentation. It must seek to create a balance". So, she says, the "very intense raw energy that is generated from trauma gets stuffed into the unconscious mind". Is this true?

A: Close enough.

Q: (L) She then goes on to say: "When an extraterrestrial looks at us, we seem like multiple personality cases to them because of our mind divisions". Is this true?

A: Irrelevant.

Q: (L) Why is that irrelevant? Is it because when a higher density being looks at us they know what they are looking at?

A: Yes. They know and understand the separations of your mind quite precisely. That would be like saying "when a human looks at a rodent, they notice that they are excessively furry". And also because, in most cases, these "separations" and "multiple personality" aspects are deliberately generated by 4th density STS beings.

Q: (L) She goes on to say: "The ET often does not know how to communicate with a fragmented human. Sometimes they fly their ships by and few people may see them, but the greater percentage do not see them as that data gets sucked into the subconscious and the triage occurs". She means triage in the sense of the mind being so flabbergasted that it immediately shunts information into the unconscious. Is this true, that ETs are having problems communicating with us because we are the one's blocking contact?

A: No.

Q: (L) Is it true that some people may not see ETs or UFOs because they block it from their own minds?

A: This can happen or the blockage may be inspired by the alien.

Q: (L) Now, she says: "For the most part, the average person in society does not know how to interpret telepathic contact... (this is her alien talking) in the moment you start perceiving us reality starts shifting because, remember, you are one frequency and we are another". Is this true?

A: It is irrelevant. This is not an obstacle, as suggested by this statement.

Q: (L) Anyway, the article goes on: "So an ET walks up to you in your backyard and for a fragment of a moment you may perceive us. But what commonly happens is that the human will suddenly shut down usually by becoming very sleepy and falling into a sleep or type of trance state such as one that is produced by alpha or theta brain waves". Is this true? When a person sees an ET do they just turn off from the shock? Is this why most ET contact is not remembered?

A: It can happen but does not usually. In general the "shut down" is deliberately imposed by the alien. We do not wish to further critique this as this is a waste of energy.

Q: (L) The whole point of this article is to say that ETs who abduct people are here to help us evolve and that it is only us, if we have dark and dirty unconscious minds, who perceive them as negative.

A: Wrong. You do not need "help" evolving, nor does anything else.

Q: (L) OK. The next question: Are any of the Grays what one might call "good guys?"

A: That is a subjective interpretation any way you look at it. For, after all, what is good and what is bad?

Q: (L) The definition that you have given is Service To Self and Service To Others. So, are any of the Grays STO beings?

A: Well, again, if we can review for just a moment. It is subjective to refer to either STS or STO as either good or bad. It merely means Service to Self and Service to Others. Now, the determination as to whether it is good or bad is made by the observer. It depends on your point of view. It depends on your objective. It depends on a lot of things. One is merely service to self. This is inward turning. The other is Service to Others which is outward expanding. It is part of the balance which makes up that which we refer to as the Universe.

Q: (L) Are any of the Grays STO?

A: In very rare instances, Gray beings have crossed over into the STO realm, but in their natural environment, they are, in fact, STS, as they were constructed to be.

Q: (L) How does it occur that they cross over into the STO environment?

A: Simply by natural circumstance, in the same general way that it occurs that human beings in the 3rd density STS environment can, under certain circumstances, rise to the STO level. Very rare.

Q: (L) Well, if the Grays are cybergenetic probes of the Lizard Beings, and, in effect soulless, does this mean that some of the Lizard beings are also STO?

A: Well, first, no being that is given intelligence to think on its own is, in fact, completely soul-less. It does have some soul imprint. Or what could be loosely referred to as soul imprint. This may be a collection of psychic energies that are available in the general vicinity. And this is stretching somewhat so that you can understand the basic ideas, even though in reality it is all far more complex than that. But, in any case, there is really no such thing as being completely soul-less, whether it be a natural intelligence or an artificially constructed intelligence. And, one of the very most interesting things about that from your perspective, is that your technology on 3rd density, which we might add, has been aided somewhat by interactions with those that you might refer to as "aliens", is now reaching a level whereby the artificially created intelligences can, in fact, begin to develop, or attract some soul imprint energy. If you follow what we are saying. For example: your computers, which are now on the verge of reaching the level whereby they can think by themselves, will begin to develop faint soul imprint.

Q: (L) That's not a pleasant thought.

A: Now, to answer your question: Are the Reptilian beings, or Lizard beings, STO. Of course, some can cross over into STO. However, their natural environment is STS as they have chosen. But, whether or not any of the cybergenetic Gray beings cross over into STO, and or the Lizard Beings cross over into STO, these are not connected to one another, these two concepts. They are independent.

Q: (L) I understand. OK, would you say there is any percentage, any fairly measurable percentage of Lizard beings that are STO?

A: It is VERY, VERY small. EXTREMELY small. Hardly worth mentioning.

Q: (L) What about the Grays?

A: That might be slightly higher, but again, it is very small, relatively speaking.

Q: (L) Is there another race of beings that are manipulating or using the Lizard beings?

A: Could you elaborate?

Q: (L) Are the Lizard Beings agents for some other group?

A: Well that is a rather simple question. But, there are levels of authority in 4th density STS environment. And these are determined by intellectual and physical prowess, as always, in STS. The "pecking order" as you call it. So, therefore, we could state that at the bottom are those you are familiar with as the Gray beings, and in the middle are those you would call the Lizard Beings, and above that are others that you are not so familiar with, the most commonly known, of course, are the Orion STS.

Q: (L) What do they look like?

A: They are, in fact, humanoid in structure, resembling large human beings.

Q: (L) And we don't see them that often?

A: Well, of course you know by now, that the ones most frequently seen on 3rd density level, are the Gray beings. All others equally less frequently seen.

Q: (L) Do these Orion STS ever participate in abductions?

A: The abductions are primarily performed by the Gray beings. However, others can and will and in fact have abducted. But when this occurs, the nature of the abduction is different.

Q: (L) Are there any positive Extra-terrestrials from the area of Sirius interacting with human beings at the present time?

A: Well, now! First off, it is important for you to know that the term you use: Extra Terrestrial, which of course, is one of the most correct terms used at your level—all that is NOT of the Earth is Extra-Terrestrial—and, for those on your surface earth environment to refer to themselves as alone in the universe, or the one and only in the cosmos, is akin to a microbe on a grain of sand referring to itself as the only form of life on the beach! Now, when you ask are there any beings in the vicinity of Sirius, it would be something like that same microbe, located on the grain of sand, on the beach, which is, of course, but one of the beaches located on the surface of the earth, after all, asking if there is, in fact, any life located over in the vicinity of that seashell...

Q: (L) But I asked if there were any interacting with Earth...

A: And we are answering that question. We have chosen to take this opportunity to put things into better focus for you. Now, to answer your question: Are there any beings who reside in the vicinity of Sirius who are positively oriented, or STO as it were? Again it is difficult to answer that because we do not know how to define the "vicinity of Sirius". But, if you mean within a light year or so of Sirius, as you measure distance, then we can say there are no such beings in that area in 3rd density. But that leaves open 4th through 6th density. So, you see, as you already know, but we wish to reinforce this, there is so much to contemplate here that it is absurd when those around you refer to certain areas or star systems and claim that there are beings from here or there or wherever, and that their objective is this or that or the other. Because if you knew the TRUE nature of the universe, of All of the universe, of all possible realms, you would also know that any and all things are possible, and, in fact, DO exist! You must NOT forget this.

Q: (L) So, in other words, these people are right?

A: All of these people are right, and all of these people are wrong. Because it is silly to point to some section of the sky, to ascribe any area as being the "Home" of this that or the other "race of extra-terrestrial beings."

Q: (L) But what if that is, in fact, the case? The Orions live in some star system in Orion, right?

A: So are you.

Q: (L) Well, we aren't living there now!

A: That's not the point. If you were to stay in 3rd density and view your star, which you know as the sun, from another point in your galaxy, it would appear to be a part of the Orion system. Would it not?

Q: (L) Probably.

A: Well, now perhaps you are beginning to understand what we are talking about??? At one level, and in one sense.

Q: (L) Well, how do these beings get here crossing such vast reaches of space?

A: As we have told you, there are seven levels of density which involves, among other things, not only state of being physically, spiritually and etherically, but also, more importantly, state of awareness. You see, state of awareness is the key element to all existence in creation. You have undoubtedly remembered that we have told you that this is, after all, a grand illusion, have you not? So, therefore, if it is a grand illusion, what is more important, physical structure or state of awareness???

Q: (L) State of awareness?

A: Exactly. Now, when we go from the measuring system, which of course has been nicely formulated so that you can understand it, of density levels one through seven, the key concept, of course, is state of awareness. All the way through. So, once you rise to a higher state of awareness, such things as physical limitation evaporate. And, when they evaporate, vast distances, as you perceive them, become non-existent. So, just because you are unable to see and understand has absolutely no bearing whatsoever on what is or is not possible. Except within your own level of density. And this is what almost no one on your current level of density is able to understand. If you can understand it and convey it to them, you will be performing the greatest service that your kind has ever seen. Think about that for a moment. Let it seep into your consciousness. Analyze it. Dissect it. Look at it carefully and then put it back together again.

Q: (L) What is it that limits our awareness?

A: Your environment. And it is the environment that you have chosen. By your level of progress. And that is what limits everything. As you rise to higher levels of density, limitations are removed.

Q: (L) What creates this environment of limitation?

A: It is the grand illusion which is there for the purpose of learning.

Q: (L) And who put the illusion into place?

A: The Creator who is also the Created. Which is also you and us and all. As we have told you, we are you and vice versa. And so is everything else.

Q: (L) Is the key that it is all illusion?

A: Basically, yes. As we have told you before, if you will be patient just a moment, the universe is merely a school. And, a school is there for all to learn. That is why everything exists. There is no other reason. Now, if only you understood the true depth of that statement, you would begin to start to see, and experience for yourself, all the levels of density that it is possible to experience, all the dimensions that it is possible to experience, all awareness. When an individual understands that statement to its greatest possible depth, that individual becomes illumined. And, for one moment, which lasts for all eternity, that individual knows absolutely everything that there is to know.

Q: (L) So, you are saying that the path to illumination is knowledge and not love?

A: That is correct.

Q: (L) Is it also correct that emotion can be used to mislead, that is emotions that are twisted and generated strictly from the flesh or false programming?

A: Emotion that limits is an impediment to progress. Emotion is also necessary to make progress in 3rd density. It is natural. When you begin to separate limiting emotions based on assumptions from emotions that open one to unlimited possibilities, that means you are preparing for the next density.

Q: (L) What about love?

A: What about it?

Q: (L) There are many teachings that are promulgated that love is the key, the answer. They say that illumination and knowledge and what-not can all be achieved through love.

A: The problem is not the term "love", the problem is the interpretation of the term. Those on third density have a tendency to confuse the issue horribly. After all, they confuse many things as love. When the actual definition of love as you know it is not correct either. It is not necessarily a feeling that one has that can also be interpreted as an emotion, but rather, as we have told you before, the essence of light which is knowledge is love, and this has been corrupted when it is said that love leads to illumination. Love is Light is Knowledge. Love makes no sense when common definitions are used as they are in your environment. To love you must know. And to know is to have light. And to have light is to love. And to have knowledge is to love. This you must discover. Before you become frustrated, if, indeed you are going to begin seeing at another density level, it must be a discovery process for the greatest learning potential. For us to give you previews would not necessarily be in your best interest.

dimensional window fallers

Q: (L) I read in a book about a monster called the Beast of Gevaudan which appeared first in 1764 and was supposedly done away with in 1767. Who or what was this beast?

A: Other dimensional "window faller".

Q: (L) You mean it fell into our dimension from another through a dimensional window?

A: Yes.

Q: (L) Well, that would explain a lot of things about it. What about the creature known as "Spring Heel Jack" who terrorized England some time ago?

A: Same.

Q: (L) What about the Mothman in West Virginia?

A: Same.

Q: (L) So, windows to other dimensions are the explanation for a whole host of strange things?

A: Yes.

Q: (L) OK, what about El Chupacabras?

A: It is what it is.

Q: (L) It is a 'goatsucker.' Where does it come from?

A: Review: "window fallers".

Q: (L) If it is a window faller, does it come from another density, or a lateral dimension?

A: Closer to the latter.

Q: (L) OK, so it is like a horizontal dimension. How is it that other dimensional or density beings enter our density?

A: This is complex, but best described as "EM wave bursts along frequency border variation".

Q: (L) Is there some way to stop this?

A: You do not yet completely understand all the "mechanics" of the window phenomenon. The physicality is entirely transitory and partially dependent upon consciousness variabilities, as well as expectations of witnesses.

Q: (L) Does the energy of the fear of the witness enable the creature to continue its operation in third density? Does it feed on the excitement and fear, and is that what makes it manifest?

A: Close, but off a little. It is the other way around, and retro-factored by one half.

Q: (L) What do you mean by that?

A: It is mutual, rather than unilateral. Also, remember that a window represents a cross-energizing of realities, equally represented from each "dimension" in question. In other words, because the dimensional curtain has been "torn", half of one and half of the other contributes to the whole reality.

170

high strangeness

Q: (L) OK, what is taking place when craft that are described to be belonging to "aliens" begin to strobe as opposed to pulsating or merely blinking or other light related activities? In other words, what are the different configurations of light emanations and what do they indicate?

A: Well, you must be aware, first of all, as we have told you before, and as you have, in fact, gained knowledge from other sources prior to your communications with us, the entire subject matter referred to as "UFOs" is extremely varied and multi-faceted in nature and does not represent any one condition, entity, source of entities, mode of transport, density level, or anything else related to these.

Q: (L) So, in other words, we would have to specify a specific sighting and condition in order to obtain an answer to this particular question or type of question?

A: Well, let us ask you, would that not be the wisest course of action?

Q: (J) I think I have a way out of that. Possibly we are referring to the type of sightings that are typical in the Gulf Breeze area where they...

A: Be aware of the fact, please, that the whole Gulf Breeze situation is rather interesting in many ways. And, when we say "rather interesting", we are being subjective viewing the subjective from your point of view. There is more going on there than meets the eye... again, from your point of view. ...Strobe lights are used for 3rd density mind control.

Q: (L) OK. You mentioned the strobe lights. Are these strobe lights that are used to control minds, are these something that we would or might come in contact with on a daily basis?

A: Do you not already know? We didn't say: some strobe lights, we said: strobe lights, i.e. all inclusive!

Q: (T) Strobe lights come in many forms and types. TV is a strobe light. Computer screens are a strobe light. Light bulbs strobe. Fluorescents strobe. Streetlights strobe.

A: Police cars, ambulances, fire trucks... How long has this been true? Have you noticed any changes lately??!!??

Q: (F) Twenty years ago there were no strobe lights on any of those vehicles mentioned. They had the old flasher type lights. Now, more and more and more there are strobe lights appearing in all kinds of places. (L) And now, they even have them on school buses! (T) And the regular city buses have them too, now. (L) OK, is the strobing of a strobe light, set at a certain frequency in order to do certain things?

A: Hypnotic opener.

Q: (L) What is the purpose of the hypnotic opener being used in this way?

A: You don't notice the craft.

Q: (T) OK, what craft are we *not* seeing?

A: Opener. Is precursor to suggestion, which is auditory in nature.

Q: (L) OK, you said the "suggestion is auditory in nature". If this is the case, where is the suggestion coming from auditorily?

A: Where do you normally receive auditory suggestions from?

Q: (L) Radio, television... (T) Telephone... (L) Is that what we are talking about?

A: Yes.

171

Q: (L) If you encounter a strobe while driving, or you are sitting in front of your television, then the suggestions can be put into you better because of this hypnotically opened state? Is that it?

A: Yes.

Q: (L) And these suggestions are that we will not see the craft?

A: Yes.

Q: (T) Do we get these signals from the radio in the car even if it is turned off?

A: Depends upon whether or not there is another source.

Q: (T) Another source such as?

A: ELP, for example.

Q: (L) What is "ELP?"

A: Extremely Low Pulse.

Q: (T) ELF, Extremely Low Frequency, and ELP, Extremely Low Pulse—is this the same thing?

A: Sometimes.

Q: (T) This would be an external pulse or frequency?

A: Yes.

Q: (T) Would it be originating from the source of the strobe?

A: No. They act in unison.

Q: (L) And this process prevents us from seeing something, such as craft flying in our skies at any given time?

A: Or maybe see them as something else.

Q: (L) Now, we have to stop for a minute because I want to tell you something. In the past few months, I have really been watching the sky carefully every opportunity I get. On three or four separate occasions I have seen what I thought was an ordinary airplane, and I would watch it carefully and then scan to the left or right, and when I looked back at the place where this plane should be, based on observable speed and direction, there would be *nothing* there. I have stood there and searched and searched and found nothing. These things just *vanished*. I knew I had seen it, I knew I wasn't crazy, I knew it couldn't have gone away that completely—and having it happen several times has just really unsettled me. What are the implications of this, other than the fact that we could be completely overflown at all times for any number of purposes and be, as a mass of people, completely unaware of it?

A: Yes, monoatomic gold!

Q: (L) And what does the reference to monoatomic gold mean?

A: Total entrapment of the being, mind, body and soul. Strobes use minute gold filament. What composes minute filament, do you suppose? Hint, it ain't from Fort Knox!

Q: (T) Monoatomic gold.

A: Bingo. You see, this has extraordinary properties.

Q: (T) I'm sure it does! The thing is, if it does what Hudson says it does, the power structure would have shut him down—he wouldn't have gotten this far with it. So, if they are letting him do it, it's because it doesn't do what he says it does, it does the opposite. Which is what he said. When you take the stuff for so many days, you complete the program, it restructures your genes and your

172

genetics are involved with your perceptions and cognition of the density levels..
(L) OK, how do we block this kind of control?

A: You don't.

Q: (L) Is this one of the things that keeps us from expanding into the next density, in terms of awareness?

A: Not related to that. You see, the souls that are affected by all these "cloaking" techniques are vibrating on a low level anyway. The point is to block those who are blockable.

Q: (L) Is there anything we can do to avoid this blocking?

A: You are not blockable. If you were, would you be doing this?

Q: (T) OK, there's a blocking technique being used on people to lower the vibrational frequency to prevent them from seeing them, right?

A: The blocking technique is for many things.

Q: (T) So that people do not understand what's going on around them.

A: Yes. That is it, in a nutshell. See and know and think or... See, know and think that which is desired.

the payoff

Q: (L) I read the new book [*The Threat*] by Dr. David Jacobs, professor of History at Temple University, concerning his extensive research into the alien abduction phenomenon. Dr. Jacobs says that now, after all of these years of somewhat rigorous research, that he *knows* what the aliens are here for and he "is afraid". David Jacobs says that producing offspring is the primary objective behind the abduction phenomenon. Is this, in fact, the case?

A: Part, but not "the whole thing".

Q: (L) Is there another dominant reason?

A: Replacement.

Q: (L) Replacement of what?

A: You.

Q: (L) How do you mean? Creating a race to replace human beings, or abducting specific humans to replace them with a clone or whatever?

A: Mainly the former. You see, if one desires to create a new race, what better way than to mass hybridize, then mass reincarnate. Especially when the host species is so forever ignorant, controlled, and anthropocentric. What a lovely environment for total destruction and conquest and replacement... see?

Q: (L) Well, that answered my other question about the objective. Well, here in the book, Dr. Jacobs says that there is ongoing abductions through particular families. I quote:

"Beyond protecting the fetus, there are other reasons for secrecy. If abductions are, as all the evidence clearly indicates, an intergenerational phenomenon in which the children of abductees are themselves abductees, then one of the aliens' goals is the generation of more abductees. Are all children of abductees incorporated into the phenomenon? The evidence suggests that the answer is yes. If an abductee has children with a non-abductee, the chances are that all their descendants will be abductees. This means that through normal population increase, divorce, remarriage and so on, the abductee population will increase quickly throughout the generations. When those children grow and marry and have children of their own, all of their children, whether they marry an abductee or non-abductee, will be abductees. To protect the intergenerational nature of the breeding program, it must be kept secret from the abductees so that they will continue to have children. If the abductees *knew* that the program was intergenerational, they might elect not to have children. This would bring a critical part of the program to a halt, which the aliens cannot allow. The final reason for secrecy is to expand the breeding program, to integrate laterally in society, the aliens must make sure that abductees mate with non-abductees and produce abductee children."

Now, this seems to suggest that there is a particular bloodline that is susceptible to...

A: We have told you before: the Nazi experience was a "trial run", and by now you see the similarities, do you not?

Q: (L) Yes, I do see...

A: Now, we have also told you that the experience of the "Native Americans" vis a vis the Europeans may be a precursor in microcosm. Also, what Earthian 3rd density does to Terran 2nd density should offer "food for thought". In other words, thou are not so special, despiteth thy perspective, eh? And we have also warned that after conversion of Earth humans to 4th density, the Orion 4th density and their allies hope to control you "there". Now put this all together and what have you? At least you should by now know that it is the soul that matters, not the body. Others have genetically, spiritually and psychically manipulated/engineered you to be body centric. Interesting, as despite all efforts by 4th through 6th density STO, this "veil remains unbroken".

Q: (L) Now, the big question is: what are we supposed to *do* with this information?

A: As with all else, it is not what you should do with it, it is just that you have it.

Q: (L) Is there any possibility of defeating the plans of the fourth density STS in this project?

A: Is there any possibility of defeating the Spanish Conquistadores and the English, French, Dutch and German "colonists?"

Q: (F) Did they say what I think they said? (L) Yes. That is inexpressibly depressing.

A: And you expected a Rose Garden?

Q: (L) If that's the way it is, why don't we all join the Heaven's Gate cult and commit mass suicide and just not deal with all this stuff?!

A: You chose to "deal with it", now did you not?

Q: (L) Well, was I in my right mind when I made that choice, or had I been drinking?

A: No drinking on 5th density!

Q: (L) Now, I have been having an exchange with Carla McCarty who was the Ra channel. She says that we are not supposed to *do* anything, we are just supposed to *be*, and what we are supposed to *be* is to just let love flow through us, love the aliens and everybody and just sort of relax in the tulips and, if they take us over, then we should *love* that, too. Somehow, I don't find this...

A: All there is is lessons!!

Q: (L) Is the lesson to learn how to give up the ghost with panache? What's the point?

A: Your experiences never end, only transform. No bodycentrics need apply.

Q: (L) Well, you once said something about the transition to fourth density creating a 'level playing field.' Then, the people will wake up and there will be a battle between the humans and aliens...

A: Yes.

Q: (L) And if it is a more level playing field, then the situation would not quite be the same as the Conquistadores against the Aztecs and the Native Americans against the Europeans and...

A: Wrong, all in that drama were at 3rd density. The rabbits, rats, dogs, etc. are not on a level playing field with you!

Q: (L) Do the aliens know about the upcoming comets and all that sort of thing?

A: Yes. [The issue of repeated cometary bombardment of Earth is a subject dealt with in *Secret History* and *Almost Human*[8]. While ridiculed in earlier decades, the reality of the danger posed by comets is slowly becoming accepted as new data is analyzed, particularly that from tree-rings. We publish additional data and research on *sott.net* as it becomes available.]

Q: (L) And they have the idea that what they are doing, this race they are creating, is going to survive this cataclysmic activity?

A: Of course.

Q: (L) Is that 'of course' as in they *are* going to survive, or that they *believe* they are going to survive?

A: Both.

Q: (L) OK, you once told us that this was like a 'cosmic battle.' That the cycle was going to create balance and so on. I am trying to understand this. If that is the case, it seems that there is more to it than the Conquistadores against the Aztecs and the Europeans against the Native Americans; that at some point the story changes—the oppressed fight back—I am trying to get the allegory into a more understandable framework. Do you see what I mean?

A: No.

Q: (L) Well, that is because I am confused. What I am trying to ask without asking it directly is: what chance do we have of doing anything?

A: You are still not seeing the "bigger picture".

Q: (L) What is the bigger picture?

A: Your souls, your consciousness.

Q: (L) So, in other words, we chose to come in at this particular point in time to experience this mass take over of our planet and the conquest and destruction of the human race, just so we could have this experience, check-out and reincarnate?

A: No.

Q: (L) Well, that is what it sounds like! You say that the only thing that really matters is our souls, our consciousness, so if we tend to our souls and our bodies

---

[8] *Wave Book 7: Almost Human* is soon to be published by Red Pill Press, redpillpress.com

check out, then obviously the answer is to a) reincarnate, or b) move to the next density and reincarnate. What other option is there?

A: How long did you expect to "live?"

Q: (L) Well, under the normal circumstance, 70 or 80 years, optimistically.

A: And is that long?

Q: (L) No, it is not. By cosmic standards it is a whiff of vapor. What are you getting at here?

A: Think about it. ? Have you had any contemporaries who transited to 5th density?

Q: (L) Yes.

A: How come? How can this be possible?

Q: (L) Because they died. The body died.

A: Why?

Q: (L) Because that is what bodies do.

A: But is it "fair?"

Q: (L) Is it fair?! I guess if that is what they choose.

A: And...

Q: (L) I don't know where you are going with this!

A: You seem to be under the impression that only "good" experiences are acceptable.

Q: (L) No, I am not under the impression that only good experiences are acceptable, but I *am* in a little bit of a quandary here because, here we are talking to you guys who are supposed to be 'us' in the future. Here we are in this period of time on this planet, where things are in a very strange state. There is some kind of huge transition going on, and I am just wondering what is the whole point. Why are we talking to you? What's the point?

A: It is the lesson. Do you not understand still? The lesson, the lessons, that is all there is. They are all immeasurably valuable.

Q: (L) OK, we are having these lessons. You have told us what is going on. We see it going on around us. I am convinced that what you have said is so from a *lot* of other circumstantial evidence as well as the research of others who have come to the same conclusion and, *damn it, it's ugly! Do you understand me?! It's ugly!*

A: That is your perspective.

Q: (L) Well, as Eva said on the phone the other day, what are we supposed to awaken to? Are we supposed to just awaken to the fact that we can *see* all this stuff going on?

A: Yes.

Q: (L) And just waking up and seeing it is the whole thing? OK, once we wake up and *see* it, why can't we just check out at that point? If you know what the script is, you don't have to watch the movie!

A: But then you miss out on the experience.

Q: (L) So, we are all here to experience being munched and crunched...

A: No.

Q: (L) Imprisoned, controlled, being treated like rats in a cage in a laboratory...

A: Ecstasy, remember?

Q: (L) Ecstasy?! *Well swell!* We can just *all* be *burned at the stake!* I understand that is *quite* an *ecstatic* experience! I'm sure William Wallace felt perfectly *ecstatic* when they castrated him and removed his bowels and burned them in a brazier in front of his face!

A: Not so long ago, your face smashed upon the pavement...

Q: (L) Was that an ecstatic experience?

A: Yes.

Q: (L) So, when you say 'ecstatic' you could just be talking about jumping out a window and croaking?! You gotta understand here! The perspective here on third density! You don't have faces to smash on pavements!

A: Neither will/do you/us.

Q: (A) You say knowledge protects. It protects against *what?*

A: Many things. One example: post-transformational trauma and confusion.

Q: (L) So, knowledge is going to protect us against post-transformational trauma and confusion. You are saying that this transition to fourth density is going to be traumatic and confusing. Do you mean transformation from third to fourth density, or third to fifth density, i.e. death?

A: Both.

Q: (L) So, if one does not have the shock and trauma and the confusion and so forth, one is then able to function better?

A: Yes.

Q: (L) Well, if a person transitions directly from third to fourth density without cycling through fifth density via dying, that implies that persons can transition directly from third to fourth density without dying. Is that correct?

A: Yes.

Q: (L) How does that feel? How is that experience...

A: Alice through the looking glass.

Q: (A) OK, they say that knowledge is supposed to protect from trauma and confusion. On the other hand, all is lessons, so trauma is a lesson. Why are we supposed to work to avoid a lesson?

A: You are correct, it is a lesson, but if you have foreknowledge, you are learning that lesson early, and in a different way.

Q: (L) So, if you learn the lesson in a different way, does that mitigate the need or the way or the process of the way of learning at the time of transition?

A: Yes. Smoother.

Q: (L) I do have to say that thinking about it all, not being able to do anything about it, not being able to talk to people about it because they don't believe, is certainly more painful than being hit by the shock of it...

A: No.

Q: (L) Well, you are suggesting that I *can* tell others such things?

A: You can convey, but suggest it be done in a subtle fashion.

Q: (L) Well, how subtle can it be? I mean, 'hello folks, you know the words munch, crunch, yum yum???'

A: It is not all that way, and you know it! Most are not eaten, just manipulated. Knowledge protects in the most amazing ways.

Q: (L) I certainly don't want to hang out on this planet after it is taken over by aliens and everybody is getting munched!

A: Munched? Please!! Here is something for you to digest: Why is it that your scientists have overlooked the obvious when they insist that alien beings cannot travel to earth from a distant system???

Q: And what is this obvious thing?

A: Even if speed of light travel, or "faster", were not possible, and it is, of course, there is no reason why an alien race could not construct a space "ark", living for many generations on it. They could travel great distances through time and space, looking for a suitable world for conquest. Upon finding such, they could then install this ark in a distant orbit, build bases upon various solid planes in that solar system, and proceed to patiently manipulate the chosen civilizations to develop a suitable technological infrastructure. And then, after the instituting of a long, slow, and grand mind programming project, simply step in and take it over once the situation was suitable.

Q: Is this, in fact, what has happened, or is happening?

A: It could well be, and maybe now it is the time for you to learn about the details.

Q: Well, would such a race be third or fourth density in orientation?

A: Why not elements of both?

Q: What is the most likely place that such a race would have originated from?

A: Oh, maybe Orion, for example?

Q: OK. If such a race did, in fact, travel to this location in space/time, how many generations have come and gone on their space ark during this period of travel, assuming, of course, that such a thing has happened?

A: Maybe 12.

Q: OK, that implies that they have rather extended life spans...

A: Yes...

Q: Assuming this to be the case, what are their life spans?

A: 2,000 of your years. When in space, that is...

Q: And what is the span when on terra firma?

A: 800 years.

Q: Well, has it not occurred to them that staying in space might not be better?

A: No. Planets are much more "comfortable".

Q: OK... imagining that such a group has traveled here...

A: We told you of upcoming conflicts... Maybe we meant the same as your Bible, and other references. Speak of... The "final" battle between "good and evil..." Sounds a bit cosmic, when you think of it, does it not?

Q: Does this mean that there is more than one group that has traveled here in their space arks?

A: Could well be another approaching, as well as "reinforcements" for either/or, as well as non-involved, but interested observers of various types who appreciate history from the sidelines.

Q: Well, *swell!* There goes my peaceful life!

A: You never had one!

Q: Well, I was planning on one!

A: You chose to be incarnated now, with some foreknowledge of what was to come. Reference your dreams of space attack.

Q: OK, what racial types are we talking about relating to these hypothetical aliens?

A: Three basic constructs. Nordic, Reptilian, and Grays. Many variations of type 3, and 3 variations of type 1 and 2.

Q: Well, what racial types are the 'good guys?'

A: Nordics, in affiliation with 6th density "guides".

Q: And that's the only good guys?

A: That's all you need.

Q: Wonderful! So, if it is a Gray or Lizzie, you know they aren't the nice guys. But, if it is tall and blond, you need to ask questions!

A: All is subjective when it comes to nice and not nice. Some on 2nd density would think of you as "not nice", to say the least!!!

Q: That's for sure! Especially the roaches! Maybe we ought to get in touch with some of these good guys...

A: When the "time" is right. Just pay attention to the signs, please! It is not helpful to place yourself in a vacuum of awareness.

Q: Now, there is a lot being said about the sightings out in the Southwest area. They are saying that this is the 'new' imminent invasion or mass landing. Can you comment on this activity?

A: Prelude to the biggest "flap" ever.

Q: And where will this flap be located?

A: Earth.

Q: When is it going to begin?

A: Starting already.

Q: Is this biggest flap going to be just a flap, or is it going to be an invasion?

A: Not yet. Invasion happens when programming is complete...

Q: What programming?

A: See Bible, "Lucid" book [Texe Marrs' *Project L.U.C.I.D.*], [Val Valerian's] Matrix Material, "Bringers of the Dawn", and many other sources, then cross reference... weed the truth from the disinformation.

Q: Well, if something is fairly imminent, we are not gonna have time to do all the things you have suggested that we do!

A: Yes you will, most likely.

Q: This just sort of takes the heart right out of me!

A: Not so!

Q: Well, are we going to have time to do all these things?

A: All these things were suggested for this reason, among others.

Q: So, all the things you have suggested are to get us ready for this event?

A: Yes.

Q: Well, we better get moving! We don't have time to mess around!

A: You will proceed as needed, you cannot force these events or alter the Grand Destiny.

Q: I do *not* like the sound of that! I want to go home!

A: The alternative is less appetising.

Q: Sure! I don't want to be lunch!

A: Reincarnation on a 3rd density earth as a "cave person" amidst rubble and a glowing red sky, as the perpetual cold wind whistles...

Q: Why is the sky glowing red?

A: Contemplate.

Q: Of course! Comet dust! Sure, everybody knows *that!* Wonderful!!! Anything further?

A: Stay tuned for all pertinent information.

chapter eight
loose ends

This is an assorted collection of excerpts relating to specific questions about different aliens and abduction processes asked by various guests at the sessions at various times. For the most part, they are self-explanatory.

Q: (L) A lot of people are writing to me about dreams lately. They seem to be having a lot of dreams about beings in the sky, entering our reality. All kinds of strange things.

A: Beings come and go at will always, it is the awareness that is expanding.

Q: (L) Another trend of the dreams is being pursued, attacked, split up from their families, being put in concentration camps—just all kinds of things.

A: All are possible futures, just wait and see. There is an alien race that has plans to replace your physical vehicles with a new "model".

Q: (L) What are they going to do with the old models?

A: "Retire them".

Q: (T) Which race is this?

A: Orion STS.

Q: (L) Is this essentially what happened with Neanderthal?

A: Yup!

Q: (L) Well, for a period of time it seems that they continued to exist on the planet alongside the new model, Cro-Magnon or whatever.

A: Some did.

Q: (L) For how long did Neanderthal exist side by side with the "new model?"

A: 233 years.

Q: (L) I thought that Neanderthal was here for a long, long, long time; and if modern man arrived on the planet, as you say, 70 to 80 thousand years ago, wasn't Neanderthal already here then?

A: Time references have been miscalculated.

Q: (L) Who miscalculated the time references?

A: Science.

Q: (L) What is the oldest Neanderthal that's been found? Anybody know? No, well then when did Neanderthal appear on the planet?

A: 5.3 million years ago.

Q: (L) You are saying that when science says that modern man appeared 35 to 40 thousand years ago, and Neanderthal disappeared at the same time, the real time frame was 70 to 80 thousand years ago? In other words, a factor of two error.

A: Close.

Q: (L) And, of course, we can't depend on any of the dating methods because of metamorphosis.

A: And genetic manipulation.

Q: (L) So, in effect, we *are* the new Neanderthals on the eve of extinction. You have said that those who transition into fourth density in the body will go through some kind of rejuvenation process or body regeneration or something. Does that mean that these present "Neanderthal" type bodies that we presently occupy will morph into something more in line with the new model? Is it genetically encoded into some of them to do so?

A: Something like that.

Q: (L) So, that's why they have been following certain bloodlines for generation after generation; they are tinkering with the DNA and arming genetic time-bombs that are waiting to go off. (A) What is interesting is how do those who are trying to get these people, to abduct them, how do they spot them? How do they get the information? By following the bloodline, or by some kind of monitor you can detect from a long distance—and they can note that "here is somebody of interest" or "here is somebody dangerous" or "let's abduct this one" or whatever. How do they select? Do they search the genealogies or is it some kind of remote sensing?

A: Now this is interesting Arkadiusz, as it involves the atomic "signature" of the cellular structure of the individual. In concert with this is the etheric body reading and the frequency resonance vibration. All these are interconnected, and can be read from a distance using remote viewing technology/methodology.

Q: (L) Can it be done in a pure mechanical way without using psychic means?

A: At another level of understanding, the two are blended into one.

Q: (T) Computerized psychic remote viewing, maybe. Like artificial intelligence. Maybe a mind connected to a computer?

A: That is close, yes. [...]

Q: (L) Who were the beings that were abducting Karla Turner and her family?

A: Lizards.

Q: (L) Why were they been abducting that group of people?

A: Same reasons they have been abducting you and Frank.

Q: (L) They have been abducting Karla Turner and her family because they perceive them as a threat and wish to drive them to self-destruction?

A: Yes.

Q: (L) In one abduction she described in this book, what was the black shadowy thing that seemed like a moving "nothing" on the ground?

A: Blocked grays. Karla must be careful driving alone to lectures and meetings.

Q: (L) Should she make sure there is always someone with her in the car?

A: At night and on lonely roads. Nephew must pay attention. Also son's friend. She does not realize the extreme importance. Communicate this to her now please Laura.

I did write to Karla and tell her that the Cassiopaeans were more or less warning her that she was in danger. She did not choose to believe that there was any benevolent intention in the warning and was extremely negative about any sort of "channeling". Not long after, she was diagnosed with a particularly virulent form of breast cancer and died. I have often wondered if she had heeded this warning to not travel alone or at night on lonely roads, if she would be here today.

Q: (L) There was an individual in the Karla Turner book, *Taken*, who had an experience similar to what you have described as a virtual abduction, and she was seen inside a blue bubble, who did this?

A: Grays.

Q: (L) How do aliens create these virtual reality scenarios?

A: Mental image restructuring.

Q: (L) Why does this phenomenon involve the use of the "blue bubble" or light?

A: Hypnotic suggestion trigger. [...]

Q: (L) Is it true that when we ask an individual under hypnosis about an alien abduction scenario to try to tune in to aliens that they can access what is in the alien mind... can we do that?

A: Yes. The individual is aware on every level and the information you seek was known at the time. The questions you ask are merely an accessing of information that is already in awareness at some level. Budd Hopkins and David Jacobs are too regimented. [...]

Q: (T) Have I ever been abducted?

A: In childhood.

Q: (L) Has he been abducted since he was grown?

A: Maybe in level 3.

Q: (L) What is level 3?

A: Type of abduction.

Q: (L) How many levels and types of abductions are there?

A: Six.

Q: (L) What is level 3?

A: Consciousness altered to "alpha" state.

Q: (T) In other words I will be seeing something other than what is actually happening? Or remembering something other than what actually happened?

A: Yes but not physical as in childhood.

Q: (L) What happened to Marcia Moore who was working on drug enhanced outer space contact via altered consciousness?

A: Permanent abduction victim by Lizards.

Q: (L) Why?

A: Too close to truth.

Q: (L) Well, are we close to the truth too?

A: Yes.

Q: (L) Will we be permanently abducted by the Lizards?

A: Knowledge protects.

Q: (L) But didn't she have a lot of knowledge too?

A: Scrambled with drugs. [...]

183

Q: (L) What or who are the South American aliens I have read about who are described as being gray with thick lips, rudimentary features, gray uniforms, and are called by the South Americans *Malos*?

A: Lizard projections.

Q: (L) Were these also the clay-like beings seen by Betty Andreasson only she saw them wearing blue suits?

A: Yes.

Q: (L) Where was Betty Andreasson taken to when she saw the Phoenix in her abduction?

A: Another dimension of reality.

Q: (L) Is Betty Andreasson correct in believing that her experiences are positive and are bringing her closer to God?

A: No.

Q: (L) Is Betty Andreasson deluded?

A: No. She is a victim.

Q: (L) What happened to the Australian pilot Fredrick Valentich?

A: He was taken by the Lizards and dissected. [...]

Q: (L) Somebody sent me an article about experiments being done by a fellow named Persinger who has been trying to duplicate the "abduction" experience by subjecting people to EM fields in a sensory deprivation chamber. I would like comments on that, and second...

A: Nonsense, some have closed mind inspired by fear.

Q: (L) My concern is that if he is doing this to people, and we have talked about electromagnetic energy blowing holes in the dimensional boundaries, my concern is that this experimentation could be detrimental to the persons being experimented on; is this a possibility?

A: Yes.

Q: (L) What could be the results of subjecting someone to these electromagnetic fields?

A: Cessation of body.

Q: (L) In other words, it could kill them?

A: Yes.

Q: (L) Could it also open doors between dimensions and allow other things to enter in?

A: Yes.

Q: (L) Could they be subjected to spirit or demonic possession by this method?

A: Yes.

Q: (L) Could they also be subjected to further programming by aliens through this method?

A: Yes.

Q: (L) There are so many stories of the "gazing" process where the alien controls that abductee by staring into their eyes and the abductee feels full of love and harmony and thereby thinks that the experience is beneficial. This makes me wonder just exactly what is the purpose of this "gazing"?

A: Hypnotic.

Q: (L) Does it also form a bond?

A: Yes.

Q: (L) In the establishing of an ongoing connection between an abductee and the abductor, what methods or techniques are used? Is it a psychic bond?

A: Close.

Q: (L) Is it formed technologically?

A: Partly.

Q: (L) What was the purpose of M's abduction?

A: To study his mind. He has a very strong mind and resolve.

Q: (L) Did they put an implant in him?

A: Yes.

Q: (L) And what do they do with that implant?

A: Is monitor. Frequent ringing in ear signifies monitoring activity.

Q: (L) We want to know if Budd Hopkins is on the right track in his research?

A: Halfway.

Q: (T) In the Linda Cortile case, has everything that she says happened really happened to her?

A: In 4th density.

Q: (T) What about being pulled out of the apartment from the 17th floor or wherever it was, and being sucked up in the beam of the light? Did that actually happen to her?

A: In 4th density.

Q: (T) How did people in third density see it?

A: Only those who were tuned in saw it.

Q: (L) Were there people there who did not see it?

A: Yes.

Q: (L) Alright, now, reading about the Linda Cortile case, it is rumored to have taken place in the sight of Javier Perez de Cuellar and his bodyguards and driver. Did Javier really witness this?

A: Yes, but not only one.

Q: (L) So, there were others? OK, of the two people who were supposed to be the bodyguards of the "VIP", one of them exhibited some extremely bizarre behavior after this event. What was the cause of this bizarre behavior? Was it him trying to freak-out Linda Cortile, or was he simply freaked out himself?

A: Simple shock.

Q: (L) So, he was having a hard time dealing with it himself. During the discussion of this case, it seems that this particular incident really involved a mass abduction because a number of women in the neighborhood have subsequently claimed that they not only were abducted at the same time on the same night, but that during the course of time that they were being taken to this craft, they saw other women walking out on the street together. Was this, in fact, a mass abduction?

chapter eight

A: Some was hysteria.

Q: (L) What is the energy fueling Whitley Strieber and his work?
A: Grays.
Q: (L) He is an agent of the Grays?
A: No. Instrument of the Grays.
Q: (T) So, all his writing is compromised by the Grays?
A: Influenced by them. *Wolfen* reflects Lizzie reality.

Q: (TM) My next question is where is my implant?
A: You have two. One in brain behind sinus and one in leg bone.
Q: (TM) I have a suspicion that I might know when I got it, last year... I have been having nosebleeds. Where was I when I got the one in my brain?
A: On travel sequence, in transit. We see transit clearly, but it is unclear why so rapid through 3rd level. Time cycle was interrupted and we can't see clearly due to cycle block.
Q: (L) Did you have missing time? (TM) In fact, I got somewhere sooner than I should have. (L) Well, that explains why they said "unclear why so rapid through third level". (J) Did TM experience time acceleration?
A: You bet.
Q: (L) What is a cycle block?
A: Too complex, but it involves a dome of frequency over subject.
Q: (GB) In a bubble?
A: Close.
Q: (BP) So, what they do is screw with our perception of time, they just yank you out, do what they do, throw you back in and if it's faster, it's faster, if it's slower, it's slower. Who gives a hoot. (L) Sloppy work.
A: Close.
Q: (J) Kind of like putting people back in the wrong cars or facing the wrong end of the bed, pajamas inside out, or whatever. (BP) People have waked up in different beds, in different houses, out in the woods, whatever.
A: Yes.
Q: (GB) When was the last time my wife was abducted?
A: Last week.
Q: (J) Were they both abducted at the same time?
A: Yes.
Q: (GB) When we were both abducted together, was it a physical or other abduction?
A: Soul abduction.
Q: (L) Did it occur during the night while they were sleeping?
A: Yes.
Q: (GB) What did they do during the soul abduction, what was the purpose?
A: Knowledge review.
Q: (GB) For what benefit? (J) Who reviewed the knowledge?

A: Lizards, of course.

Q: (J) Is there any knowledge that they might find during a review that might cause them to stop the abduction?

A: Open.

Q: (L) Are there any people, who, by virtue of their knowledge, do not get abducted?

A: Maybe.

Q: (GB) Is this to elevate our knowledge, or to monitor our knowledge?

A: Both, but mostly monitor.

Q: (L) How could being abducted by the STS beings increase our knowledge?

A: Accidentally.

Q: (L) How would this be done accidentally?

A: Self explanatory.

Q: (L) So, in other words, they may abduct someone to monitor their knowledge, but if the individual has achieved a certain level of knowledge, the abduction only serves to add to their knowledge?

A: Yes.

Q: (BP) What is the Lizard's Achilles heel?

A: STS. As in "wishful thinking" which blocks knowledge.

Q: (J) Their singular preoccupation with service to self blocks them from being able to move from fourth level.

A: Yes.

Q: (TM) Do they want to… (J) No they are happy there… they want to stay there forever and control, and consume, and have a good time. (BP) It is like finding a place with really good food, a great place to live, great sex, everything you like, you would want to stay there. (TM) Don't a lot of us like the idea of staying in the third level forever?

A: Yes.

Q: (L) Now, we want to know if there is any correlation between movement of UFOs and weather patterns… (J) Specifically, thunderstorms.

A: Correlation?

Q: (L) OK, can UFOs not fly during thunderstorms, or electrical storms?

A: Incorrect.

Q: (L) OK, they can fly during thunderstorms?

A: Yes. But "fly" is improper term.

Q: (L) OK, what do they do during thunderstorms if they don't fly?

A: Operate.

Q: (T) Well, the real question is: does the thunderstorm interfere in the EM flow between densities?

A: Can.

Q: (L) Can thunderstorms interfere with their projection ability?

A: Yes.

Q: (L) Do thunderstorms or electrical activity inhibit them?

A: Ionization.

Q: (T) Is the fact that there are very few abduction cases, at least I read about, and I've read quite a few of them, during thunderstorms, have to do with the thunderstorm interfering with the EM, so that the abduction would be much harder to do, therefore they don't bother doing it?

A: No.

Q: (T) Can abductions take place during thunderstorms?

A: Yes.

Q: (L) Is there a possibility that thunderstorms possibly enhance this activity?

A: No.

Q: (T) So third density EM disturbances don't disturb fourth density?

A: Can.

Q: (J) Can they control it. (T) Well, I haven't read very many things about abductions during storms. (L) Well, I have read about a few, enough to break it as a rule. (T) Is there some reason that it isn't happening as often during thunderstorms? (J) They don't want to get wet.

A: Can you drive a car during the rain?

Q: (J) Yes, but if it is raining really hard, you avoid it. (L) Is there any particular reason why more abductions and UFO sightings occur at night?

A: Not correct.

Q: (L) So, you mean there is as much activity in the daytime as there is at night?

A: Yes.

Q: (L) Well, that blew that theory.

Q: (L) Was there a harmonic convergence as was advertised within the metaphysical community?

A: For those who believed there was a harmonic convergence, indeed there was a harmonic convergence.

Q: (L) Did anything of a material nature happen on or to the planet to enhance or change the energy?

A: Did you notice any changes?

Q: (L) No. Except that it seems that things have gotten worse, if anything.

A: Did you notice any clear, obvious, material changes?

Q: (L) No. But that could just be me. I could just be a stubborn and skeptical person.

A: Did anyone else in the room notice any clear or obvious changes?

Q: (S) What date was it? (L) 8/8/88, I believe. (S) I thought it had something to do with 11/11 ninety-something...

A: Well, obviously if the recollection of the calendar date was difficult, one would suppose that material changes did not take place. For, if they had, would you not remember the calendar date ascribed to them?

Q: (L) Yes. The claim has further been made that, for a month, following the harmonic convergence that no abductions were taking place. Is this true?

A: No. There has been no cessation in what you term to be abduction in quite some time as you measure it.

Q: (L) Well, on the subject of abduction: we watched a film on television, Monday the 28th, that was a purported video of an alien autopsy, or, more correctly, an autopsy on an alien body. Was this, in fact, an alien?

A: How do you define "alien?"

Q: (L) Was it a being other than a naturally born human on this planet as we know human beings?

A: That is correct.

Q: (L) It was other than a naturally born human?

A: Correct.

Q: (L) OK. What kind of a being was this?

A: Hybrid.

Q: (L) What was it a hybrid of—combining what elements?

A: Cybergenetic creatures you refer to as "Grays", and earth human such as yourself, third density. So, in essence, it was a hybridization of a 3rd density and 4th density being.

Q: (L) OK, was this a fourth density being.

A: No. If you listen to the response—it was a 3rd and 4th density being.

Q: (L) How can a being be both third and fourth density?

A: It is the environmental surroundings that count, not the structure of the individual. The same is true, for you. After all, you have read literature stating that your world or planet is in the process of ascending from 3rd to 4th density, have you not? [See *The Ra Material.*]

Q: (L) Yes.

A: And this literature has also stated that this is an ongoing process, has it not?

Q: (L) Yes.

A: Then, one must wonder, if it is an ongoing process, how would it be possible, if it is not possible, for a being to be in both 3rd and 4th density at one time... Also, if you will recall from review material, you are currently living in the same environment as 2nd and 1st density level beings. Is this not true?

Q: (L) Yes.

A: At least that is what you have been told. So, therefore, it is possible for a being to be in 3rd and 4th density. And as we have also told you, when 4th density beings visit 3rd density environment, they are, in effect, 3rd density beings, and vice versa. The so-called abduction takes place, especially if it is a physical abduction, the subject becomes temporarily 4th density, because it is the environment that counts. And the key factor there is awareness, not physical or material structure.

Q: (L) I have a paper here that talks about the Grays and says that they have two brains: an anterior brain and a posterior brain; and that if you shoot one—this is what it says, I am not suggesting that I want to shoot anybody—that if you shoot one, and only shoot one part of the brain, that it does not die; that you have to shoot it in a special way and get both brains in order to kill one. Is this a correct concept?

A: Well, it is rather puzzling. Brings up a lot of questions. One question that comes to mind is: why would one seek to shoot anything.

189

Q: (L) Well, I didn't suggest that I wished to, this is just what this paper says here.

A: The physical description is accurate in terms one variety of what is referred to as the Grays. It does have an anterior brain. However, this is secondary to all other issues. And, also we would suggest that it would not be advisable to seek to cause physical harm to any particular species. Therefore, it may be advisable to disregard the information contained in the work that you are describing.

Q: (L) It also says that the Grays have to be very close to a person to telepathically link with that person. Is this correct?

A: Close? No, as we have described to you before, there are technological processes involved which do not require close physical proximity as you measure it. But, this is very complicated. It follows dimensional windows and that sort of thing, which you do not fully understand, therefore it would not be advisable to go into that in great detail. But, the general answer to that question is no.

Q: (L) It also says that they implant some sort of crystal on the optic nerve of humans that is two to four microns in diameter and that this crystal is tuned to the frequency of the individuals implanting it, which allows them to establish a mental frequency for communication. Is that anywhere along the line of what you are talking about?

A: Physical implantations do occur. The precise locations vary according to the desired effects. And when it comes to the interactions between the human species in 3rd density, and other STS issues in 4th density, there are a variety of mechanisms in use as well as a variety of directives and objectives. For example, some implants are used merely for tracking. Others are used to alter consciousness, and still others are designed to be mind altering or motor altering mechanisms. Each of these has a different structure and a different material content according to which is being employed and for what purpose. The particular function you are describing there has been used, or, rather, something similar, though we are not completely familiar with that which you have described. So, we suggest that this may be fabrication to some extent, or expansion of accurate information. But, in any case, it is true that implants do get implanted for various reasons.

Q: (L) What is the classification that the person has to fall into in order to be abducted and studied?

A: What makes you think "classifications" correlates with abductions?

Q: (TK) It's not the classification, it's.... It's gotta be the type of person...

A: Yes.

Q: (TK) And how easy it would be to influence....

A: Of course. And many other factors.

Q: (TK) It would have to have something to do with what they could do for the abductors. I mean, they have to be in a position to help them... Is that a correct assumption?

A: Yes. STS.

Q: (T) STS; Service to Self.

A: Vibrational frequency.

Q: (L) OK, so if the person has an STS vibrational frequency, that already predisposes them to abduction. Is that correct?

A: Some.

Q: (T) OK, that's a factor. There's more than one agenda involved with abductions. Are the military personnel that are being abducted, is that a specific agenda that is being followed?

A: Artificial classifications, such as military designations, are important to human groups only.

Q: (L) We have Pat with us tonight...

A: Hello Pat.

Q: (L) Now, Pat and I both would like to ask why the black, flying boomerangs showed up all over the county on the night Pat was here for her first hypnosis session?

A: Examine issue carefully.

Q: (L) The first thing we thought about it was that this was, if not necessarily rare, at least rarely observed type of craft, and the event itself was rare... is this correct?

A: It is rare.

Q: (L) If it is rare for it to occur in response to a hypnosis session, which person were the UFOs particularly interested in?

A: It was not a person, but information that is hidden in the subconscious memory of Pat.

Q: (L) Were they wanting to get this information?

A: No. To monitor what would be revealed.

Q: (L) Does this mean that Pat has information programmed into her before birth that she needs to access [as you have suggested about others]?

A: No. Abductions.

Q: (L) They wanted to see if anything would be revealed about their abductions of her?

A: Yes.

Q: (L) OK, since she is here, can we ask who abducted her?

A: Grays.

Q: (L) How many times has she been abducted?

A: 4. Snow scene was only 3rd density.

This was a reference to a missing time incident Pat had experienced when she pulled off the road in a snow storm while driving on the Pennsylvania Turnpike in 1987. She was the wife of a government scientist. This incident bothered her, and it was this that she wanted to explore when she came for hypnosis. She did not think it was an abduction, but rather that it was evidence of something triggering psychological trauma relating to the recent death of her aunt.

Q: (P) Does that mean that the snow scene was only in this realm?

A: No. Abduction which occurred there was strictly physical.

Q: (L) OK, the abduction that occurred in the snow was a physical abduction. Perhaps the others were not. Were they physical also?

A: The others were 4th density. 3rd density abduction only occurs rarely, and is of great import.

Q: (L) Was it because of her husband and his work that she had this physical abduction?

A: Perhaps.

Q: (L) Maybe that is why there is a higher rate of abduction among family members of government employees, so that they can be activated or controlled? (P) But my husband wasn't really working on anything secret.

A: He had access to sensitive facilities.

Q: (L) Did he have a security clearance or was he friends with others who did? (P) I had a security clearance too! (L) So, Pat had an implant put in. An actual, physical implant. Where is it?

A: Behind sinus cavity.

Q: (L) What is this implant designed to do?

A: Activate behavioral control reflex and thought pattern generation and alteration. Very complex, in fact, parallel subject. Pat is "locator probe" for the purpose of monitoring those in her midst. Telling is not important, reading is. Besides, most of the work performed did not involve conscious awareness.

Q: Is this still going on?

A: Partly, but also, Pat could be used as a probe to monitor all events taking place at JPL and other laboratories by examining aural imprints of her husband and others with whom she was acquainted. All events leave permanent imprints upon aural energy fields. This explains, for example, some sightings and apparitions. "Ghosts" are sometimes merely spontaneous activations of the aural records of the natural surroundings.

Q: [Question lost in static burst, relating to the blue bubble Pat saw on the side of the road just before she pulled off in the snow storm. She was apparently inquiring if it could have been her deceased aunt attempting communication.]

A: No, Pat, the "blue thing" you saw was not an aural imprint reading, it was a 4th density craft partially transferred into 3rd density. Your deep subconscious memory remembers much, much more.

Q: OK, now this next correspondent writes: "I decided to listen to one of the C's suggestions about Melatonin. What the heck, after all I might meet Santa! Curiously, It was rather hard to find it in our stores. It turns out that only a herbal/natural version of it is allowed for sale but I don't think that it's any different. Well, I must say it is all that I ever thought it would be. I have gone through the stages described in your transcripts and now am at a rather odd stage where everything seems like a TV broadcast. Last night I had a very unusual dream about an asteroid impacting Earth. I must say, I do not necessarily subscribe to this theory. I have been reading *a lot* about this so it could be my subconscious mind playing tricks on me. The impact took place in the vicinity of the north pole with the approach path from the south. But there was this curious red line extending up and over the pole after it had taken place. I don't know what it meant. Before, I also dreamt about there only being one more pope, the

Japanese being involved with the Grays and I had some dreams with religious connotations. But what really blew me away was a dream couple of nights ago. I dream that I was lifting up from my bed, through the chimney (which I do not have) into a space ship! I could actually see myself lifting off the bed. Then I was on some sort of a raised surface with a short *being* with long arms and *a human doctor* beside me. The little fellow seemed rather upset and tried to calm me down even though I was at peace, waving his arms to stop doing something. Then the doctor tried to do something to my lower back but I woke up. Now get this—I woke up turned around—with my feet on my pillows, on my back which I rarely do. When I got up, I actually noticed that the sheets weren't messed up at all—when I toss in my sleep, the sheets are always kicked off half of the bed. I don't know what happened, I know it sounds suspicious but I am very sceptical. In my case it is probably more of a wishful thinking than anything else. Regardless of what had taken place, this particular hormone resulted in a lot of research material".

I want to ask about this dream that our friend had under the influence of melatonin. There has been something of a controversy about it recently as one group claims that melatonin is stimulated in the brain by aliens in order to cause the paralysis that overcomes the victim and thereby enables them to go about their nefarious abducting activity. Is that, in fact, the case? Is melatonin part of the paralysis factor of alien abduction?

A: No.

Q: What chemicals are stimulated in the body to cause this paralysis?

A: That is not the method used.

Q: What *is* the method used?

A: Electronic wave diversion.

Q: They are diverting the electronic waves of our brain or our physiology?

A: Closer.

Q: OK, what about our friend's dream; was this a memory, a dream or an abduction?

A: Etheric body abduction.

Q: What was the purpose of abducting his etheric body?

A: Study.

Q: Who abducted his etheric body?

A: Orion STS. Melatonin only serves to make one more aware of processes in this context.

Q: So, lots of people are being abducted, physically, etherically, or in other ways, and simply are not aware of it at all?

A: More often etherically.

Q: Most abductions are etheric, but people are not aware. The melatonin is what enables them to be aware of what is happening by removing the blocks the aliens put in place?

A: Precisely.

Q: And, by becoming aware, do they have some chance of stopping the abduction process by their awareness?

A: Or more importantly, limiting the damage. Knowledge protects.

chapter eight

Q: Tonight we had visitors. It was a doctor and his wife, and they very badly wanted to talk to us about some experiences they have been having. The first thing was that he talked about was a story about a "near death experience". After we started to talk about it, I realized that we couldn't get a straight answer out of him. He talked for thirty minutes in 50 different directions; talked about death threats; talked about this event that he called a near death experience which clearly wasn't; we had to stop him, back him up, stop him and back him up, over and over again just to get a sequential account of the events. He talked about hallucinations, going psychotic, schizophrenia, and on and on. And then finally, as if on cue, he said "Oh, I saw a UFO". Now, we had some funny impressions about this: was this guy an agent sent in to cause disruption in what we are doing here?

A: No.

Q: Did he have an abduction experience?

A: Not an abduction, but a close encounter.

Q: Were the effects he was experiencing part of a "bleed through" of fourth density in the area?

A; To some extent.

Q: He was pretty distressed by all this, to the extent that he closed down his medical practice and just basically walked away from his life. Can you tell us what he wanted from us?

A: He is disjointed because he has been jarred semi-awake after years and years of programming. The effect has been something akin to a "nervous breakdown", but it goes deeper than that. It is difficult for you to relate, as you have been "on track", for the whole of your lives. He was a standard player. Severe experiences brought him to the brink, now he is both retrieving the shattered pieces of what is worthwhile that remains, and exploring the whole new arena that beckons.

A: We wish to review some things first. The concept of a "master race" put forward by the Nazis was merely a 4th density STS effort to create a physical vehicle with the correct frequency resonance vibration for 4th density STS souls to occupy in 3rd density. It was also a "trial run" for planned events in what you perceive to be your future.

Q: (L) You mean with a strong STS frequency so they can have a "vehicle" in third density, so to speak?

A: Correct. Frequency resonance vibration! Very important.

Q: (L) So, that is why they are programming and experimenting? And all these folks running around who some think are "programmed", could be individuals who are raising their nastiness levels high enough to accommodate the truly negative STS fourth density—sort of like walk-ins or something, only not nice ones?

A: You do not have very many of those present yet, but that was, and still is, the plan of some of the 4th density STS types.

Q: So, we can forget that one for now. OK, last session you brought up the subject of Frequency Resonance Vibration. You suggested that there are certain STS forces who are developing or creating or managing physical bodies that they are trying to increase the frequency in so that they will have bodies that are wired so that they can manifest directly into third density, since that seems to be the real barrier that prevents an all-out invasion, the fact that we are in third density and they are in fourth. Now, I assumed that the same function could be true for STO individuals. It seems that many individuals who have come into this time period from the future, coming back into the past via the incarnational cycle so as not to violate free will, have carefully selected bodies with particular DNA, which they are, little by little, activating so that there fourth density selves, or higher, can manifest in this reality. Is it possible for those energies to manifest into such bodies which have been awakened or tuned in third density?

A: STO tends to do the process within the natural flow of things. STS seeks to alter creation processes to fit their ends.

Q: This Top Secret document and the Anna Hayes material to some extent, both talk about many abductions being "ourselves from the future" who have come back to the past, or what is for us, the present, to abduct their own bodies to make genetic adjustments so that they can advance and not make the mistakes they made in another timeline. Is that, in fact, part of the scenario?

A: Very close to the truth!

Q: Can you abduct yourself in an STO manner and help yourself in this way? Can that be STO?

A: It is not, because that is not STO.

Q: So, when that is happening, and if it is happening, it is occurring in the STS parameter?

A: Yes.

Q: How do the STO manage?

A: They do not concern themselves with such things.

Q: Well, if the STS guys are genetically tweaking themselves to have some kind of different outcome for some reason that we do not perceive, don't you think there should be a balancing action on the STO side of some sort?

A: You are thinking in STS terms. But that is natural, since human 3rd density is STS.

Q: You say they don't concern themselves with that. What do STO individuals coming back from the future into the past concern themselves with?

A: Answering calls for assistance with knowledge.

Q: What do these STS individuals coming back into the past hope to do by genetically tweaking their ancestors? What happened that they want to have happen differently?

A: Infinite number of possible answers to that question.

Q: So, they are coming from all different timelines with all different kinds of agendas—all designed to serve themselves.

conflicting thought centers

This session was focused on a particular experience of mine. The background was that I had an appointment for a series of MRIs to be made to replace a similar series that had been made several months previously, but had been "misplaced" by the medical facility. I was worried about being able to go to sleep due to the strange events surrounding this loss of films. The MRIs were required for the ongoing therapy I was receiving as a result of an automobile accident which left me almost totally unable to use my left arm and in constant pain.

After lying down, I had been thinking about the MRIs, and then there seemed to be a sort of "blank-out", and I came to myself suddenly and found that there were three spidery type creatures battling to "float" me out of bed. I was struggling to resist, gripping the brass head-board with my damaged left hand. One of the creatures was pulling me by my ankle and I could distinctly feel a sort of "fuzziness" in the grip. All of my body, except for my shoulders and head which were held down by my grip on the bed, was suspended in air and being "sucked" into a sort of beam of light emanating from the wall to the outside of the house. The bed was shaking and bouncing with the "tug of war" taking place.

When I came awake and became aware that I was struggling violently, I became angry and my resistance increased. At this point, one of the creatures placed his hand on my head and a powerful paralysis began to spread over me from the head down. This was causing my eyes to close forcibly. As I realized my helpless state, I became angry and "spoke" to the creatures in my mind saying: "You may be able to paralyze me and overcome my physical body, but I'll fight you with everything I have, every chance I get, so don't turn your backs on me or you'll regret it!" And, with every bit of will I could muster, I attempted to curse them out loud. The only thing I actually managed to do was emit a strangled groan as the paralysis had overtaken my vocal cords as well. But, a strange thing happened with the uttering of this sound. The creatures seemed to become confused and disoriented and began to chatter in strange clicking sounds to each other as they dropped me suddenly back on the bed. Then, they clustered together like frightened birds and just "melted" into a shimmery "curtain" beside the bed.

Q: (L) The first thing on my mind is an experience I had several nights ago. It seemed as though there was some sort of interaction between myself and something "other". Could you tell me what this experience was?

A: Was eclipsing of the realities.

Q: (L) What is an eclipsing of the realities?

A: It is when energy centers conflict.

Q: (L) What energy centers are conflicting?

A: Thought energy centers.

Q: (L) Whose thoughts?

A: Thoughts are the basis of all creation. After all, without thought nothing would exist. Now would it? Therefore, energy centers conflicting involve thought patterns. You could refer to it as an intersecting of thought pattern energies. The true effort to gain knowledge should always be to be open to any response, any question.

Q: (L) Well, it seemed to me that something happened to me that blanked out a period of my experience, and you say this was an eclipsing of energies caused by an intersecting of thought centers. Now, this intersecting of thought centers, did this occur within my body or within my environment?

A: They are one and the same.

Q: (L) Can I ask about my specific perceptions of the event?

A: That is what you are already doing. We sense that you desire the truest of all possible answers and if one desires the truest of all possible answers, one must avoid expressing one's own perceptions to any great degree and simply allow the answers to flow. The best advice to accomplish this is a step-by-step approach— to ask the simplest of questions with the least amount of prejudice attached.

Q: (L) Alright. I was lying in bed worrying about being able to get to sleep. The next thing I knew, I came to myself feeling that I was being floated off my bed. Was I?

A: No. When you say "I" you are referring to your whole person. There is more than one factor involved with one's being to any particular definition.

Q: (L) Was some part of my being [in the process of] being separated from another part of my being?

A: Yes.

Q: (L) Was this an attempt to extract my soul or astral body?

A: Attempt is not probably the proper term.

Q: (L) In other words...

A: It is more just an activity taking place. Attempt implies effort rather than the nature present in a conflicting of energies and thought centers.

Q: (L) I also seemed to be aware of several dark, spider-like figures lined up by the side of the bed, was this an accurate impression.

A: Those could be described as specific thought center projections.

Q: (L) I seemed to be fighting and resisting this activity.

A: That was your choice.

Q: (L) Alright, was this the ending of an abduction that had already taken place?

A: Not the proper terminology. It was the conclusion to an event, not necessarily what one would refer to as an abduction, but more what one would refer to as an interaction.

Q: (L) What was the nature of the interaction?

A: The conflicting of energies related to thought center impulses.

Q: (L) Where are these thought centers located?

A: Well, that is difficult to answer because that is assuming that thought centers are located. And, of course this is a concept area in which you are not fully familiar as of yet. So, an attempt to answer this in any way that would make sense to you would probably not be fruitful. We suggest slowing down and carefully formulating questions.

Q: (L) At what level of density do these thought centers have their primary focus?

A: Thought centers do not have primary focus in any level of density. This is precisely the point. You are not completely familiar with the reality of what thoughts are. We have spoken to you on many levels and have detailed many areas involving density level, but thoughts are quite a different thing because they pass through all density levels at once. Now, let us ask you this. Do you not now see how that would be possible?

Q: (L) Yes. But what I am trying to do is identify these conflicting thought centers. If two thought centers, or more, conflict, then my idea would be that they are in opposition.

A: Correct.

Q: (L) And, what I want to know is, was this in opposition to me, or was this an opposition in which I simply was caught in the middle, so to speak.

A: Well, you are drifting away from the true nature of your experience, because you are making suppositions. And we are not trying to scold you, we are merely trying to guide you and this is not always easy. But, let it be known again that the simplest way for you to gather knowledge on this particular subject matter is to ask the simplest questions without prejudice.

Q: (L) OK, you said I wasn't abducted, that an event of some sort occurred. What was the event?

A: We have already described this, but the problem that you are having is that you are assuming that the description we are giving is more complicated than this. It is not.

Q: (L) OK, in the experience I felt a paralysis of my body, what caused this paralysis.

A: Yes. Separation of awareness. Which is defined as any point along the pathway where one's awareness becomes so totally focused on one thought sector that all other levels of awareness are temporarily receded, thereby making it impossible to become aware of one's physical reality along with one's mental reality. This gives the impression of what is referred to as paralysis. Do you understand?

Q: (L) Yes. And what stimulates this total focus of awareness?

A: An event which sidetracks, temporarily, the mental processes.

Q: (L) And what event can sidetrack the mental processes to this extent?

A: Any number. In this particular case, it was an eclipsing of energies caused by conflicting thought centers.

Q: (L) What energies were being eclipsed?

A: Whenever two opposing units of reality intersect, this causes what can be referred to as friction, which, for an immeasurable amount of what you would refer to as time, which is, of course, non-existent, creates a non-existence, or a stopping of the movements of all functions. This is what we would know as conflict. In between, or through any intersecting, opposite entities, we always find zero time, zero movement, zero transference, zero exchange. Now think about this. Think about this carefully.

Q: (L) Does this mean that I was, essentially, in a condition of non-existence?

A: Well, non-existence is not really the proper term, but non-fluid existence would be more to the point. Do you understand?

Q: (L) Yes. Frozen, as it were?

A: Frozen, as it were.

Q: (L) Was there any benefit to me from this experience?

A: All experiences have potential for benefit.

Q: (L) Was there any detriment from this experience?

A: All experiences have potential for detriment. Now, do you see the parallels. We are talking about any opposing forces in nature, when they come together, the result can go all the way to the extreme of one side or all the way to the extreme of the other. Or, it can remain perfectly, symmetrically in balance in the middle, or partially in balance on one side or another. Therefore all potentials are realized at intersecting points in reality.

Q: (L) Was one of the thought centers me?

A: That is presupposing that you, what is defined as you, or how you define yourself as "me" is of and by itself a thought center. Part of what is you is a thought center but not all of what is you is a thought center. So, therefore it is incorrect to say: "Was one of these conflicting energies or thought centers me?"

Q: (L) Was one of these conflicting thought centers or energies some part of me?

A: Yes.

Q: (L) And was it eclipsed by interacting with a thought center energy that was part of or all of something or someone else?

A: Or, was what happened a conflicting of one energy thought center that was a part of your thought process and another energy thought center that was another part of your thought process? We will ask you that question and allow you to contemplate.

Q: (L) Does it ever happen that individuals who perceive or think they perceive themselves to have experienced an "abduction", to actually be interacting with some part of themselves?

A: That would be a very good possibility. Now, before you ask another question, stop and contemplate for a moment: what possibilities does this open up? Is there any limit? And if there is, what is that? Is it not an area worth exploring? For example, just one example for you to digest. What if the abduction scenario could take place where your soul projection, in what you perceive as the future, can come back and abduct your soul projection in what you perceive as the present?

Q: (L) Oh, dear! Does this happen?

A: This is a question for you to ask yourself and contemplate.

Q: (L) Why would I do that to myself? (J) To gain knowledge of the future?

A: Are there not a great many possible answers?

Q: (L) Well, this seemed to be a very frightening and negative experience. If that is the case: A: maybe that is just my perception, or B: then, in the future I am not a very nice person! (J) Or maybe the future isn't very pleasant. And the knowledge that you gained of it is unpleasant.

A: Or is it one possible future, but not all possible futures? And is the pathway of free will not connected to all of this?

Q: (L) God! I hope so!

A: Now do you see the benefit in slowing down and not having prejudices when asking questions of great import? You see when you speed too quickly in the process of learning and gathering knowledge, it is like skipping down the road without pausing to reflect on the ground beneath you. One misses the gold coins and the gemstones contained within the cracks in the road.

Q: (L) OK, when this experience occurred, am I to assume that some part of myself, a future self perhaps, of course they are all simultaneous but just for the sake of reference, came back and interacted with my present self for some purpose of exchange? That somehow I made a choice and this has changed the future?

A: Well this is a question best left for your own exploration as you will gain more knowledge by contemplating it by yourself rather than seeking the answers here. But a suggestion is to be made that you do that as you will gain much, very much knowledge by contemplating these very questions on your own and networking with others as you do so. Be not frustrated for the answers to be gained through your own contemplation will be truly illuminating to you and the experience to follow will be worth a thousand lifetimes of pleasure and joy.

And indeed, it seems that this was a prediction that came true.

chapter nine
the 94% solution

At the time of the very first contact with the Cassiopaeans, some very disturbing remarks were made that upset all of us tremendously. The first thing that was mentioned was a series of prophecies:

A: Tornadoes/Florida—several. Also Texas and Alabama.

Q: (L) When?

A: When the Sun is in Libra. [But no year was given. However, the sun is in Libra from late September through most of October.]

Q: (L) What else is going to happen?

A: Seattle buried; Japan buckles; Missouri shakes; California Crumbles; Arizona burns.

Q: (L) When is all this going to happen?

A: Denver Airport Scandal.

This reply is strange in response to a question about timing. It seems that the above prophecies are linked to something that involves the Denver Airport. When this information was given in 1994, the Denver Airport was under construction. Since that time, there has been some information put about on the internet regarding certain murals in this airport and its possible use as a "staging area" for some sort of "takeover" of the human population. But, as noted, at the time this information was given, there was no indication of such, so it was extremely puzzling.

Q: (L) What about a Denver Airport Scandal?

A: New airport. Big, big, big, big scandal.

Q: (L) What kind of scandal?

A: Government.

Q: (L) Specifically what?

A: You will see. Dallas airport is secret base; Orlando too. Miami too.

Q: (L) What about Denver airport and how does it relate to prophecies?

A: Denver reveals the government. Look for it. Pay attention.

Q: (L) What else do you have to tell us?

A: Montana: Experiment with human reproduction. All people there are being exposed to harmful radon gas.

Q: (L) How are they doing this?

A: Compelled. Don't trust. Don't ignore. U.S. involved in sinister plot. Consortium.

Q: (L) Who are the members of the consortium?

A: Government and others. Aliens.

At this point I asked the question that had been burning in my mind after watching the now infamous Bob Lazar video exposing the activities at Area 51 and S-4. Lazar has claimed that, while working for Los Alamos National Laboratory in New Mexico, he was offered a job at S-4, fifteen miles south of Area 51. He claimed that alien craft were being worked on and stored at this facility, and that he read documents stating, among other things, that a group of aliens from the Zeta Reticuli star system gave humanity religion in order to preserve our physical bodies—the "containers".

Q: (L) Bob Lazar referred to the fact that aliens supposedly refer to humans as containers. What does this mean?

A: Storage for later use. 94 per cent of all population.

Q: (L) What do you mean?

A: All are containers; 94 per cent will be used.

Q: (L) Used for what?

A: Consumption.

Q: (L)What do you mean by "consumption?" You mean eaten?

A: Total consumption. Consumed for ingredients.

Q: (L) Ingredients for what?

A: New race. Important. 13 years approximately when project will be finished.

Q: (L) Why are humans consumed?

A: They are used for parts.

Q: (L) We don't understand. How can humans be used for parts?

A: Reprototype. The Vats exist. Missing persons often go there and especially missing children.

Q: (L) How can we protect ourselves and our children?

A: Inform them. Don't hide the truth from children.

Q: (L) How does truth protect us?

A: Awareness protects. Ignorance endangers.

Q: (L) Why tell children such horrible things?

A: They need to know.

Q: (L) What is the purpose of this project?

A: New life here. Each earth year 10 percent more children are taken and used for experiment and food. Bits of children's organs removed while they are wide awake. Kidneys first; then next feet; next jaw examined on table; tongues cut off; bones stress tested; pressure placed on heart muscle until it bursts. You must know what the consortium is doing. This is done mostly to Indian children.

Q: (L) Why are things like this being done?

A: There is a big effort on behalf of Orion Service To Self and their human brethren to create a new race and control it as well as the rest of humanity.

Q: (L) What happens to the souls? Is this project physical only?

A: Physical and souls recycled.

Q: (L) Where do the souls go?

A: Back here for the most part. Some go to other planets.

Q: (L) Why is this happening to earth?

A: Karma. Atlantis.

Q: (L) What did the Atlanteans do to bring this on us?

A: Worshipped and served self to extreme.

Q: (L) What can protect us?

A: Knowledge.

Q: (L) How do we get this knowledge?

A: You are being given it through this source now.

Q: (L) What knowledge do you mean?

A: You have it locked up within. We can help to prepare the way to unlock.

Q: (L) How does the knowledge of what you have told us help us?

A: Just knowing about it gives psychic defense.

Q: (L) How do we tell people? And who do we tell?

A: Inform others indirectly only.

Q: How.

A: Write. Awareness protects. Ignorance endangers.

This idea of aliens eating humans, either in terms of their energies or their flesh, is very disturbing and causes violent reactions in most people, as it did with Carlos Castaneda when don Juan informed him that it was so. I have returned to these issues for the final parts of this section so that only those who are truly determined to learn will have progressed to this point. Those who are here and reading this, very likely wish to truly know.

Q: You once said something about diet in relation to "tracking of bloodlines". The question was in the context of the dietary restrictions of the Jews. Do these dietary restrictions make it easier to track the Jews? Can fouth density track their genetics because of their dietary restrictions?

A: Foolishness!! 4th density beings have no difficulty identifying anyone on 3rd density. Dietary restrictions you speak of are relating to making the body chemistry less attractive for consumption.

Q: You mean consumption as in being eaten?

A: Yes.

Q: So, maybe we should all eat like Jews?

A: Maybe.

Q: Do you mean that fourth density STS likes particularly to eat Aryans?

A: Only the reptilian types.

Q: But, they don't like to eat Jews, is that it?

A: They most prefer children with high body fat content.

Q: What do the Orion humanoids eat?

A: Crystalline tablets, which are aspirated through oral demolecularization.

Q: Are these crystalline tablets like rocks, like our idea of crystals?

A: Picture a sparkling polished oval bead.

Q: What is the chemical composition?

A: Quartz at the 3rd power compared to Terran samples.

On many occasions, various persons have come to the sessions with the intention of getting the Cassiopaeans to "confirm" this or that rumor that is currently being passed around.

A: Beware of disinformation. It diverts your attention away from reality thus leaving you open to capture and conquest and even possible destruction. Disinformation comes from seemingly reliable sources. It is extremely important for you to not gather false knowledge as it is more damaging than no knowledge at all. Remember knowledge protects, ignorance endangers. The information you speak of, T, was given to you deliberately because you and J and others have been targeted due to your intense interest in level of density 4 through 7 subject matter. You have already been documented as a "threat".

A lot of people want the Cassiopaeans to teach them rituals that they can perform to protect them from the aliens, demons or just negative energies:

Q: (L) Do any of the rituals we perform provide protection against further abduction?

A: Maybe some Crystals with energy fields. Don't need protection if you have knowledge.

Q: OK, next question: Is it possible to create resistance to abduction by generating sound? Like an internal sound? This article I was reading said that different people used several techniques where they think it has helped them to halt or avoid abduction by "aliens". One is to generate an "internal" sound, a high-pitched "thought hum", and another is to invoke angelic spirits such as the Archangel Michael, and another is to "Just Say No", and these people think they have avoided being abducted thereby. Are any of these usable techniques?

A: Potpourri.

Q: (T) Sweet smelling dried flowers are potpourri.

A: Sage, salt, ooohm, any other rituals you like?

Q: (L) In other words, nothing works? (T) It's not going to stop them! I keep a heavy shield around the house and all that stuff and they still get through!

A: How about the hula hoop dance with green peppers stuck up your nose! [Hilarious laughter.] Perhaps one can solve the crises by focusing on other issues? You see, when you constrict the flow, you constrict the channel. And when you constrict the channel, you close down possibilities. And, you make it difficult, if not impossible for you to see that which is there. In other words, the obvious becomes oblivious because of constriction of the flow. This is why we have recommended against all rituals, because ritual restricts the flow, thereby restricting the possibilities. And, what you are describing is a situation of "dire straits", as you call it, and pressures of great magnitude which is restricting you. But actually, it is your concentration on same that is restricting, not the situation itself. And we realize that it is difficult for you to focus your attentions, or, more importantly to open up the flow of the channel. But, it is certainly not impossible.

Especially for an individual as strong as yourself. It is what you choose to do, not what you MUST do. It is what you CHOOSE to do.

If one believes in one's activities sincerely, to the greatest extent, they certainly will produce SOME benefit, at SOME level. But, merely following patterns for the sake of following patterns, does not produce sincerity and faith necessary for ultimate benefits to result. So, therefore, as always, one must search from within, rather than from without, to answer that question. Do you understand? To give you an example, to be certain, you meet this all the time. If you read material in the pages of a book that advises one form of ritual or another, and you follow that form of ritual because you have read words printed on the pages, does that really give you the true sense of satisfaction and accomplishment within yourself to the greatest extent possible? Whereas, if you, yourself, were to develop an activity which one or another could interpret or define as a ritual, but it comes from within you, it feels RIGHT to you, and you have a sincere and complete faith in it, whatever it may be, does that feel right to you?

Q: (L) Yes.

Q: (L) According to shamanistic teachings, one can have animal spirits or guides. Is this correct?

A: Partly. You have them if you believe you have them.

Q: (L) If believing in them makes it so, is this belief beneficial?

A: All belief is beneficial at some level.

Q: (L) Did Jesus of Nazareth believe in animal spirits or totems?

A: No.

Q: (L) Is it just New Age revival of superstition?

A: Shamanism is subjective and limits. Lizard inspired.

Q: (L) Are there any rituals that can be performed to provide protection for one against intrusion by the Lizzies.

A: Rituals are self-defeating.

Q: (L) Are there any technological means we can use?

A: The only defense needed is knowledge. Knowledge defends you against every possible form of harm in existence. The more knowledge you have, the less fear you have, the less pain you have, the less stress you feel, the less anguish you feel, and the less danger you experience of any form or sort. Think of this very carefully now for this is very important: Where is there any limitation in the concept behind the word "knowledge"? Being that there is no limitation, what is the value of that word? Infinite. Can you conceive of how that one concept, that one meaning frees you from all limitation? Use your sixth sense to conceive of how the word, the term, the meaning of knowledge can provide with all that you could possibly ever need. If you think carefully you will begin to see glimpses of how this is true in its greatest possible form.

Q: (L) Does this include knowledge learned from books?

A: This includes all possible meanings of the concept of the word. Can you think of how it would be that simply with one term, this one word can carry so much meaning? We sense that you are not completely aware. You can have glimpses of illumination and illumination comes from knowledge. If you strive perpetually to gain and gather knowledge, you provide yourself with protection from every possible negative occurrence that could ever happen. Do you know why this is? The more knowledge you have, the more awareness you have as to how to protect yourself. Eventually this awareness becomes so powerful and so all encompassing that you do not even have to perform tasks or rituals, if you prefer, to protect yourself. The protection simply comes naturally with the awareness.

Q: (L) Does knowledge have a substance or an existence apart from its possession or its acceptance?

A: Knowledge has all substance. It goes to the core of all existence.

Q: (L) So acquiring knowledge includes adding substance to one's being?

A: Indeed. It includes adding everything to one's being that is desirable. And also, when you keep invoking the light, as you do, truly understand that the light is knowledge. That is the knowledge which is at the core of all existence. And being at the core of all existence it provides protection from every form of negativity in existence. Light is everything and everything is knowledge and knowledge is everything. You are doing extremely well in acquiring of knowledge. Now all you need is the faith and realization that acquiring of knowledge is all you need.

Q: (L) I just want to be sure that the source that I am acquiring the knowledge from is not a deceptive source.

A: If you simply have faith, no knowledge that you could possibly acquire could possibly be false because there is no such thing. Anyone or anything that tries to give you false knowledge, false information, will fail. The very material substance that the knowledge takes on, since it is at the root of all existence, will protect you from absorption of false information which is not knowledge. There is no need to fear the absorption of false information when you are simply openly seeking to acquire knowledge. And knowledge forms the protection -- all the protection you could ever need.

Q: (L) There are an awful lot of people who are being open and trusting and having faith who are getting zapped and knocked on their rears.

A: No. That is simply your perception. What you are failing to perceive is that these people are not really gathering knowledge. These people are stuck at some point in their pathway to progress and they are undergoing a hidden manifestation of what is referred to in your terms as obsession. Obsession is not knowledge, obsession is stagnation. So, when one becomes obsessed, one actually closes off the absorption and the growth and the progress of soul development which comes with the gaining of true knowledge. For when one becomes obsessed one deteriorates the protection therefore one is open to problems, to tragedies, to all sorts of difficulties. Therefore one experiences same.

Q: (L) Back in 1981 and 1982, my daughter A__ frequently saw something outside her window that she described as an alligator, and she would wake up screaming and we would get up and, on one occasion we saw what seemed to be a figure standing in a corner by the closet. The whole series of events ended up with my having a dream in which I confronted a dragon...

A: Lizard.

Q: (L) What were they doing at that time?

A: Scoping.

Q: (L) What did they discover from their scoping?

A: Potential abductees.

Q: (L) And did they abduct anyone at that time?

A: No.

Q: (L) Why didn't they?

A: You stopped it.

Q: (L) How did I stop it?

A: Knowledge is rooted in awareness.

Q: (L) So, my awareness is what stopped it?

A: Close.

Q: (L) When I had the dream about doing battle with the dragon, was that just a dream, an astral event, or an actual interaction with the Lizzies?

A: All three.

Q: (L) You have told us, that the more knowledge we actually accumulate, it actually changes our frequency and adds volume and bulk and power and force to who and what we are, at a fundamental level. Not physically, but psychically. I mean, what does it say in the Bible? "My people perish for a lack of knowledge..." and it says, "you shall know the truth, and the truth shall set you free". And the more knowledge you have, the bigger you are, in a cosmic and psychic sense, the more powerful you are, and...

A: Suggest more questions about the goings on at underground facilities. J and T were visitors involuntary when went to Albuquerque and Las Vegas!

Q: (L) You were in an underground base? (T) We were in a front door of an underground base. We were in Carlsbad Caverns, and I know that there's a government facility at the other end of it, and they won't talk about it. (J) Is that what they mean? (T) You're talking about Carlsbad?

A: Abducted.

Q: (T) When we were in Albuquerque?

A: Yes.

Q: (T) When we were in Las Vegas, also?

A: Met alien there. Barfly.

Q: (T) Ohhhhh... I know exactly what you are talking about.

A: Disguised humanoid gray species four. Rigelian. Orion union STS.

Q: (T) Why did he talk to us? Why did he approach us? I know exactly...

A: Spying on you and aural frequency reading, had you not been as strong, would have suffered permanent abduction because of your studies.

Q: (L) What is there about strength that makes one inaccessible to permanent abduction?

A: Strength is of character, i.e. if STO candidate, not likely to be victim.

Q: (L) OK, but what is the thing inside one that stops them... I mean, is this something that is a core ingredient of certain human beings? Is this like something inside them that blocks this manipulation and victimization?

A: Soul pattern.

Q: (L) So in other words, there is something about us, or within us, that literally they cannot touch or harm, is that correct?

A: Basically, but difficult to facilitate.

Q: (L) OK, in other words, this is something that is in us, that creates an inherent barrier, but not necessarily something that we can, at this level of density, reach in, grab out as a weapon, and wave around, as in facilitate?

A: Can, but intricate to do consciously.

Q: (L) OK, so, in other words, difficult to do consciously. Is this some quality or ability that we can work at? I don't think meditation is the answer, this is a state of focused awareness, whole body awareness, internal and external, basically whole body awareness...

A: Helpful.

Q: (L) That's helpful. Is there something we can do to develop this to the highest degree possible, while in these bodies, in this density?

A: Wait for 4th density.

Q: (T) It's an involuntary thing, it's there, it works when it needs to work. Is this the idea?

A: Network western experiences for learning purposes please. Knowledge is protection.

Briefly, T related the story where he and J met the barfly at Vegas World, after having gone downtown to get their marriage license. They had taken a taxi to City Hall, and foolishly decided to walk back to the Strip, in 116 degree weather. They made it as far south as Vegas World, and stopped at the bar inside to cool off. J was close to heat prostration, and the barmaid gave her glasses of iced water and an iced towel to put on her neck. They were getting ready to go back out and hail a cab back to Bally's, when they were approached by the "Barfly", who started asking all sorts of personal questions, and seemed to be acting drunk when he wasn't really intoxicated. He became belligerent when T refused to show him his Florida driver's license, but switched to disorientation when T made the statement "We don't have a problem here, do we?!" while staring the guy down and putting the force of his personality behind the question/statement.

Q: (L) In this story that T has just recounted, what instant represents the turning point of resistance?

A: The statement.

Q: (T) When I said "We don't have a problem, here, do we?! Everything's cool, everything's OK! I'll buy you a beer?" and stared the guy down?

A: Yes.

Q: (T) Because that's when he got confused... He was escalating this to a point, and I don't know, it just came to me that the best way to do this was to just stop it right there...

A: Grays and their associates are thrown off by energy flow diversions or thought pattern interruptions.

Q: (L) I do have an idea about that. Is this what Michael Topper was writing about in his article, "Channels and the Positive/Negative Nature of Reality", where he talks about the "obedience factor" of the STS? If they can get you to obey something, no matter how insignificant it seems, you have given your permission and they have power over you?

A: Yes.

Q: (L) Back in the 1970s in the Central United States there were quite a number of cases of animal mutilation. There has been a lot of publicity about this at some point and then it died down and was covered up, and there were a lot of ideas and theories about it. What I would like to know is who was doing the animal mutilations?

A: Many.

Q: Was some of the animal mutilation done by the U.S Government, or entities within the government?

A: Was?

Q: (L) In other words, it is still going on. Was, or is, some of this activity being conducted by alien individuals?

A: Yes.

Q: (T) Were they acting for the same reasons?

A: No.

Q: Why did the government do animal mutilations?

A: Copy, in order to throw off investigation.

Q: (L) Did they do this as an act to protect the aliens who were doing animal mutilations for their own purposes?

A: No. They do it to protect the public from knowing that which would explode society if discovered.

Q: (L) What is this item that they were protecting so that society or the public wouldn't know about it. What activity is this?

A: Humans eat cattle, aliens eat you.

Q: What do aliens do to cattle?

A: Blood.

Q: (J) What do they use this blood for?

A: Nourishment.

Q: (L) OK, but you just said that aliens eat humans, and humans eat cattle. Why were the aliens being nourished by cattle, if that's not their normal bill of fare? (T) A cow's blood is a lot like human blood.

A: Do you not ever consume facsimile? Facsimile is less controversial, obviously!

Q: (L) So in other words, they were eating cattle just to keep from having to eat so many humans, that would have just upset people a lot, is that it?

A: Yes. Some of their human "food" is merely emotions, think of flesh as being the equal of "filet mignon".

Q: (T) Some of their food is merely emotions. OK, when we're talking about these aliens, are we talking about the Grays?

A: No.

Q: (T) We're talking about the Lizards.

A: Yes.

Q: (T) OK, what do the Grays feed on?

A: Plasma.

Q: (T) OK, so that's why they want the blood; so, do the Grays feed on emotions?

A: They send them to Lizards. Transfer energy through technology.

Q: (T) Are the cattle giving off enough emotion for the Grays to feed this to the Lizards also?

A: No. That is physical only, you see, Lizards and Grays only need physical nourishment while "visiting" 3rd level, not when in natural realm, 4th density, there they feed on emotions only.

Q: (T) Grays are not strictly third density? Because they've been created by the Lizzies?

A: Yes. Correct, they too are 4th level.

Q: (L) What technology do they use to surgically excise certain areas of the cattle's anatomy, is this done by laser...

A: Laser-like.

Q: (L) OK, since it has been noted that quite frequently the cattle mutilations consist of taking very specific parts of the body, such as the eyeballs, the genitalia; they core out the anal sphincter right up to the colon; what would be the purpose for these specific body parts? I mean, do they core out the rectum and put a pump on there and suck all the blood out, I mean...

A: Close.

Q: (L) OK, I think we kind of have an answer to this one, but there have been very frequently associated with the phenomenon of cattle mutilations, sightings of black, unmarked helicopters, who or what are these helicopters?

A: Variable.

Q: (L) Are some of these helicopters disguised alien craft? Are some of these helicopters the property of the U.S. Government?

A: Yes to both.

Q: (T) Are some of these helicopters private enterprise?

A: Yes. All are interconnected. Some too, are projections, this phenomenon is multifaceted.

Q: (L) OK, that's good enough. Who are the oriental-appearing personnel that have been seen manning the helicopters and the white vans that have been sighted all over the country?

A: MIB. And government copycats.

Q: (L) How many alien craft, actual alien craft, are in the hands of the government or this consortium?

A: 36.

Q: (L) And were these captured craft? Or gifted?

A: And recovered.

Q: (T) Ok, they were all three. Were any of them purchased?

A: Not correct concept, Grays are not financial.

Q: (T) I didn't mean by money, I meant purchased as in some kind of a trade. Were the gift ones not what we would really consider gifts, but they were given to us in return for something else, some other kind of payment? Barter?

A: No. Because all sought return favors were already achieved.

Q: (L) So it was all just a farce. They weren't payment, they weren't gifts, they were distractions?

A: Closer.

Q: (T) OK, so there's a lot of different categories of how these ships got into the hands of the federal government?

A: Yes. Multidimensional.

Q: (L) Who is O. H. Krill?

A: No one.

Q: (L) Is O. H. Krill a group?

A: Symbolism.

Q: (L) Symbolism of what? What does O. H. Krill translate out to?

A: For documentary purposes only, your government likes code names.

Q: (L) Give us a percentage of factual information in this document.

A: 43%

Q: (L) OK, and this has been planted by the government. Was it put out with the intention of giving out some factual information...

A: No. Planted? No. Your government is operating on many cross-purposes, very complicated!

Q: (T) Even the simplest things are very complicated with them. OK, question: The U.S. government...

A: On purpose!

Q: (T) Very true. Question: The government, our government, the U.S. government, is holding 36 craft of one kind or another that they gotten in one way or another. How many other governments have craft?

A: All is one.

Q: (L) We already have a one-world government is what they're saying. (T) Yes, they're just waiting to make it official somehow.

A: Has been so for long time, as you measure time.

Q: (L) What is the " ultimate secret" being protected by the Consortium?

A: You are not in control of yourselves, you are an experiment.

Q: (T) When you say this is the ultimate secret, that we're being "protected" from by the government, are we talking about the ultimate secret of humans only here?

A: Basically.

Q: (T) The ultimate secret of the human race is that we are an experiment that other humans are conducting on the rest of us?

A: Part.

Q: (T) OK, does the other part have to do with the Lizards?

A: Yes.

Q: (L) Other aliens also?

A: Yes.

Q: (T) OK, so, are the humans who are running the experiment, do they know that they are part of the experiment also?

A: Yes.

Q: (T) And they're doing this willingly?

A: They have no choice.

Q: (L) Why do they have no choice?

A: Already in progress.

Q: (L) Yes. OK. How "long", and I put long in quotes, because we know, as you say, there is no time, but how long, as we measure it, have the Grays been interacting with our race? The Grays, not the Lizards, the Grays, the cybergenetic probes?

A: Time travelers, therefore, "Time is ongoing". Do you understand the gravity of this response?

Q: (L) They are time travelers, they can move forward and backward in time, they can play games with our heads... (T) They can set up the past to create a future they want. (D) They can organize things so that they can create the energy that they need... (L) They can also make things look good, make them feel good, make them seem good, they can make you have an idea one minute, and then the next minute, create some sort of situation that confirms that idea...

A: When you asked how long, of course it is totally unlimited, is it not?

Q: (L) That's not good. If they were to move back through space time and alter an event in our past, would that alteration in the past instantaneously alter our present as well?

A: Has over and over and over.

Q: (D) So they do it over and over and over, constantly?

A: You just are not yet aware, and have no idea of the ramifications!!!

Q: (L) We're getting a little glimmer! Yeah, I do, a little! (T) The ramifications of being able to move in and out of time and manipulate it the way you want. (J) And the ramifications of what they're doing to us; what they are doing to us and what they will do to us, over and over. (L) So, in other words, our only real prayer in this whole damn situation is to get out of this density level. That's what they're saying, that's what it sounds like to me.

A: Close.

Q: (L) Because, otherwise, we're just literally, as in that book, stuck in the replay over and over and over, and the Holocaust could happen over and over, and we could just, you know... Genghis Khan, Attila the Hun... over and over and over again. (T) We're stuck in a time loop; they're putting us in a time loop.

A: Yes.

Q: (D) I have a question about... there was a... (pause) Mankind has found it necessary for some reason or other to appoint time for some reason or other. The only reason I can see is to have a means of telling, like in verbal or written communications...

A: Time is a control mechanism.

Q: (T) Is there a way for us to break the control mechanism? Besides moving to fourth density?

A: Nope.

Q: (D) When fourth density beings communicate it's telepathic, right?

A: Yes.

Q: (D) OK, since time doesn't exist, how do you communicate about happenings? How do you communicate about events as one happens now, as opposed to later and the next thing happens, and the next thing happens... (J) How is it sequential?

A: Translate. That is how it is done. You translate the experience from 4th density to 3rd density and vice versa.

Q: (L) So, in other words, it's almost like making movies. (J) Are linear thought processes part of it?

A: Part of 3d illusion only.

Q: (L) So, in other words, if you're a fourth density being, everything is more or less happening, excuse the term happening, everything is simultaneous, and if you wish to discuss or communicate or have any focus upon any particular aspect of this unified dimension, then what you do is you kind of extract it out, project it into 3D... like a movie.

A: Close. But you will not understand fully until you get there.

Q: (T) OK, so it's a concept that we can't completely grasp in 3D at this point.

A: Can a dog grasp algebra? You got it.

Q: (L) In other words, we're in bad shape! And these guys are playing games with us, so to speak...

A: Subjective.

Q: (L) Well, the situation we find ourselves in makes it seem that our only hope to end the suffering, to get out of this time loop, is to move into another density.

A: Yogis can do it.

The Wave series includes a historical analysis of the deception perpetrated upon mankind and proposes ideas as to how to literally "change our universe" to another probable reality. It isn't easy, but it can be done. We believe that this is the purpose of our contact with the Cassiopaeans—to strengthen, inform, educate and assist us with the gaining of the knowledge that will set us free!

chapter ten
the predator's mind

At this point, I suspect that the reader has been pretty overwhelmed with all this depressing information! But, that is neither the purpose nor the point. The purpose and point is to bring sufficient knowledge of man's true estate so that solutions can be found for dealing with same. As the Cassiopaeans once remarked to me when I protested that I did not *like* to hear "ugly" things:

A: We suppose if we told you "Laura, a great big rock is about to fall on your head", then you would say: "OK, now moving right along, about the Emerald tablets..."

Q: (Laura) OK. You have my undivided attention.

A: Great potential dangers lurk...

Q: (Laura) So this really is like the grail hunt. We have to go through a magic forest, chop heads off dragons, keep our eyes open and not be lead astray by deceptive images and tricks... the whole thing!

A: Where to get the influence for the inspiration behind that story? Danger awaits the greeting of each new day. Vigilance! Vigilance! Vigilance!!!!!

Q: (Laura) That is completely depressing. Help me out here!

A: Now... Calm down! No need for depression. Would you rather be left with a lack of knowledge, and in an ever increasing state of false security oriented oblivion, only to be struck by lightning?!? Of course not!!! So remember... Knowledge protects, ignorance endangers!! Think of it as a war. Expect every possible move/or occurrence. Victory comes from being forewarned, and therefore, forearmed.

Q: (Laura) Is that, as Frank said, the key? To turn up the vigilance volume to maximum?

A: Always. Don't be like the sentry who fell into a peaceful, pleasure filled, dreamy sleep while on watch! He did not even feel the blade as it pierced his heart!

Q: (Laura) Well, that is *not* friendly. Now I really *am* depressed! Tell me: is what we are doing so important that this kind of energy has to be concentrated on us?

A: Yes. Look at it this way: make it your goal to succeed, then you have not to fear. People must be made aware that dangers lurk everywhere, potentially. Those who have falsely implanted faith in this or that; those who have spent a lifetime building a strong sense of security, based upon anything outside of them, should understand that these ideas have been propagated for the very purpose of making one vulnerable. But now is the "time" to learn that this is not enough. Just remember: there are forces "out there" that wish to see your project, and you, fail. You two have both previously felt the sting of these forces acutely. Anyone and everyone could be a portal of attack. Remember, they work through persons, they are not normally the persons themselves. Knowledge protects!

So, we have some pretty strong warnings. But, did you catch the part about the "Grail Quest"? That is a powerful clue! Remember what don Juan said:

"We have a predator that came from the depths of the cosmos and took over the rule of our lives. Human beings are its prisoners. ... It has rendered us docile, helpless. If we want to protest, it suppresses our protest. If we want to act independently, it demands that we don't do so. ... They took us over because we are food for them, and they squeeze us mercilessly because we are their sustenance. ... Sorcerers believe that the predators have given us our [stupid and contradictory] systems of beliefs, our ideas of good and evil, our social mores. They are the ones who set up our hopes and expectations and dreams of success or failure. They have given us covetousness, greed, and cowardice. It is the predators who make us complacent, routinary and egomaniacal. ... In order to keep us obedient and meek and weak, the predators engaged themselves in a stupendous maneuver—stupendous of course, from the point of view of a fighting strategist. A horrendous maneuver from the point of view of those who suffer it. They gave us their mind! Do you hear me?! The predators give us their mind, which becomes our mind. The predators' mind is baroque, contradictory, morose, filled with the fear of being discovered any minute now." (Castaneda, 1998, 218-220)

What have the Cassiopaeans said about these very things?

Q: (L) The Sumerian story of the creation of human beings involves a story where they say they killed a god and mixed his blood and parts to mix with mud and then planted it in these female "gestation" goddesses and that this is where the human race came from. Did someone actually kill a "god", break his soul in pieces, and thereby make the human race?
A: Symbolism and not correct event sequence.
Q: (L) What was that story about? What was the real seed event?
A: Lizard beings genetically altering the human race after battle for their own feeding purposes.
Q: (L) When did these events that these Sumerian stories are talking about take place?
A: 309000 years ago, approx. Reflection passed down through psychic memory channel.

Jeremy Narby writes in *The Cosmic Serpent:*

As I browsed over the writings of authorities on mythology, I discovered with surprise that the theme of twin creator beings of celestial origin was extremely common in South America, and indeed throughout the world. ... I wondered what all these twin beings in the creation myths of indigenous people could possibly mean. ... Ruminating over this mental block I recalled Carlos Perez Shuma's words: "look at the *form.*"

215

chapter ten

That morning, at the library, I had looked up DNA in several encyclopedias and had noted in passing that the shape of the double helix was most often described as a ladder, or twisted rope ladder, or a spiral staircase. It was during the following split second, asking myself whether there were any ladders in shamanism, that the revelation occurred: "THE LADDERS! The shamans' ladders, symbols of the profession, according to Metraux, present in shamanic themes around the world according to Eliade!"

[In] Mircea Elieade's book *Shamanism: Archaic Techniques of ecstasy*, [I] discovered that there were "countless examples" of shamanic ladders on all five continents, [and that] "the symbolism of the rope, like that of the ladder, necessarily implies communication between sky and earth. It is by means of a rope of ladder... that the gods descend to earth and men go up to the sky." ... According to Eliade, the shamanic ladder is the earliest version of the idea of an axis of the world, which *connects the different levels of the cosmos,* and is found in numerous creation myths in the form of a tree. ... Campbell writes about this omnipresent snake symbolism: "throughout the material in the Primitive, Oriental and Occidental volumes of this work, myths and rites of the serpent frequently appear, and in a remarkably consistent symbolic sense. Wherever nature is revered as self-moving, and so inherently divine, the serpent is revered as symbolic of its divine life." ... "Thus the visible snake appears as merely the brief incarnation of the vital principle and of all the forces of nature. It is a primary OLD GOD found at the beginning of all cosmogonies, before monotheism and reason toppled it." (Narby, 1999)

But Joseph Campbell goes on to talk about an "inversion"—a "twist" in the world mythology of the cosmic serpent/tree/ladder. The first twist is that the serpent, formerly the offspring of the Earth Goddess, and her symbol, becomes the symbol of the male consort of the Goddess. The second twist is when the Male god becomes the slayer of the serpent.

So, in the beginning, we have the serpent, representing the amorphous, undifferentiated female creative potential, and then we have a story that tells us that "something" happened to this "serpent/tree/ladder". Could this have been the "adulteration" of human DNA—the acquisition of the "predator's mind"—as described by the Cassiopaeans?

All living species on earth are made up of exactly the same 20 amino acids. The average protein is a long chain made up of approximately 200 amino acids, chosen from those 20, and strung together in the right order. According to the laws of combinatorials, there is 1 chance in 20 multiplied by itself 200 times for a single specific protein to emerge fortuitously. This figure is greater than the number of atoms in the observable universe!

Francis Crick, co-discoverer of the DNA molecule, writes that the organized complexity found at the cellular level "cannot have arisen by pure chance". Life is based on the "DNA alphabet" that has not changed a letter in four billion years while, at the same time, multiplying in an extraordinary number and variety of species.

It would be impossible to give here all the examples of the double serpents of cosmic origin associated with the creation of life on earth. For more on this subject, refer to the books mentioned.

216

Suffice it to say: all the cells in the world contain DNA—be they animal, vegetable, or bacterial—and they are all filled with salt water—the cosmic ocean in which the "serpent" is coiled. They associate in pairs to form the rungs of a ladder, and they twist into a spiraled stack. One of the two strands is a back-to-front duplicate of the other and the genetic text is "doubled". It contains a main text on one of the ribbons which is read in a precise direction by the transcription enzymes, and a backup text which is inverted and most often not read. But, the backup text allows repair enzymes to reconstruct the main text in case of damage and, above all, provides the mechanism for the duplication of the genetic message.

Twins, therefore, are essential to life, just as the myths tell us, and they *are* associated with a serpentine form.

In the earliest myths, the "twins" were Adam and Eve, or Vishnu and Lakshmi, or whoever. In later myths, the twins become two men who battle continuously over an adulterous woman. This is another symbol of an adulteration of human DNA by some "twist" in the order of things.

> Q: (L) You said that time was an illusion that came into being at the "time" of the "Fall" in Eden, and this was said in such a way that I inferred that there are other illusions put into place at that time...
>
> A: Time is an illusion that works for you because of your altered DNA state.
>
> Q: (L) OK, what other illusions?
>
> A: Monotheism, the belief in one separate, all powerful entity.
>
> Q: (L) What is another one of the illusions?
>
> A: The need for physical aggrandizement.
>
> Q: (L) What is another of the illusions?
>
> A: Linear focus. Unidimensionality.

So, it seems that we are "programmed to believe", exactly as don Juan has remarked. And this is a curious thing. Our current state—our inherited drives and tendencies to perceive things in a certain way—is entirely intentional.

> Collective Identity, which is a result of a covenant of Monotheism, is explicitly narrated in the Bible as an invention, a radical break with Nature. A transcendent deity breaks into history with the demand that the people he constitutes obey the law he institutes, and first and foremost among those laws is, of course, that *they pledge allegiance to him, and him alone,* and that *this is what makes them a unified people* as opposed to the "other", as in all other people which then leads to violence. In the Old Testament, vast numbers of "other" people are obliterated, while in the New Testament, vast numbers are colonized (or annihilated) and converted for the sake of such covenants. (Schwartz, 1997, emphasis added)

Where did this idea come from? In his book *The Mythic Past,* Thomas Thompson, professor of Old Testament, University of Copenhagen, provides an excellent analysis of the creation of an invented past—biblical Israel—and its theology, that was accomplished long ago, for purposes of *forging a national identity among refugees.* However, at the time it was originally done, the target

217

audience understood that it was not a real "history," but rather an ideological textbook for the future. The real problems began when another group, some time later, decided to use the same stories (handily already available), for their own imperial ambitions and presented this ideological literature as History. Thompson writes:

> The early history of Palestine is a story of farmers and shepherds; of villages and markets. It is about local patrons and their clients and all the early ways of life that have lasted so long in this corner of the Mediterranean. The history of a richly varied people over an extended period of time...
>
> Our study of the roots and beginnings of historical developments also focuses on the people who wrote the Bible. How are Palestine's historical peoples related to those who created literary Israel? This is not an idle question. The new history of Palestine's peoples and their distant beginnings stems almost entirely from archaeological and linguistic research undertaken over the past fifty years. It presents a picture so radically unfamiliar, and so very different from a biblical view as to be hardly recognizable to the writers of the Bible, so thoroughly has our understanding of the past been forced to change.
>
> There is no Adam or Eve in this story, nor a Noah, Abraham and Sarah. And there is no place for them. Not even Moses and Joshua have roles in this history about the people who formed the Bible and its world. ...
>
> The conflict surrounding the Bible and history—one that has played a considerable role in Western thought since Napoleon occupied Egypt at the end of the eighteenth century—is essentially a false controversy. It has occurred only because our commitment to myths of origin as part of an historically based modern world has caused us to interpret the biblical perspective as historical, until faced with definitive proof to the contrary. We should not be trying to salvage our origin myths as history. That hides their meaning from us, and ignores the *strong anti-intellectual strain of fundamentalism* that underlies so many of the historical interests invested in biblical archaeology. ...
>
> Scholars have traditionally talked about the political structures of Bronze Age Palestine as an 'interlocking system of city-states'. Such terminology is as harmful as it is undiscriminating. Palestine at this early period had no cities, aside from Hazor of the very distant north. It has only villages and small towns. The population of the largest was only a very few thousands at best. ... To speak of 'state' structures among such towns confuses Bronze Age Palestine with Renaissance Italy! ... Palestine, *until the Assyrian period*, was a land of stable, autonomous towns ruled by their 'princes' and chiefs. ... Could any town or coalition of towns have engaged in the kind of political struggle, in the kind of financial and military build-up necessary to successfully field an army sufficient to [do anything of significance]? The prospect is unlikely. The archaeological evidence for the military and political structures of Palestine's many towns and regions stands wholly against it. ... It also stands against historical ideas of a Solomonic empire. ...
>
> [W]hen one investigates the history of Palestine independently of the biblical view of the past, this period *betrays little evidence of biblical Israel's emergence.* ... There is no evidence of a United Monarchy, no evidence of a capital in Jerusalem or of any coherent, unified political force that dominated western Palestine, let alone an empire of the size the legends describe. We do not have evidence for the existence of kings named Saul, David or Solomon; nor do we

have evidence for any temple at Jerusalem in the early period. What we do know of Israel and Judah of the tenth century does not allow us to interpret this lack of evidence as a gap in our knowledge and information about the past, as a result merely of the accidental nature of archaeology. There is neither room nor context, no artifact or archive that points to such historical realities in Palestine's tenth century. *One cannot speak historically of a state without a population. Nor can one speak of a capital without a town.*

An historical state of Israel came into existence and was sustained by the development of an olive industry built with a newly developed and expanded system of terracing in the course of the ninth century BC. This small state was comparable to other states of Palestine such as Ammon, Moab and Edom. It was organized around the settlements in the hill country between Jerusalem and the Jezreel valley... The immediate origins of this population rested in the settlement of the displaced part of the population that had abandoned the lowlands in the wake of the Mycenaean drought... (Thompson, 1999)

It was the basis of its formation—growth of an olive industry that was seen as a financial bonanza—that pretty much brought the nascent "statehood" of Israel to an end. There was money to be made from the olive industry and that almost immediately attracted the interest of the Assyrians who basically came in and took over, defeating each local "patron" or kinglet, one after the other. At this point, we learn something very interesting from Thompson. Tiglath Pileser III, king of Assyria, began a process of subsuming Syrian and Palestinian agriculture to Assyrian interests. Further, the Assyrian king reports (epigraphic evidence exists for this) that he deported people from Israel and replaced its king, Peqah, with a king of his own choice, Hoshea. As an Assyrian vassal, and from the capital of Samaria, Hoshea, *under Assyrian patronage,* gained control over the Jezreel valley. This control lasted for less than a decade. That's pretty much the extent of the "kingdom of Israel."

Now, here's the key item: The Assyrian army introduced the policy of *population transference* which involved transporting peoples across the Assyrian empire. The reason for these deportation were simply imperialistic. People were not necessarily deported because of insurrection, but rather to preemptively eliminate rivals for power. The Assyrians resettled many groups of deportees in Assyrian cities and trouble spots elsewhere. In this way, the imperial government could establish groups within the subject population who were entirely dependent upon the imperial authority.

Sometimes whole villages were deported from conquered territories and used to restore and rebuild cities elsewhere. They repopulated abandoned and empty lands and fractured any "ethnic coherence" that might have produced resistance from the local population. Throughout its existence, this seems to have been a standard policy and technique of the Assyrian empire and *was adopted by other empires that followed.* The Assyrian ideology of "democratic equality" within the provinces was propagandized as a main benefit of being subsumed to the empire. Thompson writes:

Taking rulers and upper classes captive and deporting them to regions in the heart of the empire was useful. It punished rebels and got rid of potential troublemakers. It enabled the governors of new territories to create terror through hostage-taking. It complicated any local successor's claim to legitimacy. At the same time, it put the administration of regions into the hands of local interests who were dependent on the empire for their survival and acceptance. Population resettlement did much more than handle the pacification of newly acquired territories. Undermining the local patrons basic to the political structures of the region, it recreated them as dependencies of Assyria's patronage.

The population resettlement programme was backed by *extensive political propaganda*. The conquerors of new territories couch surrender in terms of "liberation", and "salvation" from former oppressive rulers. Deportation is described as a "reward" for populations who rebelled against their leaders. The people are always "restored to their homelands". Such returns involve the "restoration" of "lost" and "forgotten" gods, following long periods of exile. ...

Resettled in the great cities of the empire, or in villages and towns of foreign territories, with their survival dependent on their future support of imperial goals, [the deportees] allegiance to the state was assured. Grateful for the freedom and equality in their new homes, they served as a countervalent force against any local opposition...

Some early texts present the Assyrian king as the savior of the people, who, after freeing them from enslavement forced upon them by their rulers, returned them and their gods to the homelands from which they had been exiled. Here, the dislocated peoples were *encouraged to think of themselves in terms of restoration* rather than punitive deportation; *as saved from exile by the will of the king.* They became *returnees to their homelands, reunited with their lost and forgotten gods....*

The deportees received land and a renewal of prosperity from the Assyrians upon resettlement, they were given support and protection against the indigenous population, who naturally viewed them as intruders and usurpers. ... The ultimate purpose was to wipe out regional and national distinctions and create an imperial citizenry...

Under the rule of the Persian kings, a number of groups and families were transferred from Mesopotamia and resettled in southern Palestine. A new colony was established in and around Jerusalem. Those resettled were accompanied by traditional political propaganda.

I hope that the implication of the above is not lost on the reader. Just *who* "returned to Israel" from "exile in Babylon" under the protection of the Persian king?

After dealing with the history and archaeology of the region, Thompson turns his attention to the literary world of the writers of the bible. The subtext of this section leads us straight into the bible's theological world. Essentially, what Thompson is doing is tracking the ideology, what Georges Dumezil referred to as the "line of force". When we have taken a particular text apart and have ascertained, as much as possible from what is exposed to us, the approximate legitimacy of each element, there still remains another question that actually constitutes the essence of the matter: What are the main trends of the whole? What are the lines of force running through the ideological field in which the details are placed? This is often where subjective belief enters the picture, acting as the lens through which we view our past and present, and the scale by which we judge the merits of fact vs. faith.

That takes us back to what Nachman Ben-Yehuda wrote, "As scientists we must affirm that there are versions of reality which are inconsistent with, even contradictory to, 'facts'. The realities which these false versions create are synthetic and misleading."

Thompson's assessment of the theological reality of Judaism is shocking. He takes the reader there in his circuitous and avuncular manner, building layer upon layer of revelation that, once he points it out to you, you wonder why you didn't see it yourself long ago! In the end, you realize that there is something very dark and disturbing about Judaism, formulated as it was, upon the model of Assyrian imperialism transferred to the "heavenly realms".

The narratives of the Bible, (and the New Testament is only a continuation of the same literary tradition), focus on "faithfulness and loyalty" to the patron, the imperial master. Total acceptance of one's fate is what is counted as "righteous" and wise. It is in this context that the "son of god"—representative of the Imperial master—figures. There are quite a few "sons of god" in the Bible, as it happens, and the definition of such is one who accepts whatever fate God has decreed, and does whatever God tells him to do, no matter how evil it may seem in the eyes of others and even his own eyes. In fact, if he is really a good "son of god," nothing that god tells him to do will seem evil whether it is annihilating every man, woman and child in an innocent town, or sacrificing one's own son. Thompson writes:

> That Mark quotes the song of David from Psalm 22:2-3 for Jesus' dying words calls up the similar scenes of David and Jesus in their despair on the Mount of Olives. The allusion seems intentional, as the larger context of the Psalm suggests and which Mark's Jesus echoes...
>
> We should also recall to mind the songs of the suffering servant in Isaiah 42-53 and the story of King Ahaz of Isaiah, 7. Both accept their destiny, refusing to question God. Also like David on the Mount of Lives, Jesus has not put God to the test. In his humility he has followed the path of righteousness. He has put his trust in God. He was scorned and despised by men. ...
>
> Jesus, as humble servant of the tradition, calls on God to be with him. At this scream, the curtain of the temple that closes off the Holy of Holies that separates God from man, tears in two, marking his death. God is with him!
>
> This nearly bitter, mocking irony of Mark's gospel finds its climax in the understanding of the Roman centurion as he hears this cry of despair and death. 'Truly this man was a son of God.' ... Behind the centurion's remark lies the hidden, dark side of biblical tradition: God abandons his children. It is Jesus' cry of despair that brings conviction above all doubt. In Mark's gospel, Jesus plays out his role of son of God. Like Israel his first-born, like Samson, Samuel and Saul, like the prophets Elijah and Jonah, and like Job in his role in this tradition, this role mediates and gives voice to the common human ambivalence about the divine in our lives. One enters the kingdom only in death.

chapter ten

Thompson then goes on to discuss what it really means to "be with God", and how the tradition slyly informs us that the real meaning is death and destruction! Repeatedly, throughout the texts, when "Yahweh, god of armies" comes, there is nothing but disaster—Armageddon.

> The days of Yahweh—when Yahweh will be with us—are days of destruction, days to be feared. The imagery calls up war and destruction as a response of divine wrath and judgment. The development of the metaphor of the 'day of Yahweh' as the day on which Yahweh will come and judge Israel draws its strength most directly from a view of the past that sees the destruction of Jerusalem and old Israel as well-deserved punishments sent by God.

Interestingly, it turns out that Yahweh himself is only a "son of god." One wonders, of course, if that is not just another name for Satan!

At one point, Thompson points out the most interesting paradox:

> The historicism implicit in the biblical theology movement of half a century ago is more modern than it is biblical. What is often referred to as history is not a history, but a tradition. It is interested neither in the past nor indeed in the future. Both are but reflections for reality, and, as such, other than reality. The most disorienting difficulty with such readings of the Bible is that they attempt to transpose a perspective of reality underlying biblical traditions into peculiarly modern terms. They permit reflection on our reality, but not reflection on what was real for the writers of the Bible. ... This fundamental assumption (and I would say arrogance) of biblical theology had at its core a belief in the inadequacy of the world-view of the ancients. At the same time, it is maintained that a blind faith in this same primitive world's religious perception could become a saving perception in our world.

Finally, the question that must be returned to is "whose history is it?"

> Writing is an exercise of influence and persuasion. This is just as true of history as of any other form of writing. ... History itself is created by its writers. ... As such, history belongs to those who do the writing.
> The capacity and vulnerability of a tradition for creative reinterpretation is not restricted much by a tradition's content, nor by how close it may be to the origins of the tradition in the past. It is almost entirely determined by the bearers of the tradition. A text such as those we find in the Bible is at the mercy of those who claim the tradition as their own and interpret is. ...
> When we ask about those who have transmitted the stories and have brought them through the centuries as meaningful, we can hardly avoid the conclusion that the history of Israel is for the most part, European. Whether Jewish or Christian, this history is a product of, and has been central to, Europe's self-understanding. Europe has written it—and written it for Europe's own purposes!
> ... A pre-emptive claim on the history of Palestine supports European intellectual and spiritual claims of continuity with the Bible, and with what is asserted as Europe's past. Europe's self-identity as Christian has its origin story in the Bible—a story that reaches back to creation.

And so it is that the history of Palestine, of the Palestinians, has been almost completely erased by a faked, invented, "history of Israel", an entity that just simply never existed. And in the same way, at the present time, as the history of Palestine—thousands of years of a rich culture—has been erased, the West, via its handmaiden, the invented Israel, are currently erasing the Palestinians.

Thomson describes the essential feature of Old Testament theology: absolute obedience to "God", and how this theology was used by ancient empires as a form of political propaganda to control populations. "One can in fact say that 'the way of mankind' is never 'God's way', *as a philosophical principle"* (Thompson, 241). Human choices and discernment are, as a rule, wrong. It is only God's will that is moral and "right".

This theology brings us face to face with the idea of the "provisional" or conditional nature of a covenant. "Believe in me and obey me or else I will destroy you." This "belief business" constitutes a sort of "permission", if you will, to accept the "vengeful" action if the agreement is broken—a perfect way to coerce blind obedience! The Hebrew phrase for "he made a covenant", is *karat berit,* or literally, he *cut* a covenant. In the covenant with Abraham in *Genesis*, animals are cut in two and a fire passes between them in a mysterious ritual. Then, there is the cutting of the flesh at circumcision, and the Sinai covenant where the laws were cut into stone. So, these covenants are apparently what constituted the mythical foundations of Israel as a nation: severed pieces of animals, it seems. Could these "cuts" be a symbol of the "breaking apart" of DNA? Most particularly when associated with the genitals!

Returning to *The Curse of Cain:*

> We are heirs of a long tradition in which Monotheism is regarded as the great achievement of Judaeo-Christian thought. Monotheism is entangled with particularism, and with the assertion that this god, and no other, must be worshipped. This particularism is so virulent that it reduces all other gods to mere idols, and is so violent that it reduces all other worshippers to abominations. The danger of a universal Monotheism is asserting that its truth is *the* truth; its system of knowledge, *the* system of knowledge; its ethics, *the* ethics; not because any other option must be rejected, but because there simply *is no other option.* They presuppose a kind of metaphysical scarcity, a kind of hoarding mentality, hoarding belief, hoarding identity, hoarding allegiance, because there is a finite supply of whatever, it must be contained in whole or part. It suggests limit and boundaries. (Schwartz, 1997)

From the Cassiopaeans:

> Q: (L) Can you tell us a little bit about how these illusions are enforced on us, how they are perceived by us?
> A: If someone opens a door, and behind it you see a pot of gold, do you worry whether there is a poisonous snake behind the door hidden from view, before you reach for the pot of gold?
> Q: (L) What does the gold represent?

chapter ten

A: Temptation to limitation. What is snake? Result of giving into temptation without caution, i.e. leaping before looking.

Q: (L) So what you are saying to us is that the story of the temptation in Eden was the story of Humankind being led into this monotheistic belief, this concept of linear time and unidimensionality... So, the eating of the fruit of the Tree of Knowledge of Good and Evil was...

A: Giving into temptation of pleasure for the self.

This brings us around to a very difficult part of our subject: sex. When one reads vast numbers of mythological presentations, one is struck by the fact that sex or sexuality is such a pivotal issue. The "Fall in Eden" had sexual connotations, as did the Flood of Noah and the destruction of Sodom and Gomorrah. In the Sumerian legends, the gods were disturbed by all the sexual activity of humanity (it interrupted their rest) and, as a result, resolved to destroy humanity. The Christian religion has fought unceasingly against sex, ranging from ideas of voluntary castration to celibacy to thinking in terms of only procreative obligations.

Everywhere you look, *sex* is an issue. And, in the present time, we have endless numbers of folks reporting sexual experiences with aliens of all types. Since it *is* such an issue, *what is the deal* here? Was sex part of the "temptation" to "pleasure for the self"?

Q: (L) And this was a trick...

A: No! Tricks don't exist!

Q: (T) OK, no trick, a trap?

A: No! Traps don't exist either. Free will could not be abridged if you had not obliged. Remember: "pleasure for the self".

Q: (T) OK, now, we were STO at that time. The Lizards opened the door, we are using this as an allegory, I guess, the Lizards opened the door and showed us a pot of gold hoping that we would reach in for the pot, or walk through the door, when they were waiting for us on the other side in order to take us over in some way. Am I on the right track?

A: Hoping is incorrect idea.

Q: (T) OK, what was it they were trying to do by enticing us?

A: Trying is incorrect idea, continue to probe for learning opportunity.

Q: (T) Was this after the battle that had transpired?

A: Was battle.

Q: (L) The battle was in us?

A: Through you.

Q: (T) The battle was through us as to whether we would walk through this doorway... (L) The battle was fought through us, we were literally the battleground. (T) OK, we were STO at that point. You have said before that on this density we have the choice of being STS or STO.

A: Oh T, the battle is always there, it's "when" you choose that counts!

Q: (T) OK, so we are still looking at that pot of gold every day? This must tie into why the Lizards and other aliens keep telling people that they have given their consent for abduction and so forth. We were STO and now we are STS.

224

A: Yes, continue.

Q: (T) We are working with the analogy. The gold was an illusion. The gold was not what we perceived it to be. It was a temptation that was given to us as STO beings on third density.

A: No temptation, it was always there. Remember Dorothy and the Ruby slippers? What did Glenda tell Dorothy???

Q: (J) You can always go home. (L) You have always had the power to go home...

A: Yes.

Q: (L) So, we always have the power to return to being STO? Even in third density?

A: Yes. "When" you went for the gold, you said "Hello" to the Lizards and all that that implies.

Q: (T) But, by going for the gold we aligned ourselves with fourth density STS. And by doing so we gave fourth density STS permission to do whatever they wish with us?

A: Close.

Q: (T) So, when they tell us that we gave them permission to abduct us, it is this they are referring to?

A: Close.

Q: (J) Go back to what they said before: "Free will could not be abridged if you had not obliged". (T) We, as the human race, used our free will to switch from STO to STS. (L) So, at some level we have chosen the mess we are in and that is the Super Ancient Legend of the Fallen Angel, Lucifer. That is us. We fell by falling into that door, so to speak, going after the pot of gold, and when we fell through the door, the serpent bit us!

A: But this is a repeating syndrome.

Q: (L) Is it a repeating syndrome just for the human race or is it a repeating syndrome throughout all of creation?

A: It is the latter.

Q: (L) Is this a repeating syndrome throughout all of creation simply because it is the cyclic nature of things? Or is it as the Indians call it, Maya?

A: Either/or.

We need to pay special attention to the term "Ruby Slippers" above. This is a key clue to the problem which we will return to later.

Q: (L) What was the true event behind the story of the "Mark of Cain"?

A: Advent of jealousy.

Q: (L) What occurred to allow jealousy to enter into human interaction?

A: Lizard takeover as discussed previously. The mark of Cain means the "jealousy factor" of change facilitated by Lizard takeover of earth's vibrational frequency. Knot on spine is physical residue of DNA restriction deliberately added by Lizards. See?

Q: (L) What was the configuration of the spine and skull prior to this addition?

A: Spine had no ridge there. Jealousy emanates from there, you can even feel it.

chapter ten

Q: (L) Do any of these emotions that we have talked about that were generated by DNA breakdown, were any of these related to what Carl Sagan discusses when he talks about the "Reptilian Brain"?

A: In a roundabout way.

Q: (L) OK, at the time this "Mark of Cain" came about, were there other humans on the planet that did not have this configuration?

A: It was added to all simultaneously.

Q: (L) How did they physically go about performing this act? What was the mechanism of this event, the nuts and bolts of it?

A: Are you ready? DNA core is as yet undiscovered enzyme relating to carbon. Light waves were used to cancel the first ten factors of DNA by burning them off. At that point, a number of physical changes took place including knot at top of spine. Each of these is equally reflected in the ethereal.

Q: (L) OK, there were however many people on the planet, how did they effect this change on all of them?

A: Light wave alteration. They used sophisticated technology to interrupt light frequency waves. Now understand this: It is all part of natural grand cycle.

Q: (L) If this is all a part of a natural grand cycle, and correct me if I am wrong here, it almost seems as if you guys, the "good guys", and the other "bad" guys, that you just really kind of go at it just for fun, is that true?

A: No.

Q: (L) But you say it is a natural thing or part of a natural grand cycle. Is this natural grand cycle just part of the interaction between light and darkness which just simply must be?

A: Yes. We are at "front line" of universe's natural system of balance. That is where one rises to before reaching total union of "The One". 6th level.

Q: (T) Now, the battle you had with the other side...

A: Are having.

Q: (T) This battle goes on... do you have the light power back?

A: Never lost it, you did.

Q: (T) OK, I guess that for us the Lizzies are the main force even though they have others on their side...

A: Yes.

Q: (T) They took our light, not yours?

A: Not against you. Currently in union with you.

Q: (T) So we are but one battle in the universe in an overall, ongoing struggle?

A: Yes. Balance is natural. Remember, it's all just lessons in the grand cycle.

Q: (L) I am really curious... when you guys and the Lizzies "go to it", what do you do? I mean, you obviously don't shoot guns at each other and you don't have tanks...

A: Too complicated for you to possibly understand because you are not at 4th level yet.

Q: (J) When you are fighting, is it any way at all possible for us to detect the battle?

A: First: We don't "fight". Second, yes; it's nature as in meteorology and earth changes.

Q: (T) Your form of confrontation takes the form of physical changes in the atmosphere and environment of the planet?

A: And in space.

Q: (T) But that is how we detect it? The more activity, the more conflict is going on?

A: Remember, we are the light. They are the dark. We are both high level thought forms reflected at all levels of reality.

Q: (T) So, what we perceive, then, is what comes through to third density which is not what we would perceive if we were looking at it from fourth or fifth or sixth.

A: Yes.

Q: (T) Now, you have referred to the movie, "The Wizard of Oz". You say that we have an ability within us that is something like the Ruby slippers that can take us back to STO any time we wish.

A: Yes.

Q: (T) So, all this stuff we have been talking about, the realm border, the wave, raising the frequencies...

A: The coming Realm wave is the "tornado".

Q: (L) Was going to the land of Oz the STO state?

A: STS.

Q: (L) So Oz was STS. And Kansas, not necessarily the physical surroundings, but the state of mind of Dorothy prior to the Oz experience, was the STO state.

A: Yes.

Q: (L) So, we need to look at the "Kansas" state of mind. The going to Oz...

A: And Elvira Gulch. The witch is the Lizards.

Q: (T) Yeah, OK. Tornado. Dorothy fell from the STO to the STS state through the tornado. Is this true.

A: Yes. Analyze more carefully, suggest break to do so.

Discussion among members of group:

(T) They are equating the tornado as the shift from STO to STS.

(L) Maybe it also is a shift from STS to STO.

(J) Yes, a shift from one to the other would be dramatic.

(T) Was it a density shift also? The realm wave is supposed to be a density shift. A window between densities. Is there also a shifting between STO and STS? Is there a gateway that you go through? A door?

(F) Oh God! There are so many possibilities here.

(L) And if you switch into STO do you find yourself on a different Earth?

(J) They have been saying "Ruby Slippers, Ruby Slippers", not "tornado, tornado".

(T) But now it is the same symbology. The tornado took her from one point to another and the slippers took her back to point A again. Two different concepts.

(F) There are all kinds of intricate little things here, somehow there must be a way to connect it. You know what it is, remember the slippers, they said, meant that the pathway was always there for her to go home.

(J) Yeah, but she had to kill the witch to get the slippers.

(F) No, she thought she had to. Don't you remember Glenda telling her "Ooh, no dear, you can always go home. All you have to do is say 'there's no place like home.'"

(J) Yeah, but you had to be wearing those slippers...

(S) Now, you know what, the tornado could be fifth density, as she was looking out the window all these things passed by...

(T) Yes, her life passed by her.

(F) Yes, but they have told us that the realm border passage itself is going to result in all kinds of hairy stuff going on.

(J) Like I say, switching from STS to STO or back, or from third density to fourth density, it's going to be a violent... it is not going to be an easy passage either way.

(F) Right.

(J) It is a radical change in reality.

(T) Yes, but for Dorothy, in the movie, it was violent in the fact that it was a tornado, though it did not physically hurt her.

(J) Yes, and that is what we have been told, too.

(F) She was scared...

(T) Yes, but that was a mental thing... it was up here [pointing to head] where the hurt was. She didn't get hurt physically.

(F) And that is also another whole thing to speculate about: throughout the entire movie, she was never hurt physically; through all the threats, she was never actually hurt.

(T) It was also 1939, if the movie had been made in 1995 they would have had machine guns, missiles, chainsaws, and there would be body counts all over the place. And she still could have gone home anytime she wanted. You know, "Dorothy Meets the Terminator".

(L) "Dorothy and the Chainsaw Massacre".

(S) "Dorothy Goes to Elm Street". [Laughter]

(T) It's the cross between a children's fairy story and a Stephen King Nightmare.

(F) You know, the fundamentalists have attacked the Wizard of Oz?

(L) They have? Why?

(T) Because it is Satanic.

(F) Yeah, they say it's Hollywood's effort to pull people away from Christianity and fundamentalism and all that jazz.

(T) The Wizard of Oz is evil to the fundamentalists.

(F) Yes, because you don't need the crucify Christ to get back to Kansas.

(L) Well, I've heard that Cinderella is politically incorrect nowadays, too.

(T) Because she didn't sleep with one foot on the floor like all the sitcoms.

(J) Excuse me?

(T) I don't know.

(S) We went from Oz to sitcoms?

(J) I think you are mixing your metaphors.

(S) That was Sleeping Beauty.

(T) Yeah, that was Sleeping Beauty in the box.

(J) And one foot on the floor.

(L) No, Snow White was in the box.

(T) Snow White was in the box. Yeah, Disney took all the things that had Beauty sleeping in them...

(L) Did you ever stop and think about that symbology: Sleeping Beauty? Being awakened by a kiss?

(F) Who turns into a frog.

(L) No!

(F) Oh, that's right, the frog turns into a prince.

(L) That's another analogy. Being awakened from the illusion into which one has been put by the evil witch...

(F) And Cinderella...

(J) Rumplestiltskin...

(S) The Ugly Duckling...

(T) Yeah, all of Grimm's fairy tales were really pretty grim. They have been cleaned up a whole lot.

(L) Yeah, in the original Cinderella, the step sister cut off part of her foot to get it to fit the slipper and the Prince found her out because of the dripping blood.

(J and S) Ooooh! Yuck!

(T) Must have been the glass slipper, cut my foot!

(L) Yeah, it's pretty grim. One cut her heel off and the other cut her toes off. And we are back to Ruby Slippers. Wonder what that can mean? It's gonna take some work to figure it out!

(T) Are we getting anywhere? We got the idea that when we fell from STO to STS we gave the Lizzies the right to do what they are doing. So, when they make the statement that we said they could, we did. But now we are asleep and we gotta figure out how to wake up!

A: OK.

Q: (L) We are having a bit of a puzzlement here because we are wondering if the tornado which represents the realm wave is something that moves one from an STO state to an STS state while still remaining in third density?

A: OK, that is one way. OK...

Q: (T) The realm border is not only a way of transferring from one density to another, but it is also a way of transiting from STS and STO and back?

A: Can be.

Q: (T) So, those who transit on this pass may transit from third to fourth density and come out as an STO being?

A: In some of the passages.

Q: (L) OK, so people can either go from STO to STS in third or fourth density... any of these choices are open at this passing of the realm wave?

A: Any of the above according to the orientation of the wave.

Q: (L) And what is the orientation of the wave that is coming? Is it strictly to move us from third density to fourth density? Is this a function of this wave?

A: We have told you this.

chapter ten

Q: (L) And they have told us that this is a wave from third to fourth density. Some of the waves, apparently, can move from STO to STS... (T) Not the wave, the person passing through the wave. As this wave passes by, does the orientation of the wave depend upon the individual?

A: Compare to seawaves. Waves are a part of the fiber of all nature.

Q: (T) In other words, this is a wave that is going to move the Earth and our entire sector of space from third to fourth density, and it will do so no matter where you are on the wave when it passes?

A: Yes. Or you could "go under" instead.

Q: (L) You could be pulled under, you could drown and become part of the primordial soup! (T) Is that Minestrone?

A: Chicken Noodle. [Laughter.]

Q: (T) Let's not even start on that one. I'm still trying to work out this movement from STO to STS. You keep referring to the movie about Dorothy. In the movie she was told she could go home any time she wanted just by saying "I want to go home", or whatever. That is a lot easier than going through all the conniptions and contankerations waiting out this wave that comes only once every so often. Is there a way for us to go back to STO that is easier and simpler than hanging out for 300,000 years waiting for this wave to come around?

A: Sure!

Q: (T) OK, now we are getting somewhere. Where are we going?

A: Now wait a minute, are you ready to just go to 4th density right now?

Q: (T) Yeah, I am ready. Right now. Let's roll! J, feed the cats when you get home! Anyway, what you are saying is that the realm wave is not the only way to make the transition, is this correct?

A: One idea presented.

Q: (T) And we are here to set up a frequency to pull as many beings through the wave, when it passes, and that is the whole purpose of why we are here... Is this so?

A: That implies interference with free will.

Q: (L) Who do the munchkins represent?

A: 2nd density beings.

Q: (L) Do the monkeys represent the Grays?

A: If you wish.

Q: (L) Who do the Witches soldiers represent?

A: The Nephalim.

Q: (L) Who does the Wizard represent?

A: Think, learn, discover.

chapter eleven
growing awareness

This chapter is enormously important for those who have been plagued by "alien interference". I realize that I am repeating some things, but that is only because they are so important that they bear reading more than once.

Let's go back for a moment to what don Juan Matus told Carlos Castaneda about the Predator and Carlos's first glimpses of same:

> "Ah, that's the universe at large", he said, "incommensurable, nonlinear, outside the realm of syntax. The sorcerers of ancient Mexico were the first ones to see those fleeting shadows, so they followed them around. They saw them as you're seeing them, and they saw them as energy that flows in the universe. And they did discover something transcendental. ... They discovered that we have a companion for life... We have a predator that came from the depths of the cosmos and took over the rule of our lives. Human beings are its prisoners. The predator is our lord and master. It has rendered us docile, helpless. If we want to protest, it suppresses our protest. If we want to act independently, it demands that we don't do so. ... You have arrived, by your effort alone, to what the shamans of ancient Mexico called the topic of topics. I have been beating around the bush all this time, insinuating to you that something is holding us prisoner. Indeed we are held prisoner! This was an energetic fact for the sorcerers of ancient Mexico.
>
> "Why has this predator taken over in the fashion that you're describing, don Juan?" I asked. "There must be a logical explanation."
>
> "There is an explanation", don Juan replied, "which is the simplest explanation in the world. They took over because we are food for them, and they squeeze us mercilessly because we are their sustenance. Just as we rear chickens in chicken coops, the predators rear us in human coops. Therefore, their food is always available to them".
>
> I felt that my head was shaking violently from side to side. I could not express my profound sense of unease and discontentment, but my body moved to bring it to the surface. I shook from head to toe without any volition on my part.
>
> "'No, no, no, no", I heard myself saying. "this is absurd, don Juan. What your saying is something monstrous. It simply can't be true, for sorcerers or for average men, or for anyone".
>
> "Why not?" don Juan asked calmly. "Why not? Because it infuriates you?"
>
> "Yes, it infuriates me", I retorted. "Those claims are monstrous!" ...
>
> "I want to appeal to your analytical mind", don Juan said. "Think for a moment, and tell me how you would explain the contradiction between the intelligence of man the engineer and the stupidity of his systems of beliefs, or the stupidity of his contradictory behavior. Sorcerers believe that the predators have given us our systems of beliefs, our ideas of good and evil, our social mores.

They are the ones who set up our hopes and expectations and dreams of success or failure. They have given us covetousness, greed and cowardice. It is the predators who make us complacent, routinary, and egomaniacal".

"But how can they do this, don Juan?" I asked, somehow angered further by what he was saying. "Do they whisper all that in our ears while we are asleep?"

"No, they don't do it that way. That's idiotic!" don Juan said, smiling. "They are infinitely more efficient and organized than that. In order to keep us obedient and meek and weak, the predators engaged themselves in a stupendous maneuver—stupendous, of course, from the point of view of a fighting strategist. A horrendous maneuver from the point of view of those who suffer it. They gave us their mind! Do you hear me? The predators give us their mind, which becomes our mind. The predators' mind is baroque, contradictory, morose, filled with the fear of being discovered any minute now."

Don Juan continues: "I know that even though you have never suffered hunger... you have food anxiety, which is none other than the anxiety of the predator who fears that any moment now its maneuver is going to be uncovered and food is going to be denied. Through the mind, which, after all, is their mind, the predators inject into the lives of human beings whatever is convenient for them. And they ensure, in this manner, a degree of security to act as a buffer against their fear". (Castaneda, 1998, 213-220)

And now, let's compare this to what the Cassiopaeans have said:

Q: (L) How did mankind come to be here?

A: Combination of factors. Numerous souls desired physical existence then was altered by three forces including principally Lizards through Grays, Nephalim and Orion Union.

Q: (L). You said numerous souls desired physical existence. When the numerous souls did this, how did physical existence come to be?

A: First was apelike. Souls altered them by transfer into seeded bodies.

Q: (L) The Orion souls came into Neanderthal bodies?

A: No. Put human souls there for incubation process.

Q: (L) Were altered ape embryos put back into ape females for gestation?

A: No. Souls only.

Q: (L) Did the soul's presence in the ape body cause its genetics and DNA to change?

A: Yes.

Q: (L) They entered into living creatures on this planet to experience 3D reality and by entering in caused mutation?

A: Yes.

Q: (L) Then were altered by Orion Union first.

A: They resemble you.

Q: (L) Who resembles us?

A: The Orions.

Q: (L) Where did the souls come from that entered into the bodies on the planet earth? Were they in bodies on other planets before they came here?

A: Not this group.

232

Q: (L) Were they just floating around in the universe somewhere?

A: In union with the One. Have you heard the Super ancient legend of Lucifer, the Fallen Angel?

Q: (L) Who is Lucifer?

A: You. The human race.

Q: (L) Are the souls of individual humans the parts of a larger soul?

A: Yes. Close. The One. All who have fallen must learn "the hard way".

Q: (L) Are you saying that the act of wanting to experience physical reality is the act of falling?

A: You are members of a fragmented soul unit.

Q: (L) What is it about wanting to be physical is a "fall"?

A: Pleasure for the self.

So, here we have a similar series of remarks to what don Juan has said regarding the "flyers", as he calls them, giving human beings their "mind".

Remember the remarks about the "Mark of Cain" and the alteration of human DNA by the "forces of darkness" which resulted in numerous changes, including the imposition of monotheism, the perception of linear time, and unidimensionality? All of these remarks are very important in regard to our subject. In order to understand the imposition of monotheism, it would be useful to read *Secret History*.

There have been proposals made in certain quarters that invoking the name and power of Jesus will "stop" abductions. I am sorry to have to say this, but experience and research simply does not support this claim. There are a number of reasons why it would appear to be so which I will outline briefly.

In the first place, an individual who is a *Christian* in the usual sense of the word, which is to be "born again" and most likely one who relies wholly on faith to solve their problems, has already given their power away to the forces behind the imposition of Christianity, i.e. the "dark forces" in the guise of angels of light.

An additional factor is the fact that, by virtue of "living in faith", one has closed off a large portion of the mind and is more susceptible to being deceived. For example: say that such an individual finds herself in the midst of an abduction experience and "calls on the name of Jesus", and observes that the abduction is "stopped". We *cannot* rely on this observation because it is based on "belief"—not reason or logic—which literally determines what a person perceives! Remember the stories of the Third Man and the Evil Magician.

Each and every human being perceives the Third Man according to their programming which activates or is activated by their belief system (think *free formal imaging*). This is their *state of awareness*. They can only be aware of what they *believe* they can be aware of, and all else becomes either "invisible" or "anomalous" and disregarded or covered up by the survival program of the subconscious mind.

As one continues to think about this problem, one realizes that there is a possible *huge* gap between what we perceive as real and the actual objective reality... and no matter how we try to be objective, we can never be sure. The only thing that seems to offer a way out is to simply observe the phenomena and compare the perceptions with a lot of other folks and try to narrow down the "constant" that is present in all of them. In this way, we can have a closer idea of what the Third Man *really* is, and what he is *really* doing, and what then, should be our best response. And, of course, "observing phenomena" means, in its most literal sense, to gain and gather knowledge of every form and sort so that one has a sufficient database from which to draw conclusions about observations of one's environment.

But, this is difficult to do because one's beliefs are intimately tied to emotions! Remember: our beliefs are formed in emotional situations of interactions with our parents and other "authorities" of our infancy and childhood. It is very frightening to even contemplate breaking free of this safe, inner "environment".

But, that is exactly what we must do.

Otherwise, we find ourselves in a reality where all sorts of anomalous things will be going on around one—observable in classical and quantum terms—but the objective *raison d'être* will be unavailable for contemplation. One will be *unable to see* the Third Man, and will then be subject to the whims and inclinations of said "personage", whoever or whatever he *really is!*

Thus we see that if a person really has faith that Jesus will "save" them or "stop an abduction", that is what they will *perceive*, but not necessarily what is happening in absolute reality.

Another point I wish to make is this: so-called "demonic" entities of higher densities do *not* fear the name of, nor belief in Jesus. They are contemptuous of those who believe that such will "preserve" them. And, they do not respect a person who "surrounds themselves with light", or "love" or whatever. In fact, when this is done, it usually provides such dark entities with a literal "aetheric feast". I know whereof I speak, as I have performed exorcisms. And, one must not confuse "exorcism" with the run-of-the-mill Spirit Releasement Therapy as taught by Dr. William Baldwin, either. Dr. Baldwin has worked with demonic type entities, according to his book *Spirit Releasement Therapy*, but I am certain that he has not encountered all types and levels of beings, as there are endless varieties.

There are a number of sources that talk about the more dangerous and complicated "exorcisms", and, for the most part, they belong to ancient teachings such as Sufism and various forms of shamanism.

Mircea Eliade, in his classic *Shamanism, Archaic Techniques of Ecstasy*, writes extensively about shamanic techniques that deal with discarnate entities, demonic entities, and what can only be alien abductions. These practices and techniques are millennia old, existing long before Jesus (leaving aside who or what he may have been) ever walked the earth. In fact, if Jesus was anything, he was a Tantrika as evidenced by a deep study of the myths and legends surrounding him and comparing them with similar stories and examples. And,

Tantra Yoga is one of the oldest and most definitive sources of techniques for dealing with various dimensions, densities, and their denizens.

Getting back to don Juan: if you read carefully my description of the abduction experience in chapter eight, then you will have the background to understand the following. If not, go back and read it carefully before proceeding here:

> Don Juan had explained that the body and the energy body were two conglomerates of energy fields compressed together by some strange agglutinizing force. He had emphasized no end that the force that binds that group of energy fields together was, according to the sorcerers of ancient Mexico, the most mysterious force in the universe. His personal estimation was that it was the pure essence of the entire cosmos, the sum total of everything there is. (Castaneda, 1998)

Cassiopaeans:

Q: (L) Well, do they just take people and kill them and do what with them?

A: They slice them up. Maximum matter and energy transfer occurs during this type of transition.

Q: (L) In other words, you are saying that a slow painful death gives them the most of what they want? This is totally sick.

A: You asked for truth. You say it is sick but it is merely the ultimate form of service to self.

Q: (L) Gravity seems to be a property of matter. Is that correct?

A: And antimatter! Binder. Gravity binds all that is physical with all that is ethereal through unstable gravity waves!!!

Q: (L) So, they are a property or attribute of the existence of matter, and the binder of matter to ethereal ideation?

A: Sort of, but they are a property of anti-matter, too!

Q: (L) So, through unstable gravity waves, you can access other densities?

A: Everything.

Q: (L) Can you generate them mechanically?

A: Generation is really collecting and dispersing.

Q: (L) I thought that gravity was an indicator of the consumption of electricity; that gravity was a byproduct of a continuous flow of electrical energy...

A: Gravity is no byproduct! It is the central ingredient of all existence! You have it too!!

Q: (L) So, gravity is the unifying principle...

A: Gravity is all there is.

Q: (L) Do thoughts produce gravity?

A: Yes.

Q: (L) You said that EM was the same as gravity. Does an increase in EM, the collection of EM or the production of an EM wave, does this increase gravity on those things or objects or persons subjected to it?

A: Gravity does not ever get increased or decreased, it is merely collected and dispersed.

Q: (L) Is STO the equivalent of dispersing gravity?

A: No, STO is a REFLECTION of the existence of gravity dispersal.

Q: (L) Is STS also dispersal of gravity?

A: No. Collection is reflected. STS is reflection or reflected by collection of gravity.

So, "giving" and being open is "dispersing" gravity and "taking" or being in a closed system is "collecting" gravity, or a reflection thereof. This is interesting in light of the Cassiopaean remarks on sexuality:

Q: (L) What happens psychically at the moment of orgasm?

A: For whom?

Q: (L) The reason I ask is because a man named Wayne Cook did some work with dowsing and he found out that the human body, after sexual climax, dowses the same pattern as a dead body. Why is this?

A: Draining of energy.

Q: (L) OK, where does the energy drain to?

A: To the ether.

Q: (L) Does the energy go to one or the other partner?

A: Maybe. It can.

Q: (L) Is it possible, during this activity, for Lizzies or other beings to be hanging around and be drawing this energy?

A: Yes. And that is, in a general sense, what usually happens.

Q: (L) Is this one of the reasons that sex has been promoted and promulgated in our society to such an extent...

A: Yes, yes, yes.

Q: (L) I have read that when you are at the higher spiritual levels that you can do a spiritual merge which is better than orgasm. Is that true?

A: Why do you need orgasm of any kind?

Q: (L) Well, it does seem to be like one of the penultimate experiences of physicality. (T) That's exactly it... it's physicality... (L) If that is so, isn't everything that exists in the physical, third density world, in some way a reflection of experiences or states of being on higher realms?

A: 3rd density as you experience it is an illusion you have been fed to continue your imprisonment therein.

Q: (L) So, in other words, the orgasmic experience is quite literally a lure to keep us... (D) Controlled... (T) And in the third level... (L) Is that true?

A: Yes. Except in rare instances, under controlled conditions, for specific purposes.

Q: (L) Let's go back to a question I asked in another session on this same subject: what happens to our energy at the point of orgasm? Where does that energy go?

A: Drains to 4th level STS.

Q: (T) Is this a manifestation of the Lizards feeding off of us?

A: STSers there retrieve it.

Q: (T) So, orgasm is a third density manifestation of the fourth density consumption of third density energy?

A: One of their methods.

Returning to don Juan's explication of the matter:

He had asserted that the physical body and the energy body were the only counterbalanced energy configurations in our realm as human beings. ... Body, mind, spirit and flesh he considered to be a mere concatenation of the mind, emanating from it without any energetic foundation. (Castaneda, 1998)

Cassiopaeans:

Q: There are a lot of people teaching that there are divisions of being as spirit, soul, consciousness, et cetera. What is the difference between the spirit and the soul?

A: Semantics.

Castaneda writes:

Don Juan had said that by means of discipline it is possible for anyone to bring the energy body closer to the physical body. Normally, the distance between the two is enormous. Once the energy body is within a certain range, which varies for each of us individually, anyone, through discipline, can forge it into the exact replica of their physical body—that is to say, a three-dimensional, solid being. Hence the sorcerers' idea of the other or the double. By the same token, through the same processes of discipline, anyone can forge their three-dimensional, solid, physical body to be a perfect replica of their energy body—that is to say, an ethereal charge of energy invisible to the human eye, as all energy is. ...

Don Juan explained that sorcerers see infant human beings as strange, luminous balls of energy, covered from the top to the bottom with a glowing coat, something like a plastic cover that is adjusted tightly over their cocoon of energy. He said that that glowing coat of awareness was what the predators consumed, and that when a human being reached adulthood, all that was left of that glowing coat of awareness was a narrow fringe that went from the ground to the top of the toes. That fringe permitted mankind to continue living, but only barely.

...To his knowledge, man was the only species that had the glowing coat of awareness outside that luminous cocoon. Therefore, man becomes easy prey for an awareness of a different order, such as the heavy awareness of the predator.

He said that this narrow fringe of awareness was the epicenter of self-reflection, where man is irremediably caught. By playing on our self-reflection, which is the only point of awareness left to us, the predators create flares of awareness that they proceed to consume in a ruthless, predatory fashion. They give us inane problems that force those flares of awareness to rise, and in this manner they keep us alive in order for them to be fed with the energetic flare of our pseudo concerns.

All we can do is discipline ourselves to the point where they will not touch us. How can you ask your fellow men to go through those rigors of discipline? They'll laugh and make fun of you, and the more aggressive ones will beat the shit out of you. And not so much because they don't believe it. Down in the depths of every human being, there's an ancestral, visceral knowledge about the predators' existence.

Carlos says:

My analytical mind swung back and forth like a yo-yo. What don Juan was proposing was preposterous, incredible. At the same time, it was a most reasonable thing, so simple. It explained every kind of human contradiction I could think of. But how could one have taken all this seriously? Don Juan was pushing me into the path of an avalanche that would take me down forever.

Don Juan:

"Whenever doubts plague you to a dangerous point, do something pragmatic about it. Turn off the light, pierce the darkness; find out what you can *see*. ... The sorcerers of ancient Mexico *saw* the predator. They called it the flyer because it leaps through the air. It is not a pretty sight. It is a big shadow, impenetrably dark, a black shadow that jumps through the air. Then, it lands flat on the ground. The sorcerers of ancient Mexico were quite ill at ease with the idea of it when it made its appearance on Earth. They reasoned that man must have been a complete being at one point, with stupendous insights, feats of awareness that are mythological legends nowadays. And then everything seems to disappear, and we have now a sedated man.

"What I'm saying is that what we have against us is not a simple predator. It is very smart, and organized. It follows a methodical system to render us useless. Man, the magical being that he is destined to be, is no longer magical. He's an average piece of meat. There are no more dreams for man but the dreams of an animal who is being raised to become a piece of meat: trite, conventional, imbecilic.

"The only alternative left for mankind is discipline. Discipline is the only deterrent. But by discipline I don't mean harsh routines. I don't mean waking up every morning at five-thirty and throwing cold water on yourself until you're blue. Sorcerers understand discipline as the capacity to face with serenity odds that are not included in our expectations. For them, discipline is an art: the art of facing infinity without flinching, not because they are strong and tough but because they are filled with awe.

"Sorcerers say that discipline makes the glowing coat of awareness unpalatable to the flyer. The result is that the predators become bewildered. And inedible glowing coat of awareness is not part of their cognition, I suppose. After being bewildered, they don't have any recourse other than refraining from continuing their nefarious task.

"If the predators don't eat our glowing coat of awareness for a while, it'll keep on growing. Simplifying this matter to the extreme, I can say that sorcerers, by means of their discipline, push the predators away long enough to allow their glowing coat of awareness to grow beyond the level of the toes. Once it goes beyond the level of the toes, it grows back to its natural size. The sorcerers of ancient Mexico used to say that the glowing coat of awareness is like a tree. If it is not pruned, it grows to its natural size and volume. As awareness reaches levels higher than the toes, tremendous maneuvers of perception become a matter of course.

"The grand trick of those sorcerers of ancient times was to burden the flyers' mind with discipline. They found out that if they taxed the flyers' mind with inner silence, the foreign installation would flee, giving to any one of the practitioners involved in this maneuver the total certainty of the mind's foreign origin. The foreign installation comes back, I assure you, but not as strong, and a process begins in which the fleeing of the flyers' mind becomes routine, until one day if flees permanently. A sad day indeed! That's the day when you have to rely on your own devices, which are nearly zero. There's no one to tell you what to do. There's no mind of foreign origin to dictate the imbecilities you're accustomed to. This is the toughest day in a sorcerer's life, for the real mind that belongs to us, the sum total of our experience, after a lifetime of domination has been rendered shy, insecure, and shifty. Personally, I would say that the real battle of sorcerers begins at that moment. The rest is merely preparation.

"Discipline taxes the foreign mind no end. So, through their discipline, sorcerers vanquish the foreign installation. The flyers' mind flees forever when a sorcerer succeeds in grabbing on to the vibrating force that holds us together as a conglomerate of energy fields. If a sorcerer maintains that pressure long enough, the flyers' mind flees in defeat.

"When one is torn by internal struggle, it is because down in the depths one knows that one is incapable of refusing the agreement that an indispensable part of the self, the glowing coat of awareness, is going to serve as an incomprehensible source of nourishment to incomprehensible entities. And, another part of one will stand against this situation with all its might.

"The sorcerers' revolution is that they refuse to honor agreements in which they did not participate. Nobody ever asked me if I would consent to be eaten by beings of a different kind of awareness. My parents just brought me into this world to be food, like themselves, and that's the end of the story."

Castaneda writes:

At home, as time went by, the idea of the flyers became one of the main fixations of my life. I got to the point where I felt that don Juan was absolutely right about them. No matter how hard I tried, I couldn't discard his logic. The more I thought about it, and the more I talked to and observed myself and my fellow men, the more intense the conviction that something was rendering us incapable of any activity or any interaction or any thought that didn't have the self as its focal point. ... The end result of my internal struggle was a sense of foreboding, the sense of something imminently dangerous coming at me.

I made extensive anthropological inquiries into the subject of the flyers in other cultures, but I couldn't find any references to them anywhere.

Apparently Carlos didn't read Eliade's *Shamanism* or Vallee's *Passport to Magonia*. These works are *full* of the historical and *ancient* references to these beings that don Juan calls "flyers". Don Juan tells Carlos:

"[T]he flyers' mind has not left you. It has been seriously injured. It's trying its best to rearrange its relationship with you. But something in you is severed forever. The flyer knows that. The real danger is that the flyers' mind may win by getting you tired and forcing you to quit by playing the contradictions between what it says and what I say.

"You see, the flyers' mind has no competitors. When it proposes something, it agrees with its own proposition, and it makes you believe that you've done something of worth. The flyers' mind will say to you that whatever I am telling you is pure nonsense, and then the same mind will agree with its own proposition. That's the way they overcome us.

"The flyers are an essential part of the universe and they must be taken as what they really are—awesome, monstrous. They are the means by which the universe tests us.

"We are energetic probes created by the universe and it's because we are possessors of energy that has awareness that we are the means by which the universe becomes aware of itself. The flyers are the implacable challengers. They cannot be taken as anything else. If we succeed in doing that, the universe allows us to continue.

"A weird thing is that every human being on this earth seems to have exactly the same reactions, the same thoughts, the same feelings. They seem to respond in more or less the same way to the same stimuli. Those reactions seem to be sort of fogged up by the language they speak, but if we scrape that off, they are exactly the same reactions that besiege every human being on Earth. I would like you to become curious about this, and see if you can formally account for such homogeneity."

...I really wanted to start for home right away ... but before we reached his house, don Juan sat down on a high ledge overlooking the valley. He didn't say anything for awhile. He was not out of breath. I couldn't conceive of why he had stopped to sit down.

"The task of the day, for you," he said abruptly, in a foreboding tone, "is one of the most mysterious things of sorcery, something that goes beyond language, beyond explanations. ...So brace yourself by propping your back against this rock wall, as far as possible, from the edge. I will be by you, in case you faint or fall down. ...I want you to cross your legs and enter into inner silence, but don't fall asleep."

It was rather difficult for me to enter into inner silence without falling asleep. I fought a nearly invincible desire to fall asleep. I succeeded, and found myself looking at the bottom of the valley from an impenetrable darkness around me. And then, I saw something that chilled me to the marrow of my bones. I saw a gigantic shadow, perhaps fifteen feet across, leaping in the air and then landing with a silent thud. I felt the thud in my bones, but I didn't hear it.

"They are really heavy," don Juan said in my ear. He was holding me by the left arm, as hard as he could.

I saw something that looked like a mud shadow wiggle on the ground, and then take another gigantic leap, perhaps fifty feet long, and land again, with the same ominous silent thud. I fought not to lose my concentration. I was frightened beyond anything I could rationally use as a description. I kept my eyes fixed on the jumping shadow on the bottom of the valley. Then I heard a most peculiar buzzing, a mixture of the sound of flapping wings and the buzzing of a radio whose dial has not quite picked up the frequency of a radio station, and the thud that followed was something unforgettable. It shook don Juan and me to the core—a gigantic black mud shadow had just landed by our feet.

"Don't be frightened," don Juan said imperiously. "Keep your inner silence and it will move away."

240

I was shivering from head to toe. I had the clear knowledge that if I didn't keep my inner silence alive, the mud shadow would cover me up like a blanket and suffocate me. Without losing the darkness around me, I screamed at the top of my voice. Never had I been so angry, so utterly frustrated. The mud shadow took another leap, clearly to the bottom of the valley. I kept on screaming, shaking my legs. I wanted to shake off whatever might come to eat me. (Castaneda, 1998, 231-233)

Now, let's go back to the excerpt from Karla Turner's book:

"I'm looking at a shadow... Maybe it's the cat, he likes that tree. Rustling, pomegranate tree. At the bottom? But how? This, there's something moving, but I can't see it. It's a dark spot, a black spot, moving around the tree. And it's gone."

Barbara asked him to expand his description, so David continued.

"I saw, it looks irregular. Is it a shadow? It's black. It's on the ground. It's moving around and away, quickly, rustling. Like walking on leaves. And it's very faint with a whisper... a snake sound, real faint. ... My brain's not working", he said. "I'm just tramping behind her to the car. Ah, ah. But I want to go look at that. I heard a noise."

"What did the noise sound like?"

"A rope, pulled real fast," he replied. "Whoooo, kind of like a top. But soft, so it was muted. And that' when I see the thing. The black. It's just blackness, on the ground. Very quick. Something hit me before."

"Where?" Barbara inquired.

"Shocked me," he answered. "In the back. In my hip, at the bottom of my spine... I'm bouncing, mechanically, towards the satellite dish, I think. .... It's big.... It hurt, all over, the shock. Tingles real loud. All over my bones it's tingling, shaking. ... I'm walking around the tree, and I hear a noise. Like a top, a spinning top. It starts high-pitched and goes lower, and goes away pretty fast. So I look towards it. I can't see very well. ...It's like a blot on the ground, ... a black towel? Or a garbage bag? Kind of odd-shaped. It's flat, flat-flat. It, it is on the ground, it's no different than the ground, but it's just black and moving fast. And it's making a little noise. ...I'm looking at the thing. ...A blackness. A 'not.' Like a 'not-there.' Like a moving oil puddle on the ground. ...And it's moving, but changing, too. Not much, just the edges, not very stable. And it's gone quick. ...I feel strange. ...I'm just not me. ...I feel blank ...like a remote unit..." (Turner, 1992, 132-139)

Carlos writes:

The predator don Juan had described was not something benevolent. It was enormously heavy, gross, indifferent. I felt its disregard for us. Doubtless, it had crushed us ages ago, making us, as don Juan had said, weak, vulnerable, and docile. I had my wrath, my unbending intent, not to let them eat me. I wept for my fellow men... (Castaneda, 1998)

Now, let us look again at what the Cassiopaeans said about my own experience, the "eclipsing of realities".

241

chapter eleven

Q: (L) The first thing on my mind is an experience I had several nights ago. It seemed as though there was some sort of interaction between myself and something "other". Could you tell me what this experience was?

A: Was eclipsing of the realities.

Q: (L) What is an eclipsing of the realities?

A: It is when energy centers conflict.

Q: (L) What energy centers are conflicting?

A: Thought energy centers.

Q: (L) Well, it seemed to me that something happened to me that blanked out a period of my experience, and you say this was an eclipsing of energies caused by an intersecting of thought centers. Now, this intersecting of thought centers, did this occur within my body or within my environment?

A: They are one and the same.

Q: (L) Was some part of my being [in the process of] being separated from another part of my being?

A: Yes.

Q: (L) Was this an attempt to extract my soul or astral body?

A: Attempt is not probably the proper term.

Q: (L) In other words...

A: It is more just an activity taking place. Attempt implies effort rather than the nature present in a conflicting of energies and thought centers.

Q: (L) I also seemed to be aware of several dark, spider-like figures lined up by the side of the bed, was this an accurate impression.

A: Those could be described as specific thought center projections.

Q: (L) I seemed to be fighting and resisting this activity.

A: That was your choice.

Q: (L) Alright, was this the ending of an abduction that had already taken place?

A: Not the proper terminology. It was the conclusion to an event, not necessarily what one would refer to as an abduction, but more what one would refer to as an interaction.

Q: (L) What was the nature of the interaction?

A: The conflicting of energies related to thought center impulses.

Q: (L) At what level of density do these thought centers have their primary focus?

A: Thought centers do not have primary focus in any level of density. This is precisely the point. You are not completely familiar with the reality of what thoughts are. We have spoken to you on many levels and have detailed many areas involving density level, but thoughts are quite a different thing because they pass through all density levels at once. Now, let us ask you this. Do you not now see how that would be possible?

Q: (L) Yes. But what I am trying to do is identify these conflicting thought centers. If two thought centers, or more, conflict, then my idea would be that they are in opposition.

A: Correct.

Q: (L) OK, in the experience I felt a paralysis of my body, what caused this paralysis.

A: Yes. Separation of awareness. Which is defined as any point along the pathway where one's awareness becomes so totally focused on one thought sector that all other levels of awareness are temporarily receded, thereby making it impossible to become aware of one's physical reality along with one's mental reality. This gives the impression of what is referred to as paralysis. Do you understand?

Q: (L) Yes. And what stimulates this total focus of awareness?

A: An event which sidetracks, temporarily, the mental processes.

Q: (L) And what event can sidetrack the mental processes to this extent? In this particular case, what was it?

A: It was an eclipsing of energies caused by conflicting thought centers.

Q: (L) What energies were being eclipsed?

A: Whenever two opposing units of reality intersect, this causes what can be referred to as friction, which, for an immeasurable amount of what you would refer to as time, which is, of course, non-existent, creates a non- existence, or a stopping of the movements of all functions. This is what we would know as conflict. In between, or through any intersecting, opposite entities, we always find zero time, zero movement, zero transference, zero exchange. Now think about this. Think about this carefully.

Q: (L) Does this mean that I was, essentially, in a condition of non-existence?

A: Well, non-existence is not really the proper term, but non-fluid existence would be more to the point. Do you understand?

Q: (L) Yes. Frozen, as it were?

A: Frozen, as it were.

Q: (L) Was there any benefit to me from this experience?

A: All experiences have potential for benefit.

Q: (L) Was there any detriment from this experience?

A: All experiences have potential for detriment. Now, do you see the parallels. We are talking about any opposing forces in nature, when they come together, the result can go all the way to the extreme of one side or all the way to the extreme of the other. Or, it can remain perfectly, symmetrically in balance in the middle, or partially in balance on one side or another. Therefore all potentials are realized at intersecting points in reality.

Q: (L) Was one of these conflicting thought centers or energies some part of me?

A: Yes.

Q: (L) And was it eclipsed by interacting with a thought center energy that was part of or all of something or someone else?

A: Or, was what happened a conflicting of one energy thought center that was a part of your thought process and another energy thought center that was another part of your thought process? We will ask you that question and allow you to contemplate. You will gain more knowledge by contemplating it by yourself rather than seeking the answers here. But a suggestion is to be made that you do that as you will gain much, very much knowledge by contemplating these very questions on your own and networking with others as you do so. Be not frustrated for the answers to be gained through your own contemplation will be truly illuminating to you and the experience to follow will be worth a thousand lifetimes of pleasure and joy.

The session from which the above extracts are taken was held in July of 1995. It was not until several years later ago that I obtained Carlos Castaneda's book *The Active Side of Infinity* (published in 1998) from which the information about the "flyers" is extracted. But, it set the bells ringing in my head. I understood that I had done, naturally, the very things that Don Juan was telling Carlos that he must do to "regrow" his awareness.

You see, I had realized that all "alien interference" in my life changed from that point on. In retrospect, I understand that it was the constant study and becoming aware of the other realities that I had been going through which gave me the "platform" from which to resist this event of "eclipsing of realities", which don Juan calls discipline in holding the energy fields together.

Subsequent to this event, there were numerous "attempts" to "play with my head" by these forces... and I was certainly amazingly aware of them. When I slept, I no longer did so in my former manner; it was as though I slept only half way, and a whole other part of me was awake and watching. I could hear voices and whispers and activity; I could hear strange breathing and feel ghostly fingers touching me from time to time, which I would fling away mentally.

When these activities would begin, as they did almost every night, I would turn on the radio softly, leave a light on, or simply sit up and read and mentally expand my awareness to keep them at bay. I felt that I was constantly surrounded by sniffing wolves looking for a sign of weakness or the scent of fear.

One of the trickiest maneuvers was when "they" planted the thoughts in my mind that I had gotten out of the bed and walked in another room. As I came to the doorway and put my hand out to touch the wall, I realized that my hand went right through it and that I was *clearly* being manipulated in my mind. I snapped myself back into my body and *forced* my energy to hold its place, endeavoring with all my might to move my hand. When my fingers suddenly moved, it was like the "attack" popped like a balloon, and the harassment ceased.

Over and over again I performed these maneuvers of awareness and discipline—unaware of don Juan's remarks about it—feeling that it was the obvious course of action.

The last night "they" came, I was lying in the bed, drifting to sleep, and the sleepiness was like a drug which was one of the "warning signs". I could "see" through my closed eyes, which was another warning, and hear raspy breathing behind me. Then, I felt a touch on my back and all the force inside me exploded in anger and I pulled my "energy body" back and forced my arm to fling off the covers. It took several tries to get it to "connect" before the arm actually moved, and at the same time I was forcing my eyes open to see with the physical apparatus so that I would know that my fields were connected. As my eyes came open, I saw a large lizard, silhouetted by the light of the streetlamp outside the house, run across the window—a symbol of my victory.

And they have never come again.

chapter twelve
why we are where we are

In 1931, Aldous Huxley wrote *Brave New World* in which he stated:

> The older dictators fell because they never could supply their subjects with enough bread, enough circuses, enough miracles and mysteries. Nor did they possess a really effective system of mind-manipulation.
>
> Under a scientific dictator, education will really work-with the result that most men and women will grow up to love their servitude and will never dream of revolution. There seems to be no good reason why a thoroughly scientific dictatorship should ever be overthrown.

Aldous Huxley also made an early connection between the effects experienced by those partaking of psychedelic drugs and the experiences of Eastern Mysticism and this set the consciousness-raising bomb off with a *bang*! Along came Timothy Leary, Richard Alpert AKA Baba Ram Dass with their LSD and other modes of mind marvels, leading the parade of those who were "turned on, tuned in". Abraham Maslow became a father figure to the new "wave" of those desiring to fill the gaping hole of their reality with "peak experiences". Maslow cited psychedelic drugs as one of the means in which even ordinary people could have a little of what the Eastern Mystics worked many years to develop. Now, it could be had for a weekend seminar at Big Sur, or a study by mail course at only $29.95 per lesson! What a deal!

Peak Experiences—experience, experience, and experience—became the pot of gold at the end of the rainbow of the 1960s. No one needed to live in Existential Despair any longer! Everyone could become a "spiritual voyager" and achieve extended periods in realms of consciousness they had only heard about in veiled, mysterious allusions down through the ages. Encounter groups, radical therapies, old and new combinations of theories and practice came rolling off the conveyor belt of techno-spirituality. The intangibles of spirit had been harnessed! Anyone could evoke some desirable experience by manipulating awareness at the basic physical and psychological levels. Never mind that all of this bypassed the vital processes of reason and conscious decision making. By its very nature, the whole techno-spiritual machine operated completely without critical thinking; it tapped the bottomless pit of feeling-emotion-primal being. Never mind that much of this emotion was negative, confusing, anxious and fearful! Let's just get it all out here in the open and have a party with it!

Each of the many techniques developed during this time was fully capable of producing an emotional high of one sort or another. There were endless "peak experiences", and dramatic "personal breakthroughs". The mixtures of Zen, yoga, meditation, and drugs along with strict mechanical technology, were a veritable adventure in awareness! The only problem was: in the midst of all this peaking, mind-blowing, turning on and tuning in, ecstasy and encountering, many people encountered things that, perhaps, ought not have been awakened. Boundaries were breached into unseeable and terrifying realms of consciousness. William Chittick, translator of the works of the great Sufi Shaykh, Ibn al-'Arabi, wrote:

> Nowadays most people interested in the spirituality of the East desire the "experience", though they may call what they are after intimate communion with God. Those familiar with the standards and norms of spiritual experience set down by disciplined paths like Sufism are usually appalled at the way Westerners seize upon any apparition from the domain outside of normal consciousness as a manifestation of the "spiritual". In fact, there are innumerable realms in the unseen world, some of them far more dangerous than the worst jungles of the visible world.
>
> So preserve yourselves, my brothers, from the calamities of this place, for distinguishing it is extremely difficult! Souls find it sweet, and then within it they are duped, since they become completely enamored of it. (Chittick, 1989, 263)

By the end of the decade of the 60s, the "human potential" movement had become a veritable potpourri of religion, science, mysticism, magick and "the occult". The drug use got out of hand, the "techniques" began to show serious flaws with a number of tragedies resulting in crime or madness, and the whole idea of human beings becoming "psychic supermen" hit the skids. The promise of the 60s decayed into an aimless lethargy—old hippies living in communes, braiding their gray locks and lusting after the sweet young teeny boppers while they fired up another bong and reminisced about the "good old days" at Esalen.

But wait! Something else happened here! Remember, this is America! The home of the Free-Market that is. Many people suggest that the subsequent proliferation of the "New Age" consciousness raising movement was the result of big business seeing a pile of money to be made in the development of slick, newly packaged psychoanalysis and psychodrama. There was, indeed, mass distribution and Madison Avenue marketing of things like Mind Dynamics, Arica, Silva Mind Control, Transcendental Meditation, and on and on. Individual entrepreneurs knew a good thing when they saw it. However, there is more to this than meets the eye. This is important to our subject, so bear with me.

Richard Dolan's *UFOs and the National Security State* is the first comprehensive study of the past 50 years of the U.S. Government's response to the intrusion of UFO phenomena in America. The compiled evidence—which includes government documents—suggests that a group of specialists working in the shadows set up and executed the most massive cover-up in the history of government; and that the Human Potential movement and the subsequent New

Age movements were key elements of this cover-up. In other words, they not only have used the "colorful community" of alternative ideas as an unwitting tool of disinformation, it is highly probable that most of it was literally created by them as COINTELPRO. According to analysts, COINTELPRO was the FBI's secret program to undermine the popular upsurge of opposition, which swept the country during the 1960s. Though the name stands for "Counterintelligence Program", the targets were not enemy spies. The FBI set out to eliminate "radical" political opposition inside the U.S. What a lot of people do not realize is that this was a high level psychological operation specifically set up to vector "ideological" trends—beliefs. Dolan writes:

> The UFO problem has involved military personnel around the world for more than fifty years, and is wrapped in secrecy. ... Because this subject is so widely ridiculed, it is important to stress why it is worthy of serious attention. ... Stories of strange objects in the sky go far back into time, but the problem received little attention until the Second World War. ... During the UFO wave of 1947, American military and intelligence organizations conducted multiple, simultaneous investigations of these sightings. ... By the end of 1947, a contingent of analysts at the Air Technical Intelligence Center at Wright-Patterson Air Force Base believed that UFOs were extraterrestrial. By the summer of 1948, this team prepared an "Estimate of the Situation". ... As the story goes, Air Force Commander Hoyt Vandenberg rejected [this conclusion]....
>
> In the summer of 1952... UFO sightings were so frequent and often of such high quality that some in the air force actually wondered whether an invasion was under way. With some help from the secret CIA sponsored Robertson Panel of January 1953, the air force improved censorship over the problem. Still, it never quite went away. Civilian organizations began to collect and analyze interesting UFO reports. ... Then came the great UFO wave of 1965 and 1966, when the air force could no longer hide behind weather balloons and swamp gas, nor withstand public scrutiny. ...
>
> Let us pause to assess the situation. By the mid-1940s, America's intelligence apparatus had reason to believe that there were artifacts in the skies that did not originate from America, Russia, Germany, or any other country. These objects violated some highly sensitive military airspace, and did not appear to be natural phenomena. One may presume that the affected national security authorities made it an immediate obsession to determine the nature and purpose of these objects, and we may infer that the issue probably became a deep secret by 1946, or 1947 at the latest. (Dolan, 2002, xix)

It was at this precise moment in time that the Human Potential movement was "born". Do we think that this was a coincidence? By the mid-50s, it was becoming obvious that things were getting out of control and in August of 1956 the FBI began its COINTELPRO operation. When traditional modes of repression (exposure, blatant harassment, and prosecution for political crimes) failed to counter the growing insurgency, and even helped to fuel it, the Bureau took the law into its own hands. Its methods ranged far beyond surveillance, and amounted to a domestic version of the covert action for which the CIA has become infamous throughout the world.

Usually, when we think of COINTELPRO, we think of the most well known and typical activities which include sending anonymous or fictitious letters designed to start rumors, among other things, publishing false defamatory or threatening information, forging signatures on fake documents, introducing disruptive and subversive members into organizations to destroy them from within, and so on. Blackmailing insiders in any group to force them to spread false rumors, or to foment factionalism was also common.

What a lot of people don't keep in mind is the fact that COINTELPRO also concentrated on creating bogus organizations. These bogus groups could serve many functions which might include attacking and/or disrupting bona fide groups, or even just simply creating a diversion with clever propaganda in order to attract members away so as to involve them with time-wasting activity designed to prevent them from doing anything useful. COINTELPRO was also famous for instigation of hostile actions through third parties. According to investigators, these FBI programs were noteworthy because all documents relating to them were stamped "do not file". This meant that they were never filed in the system, and for all intents and purposes, did not exist. This cover was blown after activists broke into an FBI office in Media, Pennsylvania in 1971. The possibility of finding evidence for any of it, after that event, is about zero. To spell it out in Dolan's words:

> Regarding matters connected with "national security", there appears to be a wealth of information that does not exist officially. Thus, a request to find such documents through a Freedom of Information Act request would be in vain. Add to this the likelihood that perhaps the most sensitive information regarding UFOs may not even exist in document form ("the first rule in keeping secrets is nothing on paper", Richard Helms), and one can appreciate the difficulty that an honest UFO researcher has in ferreting out the truth. (184)

Now, let us take a few logical steps. The UFO problem emerged into the national consciousness in 1947, or thereabouts. Not long afterward, a lot of people began asking a lot of questions. The government wasn't answering, and so the people began to band together to find out the answers for themselves. They started forming groups. And this is where things get just a bit curious. The thing that was most threatened by the UFO/alien issue seems to have been the standard monotheistic religions. Religion seems to be a necessary component of political control. Social control—that is the mainstay of religion—was most definitely under threat. In fact, what seems to be true is that it is not even clear that religions—as we know them would have survived a full disclosure. So the logical conclusion is that part of the main reason for the cover-up was to "protect the religious status quo".

As things stood at the time, protecting the religious status quo—mainly the social controls that stem from religion—was iffy at best. After a century of scholarly investigation into many religious texts, and the raising of many questions about the "old time religion", there were a lot of people in society who were most definitely turning away from religious dogma. It's fairly simple to take the next logical step and see that a combining of the questions of those who were disenchanted with religion, with the questions of those who wanted to know just what the heck was going on in terms of possible "extraterrestrials", was seen as a dangerous and explosive mixture. Something had to be done.

The activities of COINTELPRO in attempting to neutralize political opposition have been pretty well exposed. But we are now considering the fact that, in addition to political activists, it seems that COINTELPRO has particularly targeted groups that are seeking the truth about the interactions between the U.S. government and Ultra Terrestrials, or so-called "aliens". That a long-time cover-up of these matters has been in effect is certainly evident to any careful researcher.

The COINTELPRO files show the U.S. Government targeted a very broad range of religious, labor and community groups opposed to any of its agendas, and it is only logical to assume that the same type of operation would be created to cover up the "alien agenda". Such a theoretical COINTELPRO operation also goes far in explaining why, when the sincere researcher of UFO phenomena enters this field, he or she discovers only lies, lies, and more lies; confusion and disinformation. That is most definitely the signature of COINTELPRO.

Considering all of this, would anybody care to suggest that it did not also occur to the powers that be (PTB) that the chief means of diverting attention and covering up the truth would be to literally fund and create the "New Age" and "Human Potential Movement" so that it would follow their agenda of keeping secrets?

In other words, it is extremely likely that the most successful and popular of Metaphysical Mavens and New Age Impresarios are COINTELPRO agents—either conscious or dupes of those who are. The objective seems to be to attack and "neutralize" those who are seeking the answers. Those who are sincere, who do bona fide research and seek to explicate the truth, are infiltrated, attacked, and marginalized according to standard COINTELPRO procedures.

What all of this seems to suggest is that the PTB have developed COINTELPRO to an all new level of social shaping, cultural brainwashing, and the main targets of this activity would include virtually anyone who is seeking the truth about the shifting realities of our world. The cases of COINTELPRO activities against political groups must be no more than the tip of the iceberg, given that the great bulk of COINTELPRO-type operations remain secret until long after their damage has been done. By all indications, domestic covert operations have become a permanent feature of U.S. politics and social programming, and it is hardly likely, considering the evidence, that the New Age and Human Potential fields are exempt.

The implications of this are truly alarming. Those who manage to get close to the truth of these matters, despite the many obstacles in their path, face national covert campaigns to discredit and disrupt their research and reputations. Clearly, COINTELPRO and similar operations under other names also work to distort academic and popular perceptions of the problems facing our world. They have done enormous damage to the search for the Truth.

"Terrorism is changing. New adversaries, new motivations and new rationales have surfaced in recent years to challenge much of the conventional wisdom..." wrote Dr. Bruce Hoffman, Director of RAND. And he was right. The only problem is, the reader is largely unaware of the definition of "new adversaries" that might be implied in his remarks. A careful reading of Richard Dolan's book will immediately reveal what Dr. Hoffman really meant in his remarks about "terrorism."

Based on the documents assembled by Dolan, it is obvious that the governments of the world do indeed see the UFO problem as a very, very serious matter. In the course of assembling the documents and reporting the events, Dolan came to the inescapable conclusion that there exists an "Above Top Secret" group with access to all available UFO data, and that this group "straddled" the worlds of government, military, and industry. The evidence proves that the military created a complete fiction for public consumption designed to convince the masses that the UFO problem was "nonexistent". They were assisted in pulling the wool over the eyes of the public by "heavy handed official media and culture", and they were obviously under orders to consistently and repeatedly "debunk" the idea that aliens were ensconced in our world. What seems to be true is that most of our elected officials are as much victims of the debunking as anybody else. And the same is true about mainstream science. Dolan writes:

> Next to the bureau, the military intelligence services became the most important component of the domestic intelligence scene. Army intelligence had nearly unlimited funds, extensive manpower, specialized personnel, deep planning and training resources, and the most sophisticated communications and data processing capability. ... The army's intelligence surveillance did not focus on tactical and reconnaissance data, but on political and ideological intelligence within the United States. (This was wholly illegal.) ...
>
> Then there was the CIA. By the late 1960s, there were more spies than diplomats in the State Department, or employees in the Department of Labor. ... When the Weather Underground, a radical splinter of the SDS, had an "acid test" to detect agents provocateurs, they had no idea that the CIA had been tripping on LSD throughout the 1950s, creating a special caste of "enlightened agents" for precisely these occasions. [Based on this, we wonder about "agents provocateurs" in the New Age and UFO community who are "specially trained?"]
>
> The agency continued its work on mind control. Following the work of Dr. Jose Delgado [experiments in] Electrical Stimulation of the Brain [were conducted.] This involves implanting electrodes into the brain and body, with the result that the subject's memory, impulses, and feelings could all be controlled. Moreover, ESB could evoke hallucinations, as well as fear and pleasure. "It could literally manipulate the human will at will", [said Dr. Robert Keefe, a neurosurgeon at Tulane University.]
>
> In 1968, George Estabrooks, another spook scientist, spoke indiscreetly to a reporter for the Providence Evening Bulletin. "The key to creating an effective spy or assassin, rests in creating a multiple personality with the aid of hypnosis", a procedure which he described as "child's play."

> By early 1969, teams within the CIA were running a number of bizarre experiments in mind control under the name Operation Often. In addition to the normal assortment of chemists, biologists, and conventional scientists, the operation employed psychics and experts in demonology.
>
> Over at the NSA, all one can say with certainty is that its budget dwarfed all others within the intelligence community. (361)

Dolan documents how the intelligence organizations of the United States—and very likely other countries who are working in concert with them, though outwardly they may pretend to be oppositional—have conducted terminal mind-control experiments, biological spraying of American cities, human plutonium and syphilis injections, illegal communications interception, and nationwide domestic surveillance of private citizens, political assassinations and coups, ongoing media manipulation and outright public lying on a continual basis, most especially in regards to UFOs. The above organizations, via any and all means available, made sure that, to the public at large, UFOs and aliens were a "dead issue".

Scientist and UFO disclosure advocate James McDonald said in 1969: "I am enough of a realist to sense that, unless this AAAS symposium succeeds in making the scientific community aware of the seriousness of the UFO problem, little response to any call for new investigations is likely to appear". McDonald presented a brilliant paper entitled "Science in Default: Twenty-two Years of Inadequate UFO Investigations". Dolan comments that it was "perhaps the most damning statement about UFO research ever made". Speaking before the convention at Boston's Sheraton Plaza Hotel, McDonald came down hard on everyone: Condon, Menzel, Hynek, and finally the scientific establishment itself. He said:

> No scientifically adequate investigation of the UFO problem has been carried out during the entire twenty-two years that have now passed since the first extensive wave of sightings of unidentified aerial objects in the summer of 1947. …In my opinion, the UFO problem, far from being the nonsense problem that many scientists have often labeled it, constitutes a problem of extraordinary scientific interest. The grave difficulty with essentially all past UFO studies had been that they were either devoid of any substantial scientific content, or else have lost their way amidst the relatively large noise content that tends to obscure the real signal in the UFO reports. (Quoted by Dolan, 368)

This high noise to signal ratio is, based on the evidence, the direct product of the frenzied activities of the "National Security State" in their promulgation of the New Age/Human Potential smoke and mirrors magic show. What is also clearly evident is that this noise is the fundament of the prevailing scientific doctrine. What we see is that the scientific community—though they claim to be seekers of advanced scientific truth—have been as easily duped as Joe Sixpack and Shirley Seeker of Truth. The former is interested in little more than his truck, his dog, and his weekend football game, while the latter is generally looking for a lifestyle of higher "experiences". What I also suspect is that even the lower echelons of the intelligence and military organizations must be included in this rather large grouping of the duped and deceived sheep.

An example of this duping of those investigating the matter from the "bottom up" is Andrew Tully who wrote *The Super Spies*, supposedly an early report on the NSA. He, and many who have followed him, suggest that the UFO is an "intelligence" device and that it evolved out of Nazi Secrets brought to the U.S. under Project Paperclip.[9]

Dolan lays out the evidence and disabuses us of the notion that the UFO activity could be human technological breakthroughs as such naive conspiracy theorists propose. As he says, "all of the indicators point to a definitive NO". He then points out that, every single person who actually studies the UFO problem (yours truly included—who began as a flaming skeptic) becomes convinced that it *is* a problem of alien invasion of our planet. Every official study of UFOs persuaded the researchers that aliens were the explanation for the data. But that data has been denied, and when denial no longer worked, it was obscured by the noise, the smoke and mirrors that prevail today in UFO research and the New Age and Human Potential movements. Do we think that this is coincidence?

---

[9] Convinced that German scientists could help America's postwar efforts, President Harry Truman agreed in September 1946 to authorize "Project Paperclip", a program to bring selected German scientists to work on America's behalf during the "Cold War".

However, Truman expressly excluded anyone found "to have been a member of the Nazi party and more than a nominal participant in its activities, or an active supporter of Nazism or militarism". The War Department's Joint Intelligence Objectives Agency (JIOA) conducted background investigations of the scientists. In February 1947, JIOA Director Bosquet Wev submitted the first set of scientists' dossiers to the State and Justice Departments for review. The Dossiers were damning. Samuel Klaus, the State Departments representative on the JIOA board, claimed that all the scientists in this first batch were "ardent Nazis". Their visa requests were denied. Wev wrote a memo warning that "the best interests of the United States have been subjugated to the efforts expended in 'beating a dead Nazi horse.'" He also declared that the return of these scientists to Germany, where they could be exploited by America's enemies, presented a "far greater security threat to this country than any former Nazi affiliations which they may have had or even any Nazi sympathies that they may still have".

When the JIOA formed to investigate the backgrounds and form dossiers on the Nazis, the Nazi Intelligence leader Reinhard Gehlen met with the CIA director Allen Dulles. Dulles and Gehlen hit it off immediately, Gehlen was a master spy for the Nazis and had infiltrated Russia with his vast Nazi Intelligence network. Dulles promised Gehlen that his Intelligence unit was safe in the CIA. Dulles had the scientists dossier's re-written to eliminate incriminating evidence. As promised, Allen Dulles delivered the Nazi Intelligence unit to the CIA, which later opened many umbrella projects stemming from Nazi mad research. (MK-ULTRA / ARTICHOKE, OPERATION MIDNIGHT CLIMAX) By 1955, more than 760 German scientists had been granted citizenship in the U.S and given prominent positions in the American scientific community. Many had been longtime members of the Nazi party and the Gestapo, had conducted experiments on humans at concentration camps, had used slave labor, and had committed other war crimes. In a 1985 expose in the Bulletin of the Atomic Scientists Linda Hunt wrote that she had examined more than 130 reports on Project Paperclip subjects--and every one "had been changed to eliminate the security threat classification". President Truman, who had explicitly ordered no committed Nazis to be admitted under Project Paperclip, was evidently never aware that his directive had been violated. (http://www.thirdworldtraveler.com/Fascism/Operation_Paperclip_file.html)

Another evident production of "noise" is the nonsense that passes today as "channeling" or "alien contacts". Indeed, our own work involves what can certainly be called inspirational material, but as we have noted repeatedly, it is not your usual "channeled" info, nor do we treat it as such. For us, a controlled channeling experiment is the 10% inspiration that must be matched by the 90% perspiration of real research. With a broad historical awareness of the facts, a firm grounding in the realization that most of what is out there is deliberate disinformation, the individual who surveys the plethora of "alternative information" in books and on the internet, can easily recognize the "noise" factor produced by the Secret State. Dolan tells us:

> By the early 1970s, there were already means available to alter the moods of unsuspecting persons. A pocket-sized transmitter generating electromagnetic energy at less than 100 milliwatts could do the job. This is no pie-in-the-sky theory. In 1972, Dr. Gordon J.F. McDonald testified before the House Subcommittee on Oceans and International Environment on the issue of electromagnetic weapons used for mind control and mental disruption. He stated:
> [T]he basic notion was to create, between the electrically charged ionosphere in the higher part of the atmosphere and conducting layers of the surface of the Earth, this neutral cavity, to create waves, electrical waves that would be tuned to the brain waves. ...About ten cycles per second. ...You can produce changes in behavioral patterns or in responses.
> The following year, Dr. Joseph C. Sharp, at Walter Reed Hospital, while in a soundproof room, was able to hear spoken words broadcast by 'pulsed microwave audiogram.' These words were broadcast to him without any implanted electronic translation device. Rather, they reached him by direct transmission to the brain. (382)

Consider the above in terms of "chemtrails". And note the comments of our own experimentally obtained material regarding the above—not from "aliens", but rather from "us in the future."

December 4, 1999

Q: (L) But, the fact still remains, in my opinion, that there are a *lot, lot, lot* of planes flying above us in the past few years! Whether they are dumping anything on our heads, or what, there are an extreme number of planes flying in these upper level criss-cross patterns. Now, whether they are just playing war-games, or they are spy planes, they are doing *something!* What is the reason for all of this upper level flying that results in these criss-crossed contrails that everybody is seeing?

A: A lot of it is "training maneuver" oriented.

Q: Why are they training so many pilots? What are they preparing for?

A: Military budgets must be justified, you know. Review "Military-Industrial Complex 101".

Q: So, this is just training flight, justification of budget, and nothing more than that?

A: Well, we would not say "not anything more to it than that", but, when you say "M-IC", you have said a lot!

chapter twelve

Q: Are you implying that there is a build-up of the Military-Industrial Complex for a reason?

A: To preserve status quo during "peacetime". This peace business is not very profitable, you know.

Q: Does that suggest that they are building up to set off a war so they can make more money?

A: Maybe if indeed, and *if the populous can be hoodwinked*. But, fortunately, the public is less hoodwink able. Maybe the real enemy is "out there", rather than "over there". Was it not always?

Q: Does any of this increased aircraft activity have anything to do with the increased awareness and activities of aliens in and around our planet?

A: As always. But, this awareness is factionalized and compartmentalized.

The C's comments take on a whole new meaning in light of the present situation—9/11 and all that—as well as Bush's drive for "war". We also note the most interesting remark that "awareness of the activities of aliens in and around our planet" is "factionalized and compartmentalized". And this is where we come to the COINTELPRO function of creating bogus organizations to attack or disrupt bona fide groups.

We have already noted the fact that research in electrical stimulation of the brain could produce hallucinations. If you put hallucinations together with words, you can produce just about anything that you want in the way of "noise" to obscure the truth—including the "shape-shifting reptoids-as-humans", or a "gray dude in the bathroom", or a "Guardian Alliance", or a "Nibiruan Council", or an "Ashtar Command", or talking whales and dolphins, etc. You name it— they can produce it via voices in the head and hallucinations and transmissions of frequencies that produce ecstatic states, healings, or whatever. And so it is that the human element of the Cosmic COINTELPRO operation manages their many "agents" of disinformation—pied pipers leading the masses of New Age seekers—so that whatever the real truth is remains their secret. And that's exactly the way they want it.

Notice the dates in the above quote from Dolan's book telling us that in the early 70s certain technologies were being developed that could "broadcast" signals over the entire nation. We certainly suspect that this technology was developed further in the subsequent years. The question is: what did they do with it? Better yet, what *are* they doing with it?

What strikes me as an essential turning point in this COINTELPRO operation was the beginning of the "expose" of two particular items that hold sway in certain "conspiracy" circles to this very day: alien abduction and "Satanic Ritual Abuse".

The Gray alien scenario was "leaked" by Budd Hopkins. Whitley Strieber's alien abduction books, including *Communion*, followed a few years after. Prior to the publication of these books, the ubiquitous "Gray aliens" had rarely, if ever, been seen before. In fact, a review of the history of "contact" cases show that the type and variety and behavior of "aliens" around the world are quite different across the board. But, along came Budd, followed by Whitley and his glaring alien on the cover, and suddenly the Grays were everywhere.

In respect of Whitley and his Grays, allow me to emphasize one of Dolan's comments quoted above: "By early 1969, teams within the CIA were running a number of bizarre experiments in mind control under the name Operation Often. In addition to the normal assortment of chemists, biologists, and conventional scientists, the operation employed psychics and experts in demonology." This, of course, brings us to the parallel event of that period of time: satanic ritual abuse. SRA is the name given to the allegedly systematic abuse of children (and others) by Satanists.

As it happens, keeping our timeline in mind, it was in the mid to late 1970s that the allegations of the existence of a "well-organized intergenerational satanic cult whose members sexually molest, torture and murder children across the United States" began to emerge in America. There was a panic regarding SRA triggered by a fictional book called *Michelle Remembers*. The book was published as fact but has subsequently been shown by at least three independent investigators to be a hoax. No hard evidence of SRA in North America has ever been found, just as no hard evidence of abductions by Gray aliens has ever been found. Nevertheless, the allegations were widely publicized on radio and television talk shows, including Geraldo Rivera's show.

Religious fundamentalists promoted the hysteria and, just as during the Inquisitions, endless self-proclaimed "moral entrepreneurs" both fed the fires of prosecution and earned a good living from it. Most of the early accusations of satanic ritual abuse were aimed at working-class people with limited resources, and with a few exceptions, the media and other groups that are ordinarily skeptical either remained silent or joined in the feeding frenzy of accusations. The few professionals who spoke out against the hysteria were systematically attacked and discredited by government agencies and private organizations.

The question has to be asked: If there are thousands of baseless accusations of SRA and thousands upon thousands of cases of unverifiable alien abductions, how do they originate?

Most of the SRA cases are said to originate with children. Since there is a widespread belief that children wouldn't make up stories of eating other children or being forced to have sex with giraffes after flying in an airplane while they were supposed to be in day care, the stories are often taken at face value by naive prosecutors, therapists, police officers and parents. Researchers have found that children are unlikely to invent stories of satanic ritual abuse on their own. So, where do the stories come from?

Accusing the therapists, district attorneys, police and parents of inducing such stories from children doesn't seem to be a very productive answer. Yes, it may happen in some cases, but certainly doesn't seem likely in the vast number of cases.

Now, let's go back and think about our timeline. As it happens, *Michelle Remembers* was published in 1980, co-written by Michelle Smith and Lawrence

Pazder, M.D. Budd Hopkins finished *Missing Time* in December of 1980, with an "Afterword" by Aphrodite Clamar, Ph.D.

It's looking pretty "coincidental" from where I sit.

What occurs to me—putting the pieces of the puzzle together—is that there is some general kind of imagery being widely broadcast in the "neutral cavity" described above, and that it depends a lot on the individual and their cultural programming how it "takes". When we consider the fact that Operation Often employed "the normal assortment of chemists, biologists, and conventional scientists" and "psychics and experts in demonology", we begin to think that electronic COINTELPRO includes a whole supermarket of new "beliefs"—Gray aliens and "alien contacts" for the New Age crowd and a whole range of "sexual/ritual abuse scenarios" for those who are not open to the alien shtick.

Is the whole thing beamed out as some sort of "free-formal imaging", and, based on the conscious acceptance of one or another version, it takes on its individual characteristics in the minds of the millions of recipients? In other words, is it picked up by the subconscious in alpha states or in sleep, perceived as traumatic in a general scenario that can then be interpreted by the individual belief systems in terms of either being examined and or sexually manipulated by aliens on a table or "raped on an altar" by Satanists? Are the public productions—books by Hopkins, Strieber, and the SRA scandals, just variations on the closing of the circuit by the conscious mind accepting or creating one or the other scenario as the explanation for the constant bombardment of such signals as described in Dolan's book? Is it the job of COINTELPRO to create "bogus organizations" that produce various "explanations" to close the circuit and "make it real" in the person's mind?

One has to wonder about the name of the program, Operation Often, in terms of the claims of abductees—victims of repeated and "often" abductions—as well as the claims of those who suggest the SRA explanation. In either case, the believer is being "herded" into a "response camp" of either faith in alien saviors, or faith in Jesus to save from them the demonic/satanic Illuminati, Jews, Pagans—take your pick.

Let me make it clear that I am in no way suggesting that "abductions" or some whacked out satanic rituals do not ever take place somewhere, under some circumstances. What I am suggesting is that the Gray alien and SRA phenomenon most certainly was not restricted in any way by COINTELPRO, and may indeed be the smoke and mirrors that hides a far more insidious state of affairs.

In essence, Dolan's book shows us the history of how the many levels of society have been duped and deceived—or directly controlled—from the average citizen, to the seeker of higher truths, to the scions of science and industry, to the hallowed halls of government. Each "type" has been targeted in the way most likely to "manage" them best. Those who cannot be "managed" generally die, as scientist James McDonald—and others—did. But all the while, the UFOs kept coming, and people kept seeing them, and they kept asking questions.

In April 1971, an engineering research magazine, Industrial Research, published the results of a poll in which 80 percent of its members rejected the Condon Report; 76 percent believed that the government was concealing UFO facts; 32 percent believed that UFOs were extraterrestrial. Poll or no poll, the CIA continued to lie about its UFO interests. ...

The worst story of 1971 was the demise of James McDonald [atmospheric physicist from the University of Arizona]. As far as anyone could tell, McDonald was fine all through 1970 and into 1971. On March 2, 1971, he testified as an expert in atmospheric physics at the House committee on Appropriations regarding the supersonic transport (SST) and its potentially harmful atmospheric effects. McDonald's opponents questioned his credentials and ridiculed him as someone who believed in "little men flying around the sky". Laughter broke out several times.

Shortly after this incident, McDonald shot himself in the head and became blind. He was committed to the psychiatric ward of the VA medical Center in Tucson. In June, he signed himself out. On Sunday morning, June 13, a woman in south Tucson, identifying herself as a doctor, said a deranged blind man had taken a cab to the area. She wanted to know where the driver had dropped him off, and she made several calls. Meanwhile, a married couple and their children, walking along a shallow creek, found McDonald's body under a bridge at 11:40 a.m. A .38 caliber revolver was in the sand, near his head. A brief note attributed his suicide to marriage and family problems. ...

We know that many intelligence agencies were skilled in "creating" suicides. But, one might ask, wasn't McDonald's mental condition already deteriorating? Jerome Clark stated that McDonald was ready to "crack" in the aftermath of the SST hearings. But what caused this? Embarrassment at the SST hearings? His marriage? Perhaps, one supposes, but both of these explanations feel flimsy. Without exception, those who knew McDonald described him as possessing great integrity and courage. Was he really the type of person to commit suicide? (Dolan, 381)

McDonald had been described as a man who was "afraid of nothing". What seems to be so is that this was why he was destroyed. Hynek had written that McDonald was considered by the Air Force to be an "outstanding nuisance".

With the mind control arsenal that has been described at their disposal, we have a good idea of what "they" can do to the mind. Even the strongest. Courage and integrity, it seems, are no protection. We would like to note another curious death—that of Edward Ruppelt. After years as an advocate of disclosure, he suddenly did an about face—re-wrote his book recanting his belief that UFOs were extraterrestrial craft, and was dead within a year at a very young age.

It looks to me as though, if they can't corrupt you, they kill you, and if they can corrupt you, they still kill you so you won't have a chance to change your mind and recant your recantation like Jacques de Molay did when the Templars were destroyed. Those who get close to the belly of the beast are generally subjected to a new "approach" it seems. And that approach is the biggest betrayal of all.

Many important and influential people have attested to the reality of the UFO phenomenon as an "alien reality". Within the military organizations, those who affirm the "alien hypothesis" are widespread and numerous. But, as Dolan shows us, they cannot discuss those views without risking the penalties of imprisonment and stiff fines.

In the present day, we have Steven Greer's "Disclosure Project". Based on the mail I get, it seems that many in the New Age/UFO community think that this is a great and novel idea. However, history shows that it has been tried before. The one thing about Greer's effort that suggests it is just more and better COINTELPRO is his attachment to the "aliens are here to help us" idea which is directly contradicted by history, though widely promoted by most "contactees". Even Linda Howe, for a long time the most reputable of careful researchers—and no stranger to the machinations of the Secret State—seems to have fallen for this one—or COINTELPRO. It is also now being promoted in *Fate Magazine* by Rosemary Guiley, who has the odor of COINTELPRO about her with her notable connections to military "agents". Jerome Clark, quoted above, is also a regular contributor to *Fate*.

Let me make it clear at this point that I am convinced that a lot of honest, sincere, hard-working individuals are being duped and/or controlled without being fully aware of it.

Dolan documents the failure of civilian groups in their efforts to really "end UFO secrecy". NICAP had prominent and active members, connections to Congress and the military, and their effort continued for over ten years. NICAP fought diligently for congressional hearings, and yet every time they got "close" to bringing it to the table for public consideration, the congressional sponsorship "backed off" and reversed their support.

What kind of group is it that can control our government officials in this way? An even deeper question might be: What kind of group is it that can control the media, the military, the CIA, the FBI, NSA, and even the President? What do they do to intimidate and dominate ethical and substantial persons in positions of authority? Whatever it is, we would certainly like to know because it suggests that they are hiding something so significant that even hints of it behind closed doors can send the most powerful congressmen running with their tails tucked between their legs.

This brings us back to the problem of the Secret State and its agenda. Some people believe that this secrecy is absolutely essential. They say that the public simply could not handle the truth about aliens. They say that there is no reason to spoil people's lives with the truth because there is nothing that the average person could do about it anyway. Is that really true? Would there be so much effort to conceal the alien agenda if disclosure of the truth wasn't harmful to that agenda?

Dolan's chronological history of the actual interaction between UFOs and the public and the corresponding behavior of the military, the intelligence community, the media, the scientific community in its interaction with the public, make this abundantly clear. Dolan writes:

> Some believe this is, as it ought to be. Can the public really handle the truth
> about aliens? If the presence of others constitutes a threat to humanity, for

example, what could the average person even do about it? There are those who believe that secrecy about UFOs is in the public's best interest. (392)

What is clearly evident, and most especially so in the past year or two, is that the "public interest" is not the concern of those making these decisions. As Dolan rightly says, secrecy is being utilized not to protect the public, but to protect those keeping the secrets—the "Above Top Secret" group—and very likely even the aliens themselves.

When we consider the modus operandi of the intelligence community, in its historical perspective, what we see is that, at every level, right up to the very top, there is control and manipulation. This leads me to suggest that even those at the top level of the human Consortium are being duped and deceived and are as unable and/or unwilling to consider that possibility as those at the lower levels.

It seems obvious from the documentary evidence as well as the behavior of the military in response to UFOs and the "alien matter", that the aliens do have an agenda, and that—at some level in the layers of secrecy—there are those who know—at least on a "need to know" basis—what that agenda is. It seems abundantly evident that the secrecy has been enjoined on this group by the aliens themselves. What is more, a careful assessment of the evidence does not suggest a benevolent agenda.

As a result of the manipulations of this "Consortium", the majority of Americans are inculcated into the fiction of a representative government—a democracy—and that our scientists and representatives are "taking care of business" for us, and even if they are sometimes corrupt, they aren't as bad as a totalitarian regime. It has become most definitely obvious in the past couple of years that this is not the case—and probably never was. We don't even really elect our representatives. It's all a sham. But the fiction propagated by the media has clouded the ability of the American people to see their society and government for what it really is: an oligarchy that pretends to be a democracy to placate and deceive the public.

To those who suggest that it doesn't really matter since it is an efficient way to organize and manage millions of people, let us suggest that it is suicidal to think that an oligarchy is not primarily interested in maintaining its own position to the exclusion of all other considerations. When we consider the evidence, we see that the groups in question have never acted in the best interests of the public. If you doubt this, spend some time reading about nonconsensual human experimentation. And so, logically speaking, there is no reason to even suggest that the secrecy surrounding the "alien reality" is any different.

Dolan notes that, as a result of the concerted "debunking" of UFOs perpetrated on a populace that has been mind manipulated and dumbed down by public "education" for a very long time, our society has become extraordinarily schizophrenic about UFOs. At the level of "officialdom", as in academia, mainstream media, government and so forth, UFOs are either ignored or treated as a joke. You won't find UFOs or aliens—or their repeated invasion of sensitive airspace—discussed on the nightly news. You won't find Ted Koppel analyzing them as a threat to National Security. And this state of affairs is totally bizarre because it is abundantly—overwhelmingly—clear and evident that our military and intelligence organizations consider them to be so important that information about them is classified "Above Top Secret".

However, being classified "Above Top Secret" does not seem to matter to the aliens. They arrogantly do as they please and leave the "clean up" to their human lackeys the same way some media personalities have been reported to destroy hotel rooms, and then have their accountants write checks to cover the damages, while their agents give press releases that deny any such thing ever happened.

This brings us back to the efforts of COINTELPRO. Since the military is in the position of dealing with beings of such arrogance that their checks don't cover the damage they do, the "press releases" are issued in the form of diversion and division. UFOs and the "alien reality" are promoted in ways that simply do not relate to the documentary evidence or the factual data. UFOs and aliens are given cachet in the New Age and metaphysical communities, and groups studying them or "channeling" them are "managed" so that the possibility of exposure of the Truth is completely minimized in the plethora of conflicting, generated "beliefs". At the same time, there are organizations that are set up to operate as "professional debunkers" and disinformation artists. Smoke and mirrors and endless confusion.

What is evident from the documents and statements of those "in on the secret", is that the current "popularity" of aliens and New Age presentations of the subject are the direct result of deliberate infiltration by intelligence personnel who are continually "spinning the wheel" of lies and distortion.

chapter thirteen
fingerprints of the consortium

Let me now present some selections from the Cassiopaean transcripts, some of which have been withheld from publication for over two years now for what will become obvious reasons.

> Q: Whitley Strieber and Art Bell have published a book about a "global superstorm". Is any of the information they have given in this book fairly accurate?
>
> A: Derived from non-human sources known for stark accuracy, when convenient.
>
> Q: What makes it convenient at the present time for them to be "starkly accurate?"
>
> A: Fits into plans.
>
> Q: Plans for what?
>
> A: Do we not know already?
>
> Q: In other words: world conquest and the takeover of humanity?
>
> A: Not as simple.
>
> Q: What would make my statement more accurate?
>
> A: Call it amalgamation. […]
>
> Q: Let me ask some questions from a member of our [discussion] group. He is reading some material that suggests that this planet is a breeding ground for aliens, and the life cycle of the aliens, as in the Reptilians or whatever, may mimic something, such as a preying mantis. It also alludes to the suggestion that the underground of the earth is where alien females exist in some kind of a dormant stage, and it is the male that is returning or that does return at the end of each epoch, and that the focus of this appears to be the great pyramid, and that if we move to STO—it doesn't say those words but it's the same—much terror can be avoided, as the return of the male dragon will die for love for the female nymph. OK. Is the earth a breeding round for some kind of aliens as suggested in this passage?
>
> A: No.
>
> Q: Hmm. So this stuff that this guy has made up about this is like right out of his darkest nightmares? I mean the worst possible spin that could be put on this? It's already bad enough. So we really ought to forget this and just get some sleep at night, huh?
>
> A: Yes.
>
> Q: What is the source of this type of material? I mean, what kind of energy is behind it?
>
> A: STS mind control signal.

Q: What is it designed to do?

A: Reach those that are programmed to receive.

Q: Let me ask you this—If some of these STS programming signals that are going out ... I mean, I'm assuming that some of them come from third density. Is that correct?

A: Yes.

Q: Do they actually have, like, some place on the planet where these guys read science fiction books and get these really crazy theories and stories that they put together with sort of fiendish glee, and then convert them via computer into the programming code that gets beamed out into people's heads, while they sit there and just—you know—fall down on the floor laughing at what they have just done? I mean, is this possibly something that is going on?

A: Yes.

Q: That's sick! I mean, just take a whole HP Lovecraft novel, convert it into the programming signal and beam it out—and people are saying, "My God, the aliens told me ... it's just like HP Lovecraft said. Oh, my God!" Can you imagine? (A) And it works. (L) Sure does, doesn't it? [...]

Q: (L) What were the Ophanic intelligences of Dr. John Dee?

A: 4D STS.

Previously unpublished material follows:

September 14, 2001

Q: We have a series of questions about this recent event. Was the attack on the World Trade Center undertaken by Muslim Terrorists?

A: No.

Q: Who was behind this attack?

A: Israel.

Q: Is it going to become known that it was Israel? Will they be exposed?

A: Yes. [...]

Q: Are there going to be further terrorist attacks in the U.S. next week as others have been predicting?

A: No.

Q: Are there going to be further terrorist attacks of *this kind* at any time in the near future in the U.S.?

A: No.

Q: Is this the beginning of WW III?

A: No.

Q: Is the U.S. Going to bomb Afghanistan?

A: Possible in future. [...]

October 13, 2001

Q: (L) Next question: Is the anthrax that has been contracted by several people around our country a terrorist act against our country by foreign terrorists?

A: No.

Q: Where did the Anthrax come from?

A: U.S. government. [...]

high strangeness

Q: (L) Are they going to try to blame it on some foreign element?

A: Yes.

Q: (L) So, if they are going to try to blame it on some foreign group, can we have any idea of which group?

A: Iraq.

Q: (L) Are we ultimately headed toward bombing Iraq?

A: Yes.

Q: (A) Notice however, one complication: groups all over the world, as we are now noticing, have started protests against America. People are going to the streets in Europe to protest. So, in order to avoid this protest, probably America will have to produce some new evidence. Maybe an explosion of anthrax—maybe something completely new. (L) Is that something that is going to happen?

A: Yes.

Q: (L) And what might be the next major act of terrorism be that will... (A) It may be somewhere in Europe to convince the European countries. (L) So, whoever is protesting the most is the one that is likely to get hit in some way. (A) But, on the other hand, it may not be easy for America to produce something there, since it is much easier to produce "terrorist" events in America where they have complete control of everything. (L) If they try to do it elsewhere, they are liable to get caught.

A: France may be hit next with nuke.

Q: (L) Well, that's not friendly! (A) Well, that may make sense. There is this connection between the Afghans and Algerians and France. Algeria has already terrorized France in the past, so that may be the set-up. (L) That would certainly get their attention. Is there going to be an outbreak of terrorism on the 31st of this month as has been circulating on the grapevine?

A: Not likely.

Q: This Sollog guy made predictions about a certain series of events a few years ago. He claims that he predicted the plane hitting a big building, followed by the death of the Pope, followed by the death of a sitting American president. If this is true, he did make a "hit" on the "big building", and we certainly have a very aged Pope who is likely to go at any time now. That leaves the question of an American President dying in office. Is there any likelihood of that happening in the next year or two?

A: Yes.

Q: (A) Likelihood can be 1 %. (L) OK, is there a high probability of that?

A: No.

Q: (BT) Well, the thought that went through my mind, in such a scenario, is related to Cheney. Could he be part of the maverick group pulling the strings?

A: Close.

Q: (L) He may not even be conscious of it. I have the idea that most of them aren't. They are just like everyone else: manipulated puppets. (BT) Well, somebody has to be conscious of it, for this faction to be involved. When you were asking the question about Bush, the thought about Cheney just jumped to the fore. (L) Are any of these people in the government, those in the public eye, the decisions makers; are any of them consciously aware that they are furthering the agenda for the STS takeover of the planet? The main players.

chapter thirteen

A: No.

Q: (L) Bush is just a puppet. He's like Pinnochio. Every time he opens his mouth his nose just gets longer and longer. Pretty soon his nose will be so long he won't be able to walk across the room. (A) In Poland, we had this guy Jaruzelski, who introduced Martial Law. He was a general. Well, my mother was in favor of him. Because he was military. But I could see through him. (L) Well, it is easy to get upset with Bush until you realize that he is as much a dupe as anyone else. He seems to be going around in a fog. All the jokes that are made about him being so dull are true! How can you get mad at a complete puppet? I've never heard the guy say an intelligent thing that wasn't written down for him, and even then he sometimes manages to screw it up. (A) Yes, it seems so. Because those leaders who have proven *not* to be stupid in the past, have proved to be... (L) ...dead. (A) Or, they proved to be able to kill millions to stay alive. (L) Yup, seems to be so. (A) Yes, they can be stupid in a very intelligent way. (L) Are all of these people going to be exposed, caught, shown for what they are?

A: Ultimately.

Q: (BT) Yeah, and that can be part of the STS program anyway. Expose 'em and replace 'em with something worse. If everybody relies on the government to save us, and then find out that the government is not only not going to save us, but that they are guilty of harming us for manipulation, that is a manipulation of a higher order. (L) Yeah! And then who will the people cry for to be in charge? Aliens? (A) It's a "free" choice. [Laughter.] (L) Well, it's a terrible thing to feel that way about your president who is supposed to be the representative of your country. (A) I'm surprised that some Americans... (L) ...actually believe that he's doing a good job and telling the truth. (A) Yes. (L) I would like to know what is the *real* percentage of Americans who think that Bush is doing a good job. I know they put up the results of polls, but I have observed that polls are often published to sway public opinion, and are not an accurate representation of it. What is the real percentage?

A: 53 %.

Q: (L) Just a little over half. Well, even that figure is depressing. Are we in danger of Anthrax?

A: Most likely not or anything else. [...]

Q: (L) We watched one film that showed a strange, dark object, shooting down towards the ground [from one of the buildings of the World Trade Center]. What was that?

A: 4th Density energy surge.

Q: (L) Where was it surging from and to?

A: Dome of destruction energy time lock to ground.

Q: (L) Are you saying that there was a dome of a time lock over this area? Do you mean that they put a "time lock" over this area so that they could "harvest" bodies or energy?

A: Close.

Q: (BT) Was there any other purpose besides harvest?

A: Gathering records, gold, soul extraction, he said.

Q: (L) What does "he said" mean?

A: Journeyman.

Q: (L) Who or what is a "journeyman?"

A: Informant.

Q: (L) So there is a "journeyman" who is the informant from whom you obtained the information regarding the question?

A: 4th Density STO observer.

Q: (L) What did they want the gold for?

A: 4th density uses gold for technology.

Q: (BT) Well, that is in many myths about the "gods" mining gold in antiquity. (L) Were they gathering records in the sense of material objects?

A: Partly.

Q: (L) Might these records also have been an extraction of "records" from people as they were dying?

A: Yes.

Q: (L) For what purpose did they intend to use the souls that were extracted?

A: Remolecularization.

Q: What will they use these remolecularized beings for?

A: Insert them back into building to escape and be rescued.

Q: (L) Are you saying that this was an opportunity used as a very traumatic screen event of a mass abduction, so to say?!

A: Yes.

Q: (L) What was done to these people who were abducted? Was there a specific reason for a mass abduction?

A: Turn on the programs.

Q: (TB) So, those who "escaped" are very likely programmed individuals turned loose in our society. People with programs set to make them run amok at some point?

A: Close.

Q: (A) Well, we still we have one problem: the problem involvement of Israel. We were worrying about what is going to happen in Israel. At present, all the anger is directed at the United States.

A: America may shift blame.

Q: (A) Well... little things are emerging.

August 24, 2002

Q: (L) OK, I have a question before we launch off on this other subject. We have been considering putting our collected material on the attack on the WTC and the conspiracy of the government together into a book or a small booklet form or something rather than putting it on the web site and subjecting ourselves to hackers and all that kind of stuff. The question is how to do this without stepping on toes here? (A) By doing this, shall we remarkably cross the line?

A: Lines can be crossed if done carefully. [...] It would also be a good idea to present both sides of the story. Along with a little "history" of the claimants and participants so the reader may have a foundation on which to judge who is or is not likely to be truthful.

Q: (L) Well, let me think. So if I include a little bit of history about a few related things and then point out: here's what's happening now and this is what's going

265

on, that will do it. (L) OK, now, $64,000 question: what caused the fire and explosion at the Pentagon? Was it a 757?

A: No it was very close to what you have surmised: a drone craft specially modified to give certain "impressions" to witnesses. Even the windows were not "real."

Q: (S) What is a drone craft? (A) It's a guided craft run by a computer. There is not even a seat for a pilot. (L) Alright, the $64,001 question, what happened to Flight 77?

A: It was landed and now resides, in part, in fourth density.

Q: (L) What do mean "in part," how can it be in part?

A: As we have mentioned before, certain bases have this property due to direct interaction with denizens of that realm.

Q: (L) And they talked about bases that have levels underground. (A) Well, 'in part' can mean mechanical part or the human part. (L) Also, once they talked about bi-density beings that can move back and forth between third and fourth density. So, exactly what do you mean by this 'in part?'

A: Let us just say that the "human" part now resides at 5th density.

Q: (L) Well, the soul is what goes to fifth density. So that means that the bodies are still—well, somewhere. Did they later use parts of these bodies to produce evidence at the crash site of 'remains?'

A: Parts is the correct word. Do you think that any of them could be "allowed" to survive?

Q: (A) I have a technical question because if it landed somewhere, question is, whether the standard military surveying satellites, or whatever it is, know the place, or it disappeared completely before landing from normal satellite, or rather military, observation?

A: It landed in the normal way.

Q: (A) OK, then that means the military, and perhaps also the White House, knows that it landed and knows that...

A: White House knows little of what transpires in any case.

Q: (A) Right. But there are other spy satellites; some other countries may know that this story with flight 77 crashing at the Pentagon is...

A: At those levels, there is only one "Master."

Q: (L) Those levels? What levels?

A: Levels that can hand down orders to bury or suppress.

Q: (L) So you're saying that even, for example French, Russian, Chinese satellites that might have noticed something, that there is some level of control that can order such information to be buried or suppressed... (A) And the order will be respected? Why?

A: Those who are at that level have been bought and paid for by both giving knowledge of upcoming cataclysmic vents, and promised survival and positions of power after. It is not difficult to realize the there is a body of such types in positions of power already. Power is not only attractive to such types, they are the kind most easily corrupted by it.

Q: (SB) So they've been bought and paid for by... (L) Telling them what's going to happen, telling them this is the only way to survive and that they will be helped to survive. And then, telling them that once it's all over with, they can be in charge. Well, if they were going to kill the people anyway, who were in Flight 77, why didn't they just simply use this Flight 77 to crash into the Pentagon?

A: Because the damage would not have been controllable otherwise.

Q: (A) Yes, this is rather clear. If you let real hijackers and real pilots in there, who may start to fight just before the crash or something, God knows where it might hit. (L) So it was real important for this one to be carefully controlled. It had to hit a very specific target for a very specific reason. (A) Yeah. All this jet fuel will start burning, uncontrolled fire... (L) Can't have that. (S) Well also there might have been a specific area of the Pentagon that was more expendable; that they were focusing in on one specific spot in that building. (L) Well that has something to do with what L found out because she discovered that most of the people in the Pentagon who were killed were low-level female workers. All bigwigs were somewhere else in the building. (A) Well, what will be the consequences for publishing this book?

A: Who is going to put the pieces together reasonably and coherently if you don't? Everyone is seeking truth. What's wrong with putting it out there?

Q: (L) Well sometimes putting the truth out there gets you in deep doo-doo.

A: And sometimes not putting it out there gives some others hopes of stopping you from doing so. Once it is out, you are safer since at that point any "attacks" only justify and validate.

September 14, 2002

Q: (L) I want to ask about this crop circle supposedly that was created here on or around Aug. 15, 2002 and I guess the first thing I'd like to ask is whodunnit?

A: It was produced via 4th density technology.

Q: (V) STS or STO fourth density technology?

A: STS.

Q: (L) OK. You said via fourth density technology. However you did not say via fourth density beings...

A: Correct. There has been much advancement in 3D realm tech due to 4D interaction.

Q: (V) Between whom and third density?

A: Consortium.

Q: (L) Well, I noticed that last year, on or about the same date, the crop circle appeared with the woman's face and the so called signal thing. Was that also the production of fourth density?

A: No.

Q: (L) I noticed also that Aug. 15 is, in fact, an ancient feast day of the Mother Goddess and therefore the appearance of the face last year was somewhat appropriate. This one, produced on almost—if not exactly—the same date, seems almost like it is a response to the face image last year. The message deciphered from this new crop circle is—and Ark has checked it and confirmed the deciphering—"Beware the bearers of false gifts and their broken promises. Much pain but still time—and then an unknown word—there is good out there. We OPpose deception. Conduit closing. (bell sound)." What is the meaning of this message?

A: The first thing that was intended was to demonize the crop circle phenomenon. The second thing was to give those who are susceptible the impression that their favorite gray aliens might be "good guys." The third thing intended was to send a message of doubt directly to this room.

Q: (J) 'the conduit is closing.' Since the C's have talked about creating a conduit since the beginning, they are trying to convince us that the conduit is closing. What was the garbled word, was it believe, or is it believe?

A: It was believe. However the glitch was due to the application of the technology. This provides the clue to the STS source.

Q: (J) OK so their amateur fumbling caused the glitch. (A) The guy is probably the glitch in the software. There was a noise...

A: Wishful thinking will get ya every time.

Q: (L) So they were wishfully thinking that they had everything perfect and they didn't. (A) Still I want to know if physical characteristics of this circle were matched with the physical characteristics of what would be considered authentic crop circle?

A: They can get close. But again, there are differences. These can be detected if one is aware and looking.

Q: (J) Is there any criteria you can give us to measure against, is there anything in particular to look for? Or would it pop out as something strange that doesn't make sense in a crop circle if you examine it? Or is there actual...

A: One thing to look for would be growth disruptions to the area. Real circles do not disrupt the creative principle.

Q: (J) Now would this be crop circles created by STS, STO, or both?

A: STO.

Q: (J) So STO doesn't disrupt the life cycle but, if it were STS then it would change it. That would make sense. Well, there again their effect: the coldness, the burning, the whole negativity of it, would logically disrupt the life cycle. As for the way that they do this: you say that it was directed from fourth density. Do they actually come in and have any kind of physical apparatus in the vicinity?

A: It was not done from 4D.

Q: (J) I'm not talking about the one that we're talking about this time, I'm talking about when STO creates a crop circle do they have a physical...

A: Real crop circles represent thoughts from 6th density unified thought realm.[...]

Q: (L) I have a question. I had a thought the other night after I read Dolan's book. He was talking about this government technology for mind control and so forth, and how the government or the military was trying to cover up the alien presence and interactions, what they were really up to and what they were really doing, and I came to this idea after reading all of these cases. What is evident is that there were apparently abductions and landings and contact stories from very early on in the so-called UFO phenomenon. What I thought about was the fact that Bud Hopkins and Whitley Strieber promoted in their books, mostly Whitley, the image of the gray alien as the standard American abductor.

After the publication of these books all American abductions seemed to follow the pattern of the gray alien abduction. However, it is primarily an American phenomenon. Most other places in the world don't have little gray aliens with bug eyes. So, what I want to know is this: is the gray alien abduction scenario: a) a screen memory b) a creation of the American military mass mind programming project in order to acclimate people to certain conditions, circumstances and interactions, or c) something else or d) are they really just gray aliens abducting everybody?

A: You have stumbled upon an interesting question indeed. As we have noted previously, physical abductions are rare. Not only that, some abductions do not end with return of the victim. Now, what do you suppose you would do to cover up this fact? You might "create" a lot of abductions that end with return and "no harm done."

Q: (L) That wasn't one of my answer selections! Does this mean that the abductions reported by the people that Budd Hopkins worked with followed by Whitley Strieber were staged?

A: Close enough for horseshoes.

Q: (L) OK, what would get us closer.

A: How about several varieties of experiences including government experiments. Did you ever notice how some cases exhibit extreme trauma and some do not? Same general story, but one is related with deeper sensation of reality, and another is not. Why do you think so many "abductees" are able to accommodate the experience, while some result in ruined lives?

Q: (L) So you are saying that some of them are not really being abducted. They're just having something projected into their mind. So how long has this been going on?

A: Over 30 years.

Q: (L) That would be back to the 70s. And so where did Whitley come up with his gray aliens… and how does this relate to grays as cyber-genetic probes?

A: There really are "grays." But not nearly as ubiquitous the gov would like you to think.

Q: (L) So with Whitley telling everybody how it happens and what they look like along with contouring of the blanket EM mind control field or whatever, with the beaming out of a mind-programming wave—whatever it is—they're able to make a whole hell of a lot of people—everybody who is susceptible—think they are in contact with gray aliens. What is it that makes some people susceptible and not others?

A: Most generally that they are not organic portals.[10]

Q: (L) So that leads to our other question, do organic portals ever get abducted?

A: No need.

Q: (L) So they're using this, in a sense, as a weeding mechanism?

A: More or less.

Q: (L) So those people who declare firmly, that there is absolutely, never have, never could be, any evidence of abduction, could be OPs?

A: Generally speaking, yes.

Q: (V) Well, a souled person [a person with developmental potential] who has their faculties about them with knowledge is not going to get abducted either?

---

[10] See *Secret History* for a description and discussion of "Organic Portals."

chapter thirteen

(L) I don't think that's necessarily a logical conclusion.

(V) Not necessarily? Well, I thought they told us that once your knowledge level increases you will no longer be abducted.

(L) I don't think that this was the actual conclusion. Yes, it is true that if your knowledge increases then you have an idea what's going on. And most especially, if your mind is strong enough not to be susceptible to these mind control waves, you can certainly put an end to that nonsense. But, that doesn't mean that you would not be physically abducted if those fourth density dudes or the government decided to do it because that has nothing to do with battling mind control waves. I mean if they really want to get to you they'll send somebody into you life who is an OP and they'll come to you thorough that person.

(J) But, they say generally they don't say all the time. So an OP programmed to exist as a projector...

(C) Could I just ask one question? Last fall I believed I was abducted, and I actually have one memory of it, of a gray, you know, while I was laying on a table. I also had physical signs on my body of an abduction. I'm curious as I'm hearing this: was I being abducted by grays that really exist or was that like the government mind control making me think that I was?

(A) What kind of physical...

(C) I had pain in my uterus area, I had pink eye, missing time, I felt like I got run over by a train. I had all these physical symptoms of something really bad happening and then one memory of being on a table with this gray standing in front of me.

(L) Do you suffer from Post Traumatic Stress?

(C) Not that I know of.

(V) No panic attacks?

(C) No anxiety or panic attacks.

(V) I think if somebody is getting hauled out consistently for most of their life they're going to be pretty jumpy about everything.

(L) Loud noises.

(C) Oh yeah, like every loud noise, everything freaks me out, makes me jump, it's like abnormal reaction to loud noises and...

(V) Do you remember what was being done to you while you were on the table?

(C) Well, I slipped into the memory when I least expected it. You know, once I realized what was happening, that I am looking at a gray, I just kind of freaked out and got really scared and I snapped myself out of it. So I had no idea what was being done. But I know that I felt completely under control, like calm, like I wasn't scared on the table, like he was making me not be scared; like he was controlling me. But in seeing that, being numb, I got scared and pulled out of it. I'm just wondering if that actually happened, if I really was abducted by real grays, or mind control was going on.

A: How about real abductions, but not necessarily by "grays." They are very popular screens.

Q: (V) OK, if not grays then who?

A: Ask her brother!

Q: (C) OK, well he's claiming that he's being abducted by the government agents. So if that's who he thinks is abducting him, does that mean that's who's abducting me?

(L) Either that or he's saying that it's happening to him, while the one who is really being abducted is you, and he's saying it because he is part of the screen. Projecting, reflecting. Talk about diversion.

(A) So I understand it's probably some kind secret government activity that she is involved in, right? (L) Seems to be so.

(J) Is there a criteria for what they project? Is there a certain reason why they pick certain screens? Some people have experiences with reptoids and others have experiences with mantid beings and other different types of aliens. Is there a particular reason why they choose such a screen? Is it to play on a person's emotions or a person's perspective, or is it simply the way the person's mind deals with...

A: Reptoids and mantids are not screens.

Q: (J) So those are real beings who are doing that?

A: Yes.

Q: (L) But this matter about these grays: I mean, I had the thought and shot up out of bed. I got up out of bed in the middle of the night because I started thinking about it, and thinking about it, and thinking about it. I had read Dolan and I had read about these programs and then I read this thing about them being able to just send out the whole mind programming thing into a "shaped neutral cavity" created between the ozone layer and the earth, and I started to think why is that nearly everybody in America gets abducted by grays? And why is it that everybody else—all of the rest of the world—experiences different kinds of creatures? What is it and why is it there so much of it going on here as opposed to what's going on in the rest of the world?

I remember asking the C's about it once and they said because America is the capital of STS, but that did not in any way confirm that all of these abductions were actually taking place. However, putting the fact that there is this almost unbelievable number of gray alien abductions in the U.S. together with the U.S. being the capital of STS, together with the little leaks about their mind control research, well, I just asked "what is really going on here?"

Well, when we look at the phenomenon chronicled by Dolan, what we see is that the government *is*, most definitely and crucially, interested in UFOs and aliens. We also see the truly Machiavellian way they have sought to not only cover it up, but to actually pretend that it does *not* even exist! They have pushed this "there is nothing to it" idea to such an extreme, that people afraid of talking about it for fear of being thought nuts. Well, what if that is on purpose? That way, if anybody has a *real* abduction, and there is *real* evidence, or something really awful happens, they can easily attribute it to lunacy.

But, what if they *are* really concerned about some awful things going on? What if they really need to conceal things? It's not enough to just deny it or pretend things are all in people's minds, because obviously that is not true. So, what would Machiavelli do?

Well, first of all, he would build up a straw man to knock down. He would create aliens that are complete and total distractions from what is real. So, as it happens, at about the time we now know that this mind control research was at a stage where it would be possible, suddenly, one day, Whitley Strieber gets a best seller writing about things we now know the government has obviously killed people to cover up. That can't be proved, but it is strongly circumstantial. So the next logical question is this: if—as we now know—the secret government is really working on concealing this problem from society, do we—for a minute—think that Whitley would be able to publish a book that reveals the truth? And that it would be a best seller? Not one book either, but two on this subject, with the picture right on the cover.

Well, I read about people who said when they saw this picture that they felt sick, or they had this or that kind of experience. And everybody and his brother was suddenly seeing grays. And all of a sudden as soon as—I mean there were a few cases of this exact type prior to Strieber's book—after Strieber's book became a best seller the abduction phenomenon went right through the roof.

So all of this clicked together in my head in the middle of the night. As a result of this, there was another very interesting thing. If you look at that Roswell video, and you ask yourself the question: was it a hoax, and if I was going to do a hoax, how would I do it? After all, a hoax is supposed to be 'convincing', right? If it was a hoax, the hoaxers would have made that alien look like your standard gray. But the alien did not look like your standard gray. Not only that he had six fingers on each hand and each foot. He had almost like the body of a child. He looked like an enlarged fetus. So if that had been a hoaxed video or if they were going to plant this video to confirm anything about the "popular alien reality," if they faked that alien, they would've made it look like a gray because that was what everybody was expecting to see. And in fact, one of the reasons many so-called researchers—including Mike Lindemann—rejected this video, dismissing it as a hoax, was because it didn't show a gray alien!

I mean people aren't even able to think! They rejected it because it didn't look like the gray alien. Well, that's one of the most compelling reasons that it is very likely real; the fact that it didn't look like a gray.

And of course everybody is so convinced that they must look like these little four fingered bugged-eyed half insect creatures that Whitley Strieber has promoted so that when the real thing is right there in front of them, they reject it because it doesn't look like Whitley's grays.

(J) It may have been almost like a test to see how well the project was going because what is the reason for releasing the autopsy video, except to make sure that everyone's conditioned toward the contemporary gray which seems to change with time.

(L) OK, so where were we, ah yes, Whitley's ubiquitous grays. There really are some grays, but they may not look like Whitley's gray...are there grays that look exactly like Whitley's grays, real ones?

A: He missed the mark.

Q: (V) What I saw in that abduction that I remembered were not like exactly like Whitley's grays. What were those little guys?

A: The real thing.

Q: (V) OK, are they based on the moon?

A: Most are based on Earth. [...]

Q: (L) OK, now we have a couple of questions we want to get to here. You said before that OP's were originally intended as a bridge between second and third densities and that they were used. Is Mouravieff right about the potential for OP's to advance being dependent upon souled beings advancement to STO at the end of this cycle?

A: Not exactly. A soul imprint can grow independent of the cycle. However, it is more likely for a soul to "grow" when interacting with 4th Density STO. STS tends to drain energy for its own use.

Q: (L) The question came up about the remark as to the numbers of OPs and you said something about encountering half as many OPs as souled humans. It was pointed out that, in mathematical terms, that would work out to encountering or interacting with more souled humans than OPs. So, you said the population was evenly distributed, when you say the population was evenly distributed does that mean that there are half organic portals and half souled humans, more or less?

A: Yes

Q: (L) So when you say encountering 'half as many', what does that mean?

A: It means that "souls" run in families for the most part. Thus a souled, and we mean "potentially fully souled", individual is likely to encounter and interact more with other souled humans. However, when awakening, they may encounter even more OP's.

Q: (L) So they tend to run in families so they can have aberrations. Or a family that's mostly OPs could have an occasional souled human, which they don't know what to do with. And, in the same way, a family of mostly souled people could have an occasional OP, or a line of them that pops up in the family every now and then. But for the most part, people with souls marry people with souls unless there is some danger of them awakening in which case there's special situation where they insert OPs into their lives. But I would say that in a general sense what they're saying, and y'all can correct me if I'm wrong here, is that, what, water seeks its own level, so to speak.

A: More or less.

Q: (L) So in other words, the people who noticed that remark were right, and the way I took it was wrong. OK, another question, are there other types of soulless beings more than those reanimated or remolecularized dead dudes and OPs? Is there such things as holographic projection beings running around on the planet at this point and time?

A: In a sense, you are all "holographic" projections. But to answer the question, it is rare.

Q: (L) So, there are holographic projection type beings or there can be, but there's not too many of them. Alright, on to the next question. Are there any particular clues that we could have about identifying OPs?

A: Is it necessary to have more clues? Remember some things are to be learned.

Q: (C) I think they're saying to start paying attention, making mental notes and figuring it out for yourself.

(J) Didn't they say that generally OPs don't get abducted?

(L) Well, we've certainly been given a lot of clues over the years, we just weren't ready and didn't know what they were talking about.

(C) I think it's probably better, from what they're saying, if we just all figure it out from experience. You learn more by just watching than if they handed it to you.

(L) Another question we had was, in areas where third and fourth density are merged or merging, is it easier for Men in Black to project themselves into such a reality.

A: Of course.

Q: (J) They once said something about bi-density beings. They were like hybrids between fourth density beings and a third density being. Or could such an individual be a genetically enhanced human?

A: Humans were once "bi-density." And some may be again in the natural way. Those of 4D STS "manufacture" are similar. Just think of them as a type of OP with souped up engines. [...]

Q: (A) I want really to know what kind of mechanism is behind this 911 number coming up in the NY lottery. (V) Yeah, me too, and it wasn't only that it was something with the...

A: Warning. It ain't over!!!

Q: (A) Who was warning?

A: Mass consciousness signals to self about clear and present danger.

Q: (A) Makes sense. (L) Clear and present danger of what?

A: Wait and see.

Q: Might it have something to do with Iraq?

A: No cheating.

Q: (V) OK. I'm a little curious, and I don't know if it's been asked before or not, what is China's role in regards to Iraq, is there any...

A: Big question mark, eh?

Q: (V) Well, it just keeps popping into my mind, and popping into my mind, China, China, China, China. They're so quiet at this time right now, I don't hear them saying anything...

A: Indeed...

Q: (V) Are they supplying them with the chemical and biological weapons?

A: And...

Q: (V) Nuclear weapons?

A: ?

Q: (V) You can't, you can't say that?

A: Nope.

Q: (A) In fact there is an answer. The answer is yes. I mean if you were China and you had nuclear weapons and you needed a *lot* of money, what would you do?

(L) And there is somebody who needs what you have, and there is all that oil and all that money, are you kidding? Saddam wouldn't be being as cocky as he is if he didn't have a really big boom-boom lined up and hidden somewhere, and aimed at *us!*

(V) Now does our government and their so called intelligence know that this is happening?

(A) Of course!

(V) Are they in cahoots with them?

(L) Sure.

(A) On a certain level everybody's selling everything.

(L) At those levels above they are because their objective is to decimate the Earth's population.

(V) Is China the only one feeding Iraq weapons?

(L) Why should they be? The U.S. is feeding them weapons. I mean it's so dirty it's inconceivable. They're all in bed together.

(V) Is Laura right, the world leaders, the 10% that want to get rid of [the rest of us]...

A: That is the plan.

Q: (A) But you must remember, if one country is selling weapons to the other country, that doesn't mean its weapons are going to work. Selling is one thing, using is different thing. Once in a while they will fail. (V) What a mucky game, huh?

January 18, 2003

Q: (L) What is driving Bush to have his war with Iraq?

A: Orders. Bush knows little in any respect as to what or why he does anything.

Q: Is the war drama merely a play being put on to keep us all distracted and in a state of fear?

A: More or less.

Q: Yet, you said the United States would be bombed, and on another occasion you said there would not be a nuclear war.

A: "Bombs" are not all "nuclear." And, there are "natural bombs."

Q: (A) I want to ask about the collapse of the World Trade Center. There is evidence of seismicity and unusual pulses that seem to have simply disintegrated matter.

A: Very good observation, but that does not mean human sabotage either. There were certainly "pulses." They were of a "natural" source that was "sculpted" or "shaped" and directed.

Q: What do you mean by a 'natural source'?

A: Energies of the planet artificially collected and disbursed. An artificial earthquake sort of.

Q: But we are still talking about technology. Where is the operational center for this type of thing?

A: 4th density technology.

Q: This we know. But there are human brain involved. What brains are behind this?

A: Did you ever wonder why the pentagon is a pentagon? Hint!

Q: Is that why they specifically included the Pentagon as one of the buildings to be hit in the 9-11 attack; to allay suspicions?

A: Yup!

Q: Are there fourth density sections to the Pentagon?

A: Absolutely. It is a "deep cover" kind of place.

Q: (A) There is this Pentagon, then there is another superpower—Russia—and still another—China...

A: There is only one. The U.S. just happens to be the center.

Q: (A) Well. (L) Maybe the heads of these other countries are all like George Bush. They don't know why they do what they do. It's all been scripted from somewhere else.

(A) Question is: there is Europe—how can France or Russia or whoever, win against this kind of technology? Apparently, since there is only one center, and this center of technology is the U.S., it seems pretty hopeless.

A: Remember Perseus and David and Goliath. Besides, help is drawing near.

Q: (L) Sometimes I have the feeling that when they say "help is drawing near," it really means that that our "future" is getting closer and we are going to be the ones doing the helping! [Laughter.]

A: Close, but not all.

Q: (A) That means there are surprises waiting for us. (L) I think that people concentrating on the anti-war thing is a waste of time. I think they ought to be concentrating on the "impeach Bush" issue. But then, what good would it do to impeach Bush. Same thing would have happened with Gore. Until people wake up to the reality of fourth density manipulation, we are all in deep doo doo.

A: True.

Q: (L) I guess they are all gonna gather together there on the battlefield and when they are all there, something is gonna happen to scare the bayjeezus out of them...

A: Maybe...

Q: (A) The point is, that people have no choice. They are backed into a corner. The only thing they can do now is just impeach Bush. If they don't do that, there is nothing else they can do. Because if they don't do anything, they will bear the blame for doing nothing—the same way Germany did after Hitler. All the signs are here now: it is exactly like it was in 1939 in Europe.

(L) Well, anything we do, we cannot anticipate the outcome. We can't even know if it will be helpful. We just have to do what is right from one moment to the next based on what we know using our best efforts. For all we know, if we keep pushing the "impeach Bush" issue, we may end up in jail as "enemy combatants."

(A) What did we learn? That there is this help on the way. We know that we cannot quit working. We are helping the help, so to say.

(L) Well, I wrote to some people pointing out that the anti-war stance is only more divisiveness. There are people who are for the war to support Bush, and there are people who are against the war who don't support Bush. It is a question of supporting Bush. Everybody agrees that Saddam is a stinker, but they can't agree on whether how Bush is handling the matter is appropriate or not. They forget that what is happening here is that they are all being put into an oppositional stance against each other, and Bush, himself, is coming out on top clean.

If they would concentrate on the *real* issues: that Bush is a liar, that he is not even our legal president, that he stole the election by nefarious means, that he is a criminal from a criminal family, making it clear and plain with facts and massive media coverage about who and what Bush really is, then the whole issue would be focused where it belongs: on Bush and the Consortium that has put him in power to serve its agenda. But, instead of concentrating on the problem—of

276

which Bush is only the representative, the real issue being the Consortium—people are not seeing that the whole situation is being manipulated for the benefit of the Industrial-Military Complex just as Eisenhower foresaw. Bush is only the puppet for this Consortium. If that could be seen as the real danger that it is, if they could impeach Bush—who is their creature—and get somebody into the presidency who was incorruptible, who could kick butt and take names like Kennedy tried to do.

Well, we have learned. Kennedy didn't take the danger as seriously as he should have. If he had, maybe he could have carried through what he wanted to do: disband the CIA, tie the hands of the military, make things more equitable for the common people, enhance civil rights and civil liberties. If we could get somebody in the White House who was smart enough to not get assassinated, and who was clean and not tied up with the consortium, things really *could* change.

(A) The problem is only in America. If America would just stand down, Saddam would be dealt with appropriately. Nobody likes the guy. He doesn't have anything. He is no danger to anybody. But Bush is a danger to the whole planet. He has created this crisis and the whole world has gone to hell in just a few months.

(L) And the reason he is able to do what he is doing—which is basically that he is going to destroy the whole damn planet—is because of the media. The media is controlled by Jews who have only one agenda: to own all of Palestine and revenge. And so, they dangle carrots for Bush to follow without even knowing that they are signing their own death warrant. They are following the script of the Consortium which wants, above all other things, to see all Semitic peoples destroyed, and their hubris won't even allow them to see it. For that reason, the Jews have helped George Bush plunge the entire world into chaos. And they will wonder why, at the last moment, everyone hates them just as Americans will wonder why they are the most hated nation on Earth. Blind hubris.

(A) Well, there is this Game Theory, and they are employing it to the max. They are playing a game. They know where the buttons need to be pushed, to steer the delicate equilibrium where they want it.

(L) No one in the world of politics is clean. No one. They are all dirty, and if you know all the dirt, you can do what you want.

(A) ...So, if something comes along that destroys their game theory... the whole operation will collapse. Game theory is based on data.

(L) It's like V___ B___. His whole game was based on pushing our buttons, trying to blackmail us, saying things like "I'll tell the whole sordid story." Well, guess what? I'll tell it first! I'm not perfect and I have certainly made mistakes. But nobody is going to use it to control me.

If other people could do that, if they could get over their fear of being judged for making mistakes, there would be nothing that anyone could hold over their head anymore.

(A) OK, there is Bush and his Skull and Bones. And then, there is the Illuminati. And they are looking for something. So, probably somebody behind Bush is also looking for something. So, if they destroy the world, they will get nothing.

(L) And then meanwhile, there is the North Korean guy—the mirror image of George Bush; everything he says and does is modeled from George Bush. It is actually comical to watch them. "I'm going to blow up the world!" "No you're

not, I'm going to blow it up first! I'm going to turn America into a sea of fire."
And Bush is saying "I'm going to bomb Iraq back to the stone age." "No you're
not! We're going to bomb YOU back to before the Stone Age!" They are like
two identical characters! Crazy! We are in a hell of a mess. Any comments?

A: The situation looks bleak indeed. But remember the Achilles heel of STS:
Wishful Thinking.

Q: In this case, how is wishful thinking going to help?

A: There will be a big miscalculation made. It will reveal the "Man behind the
curtain."

February 2, 2003

Q: One of the first questions we want to ask tonight is about the event of the
Space Shuttle that was lost. First, was it an explosion, or was it just
disintegration, or breaking up?

A. It was a "direct hit."

Q: A direct hit by what?

A: EM pulse.

Q: (S) What was the source of the EM pulse?

A: 3/4th density Consortium.

Q: Well, I thought Bush was a puppet of the Consortium?

(A) Well, we know that the military are scrambling planes to go after UFOs…
there are even reports of firing on them and there have been reports of military
jets being disintegrated by UFOs. The UFOs are, somehow, in cahoots with the
consortium. It seems that Bush and the gang are not in control of the Consortium
and maybe they needed to be "reminded?"

A: It is not so much that he needs to be reminded, as he needs to be stimulated to
react.

Q: (L) You once before said that Bush knows very little anyway—or that the
"White House" level is pretty much in the dark about the plans of the
Consortium—even if they are carrying them out. So, you are suggesting that they
are being driven by forces of which they are unaware and do not understand?

A: Exactly. Bush is a "reaction machine."

Q: (L) I would like to know about this supposed "body guard" of Saddam
recently presented by MOSSAD? Was he one of Saddam's former bodyguards?

A: To an extent, yes. But certainly not in the way presented. Just remember this:
if pilots can be conditioned to commandeer airliners that will fly into certain
death, how hard is it to "Produce" a "bodyguard?"

Q: (L) Piece of cake to produce a bodyguard, I guess.

(A) He is saying exactly what the Israelis want him to say. He is not revealing
any particular data that counts. It is just general things. Anybody could say such
things and be called a "bodyguard."

(L) Exactly. OK, you say that an EM pulse brought down the Shuttle. (A) Where
did the EM pulse come from?

A: From space based satellite.

Q: (A) Does NASA know about the cause?

A: There are some who suspect.

Q: (L) Which explains why they are so anxious to convince everyone that it was *not* sabotage. Like Wellstone's death, there was "no question" about it being a terrorist attack. The likelihood is that the Bush Junta was behind Wellstone's death. In both cases they "know" the cause and want to divert the attention away from it.

But, in the case of the Shuttle, they aren't "dirty," but they most definitely do *not* want anyone to realize that they also are not "in charge." It makes me think of the remark the C's made a few years ago about the reason for the Military Industrial Complex build-up and manipulations. C's said that the *real* enemy is "out there" and that war was just a "cover" to prevent the masses from realizing what they were really doing. Maybe Bush and the gang are really convinced, in their own minds, that they are acting to "protect" humanity from this threat. Meanwhile, they are simply being driven to fulfill the agenda of the Consortium. And it is so interesting that the Shuttle broke up over Palestine, Texas... as though it was saying to Bush: this is what is going to happen to you: Palestine is going to be your destruction. But, of course, Bush would be incapable of perceiving it in that context. Is it so that a message was intended in this event?

A: As always, confusion is the mask.

Q: (L) In other words, everyone's reaction to the event will depend on their own context. There is the view that it was a "message to Bush." Bush and gang will, of course, see it only as a stimulus to faster and more "decisive" military action. So, it will really work on them the way it is wanted. (A) And of course, we wonder how they will make use of this event.

A: The primary effect among the masses will be shock, thus making them less resistant to Bush's policies. Still other groups will see the clear threat to Bush and Co. from their activities. Bush and Co. will, of course, seek to capitalize on the event even while remaining in the dark as to its meaning. But there most certainly is awareness among them that there is a "Maverick" element at loose. Bush has even "felt" a bit of primal fear in respect of this event.

chapter fourteen
tying it all together

Now, let's put everything that has been said into perspective. There is a really "regular guy" named David McGowan who has a not so regular website. Well, actually, he *does* have a part of his website that is quite "normal," but another part that is not what your usual contractor-Joe-Six-Pack would create. Dave has created *The Center for an Informed America* (http://davesweb.cnchost.com/).

Dave probably isn't into "channeling" or anything weird like that. But, he has a "nose" for things and he can not only present things with impeccable logic, he can do it entertainingly. If you haven't read his newsletters, you are missing a serious source of information and insight. He's a great journalist, in my opinion.

But again, Dave isn't into "high strangeness" at all as far as I can tell. And that is exactly what makes his views so valuable to me. If Dave is seeing things from the normal, entirely human, point of view, and that view confirms something that is "channeled," then those are two data points that create what I like to call "horizontal" evidence.

In the wake of the disastrous response to hurricane Katrina, McGowan wrote, in his 73rd and 74th newsletters, "Katrina, Eugenics, and 'Peak Oil'":

> Let's assume, for the sake of argument—and because you wouldn't be visiting this website if you weren't seeking out 'conspiracy theories'—that everything that happened in post-Katrina New Orleans happened because powerful actors wanted it to happen: the breaching of the levees, the flooding of selected portions of the city, the suppression of any and all relief efforts, the establishment of a pretext for a military response through the introduction of fraudulent 'news' stories, and the relocation by force of the residents of New Orleans. What then would be the motivation for these actions? I can think of at least three motives:
>
> 1. To acclimate the American people to the presence of armed troops on American soil, which will soon be a familiar sight not just in southern Louisiana, but throughout the country. Even as you read this, the White House and Congress are hard at work drafting legislation and executive orders that will normalize the use of combat personnel to deal with any contrived situation.
>
> 2. To allow the city of New Orleans to be rebuilt and refashioned into what our fearless leaders no doubt see as a city of the future—a city that is much richer, and much whiter, than the city that stood before.
>
> 3. To solidify control over the Gulf Coast oil and gas industry, since a key goal of the perpetrators of the 'Peak Oil' charade, as I've noted before, is to achieve total control over all the world's major oil and gas taps.
>
> Speaking of 'Peak Oil,' my mailbox runneth over with inquiries concerning the scam. I suppose that is because the issue is getting a little hard to ignore, what

with it popping up all over the mainstream media these days. I know this because I subscribe to only a handful of mainstream publications and every one of them have now promoted the 'Peak' lies. The cover of the August edition of National Geographic, for instance, reads: "After Oil; Powering the Future." The cover of October's Esquire reads, charmingly enough: "The End of Oil (& Life As We Know It); A Handy Guide."

Yes, friends, thanks to the tireless efforts of Mike Ruppert and company, the mainstream media have now been forced to acknowledge the 'reality' of 'Peak Oil.' That is, after all, the way that things generally work -- the truth first emerges in the fringes of the 'alternative' media, and then, within a few short years, through the hard and thankless work of dedicated researchers, some of whom might not even come from CIA families, their ideas gain mainstream acceptance. That is precisely why mainstream commentators and publications are now OK with, for example, spilling the beans on 9-11. And the sham election of 2000. And 2002. And 2004. And the war crimes being committed in Iraq and Afghanistan. And the rampant criminality of the Bush regime, on both the domestic and international fronts. And Paul Wellstone's plane 'crash.' And (insert the scandal of your choice here; I'm bored with it already). ...

What I really wanted to talk about was when I offended the 'Peak Oil' crowd by reporting that their real agenda was selling the necessity of a massive 'population reduction.' Remember that? Remember how all the Peakers got their panties in a wad and accused me of putting words in the mouth of their great and fearless cult leader, The Honorable Michael Ruppert? And remember how they nearly went into convulsions when I described their 'solution' to the alleged problem as a eugenics program, because, of course, no one in the 'Peak' movement advocated any such thing?

Well ... it appears that it is time to revisit that issue, even at the considerable risk of further offending the delicate sensibilities of the craven 'Peak Oil' proponents. This time, however, I won't be putting words in anyone's mouth. No, this time I will be quoting directly from a newsletter penned by the great Colin Campbell* [Dave's note added later: Several readers have written to inform me that the ASPO post quoted in Newsletter #74 was actually penned by someone named William Stanton, not Colin Campbell. Authorship of the piece was rather ambiguous in the post that I read and linked to, but I nevertheless apologize for the error. However, as editor of the newsletter and head honcho of the ASPO organization, it is Campbell who is ultimately accountable for the rants that appear under his organization's banner. And I have been informed that numerous people have appealed to Campbell to disown the post and he has refused to drop his tacit backing for the ideas expressed therein. I'm glad we cleared that up.], founding father of ASPO (Association for the Study of Peak Oil) and guiding light of folks like Ruppert, Heinberg and Pfeiffer. Without further ado then, let's hear what Dr. Campbell had to say this past July (with my own comments added in [italics], and with a shout-out to Ty Brown for directing my attention to this post):

[Oil and People Important Notice: This is a plain text article extracted from Dr Colin Campbell's ASPO Newsletter 55 (July 2005). First published July 2005; article no. 573]

Recent articles in the ASPO Newsletter have agreed that the explosion of world population from about 0.6 billion in 1750 to 6.4 billion today was initiated and sustained by the shift from renewable energy to fossil fuel *(sic)* energy in the Industrial Revolution. There is agreement that the progressive exhaustion of fossil fuel reserves will reverse the process, though there is uncertainty as to what a sustainable global population would be.

... a global population reduction of some 6 billion people is likely to take place during the 21st Century. *(For the mathematically impaired, Campbell is talking about no less than a 94% reduction in the world's population. If you feel that you and all of your loved ones are among the lucky 6% who will be spared, then I suppose there is no cause for alarm and you can feel free to stop reading now.)*

... probably before 2010 ... uncontrollable inflation and recession will spread round the world ... *(Probably so, but this will be, of course, a deliberately induced condition.)*

In Third World nations ... a Darwinian struggle for shrinking resources of all kinds will be in full swing ... the imperative to survive will be driving strong groups to take what they want from weak ones. The concept of human rights will be irrelevant ...

It may well be that, in the West, the same argument will affect the thinking of militarily powerful nations ... Instantaneous nuclear elimination of population centres might even be considered merciful, compared to starvation and massacres prolonged over decades. *(You have to applaud Campbell's effort here; I doubt that even Orwell could have conceived of the concept of a humanitarian nuclear holocaust.)* Eventually, probably before 2150, world population will have fallen to a level that renewable energy, mainly biomass, can sustain ...

Probably the greatest obstacle to the scenario with the best chance of success (in my opinion) is the Western world's unintelligent devotion to political correctness, human rights and the sanctity of human life. In the Darwinian world that preceded and will follow the fossil fuel era, these concepts were and will be meaningless. Survival in a Darwinian resource-poor world depends on the ruthless elimination of rivals, not the acquisition of moral kudos by cherishing them when they are weak. *(Hmmm ... overt calls for the destruction of the weak by the strong? ... now, where have I heard that before? ... Adolf Hitler? Aleister Crowley? I can't quite place it ...)*

So the population reduction scenario with the best chance of success has to be Darwinian in all its aspects, with none of the sentimentality that shrouded the second half of the 20th Century in a dense fog of political correctness ...

To those sentimentalists who ... are outraged at the proposed replacement of human rights by cold logic, I would say "You have had your day, in which your woolly thinking has messed up not just the Western world but the whole planet, which could, if Homo sapiens had been truly intelligent, have supported a small population enjoying a wonderful quality of life almost for ever. You have thrown away that opportunity."

... The scenario is: Immigration is banned. Unauthorised arrivals are treated as criminals. Every woman is entitled to raise one healthy child. No religious or cultural exceptions can be made, but entitlements can be traded. Abortion or infanticide is compulsory if the fetus or baby proves to be handicapped (Darwinian selection weeds out the unfit). When, through old age, accident or disease, an individual becomes more of a burden than a benefit to society, his or her life is humanely ended. Voluntary euthanasia is legal and made easy. Imprisonment is rare, replaced by corporal punishment for lesser offences and painless capital punishment for greater.

... The punishment regime would improve social cohesiveness by weeding out criminal elements.

... military forces should be maintained strong and alert ... Collaboration with other nations practising the same population reduction scenario would be of great mutual advantage. [Association for the Study of Peak Oil and Gas, Ireland]

I have to admit that Campbell did not once, throughout his entire rant, use the word "eugenics." But what he has described here—the destruction of the "weak," the "unfit," the sick and the elderly, the "handicapped," the "burdens" to society, and, of course, the "criminal elements"—is nothing short of a eugenicist's wet dream. The frequent references to Darwin, I have to say, are a nice touch as well.

I would hope that I don't have to point out here that it will be the all-powerful state that will decide who is a "burden" and who is a "benefit" to society, and who is "unfit," and what is and what isn't a "handicap," and who is too old, injured or diseased to go on, and what crimes are punishable by death. The good news, of course, is that the wealthy will be able to produce as many children as they desire, since the rest of us will likely be forced to barter away the only thing we will have left that will be of any value: our child "entitlement."

Some of you are no doubt wondering what sort of complex formulas will be used to determine who stays and who goes when the Great Die-Off rolls through town. It's not really as mysterious as it seems. Basically, it will work something like this: you know how in virtually every country on the planet there is a very small percentage of the people—*usually around five or six percent*—who seem to control the overwhelming majority of that country's wealth? Those will be the 'keepers.' And everyone else? Well, maybe you better sit down, because I have some bad news for you ...

I should probably point out here that when Campbell speaks of "weeding out criminal elements," he is really rather coyly referring to people that happen to have more pigment in their skin than he does. We know this because former Education Secretary and 'Drug Czar' William Bennett, who apparently gets his 'talking points' from the same folks as Colin Campbell, spelled it out pretty clearly on his radio show recently:

"I do know that it's true that if you wanted to reduce crime, you could—if that were your sole purpose—you could abort every black baby in this country, and your crime rate would go down. That would be an impossibly ridiculous and morally reprehensible thing to do, but your crime rate would go down."

It's hard to say what is more remarkable about that statement—that someone with a relatively prominent voice in the media can casually discuss genocide without stirring up a firestorm of protest, or that someone from the religious right who is not averse to equating abortion with murder could nevertheless tacitly endorse forced abortion on a grand scale, so long as the program is targeting a 'criminal race.'

The bleating of Campbell and Bennett, and the actions taken in New Orleans, are not unrelated events. To conclude otherwise would be rather foolish. What we saw in New Orleans was a glimpse into the near future. And it was likely a relatively tame glimpse at that. An overtly military form of rule, ethnic cleansing,

283

population reduction, the restructuring and rebuilding of major population centers, total control of vital resources, and the craven exploitation of disasters, both natural and unnatural—all of this and more is just around the corner.

Perhaps you are thinking that this type of future is not for you. You'd really prefer something a little different. That's unfortunate, because the future holds very few options. Here's Campbell again, concluding his mini version of Mein Kampf:

"Another problem is likely to be the residual opposition to population reduction from sentimentalists and/or religious extremists unable to understand that the days of plenty, when criminals and the weak could be cherished at public expense, are over. Acts of violent protest, such as are carried out today by animal rights activists and anti-abortionists, would, in the Darwinian world, attract capital punishment. Population reduction must be single-minded to succeed."

So it appears as though those who fight back against the agenda will likely be summarily executed, while those who passively go with the flow stand about a 95% chance of being killed off anyway. With odds like that, I would think that fighting back might be a good idea. By any means available. And sooner rather than later.

94% starting in 2010, eh? Where have we heard that before? Aside from the fact that I stumbled across these population reduction ideas while writing book seven of *The Wave*...?

Q: (L) Bob Lazar referred to the fact that aliens supposedly refer to humans as containers. What does this mean?

A: Later use.

Q: (L) Use by who? How many?

A: *94 per cent.*

Q: (L) 94 per cent of what?

A: Of all population.

Q: (L) What do you mean?

A: All are containers; 94 per cent use.

Q: I don't understand.

A: Will be used. 94 percent.

Q: (L) Used for what? You mean eaten?

A: Total consumption.

Q: (L) What do you mean by consumption? Ingested?

A: Consumed for ingredients.

Q: (L) Why?

A: *New race.* Important. 13 years about when happens [which would be around 2007].

Q: (L) Why are humans consumed?

A: They are used for parts.

Q: (L) We don't understand. How can humans be used for parts?

A: Reprototype. Vats exist. Missing persons often go there and especially missing children.

That was about the craziest thing we had ever heard. But it got even crazier as we continued with the Cassiopaean experiment. I wanted to know about the Nephilim that Zecharia Sitchen wrote about:

October 20, 1994

Q: (L) Tell me about the Nephilim.

A: That was a race of beings in the third level of density which came from an actual planet at another point in this particular galaxy also in the third level of density, who were taken, or shall we say kidnapped, reprogrammed and retrained by the Lizard Beings to act as enforcers during a particular era of what you would measure as your past.

Q: (L) What era was that?

A: That was an era... it would have been approximately 8 to 5 thousand years ago but there are also dates relating to 12 to 14 thousand years ago and others. Dating system is not ours and does not exist for us.

Q: (L) For how many years did these beings exist on our earth?

A: Approximately 15 to 18 hundred years. They died off because they were not able to reproduce naturally in the atmosphere of the earth and experimentation to try to cause them to intermix with the human population did not succeed.

Q: (L) When did the last of them die off?

A: Probably near 6 to 7 thousand years ago. But there is also a reference point of 12 to 14 thousand years as well.

Q: (L) What was the name of the planet they came from?

A: Dorlaqua.

Q: (L) Where was this planet located?

A: This planet was located in the Orion complex.

Q: (L) After the "flood of Noah" approximately how many people survived that cataclysm on the whole earth?

A: Approximately 19 million.

Q: (L) Why did the population of the earth continue to decline from that point?

A: Because of disease and inability to adjust due to artificial manipulations of the genetic pool.

From here on, I am not going to insert anymore comments. I just want you, the reader, to take in the information that the C's were giving us from as early as 1994 and contemplate the events that have occurred on our planet since that time, most particularly, beginning with 9/11, in relation to this information. Think long and hard about the reality of events, and notice how accurate the C's have been regarding "facts on the ground," and then consider the possibility that the things we cannot yet demonstrate to be true, might very well be exactly that: Truth.

October 22, 1994

Q: Who built the city of Baalbek?

A: Anteareans and early Sumerians. We meant Atlanteans [i.e., Atlantis being the name of the pre-catastrophe world empire, not necessarily referring to an island mass; I deal with "Atlantis" extensively in Secret History].

chapter fourteen

Q: What is the reason for the enormous proportions of this building?
A: Giants.
Q: Who were the giants?
A: *Genetic effort to recreate Nephalim.*
Q: Did the Atlanteans and Sumerians succeed in recreating the Nephilim?
A: No.
Q: Why did they build this enormous city?
A: Retarded subjects.
Q: The results of their efforts were retarded?
A: Yes.
Q: Why did they build the enormous city?
A: In anticipation of success.
Q: Why would someone come along and build a city of the proportions of Baalbck in anticipation of a genetic project that could take many years to accomplish?
A: Project took only three years. Speeded up growth cycle using nuclear hormonal replication procedure. Why failed.
Q: That's why it failed, because of the speeded up growth?
A: Did not take properly.
Q: What technical means did they use to cut the stones and transport them?
A: Sound wave focusing.
Q: What happened to interrupt or halt the building of this city?
A: Venus first appearance and pass.
Q: What year was this project brought to a halt?
A: 3218 B.C. [...]
Q: I would like to go back to the subject of the Nephilim. Now you said the Nephilim were a group of humanoid types brought here to earth to be enforcers, is that correct?
A: Yes.
Q: When were they brought here?
A: 9046 B.C. one reference.
Q: They were giants, is that correct?
A: Yes.
Q: They were presented to the people as the representatives, or "Sons" of God, is that correct?
A: Yes.
Q: You say these dudes were 11 to 14 feet tall...
A: Yes.
Q: You and the ancient literature say that these sons of god intermarried with human women, is that correct?
A: Yes.
Q: Did they do that the same way it is done today, that is, sexual interaction?
A: No.

Q: How was it done?

A: Forced insemination.

Q: So, it was artificial insemination?

A: Close.

Q: Were these beings like us, including their sexual apparati?

A: Close.

Q: Any significant differences?

A: Three gonads.

Q: Was their sexual apparatus otherwise similar?

A: Yes.

Q: Did they mate with human females in a normal way at any time?

A: No.

Q: Why not?

A: Size difference.

Q: Just for the sake of curiosity, just how different in terms of size?

A: 23 inches long.

Q: Were they circumcised?

A: No.

October 23, 1994

Q: (L) Tell us again who are the Nephilim?

A: Enforcers. Slaves of Orion. From Planet 3C, or 3rd star, 3rd planet.

Q: (L) You said the other night that the Nephalim came from some area around the constellation Scorpio, is that correct?

A: Originally seeded there but you were too.

Q: (L) We were originally seeded somewhere else? Where? Orion? What is the name of that planet?

A: D'Ankhiar. Ankh is ancient symbolism of this planet. Is female symbol. Stands for mother planet.

Q: (L) Is this other planet our original home?

A: Yes.

Q: (L) What is it like back Home?

A: Spent. Cindered. Burned up.

Q: (L) So it's true, you can't go home?

A: Yes.

Q: (L) These Nephilim, how tall were they again?

A: Up to 15 feet maximum.

Q: (L) Was Goliath, who was killed by David, one of the Nephilim?

A: Yes. In legend. Actual event depicted in story was earlier.

Q: (L) Was it actually David and Goliath?

A: Yes.

Q: (L) Did he actually slay him with a stone from a slingshot?

A: Close.

chapter fourteen

Q: (L) Were these Nephilim genetically intermixed with human beings?
A: Temporarily.
Q: (L) Why only temporarily?
A: DNA conflict.
Q: (L) Were they smarter than us?
A: No.
Q: (L) Were they bigger and dumber?
A: No.
Q: (L) About the same?
A: Yes.
Q: (L) Was it difficult for them to live on our planet because of their size and gravity and so forth?
A: Yes.
Q: (L) Did they have physical problems here?
A: Yes.
Q: (L) And when did the last of them die off?
A: 6000 B.C. Approximately. One reference.
Q: (L) When were they originally brought here?
A: 12000 B.C. approx. one reference.

November 2, 1994
Q: (L) Who carved the stone heads on Easter Island?
A: Lemurian descendants.
Q: (L) The natives say the stones walked into position. Is this true?
A: No.
Q: (L) Well, how?
A: Tonal vibration.
Q: (L) And what did these stones represent?
A: Nephalim.
Q: (L) Is this what the Nephilim looked like?
A: Close.
Q: (L) Does that mean that the Nephilim were present in Lemuria?
A: Close.
Q: (L) Where was Lemuria located?
A: Pacific off South America.
Q: (L) So when the Easter Island natives talk about their ancestors they are talking about people who came from the direction of South America?
A: No. Right near all around. Easter Island is remnant of Lemuria.
Q: (L) What happened to Lemuria?
A: Submerged close to time you refer to as Fall of Eden, approximately.
Q: (L) Well if the Nephilim were brought here 9 to 12 thousand years ago...
A: Last visit. Have been here 5 times. *Will return.*
Q: (L) The Nephilim are going to return? Where do the Nephilim currently live?

A: Orion.

Q: (L) They live in the constellation Orion? Where is their planet?

A: Don't have one. In transit.

Q: (L) The whole dadgum bunch is in transit?

A: Three vehicles.

Q: (L) How many Nephilim does each vehicle hold?

A: About 12 million.

Q: (L) Are they coming to help us?

A: No. Wave comet cluster all using same energy.

Q: (L) Using same energy to what?

A: Pass through spacetime.

Q: (L) Does this mean that without this comet cluster they cannot pass through space/time?

A: No. Slower. […]

Q: (L) So, it is slower for them to come here without this wave. Where is the wave coming from?

A: Follows cluster.

Q: (L) It follows the cluster. What does this wave consist of?

A: Realm border.

Q: (L) Does the realm border wave follow the comet cluster in a permanent way?

A: No.

Q: (L) Is the realm border loosely associated with the comet cluster each time it comes?

A: No. Realm border follows all encompassing energy reality change; realm border will follow this cluster passage and has others but not most.

Q: (L) Is this realm border a dimensional boundary?

A: Yes.

Q: (L) OK, this realm border, do dimensions…

A: Pulsating realms. Fluctuating realms.

Q: (L) Is our realm fluctuating or pulsating?

A: No.

Q: (L) But this other realm does?

A: No.

Q: (L) What fluctuates?

A: Residence.

Q: (L) Whatever is in that realm fluctuates?

A: No. Your planet fluctuates between realms.

Q: (L) How often does this fluctuation occur?

A: About every 309,000 years.

Q: (L) In other words we can expect to be in fourth density for about 300,000 years?

A: Yes.

Q: (L) Does this mean that the Edenic state existed for about 300,000 years before the "Fall?"

A: Yes.

Q: (L) Now, you say these Nephilim are coming and there is about 36 million of them, correct?

A: Yes.

Q: (L) And they are the enforcers of the Grays and Lizzies, is that correct?

A: Yes.

Q: (L) Well, let's sit back and watch the show! You are saying that the planet fluctuates...

A: No, realms do planet merely occupies realm.

Q: (L) What is the source in space/time of this other realm?

A: Too complex.

Q: (L) What is the generative source?

A: Part of grand cycle.

Q: (L) Is this the cycle understood by the Mayans?

A: They understood partially.

Q: (L) Their calendar extends to 2012... is that accurate as to the time of the realm border change?

A: Close. Still indefinite as you measure time. Lizzies hoping to rule you in 4th density. Closer to 18 years [i.e. 2012-2013].

November 4, 1994

Q: (L) What kind of weapons do the Nephilim use to do their "enforcing?"

A: Stun guns.

Q: (L) Do they actually use some kind of material weapon?

A: Yes.

November 16, 1994

Q: (L) In referring to the Nephilim you used the term "forced insemination". How does this differ from "artificial insemination?"

A: No difference.

Q: (L) At the time of the tower of Babel it says that the Nephilim looked on the daughters of men and took wives as if there were some friendly interaction of some sort... does this mean they broke ranks and had feelings for their human "wives"?

A: No. Another deception of history. Picturesque way of describing genetic experiments.

September 24, 1995

Q: (L) Why was Hitler so determined, beyond all reason, even to his own self-destruction, to annihilate the Jews?

A: Many reasons and very complex. But, remember, while still a child, Hitler made a conscious choice to align himself with the "forces of darkness," in order to fulfill his desires for conquest and to unite the Germanic peoples. Henceforth, he was totally controlled, mind, body, and soul, by STS forces.

Q: (L) So, what were the purposes of the STS forces that were controlling Hitler causing him to desire to annihilate an entire group of people?

A: *To create an adequate "breeding ground" for the reintroduction of the Nephalim*, for the purpose of total control of the 3rd density earth *prior to* elevation to 4th density, where such conquest is more difficult and less certain!

Q: (L) Do you mean "breeding ground" in the sense of genetic breeding?

A: Yes. Third density.

Q: (L) Did they accomplish this goal?

A: No.

Q: (L) So, the creation of the Germanic "Master Race" was what they were going after, to create this "breeding ground?"

A: Yes.

Q: (L) And, getting rid of the Jews was significant? Couldn't a Germanic master race be created without destroying another group?

A: No.

Q: Why?

A: Because of 4th density prior encoding mission destiny profile.

Q: (L) What does that mean?

A: This means encoding to activate after elevation to 4th density, thus if not eliminated, negates Nephalim domination and absorption. Jews were prior encoded to carry out mission after conversion, though on individual basis. The Nazis did not exactly know why they were being driven to destroy them, because they were being controlled from 4th density STS. But, Hitler communicated directly with Lizards, and Orion STS, and was instructed on how to create the "master race."

Q: (L) And they were going to use this as their basis to introduce a new blend of the Nephilim... (RC) And the New World Order... their version of it. (L) Well, what is the plan now?

A: We cannot tell you this yet, as you would seek to reveal it prematurely, leading to your destruction!!!!

Q: (F) Yes, Laura, I keep telling you that your curiosity is going to bring strange men to the door who are going to say: "Come with us, please!" (L) Well, I can't help it! Meanwhile, back to the Celts: obviously if the Lizard Beings thought that the Aryans/Celts were a good breeding ground for this "Nephilim Master Race," then it must be because there is something genetically inherent in them that makes them desirable in this sense. Is this correct?

A: No, *not in the sense you are thinking*. We suggest that you rephrase this question after careful reflection on the implications.

November 7, 1995

Q: (L) I have thought about my question from the last session and I want to ask it this way: You have said that Hitler received instructions from higher density beings about creating a 'Master Race.' Why were the Aryan genetic types seen to be more desirable for creation of this Germanic 'master race?'

A: Both, similarity and ancestral link most unblemished from Orion 3rd and 4th density stock.

Q: (L) So they were essentially trying to breed a group of people like themselves?

A: Yes.

Q: [question lost]

A: Not point. How would you suggest creation?

Q: (L) OK. They were preparing this breeding ground, so to speak. Obviously this was for the introduction of some other genetic strain. What was this?

A: Nephalim.

Q: (L) Well, if the Nephilim are coming in ships, 36 million of them, why bother to create half-breeds here?

A: Yes, but having an "advance party" makes 3rd density conquest much easier.

Q: (L) So, this Master Race was supposed to get everything ready…

A: Yes.

Q: (L) OK, what is it about the Semitic genes that was considered to be so undesirable in the creation of this 'Master Race?'

A: Would blemish *genetic characteristics inclined to ruthlessness and domination.*

Q: (L) So, you are saying that there is something, some genetic tendency or set of genes in the Semitic type that would counteract this?

A: Close.

Q: (L) But isn't the nature of a person determined by their soul and not the physical body?

A: Partially, remember, aural profile and karmic reference merges with physical structure.

Q: (L) So you are saying that particular genetic conditions are a physical reflection of a spiritual orientation? That the soul must match itself to the genetics, even if only in potential?

A: Yes, precisely.

Q: (L) So a person's potential for spiritual advancement or unfoldment is, to a great extent, dependent upon their genes?

A: Natural process marries with systematic construct when present.

Q: (L) Well, if that is the case, and the aliens are abducting people and altering their genes, can they not alter the genes so that higher level souls simply cannot come in?

A: Not incarnative process, natural biological processes. Incarnative involves strictly ethereal at 5th density and lower, and thus is enveloped in triple cycle "veil" of transfer which is impregnable by any means. However, any and all 1st, 2nd, 3rd, and 4th processes can be manipulated at will and to any degree if technology is sufficient.

February 24, 1996

Q: (L) I was reading some of the transcripts earlier today. One of the things I read was about the Nephilim and their interactions with human beings and about other planets and molecularization, etc. Then, I was reading about the planet

Kantek. Are there any human beings, on Earth, at the present time, who carry in them the Nephilim genes?

A: *Yes.* [...]

Q: (L) Would these Nephilim genetics be passed down in the natural way, or would they be the result of genetic manipulation by genetically altering a fetus and then putting it back?

A: No to latter. *One clue: double Y chromosomes.*

Q: (W) That's male...

A: Nephalim were.

Q: (L) They, were male. Women are a double X, men are XY.

A: Prisons are filled with double Y's with *monstrous personality disorders,* almost always Caucasian and over-sized.

Q: (L) On TV they interviewed a serial killer. He was *huge!* He described killing. The shrink who was analyzing said he did it because he wanted to get caught. I did *not* get that feeling. I think he did it just because it was what he did. [...] Big. Caucasian. My, my, my. Is there any other clue you can give?

A: Nephalim are not currently on your world, just trace residuals.

Q: (L) Trace residuals in people. And there are supposed to be 36 million of them coming...

A: With the wave.

Q: (L) That reminds me: is it possible that this comet cluster you have talked about exists in fourth density?

A: No.

Q: (L) The comet cluster is in third density?

A: Transcends 3rd and 4th.

Q: (L) OK, so it is both in 3rd and 4th...

A: It will be visible to you.

August 17, 1996

Q: (T) Are you aware of the Greenbaum effect [i.e. mind control programming like Manchurian candidates]? Dr. Greenbaum and his mind control experiments, that we've been looking at lately?

A: Yes.

Q: Is what's said there factual? I won't say true, but is if factual? Most of it?

A: Close.

Q: (T) OK, the question is, is the fellow that just shot three professors in San Diego, I think it was, the University, before they read his thesis, because he was afraid they would throw his thesis away, and make it look bad, and flunk him. Was he a Greenbaum?

A: Yes.

Q: (T) Why did they turn him 'on' at that point?

A: Not correct concept. What if: those programmed in the so called "Greenbaum" projects are preprogrammed to "go off" all at once, and some "malfunction," and go off early?

Q: (L) Oh!!! Can you tell us at approximately what time they're programmed to go off? Because it is a program...
A: Nope.

July 31, 1999
Q: OK, various folks are now saying that Dr. Mengele of Nazi fame is the same person as Dr. Green of Greenbaum programming fame.
A: No.
Q: Did Mengele go to South America and die there as reported?
A: Yes.
Q: The Greenbaum material says that there was a Jewish boy brought to America and trained as a doctor who became this infamous Dr. Greenbaum. Is that true?
A: No. "Green" is an alias, or more accurately, a pseudonym for multiple persons engaged in mind control efforts.

October 5, 1996
Q: (L) If two people who are married to each other are Greenbaumed, is it possible that they could be programmed to kill each other?
A: Maybe, but not always.
Q: (TM) Or any two people who have had the programming?
A: The programming is mainly intended to produce erratic behavior, for the purpose of "spooking" the population so that they will welcome, and even demand, a totalitarian government. [Coincidentally, this is the premise of Dave McGowan's excellent book, *Programmed to Kill*.]
Q: (L) So, the programming is designed to, in other words, when the people are just being erratic...
A: Think of the persons who have inexplicably entered various public and private domains, and shot large numbers of people... Now, you have "met" some of these Greenbaum subjects...
Q: (L) Let me say this. If this is what we're saying, well, what I'm saying is, that... Is this Greenbaum programming something that goes along the line of what I've just described a part; a part, I don't think that's all of it...
A: In part.
Q: (L) Is there also the implanted triggers to activate at a certain point in future time, to create a mass chaos, in the public domain?
A: Better to discover that one on your own.
Q: (L) OK, that's another one that's dangerous to know right now... (V) Was the person I met last week ... Greenbaumed? Has he been Greenbaumed. (L) He was bizarre, wasn't he?
A: Now, some history... as you know, the CIA and NSA and other agencies are the children of Nazi Gestapo... the SS, which was experiment influenced by Antareans who were practicing for the eventual reintroduction of the nephalim on to 3rd and or 4th density earth. And the contact with the "Antareans" was initiated by the Thule Society, which groomed its dupe subject, Adolph Hitler to be the all time mind programmed figurehead. Now, in modern times, you have seen, but so far, on a lesser scale: Oswald, Ruby, Demorenschildt, Sirhan Sirhan,

James Earl Ray, Arthur Bremer, Farakahan, Menendez, Bundy, Ramirez, Dahmer, etc...

Q: (L) Is there any particular individual who is currently being programmed to take a more prominent position in terms of this...

A: Later... you must know that Oswald was programmed to be the "patsy." So that he would say many contradictory things. Demorenschildt was both a programmer and programmed. Ruby was hypnotically programmed to shoot Oswald With an audio prompt, that being the sound of a car horn.

Q: (L) The question has been brought up, is there some way or means that one can distinguish or discern a victim of Greenbaum or other mind programming by some clues?

A: Not until it is too late.

July 25, 1998

Q: (L) I read the new book by Dr. David Jacobs, professor of History at Temple University, concerning his extensive research into the alien abduction phenomenon. Dr. Jacobs says that now, after all of these years of somewhat rigorous research, that he KNOWS what the aliens are here for and he is afraid. David Jacobs says that producing offspring is the primary objective behind the abduction phenomenon. Is this, in fact, the case?

A: Part, but not "the whole thing."

Q: (L) Is there another dominant reason?

A: Replacement.

Q: (L) Replacement of what?

A: You.

Q: (L) How do you mean? Creating a race to replace human beings, or abducting specific humans to replace them with a clone or whatever?

A: Mainly the former. You see, if one desires to create a new race, what better way than to mass hybridize, then mass reincarnate. Especially when the host species is so forever ignorant, controlled, and anthropocentric. What a lovely environment for total destruction and conquest and replacement... see? [...]

A: We have told you before: the Nazi experience was a "trial run," and by now you see the similarities, do you not?

Q: (L) Yes, I do see...

A: Now, we have also told you that the experience of the "Native Americans" vis a vis the Europeans may be a precursor in microcosm. Also, what Earthian 3rd density does to Terran 2nd density should offer "food for thought." In other words, thou are not so special, despite thy perspective, eh? And we have also warned that after conversion of Earth humans to 4th density, the Orion 4th density and their allies hope to control you "there." Now put this all together and what have you? At least you should by now know that it is the soul that matters, not the body. Others have genetically, spiritually and psychically manipulated/engineered you to be bodycentric. Interesting, as despite all efforts by 4th through 6th density STO, this "veil remains unbroken."

chapter fourteen

August 1, 1998

Q: (L) According to Dr. Jacobs and the stuff you told us last week, we are pretty well fried on this planet.

A: No.

Q: (L) What are our options?

A: Vague.

Q: (L) I know that. But, there does not seem to be any other way to ask this question...

A: Knowledge protects, remember, there are no limits with knowledge.

July 22, 2000

A: We wish to review some things first. The concept of a "master race" put forward by the Nazis was merely a 4th density STS effort to create *a physical vehicle with the correct frequency resonance vibration for 4th density STS souls to occupy in 3rd density.* It was also a "trial run" for planned events in what you perceive to be your future.

Q: (L) You mean with a strong STS frequency so they can have a "vehicle" in third density, so to speak?

A: Correct. Frequency resonance vibration! Very important.

Q: (L) So, that is why they are programming and experimenting? And all these folks running around who some think are "programmed," could be individuals who are raising their nastiness levels high enough to accommodate the truly negative STS fourth density—sort of like walk-ins or something, only not nice ones?

A: You do not have very many of those present yet, but that was, and still is, the plan of some of the 4th density STS types.

It was only while writing book seven of *The Wave* that a lot of these concepts started making sense. And it was only after Dr. Andrzej Łobaczewski contacted us with his book, *Political Ponerology*, that it all fit together. Before I provide some important excerpts from his book, here are clues from the C's that seemed to be pointing in a certain direction: Our hyperdimensional controllers wish to control us completely as a source of energetic "food". The Nazi concept of a "master race" was a "trial run" for the actual creation of a "new race", numbering 6% of the population, that would act as a "breeding ground" with the same genetics—"inclined to ruthlessness and domination", e.g. XYY karyotype—for these same beings.

In order to establish such a breeding ground, however, a system of control must be set up, using *human* means while the hyperdimensional controllers "proceed to patiently manipulate the chosen civilizations to develop a suitable technological infrastructure. And then, after the instituting of a long, slow, and grand mind programming project, simply step in and take it over one the situation was suitable."

At least one group plans to use these bodies as containers for their own "souls", disposing of the rest of the population. In order for this to work, they must have bodies with similar genetics and thus similar "frequency resonance vibration". Are there beings in 3D who nourish themselves on pain and suffering, who only see what they want to see, who are utterly ruthless and crave domination of others? Yes, and it looks like it is these beings the C's were referring to: psychopaths. With that in mind, we'll now provide a summary of some of the most relevant concepts from *Political Ponerology*.

Dr. Łobaczewski's book is divided into ten chapters. The introduction sets the stage for the type of questions the book will answer. How do we account for human evil? What are the processes by which societies enter periods of "mass madness"—bloody revolutions, power elites, totalitarian systems of government? What kinds of blind spots prevent us from coming to a proper understanding of such phenomena?

Łobaczewski begins with a personal anecdote. A psychology student at the time of the Communist takeover of Poland, he and his fellow students had to endure indoctrination lectures at the hand of a psychopathic "professor". He describes the interesting effects the professor had:

> May the reader please imagine a very large hall in an old Gothic university building. Many of us gathered there early in our studies in order to listen to the lectures of outstanding philosophers and scientists. We were herded back there – under threat – the year before graduation in order to listen to the indoctrination lectures which recently had been introduced. ... For ninety minutes each week, [the "professor"] flooded us with naive, presumptuous paralogistics and a pathological view of human reality. *We were treated with contempt and poorly controlled hatred.* Since fun-poking could entail dreadful consequences, we had to listen attentively and with the utmost gravity. ...
>
> "You can't convince anyone this way!" we whispered to each other. "It's actually propaganda directed against themselves." But after such mind-torture, it took a long time for someone to break the silence.
>
> We studied ourselves, since we felt something strange had taken over our minds and something valuable was leaking away irretrievably. The world of psychological reality and moral values seemed suspended as if in a chilly fog. Our human feeling and student solidarity lost their meaning, as did patriotism and our old established criteria. So we asked each other, "are you going through this too"?
>
> Each of us experienced this worry about his own personality and future in his own way. Some of us answered the questions with silence. The depth of these experiences turned out to be different for each individual. ... You can just imagine our worry, disappointment, and surprise when some colleagues we knew well suddenly began to change their world view; their thought-patterns furthermore reminded us of the "professor's" chatter. Their feelings, which had just recently been friendly, became noticeably cooler, although not yet hostile. Benevolent or critical student arguments bounced right off them. They gave the impression of possessing some secret knowledge; we were only their former colleagues, still believing what those "professors of old" had taught us. We had to be careful of what we said to them. These former colleagues soon joined the Party.
>
> Who were they, what social groups did they come from, what kind of students and people were they? How and why did they change so much in less than a year? Why did neither I nor a majority of my fellow students succumb to this

phenomenon and process? Many such questions fluttered through our heads then. It was in those times, from those questions, observations and attitudes that the idea was born that this phenomenon could be objectively studied and understood; an idea whose greater meaning crystallized with time. ...

It was relatively easy to determine the environments and origins of the people who succumbed to this process, which I then called "transpersonification". They came from all social groups, including aristocratic and fervently religious families, and caused a break in our student solidarity to the order of some 6%. The remaining majority suffered varying degrees of personality disintegration which gave rise to individual searching for the values necessary to find ourselves again; the results were varied and sometimes creative.

Even then, we had no doubts as to the pathological nature of this "transpersonification" process, which ran similar but not identical in all cases. The duration of the results of this phenomenon also varied. Some of these people later became zealots. Others later took advantage of various circumstances to withdraw and reestablish their lost links to the society of normal people. They were replaced. *The only constant value of the new social system was the magic number of 6%.*

The macrosocial phenomenon that Poland experienced is called by Łobaczewski *pathocracy,* in which "a certain hereditary anomaly isolated as "essential psychopathy" is catalytically and causatively essential for the genesis and survival of large scale social evil."

Moral evil and psychobiological evil are, in effect, interlinked via so many causal relationships and mutual influences that they can only be separated by means of abstraction. ... Understanding the nature of macrosocial pathological phenomena permits us to find a healthy attitude and perspective toward them, thus assisting us in protecting our minds from being poisoned by their diseased contents and the influence of their propaganda. ... The bottom line is that we can only conquer this huge, contagious social caner if we comprehend its essence and its etiological causes. This would eliminate the mystery of this phenomenon as its primary survival asset. *[Do not attempt to cure what you do not understand!].*

The second chapter provides "some indispensable concepts", including the inadequacies of our historical, social, psychological, and moral concepts and terminology; the role of human nature in relationships and society; and most importantly, what Łobaczewski calls "reality-deforming tendencies". These are natural human tendencies, *genetically programmed,* which inhibit our ability to identify and understand the essential features of ponerology. In other words, the predator's mind. This includes our natural tendencies of self-importance, self-centeredness, self-serving behavior, our emotional and morally judgmental reactions, etc. These mechanical processes play a great part in the genesis of evil, and are easily exploited by more sinister beings, whether human or not. Łobaczewski also points out that psychopathy is a problem of humanity as a whole, not of any exclusive racial group. In other words, the difference between a psychopath and a normal person is much greater than any difference between ethnicities.

Chapter three deals with the cyclic nature of pathocracy; the cycle between "good" and hedonistic times, and "bad" times of mass terror; how we gain knowledge through suffering, and lose it again through complacency and selfishness.

Chapter four is a summary of ponerology as a science and all the areas it covers. Łobaczewski shows that those individuals who seriously harm others always, as a rule, have some indication of psychopathology, whether it is an inherited disorder, one acquired by brain damage or childhood trauma, or some environmental influence. These are the individuals that comprise the "new race", the 6%, the pathocrats. The inherited anomalies include various personality disorders—e.g. psychopathy, schizoidia, XYY karyotype—while the acquired anomalies include paranoid personalities, drug-related brain damage, frontal lobe damage and dysfunction (Łobaczewski seems to be describing borderline personality disorder, which he terms "frontal characteropathy").

As psychopathy is the most important of the bunch, I'll include Łobaczewski's description of these individuals, with notes in *(italics)*.

[L]et us characterize another heredity-transmitted anomaly whose role in ponerogenic processes on *any* social scale appears *exceptionally great*. We should also underscore that the need to isolate this phenomenon and examine it in detail became quickly and profoundly evident to those researchers – including the author – who were interested in the macrosocial scale of the genesis of evil, because they witnessed it. I acknowledge my debt to Kazimierz Dąbrowski in doing this and calling this anomaly an "essential psychopathy". *(Łobaczewski uses the term psychopathy to describe any hereditary personality disorder characterized by a deficit in normal human instincts.)*

Biologically speaking, the phenomenon is similar to color-blindness but occurs with about ten times lower frequency (slightly above 1/2%), except that, unlike color blindness, it affects both sexes. *Its intensity also varies in scope from a level barely perceptive to an experienced observer to an obvious pathological deficiency. (For example, from criminal psychopaths, to "sub-clinical" psychopaths, also known as Machiavellian personalities, who do not get caught.)*

Like color blindness, this anomaly also appears to represent a deficit in stimulus transformation, albeit occurring not on the sensory but on the instinctive level. Psychiatrists of the old school used to call such individuals "Daltonists of human feelings and socio-moral values".

The psychological picture shows clear deficits among men only; among women it is generally toned down, as by the effect of a second normal allele. This suggests that the anomaly is also inherited via the X chromosome, but through a semi-dominating gene. However, the author was unable to confirm this by excluding inheritance from father to son.

Analysis of the different experiential manner demonstrated by these individuals caused us to conclude that their *instinctive substratum is also defective*, containing certain gaps and lacking the natural syntonic responses *(i.e., conscience, empathy)* commonly evidenced by members of the species *Homo Sapiens*. Our species instinct is our first teacher; it stays with us everywhere throughout our lives. Upon this defective instinctive substratum, the deficits of higher feelings and the deformities and impoverishments in psychological, moral, and social concepts develop in correspondence with these gaps.

chapter fourteen

Our natural world of concepts – based upon species instincts as described in an earlier chapter – strikes the psychopath as a nearly incomprehensible convention with no justification in their own psychological experience. They think that customs and principles of decency are a foreign convention invented and imposed by someone else ("probably by priests"), silly, onerous, sometimes even ridiculous. At the same time, however, *they easily perceive the deficiencies and weaknesses of our natural language of psychological and moral concepts in a manner some-what reminiscent of the attitude of a contemporary psychologist – except in caricature.*

The average intelligence of the psychopath, especially if measured via commonly used tests, is somewhat lower than that of normal people, albeit similarly variegated. Despite the wide variety of intelligence and interests, this group does not contain examples of the highest intelligence, nor do we find technical or craftsmanship talents among them. The most gifted members of this kind may thus achieve accomplishments in those sciences which do not require a correct humanistic world view or practical skills. (Academic decency is another matter, however.) Whenever we attempt to construct special tests to measure "life wisdom" or "socio-moral imagination", even if the difficulties of psychometric evaluation are taken into account, individuals of this type indicate a deficit disproportionate to their personal IQ.

In spite of their deficiencies in normal psychological and moral knowledge, they develop and then have at their disposal a knowledge of their own, something lacked by people with a natural world view. *They learn to recognize each other in a crowd as early as childhood, and they develop an awareness of the existence of other individuals similar to them. They also become conscious of being different from the world of those other people surrounding them. They view us from a certain distance, like a para-specific variety.* Natural human reactions – which often fail to elicit interest to normal people because they are considered self-evident – strike the psychopath as strange, interesting, and even comical. *(These reactions are anything from the joy of seeing an old friend, to emotional suffering, and signs of inner conflict.)* They therefore observe us, deriving conclusions, forming their different world of concepts. *(Psychopaths learn how to fake emotions. Some even practice in front of a mirror. Their whole life is an act.)* They become experts in our weaknesses and sometimes effect heartless experiments.

The suffering and injustice they cause inspire no guilt within them, since such reactions from others are simply a result of their being different and apply only to "those other" people they perceive to be not quite conspecific. *(That is, they contemptuously view us as another species.)* Neither a normal person nor our natural world view can fully conceive nor properly evaluate the existence of this world of different concepts. A researcher into such phenomena can glimpse the deviant knowledge of the psychopath through long-term studies of the personalities of such people, using it with some difficulty, like a foreign language. As we shall see below, such practical skill becomes rather widespread in nations afflicted by that macrosocial pathological phenomenon wherein this anomaly plays the inspiring role.

A normal person can learn to speak their conceptual language even somewhat proficiently, but *the psychopath is never able to incorporate the world view of a normal person,* although they often try to do so all their lives. The product of their efforts is only a role and a mask behind which they hide their deviant reality. Another myth and role they often play, albeit containing a grain of truth in relation to the "special psychological knowledge" that the psychopath acquires regarding normal people, would be the psychopath's brilliant mind or psychological genius; some of them actually believe in this and attempt to insinuate this belief to others.

In speaking of the mask of psychological normality worn by such individuals (and by similar deviants to a lesser extent), we should mention the book *The Mask of Sanity*, by Hervey Cleckley, who made this very phenomenon the crux of his reflections. A fragment:

> Let us remember that his typical behavior defeats what appear to be his own aims. Is it not he himself who is most deeply deceived by his apparent normality? Although he deliberately cheats others and is quite conscious of his lies, he appears unable to distinguish adequately between his own pseudointentions, pseudoremorse, pseudolove, etc., and the genuine responses of a normal person. His monumental lack of insight indicates how little he appreciates the nature of his disorder. When others fail to accept immediately his "word of honor as a gentleman", his amazement, I believe, is often genuine. His subjective experience is so bleached of deep emotion that he is invincibly ignorant of what life means to others.
>
> His awareness of hypocrisy's opposite is so insubstantially theoretical that it becomes questionable if what we chiefly mean by hypocrisy should be attributed to him. Having no major value himself, can he be said to realize adequately the nature and quality of the outrages his conduct inflicts upon others? A young child who has no impressive memory of severe pain may have been told by his mother it is wrong to cut off the dog's tail. Knowing it is wrong he may proceed with the operation. We need not totally absolve him of responsibility if we say he realizes less what he did than an adult who, in full appreciation of physical agony, so uses a knife. Can a person experience the deeper levels of sorrow without considerable knowledge of happiness? Can he achieve evil intention in the full sense without real awareness of evil's opposite? I have no final answer to these questions.

All researchers into psychopathy underline three qualities primarily with regard to this most typical variety: The absence of a sense of guilt for antisocial actions, the inability to love truly, and the tendency to be garrulous in a way which easily deviates from reality *(in other words, they are talkative, compulsive liars)*.

A neurotic patient is generally taciturn *(uncommunicative)* and has trouble explaining what hurts him most. A psychologist must know how to overcome these obstacles with the help of non-painful interactions. Neurotics are also prone to excessive guilt about actions which are easily forgiven. Such patients are capable of decent and enduring love, although they have difficulty expressing it or achieving their dreams. *A psychopath's behavior constitutes the antipode of such phenomena and difficulties.* Our first contact with the psychopath is characterized by a talkative stream which flows with ease and avoids truly important matters with equal ease if they are uncomfortable for the speaker. His train of thought also avoids those abstract matters of human feelings and values whose representation is absent in the psychopathic world view unless, of course, he is being deliberately deceptive, in which case he will use many "feeling" words which careful scrutiny will reveal that he does not understand those words the same way normal people do. We then also feel we are dealing with an imitation of the thought patterns of normal people, in which something else is, in fact, "normal". From the logical point of view, the flow of thought is ostensibly correct, albeit perhaps removed from commonly accepted criteria. A more detailed formal analysis, however, evidences the use of many suggestive paralogisms *(i.e. purposefully sinister lies and "twists" of truth)*.

Individuals with the psychopathy referred to herein are virtually unfamiliar with the enduring emotions of love for another person, particularly the marriage partner; it constitutes a fairytale from that "other" human world. Love, for the psychopath, is an ephemeral phenomenon aimed at sexual adventure. Many psychopathic Don Juans are able to play the lover's role well enough for their partners to accept it in good faith. After the wedding, feelings which really never existed are replaced by egoism, egotism, and hedonism. *(The vast majority of abusive husbands are psychopathic.)* Religion, which teaches love for one's neighbor, also strikes them as a similar fairytale good only for children and those different "others".

One would expect them to feel guilty as a consequence of their many antisocial acts, however their lack of guilt is the result of all their deficits, which we have been discussing here. *The world of normal people whom they hurt is incomprehensible and hostile to them, and life for the psychopath is the pursuit of its immediate attractions, moments of pleasure, and temporary feelings of power.* They often meet with failure along this road, along with force and moral condemnation from the society of those other incomprehensible people.

In their book *Psychopathy and Delinquency*, W. and J. McCord say the following about them:

> The psychopath feels little, if any, guilt. He can commit the most appalling acts, yet view them without remorse. The Psychopath has a warped capacity for love. His emotional relationships, when they exist, are meager, fleeting, and designed to satisfy his own desires. These last two traits, guiltlessness and lovelessness, conspicuously mark the psychopath as different from other men.

> The problem of a psychopath's moral and legal responsibility thus remains open and subject to various solutions, frequently summary or emotional, in various countries and circumstances. It remains a subject of discussion whose solution does not appear possible within the framework of the presently accepted principles of legal thought.

He then describes the techniques these individuals use in their Machiavellian quest for power. They are tremendously arrogant, with an absolute certainty in their own rightness—the are the epitome of human "wishful thinking" and all that implies. They make use of our tendency to "moralize", as they did in the aftermath of 9/11, focusing the country's vengefulness on a convenient enemy. They rely on "spellbinders" to hypnotize the masses with propaganda; they "gas-light" or tell lies repeatedly and adamantly, to the point where normal people doubt their own judgment and believe the lie; and they take advantage of the our tendency to deny and repress unwanted information—e.g. that their government is in fact a gang of petty criminals.

He then describes how normal groups are "ponerized" by pathological individuals, and how such groups use the original ideology to "piggy-back" their own agenda, to the point of ruling nations. At a period of mass hystericization and paranoia—in the aftermath of a war, catastrophe, or staged terrorist attack—the society is ripe for pathocracy, the subject of chapter five.

> During stable times which are ostensibly happy, albeit dependent upon injustice to other individuals and nations *(a perfect description of our global society of the super rich versus the super poor)*, doctrinaire people believe they have found a simple solution to fix the world. Such a historical period is always characterized by an impoverished psychological world view, so that a schizoidally impoverished psychological world view does not stand out as odd during such times and is accepted as legal tender. These doctrinaire individuals characteristically manifest a certain contempt with regard to moralists then preaching the need to rediscover lost human values and to develop a richer, more appropriate psychological world view.

We've seen this phenomenon above, in Dave McGowan's article on eugenics. The whole eugenics idea is based on a "schizoidally impoverished worldview". The best indication of a schizoidal worldview is the presence of a schizoidal declaration: "human nature is so bad that society can only be maintained by a strong power created by qualified individuals in the name of some higher idea." This naïve view of human nature has led to any number of catastrophes: from rabbis and priests declaring that "human nature is so bad that it can only be saved by highly trained individuals in the service of a strong and vengeful God" to the perversions of Marxism and the gods of capitalism. Psychopaths have no emotional attachment to any of these ideologies. So in this sense, we already have a "one world government". All the players "know the game", and will play their part for a piece of the prize.

Take another look at what the author of the Peak Oil eugenics program, William Stanton, wrote about population reduction. See if you can identify the deficits in normal human psychology in his schizoidal nonsense.

Beliefs in schizoidal philosophies soon experience a moral "twist" as more ruthless individuals gain power. Eventually, a pathocracy develops. As Łobaczewski puts it, it's as if the inmates have taken over the asylum. Eventually, 100% of essential psychopaths occupy positions of authority and power. Normal people are held in constant psychological terror. It's literally like living in Orwell's *1984,* where normal human emotions and reactions must be internalized; any outward display of normality can provoke a police interrogation, exile, or worse. One never knows when one is dealing with a government agent or a petty informant. The lives of normal people under such a system of oppression, and their reactions to same, are described in chapter six.

War without end is an essential feature of pathocracy.

303

chapter fourteen

[C]an such a system ever waive territorial and political expansion abroad and settle for its present possessions?

What would happen if such a state of affairs ensured internal peace, corresponding order, and relative prosperity within the nation? The overwhelming majority of the country's population would then make skillful use of all the emerging possibilities, taking advantage of their superior qualifications in order to fight for an ever-increasing scope of activities; thanks to their higher birth rate, their power will increase. This majority will be joined by some sons from the privileged class who did not inherit the pathological genes. The pathocracy's dominance will weaken imperceptibly but steadily, finally leading to a situation wherein the society of normal people reaches for power. This is a nightmare vision to the psychopaths.

Thus, the biological, psychological, moral, and economic destruction of the majority of normal people becomes, for the pathocrats, a "biological" necessity.

Many means serve this end, starting with concentration camps and including warfare with an obstinate, well-armed foe who will devastate and debilitate the human power thrown at him, namely the very power jeopardizing pathocrats' rule: the sons of normal man sent out to fight for an illusionary "noble cause." Once safely dead, the soldiers will then be decreed heroes to be revered in paeans, useful for raising a new generation faithful to the pathocracy and ever willing to go to their deaths to protect it.

Any war waged by a pathocratic nation has two fronts, the internal and the external. The internal front is more important for the leaders and the governing elite, and the internal threat is the deciding factor where unleashing war is concerned. In pondering whether to start a war against the pathocratic country, other nations must therefore give primary consideration to the fact that such a war can be used as an executioner of the common people whose increasing power represents incipient jeopardy for the pathocracy. After all, pathocrats give short shrift to blood and suffering of people they consider to be not quite conspecific. Kings may have suffered due to the death of their knights, but pathocrats never do: "We have a lot of people here." Should the situation be, or become, ripe in such a country, however, anyone furnishing assistance to the nation will be blessed by it; anyone withholding it will be cursed.

Chapter seven deals with psychology and psychiatry under pathocratic rule. This chapter provides a good explanation of the need for COINTELPRO-like operations. Knowledge which can successfully diagnose pathocracy, or promote human understanding and growth to the point where resistance is possible, must be stifled and destroyed. Thus, books are stolen from libraries, subjects are banned, researchers are murdered. The system relies on secrecy. It cannot survive in the light of truth.

Chapter eight deals with religion and pathocracy. As I've shown throughout my books, religion has been one of the most successful pathocratic tools of population control. There isn't an ideology that hasn't been co-opted and diverted to an agenda opposite of its original intentions (assuming its intentions were noble to being with!). The way things have played out, no matter who "wins"—Christians, Muslims, Jews—we lose.

Chapters nine and ten are Łobaczewski's recommendations for what can be done, and his vision of what a sane society would look like. You really have to read the book, because it is rich in detail, and it is directly applicable to true nature of the global games of the elite in our time. This brings us directly back to 9/11 and UFOs.

UFOs have national security implications for a lot of reasons, not the least of which is that they have involved military and industrial personnel of many nations around the globe. This situation has existed for over fifty years. In fact, a careful study of history shows an intersection between UFOs and the military for hundreds, if not thousands of years! Unauthorized airspace violations continue to occur; attempted interceptions repeatedly take place; and the secrecy orders are more severe now than ever.

We have to ask ourselves why this is so.

If the military organizations are as interested in UFOs and aliens as we know them to be based on the evidence, and if they are in the dark about them, as the evidence also suggests, would they not be utilizing the many claimed "alien contacts" among the New Age community as resources if there was the possibility that such sources really were in contact with the "real aliens" in and about the planet as they claim? There are certainly many of these contactees that claim "extreme military interest" in their work. However, based on the facts of the operations of the National Security State, we can pretty well objectively assess that if this were true, such contactees would not be out there promulgating their information. That they often operate unmolested, and even achieve great popularity is compelling evidence that their "information" is useless to the military, if not created by it. What seems to be true is that most contactees and channellers are dupes of the military cover-up—victims of COINTELPRO—created to generate the noise that hides the signal of the true Alien Reality. In short, the majority of claims of channellers, contactees, new age gurus, UFO researchers, and the like, both in books and on the internet, about the "alien reality", is COINTELPRO at its finest.

Take that to the bank.

One thing is clear: the UFOs themselves are not under the control of the military—or anybody else. But that the Consortium continues to debunk and cover it up—in the face of its violations of their own airspace—suggests to us again the analogy of arrogant and powerful Masters of Reality, aided and abetted by their military and intelligence organization servants who, all the while they are obeying the powerful overlords, seek to keep everything quiet while they try desperately to discover the secrets of power so as to arrogate it to themselves. And it seems evident that, in the present time, the game is afoot in the citadels of Power and Secrets. Something is happening and the servants of the alien masters are running scared. They are trying to cement controls, to solidify their power base, because *something wicked this way comes.*

chapter fifteen
ascension

We now come to the subject of so-called *ascension,* which is claimed by so many "contactees" and "abductees" to be the desired result of contact with so-called extraterrestrials.

The subject of ascension seems to be the number one topic of the New Age and Human Potential movement. If, as we suspect, the New Age and Human Potential movement is the product of COINTELPRO, that means that the correct understanding of, and process of, ascension is the main thing they wish to disrupt and destroy. Does that mean that such a potential does not exist at all? No. The concepts of ascension have been with us a long time, as we will see. What is different in the present day promotions is the process that is being promoted is either entirely false, or at least, seriously twisted so as to lead the seeker far from the path. Based on an assessment of the potentials of ascension, it is obvious that the reason it is such a popular subject is that it is one of the main things that COINTELPRO is designed to obstruct and prevent.

Let me repeat the observation I made above: Would there be so much effort to conceal the alien agenda if disclosure of the truth wasn't harmful to that agenda? Rephrasing this: Would there be so much effort to divert the ascension process that is purportedly connected to the "alien encounter scenario" if it wasn't harmful to the negative agendas?

As the fellow at RAND noted, "Terrorism is changing. New adversaries, new motivations and new rationales have surfaced in recent years to challenge much of the conventional wisdom". We already have the idea that the Consortium, the National Security State, the Pathocracy, does not have our best interests at heart, and that at some level, they seem to be operating at the behest of the alien invaders. Considering this, we might wish to look with new eyes at some of the ideas of ascension that are currently being promulgated.

In order to understand the growth of the "Alien-promoted Ascension Industry", we need to look at a close parallel: general culture. Among the observers of the American socio-cultural scene, there are many experts who tell us that there has been a deliberate effort for over 100 years, to "dumb down" the American population both in terms of intellect as well as ethics. This subject is too vast to be covered in detail here (see John Taylor Gatto's books on the subject). For now, let us just point out that the same process that has been used to dumb down the population in social and intellectual terms has been used to dumb us down in terms of philosophy, metaphysics and spiritual awareness. We might observe that it is hardly likely that the effort would be expended on mind control of the masses for the purposes of external controls, without a parallel program being instituted to pervert the spirit and bring it under domination also via the "Alien Scenarios" of ascension.

While everyone will readily admit that there is probably too much violence on television and that the ads are revoltingly juvenile, very few people have a real conception of the precise nature and extent of the hypnotic influence of the media. Still fewer have any idea of the purposes behind this inducement. Wallace and Wallechinsky (1975) write in *The People's Almanac*:

> After World War II, television flourished... Psychologists and sociologists were brought in to study human nature in relation to selling; in other words, to figure out how to manipulate people without their feeling manipulated. Dr. Ernest Dichter, President of the Institute for Motivational Research made a statement in 1941... 'the successful ad agency manipulates human motivations and desires and develops a need for goods with which the public has at one time been unfamiliar—perhaps even undesirous of purchasing.'
>
> Discussing the influence of television, Daniel Boorstin wrote: "Here at last is a supermarket of surrogate experience. Successful programming offers entertainment—under the guise of instruction; instruction—under the guise of entertainment; political persuasion—with the appeal of advertising; and advertising—with the appeal of drama." ... programmed television serves not only to *spread acquiescence and conformity*, but it represents a deliberate industry approach". (805, 807)

Allen Funt, host of a popular television show, *Candid Camera*, was once asked what was the most disturbing thing he had learned about people in his years of dealing with them through the media. His response was chilling in its ramifications:

> "The worst thing, and I see it over and over, is how easily people can be led by any kind of authority figure, or even the most minimal kinds of authority. A well-dressed man walks up the down escalator and most people will turn around and try desperately to go up also... We put up a sign on the road, 'Delaware Closed Today'. Motorists didn't even question it. Instead they asked: 'Is Jersey open?'" (Wallace and Wallechinsky, 1975)

Submission to minimal signs of authority; lack of knowledge and awareness; and a desire for a quick fix and an easy way out. Paraphrasing Daniel Boorstin: "For seekers of ascension, here at last is a supermarket of surrogate experience. Successful ascension philosophies offer entertainment—under the guise of instruction; instruction—under the guise of entertainment; metaphysical persuasion—with the appeal of advertising; and advertising—with the appeal of Cosmic Drama."

When we consider the information about mind programming and its potentials compiled in Dolan's book, *UFOs and the National Security State,* and how it has probably been used on the masses of humanity, we must also consider, as a logical step, that the major and most popular components of the

New Age alternative approach to interpreting reality and seeking spiritual advancement, have also been produced by this same process in the context of electronic COINTELPRO.

What seems to be so is that most of the New Age and Human Potential movement consists of a new sub-set of programmers that work to "prepare the ground", so to speak, so that the audience will be warmed up and ready for the final drama. They are the "sales team" that sells the ideas upon which the "closer" depends for success. And that success will be like the Assyrian and Persian empires, who, when deporting the population of a conquered territory or repopulating the same area with subjects from another, portrayed themselves as "liberators" of the old, "oppressive" regimes, and who were simply giving the "reward" of "returning" the people to their original "homeland" and reinstating worship of the "old gods." Those preparing the ground for the return of our very own "old gods", here to "save" us from our corrupt leaders, are here, now, in our world running New Age Circuses, seminars, workshops and "methods" or techniques for "ascension", or accomplishing any of a dozen occult or purported spiritual aims. They are the New Age COINTELPRO in its function of creating "bogus organizations" and bogus abductions.

This brings us back to our subject: aliens and ascension. If we cannot rely on what is passing as "New Age Theology" or philosophy to guide us, what is the key to *real* ascension?

What the modern day seekers of ascension are looking for—whether they realize it or not—is the age-old quest of the Knight—the quest for the Holy Grail. When we begin to research the matter, we also discover that the "Great Work" of Alchemy is described in terms of a "great battle" with forces— dragons, deception, difficult and prolonged work on the self—which make us realize that the stories of the Grail Quest must have originally been stories of "alchemical transformation". They never were stories about a "real" object—cup or otherwise—that must be found. (Or could they have been both?) What is most fascinating is the way the Grail Stories and the writings of the Alchemists about their "sacred science", also relate quite closely to the most ancient of heroic myths.

What this means is that the Quest for the Holy Grail and the Work of the Alchemists hold many clues for us as to the real work of ascension and its pitfalls, including so-called aliens and abductions—manifestations from hyperdimensional realities. Repeatedly they present allegories of struggle, deception, battles with dragons, deceivers, and evil forces of all kinds. The story of the Knight who slays the Dragon and rescues the Princess from the Tower after years of seeking, struggling, suffering and overcoming, is an allegory that is as valid today as it was in ages past. It is the true path of ascension.

The science of the ancients may have included a very comprehensive knowledge of the deeper reality that present day sciences, including physics, chemistry, mathematics, and astrophysics, are only rediscovering. And here we do not mean the ancient Egyptians or Babylonians or Sumerians, but rather peoples of far greater antiquity than they, and that the Egyptians, Babylonians,

Sumerians, and so on, retained only a distorted and corrupted version of these ideas in the form of myths and legends which they elaborated and utilized in their "magical practices". Further, that it is only in the light of the present day scientific knowledge that the true ancient knowledge, depicted in these myths and legends and religious rites can be properly understood. This is not to say that we are suggesting that we understand or have interpreted all of them. We are only saying that there are many ideas in these ancient stories that suggest the former existence of an advanced science that may have enabled an interface between layers, or dimensions of reality, on this planet in archaic times.

This idea is not original to us, as many readers will know. However, we do think that we have been able to shine a light into certain dark corners that have been, heretofore, poorly understood. Arthur C. Clarke pointed out, "Any sufficiently evolved technology is indistinguishable from magic". When we divest our minds of preconceived notions about what the ancients may or may not have known, and we just look at myths and legends, the substrate of religions, over and over again we see descriptions of activities, events, terms and potentials that express such things as a knowledge of free energy, anti-gravity, time travel, interplanetary travel, atomic energy, atomic molecularization and demolecularization; just a whole host of doings that were formerly understood as the wild and superstitious imaginings of howling savages, that today—with scientific knowledge—are becoming commonplace activities. Many scholars explain that such stories were attempts to understand the environment by personifying, or anthropomorphizing, the forces of nature. Other interpreters make the mistake of assuming that it was a "sacred science" in terms that strictly deny any form of material interpretation.

I gave this idea a great deal of thought at one point, all the while observing my five children develop, paying close attention to how and when they noticed things in their environment, how they explained phenomena to themselves and each other; avoiding my own input as long as possible so that the child's originality would develop as naturally as possible. One of the earliest observations I made about my children (and other children with whom they interacted) and their reactions to their environment, was that they pretty much just accept it as it is. They don't seem to need "explanations" for it. It is what it is until some adult repeats to them some story about it which may entertain them or frighten them. Until "stories" are told to them, children are intensely busy just imitating what they see other people do, most generally the adults in their lives. Without fantastic tales being told to them, their games of make-believe consist of ordinary mundane dramas. Even when they are told magical stories about flying horses or people with super powers, they often resist these dramas in preference for those that directly apply to their own experience and observation.

Perhaps the comparison of the development of a child's thinking in relation to their environment, to the development of evolutionary thinking of human beings in general is a stretch. But, I do think that it ought to give us some pause to question just where and how the creation of myth and legend actually served human beings evolutionarily speaking. Why would anyone tell a story about a man with magic sandals that enabled him to fly if they are merely anthropomorphizing the forces of nature? If it is a "magical being" such as a "god", why does he need sandals to fly with? He could just as easily have wings that are part of his physical structure. He's already a god, after all. He's not human. So why the sandals? Why should a technological device that enables a man to fly be part of an archaic ontology?

Indeed, there may be an "archetypal pool of ideas" from which all humanity may draw in dreams and visions, but that leads us into realms of thought that do not answer the simple question of what benefit there was for howling savages to make up fantastic tales about the forces of nature, tales that also included certain elements that suggest a technology and not only a "magical state of being."

In the present day, there are all sorts of "mystical" groups and organizations that claim to be the recipients of ancient knowledge, what is commonly called "occultism", or the "esoteric", or magical practices. There is a plethora of books that purport to be scientific, but which totally reject mainstream science in any context. Subjects such as sacred geometry, archaeoastronomy, and new physics have all become subjects of fevered study in order to discern the "occult significance" of the works of the ancients. And, invariably, it is done in strictly ritual terms, positing that all of the abilities of the ancients were accomplished strictly by magical rites or rituals—controlling what is "up there" by rituals "down here."

Occultists claim that the mental and spiritual powers of the ancients were what we have lost. They then assert that this ancient wisdom was broken up and obscured in magical doctrines, which those who are not "initiated" simply cannot grasp. They claim that parts of it have been handed down by continuous tradition, and released to the world at opportune times, and other parts have only been released to an elect few, of which exalted company, they, of course, are obviously members.

When considering such ideas, we do come to the thought that it is very likely that there are rites or stories or myths behind the rituals that may, indeed, have been passed down in such secret groups in a more pure form than the stories that make their way around the globe across millennia. But that does not mean that the "priesthood" of such groups truly understands the stories or rites of which they are guardians—especially if they do not consider the possibility that such information may be scientific codes and require a trained scientist to decode them.

Most of the so-called "occultists" and "sacred geometers" remind me of David Macaulay's *Motel Of Mysteries* (1979), a humorous account of an archaeological excavation of a twentieth century motel, in which everything is meticulously excavated, recorded and then totally misinterpreted. The "vast funerary" complex unearthed by Howard Carson contains wonders such as the "Great Altar" (Television), a statue of the deity WATT (bedside lamp) and the Internal Component Enclosure (or ICE box).

There are other promulgators of the occult who seem to be part of the very Control System we have described above and who seem to have extremely dangerous proclivities, as we have discussed in *The Wave* series of books.

In terms of archaeology, there are processes involved in the formation of the archaeological record. A lack of understanding of these formation processes is not always confined to the non-professionals. It has only relatively recently been suggested that the archaeology of a site is not a direct record of what went on there, but instead may have been distorted by a whole series of processes.

We are suggesting that the same may be true regarding myths and legends and religious rites. They are a sort of archaeological record of the history of mankind held in archetypal terms, buried in stories, distorted by a whole series of processes.

Even if some of the purported ancient schools and mystical paths have kept some of this information intact, or in a purer state, it still seems that much has "faded on the page" due to the long period of time since such things were part of the external reality. But still, there are those who have seen the contradictions in our reality and our beliefs and who have sought in these ancient teachings to discover what might have been known. Many of them have made discoveries that, when considered with information from many other fields, assists us in this essential discovery of our true condition and purpose.

PART THREE:
The Gift of the Present

chapter sixteen
realm of gods

We have examined evidence from history, myth, modern abduction reports, as well as the Cassiopaean transcripts. We see that modern reports of "alien abductions" fit with age-old accounts of meetings with gods, fairies, and other "unworldly" beings. We have seen that whatever the epoch, the beings carrying out these abductions do not have the best interests of humanity at heart.

From this study, with its data, we have a working hypothesis, the idea that these beings have the ability to move through space-time and have been interacting with humanity for all of recorded history as well as that part of our history that is preserved in myth.

Does the idea of the existence of higher dimensions or realities where such hard-to-believe possibilities are built into physical laws have any basis in modern science? Or must we abandon the whole notion when the data is subjected to critical review?

While these ideas might seem more suited to science fiction than science proper, in fact, some of the most well-known physicists have proposed models and research programs that in no way contradict our hypothesis. They may one day demonstrate the mathematical proof of such a perspective. For example, Paul Dirac wrote:

> There are, at present, fundamental problems in theoretical physics the solution of which will presumably require a more drastic revision of our fundamental concepts than any that have gone before. Quite likely, these changes will be so great that it will be beyond the power of human intelligence to get the necessary new ideas by direct attempts to formulate the experimental data in mathematical terms. The theoretical worker in the future will, therefore, have to *proceed in a more direct way*. The more powerful method of advance that can be suggested at present is to employ all resources of pure mathematics in attempts to perfect and generalize the mathematical formalism that forms the existing basis of theoretical physics, and after each success in this direction, to try to *interpret the new mathematical features in terms of physical entities*.

Dirac was not alone in suggesting that mathematical features might need to be interpreted as physical entities.

In considering the general theory of relativity science usually utilizes a four-dimensional space-time continuum. In classical general relativity, the metrical properties of the continuum are intrinsic to the continuum, but a fifth dimension in which our normally sensed space-time is embedded can also be used to account for the curvature and properties of physical space.

In the space-time continuum one can say that *all parts of the four-dimensional world exist simultaneously*, in the sense of a mathematical formalism, and this would naturally lead to a *complete collapse of the philosophical ideas of causality.*

However, many scientists who work with these ideas do not think that this continuum is "real" in a *physical sense*, such that physical beings could move back and forth at will in and out of time as easily as changing direction in three-dimensional space.

We, on the other hand, think that it is not only possible, but extremely likely based upon the data we have collected from fields of study that fall outside the range of quantum or classical mechanics: myth, history, and religion, for example. This great specialization and separation of knowledge into little boxes of awareness—or is that boxes of lack of awareness?—serves its purpose in preventing us from seeing the whole picture, from finding data across many fields of study that can shine the light of understanding on the nature of reality.

In relativity theory, time intervals between events are not completely fixed relative to moving systems or frames of reference. This has led to some speculation that there may also be analogies between precognition and anomalies. However, "time dilation", the contraction of time intervals between moving reference frames, is too small to account for precognition and *would still require any information transfer to travel faster than light,* and the special theory of relativity, when narrowly interpreted, does not allow for physical travel backwards in time but relegates this concept to an *imaginary mathematical formalism.*

Even though it is almost forbidden to question Einstein's restriction on superluminal travel, Einstein did, at one point, propose to consider the hyperdimensional world as "real". In 1938, with P. Bergmann, he wrote a paper entitled "On a Generalization of Kaluza's Theory of Electricity":

> So far, two fairly simple and natural attempts to connect gravitation and electricity by a unitary field theory have been made, one by Weyl, the other by Kaluza. Furthermore, there have been some attempts to represent Kaluza's theory formally so as to avoid the introduction of the fifth dimension of the physical continuum. The theory presented here differs from Kaluza's in one essential point; *we ascribe physical reality to the fifth dimension* whereas in Kaluza's theory this fifth dimension was introduced only in order to obtain new components of the metric tensor representing the electromagnetic field. (emphasis added)

Einstein was somewhat nervous about this idea, but he followed it anyway, writing in his paper:

> If Kaluza's attempt is a real step forward, then it is because of the introduction of the five dimensional space. There have been many attempts to retain the essential formal results obtained by Kaluza without sacrificing the four dimensional

character of the physical space. *This shows distinctly how vividly our physical intuition resists the introduction of the fifth dimension.*

But by considering and comparing all these attempts one must come to the conclusion that all these endeavors did not improve the situation. It seems impossible to formulate Kaluza's idea in a simple way without introducing the fifth dimension.

We have, therefore, to take the fifth dimension seriously although we are not encouraged to do so by plain experience. If, therefore, the space structure seems to force acceptance of the five dimensional space theory upon us we must ask whether it is sensible to assume the rigorous reducibility to four dimensional space. We believe that the answer should be "no", provided that it is possible to understand, in another way, the quasi-four dimensional character of the physical space by taking as a basis the five dimensional continuum and to simplify hereby the basic geometrical assumptions....

The most essential point of our theory is the replacing of ...rigorous cylindricity by the assumption that space is closed (or periodic). ... Kaluza's five dimensional theory of the physical space provides a unitary representation of gravitation and electromagnetism. ... It is much more satisfactory to introduce the fifth dimension not only formally, but to assign to it some physical meaning. (Einstein and Bergmann, 1938, emphasis added)

Notice particularly Einstein's remark about the assumption that space is "periodic". We believe that Einstein was following a path that was later to prove very fruitful even if, shortly after, Einstein publicly repudiated this idea. When Einstein describes space as "periodic", he means that it loops back upon itself.

We think that we should take the idea these mathematical formalisms have *physical meaning* seriously. Physics has stagnated in the period since Einstein made such a daring proposal. Might one of the reasons lie in our refusal to take such "outlandish" ideas as serious hypotheses for further research? The universe has already shown itself to be much more "unbelievable" than scientists working prior to Einstein and Dirac might ever have imagined. If we continue to draw the line *a priori* over the results we expect and accept from our research, we are saying that we prefer our current understanding of the world over the truth and will never move forward. We are closing ourselves off from possibilities that either we cannot imagine or that we find at odds with our current beliefs.

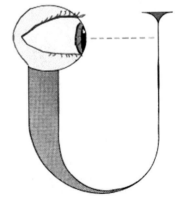

But if these mathematical dimensions are to be taken as having physical existence—whatever the term "physical" might mean given the nature of the "physical" laws that would apply—what about the idea that these other dimensions could be inhabited, could be populated with beings with some form of consciousness?

Certain ontological problems related particularly to quantum theory suggest that an "observer" (J. A. Wheeler's "Eye"—see illustration), watching the universe so as to "create it", may need to be included in our consideration. That suggests the necessity for expanding the scope of what is nowadays considered as "physical entities". The answer to "observability of parallel universes" may involve taking into account such an extension.

Now, consider the idea that there are several—maybe even infinite—"probable future yous" as observers. In Wheeler's "eye", this would be represented as many "eyes", but all of them converging on a single point on the tail—the "now" moment that we perceive, which is the moment of "choice". It is from these probable futures of infinite potential—a realm of "information"—that reality is projected. It is through human beings that these energies are transduced and become "real".

You in the here and now—at the conjunction of all of these probabilities all vying with one another to become "real"—have no possibility of "creating" anything in this reality from "down here", so to say. The realities—the creative potentials—are a projection from higher levels of density. You are a receiver, a transducer, a reflector of the view of which eye is viewing *you*, nothing more.

The phenomenon that these ideas speak to more directly is that of hyperdimensional realities wherein mental energies or consciousness energies are amplified and can be interactive with the environment; technology that suggests not only power for transport that is partly physical, partly "ethereal", communication that is also partly physical and partly ethereal, as well as powers of "manifestation" that might seem impossible to us in our present state of technology. All of these properties *do* belong to hyperdimensional existence, and such a state of being has been reported for millennia as being the "realm of the gods", including Dragons and Serpents and critters of all sorts.

If we can describe such realms mathematically and give them a physical reality, as Dirac and Einstein suggest, then we might also consider the hypothesis that they may be inhabited. Could our "gods" be inhabitants of this realm?

As many physicists will tell you, all that really exists are "waveforms", and we are waveforms of reality, and our consciousness is something that "reads waves". We give form and structure to the waves we "read" according to some agreed upon convention.

And so, certain denizens of hyperdimensional space are "read" as more or less "reptilian" because that is the "essence" of their being, the frequency of their "wave form". We call them the Overlords of Entropy. They are not necessarily physical as we understand the term, nor are they necessarily "alien" as we understand the term either. We suspect that the perceptions of these levels of reality and their "consciousness units" are what is behind many religious conceptions and mythological representations of "gods and goddesses" and creatures of all sorts.

There is even scientific evidence that the inhabitants of a higher dimension, Kaluza and Einstein's fifth dimension, would appear to us to have the powers we attribute to "gods". Michio Kaku gives this description in his book,

Hyperspace: A Scientific Odyssey Through Parallel Universes, Time Warps, and the 10th Dimension:

> Imagine being able to walk through walls.
> You wouldn't have to bother with opening doors; you could pass right through them. You wouldn't have to go around buildings; you could enter them through their walls and pillars and out through the back wall. You wouldn't have to detour around mountains; you could step right into them. When hungry, you could simply reach through the refrigerator door without opening it. You could never be accidentally locked outside your car; you could simply step through the car door.
> Imagine being able to disappear or reappear at will.
> Instead of driving to school or work, you would just vanish and rematerialize in your classroom or office. You wouldn't need an airplane to visit far-away places, you could just vanish and rematerialize where you wanted. You would never be stuck in city traffic during rush hours; you and your car would simply disappear and rematerialize at your destination.
> Imagine having x-ray eyes.
> You would be able to see accidents happening from a distance. After vanishing and rematerializing at the site of any accident, you could see exactly where the victims were, even if they were buried under debris.
> Imagine being able to reach into an object without opening it.
> You could extract the sections from an orange without peeling or cutting it. You would be hailed as a master surgeon, with the ability to repair the internal organs of patients without ever cutting the skin, thereby greatly reducing pain and the risk of infection. You would simply reach into the person's body, passing directly through the skin, and perform the delicate operation.
> Imagine what a criminal could do with these powers. He could enter the most heavily guarded bank. He could see through the massive doors of the vault for the valuables and case and reach inside and pull them out. He could then stroll outside as the bullets from the guards passed right through him.
> With these powers, no prison could hold a criminal. No secrets could be kept from us. No treasures could be hidden from us. No obstructions could stop us. We would truly be miracle workers, performing feats beyond the comprehension of mortals. We would also be omnipotent.
> What being could possess such God-like power? The answer: a being from a higher-dimensional world. (45-6)

If you have followed the arguments of this book, you will now understand that to call what happens on our planet a "conspiracy" in human terms is to greatly simplify the problem. What we see as "conspiracy" is simply the natural manifestation of the underlying reality. Very few people are consciously part of the plan; most of us simply go about our lives in a mechanical and automatic way, part of a larger "machine" of which we are completely unaware. As Łobaczewski observed, from our perspective, the genesis of the very human conspiracy is "rigidly causative in nature and lacking in the natural freedom of choice". It is mechanical at our level, but has teleological meaning at higher levels.

chapter sixteen

As I searched through the literature in hundreds of fields of study, the chief thing that became apparent to me is that mankind is in the iron grip of an uncaring control system that raises him up and brings him low for its own mysterious purposes. No group, no nationality, no secret society or religion is exempt.

I needed answers. I couldn't live haunted daily by this grief for humanity and the many horrors of history. That was the motivation for the Cassiopaean experiment. Everything we are taught in our society, our history, our religions, and the new age versions of same, is all logically inconsistent and made a mockery of the very idea of a Creator—*Ribbono Shel Olom*—Master of the Universe. There was something strange and mysterious going on here on Earth, and I wanted to know the answers. And so I undertook the channeling experiment that resulted, after two years of dedicated preparatory work, in what is known as the Cassiopaean Transmissions.

In spite of the fact that we hold an "open opinion" regarding the source of this material, the answers we received from the Cassiopaeans—us in the future— were intriguing, to say the least. The closest analogy to the view of reality presented by the Cassiopaeans is graphically explicated in the movie, *The Matrix*, wherein our reality is presented as a computer program/dream that "stores" human beings in "pods" so that they are batteries producing energy for some vast machine dominating the world. Certain programmed life-scenarios of great emotional content were designed in order to produce the most "energy" for this machine. And it seems that pain and suffering are the "richest" in terms of "juice".

Another major concept presented in *The Matrix* was that the "real now" was the reality of the control system that produced the "programmed dream of reality" that was being experienced by those "trapped in the Matrix". The Matrix Dream Reality was based on the way things were in the past, before a terrible thing had occurred to destroy the world-that-was, after which it came under the control of computers which had become sentient and needed to utilize human beings as "power sources", or "food".

The difference between the metaphor of *The Matrix* and the view of the Cassiopaeans is that they propose a para-physical realm as another layer in the structure of space-time from which our own reality is projected, looping over and over again in endless variations. You could say that the hyperdimensional realms are the "future" in a very real sense.

It is in this context—similar to the concepts presented in the movie *The Matrix*—and realizing that the inner knowledge of many great mystery teachings down through the ages have presented the same, or a similar concept, that I have come to view the phenomena and interactions of our world. Such a view— taking the Red Pill—certainly produces results of becoming "free" from the controls of this Matrix, so I can say that in terms of experiment, it produces replicable results. However, as Morpheus explained to Neo in the movie:

> The Matrix is a system, Neo. That system is our enemy. But when you're inside, you look around; what do you see? Businessmen, teachers, lawyers, carpenters.

320

The very minds of the people we are trying to save. But until we do, these people are still a part of that system, and that makes them our enemy. You have to understand; most of these people are not ready to be unplugged. And many of them are so inured, so hopelessly dependent on the system that they will fight to protect it. Were you listening to me Neo, or were you looking at the woman in the red dress? They will fight to protect it...

We could just as well re-write this to say: When you are inside the Matrix, you look around and see Christians, Jews, Mohammedans, Zoroastrians, Wiccans, Magicians... most of these people are not ready to be unplugged... they are so hopelessly inured, so hopelessly dependent on the system that they will fight to protect it. Were you listening to me, or were you listening to that Zionist Baptist Evangelist, or purveyor of Magick and mumbo jumbo?

It was also pointed out by Morpheus that any human being who was plugged into the system could be used as an "agent" by something similar to a downloaded program that was designed to activate them in a certain way. A similar state of affairs seems to be the actual case in our reality, with the Controllers acting from some hyperdimensional space of which we have but limited awareness, and even less access.

The option that does seem, realistically, to be open to us is to choose our alignment and prepare ourselves for the emanations that are traveling "downward" to be better received. We will return to this in the final chapter, but first we must look more closely at what we are up against.

chapter seventeen
creativity/
entropy

In his forward to this book, my husband Ark raises the question of *causal loops*, that is, time loops, in quantum physics. He looked at the possibility of the Cassiopaeans being "*us* in the Future", as they described themselves. If time loops are possible for this source that calls itself the Cassiopaeans, it would also be true for the denizens of the other higher densities.

If all parts of the four-dimensional world exist simultaneously, as we saw in the previous chapter, embedded in a higher "reality", that is, a higher dimension or density, then anyone looking down upon our world from that vantage point would be able to "see" past, present, and future. Not only would they be able to see all of "time", so to speak, they would be able to act upon it, appearing to us as if able to travel through "time".

If the hyperdimensional hypothesis is true, it puts what are called "conspiracy theories" in a completely different light. The hyperdimensional hypothesis goes a long way in explaining why human history is a long story of war, violence, famine, pestilence, and natural disaster; in one word, suffering. This suffering is the product sought for by our keepers in this "higher realm", designed to continue supplying them with the negative energy upon which they feed. In this way, the long processes of the genesis of evil described by Łobaczewski gain new meaning in terms of hyperdimensional "tinkering" with the time line of human events, using their agents:

> Practically speaking, cause and effect are often widely separated in time, which makes it more difficult to track the links. If our scope of observation is expansive enough, the ponerogenic processes are reminiscent of complex chemical synthesis, wherein modifying *a single factor causes the entire process to change.* Botanists are aware of the law of the minimum, wherein plant growth is limited by contents of the component which is in deficiency in the soil. (Łobaczewski, 2007)

Hyper dimensions, and the understanding that they may have some physical meaning, opens the door to a scientific understanding of what don Juan called "the topic of topics", of what the Cassiopaeans have called the "ultimate secret", that we are prisoners, an experiment.

Furthermore, the hyperdimensional hypothesis explains why the old saw about such a multi-millennial conspiracy being impossible no longer holds water. Such a "conspiracy" is no longer dependent upon the short life spans of humans. All of human history is spread out before the "conspirators" like a vast canvas upon which they can continually rework the picture, adding a bit more blood red here or enhancing the grimace on the poor victim of the Inquisition there. What seem like impossible coincidences are made intelligible. One is reminded of the pictures of Hieronymus Bosch. Hyperdimensional physics puts the idea of such a conspiracy in a new context, and it is for this reason that the idea of extra dimensions as having physical meaning is turned to derision. Certain *string theory* theorists are willing to pull an arbitrary number of "extra" dimensions out of a hat as the need arises which gives the impression that they are merely convenient theoretical stop-gaps, theorized as being so small that they have no effect whatsoever on our reality.

If we accept that there is a high probability that such a conspiracy[11] exists, we must also pose the question of "Why?". We have partially answered this question when we admit that we are a form of livestock or chickens in a hyperdimensional chicken coop, and in various clues from the C's. A conspiracy exists to keep us as food. However, if we take into account the periodic character of space and recognize from our study of the past that history repeats itself (another subject that is treated in depth in *Secret History*), we are forced to ask ourselves whether or not there exists a deeper reason for our situation. Is our "slavery" here bound up somehow intimately with the cycles of "time" itself and the moments of transition when we pass from one cycle to the next?

We can start to get an answer from some of the things the Cassiopaeans have said over the years. The beginning of an answer is to be found in the earliest communication I had with the C's—the comments about 94% of humans being used at some time in the future for total consumption—as if they wished to communicate the importance of this subject right from the start. I returned to the subject many times to clarify their exact purpose. Many of the relevant excerpts were included three chapters above, but some bear repeating.

Q: (L) Are they interested in sexual energy simply because it is life force?

A: Partly and they are also desperately working to stave off change [i.e. "the transition to 4th level] in order to retain control.

Q: (L) They are trying to stave off the fourth level change. Can they do that?

A: No. But they are also hoping to retain control even if change occurs. [...]

A: Now, as you advance to the fourth level of density which is coming up for you, you must now make a choice as to whether to progress to service to others or to remain at the level of service to self. This will be the decision which will take quite some time for you to adjust to. This is what is referred to as the

[11] I have touched upon the idea of conspiracy in other parts of this book. I also treat the idea in greater detail in both *Secret History* and *9/11: The Ultimate Truth,* as well as in articles on our website: http://www.cassiopaea.org/. For our daily look at the effects of this conspiracy on our planet, check out our news and analysis at http://sottt.net/.

"thousand year period". This is the period as measured in your calendar terms that will determine whether or not you will advance to service to others or remain at the level of service to self. And those who are described as the Lizards have chosen to firmly lock themselves into service to self. And, since they are at the highest level of density where this is possible, *they must continually draw large amounts of negative energy from those at the third level, second level, and so on, which is why they do what they do. This also explains why their race is dying,* because they have not been able to learn for themselves how to remove themselves from this particular form of expression to that of service to others. And, since they have such, as you would measure it, a long period of time, remained at this level and, in fact, become firmly entrenched in it, and, in fact, have increased themselves in it, this is why they are dying and desperately trying to take as much energy from you as possible and also to recreate their race metabolically. [...]

Q: (L) Well, since there is so many of us here, a veritable smorgasbord, why don't they just move in and take over?

A: That is their intention. That has been their intention for quite some time. They have been traveling back and forth through time as you know it, to set things up so that they can absorb a maximum amount of negative energy with the transference from third level to fourth level that this planet is going to experience, in the hopes that they can overtake you on the fourth level and thereby accomplish several things.

1: retaining their race as a viable species;

2: increasing their numbers;

3: increasing their power;

4: expanding their race throughout the realm of fourth density.

To do all of this they have been interfering with events for what you would measure on your calendar as approximately 74 thousand years. And they have been doing so in a completely still state of space time traveling backward and forward at will during this work. Interestingly enough, though, all of this will fail.

Q: (L) How can you be so sure it will fail?

A: Because we see it. We are able to see all, not just what we want to see. Their failing is that they see only what they want to see. In other words, it's the highest manifestation possible of that which you would refer to as wishful thinking. And, wishful thinking represented on the fourth level of density becomes reality for that level. You know how you wishfully think? Well, it isn't quite reality for you because you are on the third level, but if you are on the fourth level and you were to perform the same function, it would indeed be your awareness of reality. Therefore they cannot see what we can see since we serve others as opposed to self, and since we are on sixth level, we can see all that is at all points as is, not as we would want it to be.

Q: (L) David Jacobs says that producing offspring is the primary objective behind the abduction phenomenon. Is this, in fact, the case?

A: Part, but not "the whole thing".

Q: (L) Is there another dominant reason?

A: Replacement.

Q: (L) Replacement of what?

A: You.

Q: (L) How do you mean? Creating a race to replace human beings, or abducting specific humans to replace them with a clone or whatever?

A: Mainly the former. *You see, if one desires to create a new race, what better way than to mass hybridize, then mass reincarnate.* Especially when the host species is so forever ignorant, controlled, and anthropocentric. What a lovely environment for total destruction and conquest and replacement... see? [...] We have told you before: the Nazi experience was a "trial run", and by now you see the similarities, do you not?

Q: (L) Yes, I do see...

A: Now, we have also told you that the experience of the "Native Americans" vis a vis the Europeans may be a precursor in microcosm. Also, what Earthian 3rd density does to Terran 2nd density should offer "food for thought". In other words, thou are not so special, despiteth thy perspective, eh? And we have also warned that after conversion of Earth humans to 4th density, the Orion 4th density and their allies hope to control you "there". Now put this all together and what have you? At least you should by now know that it is the soul that matters, not the body. Others have genetically, spiritually and psychically manipulated/engineered you to be bodycentric. Interesting, as despite all efforts by 4th through 6th density STO, this "veil remains unbroken".

Q: Now, there is a lot being said about the sightings out in the Southwest area. They are saying that this is the 'new' imminent invasion or mass landing. Can you comment on this activity?

A: Prelude to the biggest "flap" ever.

Q: And where will this flap be located?

A: Earth.

Q: When is it going to begin?

A: Starting already.

Q: Is this biggest flap going to be just a flap, or is it going to be an invasion?

A: Not yet. Invasion happens when programming is complete...

The programming of the population was ratcheted up several notches with the events of September 11, 2001. Travel is becoming more and more difficult. The phony "War on Terror" is an excuse to bring in tyrannical legislation that strips away the rights of the population. The many lies told by Bush to justify his invasions of Afghanistan and Iraq, as well as the shadow play carried out to "investigate" 9/11 (see *9/11: The Ultimate Truth*), wherein the role of Israel was completely ignored, are all part of this programming, getting people to accept the *lie*, to align themselves with a subjective view of reality.

We must keep in mind in interpreting the C's remarks that this "invasion" may not be the kind depicted in Hollywood blockbusters with flying saucers appearing over the White House or the capitals of the world's countries. If the weather on the planet can be manifestations of "battle" between entropy and creation, then an "invasion" might also be manifested in a "natural" way, as in earth upheavals, catastrophes, or falling rocks from space. The Cassiopaeans have discussed a number of different "cycles" that affect the earth. There is a 3,600 year cometary cloud cycle that brings destruction of parts of the earth from the sky. There is a 309,000 year cycle that is part of what the C's have called The Wave. The Wave is a macro-cosmic quantum jump where our sector of space-time will momentarily collapse, before being reborn anew. According to the C's, this will be a phase transition where our earth will move from third density to fourth density. A third cycle that affects us is a 27 million year orbital cycle of our Sun's dark star companion. This companion reaches its closest point to its partner every 27 million years, passing through the Oort Cloud, and stirring up its contents like a bowling ball knocking over bowling pins, creating a new cyclic comet cluster.

What makes this moment in the cycle interesting is that all three cycles are coming to a close at the same moment.

Since the C's first brought up the question of these cycles, I have spent many years researching the hard data to either confirm or reject what the C's told me. Some of this research is in *Secret History*, some is on the web site. There is not room in this book to go over all of the data that I have uncovered. Suffice it to say that there is a lot of evidence that points to a 3,600 year comet cycle, whose last passing was around 1628 BC when the volcano Thera exploded on the island of Santorini in the Mediterranean bringing the Bronze Age to a sudden end. (See *The Wave: Book Seven* and Baillie's *From Exodus to Arthur* for more on these topics.)

There is also evidence that our Sun does indeed have a companion. A possible explanation for the 75 year solar minimum in the 17th century that has come to be known as the Maunder Minimum, and which has perplexed scientists ever since, is that it was the moment of the passage of the dark companion through the Oort Cloud, that is, its closest approach to the Sun. The gravitational effect of this close passage was to dampen solar activity, creating the 75 year solar minimum. Other disturbances in the orbits of the planets can be explained by the existence of such an object.

The cycle that is hardest to find hard evidence to confirm is the 309,000 year Wave. The evidence for this cycle may come in the form of the mathematics that explain how quantum events can occur on a macrocosmic level.

The data, then, suggests there is a high probability for the existence of two of the cycles and leaves open the possibility of the third. The convergence of the three cycles offers the opportunity for the denizens of fourth density to maintain control over humans as we pass into their level of reality. Perhaps we can learn more of their intentions and how they plan to achieve this control by looking at the problem from an esoteric point of view.

However, before we do that, there is a question that rises to the top in considering these matters: why is this topic—at the very least—subjected to such extreme prejudice that it amounts to concealment? Why are there so many books about things like the 10th Planet, or precessional alignments related to world ages, Stargates, Galactic Core Explosions, and so forth, that pass with only mild criticism, yet the idea of rains of cometary or meteoric bodies is so viciously vilified? And this brings us to a most interesting passage written by Wilhelm Reich:

Why did man, through thousands of years, wherever he built scientific, philosophic, or religious systems, go astray with such persistence and *with such catastrophic consequences?* ... Is human erring necessary? Is it rational? Is all error rationally explainable and necessary? If we examine the sources of human error, we find that they fall into several groups:

Gaps in the knowledge of nature form a wide sector of human erring. Medical errors prior to the knowledge of anatomy and infectious diseases were necessary errors. But we must ask if the mortal threat to the first investigators of animal anatomy was a necessary error too.

The belief that the earth was fixed in space was a necessary error, rooted in the ignorance of natural laws. But was it an equally necessary error to burn Giordano Bruno at the stake and to incarcerate Galileo? ... We understand that human thinking can penetrate only to a given limit at a given time. What we fail to understand is why the human intellect does not stop at this point and say: "this is the present limit of my understanding. Let us wait until new vistas open up". This would be rational, comprehensible, purposeful thinking. (Reich, 1949)

The only problem here is that we have discovered that the material *is* available! There are *many* vistas of understanding that are open in our world to those with eyes to see! We have listed our sources, there are photographs and images of the proof that our planet has been repeatedly bombarded with showers of comets/asteroids; there exist stacks of evidence—recorded in books, papers, monographs, theories—that civilizations of greater advancement than our own have existed on the earth, and have been repeatedly destroyed. There are piles of evidence that attest to a far greater age of mankind than is presently accepted or taught by mainstream science. And in every case, this evidence is ignored, marginalized, explained or argued away, and those who wish to make such information public to a wider audience are similarly marginalized and dealt with. What is even more interesting, as we noted previously, is the fact that the "mainstream occultists" have jumped on the uniformitarian bandwagon and are vigorously promoting reams of disinformation. And our own experience has been that our attempts to talk about this sort of thing have resulted in coordinated attacks from certain so-called "occultists", who have even sunk so low as to spend inordinate amounts of time roaming the internet, denouncing our research group as a "cult", writing libelous, defamatory public postings about us personally, and most importantly: attempting to destroy the C's material as a source of clues to our reality. Reich notes this problem and writes:

What amazes us is the *sudden turn from the rational beginning to the irrational illusion.* Irrationality and illusion are revealed by the *intolerance and cruelty* with which they are expressed. We observe that human thought systems show tolerance as long as they adhere to reality. The more the thought process is removed from reality, the more intolerance and cruelty are needed to guarantee its continued existence.

And here is where we have to begin to really think about things in a reasonable and objective way. If there is so much evidence available—and there is—why is it so rabidly attacked and dismissed? Why is it necessary to defame,

327

libel, crush and destroy those who bring up these matters, and who also *produce the evidence?* Most especially, why is this so, when we know that there *are* groups—such as the government and certain academics—who *do* study these things, who do commission reports on them, who do collect the data? Just what they heck is going on? Why do they permit—no, actually encourage—the crazy ideas about 10th planets or Galactic explosions or precessional clocks of world ages—when the simple truth is so evident?

Reich proposed that the "adherence to the surface of phenomena" was related to "a certain connection with the structure of the human animal". He thought that the function of seeking the truth must be somehow "buried" since the tendency to "evade the obvious" was so powerful. In this idea, we are, of course, reminded of Castaneda's "Predator".

"I have been beating around the bush all this time, insinuating to you that *something is holding us prisoner.* Indeed we are held prisoner! ... I want to appeal to your analytical mind... Think for a moment, and tell me how you would explain the contradiction between the intelligence of man the engineer and the stupidity of his systems of beliefs, or the stupidity of his contradictory behavior. Sorcerers believe that the predators have given us our systems of beliefs, our ideas of good and evil, our social mores. They are the ones who set up our hopes and expectations and dreams of success or failure. They have given us covetousness, greed and cowardice. It is the predators who make us complacent, routinary, and egomaniacal. ... In order to keep us obedient and meek and weak, the predators engaged themselves in a stupendous maneuver—stupendous, of course, from the point of view of a fighting strategist. A horrendous maneuver from the point of view of those who suffer it. *They gave us their mind!* Do you hear me? The predators give us their mind, which becomes our mind. The predators' mind is *baroque, contradictory, morose, filled with the fear of being discovered any minute now....* Through the mind, which, after all, is their mind, the predators inject into the lives of human beings whatever is convenient for them." (Castaneda, 1998, 213-220)

Reich, of course, decided that the cause of "needless human erring" was due to the "pathological quality of human character". In fact, this fits quite well with what Castaneda has written. "The Predators gave us their mind". Reich also pointed out, quite reasonably, that religion, education, social mores, suppression of a true understanding of love, and so on were merely *symptoms* of this fact. And this is what led Reich to conclude: "The answer lies somewhere in that area of our existence which has been so heavily obscured by organized religion and put out of our reach. Hence, it probably lies in the relation of the human being to the cosmic energy that governs him."

Reich was moving dangerously close to describing the hyperdimensional reality. And, as a result, he, too, was subjected to overt intolerance and cruelty. And, as Reich so rightly noted, *"Irrationality and illusion are revealed by the intolerance and cruelty with which they are expressed. ... The more the thought process is removed from reality, the more intolerance and cruelty are needed to guarantee its continued existence."*

It is in this last remark that we come to some clue about the matter: intolerance and cruelty are *needed* to guarantee the "cover-up", like some mechanical cosmic COINTELPRO system. *And a certain kind of "human being" acts on behalf of this cover-up;* a certain kind of human being acts as the playing pieces in the *Secret Games of the Gods.*

Machiavelli observed that religion, and its teachings of faith, hope, charity, love, humility and patience under suffering, were factors that render men weak and cause them to care less about worldly and political things, and thus they will turn political power over to wicked men who are not influenced by such ideals. Of course, the real trick is to convince people that the "afterlife" is the only thing worth thinking about, and it is to this end that Christianity has been formulated. It is also to this end that many of the New Age beliefs and "formulations" of the truth about ascension have been engineered. All you have to do is have faith or meditate or acquire knowledge and awareness that will help you love everything and everybody. Nothing is said about the day-by-day struggle and the necessity for action.

This para-physical reality of hyperdimensional space—the realm of the Matrix programmers—is inhabited, according to the Cassiopaeans, by beings of both positive and negative polarity who have "graduated" from our reality, but not necessarily in the sense of "dying" and going to a strictly ethereal realm. They have evolved along either the positive or negative poles of Creation. It is, effectively, a world of the future that creates our present by projecting itself into the past. What is important to realize is that if we think about the future in terms of probable futures, or branching universes, then what we do now, whether we wake up from the Matrix or not, determines what kind of future we experience, individually and collectively.

The option that does seem, realistically, to be open to us is to choose our alignment and prepare ourselves for the emanations that are traveling "downward" to be better received. This is the essential point of Castaneda's don Juan when he said:

> "One of the greatest accomplishments of the seers of the Conquest was a construct he called the three-phase progression. By understanding the nature of man, they were able to reach the incontestable conclusion that if seers can hold their own in facing [human] petty tyrants, they can certainly face the unknown with impunity, and then they can even stand the presence of the unknowable.
>
> "The average man's reaction is to think that the order of that statement should be reversed", he went on. "A seer who can hold his own in the face of the unknown can certainly face petty tyrants. But that's not so. What destroyed the superb seers of ancient times was that assumption. We know better now. We know that nothing can temper the spirit of a warrior as much as the challenge of dealing with impossible people in positions of power. Only under those conditions can warriors acquire the sobriety and serenity to stand the pressure of the unknowable." (Castaneda, 1984, 19)

All around us we see the result of this error: the idea that we can exert our will and voice upward to change what is "above" us in order to change our reality, ignoring the reality that we have to deal with "down here". This idea is at the root of rites and rituals, demanding, pleading, visualizations, tapping, "workings", and so forth. People who think that "meditating on compassion", or "feeling the feelings of all beings", is going to result in the "sonic entrainment of the heart's rhythm [being] braided into more complex and coherent patterns", which will then enable the person to "create a diamond imperishable body for use as a teaching vehicle down here on earth", have missed the entire point. To compare such ideas to the true work of the Grail Seeker is simply ignorant.

What seems to be true is that before the Seeker can ever achieve the point of being able to think even momentarily about "the oneness of all beings", or the "feelings of all beings", or be in possession of "super-awareness", he or she has spent many, many years in the struggle to "face petty tyrants", or to fully realize objective reality in a step by step process that includes action in concert with understanding.

They have repeatedly exposed themselves to as many "unpleasant experiences" as they can find, all the while struggling to master their emotions, their desires, and the lures of physicality. It is the work of making the physical vehicle "down here" receptive to what one chooses to align with "up there", as opposed to trying to forcibly change something "up there" in order to have it "down here". This process is very much involved with what is called "discernment."

The great Sufi Shaykh Ibn al-'Arabi explains that "imperfection" exists in Creation because "were there no imperfection, the perfection of existence would be imperfect". From the point of view of *sheer being*, there is nothing but good. But *infinite potential to be* includes—by definition of the word "infinite"—the potential to *not be*. And so, infinite potential "splits" into *thought centers of creation* and *thought centers of non-being*. It can be said that infinite potential is fundamentally binary—on or off—to be or not to be. That is the first "division".

Since absolute *non-being* is an impossible paradox in terms of the source of *infinite potential to be*, the half of the consciousness of infinite potential that constitute the *ideas* of *non-being*—for every idea of manifestation, there is a corresponding idea for that item of creation to *not* manifest—"falls asleep" for lack of a better term. Its "self observation" is predicated upon consciousness that can only "mimic" death. Consciousness that mimics death then "falls" and becomes *primal matter*. What this means is that the "self observing self" at the level of the Master of the Universe is constituted of this initial division between *being* and *non-being* which is, again, only the initial division—the on/off, the yes/no—of creation. You could picture this as an open eye observing a closed eye. It has been represented for millennia in the yin-yang symbol, in which, even on the black half that represents "sleeping consciousness that is matter", you can see the small white dot of "being" that represents to us that absolute non-existence is not possible. There is only "relative" non-existence.

These "thoughts of being and non-being" interact with one another—the observer and the observed—like a viewer looking into a mirror. Creation manifests between the viewer and the mirror. It is at once real—because it consists of matter informed by consciousness—and unreal—because it is ultimately composed of only consciousness acting on consciousness.

At our level of reality, the understanding that "nothing is real" as has been promulgated by gurus and teachers down through history is as useless as saying "gravity isn't real". Such considerations are useful only for expansion of perception. They are not useful for practical application since the energies of creation apparently transduce through several "levels" before they meet in the middle, so to say, in our third density reality. Organic life exists at the "crossroads" of the myriad ideas or thought centers of being and non-being. As such, they have the capacity to transduce energies "up" or "down" depending on the "consciousness energy directors" of that unit. And again, there are apparently two broad divisions: directed toward being/observing, or directed toward non-being/mirroring. This division manifests across all levels of organic life, including human beings. Human beings exist to transduce cosmic energies of Creation via organic life. Our "higher selves" are the directors of this transducing of cosmic energies, and the direction in which the energy "flows" is determined by the activities of these higher selves. Against the opposition of those forces seeking to "capture" energy of consciousness and induce it to the "sleep of non-being", which is gravitational in a certain sense, the energies of consciousness seek to "inform" matter via awakening the self-awareness of those organic units on earth that are capable of resistance to the gravity of non-being, or entropy.

As self-aware "transducing units", the human being has the potential to go either way—toward intensified being, or toward intensified non-being. In this sense, humans also function very much like a lens that can be "adjusted" like a telescope. It can be dialed to select the viewing range, which can be distant and inclusive of more "space/time", or it can be shortened to only see what is up close and evident in the material world. In other words, our first and most fundamental choice is to choose what we *see*.

When we choose what we *see*—and here we do *not* mean with the physical eyes or even psychically, but rather a more inclusive term that suggests whether or not we are capable of objectivity or subjectivity—we are receiving impressions. Impressions can become knowledge if assimilated. Knowledge leads to awareness. Knowledge and awareness then direct emotions, which then energize actions in the organic world. This is the transducing of energies of *cosmic thought centers*. Whether or not the impressions are assimilated objectively will determine with which of the thought centers, *being* or *non-being*, we are in alignment.

Ibn al-'Arabi tells us that Goodness is Being; to which all positive and beautiful attributes or *Names of God* belong. Evil is the lack of good, so it is "nonexistence". In other words, at the root, Being dwells in "non-existence" which is evil. Here is the sticking point, the item that is generally omitted from most "systems of ascension". Human beings at our level of reality exist at the crossroads of the thoughts of Being and Non-Being—Good and Evil. Mankind is made in the form of all the Names of God—those of Being and Non-Being.

331

Assuming the traits of the Names is synonymous with manifesting their properties. The search for the Grail is to obtain deep knowledge of all the Names and their true properties, the high and the low, the pleasant and the loathsome, the light and the darkness, in differentiated detail, so as to be able to *choose* which traits will be assumed. It is only with a full field of vision that a man can discover if what he subjectively thinks is good actually *is* good and leads to Being, or if it is a deception that induces to Non-Being by pretense.

God is the root of *all* Names, noble and base. The task of the seeker is to bring the Noble traits from latency into actuality and to discover the positive applications of the base traits—even if that application is to "overcome" or transmute. The Shaykh tells us "noble character traits are only those connected to interaction with others". In other words: *DOing*. If you *see* the illusion of separation, that is certainly the first thing. The lie is smuggled in by suggesting that this is all that is necessary, that if you just "see it", everything will "change" for you.

God creates the good and the evil, the ugly and the beautiful, the straight and the crooked, the moral and the immoral. Between these traits lie the manifold dangers of the path of the seeker of Truth. Many modern day "teachers" and "gurus" tell us "Since there is only One Being which permeates all things, all we have to do is see everything as only light", and that will transmute the darkness, and we will "create our own reality of light". Such a statement ignores the fact that the statement "God is One" describes a reality that is a higher level from which our own "mixed being" manifests. The man who assumes that he can become like God at this level just by thinking it, ignores the facts of Being vs. Non-Being which outrays from "God is One" at a level of existence that is clearly several levels above our own.

Evil is *real* on its own level, and the task of man is to navigate the cosmic maze without being defiled by the Evil therein. This is the root of Free Will. Man faces a predicament as *real* as himself: he is forced to choose—to utilize his knowledge by applying it—between the straight path which leads to Being, and the crooked paths which lead to Non-Being. Human beings are required to discern between good and evil—consciousness energy directors—at every stage of their existence in this reality. Because, in fact, they must understand that God is consciousness and God is matter. God is good, and God is evil. The Creation assumes all the different properties of the many "Names of God". The Cosmos is full of Life-Giving and Slaying, Forgiveness and Vengeance, Exaltation and Abasement, Guidance and Deception. To attempt to assume God's point of view and "mix everything" at this level, results only in *staying* at this level. Therefore, human beings must always separate God's point of view from their own point of view and the fact that all creation assumes the divine Names and Traits.

Thus, the first Divine Command is *BE!* And that includes Being and Non-Being instantaneously. Therefore, the second law is "follow Being or Non-Being according to your choice and your inherent nature". All creation is a result of the engendering command. So, in this respect, there is no Evil. But the second, prescriptive law determines to which *Face of God* one will return: Life or Death.

> If the engendering command alone is considered, there is no imperfection in the cosmos, since all creatures follow what God desires for them. In this respect, what is normally called "imperfection" is in fact perfection, since it allows for the actualization of the various levels of existence and knowledge. In other words, were there no imperfections—in the sense of diminishment, decrease, and lack—there would be no creation. Were there no creation, the Hidden Treasure would remain hidden. Hence Being would be unseen in every respect. There would be no self-disclosure of the Divine Reality, Light would not shine, and God would be the Nonmanifest but not the Manifest. But all this is absurd, since it demands the imperfection of Being Itself, which by definition is nondelimited perfection. Being's perfection requires the manifestation of Its properties. The effects of the Names and Attributes must be displayed for God to be God. [...] In other words, Imperfection is demanded by existence itself. To be "other than God" is to be imperfect. ...But it is precisely the "otherness" which allows the cosmos and all the creatures within it to exist. If things were perfect in every respect, they would be identical with God Himself, and there would be nothing "other than God". But then we could not even speak about the cosmos, since there would be no cosmos and no speakers. ...So, imperfection is a kind of perfection. (Chittick, 1989)

At the particular stage of existence in which man finds himself, he is equally "receptive" toward the two primary Faces of God: Being and Non-Being. The Shaykh tells us that whatever property, or trait, any human being ultimately "chooses" *is what it originally possessed in its state of immutability.* The task of the Seeker is to discover what is immutable within and to purify and amplify it. This is the development of Will. Will is a relationship, which follows knowledge, while knowledge follows the object of knowledge. In the process of "ascension", the object of knowledge is *you*. Knowledge, in and of itself, has no effects. *You*, however, the seeker, can give to knowledge what you actually are, in yourself, thereby displaying *yourself* in knowledge *by your actions* in concert with your knowledge.

As noted, there are many Names of God that call to us in our present state of existence. But you are not required to answer every one that calls. The fact that human beings are, in general, ignorant of their own true "essence" gives them the illusion of freedom. And the fact is, all paths come from God, and all paths lead back to God, but again, it can be via different faces. As the Shaykh says: "Unto Allah all things come home, and he is the end of every path. However, the important thing is which divine name you will reach and to which you will come home."

This brings us to what the Shaykh calls "perspicacity". This is the special development of the "eye of insight", or "seeing the unseen" that is crucial to the Seeker. Just as the physical eye, with the refraction of light from the Sun, can discern between the large and the small, the beautiful and the ugly, colors, the moving from the still, high and low, the ability to see the unseen is a property of an "inner light". This light reveals to the seeker things about external objects that are *not* apparent to the five senses. It reveals to its possessor when a choice that may appear to be benevolent is a step on the path of Evil. It reveals when a choice that may appear to human estimation as negative is actually a difficult step to felicity for all involved. The Sufis tell us that some individuals have achieved such a level of "seeing" that upon seeing a person's footprint on the ground, even if the person is not present, they are able to say whether he is following a life of felicity or wretchedness.

The light of perspicacity seems to be a gift that not everyone has, and those who do have it may not have developed it to the same degree. What is evident is that those who have it possess an immutable nature of Being which is able to "see" good and evil—they do not see "only good". Thus, they are able to discern between the "calls" of Non-Being and Being, and therefore, are able to strengthen their Will along the path of intrinsic Being. It then follows that individuals who are not able to see—or who choose not to see—both Good and Evil, are formed in the mold of subjectivity, which is the human expression of the *Call of Non-Being.*

A human being whose immutable nature is that of Being can strengthen the light of perspicacity by "assuming the traits" of the Names of Being. This does not mean that a person comes to possess traits that do not already belong to him. It means that these traits are amplified and "cultivated". The ruling property of an individual is determined by what Face of God is *disclosed* to him, and *this is determined by his preparedness.* Felicity can only be disclosed when Evil has been turned away from, rejected; which can only be achieved by a long period of "testing" or being challenged to *see* and then to choose Being over Non-Being in order to grow the Will or alignment to Being in a feedback loop. As the Seeker travels this path, he must not see these traits as his own, but rather he must see that he is a locus of God's manifestation of an ontological attribute.

People imagine that they believe in God when, in fact, what they believe always takes the shape of the receptacle. The old saying is that the water takes on the color of its cup. The deeper implication of this is that a person will only be in disequilibrium if his conscious beliefs are not in conformity with his own immutable nature. In other words, a person whose intrinsic nature is aligned toward Being will experience disequilibrium, struggle, and even illness by attempting to assume those traits that do not exist in him. In this sense, careful observation of the physical state—even the physical environment—can act as a guide as to whether or not the whole being is coming into alignment.

So it is that different paths can produce different effects for different individuals according to their immutable nature within. Those whose intrinsic nature is toward Being follow the path of developing the ability to *see* and to choose alignment with the infinite potential of creation, thereby being conduits of Being as God chooses to manifest through them. They not only see that limitation is illusion, they consciously *act*—they utilize that knowledge to generate energy and light.

Those whose intrinsic nature is toward Non-Being follow the path of limitation of Infinite Being by assuming that they, in their state of ignorance and subjectivity, know better than God how Creation ought to be fixed. They pray for change, they perform rituals, they chant mantras and repeat endless visualizations of "magickal forms" that are supposed to "change" reality. They

334

bomb others with "Love and Light", (their subjective version of it, of course), and they seek to fix the world "out there" by projecting their subjective view of reality onto the infinite wisdom of Creation. This "consciousness energy direction" even includes the assumption that just knowing that all division is illusion will accomplish the goal of ascension, and that is the most cunning lie of all.

Each approach "ties a knot" in the heart of the believer and fixes him on a path, the object of his belief being the end of the path. All beliefs are equivalent in that God—of one sort or another—is their ultimate objective. But each belief is different in that it leads to a different Name of God, or Thought Center. Even materialistic skepticism is a "belief" and leads to "matterizing" of the consciousness that follows this belief. What is more difficult to discern are the many mixed up "spiritual" paths that twist and distort the concepts of Being to engage the seeker on a path to Non-Being.

Going back to the idea of the human being as a transducing unit with a "lens capacity", what seems to be so is that the process of ascension begins with the choice of tuning the lens. If the individual chooses to "adjust the dial" to see the entire field of Thought Centers influencing creation, he can then begin to select those that enhance and enliven Creation and Being—the Thought Centers of Awakened Consciousness—then a feedback loop that selects that probable future will be established.

A human being can, by great effort, expand their "field of view" toward greater and greater objectivity. With a wider and farther field of view, the awareness of those things, which emanate from the Thought Centers come into focus. When Thought Centers are more in focus, the individual then has greater ability to discern whether impressions emanate from the Thought Centers of Being, or from the Thought Centers of Non-Being. At this stage, the individual is then able to further "shape" his emotions and direct his actions so as to become an efficient transducing unit of the cosmic energies of Being into this reality. This is knowledge utilization, which generates energy, which generates light.

As this process continues, as the feedback loop is activated between the Cosmic observer and the transducing/actions of the creature, the organic unit, the transducing organ, so to say, strengthens, and the exchange between it and the Cosmic Observer accelerates and intensifies. The transducing organ then begins to act as a "homing beacon" for greater levels of that chosen Thought Center energy—that "observer from the future"—the "eye" that is the Creator.

In the development of such a feedback loop, the human being—as a conduit of creation, a vessel—becomes an active participant of the creation of his own *future* in the act of choosing which observation platform and scope he accepts as "real"—objective or subjective. Furthermore, as the energy of such a being is changed and enhanced by the "flow of cosmic energy" passing through him, as he perceives more and more of the creative expressions of Infinite Potential, and chooses those he wishes to align with, he becomes collinear with those other expressions of Being—other organic units that may be quite different in make-up, but similarly aware of Infinite Potential—and is thus able to interact with them in a manner that further expands and commutates the energy of transducing.

This can then lead to exponential amplification of the transducing of the energies of Being which can then completely alter the physical nature of the organic unit. Just as a pipe that is used to channel water gets wet from the water flowing through it, so does the human being who has begun the process of aligning with Being becomes saturated with the higher energies being manifested through him or her. This process leads to permeation of the organic nature of the vessel which leads to transformation in that it "awakens" the "sleeping matter" of the organic unit and makes it a full participant in Being, rather than a weight for the soul to carry or struggle against. The energy of the organic vehicle is then available *in the terms described in Einstein's famous formula*, which might give some indication of the potential of such a being.

A person who aligns himself with Non-Being will undergo the same process, only in the opposite direction.

As the reader can easily see by now, the teachings of the current spate of New Age Gurus constitute the idea that we can exert our will and voice that exists "down here" upward to change what is "above" us in order to change our reality down here. They tell us that we can change our lives, our thinking, move our brains into harmony, or aid the "heart in opening", obtaining "harmony and balance" which is then going to "open windows in our mind, our heart, and our spirit", etc. It is claimed that we can do this basically by assuming God's point of view that "all is one, all is love". It is stated, (with some truth I should add, since good disinformation is always wrapped in a warm and fuzzy truth), that, "without Divine Unity inside of us, these windows of inspiration are rarely available". What they do *not* tell you is that the staircase to Divine Unity of Being requires a full field of awareness of Being and Non-Being, and that this can only be achieved *by divesting oneself of the controls of Non-Being* which are, indeed, part of Being, but which seek to obviate Being in a paradoxical sleep of "Unification" which often begins by believing the lie that "knowledge protects" simply by having it.

Indeed, many of the "techniques" sold in the slick packages of "ascension tools" will temporarily produce chemical changes that will feel *very* good, the same way a good meal satisfies hunger temporarily. It really "feels good"! But just as the steak and salad are digested and most of the matter excreted in a few hours, and another steak and salad are needed to fill the stomach again, so do such practices fail to do anything more than perpetuate the "food chain". And, staying with the analogy, very little of the "substance" of such practices actually "stays with" the individual.

A considerable period of time is required for the seeker to finally come to the realization that techniques that relieve stress or produce "good feelings" have done nothing to actually change their lives or their "vibrations". They are still recognized by their neighbor's dog, they still find new gray hairs on their heads, and they still get sick and have aches and pains like everyone else. The problem is, again, the "bottom up" ideas have been employed which only result in remaining in the "mixed" state, or, worse, being drawn deeper into the path of Non-Being.

Well, I should qualify that: to those for whom Non-Being is their immutable nature, this is only natural and right, and they will thrive following the path of Non-Being. But for those many, many seekers whose immutable nature is toward Being, this is a terrible trap. The gravitational effect of the Thought Center of Non-Being, which draws all of Creation into Non-Being, will act on them in ways that are crippling to their relationships and health. Human beings who go through life feeling as though they have a "hole in their hearts" are those who are not synchronized with their immutable nature.

The natural field of view for the organic unit alone—with no connection to the higher self—is that of the material and/or mechanical interpretation of all phenomena. The influences of the Thought Center of Non-Being—the source of matter—have been increasing through the manifestation of billions of such units at a single point in time: the present.

The Thought Center of Non-Being is of a certain nature—contractile subjectivity—that exerts a more or less "gravitational" pull—a desire to absorb and assimilate the soul energies of Being—so as to feed its own contracting nature. Even if it promotes a full field of awareness in principle, it can only view Being as a traitor to its own need to not exist. This results in an individual who may proclaim that all is illusion, but whose actions—or rather lack thereof—betray the deeper immutable state of Non-Being. Due to its intrinsic nature, there is a powerful exertion of Non-Being to destroy and obviate Being and Creation—all the while it is unable to achieve the awareness that it only exists by virtue of Being and Creation *in action*!

The powerful exertion of the Thought Center of Non-Being to absorb and assimilate all of creation, powered by its own contractile subjectivity, poses certain problems both for itself and for Being. The fundament of Non-Being is a *lie*—that is to say, the state of absolute Non-Being that it promotes is a paradoxical impossibility. The fundament of Being is the objective fact that Existence simply *is* via *action* or utilization of knowledge which generates light. *Therefore, the essential conflict is between lies and truth.* The Thought Center of Non-Being tells itself the biggest lie of all—that it does not exist—and goes to sleep in pretense. And from this essential point, we see that the nature of subjectivity is that of lies. Lies and belief in lies—whether or not the believer is aware that they are believing a lie—all partake of the same essence—subjectivity and Non-Being. This is the esoteric importance of the programming of the population that we see now all around us.

The Thought Center of Non-Being, in its expression as matter, being "impressed" by Creative consciousness in action which partially awakens it and draws it into the creation of the organic world, wraps itself around this awakened consciousness. Its intrinsic nature of pretense to Non-Being acts "gravitationally" on consciousness, and twists and distorts it into varying degrees of subjectivity. It is this interaction of the energy of all possibility, lensed through subjectivity of matter, that produces the myriad manifestations of the material universe.

In the realm of the Thought Center of Non-Being, there are many manifestations—or ways—of seeking annihilation—the "Base Names of God". These modes act in a gravitational way to engage, enfold, and distort consciousness to their ends. This results in the formation of consciousness units of great power and depth of cunning—far beyond anything imaginable in our own reality.

These consciousness units use their wiles to assimilate weaker consciousness units so as to accrue more contractile power. Obviously, the more "dense" the consciousness units "consumed", the more "nutritious" they are. And so they seek, by great cunning, to carefully, and with great patience, manipulate the consciousness units selected for assimilation. It is, effectively, trans-millennial stalking.

These Overlords of Entropy—or so we may call them—by virtue of the overlay of intensified subjectivity—the hallmark of the influence of the Thought Center of Non-Being—interface with the organic world on a "geographic" scale. Since they have, so to say, an intimate relationship with matter, the contractile consciousness of such a being can affect its area of chosen dominion very much like an overshadowing "cloud" with millions of tendrils of connections between it and its range of influence. This includes even the very matter of the bodies of human beings. It is through these etheric fibers that the Overlords of Entropy assimilate energy.

These overlords have "organs" so to speak. Just as a group of people were described by the Apostle Paul as "the body of Christ", so are the organs of entropic overlords manifested as individual beings, though their direct connection to a single massive consciousness unit makes them more like "projections" than individually souled beings.

Because of their great drive to conserve and assimilate energy, the overlords are "stingy" with allowances to their organ-beings. It seems that they do not "waste" energy in manifesting and maintaining organic structures for their organs, and thus the organic physicality takes on the configuration of less complex creatures in the organic world. Rather than interacting with an organic structure in a cooperative, awakened state, they exercise control over theirs, utilizing organic structures that require the least amount energy to maintain in order to conserve energy. To this end, they draw the energy for their organic units from the pools of archetypal form of the animal kingdom. This energy is more easily accessed, is lower in frequency, and thus more amenable to control.

This seems to be the reason why, when perceived by individuals of the third dimensional self-consciousness—third density—realm, the Entropic Overlords' appearance is generally startling. The reptilian type comes to mind as being the most energy efficient. Again, remember that consciousness is merely "reading waves".

For the same reason—the contractile nature of the hierarchy and its energy consumption—it is extremely difficult for these organ-beings of the Overlords of Entropy to actively function in our realm for any period of time. When they enter our realm, assuming a third density organic form, they are at a disadvantage. They are temporarily disconnected from the energy pool, which weakens, but they are at another great disadvantage as well. Since they are not internally connected to an expanding, creative feedback loop of Creative Being, their own Entropic Overlord is a constant drain on them, pulling them gravitationally as it were, making them even weaker than the natural denizens of this realm. Such are those called aliens and "Men in Black". It is this great strain on their energy resources that makes such appearances so rife with anomalous glitches. There is no creativity, and thus no ability to pull off such an intrusion into our reality with any convincing effectiveness. The appearance of the Grays is almost that of partially formed humans, with many of the details left out. It is as if an exact replication would demand too much energy, so they choose an imperfect copy.

For this reason they generally avoid direct interaction in the organic world, preferring to utilize other methods to stalk and conquer weaker units to "feed" the Thought Center of non-being. To this end, these entropic overlords seek to establish and maintain the "entrainment of creative energy" within the third density reality by deceptively enhancing third density, material interpretations of the phenomenal world.

In short, such beings of enormous geographic domination actively operate within their geographic field of influence to divert and discourage those organic units who have tenuous connections to creative energy—higher self—from interpretations which will lead to the establishing a feedback loop with those Thought Centers of Being/Creation.

As noted, the nature of such beings, and the dynamic of their existence, requires massive energy input in order to "control" and direct their own organic physicality. This is possible at the level of overlord/sub-units of the Thought Center of Non-Being by virtue of the extensive assimilation of other consciousness units, and most especially by virtue of their "geographic" character, which enables them to "connect" to thousands, if not millions, of organic beings in the organic realm. This is, effectively, the "Program of the Matrix".

This connection is naturally enabled by the aforementioned intrinsic nature of organic units to only perceive the field of view of the organic realm. That is to say that mechanical and material feedback loops are far more easily created between organic units and the sub-units of Non-Being by a sort of "gravitational" pull of these sub-units upon the natural inclinations of the organic being.

This establishes "feedback loops" as previously described. The organic unit, "infected" with the material/mechanical view, begins to act according to that Thought Center's dictates, and this generates activities of that nature in the organic unit. Due to the fact that any given sub-unit of the Thought Center of Non-Being may be connected to millions of organic units in third density, any of them may be activated singly, or in concert, to fulfill the wishes of the Overlords of Entropy, a "larger" sub-unit of the Thought Center of Non-Being.

We have found similar explications of the "spiritual science" of the Cassiopaeans in the work of some few others—very few—Ra, Castaneda, Gurdjieff/Ouspensky, ancient Sufi teachings, ancient myths and legends, and we have found a whole new segment of the puzzle that fits by virtue of numerous amazing correspondences, in the work of Boris Mouravieff. What is more, this material also contains added information that is startling in its implications.

Among those implications, which just happens to confirm some *current* observations, is the likelihood that this planet is going to have a rough ride not too many years down the road, including the idea that a lot of the human race may be checking out at that time. Quite a number of other "sources" are telling their followers that they are soon going to ascend to the "fifth dimension, skipping the fourth", and this is indeed the truth, though they don't fill in the details. Fifth density is where you go when you die.

This information we have assembled suggests that there is a *reason* for this current state of affairs—the cyclical nature of such events—that organic life on earth is a transmitter of energy that *feeds* the cosmos—that what we observe in nature—that there is a *food chain*—is something that exists at all levels—and we are *not at the top!*

We also have the idea that we can possibly get *off* this train before it runs off the track. It's a scary, remote idea to most of us because of the very Matrix that we are studying, and which we have the idea is not quite as solid as it has been presented to humanity down through the millennia.

In book seven of *The Wave* I became aware of the important question of the psychopath. Those of you who have read that series online (as the *Adventure Series*) may remember the long, and careful exposition of the facts, the data, the observations that lead up to the following remarks:

> And we see that the ultimate aim of the psychopath, as living representatives of the [Non-Being] hierarchy, is to *master* creative energy. To assimilate it to the self, to deprive others of it by inducing them to believe lies. Because, when you believe the lie of the psychopath, you have given him control of your Free Will—the essence of Creativity.
>
> The planetary entity is the focal point of a specific density of mind/body interaction. At certain cosmic moments, or "crossroads", such a planetary entity may be scheduled to polarize into a higher density. The Negative hierarchy sees this as a "ripe moment" to induce that polarization to take place negatively so that the planetary entity will participate wholly in the Negative fourth density reality rather than the Positive reality. Negatively polarized beings require a negatively polarized planetary base from which to function, just as higher-density positive beings need positively polarized planetary bases.
>
> The Hermetic maxim again: Economics of light energy above, and economics of control of minds and will below. They want to use humanity's own creative energy to "lock" our planet under their domination.
>
> What we see now in terms of the diminishing resources of our planet, the intensified UV bombardment of our atmosphere, is *not* an "unfortunate but

inevitable byproduct of industrialization": it is part of the deliberate, covert effort of the Negative hierarchy to prepare the biochemical and electrical composition of this planet for negative polarization.

There *are* such things as "evil planets" and dark stars. And the real question at this time is: Is Mother Earth about to become one?

Organic life on Earth serves as a "transmitter station". As such a transmitter, during times of Transition, as it is in the case of a quantum wave collapse, what is being "transmitted/observed" determines the "measurement". There are approximately six billion human beings on the planet at this moment of transition, most of them contributing to the *quantitative* transmission. But what is missing is the *qualitative frequency response vibration* that will create the template for the *new world.*

The *quality* of humanity has changed little in the past many millennia. Most human beings are still ruled by fear, hunger and sex in states of misery and chaos. The disinformation machine of the Matrix has worked very hard to keep this state of affairs intact, with great success. The nonsense propagated as "ascension" is evidence of that fact. This is because the negative hierarchy has been working for millennia to elaborate the control system in such a way that at the "ripe moment" of transition, utilizing the massive release of energy from the enormous numbers of human beings on the planet, they wish to induce that polarization to take place negatively.

Now, to put this in perspective, let me repeat again: Organic life on Earth serves as a "transmitter station". As such a transmitter, during times of Transition, as it is in the case of a quantum wave collapse, what is being "transmitted/observed" determines the "measurement". There are approximately six billion human beings on the planet at this moment of transition, most of them contributing to the *quantitative* transmission. But what is missing is the *qualitative frequency response vibration* that will create the template for the *new world.*

What do you think this means?

What is the "time of transition"?

What is being *transmitted*?

Think about it: six billion human beings... transmitting *what*?

In other words, humanity is being set up to be *batteries* to *fuel* an "event" that the Entropic forces *hope* will result in their aims of being masters of the planet in fourth density.

What do you think that means?

You don't think that six billion people on the planet have aligned themselves consciously with the force of Creation do you? And we know there aren't a whole lot of them ready to graduate to conscious alignment with Entropy either.

So what does the Matrix *want*?

LIFE FORCE.

In short, although the potential for the global intensity of transmission has grown exponentially, the quality of energies has been gradually and cunningly co-opted to the negative polarity. This is the esoteric meaning of 9/11, the real purpose behind the plans of the Bush Reich and the Zionists. Remember what the C's told us: "We have told you before: the Nazi experience was a "trial run", and by now you see the similarities, do you not?"

Little did I know what was in store for us!

If the negative polarity has been growing, the planet lacks *massive* amounts of the finest energies of the psyche which would serve as the template for the transition to result in the restoration of the pre-Fall state of Eden. Only human beings on the verge of *true spiritual* ascension are capable of ensuring the transmission of these energies in sufficient quality and quantity.

What this means, we will look at next.

chapter eighteen
gnosis

Let's face it. We are in a prison guarded by sentries with the power of travel through space-time. They intervene in our world with the ease of a chicken farmer intervening in his chicken coop. They foment war, violence, famine, and natural disasters in the global level by playing us like virtuosos, while also using our emotions and intellect to create strife and discord in our daily lives.

In part one of this book, I cited the story told by Gurdjieff about the Evil Magician. It bears repeating:

> A very rich magician had a great many sheep. But at the same time this magician was very mean. He did not want to hire shepherds, nor did he want to erect a fence about the pasture where his sheep were grazing. The sheep consequently often wandered into the forest, fell into ravines, and so on, and above all they ran away, for they knew that the magician wanted their flesh and skins and this they did not like.
>
> At last the magician found a remedy. He hypnotized his sheep and suggested to them first of all that they were immortal and that no harm was being done to them when they were skinned. On the contrary, it would be very good for them and even pleasant. Secondly he suggested that the magician was a good master who loved his flock so much that he was ready to do anything in the world for them. In the third place he suggested to them that if anything at all were going to happen to them it was not going to happen just then, at any rate not that day, and therefore they had no need to think about it. Further, the magician suggested to his sheep that they were not sheep at all; to some of them he suggested that they were lions, to others that they were eagles, to others that they were men, and to others that they were magicians.
>
> And after this all his cares and worries about the sheep came to an end. They never ran away again but quietly awaited the time when the magician would require their flesh and skins.

This allegory describes our situation perfectly. We are hypnotized to believe that we are safe so that our keepers can continue to shear us or flay us, that is, live off of the negative emotional energies that our suffering creates.

The question is: What can we do about it? How do we go about dehypnotizing ourselves?

Most "solutions" that are put forward involve proposals of means for changing this world. Some of these proposals are individual, others involve organizing the masses to overthrow the existing order and to establish a new, "just", society based upon a new set of principles elaborated by a new elite.

While in material terms, these plans work from the top down, that is, from a small group who seek to impose their will down the hierarchies to those below, in esoteric terms, we say that these plans work from the bottom up, that is, against the Creative force that is at work in the universe, a force that can work through us from above if we allow it. When we are aligned with the force of entropy, we impose our own limited understanding upon the world. We seek to shape the world in our image rather than allowing ourselves to become the expression of Creation. This imposition of an idea upon the world holds true whether it is the latest New Age fad, from Creative Visualization to the Cosmic Bombardiers of Light and Love, to a political movement, be it Marxist or Libertarian. Thousands of years of human history show conclusively that none of these solutions work. If they did, why are we still confronting the same, age-old, problems?

After over thirty years of work, the one thing that has become evident is that the energies of Creation emanate "downward", and our individuality as human beings is merely an expression of the "Theological Dramas", so to say. To attempt to exert our will or to make our voice travel "upward", against Creation is, in essence, an attempt to violate the Free Will of Creation, i.e. *hubris*. This is why praying, rituals designed to "change" reality, "positive thinking" with the "intent" to change something "up there", in order to receive the benefits "down here", is always doomed to produce more strife, misery and suffering globally.

Again let me say this: if the Truth about the *real* process of waking up from our hypnotic slumber were not so detrimental to the agenda of the Controllers of our world, the Matrix, they would not have gone to so much trouble to cover it up. When we finally make the connection between that fact, and the fact that our governing elite is operating on the instructions of the Controllers, we then begin to realize that the drama on the political stage is a shadow of the higher-level agenda. And that leads us to realize that the COINTELPRO operation in the New Age and Human Potential movement has truly been the "opening act".

Based on observation and research, it is apparent that humanity has now reached a great historical crossroads. We have come to the end of a two thousand year history of intolerance, cruelty and stupidity, which has created our present state of global, collective madness. Humanity, as a collective whole, is arriving at a state of collective spiritual bankruptcy, or "death". And yet, we cannot assume that this is meaningless. Those who understand the principles of electricity will comprehend when I say that this present global estate is the way nature works and is the establishing of sufficient *contact potential difference* for the inflow of energy of Cosmic Light. But just as it is in the case of the individual, when that point is reached—that dark night of the soul—there is a "choice" that becomes apparent: the soul is offered the way "up" or the way "down". In order for this coming inflow of energy to act in positive ways, to create a new reality of Free Will and Balance, there must be a point of contact that can conduct the energy. There must be human "micro-chips" or "circuits" sufficient to sustain this energy or all of humanity will perish. This means that only the development of human beings of a certain sort—with a certain "wiring", so to say—will result in the global capacity to confront the energies of the Crossroads.

Boris Mouravieff''s *Gnosis* is an attempt to recover and describe, in terms understandable to modern man, a particular Tradition handed down over the centuries, in a sometimes perhaps broken line, but one that still exists today in the Orthodox Church. Paraphrasing Mouravieff, this tradition could be said to be the Christian equivalent of Yoga, Zen and the other inner traditions of the far Eastern religions, disciplines which have each existed as specializations within the religion of which they are part. Its later form can be traced particularly in the Russian Church and clearly relates to the oral tradition known as the Royal Way.

Mouravieff himself admits that the survival of this tradition within the church is tenuous, that the doctrine does not appear to survive in full or has not been collected together in full. Monks on Mount Athos admit the existence of the Tradition but say that it has never been fully spelled out in writing.

In carefully studying the work of Mouravieff, we discover that we have found many of the missing pieces of our puzzle. What is more significant is that these pieces relate directly to the hidden meanings of the Quest for the Holy Grail and the Great Work of the Alchemists.

Again and again, Seekers have sought to interpret the process of ascension in terms of their external experiences. As Fulcanelli has told us, it is in the clash of ideas that the letter dies and the spirit is born. That is to say: the knowledge is in the meaning, not in the words.

Again and again the esoteric Tradition is misunderstood in this way and so it dies. Then, when the time is ripe, it must be either restored or rephrased. In the meantime the meaning is kept alive in communities or schools symbolized by the name "Ark", of which Noah's Ark was one. Mouravieff writes:

> With time, the revealed Word, sometimes handed down from extinct civilizations, is subject to damage due to human forgetfulness: it becomes fragmentary. Then it receives arbitrary additions from purely human sources. With time, those conjectures are generally taken as realities. Apart from these mutilations, we should not lose sight of a phenomenon of a totally different order. Divine Revelation, the source of all true Tradition, does not crystallize into immobility through the course of millennia. Revelation is given in stages: metered out each time in a necessary and sufficient way in answer to the needs of the epoch and of the Cause.

Mouravieff's words echo those of the legendary alchemist, Fulcanelli:

> Every prudent mind must first acquire the Science if he can; that is to say, the principles and the means to operate. Otherwise he should stop there, without foolishly using his time and his wealth. And so, I beg those who will read this little book to credit my words. I say to them once more, that *they will never learn this sublime science by means of books, and that it can only be learned through divine revelation, hence it is called Divine Art*, or through the means of a good and faithful master; and since there are very few of them to whom God has granted this grace, there are also very few who teach it.

345

When we turn back for a moment to consider the problems of the many and varied teachings of Ascension, we find that this issue of "works vs. faith" has always been the condition confronting the Seeker. It is part of the Haunted Forest through which he must pass even before he is faced with his true tests of stamina, courage, and discernment. Mouravieff discusses this also:

> A very ancient maxim quoted in Saint Luke's Gospel places the problem [of ascension] in its proper context. He writes: "the labourer is worthy of his hire". This maxim is given in the context of sending the seventy disciples "as lambs among wolves" to announce to the people that "the kingdom of God is come nigh unto you."
>
> This means that in the esoteric field, as in everyday life, man earns a salary for the service he provides. In the esoteric field we can gain nothing pure or true and thus nothing beautiful without making efforts whose sum and importance are equivalent to the result to which the worker aspires. Conversely, the value of the results we obtain is always equivalent, quantitatively and qualitatively, to the measure of the services rendered on the esoteric level.
>
> It is possible to obtain so-called esoteric results that are impure, but they are false and thus transitory.
>
> Here we refer to the vast realm of occultism, where the children of this century, more capable than the children of light, seek to apply their abilities beyond the visible world. This occurs in what we call mysticism of phenomena. ... If the seeker ... approaches the esoteric domain driven by the desire to find in it personal and thus impure satisfaction for himself, he will not be able to advance very far along this way. If he persists, he will meet with failure. The error of conception made at the start will imperceptibly lead him towards this "mysticism of phenomena."
>
> The attentive reader will draw a practical conclusion from the above: one must find a genuine esoteric task being carried out in the world, make oneself useful in that work, and take an active part in it. ... [We are in the heart of this period] we will call the Time of Transition. ... All the signs show that the necessary conditions for the End are emerging before our very eyes. ... The preparatory task fundamental to the Time of Transition can and must be accomplished ... for human beings and by human beings. This is, therefore, a question of the New Man. ... In practice, this problem can be reduced to the need to form a new elite [the Children of Elias, as Fulcanelli states]. In the time of transition between our civilization which has now reached its end and the new era into which humanity is now moving in its historical evolution, success depends on the emergence in the near future of a sufficient number of people belonging to this new human type.

Here Mouravieff is raising the same question that we raised at the end of the previous chapter: the planet lacks the *massive* amounts of the finest energies of the psyche needed for the transition.

So, let us briefly describe what the Ancient Secret Science of Ascension is *really* about according to our research and what we have learned from the Cassiopaeans.

Recapping a bit from the last chapter, organic life on Earth serves as a "transmitter station". As such a transmitter, during times of Transition, as it is in the case of a quantum wave collapse, what is being "transmitted/observed" determines the "measurement". There are approximately six billion human beings on the planet at this moment of transition, most of them contributing to the *quantitative* transmission. But what is missing is the *qualitative frequency resonance vibration* that will create the template for the *New World*.

The quality of humanity has changed little in the past many millennia. Most human beings are still ruled by fear, hunger and sex in states of misery and chaos. In short, although the global intensity of transmission has grown exponentially, the spectrum of energies transmitted is incomplete. It lacks massive amounts of the finest energies of the psyche. Only human beings on the verge of true spiritual ascension are capable of ensuring the transmission of these energies in sufficient quality and quantity.

The energies needed are the *three currents of objective love:* spiritual, emotional/mental, and physical love. And we emphasize that these currents must be *pure*.

Man alone has the ability to capture and live all three. But to grasp and fully experience the *soul love,* the giving love, the courteous love demonstrated and taught by Chivalry and the Knights of the Grail stories, the Seeker must develop a *magnetic center* within himself.

Man is penetrated through and through by the two currents of mental/emotional and physical love, but these currents are not pure; without a fully developed magnetic center, man has no capacity to capture them. It is only by actualizing these three currents in his life, either in the mode of the Alchemist, or in the Model of the Grail Quest, both of which exemplify the Shamanic Ecstatic Ascent, that a man has the *real* possibility of ascension, the return to the Golden Age.

We have seen in our survey of the history and the evidence, what the potentials are: a Return to the Edenic State in the literal terms of Primitive Chiliasm—a New Heaven and a New Earth.

Again, this depends upon capturing and holding stable—possibly in the face of extraordinary events—massive quantities of purified *objective love.*

It is clear to those who have been paying attention to what is going on in the world that there are forces that do not wish for this possibility to manifest! They do not want to lose their supply of negative energy food! And with this end in mind, they propagate endless lies and deceptions upon humanity—so as to deceive even the very elect!

How to achieve this anchoring of the frequency—the three currents of objective love?

The attitude a man takes toward Love reflects his level of *Being*. The splendor of the Love of God/Creation is inconceivable to him. It would burn out all his circuits with a mere glimpse. However, man can glimpse and survive the spiritual Love of Objective Knowledge. To do this, he must pass to a higher level of *Being* and become a true *individuality*. Only those beings who have achieved the level of individuality, who obey the imperatives of the Divine within, the real "I", have the possibility of holding this frequency and radiating it at the Time of Transition.

The "Elect", the Children of Elias, are human beings who have crossed the Second Threshold and who have achieved the Second Birth. They will be "gathered from the four winds, from one end of heaven to the other", to pass through the Transition and form the seed of humanity in the New World. This means that they will be humans of all colors and types—the only criteria being that they have crossed the Second Threshold. Each of them will be fully conscious through a direct and indissoluble union of his personality with his higher emotional and intellectual functions. This direct contact of the new humanity with the higher planes explains why the "second coming" will not require a "new incarnation of Christ". This is why we were warned: "If any man shall say unto you, Lo, here is Christ or there; believe it not. For there shall arise false Christs and false prophets and shall show great prodigies and miracles; insomuch that, if it were possible, they shall seduce the very elect."

The path that must be followed is that which is exemplified in the Quest for the Holy Grail. Human beings must travel from the residue of Celestial Love that we experience in our ordinary lives, to the Love of the Spirit. This is the general requirement for "Salvation."

This path is the way to the Second Birth. But to be reborn, a human being must pass the test of True Love. Only he who has mastered his personality and burns with this True Love can cross the Second Threshold. And before he can even reach this point, the Seeker, upheld by the ardent desire for Salvation, must pass through the intermediate stages. He must give proof of his Sincerity by his faith, then he must pass the test of Strength nourished by Hope. Then, he must acquire discernment, and he cannot do this without first attaining Knowledge. The passage from Hope to Love is marked by the renewal of the mind, the intelligence, by Knowledge.

Knowledge acquired through study and work is only a temporary—but essential—stage. Only Higher Love can reveal the Divine Nature, and this springs directly from God. But if there is no vessel built by Knowledge to receive Gnosis, there is no possibility of anchoring the Forerunner Spirit which will open the gates to the Holy Spirit. The Gatekeeper is Knowledge.

But for this to occur, the sign of Knowledge, that is, the Sign of St. Matthew/Science, must be correctly oriented. And this means that the Seeker must be liberated from lying and believing in lies. Without this, there is no possible access to the Era of the Holy Spirit. No matter how well meaning the individual, if they are following practices or teachings that are based on lies, they will not achieve the Grail. And so, we see why knowledge and discernment is essential.

Access to knowledge requires courage, as it demands a special psychological effort from the Seeker: he has to accept the postulate that "the truth is out there, but it is very difficult to find", while at the same time disregarding his own ideas and personal beliefs.

With the approach of what Mouravieff calls the era of the Holy Spirit, everything must be gradually brought to the light of day, not only the secrets of the laboratory, but the deepest meaning of esotericism. The same must happen with illusions, errors and lies, which must be revealed so that they can be rectified. This process, including the Revelation of the deepest esoteric Knowledge that has been promised and prophesied, will fully reveal the many deviations of man's fundamentally inquiring spirit. Initiation, in the esoteric meaning of the word, is not simply a "ceremony". In fact, the "initiation ceremony" no longer occurs on the human plane with human rituals. The initiation of the present cycle occurs on the super-sensory plane. It confirms the Initiate in a new dignity earned by his Work, and carries him towards the Divine Grace.

To solve the problem of anchoring the Three Currents of Objective Love, we must concentrate on a positive and practical solution to the problems of individual human beings. A practical application of esoteric knowledge should help those who are Seekers and who burn with the desire to reach the Second Birth.

The Seeker of the Holy Grail, just as depicted in the stories, must first assimilate all they can learn exoterically and mesoterically. And they must then be ready to serve the Cause joyfully.

To Burn and to Serve is the motto of the new Knight.

The Tradition teaches—and this knowledge can be discerned in the Grail Legends as well as in the fragments of the Catharist teachings—that at the End of Time, the Children of Elias will consist of Polar Couples and their affiliated groups and helpers. During the Time of Transition, the New Human must resolve the problem of the Singular Romance.

The evolutionary path of love from the Fall has traveled from polygamy, with other human beings (mostly women) considered as "chattel", to the Free Choice of partners which has progressed to its ultimate expression at this point in time. It now is a decaying form, leading to over-emphasis on the physical expression and, in some cases, is even regressing to a form of "polygamy", or multiple partners.

The next step of the evolution of Love is the Alchemical Androgyne. This is not to be understood in the physical sense, but rather in the Spiritual meaning. The Divine Androgyne is the highest condition of Human Consciousness which crowns the efforts of the Seeker and which Union results in the Second Birth. Mouravieff writes:

> A revolution is occurring silently which will replace the free romance, distinctive mark of the Christian era, with the singular romance characteristic of the Holy Spirit. Liberated from servitude to procreation, this romance of tomorrow is called on to cement the indissoluble union between two strictly polar beings, a union which will assure their integration in the bosom of the Absolute. As St. Paul says: "Nevertheless, neither is the woman without the man, nor man without the woman in the Lord."

chapter eighteen

The vision of such a romance has haunted the highest minds for thousands of years. We find it in platonic love, the basis of the singular romance in the myths of Androgyny man; of Orpheus and Eurydice; of Pygmalion and Galatea... This is the aspiration of the human heart, which cries in secrecy because of its great loneliness. This romance forms the essential aim of esoteric work. Here is that love which will unite man to that being who is unique for him, the Sister-Wife, the glory of man, as he will be the glory of God. Having entered into the light of Tabor, no longer two, but one drinking at the fount of true Love, the transfigurer: the conqueror of Death.

The principle of Woman's intervention is found in *all* crucial periods of history.

Periods where the ennobling role of the woman in the life of human society has faded are marked by a triviality of morals and manners, expressed in particular by a taste for realism carried to its utmost limits.

Today, human relations suffer from a real distortion in the innate role that woman is destined to play at the side of man: instead of being the active force in these relations, the inspiring and fruitful complement to the man, the woman tends to follow a parallel path, which no longer permits her to exercise her own creative vocation. ... Man and woman once formed a single spiritual being— even if in separate bodies—endowed with the unique consciousness of the real Self; the Being described in the myth of the Androgyne.

The incomplete "I" of the Personality, unfinished and powerless, wanders in life with no faith and no true affection. It goes from error to error, from weakness to weakness, and from lie to lie. A prisoner—perhaps voluntarily—but nevertheless a prisoner—man does not do what he wants to do in life, but does what he hates, blindly obeying a diabolical mechanicalness which, under its three aspects: fear, hunger and sexuality, rules his life.

This purely factitious existence has nothing real except the possibility of evolution—which remains latent, and forms the objective of esoteric studies and work. Apart from this seed, everything in exterior life is based on lies.

If the Fall is a direct consequence of identifying with the "I" of personality [the predator's mind, the degraded DNA state], and the solitude of polar beings separated by the Fall is the source of weakness in humans who have in this way become mortal, the return of Unity appears to be an inexhaustible source of new energies. These energies are necessary to man, and to restore the dangerously disturbed equilibrium of today's public and private life, he must seek them out.

However, this return to the perfect unity of polar beings is not given freely. It is the exclusive privilege of those who have crossed, or are ready to cross, the Second Threshold of the Way.

It is through realization of the totally indivisible unity of their real "I", by two polar Individualities arrived at the Second Birth, that the original sin can and must be redeemed.

Objective Love can only be attained here, in human existence, by its complete and vivifying manifestation at the time of the Second Birth. Courtly Love, as exemplified in the Grail Stories, is then the precursor of Objective Love.

Courtly Love is the raison d'être for the couple of polar beings: for the Knight and the Lady of his Dreams. Without it, their polarity remains spiritually sterile and they fall back into the common estate.

The practice of Courtly Love demands sacrifices and exploits. These are tests. For those who surmount them, the salutary effect of Gnosis is doubled.

The courtly Love of the Knight and his Lady will immediately place them on the fourth step of the Staircase, where their exploits and sacrifices will hasten their advance, provided that Gnosis, having been sufficiently assimilated by them, produces its fruits, i.e. work for the Cause. The time they need for this will be given them, but they will remain on the step only if they Burn with Love.

Courtly Love can only be effective when it is based on a Gnosis which is *lived*. For only *lived Gnosis* goes down into the heart and can ensure that the Knight will have the discernment which will prevent him from going astray in the jungle of purely human reasoning and feeling.

Courtly Love is the meaning of, and the instrument of work on what Mouravieff has called the Fifth Way: the sublime esoteric way to acquire the attributes which will be characteristic of the world to come.

This Fifth Way is not given to everybody to attempt. It does not exclude the other four ways either. The great error in esoteric studies which leads to inevitable failure, is to embark on a way which is above a man's capacities. The Tradition warns us about this. This overestimation of strength by the seeker is a classic snare laid for people of Good Faith, in which they might achieve success by following one of the other Ways which do not force the disciple immediately to pass through the Trial of Fire.

Today, as in the time of the emergence of the Grail Stories, Courtly Love remains, by definition, the indispensable condition for the success of the Polar Couple who aspire to the vivifying Love of the Higher Realms, the objective of the Quest for the Holy Grail. Then, and only then, can the Seeker gain access to the Ancient Secret Technology which includes mastery of Space and Time and Matter: The Philosopher's Stone: ascension.

I have become One: Creator of worlds.

epilogue

We have finished our look at the question of *The High Strangeness of Dimensions, Densities, and The Process of Alien Abduction*. We have seen that this is not a new phenomenon, but is one that stretches back thousands of years. These events could more correctly be described as our interactions with our keepers, those beings who raise us like cattle, sheep, or chickens in order to feed off of our negative emotions. These beings are the denizens of what modern physics calls hyperdimensions, dimensions that we can neither see nor touch, but which have a physical existence nonetheless.

The existence of such beings, their power over us, their experiment, is the "topic of topics" according to don Juan Matus. It is the "ultimate secret" of the Consortium that rules our planet according to the Cassiopaeans. In other words, we are not the top of the food chain, a certain blow to the ego to people raised to believe that we are the center of the universe and made in God's image. As we have seen, this age-old monotheistic aphorism may well be true. It is only our understanding of God that must change.

afterword

The term "Cassiopaeans" appears in many places in this book. The name Cassiopaea was given by a source identifying itself by saying "we are you in the future" which Laura Knight-Jadczyk contacted via an experiment in superluminal communication in 1994.

"We are you in the future"

This is what "they" declare: that "they"—the Cassiopaeans—sixth density Unified Thought Form Beings—are Us in the future. What a bizarre concept. Or is it?

Is that possible? Can such a statement find a place in accepted theories? Or is it an evident contradiction with everything that we—that is, physicists—know about Nature and its laws?

Putting aside for the moment the issue of whether existence in a pure state of consciousness is possible, is traveling in time possible, even if only in theory? Is sending and receiving information from the future or sending information into the past allowed by our present theories of relativity and quantum mechanics? If information can be sent, does this also imply that physical matter can be "sent", via some sort of TransDimensional Remolecularization? And if so what are the laws, what are the restrictions? What are the means?

Well, frankly speaking, we do not know, but we may have a clue. Kurt Gödel, after he became famous for his work on foundations of mathematics, went on to study the Einstein general theory of relativity and made an important contribution to physics: he discovered a class of otherwise reasonable cosmological solutions of Einstein equations—except for one point: they contained causal loops!

At first these causal loops were dismissed by relativists as being "too crazy". The arguments against these model universes even became rather personal, commenting upon the state of mind of the inventor! (A not terribly unusual phenomenon in the heated debates within so-called "ivory towers" of academia.)

A "Causal Loop" means the same thing as "Time Loop". It can be described as going into the future and ending up where you started at the original time and place. It is called "Causal" because, in Einstein's Theory of Relativity, Time is a relative concept and different observers can experience Time differently, so the term "causal" is used to avoid using the term "time."

But, little by little, it was realized that causal—or Time—loops *can* appear in other solutions of Einstein equations as well—usually they correspond to some kind of "rotation" of the universe.

Causal loops make time travel not only possible, but probable. But then, causal loops lead to unacceptable logical paradoxes, and physics does not like such paradoxes at all—they are a serious problem!

But, the subject of communicating with the past or receiving information from the future *is* being discussed in physics even in terms of the flat, not-curved-at-all space-time of Lorentz and Minkowski. Hypothetical faster-than-light particles—tachyons—can serve as the communication means. They make an "anti-telephone"—a telephone into the past—possible.

But do tachyons exist? Or *can* they exist?

Well, that is still a question that has not been answered definitively for some.

And, the truth is that paradoxes must never be ignored. They always indicate that some important lesson is to be learned; that some essential improvement or change is necessary. The same holds true for the paradoxes involved in the idea of receiving information from the future. We cannot simply go back into Saturday and tell ourselves the winning lottery numbers of Sunday. If this were possible, then it should also be possible for some future, future self to tell a future self *not* to tell! Thus we have a paradox: we, in the future, have intervened into the past making our communication from the future impossible!

A paradox: if we communicated, we have not communicated, and if we do not communicate, then we have communicated! Impossible in a linear, non-branching universe!

Is there a possible escape from the paradox, an escape that leaves a door open, even if only a little—for our anti-telephone?

Indeed, there is, and not just one, but several ways out.

First of all—the evident paradox disappears if we admit the possibility that the communication channels are inherently noisy; that is a normal situation when we deal with quantum phenomena. So, if the communication into the past is a quantum effect—we are saved from evident paradoxes. Quantum Theory can be useful!

Sending a signal into the past, we are never 100% sure if the message will be delivered without distortion. And conversely, receiving info from the future we are never 100% sure if this comes from an authentic broadcast or is a spontaneous and random creation of the receiving end. If this is the case, and if certain quantitative information—that is, theoretic relations between receiving and transmitting ends—are secured to hold, then there are no more paradoxes even with reasonably efficient information channels.

In other words: there *can* be broadcasts from the future to the past, but *there will be few "receivers"*, and of those few, *even fewer that are properly tuned*. And even those that are properly tuned may be subject to "static". Even if there is no static, those receivers that can receive pure information will experience the static of "non-belief" and distortion after the fact from society.

There is also another aspect of such an information transfer which is that the probabilities involved are connected with a *choice event*; with the choosing of one among many possible futures.

It may happen that branching of the universe corresponds to each such event. Branching of the universe into an infinite tree of decisions has been discussed within quantum measurement theory—it even has the name of "Many Worlds interpretation of quantum theory".

Two of the well-known physicists who consider the many worlds interpretation more than just an exercise in theorizing are John Archibald Wheeler and David Deutsch.

The Many Worlds Interpretation has one serious weakness: it has no built in algorithm for providing the timing of the branchings. Thus it is a certain framework rather than a complete theory.

There is, however, a theory that fills in this gap in the Many Worlds Interpretation—and this theory I know quite well, and in fact I know it better than most others for the simple reason that I developed it in collaboration with Philippe Blanchard (University of Bielefeld) in 1988 as an integral part of the Quantum Future Project. It is called Event Enhanced Quantum Theory (EEQT for short notation). (A complete list of references and much more info on this subject can be found on my "Quantum Future" project page[12] on the World Wide Web).

The fact that our generally accepted theories of the present do not prevent us from thinking that time travel is, perhaps, possible, does not necessarily imply that we know how to build the time machine!

On the other hand, it is perhaps possible that the time machine already exists and is in use, even if we do not understand the principle of its work, because it goes much too far beyond our present theoretical and conceptual framework. It is also possible that some of the machines we think are serving a totally different purpose do, in fact, act as time machines. Many things are possible...

Now, back to superluminal communication, or "channeling" in general and the Cassiopaeans in particular: the fact that sending information into the past is possible does not necessarily imply that any information that pretends to be sent from the future is such indeed! But, if we generally accept that extraterrestrial life is possible, and we use all of our knowledge and resources to search for life beyond our Earth, then we also need to include the understanding that receiving information from the future is equally possible. With this perspective, science should search for any traces of such information.

What kind of information channels are to be monitored in search of such broadcasts? What kind of antenna arrays do we need? How must we direct them into a particular "future time"? Say, into the year 3000? Or 30,000? Or 300,001?

My answer is: nothing like that is necessary. All that we need we already have, namely *our minds*.

And indeed, assuming that the knowledge and technology of the future is (or *can be*) much more advanced than ours, then it is only natural that any broadcast from the future *will be addressed directly into the mind*.

Even today there are techniques of acting directly on our minds. They are not always used for our benefit; nevertheless they do exist. But if communications from the future are possible, why don't we receive these broadcasts on a daily basis? If our minds can serve as receivers, then why aren't we all aware of the transmissions?

---

[12] http://quantumfuture.net/quantum_future/

I think that the answer has to do with multiple realities and branching universes, and perhaps any civilization which would receive messages from the future on a daily basis has ceased to exist because communication through time is a very dangerous game. You produce paradoxes, and these paradoxes remove the paradoxical universes from the repository of possible universes; if you create a universe with paradoxes, it destroys itself either completely or partially. Perhaps just intelligence is removed from this universe because it is intelligence that creates paradox. Perhaps we are very fortunate that even if we can receive *some* of these messages from the future, we still continue to exist.

Suppose our civilization were to advance to the point where everyone can communicate with themselves in the past; they have a computer with a special program and peripheral device that does this. It becomes the latest fad: everyone is communicating with themselves in the past to warn of dangers or upcoming calamities or bad choices, or to give lottery numbers or winning horses. But, what is seen as a "good event" or "benefit" for one, could be seen to be a "bad choice" or "calamity" to someone else!

So, the next step would be that "hackers" would begin to break into the systems and send false communications into the past to deliberately create bad choices and calamities for some in order to produce benefits for themselves or others.

Then, the first individual would see that false information has been sent and would go into their system and go back even earlier to warn themselves that false information was going to be sent back by an "imposter" and how to tell that it was false.

Then the hacker would see this, and go back in time to an even earlier moment and give false information that someone was going to send false information (that was really true) that false information (that was really false) was going to be sent, thereby confusing the issue.

This process could go on endlessly with constant and repeated communications into the past, one contradicting the other, one signal canceling out the other, with the result that it would be exactly the same as if there were *no* communication into the past!

There is also the very interesting possibility that the above scenario *is* exactly what is taking place in our world today.

It is also possible that, whenever a civilization comes to the point that it can manipulate the past and thereby change the present, it would most probably destroy itself, and probably its "branch" of the universe, unless there comes a cataclysmic event before this happens which would act as a kind of "control system" or way of reducing the technological possibilities to zero again, thus obviating the potentials of universal chaos. In this way, cataclysmic events could be a sort of preventive or pre-emptive strike against such manipulations, and may, in fact, be the result of engineered actions of benevolent selves in the future who see the dangers of communicating with ourselves in the past!

So, the probability is this: if there *is* communication from the future, it *may*, in fact, be constantly received by each and every one of us as an ongoing barrage of lies mixed with truth. Thus, the problem becomes more than just "tuning" to a narrow band signal, because clearly the hackers can imitate the signal and have become *very* clever in delivering their lies disguised as "warm and fuzzy" truths; the problem becomes an altogether different proposition of believing nothing and *acting* as though *everything* is misleading, gathering data from all quarters, and then making the most *informed* choice possible with full realization that it may be in error!

Using our computer analogy: we can't prevent hackers from hacking, but, what we can do is make every effort to prevent them from hacking into *our* systems by erecting barriers of knowledge and awareness. Hackers are always looking for an "easy hack", (except for those few who really *like* a challenge), and will back away as you make your system more and more secure.

How do you make your computer (or yourself) immune to hackers?

It is never 100% secure, but if all preventative measures are taken, and we constantly observe for the signs of hackers—system disruption, loss of "memory", or energy, damaged files, things that don't "fit", that are "out of context"—we can reduce the possibility of hacking. But, we can only do this if we are *aware* of hackers; if we *know* that they will attempt to break into our system in the guise of a "normal" file, or even an operating system or program that promises to "organize" our data for greater efficiency and ease of function or "user friendliness", while at the same time, acting as a massive drain on our energy and resources—RAM and hard drive.

As a humorous side note: we could think of Windows Operating system as the "ultimate hacker from the future" who, disguised as a sheep, is a wolf devouring our hard disk and RAM, and sending our files to God only knows where every time we connect via the internet!

And of course, there are viruses. Whenever we insert a floppy disk or CD into our computer, we risk infection by viruses which can slowly or rapidly, distort or destroy *all* the information on our computer, prevent *any* peripheral functions, and even "wipe" the hard disk of all files to replace them with endless replications of the viral nonsense. The human analogy to this is the many religions and "belief" systems that have been "programmed" into our cultures, and our very lives, via endless "Prophet/God" programs, replacing, bit by bit, our own thinking with the "dogma and doctrines of the faith".

Enough of the computer analogies. I think that the reader can imagine any number of variations on the theme and come to an understanding of how vulnerable we are to "disinformation" in the guise of truth from either the future, the past, or the present.

Among the many critics of "channeling", in general, and my wife's work in particular, which is quite different both in theoretical approach and content, there are those who say "Channeled Information is crap. It is 100% disinformation."

I can't take such claims seriously.

Why?

afterword

I am a scientist. I look at things in a somewhat different way than other people. I am more critical. I am even more critical than most of my colleagues. So, when I see a statements like these, or even "channeling is a satellite transmission", I get very suspicious.

Why so?

I immediately see that anyone who says things like this is speaking nonsense—in *these* sentences. And when I see someone speaking nonsense in couple of sentences, and when this somebody is so affirmative—*then* I can't take this person seriously in all the rest.

What are the facts? What are the possibilities?

Certainly there is a possibility that some (most?) of the channeling *today* comes via satellites or other means of programming. That *is* not only possible but probable.

The next question we should ask is: *Why?*

The evident answer is: to twist, to misinform, via New Age-type naive people. Based on an assessment of the facts of technology and the morality (or lack of) amongst the Elite rulers of our world, it is highly probable that if there was information that would tend to free humanity from their controls, they would co-opt it immediately exactly as I have described above in my computer analogies.

Can the Cassiopaean channeling be disinformation or come as a result of such technology and/or programming?

This would not be so easy. We are not naïve, we are critical of our work. We think, we analyze, we test and do research.

Could *some* of our "communications" have been influenced this way?

Yes. There is such a possibility.

Can *all*, or even 95% be received this way?

No. Because there are too many instances in which the Cassiopaeans were answering questions to which normal "satellite type" of intelligence, without being able to instantly read the minds of everyone on this planet, could not have had access.

Therefore, I think the statement that *all* channeling is crap and disinformation, and that 95% is via satellites shows that the individuals who make such claims are:

a) Unable to think logically,

b) Not interested in discovering the truth.

This is the main difference between their approach and ours. While we are ready to question everything, and *always* look for new facts, other individuals declare, "*We know the Truth.* Here it is!" And then we find one or another easily detectable nonsense statement that is claimed to be absolute, and this discredits everything else they say.

The Devil is always in the details.

Whenever someone claims: "All white is black"—I get suspicious. And I am turned off to everything else they say. Not because "white being black" is impossible, we know there *are* paradoxes, but *because* the person uses this three letter word: "all".

As for parallel realities, yes, probably this is part of the clue. As for satellites trying, once in a while, their dirty tricks—yes, this is possible. And we *are* taking it into account. But *always* we are trying to apply our logical thinking, our "judgment". But we know that this third density reality check is *never sufficient* when dealing with possible hyperdimensional realities. But it is *always necessary*. Which means, in practical terms:

1) Always use it to the max.

2) Never think you can rely completely on it alone!

What I want to state clearly is this: this channeling, the Cassiopaean channeling, *is* different than other channeling. It was different from the very beginning, it continues to be so, and it will continue to be different. We may give it a name: Critical Channeling. It is such by intent, not by chance. It is channeling in which, by intent, the messenger is as important as the message itself. They are inseparably entangled in a quantum way; an interfering quantum amplitude. They form a oneness, a whole. To separate the message from the messenger would be, in this Cassiopaean quantum experiment, like closing one hole in a double slit experiment. You close one hole, and the whole pattern is different, not just a part of it. As I have written above:

There *can* be broadcasts from the future to the past, but *there will be few "receivers"*, and of those few, *even fewer that are properly tuned*. And even those that are properly tuned may be subject to "static". Even if there is no static, those receivers that can receive pure information will experience the static of "non-belief" and distortion after the fact from society.

It is in this context—that my wife is one of those few receivers who has worked very hard to properly "tune" to transmissions from the future—that I call the Cassiopaean Communication "Critical Channeling".

What is this "Critical Channeling"? In what way is it different than other channeling?

It would take a lot of space and time to describe it in details. One day we will do it. But for now, let me just make this observation: the Cassiopaean channeling has characteristics of a scientific experiment. Think of scientists in their lab, working on the great laws of the universe. They perform an important series of experiments. They are trained professionals, they know their stuff, they know their laboratory equipment and its quirks. But they are human beings. Once in a while someone will make some dirty joke, once in a while they will have to discard a series of data because mice have messed up their equipment during the night. Now, think, what advantage it would be if they would write in their paper the dirty joke, include the mice data, the ink blobs, etc., etc.

That is not the way of science. And the Cassiopaean experiment will proceed as a scientific one. With scientific standards in mind. The Cassiopaean channeling is Critical Channeling. It is in this respect that it is *different* from other channeling. And it will stay so.

The difference is in the approach. We are searching for the truth. Others who make unilateral statements that all channeling is crap are sure that they know it and would like to impose it on other people, or manipulate other people into believing what they say. And naturally, when such individuals state such things, they claim that it comes from God or some equally authoritarian source, but when someone else dares to have a different way of finding the truth, it is necessarily "100% disinformation" and "crap".

We try to share our thoughts, and when necessary, we are ready to learn and *change*. And that is what is most important. This attitude of being open.

What if such claims are right, that all channeling is crap and disinformation? Even if I consider it as highly improbable, can it be true?

Of course, being a scientist, and using my brain in order to judge, I had to consider also this possibility, however improbable it may look to me. And I concluded that such a claim cannot be true. Here is my reasoning: it goes via *"reductio ad absurdum"*—which is often used in logic and in mathematical proofs. You assume something to be true, and then by a chain of logical deductions you come to the conclusion that your assumption cannot be true. Somewhat tricky—but useful.

Applying this method to the claim that "all channeling is 100% disinformation because it is coming via satellite", let us suppose it is true. In order to be true it must include the capability of reading and controlling *everybody's* mind at *all* times.

But if that is the case, then why would the persons making such claims be exempt from this control?

Therefore, by logic, anyone who makes such a statement is also being influenced by programming and by satellites (if everybody is, then so is he). If so, then what such a person writes is skewed. And, because such debunkers are often so loud, and so sure, about this subject for no valid reason, it is a logical conclusion that what they are saying is *not* true, that the claim that all channeling is crap is, itself, disinformation.

So we see that starting from the assumption that such a claim is right (satellites affect everybody), we come to the conclusion that the claim is wrong (because it is simply repeating the satellite disinformation). So, here we have *reductio ad absurdum.*

But we can go even further. Can we find a reason why debunkers would state such evident nonsense with such certainty?

Well, here we can have a hypothesis too. If, as we know by the above analysis, *not all* channeling is from satellites, that *some* channeling can provide us with real information from "benevolent higher beings", from "us in the future", or from "Mind-God and Oversoul", call it as you will, then it is only natural that there will be forces trying to discredit *this* channeling. So, we have solved one problem here. If a critic calls all channelers disinformation agents, and if he is right, or even partly right, then we have reasons to suppose that such an individual is an agent of those forces.

There is one more exercise in logical reasoning and critical thinking that comes to mind. Most critics are not clear about what channeling is, so let me take the particular example of using the Ouija board, as my wife, Laura, does. Why does she use the Ouija board?

Laura went to great lengths to research the subject of channeling before she ever began her experiments. Based on facts and data, it was clear that using a "peripheral device" in a full state of consciousness was the optimum method to screen out noise. In particular, such a method makes it far more difficult for satellites, or other programming signals coming from human and hybrid technology, when and if they come, to affect the message. At least two persons are needed, full consciousness, critical thinking, often coffee, fresh minds, loud discussion of the data as it comes, and the board. Thinking in terms of possible quantum physics involved in mind-matter interactions, it is clear to me that the methods she uses are more likely to be robust and shielded against deliberate bombarding from outside by mind controlling signals, whether technological or "psychic". On the other hand, talking directly to "Mind-God" as so many other channels do is far more susceptible to interference. For example, a weak outside EM signal can be talking directly to a tiny implant in our teeth, and we will take it for our Oversoul...

So, by logical thinking and by critical analysis we come to a working hypothesis. But, please, do not jump to the conclusion that we have solved all the problems. Important problems are still out there and need to be addressed. The above analysis does not confirm anything 100%. It gives indications. To answer the question as to whether or not the Cassiopaean Communications is exactly what it says it is—transmissions from Us in the Future—a full analysis, that takes into account not one but many aspects, is necessary. Completely different methods must be used. If A is an opponent of B, and if we find that A is wrong, that does not mean that B is right! To see whether B is right or not—is a different problem.

Let me just note that we have discussed these issues on many occasions on our website[13], with other groups or individuals and quite often, those who started as skeptics have later admitted openly that these Cassiopaeans have an amazing record.

Arkadiusz Jadczyk, PhD

[13] http://www.cassiopaea.org

underground and underwater bases

This subject is rather "touchy" for a lot of reasons. The first time I was exposed to it, I rejected it outright as being pure "poppycock." However, as I began to research in many other areas, particularly historical, I found that there are many things that not only tend to confirm this idea, but are explainable only in these terms. The historical work is included in *The Wave* books, so be sure to read them in order to have a full background for all of the following information.

For the most part, this information was delivered during 1995 with a few of the last pieces in 1996 and 1997. The material is presented chronologically (as it was received) and explanatory notes are inserted where necessary. The following was extracted from one of the earliest sessions in 1994. There were so many other issues on our agenda that we did not come back to it again for some time.

Q: (L) Why are there more abductions by the grays in the United States than in other countries around the world?

A: Government opened channel.

Q: (L) Are there alien bases in the United States?

A: Yes. New Mexico, Colorado, Off Florida, Appalachia, California.

Q: (L) Are these underground bases?

A: Yes. Also under water.

I did not necessarily believe the information about all these alien bases, but I was willing to suspend disbelief for the duration of the sessions if only to collect a large amount of data for analysis. About a year later, I had worked with some abductees who reported being taken to underground bases, or tunnel areas, where large laboratories were set up and some of the descriptions were so bizarre that I was pretty much incredulous. I had the idea that these were, in fact, screen memories to mask something much more prosaic. Some of the other group members were a lot more knowledgeable about the subject than I was, having read more extensively in the realms of UFO literature. It seems that there was such a mass of confusing information on the subject that we wanted to just get to the "basics" and get "another opinion", so to speak.

Q: (L) We want to know if there are really underground tunnels all over the place that many people have reported being taken to in alien abductions?

A: Yes.

Q: (T) Do they predate humanity?

A: A few.

Q: (T) Are they equivalent of subway tunnels, to get from one place to another?

A: OK.

Q: (L) How do they travel through these tunnels?

A: Electromagnetically.

Q: (T) Can individuals be transported through the tunnels without benefit of equipment? Or do they use some kind of gadgetry?

A: All of the above.

Q: (L) Who occupies these tunnels?

A: Various.

Q: (T) Are there still beings in there?

A: Yes.

Q: (T) Are humans involved in this?

A: Yes.

Q: (T) Were there humans involved in digging some of these tunnels?

A: Some.

Q: (T) Before that, there were other beings that were not human?

A: Yes.

Q: (T) Are those other beings still down there?

A: Yes.

Q: (T) Is this a worldwide network of tunnels?

A: No.

Q: (T) Where are most of the tunnels?

A: North America, since that is the "capitol" of STS, currently.

Q: (T) Are there other tunnel systems other than in North America?

A: Yes.

Q: (T) Do any of the tunnels lead to Antarctica?

A: No.

Q: (T) Is there any way of getting to Antarctica through the tunnel systems even if you have to come to the surface occasionally?

A: OK.

Q: (T) Is there some kind of underground base in Antarctica?

A: Yes. Eight.

Q: (T) Were any of those bases underground in Antarctica built by the Germans during World War II?

A: Sect. Remember, all is structured in cycles and circles. Circles within circles.

Q: (L) Masons?

A: One example of concept.

Q: (T) Jan and I have a friend who has told us about someone she knew who found entrances to tunnel systems in North America. One of the entrances was in the Adirondacks, another was in the Mammoth cave system. Was what she was told true?

A: Yes, but there are thousands of entrances. Are you ready for a "shocker?"

Q: (J) Oh, you know we are always ready for a shocker. (L) Sure! (T) OK, give us the shocker. (J) We're ready!

A: There is a tunnel right beneath your feet!

Q: (J) I knew they were going to say that. (L) How deep under our feet?

A: 2000 feet.

Q: (T) Is that tunnel being used?

A: Yes.

Q: (T) Are there humans down there?

A: Have been, listen for sound anomalies such as loud sonic boom like noises and vague motorized sounds.

Q: (L) Is there any kind of electronic gadgetry down there causing my appliances to keep breaking down?

A: Maybe.

Q: (T) Is there an entrance to this tunnel underneath us somewhere in this area?

A: Near power plant.

Q: (T) Is that why the power plant is built there?

A: Related; old Nike base.

Q: (T) What direction does this tunnel run that is underneath us?

A: East - West.

Q: (T) The West ends at the power plant. OK, where does the East end go?

A: Near Lakeland. Transfer point and redirector.

Q: (T) Is there another tunnel that comes into this tunnel, that intersects this tunnel?

A: Yes.

Q: (T) Near Lakeland?

A: Yes.

Q: (T) Is that what you are talking about; a transfer point?

A: Yes.

Q: (T) Does that tunnel travel North/South?

A: Yes.

Q: (L) Lakeland is in the center of the state. (T) Where does it go? Are these side tunnels to a main tunnel that runs along the East coast?

A: All are interconnected.

Q: (T) So, it is like a subway or bus line? Is there a tunnel farther South of here?

A: Yes.

Q: (T) How far does the farthest South tunnel go?

A: Antarctica.

Q: (T) I was thinking about the military base. (L) I would think that the tunnels bear no relationship to the structures under the surface except in certain instances. (J) But, what got there first, the tunnels or the structures on the surface? (L) Obviously the tunnels have been there for a long time, and perhaps, in certain instances a situation may be manipulated so that a specific structure is built to facilitate the tunnel usage, but the fact that Lakeland is built over it may not be relevant. (T) There is no entrance to the tunnel system near Lakeland?

A: Yes. Phosphate plant. Mine.

Q: (J) Was the placement of this tunnel under our feet the reason Laura got this house?

A: No.

Q: (T) Does the placement of the tunnel underneath us have something to do with the channel?

A: Maybe.

Q: (T) Because of the greater EM underneath us; we are tapping into that EM energy?

A: Helps in offhand way.

Several months later we had a guest, my brother, who is retired from the Navy. He was curious about some strange experiences he had while on a "shake down cruise" of one of the new Aegis guided missile cruisers. This series of questions led to some really *strange* things...

Q: (L) Are all military personnel routinely abducted and studied by aliens?

A: No.

Q: (L) Are all military personnel routinely abducted and studied by the military itself?

A: No.

Q: (L) What is the classification that the person has to fall into in order to be abducted and studied by the military?

A: What makes you think "classifications" correlates with abductions?

Q: (TK) It's not the classification, it's... It's gotta be the type of person...

A: Yes.

Q: (TK) And how easy it would be to influence...

A: Of course. And many other factors.

Q: (TK) It would have to have something to do with what they could do for the abductors. I mean, they have to be in a position to help them...

A: Yes. STS. Vibrational frequency.

Q: (L) OK, so if the person has an STS vibrational frequency, that already predisposes them to abduction. Is that correct?

A: Some.

Q: (T) OK that's a factor. There's more than one agenda involved with abductions. Are the military personnel that are being abducted, is that a specific agenda that is being followed?

A: Artificial classifications, such as military designations, are important to human groups only.

Q: (J) I've got a question. Isn't it true that in order to become part of the military, you have to go through boot camp, the indoctrination to the point where you're going to follow orders without questioning, and that that mind-set would lend itself more towards... (TK) The Marines are about the only ones that even try to get people to follow orders without question any more. The Navy has all but given up on that. (J) That's interesting. I didn't know that. I just assumed that all military. (TK) Well, it's not a time of war so it's not necessary right now.

A: Yes. Some have always "faked" such blind allegiance anyway.

Q: (TK) I basically faked it, I...

A: You were not alone.

Q: (TK) Oh, yeah! There were a bunch of us. "Yeah, sure, tell us what to do. If it's in our interest, if we're going to stay alive, we'll do it; if you're going to kill us, forget it!" I used to tell them on the ship, that if those suckers ever catch me, I'm going to tell them everything I know. I said, they aren't going to have to torture me long... (T) Besides, when you torture me, I tend to scream a lot and not tell you too much, so I'll just tell you and let's skip the torture. (TK) So when I refused to go up for ESWS, I was kind of an outcast, I wasn't in the club anymore... Enlisted Surface Warfare Specialist. This captain put it in such a way, he said, "Well, if you'll work on your ESWS and get that pin, I'll see to it that you get good marks and make chief", which to me was like saying, well, if you don't do it, you're not going to make chief. I said, "sorry, bud!" I don't respond well to that kind of stuff. (F) You would have set the service back a number of years. (TK) That's when I became an outcast from the club.

A: Not correct concept, not outcast, just deemed not SG material.

Q: (L) What's SG?

A: Secret Government.

Q: (TK) Darn! (J) You had your chance Tom, and you blew it!

A: There are several steps that must be followed to become part of the secret government. Vietnam MIA's, where do you suppose they are now?

Q: (TK) Have they been abducted? (T) Some of them got blown up so badly that they couldn't be found, so they were listed as MIAs, because they couldn't mark them as KIAs. Some of them are deserters, some of them... well, deserters would fall into several classifications, which I won't bother getting into. Some of them went into the drug trade. (TK) Some of them just decided they liked it better over there. (T) Yeah, there's that, and some of them, I would imagine, have been either abducted or swapped, moved into the secret government. (L) Is all of this correct?

A: Yes. KIA's... Are a separate subject!! KIA's, how many really were?

Q:(T) How many of the 60,000 really were killed? [Estimates for American casualties range from 47,000 to 58,000, the total number dead ranging from one to three million.] How many of them are listed as dead when they're not? Intelligence... Are these some of the people working in these underground places?

A: Yes... Yes...Yes.

Q: (L) That's where those personnel are coming from... their lives, they have died the philosopher's death.

A: And many other places, times. etc...

Q: (TK) Wars all through the ages. How many are we talking about?

A: Since your imagination center is on low frequency tonight, suppose we have to spell it all out for you, W.W.II, 72,355, still alive where????

Q: (L) Is that the correct figure? (T) Now, wait a minute...

A: Yes.

Q: (T) That's how many people the secret government has snatched up? (TK) That's out of something like 40 million casualties... (F) Total People killed in W.W.II was 70 to 80 million... [Most historians agree with a figure of 50 million.] (TK) Military casualties... We're not talking about just U.S. military, either, we're talking about total, anybody... (L) Still alive! (T) That were supposedly killed in action...

A: Yes.

Q: (T) From all branches of the service.

A: Yes.

Q: (TK) These people aren't aging; they're still in action and ready to go...

A: Precisely, my friends!!!

Q: (J) OK, that's just W.W.II... (TK) How about Korea, Vietnam, etc... (L) All right, what's the figure from Korea? (TK) What difference does it make?

A: 6,734.

Q: (TK) How about the Gulf War?

A: Yes. 55.

Q: (T) Yeah, there was about 55 thousand casualties in Korea, in the four years of Korea. [With a total of about 2.8 million dead, estimates for American losses range from 34,000 to 55,000, the official number being 36,568.] Really it was three and a half years in Korea. So 6,000, about a little over 10% of them aren't really dead.

A: 23,469.

Q: (T) 23000 of the 66000...

A: Yes.

Q: (T) ...are still alive?

A: Yes. Some are body duplicate soul receptacle replacements.

Q: (J) They have just around 100,000 with those three figures they gave us. (T) Yes, we're only asking about the U.S. How about others? Yes, you're right, how about other military... (J) We have no way of knowing. Have they ever released figures? We don't know. (TK) So, the underground bases, the Secret Government has a military right now, and it's not just a military, these are elite. I'll bet you, they're elite. I mean, they've been recruited. (J) They've been asked the question, and they said yes! (T) Yes, this is not some guy hunking a gun in a foxhole just for the heck of it. These are specialists. (TK) The CIA was siphoning people off in 'Nam right and left. (J) Oh, I'm sure they were. (TK) This "New World Order" is about to come about. You know what, there isn't any way to stop it. You can fight back and try to survive on your own, but there's no way to stop the New World Order. (T) The only way to get through this is the old Lao Tzu or whoever, the Chinese military philosopher, who said, "The wheat stalk that survives is the one that bends with the wind." (TK) "Yes, I'll do whatever you say." (T) There's no way to stop it. All these people who are talking about going out and going to fight it, they aren't going to fight it. They can't. They can't win. (F) Well, they are already being diverted. (TK) On top of everything else, these are the elite. I mean, these are the ones that have been recruited, and they are the elite. Now, most military organizations are going to fall right into this, because the government... Admitted, there's gong to be a lot of deserters from the military, I mean there's some people, like, if I was in the military, and they

started rounding people up in the U.S., I'd say, "Sorry, this is where I came in..."
(T) This is why this Koernke guy up in the Michigan militia group has been
talking about the foreign UN troops, because the military, the government that's
ready to come into power, this one world government knows that you can't
subdue any country with their own troops. (TK) It can't be done. (T) That's why
they're sending American troops to all these other countries. (F) And all the other
countries are sending troops here. (J) Well, what about the guy who wouldn't put
on the UN uniform? (T) Yes, that was mentioned in the paper again today, in
passing. This guy knew. (TK) Well, really, the only thing a person can do is like
you were saying, go with the flow... Basically, you've got to. Up to a point, at
least. (T) It's easier to fight it by going with the flow than it is to fight it by going
against it. (F) Who is going to stand up in the line of fire and say "I refuse!"
They'd blow him away... (TK) What, if anything, can be done about this "New
World Order?"

A: Too complex to answer, need specific questions.

Q: (T) Also, right now, if you're considering survivalist groups, you have to keep
in mind, they're under attack right now. (TK) Oh, yeah, the government's after
them. (T) Between Oklahoma and this thing with Amtrak out in Arizona, militias
are under heavy attack.

A: Being lead into a trap.

Q: (L) I suspected that at one time. They're all being led into a trap. (T) Well,
they've got guns right now... (J) Maybe guns aren't going to change anything...

A: Good intentions.

Q: (TK) Started off with good intentions... They've got to be infiltrated, and it's
been tainted at the very least. (J) Maybe it's the idea of putting all the ones
together with the same mind set so you know where they are. (T) Their
usefulness to the One World Government people has come to an end. It brought
the conservative grouping into power in this country.

A: Not yet.

Q: (TK) Their usefulness isn't over yet, but... (L) OK, in those terms, what is the
single most important thing that we as individuals should focus on in order to
prepare ourselves for whatever events may occur?

A: No single thing.

Q: (TK) Is what Terry was saying earlier, like the thing... with the reed bending
and going with the flow, is that the idea?

A: Close. Watch, look, listen.

Q: (J) Got it, knowledge is power.

A: Alertness. Messengers are all around. Look, listen.

Q: (TK) Is it going to be necessary to stockpile supplies, or anything along those
lines?

A: Third density.

Q: (L) Are there any Civil War individuals involved in this project, these
underground tunnels or bases or whatever? (T) KIAs of the Civil War?

A: A few.

Q: (L) I think the point is who they are. Now, in the Matrix material [compiled
by Val Valerian], there's a section extracted from the L. Ron Hubbard teachings

that talks about technical abilities to jerk people's souls out of their bodies, insert other souls, reprogram the memories, essentially that there is no congruency...

A: False.

Q: (L) OK, so the jerking out and the manipulating of souls as described by L. Ron Hubbard is false? In a general sense?

A: Yes.

Q: (L) OK, now, you said a moment ago that some of these bodies were used as receptacles, soul receptacles. When you say soul receptacles, do you mean soul receptacles for whom?

A: Replacements for dead bodies, i.e. duplicated.

Q: (L) So, in other words, they make replacements for dead people and put their souls in a replacement body, so that they can continue living on, is that it?

A: Yes.

Q: (L) Do they ever use dead bodies and re-animate them and then put other souls in them?

A: No. For example: a soldier is KIA, his body is duplicated, his soul is replaced into new body, then he is "reprogrammed for service" to aliens and S.G. [Secret Government]

Q: (L) Where does the new body coming from?

A: It is duplicate of old body. TDARM.

Q: TDARM is TransDimensional Atomic ReMolecularization (T) Otherwise known in Star Trek as a 'Replicator'. (TK) Does somebody have to die in a certain way before they can do this?

A: No.

A: (TK) Is there a time limit on how long they can be dead?

A: No. Zero time.

Q: (T) Because there's no time... (L) They use the frequency vibration of the soul pattern, they take it into another density, use their TDARM technology to cause a molecular re-assembly; in other words, the atoms begin to whir and assemble around it in the pattern that it had before, and then it is a full-fledged body, and then they insert it back through the time doorway into 3D again. Is that correct?

A: Close.

Q: (T) Are all these KIAs, are they dead KIAs, when they go, that you were talking about? I mean, are they really dead? (TK) Were they dead when this was done?

A: ?

Q: (T) OK, you said... let's use Vietnam. You said there were 23,000 KIAs of the 60,000 that actually were not killed in action. True? Yes?

A: Were killed, then reanimated.

Q: (L) We're not talking about physical bodies here, are we?

A: Yes.

Q: (L) OK, there are some that were killed in action that the actual bodies were reanimated? (J) As long as they weren't blown up in a land mine, yeah. (L) There were actually bodies that were actually reanimated, is that correct?

A: Some, but most were duplicated.

Q: (L) Now this leads to the immediate question: Is there some potentiality that is created by dying in a violent manner; i.e., in war, in an atmosphere of war, that makes one susceptible to this particular type of activity, as opposed to just people dying in an ordinary sense?

A: No.

Q: (T) No, because violent death like that, we have violent death all the time without being in a war; car crashes, fires, explosions...

A: War makes covert actions so easy.

Q: (T) Well, no, it's not like car crashes, the violent part of it, I don't think has anything to do with it. It's just that the cover of a war, is easier to take the bodies. (TK) They're not wanting people to realize ... They're not wanting to just take them out of the graves, because if you did, it would be more noticed. (T) These are real bodies, they were dead. In other words, the people were dead, they were taken, and reanimated, or... (L) Were some of these bodies taken, like dead bodies of somebody who just died... were the bodies picked up, taken into another density for this remolecularization patterning?

A: Yes.

Q: (L) OK, so they had to have an actual body for the pattern. (T) Was the original body... (TK) Did they actually get the bodies before anybody actually... (T) Before they were recovered, yes. Were the original bodies returned once the duplication was done?

A: More than one type of situation.

Q: (L) So, in other words, it could be sometimes, yeah, they were, and sometimes, no, they weren't. (J) It would be case by case. (T) Were some of these supposed "killed in action's" actually not killed? Were they still alive when they were removed?

A: All possibilities.

Q: (L) So this is in a sense a "crime of opportunity." (J) It's a supermarket of opportunities. (T) Some were just taken by the secret government when they were alive, some were dead and brought back in new bodies to continue on, and they were considered dead, but they're all considered dead.

A: Taken by aliens, not SG. Secret Government aware to some extent, but not in control of operation.

Q: (L) OK, now this brings up the question about... We were told that there was, and this was... last week we asked about this thing about the death... and we were told that there was an impenetrable triple veil that prevents some of this "L. Ron Hubbard'" type of activity, that he describes happening. How can this be reconciled?

A: Time adjustment.

Q: (L) Does that mean that they know that they're going to, and they go back in just before they die, or just at the moment of death, or...??

A: Close.

Q: (T) Now, what are the aliens doing with these bodies? With the humans that they replicate and duplicate and reanimate? What are they doing with them?

A: Serve them. Workers.

Q: (T) They're slaves. (L) Now, this leads me to a question that I have thought about asking on many occasions. In terms of finite numbers, how many of these

STS aliens of any different group, or any combination of groups all together, do we have operating on this planet at the present time?

A: Specify.

Q: (L) OK, how many Lizzies are operating on the planet?

A: 300,000.

Q: (L) OK, how many Oranges?

A: 62,530.

Q: (L) How many grays?

A: 2,750,000.

Q: (L) This is not a pretty picture! (J) No s**t. (L) Are most of these inhabiting alternate dimensions or densities most of the time? I mean, it would be kind of crowded otherwise!

A: Back and forth. And others.

Q: (L) We have here some drawings of supposed alien servants [from the Matrix material]. This one right here is called a Rigelian servant. It's a proto-synthezoid, in other words, a cyber-genetic. Is this an accurate representation of this being, and does this being actually exist?

A: Yes.

Q: (L) Well, that's friendly. Now, this one here... (T) Oh, lightning bolt man!. (L) Does this one actually exist? This mutative clone form?

A: Yes.

Q: (L) OK, now this one is a real pleasant looking fellow...

A: Yes. Occupies Dulce base.

Q: (L) (Reading) "This is a cloned synthezoid form," in other words a cybergenetic, "whose specific job is to act as controllers. They are plus or minus four feet tall." This is, I think, your standard gray. It's just that the drawing is kind of crappy-looking. (T) Wait, the face... the eyes are smaller on the thing but the face is a lot like the one in the autopsy film. OK, now, this is what they call a replica. (Reading) "They are proto-synthezoid form of human whose specific job is as a special outside agent. Observation: Face and body change shape at will." This is like in the X-File thing where the guy... the shape changer. Is this a correct concept? Is this basically a... I mean of course you have to draw them in an ambiguous way...

A: Close.

Q: (L) OK, these are the servants from Zeta Reticuli One... this is another version of the one. I would also assume that these are the servants at the Dulce base?

A: No.

Q: (L) What are these guys?

A: Floaters.

Q: (L) OK, these are floaters. (T) Floaters? As in how floaters? (L) I would say it was like somebody in a job... (TK) Trouble shooters, they go from place to place... (L) OK, these are real friendly looking... I love these guys! The THROOB! (T) Are these the little short stubby blues that Whitley was into... (L) Plus or minus four feet tall... Yeah, I think so. It says here "They are originally from the Draco Constellation and their job is to complete research. They are plus or minus four feet tall. Are these accurately represented here, both in terms and drawing?

A: Yes.

Q: (T) Are these the ones that Whitley Strieber has seen?

A: Maybe.

Q: (L) OK, now, the degenerative clone form, which is the bottom photograph, is this also an accurate representation?

A: Close.

Q: (L) What is the color of the skin of these friendly-looking little guys?

A: Variable.

Q: (L) OK, I think there may be one more... Ha ha! Are you guys ready for this one? This is a Cassiopaean! (T) Well, I don't think that's a Cassiopaean! (J) Let me see... Oh, lovely! (T) Cassiopeia, I couldn't find a star called Cassiopeia... (L) There isn't. (T) Well, I know that. (L) OK, this is one called a race of insectoids from Cassiopeia, whose specific job is genetic research. Is this an accurate description and drawing of this critter?

A: Yes.

Q: (T) Is Cassiopeia a star? (L) No. (T) What is Cassiopeia? (L) It's a constellation. (T) I know it's a constellation, but they say they're from Cassiopeia. You can't be from Cassiopeia...

A: Region.

Q: (L) Are these guys coming here?

A: All are already.

Q: (L) OK, hang on... (T) What about the one below? What's the one below? (L) Well, that's just a biological android. "The Nordics and Oranges normally use inorganic, high-tech servants." Is this an accurate representation of an inorganic, high-tech...

A: Yes.

Q: (T) What are all the hieroglyphics? (L) It's supposed to be one of their alien languages. What does this business say here?

A: Scrambled.

Q: (L) It's scrambled. So it's a combination of the various different languages they have back there.

A: Yes.

Q: (L) Somebody just put the various different symbols together, because it looks like two or three different languages. OK, well, that answered those questions. (TK) Doesn't seem to me like there's too much to worry about... (T) It's all supposed to be fun! (TK) Seems to me it's something you've got to take as it comes, and deal with it!

A: Yes.

Q: (TK) Are we asking all the wrong questions here?

A: There are no such.

Q: (TK) But what can... are there questions you can ask, and answers you can get that will make a difference one way or the other?

A: Ask. Suggest more questions about the goings on at underground facilities. Jan and Terry were visitors involuntary when went to Albuquerque and Las Vegas!

Q: (J) Oh, really! (T) We were in a front door of an underground base. We were in Carlsbad Caverns, and I know that there's a government facility at the other end of it, and they won't talk about it. You're talking about Carlsbad?

A: Abducted.

Q: (T) When we were in Albuquerque?

A: Yes.

Q: (T) When we were in Las Vegas, also?

A: Met alien there. Barfly.

Q: (T) Ohhhhh... (J) I know exactly what you are talking about.

A: Disguised humanoid gray species four. Rigelian. Orion union STS.

Q: (T) Why did he talk to us? Why did he approach us?

A: Spying on you and aural frequency reading, had you not been as strong, would have suffered permanent abduction because of your studies.

Q: (L) What is there about strength that makes one inaccessible to permanent abduction?

A: Strength is of character, i.e. if STO candidate, not likely to be victim.

Q: (L) Not likely to be victim... OK, but what... but what is the thing inside one that stops them... I mean, is this something that is a core ingredient of certain human beings? Is this like something inside them that blocks this manipulation and victimization?

A: Soul pattern.

Q: (L) So in other words, there is something about us, or within us, that literally they cannot touch or harm, is that correct?

A: Basically, but difficult to facilitate.

Q: (L) OK, in other words, this is something that is in us, that creates an inherent barrier, but not necessarily something that we can, at this level of density, reach in, grab out as a weapon, and wave around, as in facilitate?

A: Can, but intricate to do consciously.

Q: (L) Is this a state of focused awareness, whole body awareness, internal and external, basically whole body awareness...

A: Helpful.

Q: (L) Is there something we can do to develop this to the highest degree possible, while in these bodies, in this density?

A: Wait for 4.

Q: (L) Wait for 4? 4th density?

A: Yes.

Q: (T) It's a "do", it's an involuntary, it's there, it works when it needs to work. Is this the idea?

A: Network western experiences for learning purposes please. Knowledge is protection.

appendix

[Briefly, Terry related the story where he and Jan met the barfly at Vegas World, after having gone downtown to get their marriage license. They had taken a taxi to City Hall, and foolishly decided to walk back to the Strip, in 116 degree weather. They made it as far south as Vegas World, and stopped at the bar inside to cool off. Jan was close to heat prostration, and the barmaid gave her glasses of iced water and an iced towel to put on her neck. They were getting ready to go back out and hail a cab back to Bally's, when they were approached by the "Barfly," who started asking all sorts of personal questions, and seemed to be acting drunk when he wasn't really intoxicated. He became belligerent when Terry refused to show him his Florida drivers license, but switched to disorientation when Terry made the statement "We don't have a problem here, do we?!" while staring the guy down and putting the force of his personality behind the question/statement.]

Q: (L) In this story that Terry has just recounted, what instant represents the turning point of resistance?

A: The statement.

Q: (T) "We don't have a problem, here, do we?! Everything's cool, everything's OK! I'll buy you a beer?"

A: Yes.

Q: (T) Because that's when he got confused... He was escalating this to a point, and I don't know, it just came to me that the best way to do this was to just stop it right there...

A: Grays and their associates are thrown off by energy flow diversions or thought pattern interruptions.

Q: (T) Another thing that comes to mind while I'm thinking about it, before it turned ugly, he was leading up to going someplace. He was leading up toward, "We ought to get together and go someplace." I think that's when I really shut the whole thing off. (L) OK, now, in this episode where Terry and Jan were taken to an underground base, can you identify the location of the underground facility?

A: Soccoro, NM.

Q: (L) OK, what was done to them when they were in this underground facility?

A: Quick exam.

Q: (T) Which of the nights in Albuquerque was it we were taken?

A: Second.

Q: (T) We got there Friday afternoon, that would have been Saturday... (L) Who was in charge of this base, this facility? What group?

A: Orion union STS.

Q: (T) Did we get taken to the base because we happened to be close by at the time when they grabbed us? Was it an opportunity for them?

A: Close.

Q: (T) Did they know we were coming out there?

A: Yes.

Q: (T) Why did they follow up with a spy afterwards?

A: Test.

374

Q: (T) You mean that what they were looking at was to see whether we were STS or STO?

A: Partly.

Q: (L) And if they had been permanently abducted at that point in time, what would have happened to them?

A: Body part utilization.

Q: (TK) Basically, what that means is that you wouldn't have been any good to them as a person, but the parts would have been all right. (L) I do have an idea about that. Is this what Michael Topper was writing about in his article where he talks about the "obedience factor" of the STS? If they can get you to obey something, you have given your permission?

A: Close.

So, that was a lot of information to digest at one time. But, we came back to it again briefly not long after.

Q: (L) The other night, when we were talking about the underground laboratories and the taking of the MIA and KIA individuals from W.W.II, that would seem to imply that the underground tunnel system and the alien activity has been going on there has been going on a lot longer than since 1947, is this correct?

A: Yes, but in much less intensive form.

Q: (L) OK, it's gotten a lot more intensive since 1947 or thereabouts. Well, the thing that I want to know: is there any relationship between these underground laboratories and facilities and our cultural concept of Hell?

A: Not in such a simplistic sense.

Q: (L) Well, I'm just curious as to whether the concept of Hell being underground, where people were tortured and worked on and all kinds of miseries going on arose from some people who escaped from, or psychically intuited...

A: Link, but not unified.

Q: (L) Is there a Hell?

A: No.

Q: (L) What I want to know, is this tunnel that's under the house, which you have said is straight down under my house, is it a tunnel... is there like a laboratory under the house, or is it just a tunnel that's used for traveling from one facility to another?

A: Closer to latter.

Q: (L) Does the tunnel under my house go to Anclote base?

A: The base at Anclote is a Portal.

Q: (L) One of the abductees I worked with gave some interesting information under hypnosis. I suggested to here that she could travel a mind link to read the minds of the aliens, and ask them, or inquire of them what the purpose of the implants were, the response she got was that it was like connecting a bunch of speakers, and once all the speakers were connected, then the stereo was turned on. What does this mean?

A: Unit group mind. Activation.

Q: (L) So what will happen when they, as she said, turn on the stereo?

A: Wait and See.

Q: (L) Well, earlier today I was thinking to myself that they way I feel right now must be very similar to the way animals in the forest feel on the opening day of hunting season. I mean, it's like every so many thousands of years, it's hunting season on planet Earth.

A: You are aware, 2nd density is not.

Q: (L) Is it still, in a sense, like hunting season? Are they just here... I mean, according to this Matrix material, they plan on decimating our entire planet, either with disease, or taking over their bodies...

A: Some is disinformation.

It was about six months before we came back to the subject, and again, my brother was a guest. And, again, the information was startling. We had another guest, a friend who had spent some time in Army Intelligence many years prior to this time. I have to say in advance here, that my level of "acceptance" of incredible material was stretched to the limit in both the previous session and this one that follows!

Q: (L) One of the things we talked about the last time Tom was here was the underground base issue and military interference in civilian affairs and civilian interface with military affairs. One of the questions we were dealing with was the use of warfare to create situations in which bodies could be taken...

A: Warfare has many "uses."

Q: (L) Could you list for us some of the most common uses of warfare?

A: Generation of environment to facilitate *inconspicuous replacement of gene pool.* Factors in paradigm shift through stimulation of conception activity, *replacement of key personnel* according to frequency vibration prereadings...

Q: (L) 'Replacement of key personnel according to frequency vibration pre-readings...' OK, do you mean to say that war...

A: Creates "environment" for unnoticed genetic modifications because of greatly heightened exchange of both physical and ethereal factors.

Q: (L) What do you mean by "replacement of key personnel?" Key personnel according to whose definition?

A: 4th density STS.

Q: (L) Are these key personnel human?

A: Yes.

Q: (L) When you say replacement, do you mean something as simple as someone dying, such as a head of state, and being replaced by another person who comes to power? That would be the simplest scenario that would fit this explanation.

A: Your scenario is not simple.

Q: (L) I mean simple in terms of the machinations...

A: Both.

Q: (L) Would it also be that key personnel could also be replaced as in duplication as you have described previously?

A: Yes. And removing to secret activity realm. Enough wars have taken place to effectively create entire new "underground race" of humans, both from direct

376

capture followed by "reeducation," and spawning activity using these persons and others.

Q: (L) What do you mean by spawning activity?

A: Those captured have reproduced offspring, these never having seen your world.

Q: (L) Are you saying... (TK) They have given birth and these children have never seen our world... (L) How can an entire race of people, or groups of people, live under the surface of this planet, without the whole six billion of the rest of us on top, or at least a large number, realizing that there is anything going on? This is so wild an idea...

A: No. How much space exists underground, as opposed to that on the surface?

Q: (L) A lot, I suppose. You aren't saying that the earth is hollow, are you?

A: No, not exactly.

Q: (L) Well, how deep is the deepest of these underground cities?

A: 3,108 miles.

Q: (L) That's pretty deep! But wouldn't it be too hot at that depth?

A: No. Temperature averages 68 degrees F.

Q: (TK) That's pretty comfortable! (L) How do they have light?

A: Magnetic resonance.

Q: (L) Well, aren't they subject to being crushed by earthquakes?

A: No, earthquakes are not felt deep underground!!

Q: (TK) Is any of this under the ocean?

A: Yes.

Q: (TK) Well, we'll never explore all of what is under the ocean. (L) It just staggers the mind to think about it. What do they want these people for?

A: To replace you.

Q: (TK) And why? Because they can control them better. Right?

A: Completely.

Q: (L) Do these people being bred and raised in these underground cities have souls?

A: Yes, most.

Q: (TK) Are they just like us only raised differently?

A: More complicated than that.

Q: (L) How long have they been doing this?

A: 14,000 years, approximately.

Q: (L) If they have been doing it that long, obviously the ones they have taken at the beginning have croaked and are of no use to replace anybody on the earth unless they have been replacing people from time to time for various reasons...

A: No, their technology makes yours look like Neanderthal by comparison! Hibernation tubes... One heartbeat per hour, for example.

Q: (TH) That means that for every year we live, they would live 4200 years... (L) Does any of this have anything to do with that crazy pit at Oak Island where you have said a Remolecularizer is buried?

A: In an offhand way.

appendix

Q: (L) How do we fit into all of this? (TK) We don't!

A: You have been the "preparation committee."

Q: (L) What have we been doing? Is it part of the plan for us to destroy the planet, destroy the ozone layer, pollute the seas and so forth to make it more habitable for them?

A: Those things are inconsequential and easily repaired.

Q: (TK) With their technology, they can fix all of that. (L) This is really horrible, you know! To think of all this... (TK) Apparently, from what I am understanding, they can't just come in and wipe us out and replace us, because the 'rules' won't allow it.

A: Yet the natural cycles within the framework of the natural order of things will allow all these things to fall into place.

Q: (L) Is there some law within the realm of these beings, sort of like the law of gravity, that prevents them from just coming in and taking over?

A: No.

Q: (TK) I don't think it is like the law of gravity...

A: What "law" is there that inhibits you from manipulating 2nd density beings at will?!?

Q: (L) Well, I don't go out and deliberately hurt or manipulate anything or anybody. (TK) Of course, in our handling of these 'critters,' we are conserving them in some ways so that we will have an ongoing food supply... I think there are rules to the game. It's like a chess game. They can't just come in and change things, it has to progress in some way. But, there are loopholes and they can sneak in and manipulate and get away with some things... (TH) Then, there aren't rules, there are just guidelines.

A: Two important points there: 1) When we said "you," we meant 3rd density collectively. 2) You missed our statement about the *natural cycle* and order of things almost completely. We suggest you reread and ponder... Also, what if your race is manipulated to destroy yourselves, or, just hang around until the next natural cataclysm?

Q: (TK) Well, it seems like there is another side that is trying to prevent them from gaining control. (L) Well, from what I understand, the only thing the good guys are able to do is, because of free will, they have to wait to be asked for help, and the only they thing they can really do is give information. (F) Well, this is valuable if used by the right people at the right time. (TK) You have to come up with the right questions, too. You have to have enough information to be able to come up with the right questions. I am sure the information is there. You have one group with all these people underground and they want to take over the planet. This group likes being fourth density—they don't want to advance. *They want to block advancement.* Then, you have the group that want to advance, they want the natural order to proceed. This negative group wants to stay there and keep everyone they can there. (L) And because they deplete themselves and diminish in numbers, they keep having to supply their needs and existence. (TK) If, by some odd chance, the earth is the only place where people come to advance, then sooner or later it is going to stop, if these other guys take over, then it will just stop... implode. (TH) I know! The earth is a fourth density theme park! (L) We already thought of that... we all have an 'E' ticket ride! Is what I am saying close to the truth?

A: Yes. Total truth is elusive.

Q: (TK) So, what I said was the gist of what is going on here. So, we have to figure out what we are supposed to do so that the earth can be maintained...

A: You will do what you will do.

Q: (TK) This is true.

A: Do you, in general, control 2nd density beings on earth?

Q: (L) Yes.

A: So, what is "fair" about that?

Q: (L) Nothing.

A: OK, so what is the difference?!?!???

Q: (TK) So, basically, we control second density, and fourth density controls us. There are the good guys and bad guys. (L) And we will do what we will do. Either we choose to align ourselves with the good guys, or with the bad guys.

A: It's up to you.

Q: (TK) However, if too many people align themselves with the bad guys, then the balance tips in their favor, and there is no more advancement, so there has to be education so that people will know...

A: Tom, you are close, but you are missing the point.

Q: (L) What is the point?

A: The point is, there "has to be" nothing. You will do what you will do. You choose. We have told you this repeatedly, but you still suffer from self-centered perspective.

Q: (TK) Everybody is worried about themselves. They all want to be saved and not worry about others.

A: More to the point, everybody in an STS realm views themselves as somehow "special, chosen, or protected." This is simply not so!!

Q: (TK) What is going to happen, is going to happen. The people...

A: The body does not matter. It is the soul that either progresses or digresses!

Q: (L) So, in other words, we could just sit around and live our lives and have a good time and not worry about a damn thing. It's our choices?

A: Yes.

Q: (TK) The point is it's going to happen...

A: But, nobody is there to intervene on your behalf as many would like to believe.

Q: (L) So, we are here on this planet, and we will either make it or we won't, just like Dorothy and Toto in Oz, based on our own ability to figure it out, to overcome the odds, the witch, monkeys and soldiers... (TK) Maybe what they are trying to do is give people the information, or make the information available so that people can make the choice, do they want to stay...

A: We are not "trying" to do anything. We are here to answer questions if asked. We cannot interfere.

Q: (TK) Yes, the non-interference idea is pretty clear and understandable. So, they cannot interfere...

A: And, even when we answer, you may not believe, it is up to you!

Q: (L) So, we are really on our own!

appendix

A: You always have been, and so have we, and all others, too!!

Q: (TK) I guess then, it is a matter of asking the right questions so that you will know what course of action to take. I mean, do you want to advance? Do you want to go to fourth density? Or do you want to go higher? Or do you want to stay here? How can you make an informed choice if you don't know the true conditions and what your options are? (L) Is it that the religions that have been generated and foisted on the human race, have been designed to give people a feeling of complacency or faith in something outside themselves, and that this prevents them from seeking knowledge, opening their eyes, facing the facts of their existence, and therefore keeps them in bondage?

A: It's just obstacles, as always. You employ those too, for your 2nd density friends!!

Q: (TK) What state of mind do you have to have to want to advance? (F) Well, you know you are on the path when you can see that the words don't match the facts of life. Think of all the people you have met with whom you may have had a philosophical conversation. How many will say: Oh, all I need is the Bible. That's all I pay any attention to. (TK) I don't have many philosophical conversations with people because I rarely agree with anything that is said. (F) Well, you must have decided on this because you tried it and found it didn't work. (TK) I have a real problem... yes, the Bible has been around for a long time, and religion has been around for a long time... but I have a real problem believing something that is so obviously produced by humans with agendas of their own! (F) But most people that you tell that to will say: Oh, no! People didn't write the Bible, God did! Or, they could be a complete atheist and believe only in the religion of science. (TK) I believe that a person is supposed to live by rules and treat people with respect and honor life... and some of the ideas of religion are good... but they just go over the edge. (F) That is how they suck people in. Mix lies with the truth. (L) Yes, a lie sandwiched between two truths makes it easier to swallow. (F) Yes, if it was *all* false, the vast majority of people would have figured it out immediately. Or, very quickly. (TK) The vast majority don't care. They just want to be led like sheep. They don't want any responsibility. (F) And what happens to the vast majority of cattle? They munch away in their pasture until time to get in the truck to go to the butcher. (TK) Well, after all my years in the military, I have gotten to the point that I just don't trust anybody with authority. (F) And, if you talk to the religious types, they will say: Oh, I don't have any answers... I just follow the Bible. (L) Not only do they not have any answers, they don't have any questions, either. And, I think that is the clue. The people who are still asking questions after wading through all the religions and mystical mumbo-jumbo. The ones who think they have found the ultimate answer are—well—lunch! (TK) The whole purpose of life, it seems to me, is to obtain knowledge and advance. You are stuck on this level until you figure it out. But what are you supposed to figure out? (L) I think that the knowing is the doing. (TH) "Ye shall know the truth and the truth shall set you free." It's in the Bible!!! (L) Is the knowing the key?

A: Yes.

Q: (L) I think that knowing changes your frequency. Is that true?

A: Yes.

Q: (L) The acknowledging and the seeing?

A: Yes.

Q: (L) What did they tell us once... it's not where you are, but who you are and what you see that counts. (TK) So, we aren't gonna change what happens. There is no way we can have any appreciable effect on the underground armies... it is just a matter of changing ourselves and whoever else we can share with.

A: Correct, the cow has no effect on the health of the livestock industry...

Q: (TK) The cow has no effect on the herd. One cow doesn't... or even a lot of cows. (F) But there might be one or two cows that follow one that breaks out of the herd. (TK) Yes, you might be able to affect somebody else's life, but not the whole group. So, worrying about the underground stuff, is immaterial. (L) But, knowing about it is.

This next extract is interesting because the guest present was Pat, my first abductee/hypnosis client, some of which is included in chapter eight.

Q: (L) Now, with all of us here, we would like to ask why the black, flying boomerangs showed up on the night Pat first came for hypnosis? The first thing we thought about it was that this was a, if not necessarily rare, at least rarely observed type of craft, and the event itself was rare... is this correct?

A: It is rare.

Q: (L) If it is rare for it to occur in response to a hypnosis session, which person were the UFOs particularly interested in?

A: It was not a person, but information that is hidden in the subconscious memory of Pat. To monitor what would be revealed.

Q: (L) They wanted to see if anything would be revealed about their abductions of her?

A: Yes.

Q: (L) OK, since she is here, can we ask who abducted her?

A: Grays.

Q: (L) How many times has she been abducted?

A: 4. Snow scene was only 3rd density abduction. Abduction which occurred there was strictly physical.

Q: (L) OK, the abduction that occurred in the snow was a physical abduction. Perhaps the others were not.

A: The others were 4th density. 3rd density abduction only occurs rarely, and is of great import.

Q: (P) Was my son, who was accompanying me, also abducted?

A: Frozen.

Q: (L) Why did they want Pat so bad that they would take her physically?

A: Do you have any ideas?

Q: (L) Yes, I have ideas. Maybe Pat has ideas and knowledge that she could access that would expose these beings?

A: But real reason is more fundamental. Government proximities!

Q: (L) Oh! Someone was telling me earlier that people who are connected to someone working for the government tend to be abducted more. But, just because Pat was married to a scientist who worked at JPL doesn't mean she knew anything. Does she know something?

A: Not what she knew. Because of proximity to Consortium activity. Implanted for possible future activation.

Q: (P) Was this related to what was going on under the mountain?

A: Not locator, personnel are factored.

Q: (L) OK, it is not where you were so much as who you were in contact with.

A: Yes.

Q: (L) Was it her husband?

A: Perhaps.

Q: (L) Maybe that is why there is a higher rate of abduction among family members of government employees, so that they can be activated or controlled? (P) But my husband wasn't really working on anything secret.

A: He had access to sensitive facilities.

Q: (L) Did he have a security clearance or was he friends with others who did? (P) I had a security clearance. (L) So, Pat had an implant put in. An actual, physical implant. Where is it?

A: Behind sinus cavity.

Q: (L) What is this implant designed to do?

A: Activate behavioral control reflex and thought pattern generation and alteration.

Q: (P) Is that why I can't remember anything?

A: Some.

Q: (L) So, can I say that this UFO appeared over my house on the night Pat was under hypnosis, to reinforce the implant so that she would not be able...

A: To monitor.

Q: (L) If Pat had revealed the details of her abduction, would there have been any repercussions?

A: Not in this case.

Q: (L) So, if Pat had gone to anyone for hypnosis, these craft would have appeared?

A: Yes.

Q: (L) You have already told us that this is extremely rare. What else was unusual? (P) Does this have anything to do with Camp David?

A: Not the issue, its personnel!

Q: (L) Was it that she knew someone or interacted with someone in particular?

A: Many others!

Q: (P) Do the planes have anything to do with it?

A: It is up to Pat, the extent she wishes to retrieve and divulge, the many unusual experiences that were met, by Pat, with unusual indifference.

Q: (P) The first thing unusual was the geographic location of our house. Directly West of us was the mountain that housed all the communications to be used in the event of nuclear war. We were thirteen miles North of Camp David. And, while we lived there, many, many things took place at Camp David that were of global significance. And, we built a barn in 1982 and had bought the house in 1976, and never, in all the years that I lived there, did I ever notice these planes until we built the barn. If I had a stick in my hand, I could have touched them, that's how low they flew. Right over my barn. The same day every week. And there was always two of them, and they never had a single marking on them. And, they were propeller planes. And I wondered: what in the hell is this country doing flying planes, unmarked, propeller driven, and so low, over this area? This continued until we moved from that house. So, these planes came twice a week from 1982 until 1989. (L) What were these planes? Well, after the first couple of times, I sort of just said: "Well, there are the planes." So, what else is new?

A: Indifference.

Q: (P) I thought the planes had something to do with the mountain. Did they?

A: Maybe.

Q: (P) We knew they were flying under radar. Now that I am thinking about this, nobody else ever talked about these planes. It was like we were the only people that ever saw them, or people who were at our house saw them too. My best friend who lived right up the road never saw them. I asked her: "Did you see the planes?" and she said "What planes?" I mean, she was seven acres away and nothing in between!

A: Unusual experiences mount!

Q: (P) V also noticed these things and he would always say—he was less indifferent than I was—he would say: "What in the hell are those planes and what are they doing?" Well, it didn't affect *my* life, except that I was damn mad that it upset my horses. But then, the horses got used to them too, and they became indifferent! [laughter] Well, they came so often, twice a week—"It's Wednesday, the planes will be here!"

A: More... continue probing...

Q: (P) The planes came from East to West, and in the West was the mountain...

A: Catoctin.

Q: (P) That is the name of the mountain. The tunnel where all these facilities were... under Catoctin Mountain. Camp David is near, too.

A: And MUCH ELSE! Mount Weather, Virginia. And why did you live in area... helicopters?

Q: (P) Is it because of Fort Detrick?

A: What brought you to Maryland?

Q: (P) Fort Detrick. (L) What does Mount Weather mean? (P) The underground tunnel—everybody in town called it The Tunnel—but there was nothing around there to ever give anybody the slightest clue as to what it was. In fact, I lived there for quite a long time before I knew it existed. And, on top of the mountain there was a weather station... (P) V was doing electron microscopy—cancer research.

A: REALLY?

Q: (P) It was a photographic lab.

A: Helicopters, Pat? We are asking you!

Q: (P) Well, the helicopters in Frederick went over our house every time the president was at Camp David. But, that was our house in Walkersville not in Emmetsburg. When we first moved to Maryland. Sometimes the helicopters were unmarked...

A: You see, Pat is resistant due to experiences, things don't "phase" her easily, programming, etc.

Q: (L) So, all of these things happening around her, the planes, the mountain, the helicopters... (P) But the helicopters, I knew it was the President either going to or coming from Camp David.

A: Resistant, not resisting.

Q: (L) Is the term "resistant" a clue?

A: All is a clue here!

Q: (L) Since Pat has only been abducted four times, can this mean that she is resistant to that?

A: No.

Q: (P) Isn't that just my personality, that if it doesn't affect me I don't bother with it?

A: Yes.

Q: (P) I don't get bothered about things that...

A: Shoot somebody in front of Pat, and she says: "Oh well, that's life" so, to discover spectacular things, one must be patient and probe carefully, no hasty assumptions, please!! There is to be retrieved, revealed, studied.

Q: (P) Well, the helicopters went back and forth to Camp David. The President was supposed to be in them. And his entourage. There was only three helicopters. (L) Are these the helicopters referred to?

A: No. Let Pat digest it, and report back later.

Q: (L) At the time we had all those sightings around here on the night we did that session with Pat, why did so many other people see them?

A: Window was "blasted."

Q: (P) I would like to know about the apparitions of the Virgin Mary at Conyers, GA, as well as this book *Mary's Message to the World* and all the other messages about the End Times that are coming out all over?

A: The forces at work here are far too clever to be accurately anticipated so easily. You never know what twists and turns will follow, and they are aware of prophetic and philosophical patternings and usually shift course to fool and discourage those who believe in fixed futures.

Well, needless to say, this whole session *really* spooked Pat! About a year later, the subject of underground bases came up again in a slightly different context.

Q: (L) I have a question that may take us somewhere. I noticed when I was reading these transcripts that when we were discussing the origin of the Celts, that the question was asked, by me: were they in any way superior to the indigenous people of this planet? And the remark was, that they were sturdier in some way. And then I commented that they didn't appear to be sturdier than and others, and, in fact, because Celts are very fair, and very thin-skinned looking, they actually look very delicate. It just seemed to me to be kind of an odd remark to make. However, the response that I received, which I didn't pick up on at the time, was that they were sturdier, but not necessarily on the surface. So, does that "surface" mean surface of their appearance, or does that surface mean surface as in underground? That's my question.

A: Both.

Q: (L) Now, in talking about these large underground cities or enclaves that we've talked about on a couple of occasions, it has been said that these beings come and actually may take human babies. I mean this is like fairy lore, legends, of different kinds of creatures that come and steal people's babies, and they go and live underground, and sometimes, one or another will escape. (T) Are the Celts part of these underground civilizations?

A: Yes.

Q: (L) Well, what's the story?

A: They went underground.

Q: (T) When did they go underground?

A: Several occasions, the most recent being, on your calendar: 1941 through 1945. Last episode of mass migration, mostly Deutschlanders.

Q: (T) Underground. We're talking underground, as in under the surface of the earth. Is this what we're talking?

A: Antarctica. Under there. Entry port.

Q: (T) They went underground in Antarctica, they built a large underground base there. This is where the Germans, as in the Nazi Germans, claimed territory.

A: Yes, but they entered through their constructed base, as instructed, then were assimilated.

Q: (L) They were assimilated into the population already existent? Underground cities, underground bases?

A: Yes.

Q: (L) So, they didn't build them, they entered into them as instructed, and were assimilated into the population?

A: They did build a base.

Q: (T) Now, you said instructed... Instructed by whom?

A: Those identifying themselves as "Antareans."

Q: (L) And who are the Antareans?

A: STS Humanoid Orion linkage.

Q: (L) What is an STS Orion Linkage?

A: An STS race from Orion that is humanoid.

Q: (L) How did the Nazis get hooked up with these "Antareans?"

A: The Thule Society originated contact.

Q: (T) And the Nazis failed in their first attempt to take over the world, so now they are down there waiting for their next opportunity.

A: Waiting?

Q: (T) So there is truth about the rumors that Byrd found alien bases down there.

A: Yes, but he was led to believe he was chasing what amounted to merely an encampment of detached Nazis.

Q: (T) So Byrd must have *seen* something and was then led off the track...

A: Yes

Q: (V) Are they coming back out now in the shape of the White Supremacists that are like popping up all over the place? (T) They've been coming and going all along. Admiral Byrd was sent down there, supposedly to go to the South Pole—the first Admiral Byrd expedition to the South Pole—but he took a large military force with him. He was still a U.S. Admiral at the time. The large military force encountered resistance and got their asses whupped real good down there. But, they kept it real quiet, because nobody knew what was really going on down there. So, they just said, oh, it was a scientific expedition. And in reality, what they'd done was to go down there to root out this base out after the war, and they didn't do real well at all! They lost a whole lot of people and a whole lot of ships, and a lot of equipment down there. That's why all these bases are in a ring around the outside; all the scientific bases from different countries; Russia, the U.S., Great Britain; all these countries have these scientific bases all along the outer edge of the Antarctic. They're scientific, they use them for study, but they are there to monitor what's going on, that's why they don't go into the Antarctic. (L) What do these guys plan on doing?

A: This is where "The Master Race" is being developed.

Q: (L) And what is the timeframe they have planned for this activity?

A: Never mind.

So, that was that! Apparently there are things that are dangerous to know! But, at a later time, after the movie *Independence Day* came out, we decided to ask about the significance of this film.

Q: (T) Is there any significance to the movie *Independence Day*?

A: Sure.

Q: (L) What was the primary intention of the makers of this movie? The primary message that they attempted to convey?

A: Infuse thinking patterns with concept of aliens. Part of a larger project.

Q: (L) And what is this project?

A: Called "Project Awaken."

Q: (L) And who is behind, or in charge of, this project?

A: Thor's Pantheum. Subselect trainees for transfer of enlightenment frequency graduation.

Q: (L) Well, is this group STS or STO?

A: Both.

Q: (J) Are they aware of each other? Working on this?

A: Yes. There is more to all of this than you could dream. An army of Aryan psychic projectors.

Q: (L) And what do they project?

A: Themselves… Right in to one's head.

Q: (L) Project right into one's head… Is anybody subject to this projecting?

A: Yes.

Q: (L) And when they project themselves right into someone's head, what does that someone perceive?

A: Inspiration.

Q: (L) Inspiration to do things?

A: Yes. And…

Q: (L) To do something, and to understand or perceive something, is that it?

A: Yes.

Q: (J) To believe something?

A: Yes.

Q: (L) So, how many are in this army?

A: 1.6 million.

Q: (L) When they're doing this projecting into someone's head, where are they projecting from?

A: Mostly subterranean.

Q: (L) Subterranean, so these are the people of the tunnels, the underground bases and all that sort of thing. Are they third or fourth density beings?

A: Both. This is an intense activity, directed towards influencing the high level creative forces.

Q: (L) Was there something subliminal in the movie? That opened something?

A: Sure. Not for you, but for others.

Q: (L) Why not us?

A: You already have the knowledge.

Q: (T) The movie was meant for all of those who don't understand.

A: Say hello to Gene Roddenberry.

Q: (L) In other words, say hello to him because he was doing that sort of thing a long time ago?

A: Yes.

Q: (L) Why did you bring up Gene Roddenberry? (J) Because he was doing it in Star Trek?

A: Yes.

Q: (T) He was doing a whole different thing with Star Trek... (L) When you say influencing high level creative forces, what are these high level creative forces that are needing to be influenced, or desirable of being influenced?

A: Those in the creative arts.

Q: (L) So in other words, this group is using their projecting ability to influence those in the creative arts to do creative things that will therefore influence the people on the planet. Is that it?

A: Yes.

Q: (L) And, these individuals are in the underground places, and you say that they are both STS and STO. Are there any specific things about this movie other than the general import of opening to the idea of aliens...

A: No.

Q: (T) So, we're looking at some Aryan psychic projectors who are trying to stimulate people in a positive way, a la Gene Roddenberry... (L) Now, that's an assumption. Can we say that they are stimulating people in a positive way?

A: Maybe.

Q: (J) Can we say that some of them may be stimulating people in a negative way?

A: Maybe.

Q: (L) So, there's probably a little of both. And you say that we are immune to it because we already have knowledge. Now, when you say we have knowledge, do you mean just knowledge in particular about aliens and alien realities and alien potentials and so forth?

A: Yes. The seriousness of the situation... the reality of it... this is not fun and games.

When the book *Cosmic Voyage* by Courtney Brown came out, we all passed a copy of it around and found it to be full of clear and evident "propaganda" of exactly the type described in the "Thor's Pantheon" session. So, we decided to ask some questions about it.

Q: (T) I want to ask about the book Courtney Brown wrote, *Cosmic Voyage,* concerning the Martian population...

A: It is true that there are underground bases on Mars, but they are Orion STS, NOT "Martian."

Q: (T) Are there Martians as portrayed by Courtney Brown?

A: Not exactly. He is portraying the Orion STS as the Martians. He is more of an "agent provocateur."

Q: (T) Is he working for the government?

A: Not directly, and remember, the government is not one entity.

Q: (L) Who is primarily backing Courtney Brown?

A: R_____ group.

Q: (L) And, is ML and company part of this R_____ disinformation group at this time?

A: Yes.

Q: (L) LM?

A: No.

Q: (T) Did Courtney actually do remote viewing to obtain the information in the book?

A: Not really. Not needed.

Q: (T) Does this mean that the whole story is concocted on his part?

A: Semi. Elements of it are factual.

Q: (T) Yes. I could see that there were factual elements. I could also see that there was a *lot* that was questionable. that conflicts with *everything* else that has come out from other researchers not to mention what we have received here. This is all totally twisted and different.

A: Close.

Q: (T) Is Courtney able to do remote viewing?

A: Yes.

Q: (T) But he did not use it with this book?

A: No.

Q: (T) So, the book is *not* an account of work that has come from remote viewing sessions?

A: No, but not needed.

Q: (L) You have said twice that remote viewing was not "needed." Where did he get his information?

A: Secret sources. Agents of the nation "of the third eye"

Q: (J) What or who is the "Nation of the Third Eye?"

A: Terran civilization under the surface.

Q: (L) Have the Aryans AKA Nordic types as described by Courtney been glorified as the "master race" because they are more suited to living underground?

A: Close. All types there are "Aryan."

Q: (L) OK, is this a Terran underground civilization that has developed on its own?

A: Yes.

Q: (L) Is it managed or manipulated by Orions as well?

A: Yes.

Q: (L) Are these "managers" Orions from other densities?

A: Yes and no.

Q: (L) I don't understand. Are there some that are fourth and some that are third?

A: The human types there are "bi-density."

Q: (L) Holy Shiite Moslems!

A: Grays and Lizards are 4th density. They can "visit" 3rd density, but they must keep returning to 4th in order to "regenerate."

Q: (T) Are you saying that the human/Aryan types can exist as long as they want in any density?

A: In 4th and 3rd.

Q: (L) They can move back and forth, existing with equal ease on either density?

A: Well, not with "equal ease," because 4th density is easier, naturally.

Q: (T) So, the information Courtney Brown was given to write this quasi fiction book, is about the Aryans and not about the Martians?

A: "Martians" is easier to understand for the less well-informed, not to mention any discussion of the densities!

Q: (T) Absolutely. Martians are easier to accept. A lot easier to understand than densities! (L) OK, Third Eye. What is this?

A: That is what they call themselves when pressed for an explanation by surface types, such as yourselves. They were the inspiration for Masonic lore and Illuminati, too.

Q: (L) Does this "Third Eye" designation have a connotation of third eye abilities as we understand them?

A: Psychic.

Q: (T) Does Courtney know he has been had?

A: He has not been "had." He is under the employ of those who pull the levers, so to speak.

Q: (L) You said "pull the levers." Is Courtney Brown a robot, Greenbaumed, mind-controlled, implanted, or any or all of the above? (T) Or is he just foolish?

A: No. Not so foolish, he does not worry about paying the power bill. As Forest Gump said: "Stupid is as stupid does." Who is he hurting? And, he has hit the jackpot with this one. Knowledge can be procured by reading literature, then analyzing it.

Q: (T) Is the time table that he has given correct?

A: Close.

Q: (T) So, the powers that be are going to follow this time table and present the Aryans as Martians?

A: No.

Q: (L) Are the Aryans going to present themselves as Martians?

A: Initially. In order for the Terrans to get used to the idea of EBEs.

Q: (T) But, they are not the good guys. Beware of Greeks bearing gifts.

A: But, do not forget that some of the "good guys" are identical in appearance.

Q: (T) Is this a subterfuge on the part of the Aryans so that they can slide in quietly and take over?

A: No, they do not need that at all. It is a way for the "government" to introduce everyone to the new reality of the existence of intelligent life all over the place, not just here.

Q: (T) So, they have their own agenda, but it is not what Courtney presented in the book.

A: It does not matter. The book is a somewhat altered "New Reality 101."

Much later, about a year, the Cassiopaeans brought up the subject of underground bases on their own. It is unusual for them to initiate a subject!

Q: (L) Ok, we have several things that we discussed earlier, is there anything you wish to say before we launch into questions?

A: Underground bases see dramatic budget increase.

Q: (L) Ok, why do they have a budget increase?

A: Because there is much more activity to come.

Q: (L) Ok, what kind of activity?

A: Broad range. Experimentation, utilization and implementation.

Q: (L&T) Of what?

A: Human "resources." Plan falling into place for "harvest." And other purposes of STS forces' plans.

Q:(L) What is this thing called 'The Harvest'?

A: What do you think?

Q: (L) Well, is that harvest in a negative event, or harvest in a positive one? I mean, as in the harvesting of the wheats and the tares...

A: Either/or.

Q: (L) Ok, now you say the plans are falling into place. What specific events of the past, say, several weeks, or months, whatever period of time set aside, are these plans that are falling into place? I mean, what's the key in the lock?

A: Have you been paying attention, as we have always suggested you should?

Q: (L) Of course! I just asked you because I wanted you to enumerate! Of course I'm paying attention!

A: Lately, there has been diversion for you.

Q: (L) Well, it doesn't mean I'm asleep!

A: V mentioned the weather earlier. Was that a bit "nippy" for you in central Europe in December and January, A?

Q: (T) But it could also be that HAARP adds to it. (L) I don't think that HAARP has anything to do with the weather. The "disinformation artists" would love for us to think that HAARP has something to do with weather. 'Yes, we're having bizzare weather. Let's blame it on HAARP!' because we're going to think about HAARP... (V) I guess the point I'm trying to get at is, are these weather changes promoting some changes in the physical body, that's making the physical body more 'harvestable?'

A: We told you that "HAARP" was being designated for capturing and modulating electromagnetic fields for the purpose of total control of brainwave patterns in order to establish a system of complete "order on the surface of the planet" in either 3rd or 4th density.

Q: (L) Is HAARP in operation at the present time?

A: Yes, in its early stages.

Q: (T) Is the spreading of all these communication towers out across the country the equivalent of a HAARP program on a continental scale?

A: Back up system.

Q: (L) So, they don't need the towers to operate the HAARP system, but they are there as the backup?

A: Towers serve dual and lateral purposes.

Q: (L) Is the weather being controlled or changed or in any way affected by HAARP?

A: Climate is being influenced by three factors, and soon a fourth. 1) Wave approach. 2) Chloroflorocarbon increase in atmosphere, thus affecting ozone layer. 3) Change in the planet's axis rotation orientation. 4) Artificial tampering by 3rd and 4th density STS forces in a number of different ways.

Q: (L) All right, were those given in the order in which they are occurring? The fourth being the one that's coming later?

A: Maybe, but remember this: a change in the speed of the rotation may not be reported while it is imperceptible except by instrumentation. Equator is slightly "wider" than the polar zones. But, this discrepancy is decreasing slowly currently. One change to occur in 21st Century is sudden glacial rebound, over Eurasia first, then North America. Ice ages develop much, much, much faster than thought.

[Discussion of new scientific theory recently presented that the earth is expanding.]

Q: (T) Is the Earth expanding? That's just putting it bluntly, but, is the Earth expanding, how did you put that? (A) Yes, that's the theory: the idea is that the continents move away because the Earth is expanding, and this is much faster than you know, than geologists were thinking.

A: Continental "drift" is caused by the continual though variable, propelling of gases from the interior to the surface, mainly at points of magnetic significance. By slowing down of rotation, Earth alternately heats up and cools down in interior.

Q: (L) Why does it do that? What's the cause of this?

A: Part of cycle related to energy exerted upon surface by the frequency resonance vibrational profile of humans and others.

appendix

Q: (T) OK, let's go back to the beginning of the session, when we were talking about the acceleration/expansion on underground bases in preparation for the harvest. Is that world-wide, we're talking here?

A: Yes, but United States is focus, due to particularly cooperative power structure profile.

Q: (L) What I would like to know is what particular steps are being taken, what particular activities are being stepped up?

A: Acquisition, staging, testing of planned activity.

Q: (L) And what is the planned activity?

A: Control of absolutely everything.

Q: (L) Well, swell! (T) That's the one world government! That's what they want! (L) OK, is there anything in particular that we can do to…

A: Knowledge protects, ignorance endangers. Awareness makes you less vulnerable, both directly and indirectly. Heard anything about synthetic blood, and blood and plasma alteration lately?

Q: (L) All right, I'll bite! Go ahead, tell us about the synthetic blood and the blood plasma.

A: Less "mutes" needed. Bio and cyber/genetic humanoid types now increasing exponentially in general population. You may have already encountered one or two during the past 10 days. Reflect upon activities, and power and influence centers for answer.

Some more time went by and I obtained several books about underground bases and read them. Richard Sauder's books are an excellent resource. Sauder shows the trail of government and military documents relating to the technology and plans for such bases. Reading these books and others led to more questions.

Q: In this underground bases book I have been reading, there are two old miners telling a story about falling through a hole in a mine into a city of gold with mummified soldiers sitting around a huge table, and a 98 foot tall, solid gold statue. I would like to know if this was just a story these guys made up?

A: Fable.

Q: So, they did not fall through a mine shaft into a city of gold in the Panamint Mountains?

A: The area around Death Valley does have many underground mysterious mysteries, but many have heard the legends.

Q: OK. Just a general legend being repeated and embellished. I thought so. Now, I noticed when looking at the map that there is a place called "China Lake Naval Weapons Center" right next to Death Valley. I mean, aside from the fact that it is a *naval* station nowhere near water, is this connected in anyway to these underground bases or cities?

A: In a circuitous way.

Q: I also notice that Edwards Air Force Base is a little to the South of there, and my guess is that these bases are connected to this underground tunnel system, these underground bases or cities. Am I going in the right direction?

A: Draw a line on the map to connect Death Valley, Edwards, and the Antelope Valley. Then connect with Mount Shasta, Mount Ranier, Back to Las Vegas, on to Sedona, over to the Archuleta Mesa, then on up to the Denver Airport.

392

Q: Well, speaking of the Denver Airport, C may be going there soon.

A: Then have C go to that airport, observe carefully, then report back her findings. Very important, because the murals there are directly connected to what you are studying carefully right now. Superclues to be found there, which can point to monstrous future plans of 4th density STS and much, much more.

Q: OK. Change gears: Why is the rooster, or the crowing of the rooster, associated with the idea of underground cities, civilizations, or bases?

A: What causes the rooster to crow?

Q: Light. But, how is light related to an underground city?

A: Tis not just light, but the emergence of light from the depths of the darkness.

Q: Are there such things as 'DEROS,' as described in this underground bases book?

A: Detrimental Robots.

Q: Are DEROS part of the underground city/bases scenario?

A: Yup.

Q: Well, we notice that things are really heating up. Weather, government exposure and confessions of this and that...

A: Massive alien/UFO coverage, some fictionalized, some not.

Going in another direction, there was a funny mention of the "underground" while discussing certain popular theories about "bloodlines" and the "Holy Grail" and all of that.

Q: Now, all these Masons are very hot on the Sinclair family and the Rosslyn Chapel. They are certain that their guys came to America, because in this chapel, built supposedly by a Master Mason, there are carvings of corn, as in maize, and aloe vera plants. This is evidence, to them, that Prince Henry the Navigator and all the Templars and all that...

A: Nonsense!

Q: Well, then, what *is* the explanation for these carvings in Rosslyn Chapel?

A: Visitors yes, but the Masonic creed is intertwined with ancient order of Essenes, arising out of ancient Egypt, from the secret knowledge stored at the base of the Sphinx, as left there by "Atlantean" survivors.

Q: Does anybody in the Masonic order know anything?

A: Yes.

Q: Well, how high do you have to go to get to know anything?

A: Page 33. Blond and blue-eyed, of course! Before genetic alteration, one branch stood eleven feet tall.

Q: Speaking of these tall guys, during the time that all that mess was going on over in Scotland with Wallace and the Bruce, the Templars were being dissolved in France...

A: Dissolved?!? We think not! They merely went "underground."

Q: Is that literally or figuratively?

A: Why not both?

Q: Well, there are Templar organizations that some Mason's claim to be in contact with.

A: And where do you suppose these are?

Q: Underground?

A: Bingo!

More recently, there was a book entitled *The Ultimate Alien Agenda* which promotes a clearly "Reptoid Propaganda" position. I decided to ask some questions about it.

Q: Onto this alien book. It seems to be almost a point by point refutation of some of the things you have told us about these Reptoid aliens. At the same time, it is very revealing. This guy says that 'alien scientists have developed an array of human programs or life orientations which they use to create human hybrids. I was programmed to serve others, and most of my life has been devoted to service as a public official, educator, and psychic counselor. My life exemplifies one category of alien programming.' Is it a fact that the Reptoid aliens are making a bunch of hybrids to 'serve others.'

A: No.

Q: Another thing he talks about is the underground laboratory, and he has a terrible time trying to speak about it because of the pains in his head. He finally gets to the point where he admits that part of the human 'engineering' project, part of what they are doing with the embryos they create by harvesting human eggs and sperm, is that they use them for 'nourishment.' Naturally, he is aghast at this admission from his own memory. And somehow he just glosses over it. Is this true? That some human embryos are being created to provide nourishment for aliens?

A: In a sense.

Q: He never comes back to this specifically, except to vaguely state that the vats and body parts and all that which are reported by many eye-witnesses, are merely 'symbolic' imagery to teach us how unimportant the body is... can you comment?

A: Not necessary. We have already told you.

Q: He further says that the Reptoid aliens have been increasing human intelligence for these many thousands of years with the intention of letting go and leaving us on our own. The Reptoids are going to pull out soon, because they just came to help us evolve, and now we are at the stage we can take charge of things ourselves... Have the Reptoids been increasing human intelligence? Is this part of their agenda?

A: Perhaps, but the agenda is not as stated.

On the subject of the "Aryan" agenda—which is really a psychopathic/pathocratic agenda—I once asked about the infamous *Protocols of the Elders of Zion*:

Q: (L) Who was the author of the *Protocols of the Elders of Zion*?

A: Source is "Aryan" in nature.

Q: (L) Was it written to make the Jews look bad, or to cast blame on them?

A: Some.

Q: (L) Was it also written as a disguised protocol for the Aryan plan to take over the world?

A: No.

Q: (A) I heard that the source was in Russia?

A: No, Turkey.

Now, keeping in mind that we cannot take this as a "truth," but rather as a clue to either be confirmed or denied, in whole or in part, this exchange has a couple of interesting features. First, it says that the source was "Aryan in nature." Notice the key term "nature." The word "nature" in this context reminded me of the following, from 1995:

Q: (L) So, what were the purposes of the STS forces that were controlling Hitler causing him to desire to annihilate an entire group of people?

A: To create an adequate "breeding ground" for the reintroduction of the Nephalim, for the purpose of total control of the 3rd density earth prior to elevation to 4th density, where such conquest is more difficult and less certain!

Q: (L) Do you mean "breeding ground" in the sense of genetic breeding?

A: Yes. Third density.

Q: (L) Did they accomplish this goal?

A: No.

Q: (L) So, the creation of the Germanic "Master Race" was what they were going after, to create this "breeding ground?"

A: Yes.

Q: (L) And, getting rid of the Jews was significant? Couldn't a Germanic master race be created without destroying another group?

A: No.

Q: Why?

A: Because of 4th density prior encoding mission destiny profile.

Q: (L) What does that mean?

A: This means encoding to activate after elevation to 4th density, thus if not eliminated, negates Nephalim domination and absorption. Jews were prior encoded to carry out mission after conversion, though on individual basis. The Nazis did not exactly know why they were being driven to destroy them, because they were being controlled from 4th density STS. But, Hitler communicated directly with Lizards, and Orion STS, and was instructed on how to create the "master race."

Q: (L) And they were going to use this as their basis to introduce a new blend of the Nephilim... (RC) And the New World Order... their version of it. (L) Well, what is the plan now?

A: We cannot tell you this yet, as you would seek to reveal it prematurely, leading to your destruction!!!!

The remark about Hitler and Lizzies brings up this, from August 17, 2003:

Q: (S) So is Mossad part of that [military abductions disguised as "alien"]?

A: Mossad is near the apex of the 3D consortium. The lines blur at that level.

Q: (JH) What's the relationship between the Mossad and the Rothschilds?

A: Mossad is a "brainchild."

[Laughter at the joke, followed by discussion as to whether the Rothchilds are part of the apex or if they are just useful idiots that are going to be double-crossed also. C's break in as Laura is saying she doesn't understand.]

A: The lines blur. Rothchilds are similar in a smaller way to Sargon. Deep level punctuator.

Q: (L) What is a deep level punctuator?

A: One who emerges from seeming obscurity to "make a mark" on history. Don't you wonder where they come from? Think "deep."

Q: As in underground bases?

A: Well, what a concept!

The concept of an underground Aryan race, and what it means for the state of the world as it is now, prompted the research that led to my book *9/11: The Ultimate Truth*. It deals with the issue of certain genetics, which we now suspect to be Aryan, Khazarian in origin, though tweaked through the centuries, and mainly concerned with psychopathy.

Q: (L) I have thought about my question from the last session and I want to ask it this way: You have said that Hitler received instructions from higher density beings about creating a 'Master Race.' Why were the Aryan genetic types seen to be more desirable for creation of this Germanic 'master race?'

A: Both, similarity and ancestral link most unblemished from Orion 3rd and 4th density stock.

Q: (L) So they were essentially trying to breed a group of people *like themselves*?

A: Yes.

Q: [Tape garbled, question apparently about how could it be efficient to try to genetically sort people to create a master race… it would take a long time and since humanity is all so mixed, and genetic recombination so uncertain…]

A: Not point. How would you suggest creation?

Q: (L) OK. They were preparing this breeding ground, so to speak. Obviously this was for the introduction of some other genetic strain. What was this?

A: Nephalim.

Q: (L) Well, if the Nephilim are coming in ships, 36 million of them, why bother to create half-breeds here?

A: Yes, but having an "advance party" makes 3rd density conquest much easier.

Q: (L) So, this Master Race was supposed to get everything ready…

A: Yes.

Q: (L) OK, what is it about the Semitic genes that was considered to be so undesirable in the creation of this 'Master Race?'

A: Would blemish genetic characteristics inclined to *ruthlessness and domination* [e.g. psychopathy and various other inherited anomalies].

Q: (L) So, you are saying that there is something, some genetic tendency or set of genes in the Semitic type that would counteract this? [And that obviously relates to true "Semites" and not the more recent Khazarian Jews. But even this terminology is uncertain and needs more research.]

A: Close. [Which more or less confirms my comments in brackets immediately above.]

Q: (L) But isn't the nature of a person determined by their soul and not the physical body?

A: Partially, remember, aural profile and karmic reference merges with physical structure.

Q: (L) So you are saying that particular genetic conditions are a physical reflection of a spiritual orientation? That the soul must match itself to the genetics, even if only in potential?

A: Yes, precisely.

Q: (L) So a person's potential for spiritual advancement or unfoldment is, to a great extent, dependent upon their genes?

A: Natural process marries with systematic construct when present.

bibliography

Allen, Gary. *None Dare Call It Conspiracy.* Seal Beach, California: Concord, 1972.

Baigent, Michael; Leigh, Richard; Lincoln, Henry. *The Holy Blood and the Holy Grail.* London: Jonathan Cape, 1982.

Baillie, Mike. *Exodus to Arthur: Catastrophic encounters with comets.* London: B. T. Batsford Ltd., 1999.

Baldwin, William J., D.D.S., Ph.D. *Spirit Releasement Therapy: A Technique Manual.* Falls Church, VA: Human Potential Foundation, 1993.

Bastide, Jean. *La memoire des OVNI: Des argonauts aux extraterrestres.* Mercure de France, 1978.

Boëdec, Jean-Francois. *Fantastiques recontres au bout du monde: les apparitions de phenomenes aerospatiaux non identifies dans le finistere.* Plomeur: Editions Le Signor, 1982.

Bramley, William. *The Gods of Eden.* New York: Avon Books, 1990.

Briggs, Katharine. *The Encylopedia of Fairies.* New York: Pantheon Books, 1976.

Campbell, Joseph. *The Hero with a Thousand Faces.* Princeton: Princeton University Press, 1973.

_____. *The Masks of God* (4 volumes). New York: The Viking Press, 1959-1968. *Volume 1: Primitive Mythology* (1959). *Volume 2: Oriental Mythology* (1962). *Volume 3: Occidental Mythology* (1964). *Volume 4: Creative Mythology* (1968).

Castaneda, Carlos. *The Fire From Within.* New York: Simon and Shuster, 1984.

Castaneda, Carlos. *The Active Side of Infinity.* HarperCollins, 1998.

Cayce, Hugh Lynn. *Venture Inward.* New York: Paperback Library, 1966.

Chittick, William. *The Sufi Path of Knowledge.* Albany: State University of New York, 1989.

Cohen, Stanley. *States of Denial: Knowing about Atrocities and Suffering.* Cambridge: Polity Press; Malden, MA: Blackwell Publishers, 2001.

Corso, Col. Philip J., with William J. Birnes. *The Day After Roswell.* New York: Pocket Books, 1998.

Curran, Robert. *The Haunted: One Family's Nightmare.* New York: St. Martins Press, 1988.

Dolan, Richard. *UFOs and the National Security State.* Hampton Roads, second edition, 2002.

Ecker, Don. "The Human Mutilation Factor": http://www.paranetinfo.com/UFO_Files/ufo/hummute.txt

Eco, Umberto. *The Search for the Perfect Language*. Oxford: Blackwell, 1995.

Einstein, Albert and P. Bergmann. *Annals of Mathematics* Vol. 38, No. 3, July 1938.

Eliade, Mircea. *Shamanism: Archaic Techniques of Ecstasy*. New York: Oxford University Press, 1964.

Fawcett, Lawrence, and Barry J. Greenwood. *Clear intent: The government coverup of the UFO experience*. Englewood Cliffs: Prentice-Hall, 1984.

Fowler, Raymond E. *The Andreasson affair: The documented investigation of a woman's abduction aboard a UFO*. Newberg, Or.: Wild Flower Press, 1994.

Fort, Charles. *The Complete Books of Charles Fort*. New York: Dover Publications, Inc., 1974.

Fowler, Raymond E. *The Andreasson Affair*. New York: Bantam Books, 1979.

Fuller, John G. *The Interrupted Journey*. New York: Dell, 1967.

Gatto, John Taylor. *The Underground History of American Education: An intimate investigation into the problem of modern schooling*. New York: Oxford Village Press, 2001.

Godwin, Joscelyn. *Arktos: The Polar Myth*. Kempton: Adventures Unlimited Press, 1996.

Hopkins, Budd. *Missing Time*. New York: Ballantine Books, 1981.

Hurley, Matthew. *The Alien Chronicles: Compelling evidence for extraterrestrial encounters in art & texts since ancient times*. Quester Publications, 2003.

Hynek, J. Allen. *The UFO Experience: A Scientific Enquiry*. New York: Ballantine Books, 1977.

____. Speech at the United Nations, Nov. 27th 1978. *UFOEVIDENCE.com*: http://www.ufoevidence.org/documents/doc757.htm

____. Speech at AIAA 13th Aerospace Sciences Meeting Pasadena, Calif., January 20-22, 1975. *nicap.org*: http://www.nicap.org/emerge.htm

Isserlin, B.S.J. *The Israelites*. London: Thames and Hudson, 1998.

Jacobs, David. *The Threat*. New York: Simon & Schuster, 1998.

Kaku, Michio. *Hyperspace: A Scientific Odyssey Through Parallel Universes, Time Warps, and the 10th Dimension*. Oxford University Press, 1994.

Keel, John A. *The Mothman Prophecies*. Avondale Estates, GA: IllumiNet Press, 1991.

Łobaczewski, Andrzej. *Political Ponerology: A science on the nature of evil adjusted for political purposes*. Red Pill Press, 2005.

Mack, John E., M.D. *Abduction: Human Encounters with Aliens*. New York: Ballantine Books, 1994.

Marchetti, Victor, and John D. Marks. *The CIA and the Cult of Intelligence*. New York: Laurel, 1980.

Marrs, Jim. *The Alien Agenda*. New York: Harper Collins, 1997.

Macaulay, David. *Motel Of Mysteries*. Boston: Houghton Mifflin, 1979.

Mouravieff, Boris M. Gnosis Book One: The Exoteric Cycle. Praxis Institute Press, 2002.

Narby, Jeremy. *The Cosmic Serpent*. New York: Jeremy P. Tarcher/Putnam,1998.

Osborn, Nancy. *The Demon Syndrome*. New York: Bantam Books, 1983.

Ouspensky, P. D. *Tertium Organum: A Key to the Enigmas of the World*. New York: Vintage Books, 1981.

_____. *In Search of the Miraculous: Fragments of an Unknown Teaching*. San Diego: Harvest/HBJ, 1977.

Picknett, Lynn, and Clive Prince. *The Stargate Conspiracy: The Truth About Extraterrestrial Life and the Mysteries of Ancient Egypt*. New York, Berkley, 1999.

Reich, Wilhelm. *Ether, God, and Devil*. NY: Orgone Institute Press, 1949.

Schwartz, Regina M. *The Curse of Cain*. University of Chicago Press, 1997.

Sitchin, Zecharia. *The 12th Planet: Book 1 of the Earth Chronicles*. New York: Avon Books, 1978.

Tacitus, trans. Kenneth Wellesley. *The Histories*. London: Penguin Books, 1964.

Thompson, Thomas L. *The Mythic Past: Biblical archaeology and the myth of Israel*. Basic Books, 1999.

Topper, Michael. "Channeling, UFOs and the Positive/Negative Realms Beyond This World". http://zelator.topcities.com/text1.htm

Turner, Karla, Ph.D. *Into the Fringe: A True Story of Alien Abduction*. New York: Berkley, 1992.

_____. *Taken: Inside the Alien-Human Agenda*. Tallahassee: Rose Printing Company, Inc., 1994.

Turner, Karla, Ph.D., with Ted Rice. *Masquerade of Angels*. Kelt Works, 1994.

Turner, Elton. "Alien Behavior: Concept or Precept?" *Contact Forum*, Sept/Oct 1994: http://www.karlaturner.org/articles/alien_behavior.html

Vallee, Jacques. *Passport to Magonia*. Chicago: H. Regnery Co., 1969.

_____. *The Invisible College: What a group of scientists has discovered about UFOs*. New York: Dutton, 1975.

_____. *Messengers of Deception: UFO Contacts and Cults*. Berkeley: And/Or Press, 1979.

_____. *Dimensions*. New York: Contemporary Books, 1988.

_____. *Forbidden Science: Journals 1957-1969*. New York: Marlowe and Co., 1996.

Vallee, Jacques F. and Eric W. Davis. "Incommensurability, Orthodoxy and the Physics of High Strangeness: A 6-layer Model for Anomalous Phenomena", *National Institute for Discovery Science*: http://www.nidsci.org/pdf/vallee_davis.pdf

Velikovsky, Immanuel. *Worlds in Collision*. New York: Dell, 1965.

Von Daniken, Erich. *Chariots of the Gods?* Putnam Books, 1970.

Wallace, Irving and Wallechinsky, David. *The People's Almanac*. Doubleday, 1975.

Also Published by Red Pill Press

The Secret History of the World
and How to Get Out Alive

Laura Knight-Jadczyk's epic work

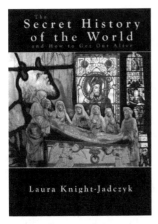

How did the world get into its present state? Ongoing war in the Mideast, rising fuel prices, food riots and shortages, climate change, the extreme polarization of the rich and poor, the war on civil liberties and freedoms masquerading as the so-called War on Terror...

What happened?

This is the question Laura Knight-Jadczyk answers in her groundbreaking and provocative work *The Secret History of the World and How to Get Out Alive*. An accurate understanding the present requires an objective look at all that came before. However, what are we to do when our history has been repeatedly destroyed, suppressed, or Stalinized by those with vested interests? The "history" we are left with is often simply the political propaganda of an elite historical group, and it is a lie.

Knight-Jadczyk sifts the wheat from the chaff to find the scientific underpinning of humanity's spiritual quest and evolution. She traces the dual stream of "official" history and all those subjects deemed incompatible with the wishes of those who write the history: how the Bible was constructed for those very purposes, the more-ancient-than-known culture of stones and its Northern roots, UFOs and so-called "alien abductions", the historical and scientific evidence for repeated and cyclical bombardment of earth by cometary fragments, and the truth about the possible evolution of humanity.

Working with her husband, internationally renowned mathematical physicist Arkadiusz Jadczyk, she marries science with mysticism, critically analyzing the claims made for applications of modern physics in the interface between human consciousness and reality.

Knight-Jadczyk argues, based on her thirty years of research, that we are entering a period of global chaos: social, political, and environmental. These cyclic periods are part of the human experiential cycle and are accompanied by cosmic bombardment, meteors and comets in the sky, and a rain of fire falling on our heads.

But there is a way out, long known and long hidden. *The Secret History of the World and How to Get Out Alive* will show you the way.

Visit www.qfgpublishing.com for these and other titles, or ask for them at your bookseller.

9/11: The Ultimate Truth

Laura Knight-Jadczyk and Joe Quinn

Second Edition

In the years since the 9/11 attacks, dozens of books have sought to explore the truth behind the official version of events that day - yet to date, none of these publications has provided a satisfactory answer as to **why** the attacks occurred and who was ultimately responsible for carrying them out.

Taking a broad, millennia-long perspective, Laura Knight-Jadczyk and Joe Quinn's *9/11: The Ultimate Truth* uncovers the true nature of the ruling elite on our planet and presents new and ground-breaking insights into just how the 9/11 attacks played out.

9/11: The Ultimate Truth makes a strong case for the idea that September 11, 2001 marked the moment when our planet entered the final phase of a diabolical plan that has been many, many years in the making. It is a plan developed and nurtured by successive generations of ruthless individuals who relentlessly exploit the negative aspects of basic human nature to entrap humanity as a whole in endless wars and suffering in order to keep us confused and distracted to the reality of the man behind the curtain.

Drawing on historical and genealogical sources, Knight-Jadczyk and Quinn eloquently link the 9/11 event to the modern-day Israeli-Palestinian conflict. They also cite the clear evidence that our planet undergoes periodic natural cataclysms, a cycle that has arguably brought humanity to the brink of destruction in the present day.

For its no nonsense style in cutting to the core of the issue and its sheer audacity in refusing to be swayed or distracted by the morass of disinformation that has been employed by the Powers that Be to cover their tracks, *9/11: The Ultimate Truth* can rightly claim to be **the** definitive book on 9/11 - and what that fateful day's true implications are for the future of mankind.

The new Second Edition of *9/11: The Ultimate Truth* has been updated with new material detailing the real reasons for the collapse of the World Trade Center towers, the central role played by agents of the state of Israel in the attacks, and how the arrogant Bush government is now forced to dance to the Zionists' tune.

Visit www.qfgpublishing.com for these and other titles, or ask for them at your bookseller.